Michael Rösser

Prisms of Work

Work in Global and Historical Perspective

Edited by
Andreas Eckert, Sidney Chalhoub, Mahua Sarkar, Dmitri van den Bersselaar, Christian G. De Vito

Work in Global and Historical Perspective is an interdisciplinary series that welcomes scholarship on work/labour that engages a historical perspective in and from any part of the world. The series advocates a definition of work/labour that is broad, and especially encourages contributions that explore interconnections across political and geographic frontiers, time frames, disciplinary boundaries, as well as conceptual divisions among various forms of commodified work, and between work and 'non-work'.

Volume 21

Michael Rösser

Prisms of Work

Labour, Recruitment and Command
in German East Africa

DE GRUYTER
OLDENBOURG

This publication was accepted as dissertation thesis of the Max Weber Centre for Advanced Cultural and Social Studies of the University of Erfurt.

The Open Access publication has been kindly supported by the OA publication fund of the Otto Friedrich University of Bamberg.

ISBN 978-3-11-120462-8
e-ISBN (PDF) 978-3-11-121809-0
e-ISBN (EPUB) 978-3-11-121896-0
ISSN 2509-8861
DOI https://doi.org/10.1515/9783111218090

Library of Congress Control Number: 2023941344

Bibliographic information published by the Deutsche Nationalbibliothek
The Deutsche Nationalbibliothek lists this publication in the Deutsche Nationalbibliografie; detailed bibliographic data are available on the internet at http://dnb.dnb.de.

Cover image: Indian Craftsmen Riveting Bridge Parts Using Modern Machinery at the Malagarassi-Bridge 1912–1913; holzmann-bildarchiv.de/BBWA U5/03/17, Nr. 177. Bildarchiv der Philipp Holzmann AG / Hauptverband der Deutschen Bauindustrie e.V. im Berlin-Brandenburgischen Wirtschaftsarchiv.
Typesetting: Integra Software Services Pvt. Ltd
Printing and binding: CPI books GmbH, Leck

www.degruyter.com

To Eleo and Tina

Preface

This book is the revised and shortened version of my PhD thesis titled *Prisms of Work – Labour, Recruitment and Command in German East Africa*. The thesis was submitted in March 2022 and defended successfully at the Max Weber Centre for Advanced Cultural and Social Studies of the University of Erfurt (Germany) on 20 October 2022. The board members of the doctoral colloquium were Prof. Dr Iris Schröder, Prof. Dr Andreas Eckert, Prof. Dr Omar Kamil, PD Antje-Linkenbach -Fuchs and Prof. Dr Hartmut Rosa. I thank all the board members and all those who largely contributed to the completion of my PhD (cf. acknowledgements).

For the publication process, I would like to express my thanks to Rabea Rittgerodt working for the publishing house of de Gruyter for her support and the acceptance in the publisher's series *Work in Global and Historical Perspective.* I would also like to express my thanks to the *Klett-Stiftung* and the University Library of the Otto-Friedrich-University of Bamberg which both supported the publication of this book financially.

In the publishing process, German quotations from literature and sources, originally provided in the footnotes, have been removed. All quotes now provided in English from the original German sources or literature are my own translations. Although the manuscripts have been proofread by native speakers, any flaws or failures therein are my own mistakes.

https://doi.org/10.1515/9783111218090-202

Acknowledgements

This work would have been impossible without a great number of people. First and foremost, I would like to thank my supervisors Prof. Dr Iris Schröder and Prof. Dr Andreas Eckert for their constant support and advice for this PhD thesis. Further thanks go to all my colleagues and seniors at the University of Regensburg and the University College Dublin during and after my undergraduate studies: Prof. Dr Mark Spoerer, Kathrin Pindl, Lino Wehrheim, Sebastian Pößniker, Anna Pauli and Tobias Jopp as well as Prof. Dr Mary E. Daly, Declan Downey and Paul Rouse. Special thanks go to my former colleagues and seniors at the Heinrich-Heine-University of Düsseldorf, Prof. Dr Stefanie Michels, Yagmur Karakis, Caroline Authaler and Tristan Oestermann. Of course, this PhD would have been impossible without the funding provided by the Max Weber Centre for Advanced Cultural and Social Studies as well as the *Stabsstelle Forschung und Nachwuchsförderung* of the University of Erfurt. I would like to thank all the people I met at the University of Erfurt in general, at the Chair for Global History and at the Max Weber Centre in Erfurt in particular. They are: Benjamin Sippel, Felipe Torres Navarro and Valeria Vergara, Urs Lindner, Prof. Dr Cécile Stehrenberger, Peter Schröder, Prof. Dr Rana Behal, Cornel Zwierlein, Juhi Tyagi, Sarah al-Taher, Marco Pasi, Prof. Dr Christiane Kuller, Prof. Dr Kornelia Kończal, Bettina Hollstein, Alexander Nathan, Christoph Henning, Beatrice Renzi, Friedrich Cain, Tomás Bartoletti, Eleonor Marcussen, Hannah Peaceman, Julia Seeberger, Tanja Visic, Stella Rehbein, Michael Wutzler, Prof. Dr Omar Kamil, Christian Methfessel, Claudia Gatzka, Florian Wagner, Sonja Dolinsek, Maria Framke, Felix Schürmann, Ned Richardson-Little, Reiner Prass, Prof. Dr Alf Lüdtke (†), Tobias Mörike, Elisa Schaarschmidt, Claudia Berger, Carolyn Taratko, Andrew Tompkins and Sarah Frenking. Many thanks go also to my former colleagues and seniors at the FernUniversität in Hagen: Prof. Dr Jürgen G. Nagel, Fabian Fechner, Barbara Schneider, Dennis Schmidt, Tabea U. Buddeberg, Pascal Hirschberg, Mareen Heying, Arndt Neumann, Prof. Dr Wolfgang Kruse, Prof. Dr Felicitas Schmieder, Prof. Dr Reinhard Wendt and Karin Gockel. Also, many thanks to all the helpful advice of those colleagues I have met at several conferences, in archives or anywhere else: Christian Westerhoff, Jens Thiel, Friedrich Ammermann, Norman Aselmeyer, Jürgen Dinkel, Prof. Dr Nina Kleinöder, Andreas Greiner, Jürgen Schmidt, Stefan Noack, Stephanie Lämmert, Erich Friedlein, Gerlinde Simon, Reinhard Frost, Kathleen Rahn, Malte Fuhrmann, Konrad Steinert and Steffen Dörre. For bed, breakfast, dinner and friendship, many thanks go to Andreas Boos and Michael Wenzler. For their support when researching in Tanzania and beyond, special thanks go to Osmund Kapinga, Andrew Kasambala, Jana Sahre and Jan Kuever. Particularly during the Covid-19 pandemic, the joint *virtuelle Schreibzeit* sustained

https://doi.org/10.1515/9783111218090-203

my eagerness to finish the dissertation. For our regular online meetings featuring great discussions, help, advice, and motivation, special thanks go to my colleagues in Erfurt, Gotha and Osnabrück Verena Bunkus, Anna-Maria Hünnes, Annika Dörner, Erik Liebscher and Julia Fesca. For always reminding me of the bright sides of life, many thanks go to Vincent Berger, Marie Berger and Eleo Rösser. For his countless and tireless proofreading of my drafts, papers, and chapters since 2013, I am deeply grateful to Frederick Myles. The final proofreading was generously financed by the SFB *Transregio SFB TRR 294 Strukturwandel des Eigentums,* powered by the Max Weber Centre of the University of Erfurt and carried out by Linda Finnigan – I owe many thanks to both the SFB's financing and Linda's final proofreading. For her ongoing support and love, I am deeply grateful to Tina Czada.

Regensburg, March 2022

Contents

List of Figures

https://doi.org/10.1515/9783111218090-205

1 Towards a Global History of Labour

1.1 Labour and Non-work in Global History

> But what is work and what is not work? Is it work to dig, to carpenter, to plant trees, to fell trees, to ride, to fish, to hunt, to feed chickens, to play the piano, to take photographs, to build a house, to cook, to sew, to trim hats, to mend motor bicycles? All of these things are work to somebody, and all of them are play to somebody. There are in fact very few activities which cannot be classed either as work or play according as you choose to regard them. The labourer set free from digging may want to spend his leisure, or part of it, in playing the piano, while the professional pianist may be only too glad to get out and dig at the potato patch. Hence the antithesis between work, as something intolerably tedious, and not-work, as something desirable, is false.
>
> George Orwell. *The Road to Wigan Pier*. London: 1937.[1]

George Orwell's biography and his thoughts on work reflect the fault lines of global labour history.[2] They thus inspire the present study on global labour history in the context of colonial German East Africa between ca. 1900 and 1920. In this respect, the title of the present study – *Prisms of Work* – reflects its programme. As soon as work is investigated, it fans out in multiple directions. As the manifestation of labour is thus inherently context-dependent, complex, and ambiguous, work is characterised as a prism. Keeping in mind that colonial labour contexts were always prone to various forms of coercion, the study primarily approaches the phenomenon of labour as a product of multifaceted negotiations on behalf of all protagonists involved, in this case at three individual working sites. These workplaces in German East Africa are the construction sites of the *Central Railway* (ca. 1905–1916), the *Otto* cotton plantation near Kilossa (ca. 1907–1916) and the palaeontological excavation sites of the Tendaguru Expedition in the colony's southern region of *Lindi* (ca. 1909–1911).

Central to the investigation of labour at these three places are therefore the following questions: What is the overall setting of each particular place of work and how far are their respective characteristics shaped by global and/or local parameters? Who are the decisive protagonists of labour at each working site that manifest the phenomenon of work through their actions and abilities? Do skills

---

1 Orwell, George. *The Road to Wigan Pier*. Ed. Selina Todd. London: 2021, pp. 135–136.

2 Touching on the connection of Orwell to global labour history cf. Hofmeester, Karin and Linden, Marcel van der. 'Introduction'. *Handbook The Global History of Work*. 1–12. Eds. Karin Hofmeester and Marcel van der Linden. Berlin and Boston: 2018, p. 2. Cf. Orwell, George. 'Marrakech'. *The Orwell Foundation*. Web. https://www.orwellfoundation.com/the-orwell-foundation/orwell/essays-and-other-works/marrakech/ (25 May 2021).

https://doi.org/10.1515/9783111218090-001

enhance the opportunities to become more autonomous when at work? Are those who have long been perceived as 'the colonisers' really a homogeneous group particularly in the daily context of work? Were there lines of conflict between them? If yes, which conflicts occurred, and finally, how did each party justify its point of view? Approaching the prisms of work accordingly, this study deliberately does not investigate topics that have long been broadly discussed either in colonial history or in labour history. First of all, this applies especially to discussions centring on the trope of 'educating' the African population to work in the colonies. This study presupposes the omnipresence of such discourses in colonial Africa. It takes such discourses as a given to be always kept in mind especially when interpreting sources in the colonial archives. Secondly, questions of whether colonial labour has to be classified as forced work or not or whether tax work is to be regarded as (un-)free labour are not examined in detail. Rather, this study presupposes that a certain degree of force always lingered in any colonial working relationship, oscillating between the two poles of coercion and voluntariness.

All the questions asked by this study are central for global labour history. Although having greatly expanded in recent years, the research subject of global labour history is still blurry. The genesis of its historiography may be traced back in analogy to George Orwell's biography and his thoughts on work quoted above. Investigating Orwell's biography and his *œuvre* more closely, it is striking that Orwell's career in the service of the British Imperial Police Forces preceding his work as an author has found so little attention, although this period was a fundamental facet of Orwell's life. After all, Orwell worked as an officer of the Indian Imperial Police in Burma between 1922 and 1928. Despite the fact that Orwell decided to become a writer directly after his return from Burma to England just before the 1930s, Orwell's Burmese experience as a colonial police officer has only been treated as a sideshow that allegedly had little influence on Orwell's second career as a writer.[3] This general negligence is even more surprising as many of Orwell's initial, but also later (and longer) writings drew a lot on his experience as a police officer in the British colony.[4] Undoubtedly, many events in the twenti-

3 Cf. Lynskey, Dorian. *The Ministry of Truth: A Biography of George Orwell's 1984.* London: 2021, Introduction. Cf. Bowen, John. 'Introduction'. Orwell, George. *Nineteen Eighty-Four.* vii–xxxi. Ed. John Bowen. Oxford: 2021. Cf. Hofmeester and Linden. 'Introduction', p. 2.

4 Clearly, Orwell processed his experience and feelings about (colonial) despotism, racism and the absurdity of white supremacy in essays such as "A Hanging" (1931), "Shooting an Elephant" (1936) or "Not Counting Niggers" (1939), not to mention his very first novel *Burmese Days* published in 1934. For historical research inspired by George Orwell's *Shooting an Elephant,* cf. Saha, Jonathan. 'Colonizing elephants: animal agency, undead capital and imperial science in British

eth century were important to Orwell, but Eric Blair (Orwell's given name) still indeed has something to say about the global history of labour.[5]

Thus, Orwell's thoughts on work quoted above must be linked to the historiography of global labour history. This applies also to his book, *The Road to Wigan Pier*, containing his thoughts on work. This quasi-investigative journalistic book about the hardships of the daily lives of the working class in northern England is not exclusively about the English working class(es). Rather, Orwell drew a lot on his colonial experience in British imperial Burma and links his thoughts about the English working classes to labour and work in colonial Asia. *The Road to Wigan Pier* is generally known for its description of the wretched life of individuals of the working class during the 1930s. Orwell describes the misery of both unemployed people and the working poor in the industrial centres of 1930s England and urges them to overcome this distress by his individual vision of socialism. Yet, laying bare the sufferings of the English working class, who still regarded themselves as citizens of the British Empire at that time, Orwell often explicitly links the hardships of the working classes to British colonialism in *The Road to Wigan Pier*.[6] But it was not only George Orwell's own experience as an imperial police officer in Burma between 1922 and 1928 that was strongly linked to British colonialism. In fact, Orwell himself was even born in India's Motihari (Bihar) in 1903, as his father Richard Blair worked for the Indian Civil Service. Orwell's father's family had further owned Jamaican sugar plantations and his grandfather had been a deacon in Calcutta, while his mother's family had run a thriving business in shipping and teak for generations in Burma.[7] Besides these familial aspects of Orwell's background that influenced all of his later writings, Orwell himself connected his early occupation as an imperial police officer to the subject matter of *The Road to Wigan Pier*.[8] In this very work, Orwell himself is very clear on this interrelationship:

> When I came home [from Burma] on leave in 1927 I was already half determined to throw up my job, and one sniff of English air decided me. I was not going back to be a part of that evil despotism. [. . .] I felt that I had got to escape not merely from imperialism but from every form of man's dominion over man. I wanted to submerge myself, to get right down

Burma'. 169–189. *BJHS: Themes 2*. 24 April 2017. Web. https://www.cambridge.org/core/journals/bjhs-themes/article/colonizing-elephants-animal-agency-undead-capital-and-imperial-science-in-british-burma/34A559317F45848054C76C384BEEB8F3/core-reader (18 June 2018).

5 Cf. Hofmeester and Linden. 'Introduction', pp. 5–6.

6 Cf. Todd, Selina. 'Introduction'. George Orwell. *The Road to Wigan Pier*. vii–xxxiii. Ed. Selina Todd. Oxford: 2021, pp. vii–xxxiii.

7 Cf. Chaudhuri, Rosinka. 'Introduction'. George Orwell. *Burmese Days*. vii–xxxii. Ed. Rosinka Chaudhuri. Oxford: 2021, p. x.

8 Cf. Chaudhuri. 'Introduction', pp. xiii–xv.

> among the oppressed, to be one of them and on their side against their tyrants. [. . .] It was in this way that my thoughts turned towards the English working class. It was the first time that I had ever been really aware of the working class, and to begin with it was only because they supplied an analogy. They were the symbolic victims of injustice, playing the same part in England as the Burmese played in Burma.[9]

Indeed, there are a lot more passages in *The Road to Wigan Pier* where Orwell draws connections to British imperialism.[10] It is therefore correct to stress that it is important "to realize today how closely linked Orwell's understanding of the 'class question' [. . .] was to his experience of imperialism".[11] With Orwell being not only a brilliant writer, but also a sharp observer of his times, some of his further thoughts on labour and working life are also worth noticing, and indeed supply a basis for taking his ideas in *The Road to Wigan Pier* one step further. Accordingly, I argue that Orwell's thoughts can not only inspire research on the working classes of 1930s England, but they also go to the very heart of current research questions asked by global labour history.

This is because there are striking parallels between the general perception about Orwell's *The Road to Wigan Pier* and the historiography of labour done in Europe and North America. Just as *The Road to Wigan Pier* has largely been perceived as a work merely reporting about England's unemployed and working poor, so too labour historians have devoted their energy primarily to analysing labour and the working classes in various nation states of the Global North. During its gilded age in the 1970s, labour history generally investigated the phenomenon of labour by means of the methodology of social and economic history. In this type of research, labour and work were primarily presented as something taking place within the boundaries of individual industrial nation states. In addition, the historians perceived working people as a comparatively homogeneous group, who had similar interests and generally stood up for their interests by collective action and trade union activism. Yet, by the end of the same decade, political developments and new research approaches all around the world facilitated the decline of this approach to doing labour history. First of all, the world experienced the decolonisation of many territories around the globe from the 1940s onwards. This development accelerated in the 1960s with the independence of many former colonies particularly in Africa. With the end of colonial rule, scholars of the Global South now had the opportunity to study the labour history of their newly independent states. Their insights differed significantly from labour historians of the Global North, as they

---

9 Orwell. *The Road to Wigan Pier*, pp. 101–102.

10 Cf. Orwell. *The Road to Wigan Pier*, pp. 41, 58, 69, 76, 85–89, 94–102, 109–110, 123–124, 132–136, 146–148, 155.

11 Chadhuri. 'Introduction', p. xx.

highlighted the central role of forced labour in contrast to the free-wage labour paradigm propagated by old-established labour history. “At the same time, they discovered that the ‘national’ historiography that predominated in Europe and North America was impossible in former colonial territories since their history was inextricably linked with that of the colonial metropoles.”[12] Noticing the research results of their colleagues working in the Global South, labour historians of the Global North thus increasingly acknowledged their methodological nationalism as their primary blind spot in their own historiography of labour. With historians of the Global South pursuing labour history that also took European developments into account, scholars of the Global North realised that it was impossible to write a history of labour by exclusively investigating European or North American nation states. Furthermore, they realised that they had neglected the Global South almost entirely in their research. The second blind spot of conventional labour history was laid bare by feminist historical investigations that illuminated the centrality of female work especially in the domestic sphere. Usually subsumed under the terms ‘reproductive’ and ‘care work’ and generally unpaid work, intense debates from the 1960s to the 1980s clearly showed that (female) work without any salary was indeed also a form of labour.[13] Other developments further contributed to the decline of this type of labour history. By the fall of ‘the iron curtain’ and the alleged ‘End of History’,[14] labour historians generally took the view that countless works on the history of labour had said everything there was to say about their subject. This trend further accelerated with the decline of the Soviet Union contributing to the understanding that research inspired by Marxist theory – broadly speaking – could neither lead to a better understanding of the past nor the present. Consequently, historical research on labour had slowly but surely lost its significance by the 1990s. Instead, historians increasingly took up research inspired by ‘the cultural turn’ and post-colonialism. As both of the newer approaches rather shied away from ‘materialism’ and the methodology of social and economic history, an analysis of the working ‘masses’ appeared even more outdated. Instead, cultural representations, discourse analysis and corresponding individual practices came to the forefronts of historical investigations.[15]

12 Hofmeester and Linden. ‘Introduction’, p. 2.

13 Cf. Hofmeester and Linden. ‘Introduction’, pp. 1–3. Cf. Eckert, Andreas. ‘Area Studies and the Development of Global Labor History’. *The Lifework of a Labor Historian: Essays in Honor of Marcel van der Linden.* 156–173. Eds. Ulbe Bosma and Karin Hofmeester. Leiden: 2018, pp. 156–160. For a longer perspective on the historiography of labour since antiquity cf. Lucassen, Jan. ‘Workers. New Developments in Labor History since the 1980s’. *The Lifework of a Labor Historian: Essays in Honor of Marcel van der Linden.* 22–46. Eds. Ulbe Bosma and Karin Hofmeester. Leiden: 2018.

14 Cf. Fukuyama, Francis. *The End of History and the Last Man.* New York: 1998.

15 Cf. Eckert, Andreas. ‘Why all the fuss about a Global Labour History?’. *Global Histories of Work.* 3–24. Ed. Andreas Eckert. Berlin and Boston: 2016, pp. 3–24. Cf. Cooper, Frederick. ‘The ‘La-

But there was life in the old dog yet. During the last two decades, labour history has increasingly integrated approaches of global history and focused on labour in areas other than the Global North. Just as Orwell's biography now starts to be associated with colonialism and the British Empire, global labour history reassessed the phenomenon of work largely via the analysis of labour in colonial contexts. In these last few decades, the emerging global labour history has expanded its field of research particularly to Africa, Asia, (Latin) America and Oceania. As the overwhelming part of these regions had been areas colonised by western Empires by the 'long nineteenth century' (Eric Hobsbawm) at the latest, global labour history reassessed the old-established works on colonial history. One prominent strand of global labour history took the 'bird's eye-view' and jumped on the bandwagon named 'globalisation'. With the rise of the USA as the only remaining global superpower in the 1990s after the failure of the non-capitalist 'Soviet Bloc' for the time being, globalisation became the omnipresent buzzword permeating not only public discourse but also historical research. As global history of this fashion was thus primarily carried out as the history of globalisation, global labour history too largely focussed on topics strongly related to the trope of 'globalisation' and the Global North as the latter's major perpetrator. In this respect, scholars regarded globalisation as a phenomenon marked by ever increasing goods production, goods consumption, and the global circulation of products, people and ideas. 'Globalisation' was further seen as a process that not only compressed time and space by modern means of communication and transportation, but many historians also took the view that globalisation entailed ever closer interconnections between the most distant parts of the world, mobilising – largely in the literal sense – the global population(s) who were equally and ever more comprehensively integrated into an increasingly globalising world.[16] Highly mobile protagonists of labour thus became the major field of interest. Global labour historians reassessed unfree labour relationships ranging from slavery to

---

bour Question' in Africa and the World'. *General Labour History of Africa. Workers, Employers and Governments, 20th–21st Centuries.* 617–636. Eds. Stefano Bellucci and Andreas Eckert. Exeter: 2019, pp. 617–623. Cf. Bellucci, Stefano and Eckert, Andreas. 'The 'Labour Question' in Africanist Historiography'. *General Labour History of Africa. Workers, Employers and Governments, 20th–21st Centuries.* 1–16. Eds. Stefano Bellucci and Andreas Eckert. Exeter: 2019, pp. 1–9. Cf. Linden, Marcel van der. *Workers of the World. Eine Globalgeschichte der Arbeit.* Frankfurt o.M. and New York: 2017, pp. 17–31.

16 Cf. Osterhammel, Jürgen. *Die Flughöhe der Adler: historische Essays zur globalen Gegenwart.* Munich: 2017, pp. 11–53, 203–214. Cf. Bayly, Christopher. *The Birth of the Modern World. 1780–1914. Global Connections and Comparisons.* Oxford: 2014. Cf. Osterhammel, Jürgen. *Die Verwandlung der Welt. Eine Geschichte des 19. Jahrhunderts.* Munich: 2009. Cf. Conrad, Sebastian. *Globalisation and the Nation in Imperial Germany.* Cambridge: 2010.

indentured labour and other highly mobile 'free' wage workers such as crewmen on ocean steamers. Later, also comparatively immobile workers such as dock workers and railway workers came into focus as their workplaces were particularly influenced by the global circulation of goods.[17]

Yet, there was criticism of the global history approach from the very beginning. With its major focus on highly mobile people and various forms of worldwide interconnectedness, global labour historians lost sight of the majority of the global population, who lived comparatively sedentary and immobile lives. Furthermore, the focus on mere mobility failed to assess that there were accepted forms of 'global' mobility such as tourism or the global circulation of goods, whereas other forms of movement like those of nomadic people living in colonial territories were subject to restrictions or colonial control and therefore not sanctioned by the imperial powers.[18] Among others, the historian of Africa, Frederick Cooper, was one of the most prominent critics of global history pursued merely as the history of globalisation.[19] In his view, there was neither coherence nor any unilateral direction of what so many people perceived as an ever progressing 'globalisation'. Acknowledging that there were border crossing flows of information, goods, people and ideas, Cooper still urged for them neither to be taken for granted nor as universal. Instead, any historian of global history must focus on a comprehensive analysis of 'global' processes to avoid the danger of teleological research. As a matter of fact, Cooper argues, there certainly is global interconnectedness,

---

17 Cf. Linden. *Workers of the World.* Cf. Varela, Raquel et al. (Eds.). *Shipbuilding and Ship Repair Workers around the World. Case Studies 1950–2010*. Amsterdam: 2017. Cf. Callebert, Ralph. *On Durban's Docks. Zulu Workers, Rural Households, Global Labor.* Rochester: 2017. Cf. Castryck, Geert (Ed.). 'From Railway Juncture to Portal of Globalization: Making Globalization Work in African and South Asian Railway Towns'. *Comparativ. Zeitschrift für Globalgeschichte und vergleichende Gesellschaftsforschung,* 25, 3. Leipzig: 2015. Cf. Damir-Geilsdorf, Sabine et al. (Eds.). *Bonded Labour. Global and Comparative Perspectives (18th–21st Century).* Bielefeld: 2016. Cf. Behal, Rana and Linden, Marcel van der (Eds.). *Coolies, Capital, and Colonialism: Studies in Indian Labour History.* New York: 2006. Cf. Lambert, David and Lester, Alan (Eds.). *Colonial Lives Across the British Empire: Imperial Careering in the Long Nineteenth Century.* Cambridge: 2010. For a 'state of the art' summary of the field cf. Cole, Peter and Hart, Jennifer. 'Trade, Transport, and Services'. *Handbook The Global History of Work.* 277–298. Eds. Karin Hofmeester and Marcel van der Linden. Berlin and Boston: 2018.

18 Cf. Huber, Valeska. 'Multiple Mobilities. Über den Umgang mit verschiedenen Mobilitätsformen um 1900'. 317–341. *Geschichte und Gesellschaft,* no. 36. Göttingen: 2010, pp. 317–335.

19 Cf. Cooper, Frederick. 'What Is the Concept of Globalization Good for?. An African Historian's Perspective'. 189–213. *African Affairs,* vol. 100, no. 399. Oxford: 2001. Web. *Jstor.* https://www.jstor.org/stable/3518765 (12 March 2021), p. 189.

but at the same time, there are certainly also disruptions and stoppages in this process, which tend to be overlooked when focussing solely on global interconnectedness.[20] In the meantime, such criticism was taken up by many scholars – particularly trained in African history – who largely observed these warnings. Although others still regard the concept of globalisation as an important analytical category of global history, they refined their approach according to the criticisms and often prefer to speak about 'globalisations' (plural), to stress the many facets and characteristics of 'globalisation'.[21] On the whole, global labour history has certainly observed the critique and there is now an emerging field of historical research explicitly dedicated to the investigation of global disconnections in global history, for instance.[22]

In the wake of this criticism of global history in general and global labour history in particular, other certainties about labour also thought to be safe slowly but surely eroded. Historians increasingly wondered whether labour could exclusively be perceived as mere wage labour and nothing else. With the slow but continuous erosion of social security services since the 'neo liberal' 1980s, this perception has changed fundamentally, however. By now, the image of such wage labour typical of the industrial countries as the prototype defining labour as such has certainly waned. Instead, historians sensed that the type of wage labour that had dominated the Global North during the twentieth century was rather the global and historical exception than the rule. With global (labour) his-

20 Cf. Cooper. 'What Is', pp. 189–213. Cf. Drayton, Richard and David Motadel. 'Dicussion. The Futures of Global History'. 1–21. *Journal of Global History,* 13. Cambridge: 2018. Web. https://www.cambridge.org/core/terms. https://doi.org/10.1017/S1740022817000262. (1 August 2018).

21 Cf. Epple, Angelika. 'Globalisierung/en'. *Docupedia-Zeitgeschichte*. 11 June 2012. Web. http://docupedia.de/zg/epple_globalisierung_v1_de_2012 (21 January 2021).

22 The Kru people are a fascinating example of accepted mobility in an overall framework of forced mobility and slavery. As African people originating in west Africa where most humans were enslaved, the Kru – among many other occupations – worked on European slave ships and thus facilitated slavery while rarely being taken into slavery themselves. Cf. Gunn, Jeffrey. *Outsourcing African Labor. Kru Migratory Workers in Global Ports, Estates and Battlefields until the End of the 19th Century.* Berlin and Boston: 2021. Cf. Glasman, Joel and Gerstenberger, Debora (Eds.). *Techniken der Globalisierung. Globalgeschichte meets Akteur-Netzwerk-Theorie.* Bielefeld: 2016. Cf. Hofmeester, Karin et al. 'No Global Labour History without Africa: Reciprocal Comparison and Beyond'. 249–276. *History in Africa,* vol. 41, n.p.: 2014. *JSTOR.* Web. www.jstor.org/stable/26362091 (12 March 2021). Cf. Freund, Bill. 'Sub-Saharan Africa'. *Handbook The Global History of Work.* 63–82. Eds. Karin Hofmeester and Marcel van der Linden. Berlin and Boston: 2018. Cf. Bellucci and Eckert. 'The Labour Question'. Cf. Adelman, Jeremy. 'What Is Global History Now?'. *Aeon.* N.d. Web. https://aeon.co/essays/is-global-history-still-possible-or-has-it-had-its-moment (1 December 2020). Cf. "Global Dis/Connections". *CAS LMU. Center for Advanced Studies.* N.d. https://www.cas.uni-muenchen.de/schwerpunkte/global_dis_connections/index.html (12 March 2021).

tory having focused predominantly on male protagonists of work, gender has become a decisive desideratum of research. With the dominance of wage labour pushing reproductive and care work into the background, global labour history has largely been a masculine affair. As a lot of care work was done by women or feminised men like personal servants (so-called *boys*), this research gap largely persists.[23] Moreover, doubts about the classical understanding of labour as wage labour especially evolved when scholars attempted to apply the wage labour paradigm of the Global North to analyse labour in the Global South. Particularly in the second half of the twentieth century, scholars realised that the prototypical wage labour dominating the industrial countries rarely existed in so-called developing countries. Trying to overcome their methodological deficiencies, scholars thus readjusted their approach to labour in countries outside the Global North and introduced concepts such as the 'informal urban sector' to their research. Although the concept of the 'informal urban sector' proved to be an inspiring approach, it soon turned out that this 'informal urban sector' was neither informal nor limited to urban spheres. Rather, the 'informal urban sector' permeated not only cities and larger towns, but its connections also reached right into rural areas and the labour relations involved followed implicit and explicit rules that mutually bound all labour market participants to each other. Hence, both the two major ideas so central to the concept had to be dismissed.[24] Likewise, scholars increasingly refrained from taking the twentieth-century wage labour of the Global North as the yardstick that determined how labour should be measured. Shifting their focus away from the Global North, and particularly away from Eu-

---

23 Cf. Boris, Eileen. 'Subsistence and Household Labour'. *Handbook The Global History of Work.* 329–344. Eds. Karin Hofmeester and Marcel van der Linden. Berlin and Boston: 2018. Cf. Bryceson, Deborah Fahy. 'Domestic Work'. *General Labour History of Africa. Workers, Employers and Governments, 20th–21st Centuries.* 301–332. Eds. Stefano Becllucci and Andreas Eckert. Exeter: 2019. Cf. Huws, Ursula. 'The reproduction of difference: gender and the global division of labour'. 1–10. *Work Organisation, Labour & Globalisation,* Vol. 6, no. 1, n.p.: 2012. Web. *Jstor.* https://www.jstor.org/stable/10.13169/workorgalaboglob.6.1.0001 (4 June 2021). Cf. Cobble, Dorothy Sue. 'The Promise and Peril of the New Global Labor History'. 99–107. *International Labor and Working-Class History,* Fall 2012, no. 82. Cambridge: 2012. Web. *Jstor.* https://www.jstor.org/stable/23391672 (4 June 2021). Cf. Vigna, Xavier et al. 'Gender history and labour history'. 176–203. *Clio. Women, Gender, History,* no. 38, Working women, working men. N. P.: 2013. Web. *Jstor.* https://www.jstor.org/stable/10.2307/26273601 (4 June 2021). Cf. Aitken, Robbie. 'Forgotten Histories: recovering the precarious lives of African servants in imperial Germany'. *Locating African European Studies. Interventions, Intersections, Conversations.* 139–150. Eds. Felipe Espinoza Garrido et al. London: 2020.

24 Cf. Cooper, Frederick. 'Von der Sklaverei in die Prekarität? Afrikanische Arbeitsgeschichte im Globalen Kontext'. *Re:work. Arbeit Global – Historische Rundgänge.* 4–29. Eds. Andreas Eckert and Felicitas Hentschke. Berlin and Boston: 2019, pp. 3–11.

rope, they tried to generate a better understanding of labour in the Global South. In doing so, labour historians consequently attempted to transcend not only the concept of wage labour as such, but also asked larger questions about what labour and work actually meant.[25]

The subsequent considerations of global labour historians largely echoed George Orwell's thoughts quoted at the very beginning of this study. The fundamental question was this: if labour was not necessarily wage labour, how could you possibly define labour? Hence, scholars reassessed labour by its alleged counterpart or rather complement: leisure. Perceived as the other side of the coin of labour, free-time activities and the innumerable and seemingly ever-increasing offerings of the consumer societies came to the limelight as forms of non-work. In this respect, not only current phenomena of mass consumerism in the Global North after WWII received recurring attention, but also its beginnings in the rapidly industrialising societies of the *fin du siècle.*[26] Discussing whether leisure and free time really were the opposite of wage labour, the question arose whether this approach was not too dichotomic and narrowly defined. Thus, even larger questions about labour, leisure and non-work were raised to scrutinise further what work was and how labour could be defined and by which parameters.[27] So far, there has not been a clear consensus about the definition of labour among historians. Therefore, the global history of labour should neither be regarded as a uniform new narrative nor as a new historical theory demonstrating how to pursue this kind of research. It rather aims at synthesising various examples of empirical research and is generally open to multiple academic interpretations.[28]

---

25 Cf. Eckert. 'Area Studies', pp. 156–173.

26 Cf. Bänziger, Peter-Paul. *Moderne als Erlebnis. Eine Geschichte der Konsum- und Arbeitsgesellschaft. 1840–1940.* Göttingen: 2020. Cf. Hentschke, Felicitas. 'Labour and Leisure in Global History. Summer Academy'. Cfp. 27 March 2018. *HSozKult.* Web. https://www.hsozkult.de/searching/id/event-86591?title=labour-and-leisureleisure-in-global-history-summer-academy&q=Labour%20and%20Leisure%20in%20Global%20History&sort=&fq=&total=39&recno=10&subType=event (12 March 2021). Cf. Burke, Peter. 'The Invention of Leisure in Early Modern Europe'. 136–150. *Past & Present,* no. 146. Oxford: 1995. *Jstor.* Web. https://www.jstor.org/stable/651154 (1 August 2018). Cf. Akyeampong, Emmanuel and Ambler, Charles. 'Leisure in African History. An Introduction'. 1–16. *The International Journal of African Historical Studies,* Vol. 35, no. 1. Boston: 2002. Web. *Jstor.* https://www.jstor.org/stable/3097363 (1 August 2018).

27 Cf. Genner, Julian et al. 'Muße und Arbeit'. Conference Report 12th–14th April 2018. *HSozKult.* Web. https://www.hsozkult.de/searching/id/tagungsberichte-7814?title=musse-und-arbeit&q=mu%C3%9Fe&page=2&sort=&fq=&total=163&recno=29&subType=fdkn (25 May 2021).

28 Cf. Re:work. *International Research Center. Work and Human Lifecycle in Global History.* Web. https://rework.huberlin.de/de/aktuelles.html. (21 July 2017). Cf. Eckert. 'Why all the fuss', pp. 5–9. Cf. Kocka, Jürgen. 'Arbeit im historischen Grundriss'. *Alltag, Erfahrung, Eigensinn. Historisch-anthropologische Erkundungen.* 445–457. Eds. Belinda Davis et al. Frankfurt o.M. and New York:

This general openness also includes fundamental questions about the inherent meaning of work, labour and employment. More precisely, the semantics of the terms 'work' and 'labour' have come under thorough scrutiny and must be reflected in any (global) history of labour. There must therefore be some reflection about the terms of 'labour' and 'work'. Already shimmering through George Orwell's reflections about work cited above, Hannah Arendt described 'work' as an activity that is pursued rather autonomously and for its own sake. In contrast to such a high degree of autonomy, 'labour' is restricted to those activities pursued to survive or to make a living. Although this rough division between 'labour' and 'work' is legitimate, it remains too vague for closer historical investigations. In their *Semantiken von Arbeit* (semantics of work), Thomas Sokoll, Jörn Leonhard and Willibald Steinmetz therefore advocate using the terms 'labour' and 'work' pragmatically. They therefore use the terms interchangeably, which is also done in this study.[29]

In addition, there are two other aspects to be observed, which are particularly important for the analysis of labour in colonial contexts. First of all, the fundamental understanding that the meanings of the terms 'labour' and 'work' may change in colonial contexts through the introduction of new labour regimes by the colonisers. Secondly, the insight that a genuine understanding of what labour is may be fundamentally different depending on the views of either the coloniser or the colonised. Julia Seibert has traced back how the meaning of the Swahili word *kazi* changed over the course of Belgian colonial rule in the region of Congolese Katanga between 1908 and 1960. Swahili is the most widespread language in East Africa, spoken from southern Somalia to northern Mozambique and from the shores of the Indian Ocean to the eastern parts of the Congo. Generally, *kazi* translates into both 'work' and 'labour' and still has the same meaning today. With nuances of meaning differing locally, especially in the Congolese region of Katanga, *kazi* primarily denotes wage labour in industrial contexts. In contrast to *kazi*, there is the verb *kulima*, which is related primarily to agricultural means of

2008, pp. 447–449. Cf. Linden, Marcel van der. 'The Promise and Challenges of Global Labor History'. *Global Histories of Work.* 25–48. Ed. Andreas Eckert. Berlin and Boston: 2016, p. 30.

29 Finally, Arendt uses the term 'action' to describe any voluntary activities pursued for or on behalf of the civil society. As the civil society is irrelevant to the present study it is left out here. Cf. Leonhard, Jörn and Steinmetz, Willibald. 'Von der Begriffsgeschichte zur historischen Semantik von 'Arbeit''. *Semantiken von Arbeit: Diachrone und vergleichende Perspektiven.* 9–59. Eds. Jörn Leonhard and Willibald Steinmetz. Cologne et al.: 2016, pp. 30–59. Cf. Sokoll, Thomas. 'Alteuropäisches Erbe, moderne Ausprägung und postmoderne Verwerfungen im Arbeitsbegriff'. *Semantiken von Arbeit: Diachrone und vergleichende Perspektiven.* 393–409. Eds. Jörn Leonhard and Willibald Steinmetz. Cologne et al.: 2016, pp. 393–397. Cf. Kocka. 'Arbeit', pp. 445–449.

production. As the imposition of wage labour, i.e. *kazi*, was the result of Belgian colonial labour regimes in the Congolese region of Katanga, Seibert traces back shifting meanings of *kazi* by analysing contexts of labour in Congolese mines throughout Belgian colonial rule (1908–1960). Around 1900, *kazi* described forms of coerced labour. Although the slow yet constant imposition of wage labour was a global process closely related to the establishment of capitalist modes of production, it was never a natural process. Instead, wage labour had to be introduced actively. This process was generally marked by conflicts, and the imposition of wage labour was most violent in colonial territories in the period between 1885 and 1960. Nevertheless, it was a very complex process that also included the introduction of more liberal forms of wage labour at the same time. With Katanga being very rich in natural resources and therefore constituting the most important industrial region of central Africa, both the Belgian colonial administration and the Belgian mining industries joined forces to maximise the profits of the region. Key to this undertaking was to stabilise the labour market. To make wage labour more attractive to the local population, the colonial state and the companies thus introduced incentives such as constant pay, company dwellings or medical care for those employed in the industrial sector from the 1920s onwards. These labour policies enhanced the workers' capacities to take an active role in the arrangement of employment relationships and working conditions. Despite numerous conflicts in such labour negotiations, the increasing power of Katanga's mine workers led to comparatively liberal wage labour conditions. These transitions with respect to labour conditions on the spot were also reflected in language and the meaning of the word *kazi*. While *kazi* was still associated with slavery and forced labour at the beginning of the twentieth century, it had fundamentally changed its meaning by the 1930s: *kazi* was increasingly associated with the appreciation of individual work performance and opportunities for upward mobility within the social order of the copper mining industry. Therefore, Katanga's concept of *kazi* still bears connotations of freedom and modernity today and has lost its original connotation of forced labour and slavery.[30]

Besides this semantic analysis of *kazi* in Belgian colonial Katanga, football provides for another illustrative example. It shows how blurry the line between labour and non-work may prove to be in colonial contexts. Like almost anywhere else in the world, football is one of the most popular sports on the African continent today. At the beginning of the twentieth century, however, the sport was

---

30 Cf. Seibert, Julia. 'Kazi. Konzepte, Praktiken und Semantiken von Lohnarbeit im kolonialen Kongo'. *Semantiken von Arbeit: Diachrone und vergleichende Perspektiven.* 209–223. Eds. Jörn Leonhard and Willibald Steinmetz. Cologne et al.: 2016, pp. 209–211, 223. Cf. Eckert. 'Why all the fuss', p. 18.

largely unknown in Africa. Emmanuel Akyeampong and Charles Ambler have analysed an incident that took place at the compound of the Rhodesian *Roan Antelope Mine* in 1932 when the company attempted to benevolently offer their staff leisure activities. This incident reveals a lot about clashing views on colonial labour:

> The compound manager [. . .] bemoaned the mine workers' lack of enthusiasm for the soccer and the drill teams organized by the mine management to occupy employees in their non-working hours. The manager showed particular irritation at the failure of the African workers to recognize 'leisure' when they saw or experienced it: 'they have the idea', he wrote, 'that whatever is required of them, whether it be an exhibition of Physical Drill or game of football, it is required of them solely for the amusements of the Bwanas [here: colonizers].' He continued incredulously: 'We have had several instances of natives having failed to turn up for a game of physical drill and putting forth the excuse that they did not get overtime pay for doing the 'work'.'[31]

In this incident, the attempt to privilege wage labour by means of after-work opportunities for leisure failed. Instead of making wage labour more agreeable to the local workforce, the mine workers in Rhodesia protested the unpaid 'extra work', which was solely a leisure activity in the colonisers' eyes. Both this example about conflicting views about work and leisure as well as that of the transforming semantics of *kazi* in Congolese Katanga show that there may be a thin line between labour, leisure and non-work. Furthermore, they reveal that the parameters that constitute the meaning of labour are fundamentally dependent on the context and on all protagonists involved in any labour relationship. Hence, an analysis of labour must always be an analysis of one particular site of work that takes the agency of all individuals involved in the process of labour into account. Historically speaking, research on labour should focus on individual case studies that seek to include the perspective on the micro-level as well in general.[32] In this respect, the buzzword for historical investigation has long been, and still is, 'agency'.

With historians having used agency predominantly as another cipher for any acts of resistance against slavery or colonialism, scholars criticising such a narrow understanding of agency remained unheard for a very long time.[33] In the

---

31 Roan Antelope Consolidated Mines (RACM), Monthly Compound Report, ZCCM, Box 10.7.10c. Qutd. in: Akyeampong and Ambler. 'Leisure in African History', p. 5. Generally, 'bwana' (Swahili) translates into 'sir'.

32 Cf. Sokoll. 'Alteuropäisches Erbe', pp. 393–409. Cf. Kocka. 'Arbeit', pp. 453–455.

33 Cf. Johnson, Walter. 'On Agency'. 113–124. *Journal of Social History*, vol. 37, no. 1. Oxford: 2003. A very recent example on reading (largely African) agency overwhelmingly as resistance cf. Daughton, J.P. *In the Forest of No Joy. The Congo-Océan Railroad and the Tragedy of French Colonialism.* New York: 2021, pp. 172–213. For a broader application of (African) agency cf. Lawrence, Benjamin N. et al. (Eds.). *Intermediaries, Interpreters, and Clerks. African Employees in the Making of Colonial Africa.* Wisconsin: 2006. Cf. Iliffe, John (Ed.). *Modern Tanzanians. A Volume of Biographies.* Dar es Salaam: 1973. Cf. Auslander, Leora. 'Accommodation, Resistance, and *Eigensinn.*

background of the rise of global history, this has changed to a certain degree. A growing number of historians have been insisting on an understanding of agency beyond mere acts of resistance on the part of the enslaved, colonised or subalterns. Lynn M. Thomas, for example, highlights the fact that the genuine question for a historian is not to reveal whether any individual under investigation possessed agency or not. Thomas rather takes the general capacity for agency as a foundational assumption, "while posing the *form, scale and scope* of that capacity and those forces as research questions to investigate."[34] Naturally, this understanding of agency may include acts of resistance against colonial rule, for example. But historical investigation has not only to reveal that there was agency to acts of resistance. It must go beyond to the questions of how such resistance was carried out in detail and under which circumstances. Naturally, an understanding of agency beyond resistance also includes forms of cooperation or collaboration between the colonised and the colonisers, for instance. Of course, the capacities to agency vary greatly according to the circumstances. But if any individual has at least "some capacity to shape the world around [him or her]",[35] there is no doubt that an individual has not only agency to resistance, but also to cooperation or collaboration. Historical research therefore must examine the circumstances and parameters in which any form of agency is exerted and investigate why, when and how an individual chooses a specific action from the broad spectrum ranging from resistance to collaboration and beyond. For this global history of labour, adopting both this broader understanding of agency and the central threads of global labour history has numerous consequences.

First of all, this research project chooses to investigate the global history of labour by examining three sites of work in the colony of German East Africa: the construction sites of the *Central Railway* (1905–1916), the *Otto* cotton plantation near Kilossa (ca. 1907–1916) and the palaeontological Tendaguru Expedition between ca. 1909–1911. Each of these places of labour had dynamics of its own and followed its own logics. At all three sites of work, labour was not only prone to various forms of coercion, but it was also the result of constant negotiations of all protagonists involved in the process of work. Secondly, the overall setting of each work site must be examined thoroughly as it is the background setting for any agency on the part of all those involved in labour. Generally, the topography of

Évolués and Sapeurs between Africa and Europe'. Alltag, Erfahrung, Eigensinn. Historisch-anthropologische Erkundungen. 205–217. Eds. Belinda Davis et al. Frankfurt o.M. and New York: 2008.

34 Thomas, Lynn M. 'Historicising Agency'. 234–239. *Gender & History,* vol. 28, no. 2. Oxford: 2016, p. 235.

35 Thomas. 'Historicising Agency', p. 325.

each workplace underpins the colonsers' claim to control any events on the spot. If transgressions to this colonial rule *en miniature*[36] occur, the clash between claim and reality becomes obvious. If no transgressions occur, one must wonder why this is the case. Thirdly, in any case the capacities for action of the individual protagonists of labour must be considered, asking the question why an individual carries out a specific action of resistance, cooperation, collaboration, or anything else. Naturally, an individual does not act in a vacuum. He or she always has to adjust his or her actions not only to the (societal) circumstances, but also to his fellow human beings. Any action is therefore always the result of a complex process also valid in any context of labour. Thus, the inter-individual relationships of all protagonists involved in each work site under investigation must be examined closely. All in all, decent investigation in global labour history demands the usage of macro- and micro-perspectives to grasp the multifaceted phenomenon of work.[37]

1.2 Current State of Research

The three places of work under investigation have been selected for the following reasons. Each of them has been central to studies investigating the history of German East Africa. At the same time, studies on them have neglected decisive aspects as far as the history of labour is concerned. This holds true not only for the historiography on German colonialism in general, but also for works of global history. Although imperial infrastructures and railway building have featured prominently in global and colonial historiography, colonial railways have predominantly been perceived as 'tools of empire' that were anonymously established in a colony. In existent research, it mostly appears that they were built by invisible hands and the existing studies on colonial infrastructures neglect those people who actually made the infrastructure become a reality.[38] As far as labour at the construction sites of the *Central Railway* in German East Africa is concerned, if at all, two groups of people were considered. Recently, Sebastian Beese has investigated the roles of Euro-

36 Cf. Stoyke, Michael. 'Suche nach einem Europa *en miniature:* Chinas Städte in den Augen europäischer Reisender um 1900'. *Welt-Räume. Geschichte, Geographie und Globalisierung seit 1900.* 147–174. Eds. Iris Schröder and Sabine Höhler. Frankfurt o.M. and New York: 2005.

37 Cf. Sokoll. 'Alteuropäisches Erbe', p. 401.

38 Cf. Headrick, Daniel R. *The Tools of Empire. Technology and European Imperialism in the Nineteenth Century.* New York and Oxford: 1981. Cf. Laak, Dirk van. *Imperiale Infrastruktur. Deutsche Planungen für eine Erschließung Afrikas 1880 bis 1960.* Paderborn et al.: 2004. A recent exception is Daughton's study on the *Congo-Océan Railroad* built after WWI in French colonial Congo. Cf. Daughton. *In the Forest of No Joy.*

pean railway experts like engineers, while the remaining research has investigated the role of African men and women in charge of manual railway construction. Other protagonists of labour involved in the construction process working every day with the African workforce have largely been ignored. As research on business history in Africa before WWI is still scarce in general,[39] little is also known about the railway construction companies and their engineering personnel working and interacting with other personnel on the spot. In this respect, the decisive presence of Indian artisans and South(-East) European railway sub-contractors or rather labour recruiters, who were all decisive in building the railway, has largely been overlooked. Likewise, apart from the engineers, whether persons occupied at the railway were regarded as skilled workers or not, and whether their skills influenced their standing in the context of colonial labour have generally not been considered. If there is research on these issues, it is still very much work in progress.[40]

---

39 Cf. Austin, Gareth. 'African Business History'. 141–158. Ed. John F. Wilson. *The Routledge Companion to Business History.* London: 2017, p. 145. Cf. Oestermann, Tristan. 'Review on: Samarin, William J. *The Black Man's Burden. African Colonial Labor on the Congo and Ubangi Rivers, 1880–1900.* New York: 2019'. *HSozKult.* 30 August 2021. Web. https://www.hsozkult.de/searching/id/reb-96367?title=w-j-samarin-the-black-man-s-burden&q=oestermann&sort=&fq=&total=21&recno=1&subType=reb (6 September 2021).

40 Cf. Koponen, Juhani. *Development for Exploitation. German Colonial Policies in Mainland Tanzania, 1884–1914.* Helsinki and Hamburg: 1994, pp. 297–314, 410–413. Cf. Tetzlaff, Rainer. *Koloniale Entwicklung und Ausbeutung. Wirtschafts- und Sozialgeschichte Deutsch-Ostafrikas 1885–1914.* Berlin: 1970, pp. 81–100. Cf. Reichart-Burikukiye, Marianne. *Gari la Moshi – Modernität und Mobilität. Das Leben mit der Eisenbahn in Deutsch-Ostafrika.* Münster: 2005, pp. 24–72. Cf. Biermann, Werner. *Tanganyika Railways – Carriers of Colonialism. An Account of Economic Indicators and Social Fragments.* Münster: 1995. Cf. Divall, Colin. 'Railway Imperialisms. Railway Nationalisms'. *Die Internationalität der Eisenbahn. 1850–1970.* 195–210. Eds. Monika Burri et al. Zürich: 2003. Cf. Hertsch, Florian M. and Mutlu, R. (Eds.). *Die Bagdadbahn. Ein Umriss deutsch-türkischer Beziehungen. Gesammelte Beiträge.* Hamburg: 2016. More nuanced and inspiring the latest approaches cf. Monson, Jamie. *Africa's Freedom Railway. How a Chinese Development Project changed Lives and Livelihoods in Tanzania.* Indiana: 2009. Cf. Panel "Railway Imperialism Reconsidered" of the Society for the History of Technology (SHOT) in Milan (Italy) in November 2019. Cf. "Changing Track. Redirecting Research on Colonial Railways. Workshop on Colonial Railways in Africa c. 1880–1960". *EUI Florence* (Online): 9 November 2020. Cf. Decker, Julio. 'Lines in the Sand. Railways and the archipelago of colonial territorialization in German Southwest Africa, 1897–1914'. 1–36. Web. *Sciencedirect.com.* https://doi.org/10.1016/j.jhg.2020.09.002 (15 March 2021). Cf. Kleinöder, Nina. 'A Place in the Sun'? German Rails and Sleepers in Colonial Railway Building in Africa, 1905 to 1914'. 1–23. *Zeitschrift für Unternehmensgeschichte,* 65, no. 1. Berlin: 2020. Cf. Beese, Sebastian. *Experten der Erschließung. Akteure der deutschen Kolonialtechnik in Afrika und Europa 1890–1943.* Paderborn: 2021. Cf. Todzi, Kim Sebastian. 'Colonial Capitalism in Action. The New Social and Economic History of German Colonialism'. *HSozKult.* 14 April 2021. Web. https://www.hsozkult.de/searching/id/event-97072?title=colonial-capitalism-in-action-the-new-social-and-economic-history-of-german-colonialism&q=colonial%20capitalism%20in%20action&sort=&fq=&total=139&recno=1&subType=event (31 May 2021).

Likewise, the *Otto* cotton plantation near Kilossa is not unknown in historiography on German colonialism. Moreover, it is especially Thaddeus Sunseri who has stressed the significance of German colonial cotton schemes in East Africa and highlighted large-scale plantations like *Otto's*. With Sunseri considering African labour and the workers' individual agency at such cotton plantations, he even touched upon the decisive role of labour recruiters providing for the workforce necessary in the colonial labour market. As a matter of fact, Sunseri's research largely remained within the boundaries of the German East African colony and has not addressed the typical questions asked by global (labour) history. Especially since Andrew Zimmerman's seminal work *Alabama in Africa* on the global dimension of colonial cotton schemes that linked cotton production of the southern US American states to German colonial Togo, and Sven Beckert's new history of global capitalism *Empire of Cotton*, it is not enough to remain within the boundaries of one single African colony when it comes to the history of cotton cultivation and textile production. As any history of global textile and cotton production has "given little space to labour",[41] the present study thus investigates labour at the *Otto* cotton plantation from a global perspective without neglecting decisive parameters on the spot. Furthermore, it reinvestigates the central role of the Indo-German plantation manager in Kilossa, Ranga Kaundinya, who was not only confronted with discriminatory discourses when at work, but also with profound management failures of his boss. Another issue concerns technological innovations intended to reduce manual African labour in Kilossa. Although *Otto* tried to cultivate the cotton plantation by huge steam ploughs, the attempt failed miserably. Thus, the skill of the African workforce remained decisive to grow and harvest this cash crop. Describing the mode of cotton plantation using African labour as 'the living machine', Kaundinya soon realised that this machine of manual African labour had defeated the modern engines of the steam ploughs.[42]

Labour features only little in research about the Tendaguru Expedition. While research about the palaeontological Tendaguru excavations has been widely no-

---

41 Riello, Giorgo. *Cotton: The Fabric that made the Modern World.* Cambridge: 2013, p. 11.

42 Cf. Sunseri, Thaddeus. *Vilimani. Labor Migration and rural Change in early colonial Tanzania.* Oxford: 2002. Cf. Bleifuß, Gerhard and Hergenröder, Gerhard. *Die "Otto-Plantage Kilossa" (1907–1914). Aufbau und Ende eines kolonialen Unternehmens in Deutsch-Ostafrika.* Wendlingen am Neckar: 1993. Cf. Beckert, Sven. *Empire of Cotton. A New History of Global Capitalism.* New York: 2015. Cf. Riello. *Cotton.* Cf. Zimmerman, Andrew. *Alabama in Africa. Booker T. Washington, The German Empire, and the Globalization of the New South.* Princeton: 2010. Cf. Robins, Johnathan E. *Cotton and Race Across the Atlantic. Britain, Africa, and America, 1900–1920.* Rochester: 2016. Cf. Powell, Jim. *Losing the Thread. Cotton, Liverpool, and the American Civil War.* Liverpool: 2021. Cf. Dejung, Christof. *Commodity Trading, Globalization and the Colonial World. Spinning the Web of the Global Market.* New York and London: 2018.

ticed by historians, this research has been rather situated in research fields on the history of colonial objects as well as in research on the history of science and imperialism. Regarding work, only one article explicitly deals with labour at the dinosaur fossil excavation sites. Examining visual sources, Mareike Vennen analysed how labour was captured by the view of the colonial camera and subsequently orchestrated to celebrate the industrious and well-organised excavation works. Particularly, East African fossil preparators and porters, who transported tons of petrified bones hundreds of kilometres from the Tendaguru Mountain to the coastal town of Lindi on the Indian Ocean, were staged in contemporary photography. Yet, there were also other profoundly skilled people working at the Tendaguru, whose roles have so far been neglected both in research on palaeontological excavation sites and in (colonial) history and who were indispensable for the success of the expedition. Although acknowledged in published and widely read books on the Tendaguru issued around 1912, the role of African labour has not been studied in detail. In this respect, two groups are of special interest. These are the personal servants working for the colonisers, such as the so-called *boys* who were especially in charge of housekeeping, as well as the East African chefs responsible for the daily meals of the Europeans. As there were generally only two German palaeontologists present at the Tendaguru, their personal servants were central for the smooth functioning of the excavations. Moreover, apart from the article by Vennen, the remaining literature on the Tendaguru Expedition was published only a few years after the millennium, and it therefore does not address the more recent questions raised by global (labour) history. Apart from such research on the excavations at the Tendaguru proper, several recent studies have been released that ascertained a widespread 'dinomania' which captured North American and European societies in the 'long nineteenth century'. The dimension of the West's longing for ever greater and more spectacular fossil finds all around the world must be included into research on labour at the Tendaguru Mountain, of course.[43] Taken together, the present study investigates global labour history by means of these three profoundly individual places of work, each with its own dynamics. Although all of them were

43 Cf. Vennen, Mareike. 'Arbeitsbilder – Bilderarbeit. Die Herstellung und Zirkulation von Fotografien der Tendaguru-Expedition'. *Dinosaurier Fragmente. Zur Geschichte der Tendaguru-Expedition und ihrer Objekte. 1906–2018.* 56–77. Eds. Ina Heumann et al. Göttingen: 2018. Cf. Vennen, Mareike. 'Träger-Arbeiten. Die Zirkulation kolonialer Dinge und Bilder der Tendaguru-Expedition (1909–1913)'. *Der Träger. Zu einer 'tragenden' Figur der Kolonialgeschichte.* 157–180. Eds. Sonja Malzner and Anne D. Peiter. Bielefeld: 2018. Cf. Maier, Gerhard. *African Dinosaurs unearthed. The Tendaguru Expeditions.* Indiana: 2003. Cf. Mogge, Winfried. *Wilhelm Branco (1844–1928). Geologe – Paläontologe – Darwinist. Eine Biographie.* Berlin: 2018, pp. 199–222. Cf. Rieppel, Lukas. *Assembling the Dinosaur. Fossil Hunters, Tycoons, and the Making of a Spectacle.* Harvard: 2019. Cf. Nieuwland, Ilja. *American Dinosaur Abroad. A Cultural History of Carnegie's Plaster Diplodocus.* Pittsburgh: 2019.

part of the 'colonial globality' taking place around 1900 (S. Conrad), each remained strongly dependent on local parameters. This field of tension between the local and the global set the stage for all the protagonists who together created the phenomenon of labour at each place of work.

The publication of handbooks generally indicates when historiography has reached a new state of research. Regarding global labour history, two works especially are fundamental: Hofmeester and van der Linden's *Handbook The Global History of Work*, and Bellucci and Eckert's *General Labour History of Africa.* While disagreeing about the historical applicability of the concept of 'globalisation', both handbooks nevertheless take a broad approach to labour. This approach includes consideration of, among others, forms of free and unfree labour, the military and police, crime and illegal work, sport, tourism and entertainment, entrepreneurship, international organisations, domestic work, and gender, as well as forms of labour protest and (trade union) activism, and micro- versus macro-perspectives.[44] Given this vast research scope, it is of course impossible to assess the entire state of research of all research subjects and all areas of interest to global labour history. Besides the larger questions of global labour history outlined above, I therefore first concentrate on the state of research regarding labour and work in German colonial East Africa. Subsequently, I outline the existent studies that have been done on the three places of work under investigation, checking whether they had anything to say about labour at the (construction sites of the) *Central Railway*, the *Otto* plantation in Kilossa and the Tendaguru Expedition.

In old-established works of German colonial history, labour and work usually feature as a sub-chapter. Generally, these works assess the colonial administration's labour policies and their implementation. Themes such as direct and indirect policies of forced labour on the part of the German colonial administration feature prominently. Thus, convict labour during warfare, e.g. during the Maji Maji War 1905–1908 or the introduction of taxation or labour card systems to provide indirect incentives compelling the East African population to work for the colonisers are fundamental to this research. Furthermore, these studies focus on legal reforms of labour policies or labour as a component of general colonial economic policies.[45] In regards to both, the most comprehensive work on German

44 Cf. Hofmeester and van der Linden. 'Introduction', pp. 1–12. Cf. Cooper. 'The 'Labour Question'', pp. 617–623. Cf. Bellucci and Eckert. 'The 'Labour Question'', pp 1–16.

45 Cf. Gründer, Horst. *Geschichte der deutschen Kolonien.* Paderborn: 2004, pp. 157–160. Schinzinger, Francesca. *Die Kolonien und das Deutsche Reich. Die wirtschaftliche Bedeutung der deutschen Besitzungen in Übersee.* Stuttgart: 1984, pp. 83–94. Cf. Iliffe, John. *Tanganyika under German Rule. 1905–1912.* Cambridge: 1969, pp. 49–81, 166–200. In his *A Modern History of Tanganyika,* Iliffe generally puts the results of his study of the German colonial period in a broader frame-

colonial policies in East Africa certainly is Juhani Koponen's *Development for Exploitation,* which deconstructed the development and progress paradigms towards 'Third World' Tanzania. In Koponen's view, the concept of (wage) labour is exported to the German colony to integrate the latter into the world market. Primarily serving heterogeneous German economic interests, Koponen names this process 'the creation of labour'. It consists largely of the colonial state's pursuing active labour policies and creating a modern labour market. Thereby, besides economic incentives, direct forms of forced labour such as convict or compulsory labour, as well as indirect forms of forced labour, such as taxation, were integral.[46] Written thirty years ago, Koponen's research approach and the corresponding discourses around the 'development paradigms' are certainly not up to date. His work is nevertheless extensive and covers a wide range of colonial policies on labour and thus acquires almost the status of a handbook on German colonial policies in East Africa. Remarkably, it also seems that Koponen's concluding thoughts on the "indirect and complex [. . .] links between colonialism and capitalism" that were "mediated through the colonial state" and its "creation of labour" may well be connected to the latest discussions around the (new) history of global capitalism.[47] Especially connected to global labour history, various questions about the manifold forms of free and unfree labour in relation to the global expansion of capitalism are currently being reassessed; not least regarding labour regimes in (colonial) Africa.[48]

---

work of social and economic history in mainland Tanzania from 1800 to Tanganyikan independence in 1961. On this occasion however, he highlights the role of the African population. Exemplifying several population groups like the Wanjamwezi, he illustrates their integration to the colonial labour market. Cf. Iliffe, John. *A Modern History of Tanganyika.* Cambridge: 1979, pp. 135–162. Cf. Tetzlaff. *Koloniale Entwicklung,* pp. 193–279.

46 Cf. Koponen. *Development,* pp. 321–437.

47 Koponen. *Development,* p. 665, cf. pp. 663–677.

48 For a summarising discussion on the relationship of global labour history and the history of capitalism cf. Edwards, Andrew David et al. (Eds.). 'Capitalism in Global History'. E1-e32. *Past and Present,* vol. 249, Issue 1, November. Oxford: 2020. Web. https://academic.oup.com/past/article/249/1/e1/6007772 (15 May 2023). Cf. Kocka, Jürgen. 'Introduction'. *Capitalism. The Reemergence of a Historical Concept.* 1–12. Eds. Jürgen Kocka and Marcel van der Linden. London et al.: 2016. Cf. Komlosy, Andrea. 'Work and Labor Relations'. *Capitalism. The Reemergence of a Historical Concept.* 33–70. Eds. Jürgen Kocka and Marcel van der Linden. London et al.: 2016. Cf. Eckert, Andreas. 'Capitalism and Labor in Sub-Sahara Africa'. *Capitalism. The Reemergence of a Historical Concept.* 165–186. Eds. Jürgen Kocka and Marcel van der Linden. London et al.: 2016. Cf. Austin, Gareth. 'The Return of Capitalism as a Concept'. *Capitalism. The Reemergence of a Historical Concept.* 207–234. Eds. Jürgen Kocka and Marcel van der Linden. London et al.: 2016. Cf. Beckert, Sven. 'The New History of Capitalism'. *Capitalism. The Reemergence of a Historical Concept.* 235–250. Eds. Jürgen Kocka and Marcel van der Linden. London et al.: 2016. Cf. Linden, Marcel

Overwhelmingly ignored by recent studies on German colonial East Africa have been regional studies. This is contrary to their value, as especially Norbert Aas' work investigates the economy and East African workers in the colony's south. It is particularly revealing regarding the general context of labour regarding the Tendaguru Expedition, as the palaeontological excavations took place in the southern region of *Lindi*.[49] The African workers' legal status in the context of labour is illustrated by the works of Schröder, Aas and Sippel.[50] With respect to the African workers' recruitment and their relationship as (forced) labourers towards European settlers, Söldenwagner provides some insights besides Aas and Sunseri.[51] A few passages of Horst Gründer's works deal with (forced) workers at Protestant and Catholic missions, while Rebekka Habermas rightly demanded to include the history of Christian missions in global history and to stress the perspectives and actions of the colonised populations involved in the Christian missions. This applies to mission pupils or members of the Christian churches who worked on the construction sites of the *Central Railway*, for instance.[52]

For the interconnectedness of the ideology of 'educating to work' in the German *Reich* and its colonies, Sebastian Conrad's research has induced scholarly debates. Although it is yet "far from clear whether the radicalization of the labour

---

van der. 'Final Thoughts'. *Capitalism. The Reemergence of a Historical Concept.* 251–266. Eds. Jürgen Kocka and Marcel van der Linden. London et al.: 2016.

49 Cf. Aas, Norbert. *Koloniale Entwicklung im Bezirksamt Lindi (Deutsch-Ostafrika): Deutsche Erwartungen und Regionale Wirklichkeit.* Bayreuth: 1989. Cf. Arnold, Bernd. *Steuer und Lohnarbeit im Südwesten von Deutsch-Ostafrika 1891–1916.* Münster and Hamburg: 1994.

50 Cf. Aas, Norbert and Sippel, Harald. *Koloniale Konflikte im Alltag. Eine rechtshistorische Untersuchung der Auseinandersetzungen des Siedlers Heinrich Langkopp mit der Kolonialverwaltung in Deutsch-Ostafrika und dem Reichsentschädigungsamt in Berlin (1910–1929).* Bayreuth: 1997, pp. 29–71. Cf. Schröder, Peter, J. *Gesetzgebung und "Arbeiterfrage" in den Kolonien. Das Arbeitsrecht in den Schutzgebieten des Deutschen Reiches.* Berlin: 2006, pp. 609–613. Cf. Sippel, Harald. '"Wie erzieht man am besten den Neger zur Plantagen-Arbeit?" Die Ideologie der Arbeitserziehung und ihre rechtliche Umsetzung in der Kolonie Deutsch-Ostafrika'. *Arbeit in Afrika.* 311–333. Eds. Kurt Beck and Gerd Spittler. Hamburg: 1996. Cf. Heyden, Ulrich van der and Becher, Jürgen (Eds.). *Mission und Gewalt. Der christliche Umgang mit Gewalt und die Ausbreitung des Christentums in Afrika und Asien in der Zeit von 1792 bis 1918/19.* Stuttgart: 2000. For colonial law and African agency when at court cf. Schaper, Ulrike. *Koloniale Verhandlungen. Gerichtsbarkeit, Verwaltung und Herrschaft in Kamerun, 1884–1916.* Frankfurt o.M. and New York: 2012, pp. 205–227. Cf. Habermas, Rebekka. *Skandal in Togo. Ein Kapitel deutscher Kolonialherrschaft.* Frankfurt o.M.: 2016.

51 Cf. Söldenwagner, Philippa. *Spaces of Negotiation. European Settlement and Settlers in German East Africa. 1900–1914.* Munich: 2006, pp. 147–206. Cf. Aas. *Koloniale Konflikte.*

52 Cf. Gründer, Horst. *Christliche Mission und deutscher Imperialismus. Eine politische Geschichte ihrer Beziehungen während der deutschen Kolonialzeit (1884–1914) unter besonderer Berücksichtigung Afrikas und Chinas.* Paderborn: 1984, pp. 239–254. Cf. Habermas, Rebekka and Hölzl, Richard (Eds.). *Mission Global. Eine Verflechtungsgeschichte seit dem 19. Jahrhundert.* Cologne et al.: 2014.

discourse in Germany has anything to do with colonial experiences and practices",[53] Conrad takes the view that the godlike status of work in German society at the *fin du siècle* led to discourses demanding forced labour in Germany and in East Africa, and vice versa.[54] Building largely on Conrad's insights and further discourse analysis, Minu Hashemi Yekani has recently reinvestigated labour in German East Africa by taking a closer look at Indian and (southeast) Asian indentured labourers at colonial plantations, on discourses about work and Islam in colonial schools and on destitute middle class Central Europeans whom Yekani described as precarious whites.[55] Like Philippa Söldenwagner, Yekani emphasised by her concept of 'precarious whites' that the colonisers were not a homogeneous group, but a society with various gradations. The same applies to the colonised populations, of course, and Yekani also stresses that there were special discourses directed against Indian or Chinese workers in German East Africa, for example.[56]

The fact that German colonial society in general and the colonial administration in particular was heterogeneous is decisive for analysing labour at all three places of work under investigation herein. As not only global but also social and economic history are rediscovering their interest in infrastructure, this applies first to the construction of the *Central Railway* in German East Africa between ca. 1905 and 1916. Deconstructing colonial infrastructure as mere 'Tools of Empire', historians focus on various individual protagonists and groups involved in such large-scale infrastructure construction processes. In the first place, this focus needs to consider the railway construction companies and the banks financing such large-scale endeavours.[57] In German East Africa, this was the company of *Philipp Holz-*

53 Eckert. 'Why all the fuss', p. 17.

54 Cf. Conrad. *Globalisation*, pp. 77–143. Connected to Conrad's ideas but widening the approach cf. Axster, Felix and Lelle, Nikolas (Eds.). *«Deutsche Arbeit». Kritische Perspektiven auf ein ideologisches Selbstbild.* Göttingen: 2018.

55 Cf. Yekani, Minu Hashemi. *Koloniale Arbeit, Rassismus, Migration und Herrschaft in Tansania (1885–1914).* Frankfurt o.M. and New York: 2019. Yekani's insights about indentured labour and the colonial school system largely correspond with Koponen's. *Development*, pp. 321–365. The same applies for colonial schools; her insights largely correspond with Krause's cf. Krause, Ingo Till. *"Koloniale Schuldlüge"? Die Schulpolitik in den afrikanischen Kolonien Deutschlands und Britanniens im Vergleich.* Hamburg: 2007, pp. 66–99. Cf. Yekani, Minu Hashemi. '"Inder und Chinesen werden unsere Kolonie nicht in die Höhe bringen". Arbeit, Klima und der 'Rasse'-Diskurs in Tansania (1885–1914)'. 209–225. Eds. Felix Axster and Nikolas Lelle. *«Deutsche Arbeit». Kritische Perspektiven auf ein ideologisches Selbstbild.* Göttingen: 2018.

56 Cf. Söldenwagner. *Spaces*, pp. 53–69, 207–242.

57 Cf. Headrick. *The Tools of Empire.* Cf. Biermann. *Tanganyika Railways.* Cf. Divall. 'Railway Imperialisms', pp. 195–210. Cf. Hertsch. and Mutlu (Eds.). *Die Bagdadbahn.* Cf. Monson. *Africa's Freedom Railway.* Cf. Panel "Railway Imperialism Reconsidered". Cf. "Changing Track." Cf. Decker. 'Lines in the Sand'. Cf. Kleinöder. '"A Place in the Sun"?' Cf. Todzi. 'Colonial Capitalism in Action'.

mann from Frankfurt on Main, which was, under the umbrella of the *Ostafrikanische Eisenbahngesellschaft* (*OAEG*), the company in charge of planning and carrying out railway construction on the spot. One of the large-scale infrastructure's most prominent perpetrators and largest financial player was the *Deutsche Bank*, which had already been involved in infrastructural planning work in German East Africa since ca. 1900. Previously and simultaneously, the *Deutsche Bank* financed the famous *Bagdadbahn* in the Ottoman Empire, which was likewise constructed by *Philipp Holzmann*. Both the construction company and the bank from Frankfurt had also been involved in various other infrastructure projects in the Americas, Africa and Asia. With business history in (colonial) Africa only scarcely investigated,[58] general research on these companies focussed either on a broader audience or followed classic narratives of business history that focussed on individual companies or banks, neglecting their impact on their colonial fields of activities or their connection to the (new) history of capitalism.[59]

With social and economic historians rediscovering their interest in German colonialism especially with respect to railways,[60] historians have still disregarded the central role of outsourcing in the colonial tracks' construction process. This is in

---

58 Cf. Austin. 'African Business History'. Cf. Oestermann. 'Review on: Samarin, William J'. In Daughton's work, the decisive role of the construction company *Société de Construction des Batignolles* remains largely in the background and its stakeholders remain overwhelmingly anonymous. Instead, Daughton focusses on men, who were central for French colonialism or its governmental administrations like Pierre Savorgnan de Brazza or "Governor-General Raphaël Antonetti [. . .] who built it [the railway]" and local governmental administrators like Georges Pacha. Daughton. *In the Forest of No Joy*, p. 57, cf. 23–92.

59 Cf. Franzke, Jürgen (Ed.). *Bagdad- und Hedjazbahn. Deutsche Eisenbahngeschichte im Vorderen Orient.* Nuremberg: 2003. Cf. Pohl, Manfred. *Von Stambul nach Bagdad. Die Geschichte einer berühmten Eisenbahn.* Munich: 1999. Cf. Rösser, Michael. 'Transimperiale Infrastruktur? Personal, Unternehmer und Arbeit beim Bau der Zentralbahn in Deutsch-Ostafrika'. *Moderne Transimperialitäten. Rivalitäten, Kontakte, Wetteifer.* 274–289. Eds. Laurent Dedryvère et al. Berlin: 2021. Cf. Rösser, Michael. '"*Shenzi Ulaya*". Deutsch griechische Verflechtungen von der Bagdadbahn zum kolonialen Deutsch-Ostafrika'. *Online-Compedium der deutsch-griechischen Verflechtungen.* Zentrum Modernes Griechenland der Freien Universität Berlin: 02 March 2022. Web. https://comdeg.eu/compendium/essay/109893/. (02 March 2022). Also published in Greek as '«Shenzi Ulaya» — Ελληνογερμανικές Διασταυρώσεις: Από τον Σιδηρόδρομο της Βαγδάτης στην Αποικία της Γερμανικής Ανατολικής Αφρικής'. *Online-Compedium der deutsch-griechischen Verflechtungen.* Zentrum Modernes Griechenland der Freien Universität Berlin: 02 March 2022. Web. https://comdeg.eu/el/compendium/essay/109893/ (02 March 2022). Cf. Pohl, Manfred. *Philipp Holzmann. Geschichte eines Bauunternehmens. 1849–1999.* Munich: 1999, pp. 81–140. Cf. Bähr, Johannes et al. *MAN. The History of a German Industrial Enterprise.* Munich: 2009. Cf. Plumpe, Werner et al. *Deutsche Bank. Die globale Hausbank 1870–2020.* Berlin: 2020, pp. 79–164. Cf. Gall, Lothar et al. *Die Deutsche Bank. 1870–1995.* Munich: 1995, pp. 52–82.

60 Cf. Kleinöder. ' "A Place in the Sun"?'. Cf. Todzi. 'Colonial Capitalism in Action'.

stark contrast to the fact that outsourcing is one of the central elements of capitalism to lower costs and to externalise liabilities that might apply in any business operation.[61] Indispensable for both prestigious infrastructural projects – the *Bagdadbahn* in the Ottoman Empire and the *Central Railway* in German East Africa – were first and foremost South(-East) European sub-contractors, who not only carried out construction work as such. They also recruited the largest share of the East African workforce necessary to build the *Central Railway* in the German colony. In addition, they occupied a conflict-laden intermediate position in the colonial society of German East Africa as the European population was very heterogeneous. Divisions amongst the colonisers with each other had three major fault lines. These were, firstly, class and standard of living; secondly, nationality; and thirdly, discourses about race. Often these three categories intersected. According to the German colonial discourses dominating German East Africa, citizens of the German *Reich* generally regarded themselves as not only superior to the African populations, but also looked down on white people who were not genuine *Reichsdeutsche,* such as several Boer or Russian-German families who had migrated to the German colony along the Indian Ocean. In this respect, both Yekani and Söldenwagner also make short references to the role of South(-East) Europeans, and especially Greek residents in German East Africa, but only treat them as a sideshows.[62] Yet, these South(-East) European railway sub-contractors and labour recruiters, especially Greek sub-contractors, were judged as *shenzi ulaya* ('white negroes').[63] In addition, their role was decisive as far as labour is concerned. Either as railway sub-contractors or free-lance labour recruiters, Greeks, especially, were indispensable players not only for railway construction but also for the entire colonial labour market. Investigating their

61 Cf. Komlosy. 'Work and Labor', pp. 39–63. Cf. Grazia, Victoria de. 'The Crisis of Hyper-Consumerism: Capitalism's Latest Forward Lurch'. *Capitalism. The Reemergence of a Historical Concept.* 71–106. Eds. Jürgen Kocka and Marcel van der Linden. London et al.: 2016, pp. 80–96.
62 Cf. Söldenwagner. *Spaces,* pp. 53–69, 207–242. Cf. Yekani. *Koloniale Arbeit,* pp. 197–264. Cf. Dejung, Christof et al. 'Worlds of the Bourgeoisie'. *The Global Bourgeoisie. The Rise of the Middle Classes in the Age of Empire.* 1–40. Eds. Christof Dejung et al. Princeton: 2019. Cf. Hunter, Emma. 'Modernity, Print Media, and the Middle Class in Colonial East Africa'. *The Global Bourgeoisie. The Rise of the Middle Classes in the Age of Empire.* 105–122. Eds. Christof Dejung et al. Princeton: 2019. Cf. Dejung, Christof. 'From Global Civilizing Missions to Racial Warfare: Class Conflicts and the Representations of the Colonial World in European Middle-Class Thought'. *The Global Bourgeoisie. The Rise of the Middle Classes in the Age of Empire.* 251–272. Eds. Christof Dejung et al. Princeton: 2019. Cf. Drayton, Richard. 'Race, Culture and Class: European Hegemony and Global Class Formation, circa 1800–1950'. *The Global Bourgeoisie. The Rise of the Middle Classes in the Age of Empire.* 339–358. Eds. Christof Dejung et al. Princeton: 2019.
63 Cf. Rösser, Michael. *'Shenzi Ulaya'.* On white subalternity cf. Fischer-Tiné, Harald. *'Low and Licentious Europeans'. Race, Class and "White Subalternity" in Colonial India.* New Delhi: 2009. Cf. Ignatiev, Noel. *How the Irish Became White.* New York and London: 2012.

role illuminates another recent field of research about the history of work: the history of labour intermediation. Especially because the history of labour intermediation has primarily focussed on the Global North, asking larger questions about Greek railway sub-contractors and labour recruiters in German East Africa contributes to a better understanding of global labour history and the workings of 'colonial capitalism in action'.[64] The Greek role in global labour history is especially relevant, because the latest publications about the global history of labour have considered the Ottoman Empire and South-East Europe, but neglected Greek involvement in general, and in (East) Africa in particular. The same applies to historians of South-East Europe who have included global approaches and colonialism into their research, but generally neglected the Greek perspective. Overwhelmingly, historiography on Greece still focusses on the history of the nation state itself, or on the Greek diasporas especially in North America emerging in the late nineteenth century.[65]

---

64 Cf. Wadauer, Sigrid et al. 'Introduction: Finding Work and Organizing Placement in the Nineteenth and Twentieth Centuries'. *The History of Labour Intermediation. Institutions and Finding Employment in the Nineteenth and Early Twentieth Centuries.* 1–22. Eds. Sigrid Wadauer et al. New York and Oxford: 2015. Cf. Wadauer, Sigrid et al. 'Concluding Remarks'. *The History of Labour Intermediation. Institutions and Finding Employment in the Nineteenth and Early Twentieth Centuries.* 415–420. Eds. Sigrid Wadauer et al. New York and Oxford: 2015. Exception to the dominance of the Global North cf. Mishra, Amit Kumar. 'Sardars, Kanganies and Maistries: Intermediaries in the Indian Labour Diaspora during the Colonial Period'. *The History of Labour Intermediation. Institutions and Finding Employment in the Nineteenth and Early Twentieth Centuries.* 368–387. Eds. Sigrid Wadauer et al. New York and Oxford: 2015. Cf. O'Donnell, Anthony. 'Organizing the Labour Market in a Liberal Welfare State: The Origins of the Public Employment Service in Australia'. *The History of Labour Intermediation. Institutions and Finding Employment in the Nineteenth and Early Twentieth Centuries.* 388–414. Eds. Sigrid Wadauer et al. New York and Oxford: 2015. Cf. Sunseri, Thaddeus. 'Labour Migration in Colonial Tanzania and the Hegemony of South African Historiography'. 581–598. *African Affairs*, Vol. 95, no. 381. Oxford: 1996. Web. *Jstor.* http://www.jstor.org/stable/723445 (11 April 2018), pp. 593–598. Cf. Hill, M.F. *Permanent Way. Vol II. The Story of the Tanganyika Railways.* Nairobi: 1957, pp. 77–90.

65 Cf. Papastefanaki, Leda and Kabadayi, Erden M. (Eds.). *Working in Greece and Turkey. A Comparative Labour History from Empires to Nation States, 1840–1940.* New York and Oxford: 2020. Cf. Papastefanaki, Leda and Potamianos, Nikos (Eds.). *Labour History in the Semi-periphery. Southern Europe, 19th-20th centuries.* Berlin and Boston: 2021. Cf. Lockman, Zachary (Ed.). *Workers and the Working Classes in the Middle East: struggles, histories, historiographies.* Albany (NY): 1994. Cf. Calic, Marie-Janine. *Südosteuropa. Weltgeschichte einer Region.* Munich: 2016. Cf. Brunnbauer, Ulf and Buchenau, Klaus. *Geschichte Südosteuropas.* Stuttgart: 2018, pp. 13–36, 108–230. Cf. Rösser. *'Shenzi Ulaya'.* Cf. Kaloudis, George. *Modern Greece and the Diaspora Greeks in the United States.* Lexington: 2018. Cf. Gallant, Thomas W. *Modern Greece. From the War of Independence to the Present.* London: 2016. Cf. Frangos, Stavros K. *Greeks in Michigan.* Michigan: 2004. For the Greek Diaspora cf. Clogg, Richard (Ed.). *The Greek Diaspora in the Twentieth Century.* Basingstoke:

Furthermore, there is another group of protagonists involved in railway construction in German East Africa that has not received sufficient historical attention yet. Regarding colonial labour in general, Indians have played a pivotal role as indentured labourers on plantations all around the globe or as railway workers constructing the *Uganda Railway*, for instance.[66] However, their role as skilled workers who were indispensable to the construction of German East Africa's *Central Railway* has not been considered in any detail. Working especially as carpenters and smiths at the construction sites or as clerks in the offices of the railway companies, their involvement has either been treated as a sideshow or even denied by old-established works on German colonial history.[67] Moreover, skilled labour was not only decisive regarding Indians; skill also mattered for other groups involved in railway construction. The East Africans themselves comprised the majority of people involved in railway construction in the German colony, and they actively shaped their working environments, of course. Although there are studies that acknowledge the African role in labour at the *Central Railway*, they generally disregarded the Africans' relationship to the great variety of other stakeholders of labour in the colonial context of German East Africa. Usually, the East African perspective on work has been analysed only in relation to actions or legislation of the colonial administration. In contrast, their relationship to (South-East) European railway sub-contractors, for example, has not been considered. Furthermore, historical research has generally limited its focus to published or printed sources in this respect.[68]

2001. Cf. Tziovas, Dimitris (Ed.). *Greek Diaspora and Migration Since 1700. Society, Politics and Culture.* Ashgate: 2009.

66 Cf. Behal and Linden (Eds.). *Coolies, Capital, and Colonialism.* Cf. Yekani. *Koloniale Arbeit,* pp. 44–50. Cf. Yekani. 'Inder und Chinesen'. Cf. Hill, M.F. *Permanent Way. The story of the Kenya and Uganda railway, being the official history of the development of the transport system in Kenya and Uganda.* Nairobi: 1976, pp. 141–246. Cf. Mangat, J.S. *A History of the Asians in East Africa c. 1886 to 1945.* Oxford: 1969, pp. 1–96.

67 Cf. Reichart. *Gari,* p. 66. Cf. Tezlaff. *Koloniale Entwicklung,* pp. 88. Cf. Hill. *Permanent Way. Vol. II,* pp. 57–108.

68 Cf. Sunseri, Thaddeus. '"Dispersing the Fields": Railway Labor and Rural Change in Early Colonial Tanzania'. 558–583. *Canadian Journal of African Studies/Revue Canadienne des Études Africaines,* vol. 32, no. 3. N.P.: 1998. Web. https://www.jstor.org/stable/pdf/486328.pdf?refreqid=excelsior%3A219c27ca837ae53f96b249dce27189f7 (20 June 2018), pp. 558–565. Cf. Sunseri. 'Labour Migration'. Cf. Sunseri, Thaddeus. *Vilimani.* Cf. Reichart. *Gari.* Cf. Tetzlaff. *Koloniale Entwicklung,* pp. 143–279. Cf. Koponen. *Development,* pp. 321–440. Cf. Iliffe. *Tanganyika under German Rule,* pp. 66–108, 134–139, 203. Cf. Iliffe. *A Modern History,* esp. pp. 41–163. Cf. Gottberg, Achim. *Unyamwesi. Quellensammlung und Geschichte.* Berlin: 1971, pp. 69–92.

Skill also mattered at the *Otto* cotton plantation near Kilossa. At this large-scale plantation, the southwest German company *Otto* attempted to follow the topical call for German cotton autarky around 1900. Failing to cultivate the cotton monocultures by modern steam ploughs intended to save labour costs, *Otto* consequently remained dependent on the manual labour of the East African workforce. Although there are some studies about the *Otto* plantation and labour, they have several shortcomings. They are either limited in scope or neglect the aspect of the Pietist global company networks of *Otto*. Moreover, they disregard the overall global dimension of colonial cotton around 1900, linking numerous spheres of cotton cultivation and textile production between Europe, colonial Africa and the USA.[69] With skill thus also mattering in cotton cultivation, the biography and family background of the Indo-German plantation manager working in Kilossa, Ranga Kaundinya, is crucial. Recruited through the Pietist networks of the Swabian company, *Otto* hired the supposed cotton expert Kaundinya, whose family had had links to the Ottos for two generations, for their newly established enterprise in German East Africa. Although there is some research available that investigates *Otto's* Pietist company networks and the history of the Kaundinya family, they still neglect Ranga Kaundinya's position as a white subaltern in colonial East Africa and his place in the Pietist networks of the *Otto* company. Analogous to the societal standing of the Greeks in German colonial East Africa, the Indo-German was not only vilified as 'half-Oriental' by top ranking representatives of the German colonial administration, but also discriminated against by his own European employees at *Otto's* cotton plantation in Kilossa.[70]

Functioning as a quasi-counter case to both the construction of the *Central Railway* and the *Otto* plantation, the Tendaguru Expedition was distinct from the dynamics and realities of labour relationships at the other two places of work in many ways. Conducting palaeontological excavations at the remote Tendaguru Mountain in the southern district of *Lindi* in German East Africa, there were generally only two leading German palaeontologists consistently present at this place of work. The vast majority of ca. 500 workers were East Africans who thus obtained an employment with substantial autonomy. With individual excavation

69 Cf. Sunseri. '"Dispersing"'. Cf. Sunseri. 'Labour Migration'. Cf. Sunseri. *Vilimani*. Cf. Bleifuß and Hergenröder. *Die "Otto-Plantage"*. Cf. Beckert. *Empire of Cotton*. Cf. Riello. *Cotton*. Cf. Zimmerman. *Alabama in Africa*. Cf. Robins. *Cotton and Race*. Cf. Powell. *Losing the Thread*.

70 Cf. Konrad, Dagmar. *Missionsbräute. Pietistinnen des 19. Jahrhunderts in der Baseler Mission*. Münster et al.: 2001, pp. 45–47, 87–89, 308–309, 338–340, 469–470, 475. Cf. Eggers, Erik (Ed.). *Handball. Eine deutsche Domäne*. Göttingen: 2007, pp. 73–76. Kaundinya, R. *Erinnerungen aus meinen Pflanzerjahren in Deutsch-Ostafrika*. Leipzig: 1918. Cf. Brahmputr, Gango Rao. *Indien. Seine Stellung zum Weltkrieg und zu seiner Zukunft*. Tübingen: 1916.

sites being several day's march away from each other, the two German palaeontologists could hardly ever supervise their workers comprehensively. They rather had to rely on the knowledge, skill and reliability of their excavators and preparators at any time. Yet, research on the Tendaguru and other palaeontological excavations has only either presented the general history of the expeditions as such, the widespread 'dinomania' of the western societies around 1900, or used the excavations to illuminate the object history of the dinosaur fossils. So far, research on the Tendaguru has treated labour as a sideshow.[71] Although corporal punishments of East African workers also occurred at the Tendaguru, violence, normally typical of any colonial employment, was largely absent there. Investigating the specific reasons for this very special labour relationship, the role of the German palaeontologists' generally experienced and skilled personal servants – their so-called *boys* and chefs – is also examined in more detail. Also, the role of women at all three sites of work is considered. Even though many women[72] at the *Central Railway*, the *Otto* plantation, and the Tendaguru were in charge of reproductive labour, there is also clear evidence that they were likewise constructing the railroad, working the cotton fields and contributing to the excavations at the Tendaguru. With this great variety of protagonists involved in labour and labour relationships at the three different sites of work, a great variety of historical sources required consultation. Their spectrum, value and shortcomings, as well as the methodological approach to them are outlined in the following sections.

---

71 Cf. Vennen. 'Arbeitsbilder'. Cf. Maier. *African Dinosaurs*. Cf. Mogge. *Wilhelm Branco*, pp. 199–222. Cf. Rieppel. *Assembling*. Cf. Nieuwland. *American Dinosaur*. Cf. Roolf, Christoph. 'Dinosaurier-Skelette als Kriegsziel: Kulturgutraubplanungen, Besatzungspolitik und die deutsche Paläontologie in Belgien im Ersten Weltkrieg'. 5–26. *Berichte zur Wissenschaftsgeschichte*, 27. Weinheim: 2004.

72 Cf. Dennis, Carolyne. 'Women in African Labour History'. 125–140. *Journal of Asian and African Studies*. XXIII, 1–2. Leiden: 1988. Cf. Akurang-Parry, Kwabena Opare. 'Colonial Forced Labor Policies for Road Building in Southern Ghana and International Anti-Forced Labor Pressures, 1900–1940'. 1–25. *African Economic History*, no. 28. N.P.: 2000. Web. *Jstore*. http://www.jstor.org/stable/3601647 (12 November 2017). Highlighting the role of women and families within Askari households also cf. Moyd, Michelle R. *Violent Intermediaries. African Soldiers, Conquest, and Everyday Colonialism in German East Africa*. Athens (Ohio): 2014, pp. 148–206. For an ethnological approach to late twentieth-century skilled women in Nairobi cf. Wurster, Gabriele. '*You have to balance*. Über die Verknüpfung von Beruf und Familie bei qualifizierten Frauen in Nairobi'. *Arbeit in Africa*. 275–287. Eds. Kurt Beck and Gerd Spittler. Hamburg: 1996.

1.3 'Double Geographies', Self-Narratives and the Colonial Archive(s)

The historian of Africa Michael Pesek used the metaphor *Inseln von Herrschaft* ('Islands of Sovereignty') to describe the ephemeral character of the German colonial state. Accordingly, German colonial rule remained precarious throughout German formal colonialism and the colonial administration could, at best, exert comprehensive rule only in the direct environments of governmental strongholds.[73] Whereas the German term *Inseln* means 'islands' in English, the German term *Herrschaft* does not translate well. In English 'sovereignty' means primarily legal superiority, whereas *Herrschaft* implies also cultural aspects of dominance that go beyond the legal sphere. Keeping this remark in mind, I argue in the following that colonial economic or scientific endeavours such as the three places of labour under investigation may also be interpreted as 'Islands of sovereignty'. Besides political and military centres of the colonial administration, it was also colonial economic undertakings that established and maintained the power of the coloniser over the colonised. Pesek himself stresses that places such as Tabora or Kilossa were devoid of significant colonial penetration before colonial economic endeavours were established there. Governmental strongholds or military stations, and with it the 'colonial state's' representation, had only been rudimentary during the first half of colonial rule in Tabora or Kilossa. This only changed when economic activity was stirred in Tabora by the construction of the *Central Railway* and the establishment of large-scale plantations, such as the *Otto* plantation in the region around Kilossa. Indeed, such colonial economic endeavours must also be regarded as representatives of colonial rule; and as representatives of colonial rule, they may also be regarded as 'islands of sovereignty' that adapted, renegotiated, and integrated pre-colonial power structures and thus also constituted centres of colonial agitation.[74] The same holds true for the Tendaguru Expedition, which took place in a very isolated area in the *Lindi* region of German East Africa. As

73 Cf. Pesek, Michael. *Koloniale Herrschaft in Deutsch-Ostafrika. Expeditionen, Militär und Verwaltung seit 1880.* Frankfurt o.M.: 2005, pp. 19–21. Stressing the precarity of colonialism on a rather discursive level and particularly for the Cameroonian case cf. Hamann, Ulrike. *Prekäre Koloniale Ordnung. Rassistische Konjunkturen im Widerspruch. Deutsches Kolonialregime 1884–1914.* Bielefeld: 2016. For a sociological-historical approach for the case of Togo cf. Trotha, Trutz von. *Koloniale Herrschaft. Zur soziologischen Staatsentstehung am Beispiel des «Schutzgebietes Togo».* Tübingen: 1994.
74 Cf. Pesek. *Koloniale Herrschaft,* pp. 244–259. Cf. Kundrus, Birthe. 'Die Kolonien. Kinder des Gefühls und der Phantasie'. *Phantasiereiche. Zur Kulturgeschichte des deutschen Kolonialismus.* 7–18. Ed. Birthe Kundrus. Frankfurt o.M.: 2003, pp. 7–16. Cf. Sabea, Hanan. 'Pioneers of Empire? The Making of Sisal Plantations in German East Africa, 1890–1917'. *German Colonialism Revisited. African, Asian and Oceanic Experiences.* 114–129. Eds. Nina Berman et al. Ann Arbor: 2017, pp. 114–126.

the only colonial stakeholder in a vast area, the excavation camp must also be regarded as representative of German colonial rule. As an 'island', each contested place therefore also bore its individual characteristics and dynamics that shaped the daily realities of labour, which were dependant on the presence and actions of all actors involved in work.

Characterising the German colonial sphere of influence as ephemeral and incomplete, it must be stressed that any island – whether taken only metaphorically or geographically – is never a completely cut-off entity that has no connections to the outer world. Rather, analysing the history of Sri Lanka, Sijut Sivasundaram has coined the term *islanding* to express his view that an island's (dis)connections to its surrounding waters and its neighbouring as well as faraway land masses are constantly made, adapted and rearranged.[75] Such an understanding of an island, that stresses the multiple relationships featuring their immediate and faraway surroundings, concords with the major insights about space and global labour history. Andreas Eckert and Angelika Epple similarly emphasise the multiple intersections between research approaches of area studies and global labour history. These observations are also pertinent for the present research. At the heart of these discussions is the presupposition that any spatial entity may never be regarded as a stable and fixed container, which can be analysed without considering its connections to other areas.[76]

An analysis of spatial entities must therefore understand space as a relational category and differentiate between *space* (Raum), *place* (Ort) and *location* (Stelle). Following the sociologist Martina Löw's understanding of *spaces* as relational concepts means that the concept of *space* goes beyond one specific *location* and one specific *place*. Still, a specific *location* as well as a specific *place* are fundamental features to constitute the more comprehensive and relational concept of *space*.[77] Moreover, the constitution of a *space* is very much dependent on the presence of individual protagonists, their actions and the specific arrangement of a *space's* overall structure.[78] This understanding of space is highly relevant for

75 Cf. Sivasundaram, Sujit. *Islanded. Britain, Sri Lanka, and the Bounds of an Indian Ocean Colony.* Chicago and London: 2013, pp. 5–17, 24–27.

76 Cf. Eckert. 'Area Studies', pp. 156–173. Cf. Epple, Angelika. "Global History' und 'Area Studies'. Plädoyer für eine weltgeschichtliche Perspektivierung des Lokalen'. *Area Studies und die Welt. Weltregion und neue Globalgeschichte.* 90–116. Ed. Birgit Schäbler. Vienna: 2007, pp. 92–113. Cf. Middell, Matthias and Naumann, Katja. 'Global history and the spatial turn: from the impact of area studies to the study of critical junctures of globalisation'. 149–170. *Journal of Global History.* 5. London School of Economics and Political Science: 2010. Web. https://cambridge.org/core/terms.https://doi.org/10.1017/51740022809990362 (27 March 2019), pp. 149–156.

77 Cf. Löw, Martina. *Raumsoziologie.* Frankfurt o.M.: 2015, pp. 9–68, 263–273.

78 Cf. Löw. *Raumsoziologie,* pp. 9–68, 152–157, 224–230, 263–273.

historical research as the historian can only pick one history out of many histories to reveal the connections between the local and the global. Quite often, it is not clear whether these connections can really be judged as representative and if there is any linear transfer between the local and the global or the other way around.[79] Global history should therefore seek the global through the specific, i.e. through the local.[80] An adequate means to reveal the global through the local is to highlight the autonomy of individual protagonists on the local level while simultaneously considering global processes. Accordingly, people and therefore also historical protagonists have never been passive recipients of global processes, but certainly obtained opportunities for agency ranging from resistance to collaboration to act out on the local level. Of course, they do not live in a vacuum, but rather within certain structures that pose limitations on their actions. Thus, historical events have always been the result of constant negotiation of individuals with their fellow human beings, societal structures, and their environment.[81] The *space* of the colonial globality around 1900 must therefore be seen through the lens of local *places* especially regarding labour. That is why this research investigates labour through the lenses of the construction sites of the *Central Railway*, the *Otto* plantation in Kilossa, and the palaeontological excavations at the Tendaguru. As these three *places* of work had each its own characteristics and dynamics, they were individually embedded in the global *space*. At each place of labour, local parameters as well as the protagonists' actions and labour relationships constituted what work meant in the overall global context. Approaching global labour history accordingly has therefore fundamental consequences for the selection and analysis of the historical sources under investigation. This applies first to the analysis of the self-narratives that have been studied to analyse the global history of labour at the three selected sites.

Schröder and Höhler have already considered Löw's sociological concept of *space* in their research about the global practice of geographies, the craft of mapping, and maps as historical sources.[82] In this respect, one map represents one particular world view, and it is therefore not surprising that there can be numer-

79 Cf. Conrad, Sebastian. *Globalgeschichte. Eine Einführung*. Munich: 2013, pp. 27–28. Cf. Conrad, Sebastian. *What is global History?* Princeton: 2016, pp. 115–141.

80 Epple. 'Global History' und 'Area Studies', pp. 92–112, p. 113.

81 Cf. Rothermund, Dietmar. 'Globalgeschichte als Interaktionsgeschichte: Von der Außereuropäischen Geschichte zur Globalgeschichte'. *Area Studies und die Welt. Weltregion und neue Globalgeschichte*. 194–216. Ed. Birgit Schäbler. Vienna: 2007, pp. 194–199.

82 Cf. Schröder, Iris and Höhler, Sabine. 'Welt-Räume: Annäherungen an eine Geschichte der Globalität im 20. Jahrhundert'. *Welt-Räume. Geschichte, Geographie und Globalisierung seit 1900*. 9–50. Eds. Iris Schröder and Sabine Höhler. Frankfurt o.M. and New York: 2005, pp. 20–30.

ous maps to describe just one location, region or phenomenon. Besides these world views cast into maps, there are also mental maps or imagined geographies of particular territories and phenomena that represent an individual's view not only of the local, but also of the global.[83] These mental maps were and are often cast into self-narratives, which are important sources for the analysis of labour at all three places of work under investigation. Analysing travel writings, David Gregory first examined self-narratives in accordance with a relational understanding of *space*. In this respect, he coined the term *double geography* to characterise how individual mental maps of European travellers to Egypt were (re)produced and (re)imagined when encountering the (colonial) 'other'.[84] Travelling to 'the Orient', nineteenth-century tourists had a twofold experience. On the one hand, they modelled their experience in Egypt around their own expectations, which were strongly influenced by contemporary discourses of the metropole. On the other hand, the tourists' Egyptian experience was not merely a matter of European phantasy. They also interacted with the Egyptian population, every now and then, and published on this experience, which included their anticipated experience, in various travel writings. Thus, Gregory stresses the real dimension of nineteenth-century tourism to Egypt as these travels and literary productions were not merely the results of unrealistic colonial phantasies but had a basis in reality as well.[85]

The concept of *double geographies* thus enables us to illustrate the relationships between colonisers and the colonised in more detail. Reading self-narratives through the lens of *double geographies* generates new perspectives on the coloniser, the colonised, their interrelationship and the colonial *places* where such encounters occurred.[86] The encounter with the new, unknown and unfamiliar always required strategies to cope with 'the other'. As such attempts always remained disputed, they required constant confirmation to ease the coloniser's mind and functioned as an attempt to affirm the claims of colonial superiority. The fact that such attempts required constant repetition to have any effect shows how difficult the

83 Cf. Schröder and Höhler. 'Welt-Räume', pp. 33–34. Cf. Struck, Wolfgang. 'Einleitung'. *Karten-Meere: eine Welterzeugung*. 7–21. Eds. Wolfgang Struck et al. Wiesbaden: 2020. Cf. Schröder, Iris. 'Von der Ordnung zur Unordnung zur Umordnung'. *Karten-Meere: eine Welterzeugung*. 87–107. Eds. Wolfgang Struck et al. Wiesbaden: 2020. Cf. Struck, Wolfgang. 'Von der Schwierigkeit, eine Linie zu ziehen'. *Karten-Meere: eine Welterzeugung*. 125–135. Eds. Wolfgang Struck et al. Wiesbaden: 2020.

84 Cf. Gregory, David. 'Scripting Egypt. Orientalism and the Cultures of Travel'. *Writes of Passage. Reading Travel Writing*. 114–150. Eds. James Duncan and David Gregory. New York: 1999, p. 119.

85 Cf. Gregory. 'Scripting Egypt', p. 146.

86 Cf. Stoyke. 'Suche', pp. 148–149.

maintenance of colonial rule proved to be, not only in material, but also in symbolic terms. That is why reading self-narratives by means of *double geographies* helps to uncover ambivalences, insecurities, ruptures and contradictions in the European narrator.[87] Uncovering such contradictions is not only relevant with respect to analysing the (work) relationship between coloniser and the colonised. Contradictions, ambivalences, insecurities, and ruptures are central to analysing the conflict-laden intermediate position of white subaltern South(-East) European railway sub-contractors working at the *Central Railway* and that of the Indo-German plantation manager Ranga Kaundinya at the *Otto* plantation in Kilossa. They are equally important for the analysis of the labour of precarious white railway sub-contractors and precarious white German plantation employees in Kilossa.

It is crucial to understand that *double geographies* are not only valid for published self-narratives such as colonial travel writings. Self-narratives should not merely be used as sources to investigate an individual's inner self. Quite on the contrary, investigating the spatiality of self-narratives presupposes that a person's self-concept derives not merely from his or her closed-off 'inner life', but is decisively shaped by his or her own body, actions, social relationships, individual senses of belonging and cosmological or religious worldviews.[88] Hence, self-narratives presuppose 'relational-selves' to highlight that individuals constitute *space* through their actions, while individuals and their writings are themselves constituted by the *space* that surrounds them.[89]

87 Cf. Stoyke. 'Suche', pp. 169–171.

88 In contrast to the old-established source category of ego-documents (*Ego-Dokumente),* the approach of self-narratives denies the seclusion of the inner life of an individual from the 'outer' world and the production of self-narratives as a phenomenon of the process of western individualisation starting with the early modern enlightenment era. The allegedly separated sphere of an individual mind that commands the production of ego-documents and an independent exterior world surrounding this lonely mind are dismissed. Self-narratives rather entail that an individual mind is intertwined with its environment and that these two spheres mutually influence each other. Cf. Bähr, Andreas et al. 'Räume des Selbst. Eine Einleitung'. *Räume des Selbst. Selbstzeugnisforschung transkulturell.* 1–25. Eds. Andreas Bähr et al. Cologne et al: 2007, pp. 1–5.

89 Cf. Ulbrich, Claudia et al. 'Selbstzeugnisse und Person. Transkulturelle Perspektiven'. *Selbstzeugnis und Person. Transkulturelle Perspektiven.* 1–20. Eds. Claudia Ulbrich et al. Cologne et al: 2012, pp. 1–9. Cf. Medick, Hans. 'Introduction. Relational Selves'. *Selbstzeugnis und Person. Transkulturelle Perspektiven.* 75–77. Eds. Claudia Ulbrich et al. Cologne et al: 2012, pp. 75–77. Cf. Ulbrich, Claudia. 'Europäische Selbstzeugnisse in historischer Perspektive – neue Zugänge'. 1–20. *FU-Berlin.* Web. https://www.geschkult.fu-berlin.de/e/fmi/institut/arbeitsbereiche/ab_ulbrich/media/UlbrichEurop_ische_Selbstzeugnisse.pdf (10 May 2019). Cf. Watson, Julia. 'The Spaces of Autobiographical Narrative'. *Räume des Selbst. Selbstzeugnisforschung transkulturell.* 13–25. Eds. Andreas Bähr et al. Cologne et al: 2007, pp. 15–25.

Having been predominantly used to analyse the history of the Early Modern period, self-narratives claim to offer an approach that may be applied to various periods, for example to sources of the nineteenth and twentieth centuries. In this respect, self-narratives encompass a great variety of sources such as autobiographies, diaries, personal correspondence and memoirs. While some scholars would exclude (in)voluntary testimonies of defendants and witnesses at court from the corpus of files that may be regarded as self-narratives,[90] other historians do indeed regard files that were produced during legal proceedings as self-narratives. In this respect, it is of course crucial to highlight that court testimonies may well have been the product of varying degrees of force. Moreover, their character is less immediate and more indirect, as court files are usually not produced by the testifying individual him- or herself, but by court officials.[91] Although a similar intermediation between the reporting individual and the resulting self-narrative may also occur when writers are employed to, e.g. take dictation of an individual's diary, the indirect character of especially court testimonies always has to be made explicit.[92]

Generally, self-narratives do certainly have their shortcomings, just as all sources do. Their acknowledged potential for spatial analysis, as well as the opportunity to provide a micro-perspective on events of global history, appears promising, however. This is enhanced by the fact that they provide the opportunity to investigate actual protagonists in transcultural settings, living in an environment characterised by the tension between the local and the global. In colonial environments, multiple feelings of belonging to various social and cultural groups often emerge, and self-narratives are fitting source material to highlight such diverse and constantly contested senses of belonging that are central to the conflict-laden intermediate position of white subalterns and precarious whites in German East Africa. Moreover, self-narratives often enable insights into the (world) views of people who did not belong to the groups of elites or experts. This holds particularly true for files pro-

90 Cf. Sauer, Michael. 'Selbstzeugnisse als historische Quellen'. 2–11. *Geschichte Lernen.* Heft 156. Seelze: 2013, pp. 2–3.

91 Cf. Preuss, Monika. 'Das Unsagbare sagen. Aussagen über Sexualität von Jüdinnen und Juden in amtlichen Verhörprotokollen'. *Selbstzeugnisse und Ego-Dokumente frühneuzeitlicher Juden in Ashkenas. Beispiele, Methoden, Konzepte.* 167–184. Eds. Birgit E. Klein and Rotraud Ries. Berlin: 2011, pp. 167–170. Cf. Jancke, Gabriele. 'Jüdische Selbstzeugnisse und Ego-Dokumente der frühen Neuzeit in Ashkenas. Eine Einleitung'. *Selbstzeugnisse und Ego-Dokumente frühneuzeitlicher Juden in Ashkenas. Beispiele, Methoden, Konzepte.* 9–26. Eds. Birgit E. Klein and Rotraud Ries. Berlin: 2011, pp. 12–15.

92 For the case of an employed writer who changed the content of the diary of the German merchant Heinrich Witt cf. Wetzel, Christa. 'Schreibend leben (1799–1892). Heinrich Witt und sein Tagebuch im Lima des 19. Jhs.'. *Selbstzeugnis und Person. Transkulturelle Perspektiven.* 139–154. Eds. Claudia Ulbrich et al. Cologne et al: 2012, pp. 144–146.

duced in legal proceedings, as most of the defendants and witnesses at court were ordinary people, who would generally not produce any self-narratives on their own.[93] Last but not least, regarding (German) colonial history in East Africa and global history as such, self-narratives have not been exhaustively incorporated into investigating the phenomena of labour. Often the focus lies on the elite and standard works of German colonial history in East Africa, which rarely quote self-narratives, while they also disregard colonial court files if they are not about legal history.[94] This is why self-narratives such as Clement Gillman's and Edwin Hennig's diaries, published autobiographical sources like those of Ranga Kaundinya and the German labour recruiter Heinrich Langkopp, and (in-)voluntary court testimonials of (African) witnesses and defendants at court in German East Africa provide for a significant corpus of sources in this study. The production of these sources is strongly tied to the three places of labour, which are analysed in the following. They serve to reveal the contested character of the places of labour, but also provide for an adequate picture of collective and intra-individual *spaces*. Of course, special attention must always be paid to the question of whether any self-narrative was published or not.

All other sources consulted herein are held in colonial archives. Investigating colonial archives "as a process rather than [. . .] as things", Laura Ann Stoler has placed influential emphasis on the fact that any archive does not simply offer content via sources, but that especially colonial archives were "epistemological experiments" that represent "cross sections of contested knowledge". Applying this view to the sources under investigation, any colonial archive does not only contain content about colonial rule, but as colonial rule inscribed itself into this very institution, the colonial archive also served as an "intricate technolog[y] of rule" itself.[95] This does of course not mean that Stoler generally rejects the usage of the colonial archive. In fact, she urges us to treat especially colonial archives as "cultural artifacts of fact production, of taxonomies in the making, and of disparate notions of what made up colonial authority".[96] The consequence of such an approach to the colonial sources held in the archives is not to judge whether information from the archives is fiction or fact. This more profound approach to the colonial archive intends to trace back the production and consumption of the alleged 'facts' contained in the sources. To her, this is especially relevant as reading any colonial source against the grain presupposes the understanding of how

93 Cf. Ulbrich. 'Selbstzeugnis und Person', pp. 1–19.
94 Cf. Koponen. *Development*, pp. 678–686.
95 Stoler, Ann Laura. 'Colonial Archives and the Arts of Governance'. 87–019. *Archival Science*, 2. N.P.: 2002, p. 87.
96 Stoler. 'Colonial Archives', p. 91.

an archive works in the first place and how any representative of the colonial administration used the files held in this archive to actually exert colonial rule. Only after this precondition is observed may the historian read sources and entire archives against the grain, checking for irregularities, misconceptions, flaws and other disturbances, which are pivotal to identify those themes that were crucial to the colonial administration and therefore also pivotal to illuminate the workings of colonial rule.[97] Such disturbances in the colonial archives and their reading against the grain are not only important to generate a better understanding for the workings of the colonial archives and colonial rule. They are also key for the attempt to access the perspective and room for manoeuvre of the colonised and subalterns, who were rarely ever recorded in the colonial archives at all. Although even prominent representatives of the subaltern studies group soon voiced the criticism that it will hardly ever be possible to regain such genuine subaltern voices, any historian investigating global or rather colonial history must always remain attentive to voices unheard and groups of people and individuals neglected by historical research.[98] Just as the reliability of any historical source always has to be questioned, the colonial archive thus urges any historian to even more thorough investigation, and the usage of a great variety of sources beyond just one single colonial archive.

1.4 Sources

Even though the colonial administration had an ephemeral character, it was of course a decisive player in German East Africa. Gradually expanding the structures of the colonial state by enhancing bodies of civil administration at the expense of quasi-military rule especially after the Maji Maji War, many more files were produced from ca. 1908 onwards. This is relevant not only for files produced

97 Cf. Stoler. 'Colonial Archives', pp. 92–109. Cf. Stoler, Laura Ann. *Along the Archival Grain. Epistemic Anxieties and Colonial Common Sense.* Princeton: 2009, pp. 17–54, 237–278. Cf. Nagel, Jürgen G. *Die Kolonie als wissenschaftliches Projekt. Forschungsorganisation und Forschungspraxis im deutschen Kolonialreich.* Habilitationsschrift an der FernUniversität in Hagen. Fakultät für Kultur- und Sozialwissenschaften. May 2013. Web. https://www.academia.edu/41830319/Die_Kolonie_als_wissenschaftliches_Projekt_Forschungsorganisation_und_Forschungspraxis_im_deutschen_Kolonialreich (21 June 2021).

98 Cf. Büschel, Hubertus. 'Das Schweigen der Subalternen. Die Entstehung der *Archiv*kritik im Postkolonialismus'. *Archiv – Macht – Wissen. Organisation und Konstruktion von Wissen und Wirklichkeiten in Archiven.* 73–88. Eds. Anja Horstmann und Vanina Kopp. Frankfurt o.M.: 2010. Cf. Spivak, Gayatri Chakravorty. 'Can the Subaltern Speak?'. *Can the Subaltern Speak? Postkolonialität und subaltern Artikulation.* 17–118. Ed. Hito Steyerl et al. Vienna and Berlin: 2020.

by the colonial administration regarding colonial labour policies in general, but also regarding railway construction in particular. With the colonial administration enhancing its labour laws during State Secretary Bernhard Dernburg's assumption of office in the newly established Colonial Department in Berlin from 1907 onwards, not only new labour legislation was issued, but also governmental bodies to supervise railway constructions were established and significantly enhanced by 1911. As far as the files of the colonial administration held in the Tanzania National Archives in Dar es Salaam regarding labour policies are concerned, there are consequently many more sources available from ca. 1909 onwards. This is primarily because there were more governmental bodies existent that could genuinely produce any files. With more labour laws established in German East Africa, more legal transgressions also occurred. In turn, these legal transgressions in the context of labour also found their way into files produced by colonial courts. Thus, especially regarding the construction of the *Central Railway* and the *Otto* plantation in Kilossa, the files of the colonial administration held in Dar es Salaam are the major sources under investigation in this study. In particular, the records of the colonial governmental bodies supervising railway construction, like the railway commissioners (*Eisenbahnkommissare*), have been pivotal to analysing labour at the railroad's building sites. They are accompanied by court files that report about the transgressions regarding labour legislation not only at the *Central Railway*, but also at the *Otto* plantation in Kilossa. With railway construction being a very complex endeavour, other bodies of the colonial administration also document various aspects relevant for railway construction. This applies to those governmental bodies in charge of the health sector, labour in general, but also those responsible for foreign relationships to other colonies like neighbouring British East Africa. Their records include considerations about inter-colonial competition with the *Uganda Railway*, or settlement and migratory schemes of Indians who had been targeted to migrate from British colonies as settlers or railway employees for German East Africa since the late 1890s.

Other significant source material about labour at the *Central Railway* produced after 1909 is held in the Railway Museum in Nairobi. Individually stored in the archive, when examining the sources in Nairobi in March 2020 I had the impression that they have largely been unknown or at least scarcely used by historians so far. The reason for this neglect derives probably from the fact that there is hardly any information available that provides for the files' provenance. The most plausible explanation for the German colonial files' location in today's Kenya are probably the territorial reorganisations of the East African colonies after WWI and WWII. As those files produced by German colonial bodies in East Africa between 1890 and 1918 are generally held in the Tanzania National Archives in Dar es Salaam, files about the *Central Railway* in Nairobi's railway museum might have been relocated to Kenya after WWI for the first time. With the Treaty of Versailles deciding to transform the vast majority of German East Africa into a Mandate of the League of Nations, Tanganyika Territory, as the German colony was called subsequently, fell under British administration. This remained the case until Tanganyika's independence in 1961, although the East African territory was now a British Mandate under the United Nations after WWII in 1948. In charge of the Mandate, British rule in East Africa included also taking over the formerly German colonial railways, of course. Whether any circulation of railway files between Tanganyika Territory and Kenya had taken place in the interwar period is difficult to assess. In any event, it seems most likely that the files of the *Central Railway* were transferred from Dar es Salaam to Nairobi in the 1950s after the establishment of the East African High Commission in 1948. Deriving from administrative actions to delegate war efforts more effectively, the British idea behind the High Commission was to put railways and harbours, telecommunications, postal services and the collection of certain taxes under one umbrella. While the territories of Kenya, Tanganyika and Uganda kept their integrity and their individual governors, their combined territory was largely administrated through the High Commissioner resident in Kenya. With this administrative centralisation of the railway infrastructure in the Kenyan capital, the East African Railways and Harbours Administration probably ordered some German colonial files, apparently arbitrarily, from Dar es Salaam to be transferred to Nairobi. Today, they are still held in the city's railway museum. With the publication of M.F. Hill's *Permanent Way: The Story of the Tanganyika Railways* on behalf of the East African Railways and Harbours Administration in Nairobi in 1957, it is very likely that the files were taken to the Kenyan capital for the purpose of the book's production.[99] Whether this was all really the case, must remain unclear, however.

As the files of colonial railway construction held in Germany were almost entirely burnt during WWII, there remain only a few scattered and unsystematic folders in the *Bundesarchiv* in Berlin. Thus, the *Bundesarchiv* has been consulted primarily to access a few files produced by the Colonial Department from 1907 onwards and for microfilms of files of German East Africa's district offices. In respect of the *Central Railway*, a few patchy files of the construction companies *Philipp Holzmann, Krupp* and *MAN* also survive in the *Stadtarchiv Frankfurt am Main* as well as in *Krupp's* archives in Essen and in the company archives of *MAN* in Augsburg. Moreover, there is extensive inventory held by the archives of the *Deutsche*

---

99 Cf. Banfield, Jane. 'Federation in East Africa'. 181–193. *International Journal*, Vol. 18, No. 2. N.P.: 1963. Web. *Jstor*. https://www.jstor.org/stable/40198786 (14 June 2021). Cf. Hill. *Permanent, Way. Vol II.* pp. v–vii.

Bank, which have especially been consulted for the railway's planning stage. As financing the railway and its profitability are generally of no interest in this research, many files sighted were not interpreted for this study. Especially regarding the issue of skilled African labour, the mission archives of the Moravians in Herrnhut have proven to provide precious material. Particularly, the files and reports of the railway mission, which targeted East African railway workers as future Christians, were consulted. In addition, other mission files produced by numerous individual Moravian missionary stations in German East Africa as well as the correspondence of the mission's board, e.g. with *Philipp Holzmann*, were consulted. Finally, Nairobi's newspaper *The Indian Voice of British East Africa, Uganda and Zanzibar* provided significant information highlighting the role of Indian (skilled) labour at the railway between 1909 and 1911. Moreover, the newspaper provides for the Indian point of view regarding colonial labour. It therefore balances those anti-Indian and anti-Greek discourses primarily revealed by the German settlers' press organ, *Deutsch Ostafrikanische Zeitung* (*DOAZ*), which has been consulted thoroughly.

Apart from the articles about railway construction published by the *DOAZ*, there is thus an obvious source gap for the initial period of railway construction between ca. 1905 and 1908. With the colonial administration following a *laissez-faire* approach in these initial years of railway construction, it hardly ever produced any files about labour conditions along the railroad. As the files of the construction companies were furthermore destroyed during WWII, the close examination of the self-narratives of the Anglo-German railway engineer Clement Gillman, employed by *Philipp Holzmann* from 1905 until WWI, bridges this gap. Throughout his career, Clement Gillman kept extensive and detailed diaries, which are stored in the Bodleian Library at the University of Oxford. Working as a railway engineer and geographer as well as living through many decades of German and British colonial rule in East Africa until his death in 1946, his self-narratives are precious to any historian who attempts to study colonial railway construction in this region. Gillman's self-narratives are of particular importance, as recent studies on the role of colonial railway engineers in German East Africa have neglected this source material entirely. Even though he wrote a history on the European railway engineering personnel in German colonial (East) Africa and mentioning Gillman repeatedly in his study, Sebastian Beese only consulted Gillman's published accounts, for example. By contrast, in this research project about global labour history, Gillman's diaries and personal correspondence produced until the early 1920s are examined thoroughly.[100]

100 Cf. Hoyle, B.S. *Gillman of Tanganyika 1882–1946. The Life and Work of a Pioneer Geographer.* Avebury: 1987. Cf. Beese. *Experten*, pp. 12, 61, 79, 87, 91, 110–120.

Regarding the *Otto* cotton plantation in Kilossa, several archives were consulted. First of all, there are two folders in the Tanzanian National Archives that document the correspondence between the textile company, the *Gouvernement*, and the local bodies of the colonial administration. They are accompanied by files held in the *Stadtmuseum Wendlingen am Neckar* near Stuttgart, the place where the company was founded, and the company files held in the *Technoseum – Landesmuseum für Technik und Arbeit* in Mannheim. In Wendlingen, especially the diary of one of the company's senior members, Fritz Otto, who travelled to German East Africa to inspect his plantation in Kilossa, was consulted. In Mannheim, especially the company's chronicles produced in the 1930s are precious for this study. Besides, further files about other economic activities of *Otto* in German East Africa as well as correspondence between ca. 1900 and 1930 were of special value. Of course, the published autobiography of Ranga Kaundinya, reporting about his time as an Indo-German plantation manager in Kilossa, is a pivotal source – which can be classified as self-narrative – for this study.[101] Regarding the Tendaguru, besides the diaries and personal correspondence of the palaeontologist Edwin Hennig held at the University Archives in Tübingen, the Natural History Museum Berlin holds all remaining files informing about the paleontological excavation works. They are completed by quasi-autobiographical works by Edwin Hennig published a few months after his stay in German East Africa, and others with longer temporal distance released in the 1950s.[102]

1.5 Outline

Any global labour history is not only embedded in global, but also in regional and local contexts. Chapter 2 thus situates this global history of labour in the Indian Ocean Area to illustrate the region's interconnections especially with the Arabian Peninsula and India. While the characteristics of the Indian Ocean Area had largely been independent from Europe and North America, this began to change during the nineteenth century. Gradually, the seas between the East African coast and western Oceania came under British dominance. In the first two-thirds of the nineteenth-century German influence was negligible, while Britain dominated trade and politics between India and East Africa centred on the Zanzibar Archipelago. This situation first changed when the German *Reich* intensified its imperial ambi-

101 Cf. Kaundinya. *Erinnerungen.*

102 Cf. Hennig, Edwin. *Am Tendaguru. Leben und Wirken einer deutschen Forschungsexpedition zur Ausgrabung vorweltlicher Riesensaurier in Deutsch-Ostafrika.* Stuttgart: 1912. Cf. Hennig, Edwin. *Gewesene Welten. Auf Saurierjagd im ostafrikanischen Busch.* Rüschlikon bei Zürich: 1955.

tions in East Africa and the German chartered company *Deutsch Ostafrikanische Gesellschaft* (*DOAG*) eked out territorial possessions on the East African mainland in the 1880s. When Britain and Germany reached an agreement about their imperial spheres of influence in the western Indian Ocean, German East Africa was founded as a German colony and Zanzibar became a British Protectorate in the 1890s. As Zanzibar, the economic centre of the region, was now cut off from its major trading hinterland, German colonial policy makers planned to readjust the colonial economy primarily by large-scale infrastructure policies, i.e. railway building. In the context of the heyday of European imperialism, the construction of large-scale infrastructure, especially railways, was seen as the most important tool to not only exert influence beyond a nation's boundaries, but to make any colony an economic success. In this respect, the German *Reich's* most prestigious imperial railway was the *Bagdadbahn* in the Ottoman Empire, which sought to connect Berlin to Bagdad via Constantinople not only to emphasise German imperial claims, but also to challenge the British privileged access to the Indian Ocean via the Suez Canal and the Strait of Hormuz. In German East Africa, too, railway construction was the decisive strategy to open up the territory and make the colony an economic success, especially once Colonial State Secretary Bernhard Dernburg took office in 1907. As historical investigations on imperial infrastructure have regarded large-scale infrastructure as mere 'tools of empire', hardly anything is known about the railroads' construction, however.

Chapter 3 thus investigates the prisms of work at the construction sites of the *Central Railway*. In German East Africa, the *Central Railway* from its coastal capital Dar es Salaam to Lake Tanganyika was the largest and most important infrastructural project in the colony. Its construction and especially the labour relationships of all protagonists involved in railway building are thus analysed. Between the colonial administration and its supervising bodies, and the construction company *Philipp Holzmann*, there were constant disputes over respective areas of authority and a tendency to veil controversial information about labour conditions. Supervising deficiencies increased as *Holzmann* outsourced the majority of railway building to numerous South(-East) European sub-contractors, who themselves outsourced track sections to sub-sub-contractors. Moreover, these predominantly Greek sub-contractors were not only indispensable for railway construction as such, but also for the recruitment of the African workforce. With the background of Greek people in East Africa being largely unknown, a section investigates the general history of Greeks in (East) Africa and their migration from the Ottoman Empire, working for the *Bagdadbahn*, to the railway construction sites in German East Africa. Generally, South(-East) Europeans were judged as white subalterns according to the hegemonic colonial discourses, ranking them between coloniser and the colonised. Although colonial discourse claimed them responsible for almost any shortcomings regarding labour conditions at the *Central Railway*, a closer analysis shows that German and Greek railway sub-contractors treated the African workers equally badly. Likewise unknown is the decisive role of skilled Indian craftsmen, who came to work at the *Central Railway*'s construction sites in German East Africa not only from India, but also from British East Africa, where some of them had previously worked at the *Uganda Railway*. Especially in the initial years of railway construction their skilled labour was in high demand. Slowly but surely, their comparatively expensive labour was replaced by that of skilled East Africans, although some Indians certainly remained at the railroad's construction sites until the completion of the railway. Despite there being general African agency at the railway construction sites, skill development enhanced especially the East African workers' abilities to resist (physical) abuse and to eke out advantages in the colonial labour market. This analysis not only applies to Indian craftsmen working at the *Central Railway*, but also to skilled East Africans who had received their training at missionary schools of the Moravians. As there is hardly any source material for the railway available between 1905 and 1907, the diaries of the Anglo-German railway engineer Clement Gillman substitutes for the missing evidence on a micro-level. It also serves as a valuable source to illuminate the daily labour relationships of all protagonists involved in individual construction camps. Here, the role of female labour is also analysed thoroughly.

Although Bernard Dernburg's allegedly 'reformed colonial policies' only scarcely enhanced colonial labour conditions, the Colonial State Secretary's call for determined colonial policies and large-scale investments in German East Africa was answered. The construction of the *Central Railway* stirred economic expectations and contributed to the German textile industry's investment in cotton plantations in German East Africa. That is also why the second case study investigates the history of the *Otto* cotton plantation in Kilossa. Chapter 4 thus examines the company's cotton enterprise in German East Africa within the logics of the 'empire of cotton'. The analysis here of the global textile industry intermingles with Pietist networks of the *Otto* family in India, where they recruited an Indo-German planter as manager for their enterprise in German East Africa. When at work, he faced not only prejudice as a white subaltern by the colonial administration and his German employees, but also had to grapple with the mismanagement of his superiors. Of course, the role of the African workers is also illuminated, suggesting that their skill in plantation labour helped them to eke out advantages in the racist colonial labour market. In addition, African labour remained indispensable at the cotton plantation as the introduction of modern steam machinery proved disastrous for the company's production. Furthermore, the chapter sheds light on precarious white German plantation workers in Kilossa, investigating their role against the backdrop of other white subalterns like South(-East) European railway sub-contractors in the colony.

With sensational discoveries in science boosting an empire's prestige, the Tendaguru Expedition handily refurbished the reputation of German colonialism. With colonial warfare, especially in German South West Africa and German East Africa between 1904 and 1908 initially damaging the reputation of German colonialism, the exceptionally successful dinosaur fossil finds in German East Africa's south excited the German public and boosted the *Reich*'s prestige as a colonising power at home and internationally. Chapter 5 thus deals with the third case study of this global labour history and investigates work relationships at the Tendaguru Mountain in the colony's region of *Lindi*. In comparison to the *Central Railway* and the *Otto* plantation, the palaeontological excavation site at the Tendaguru is even more characterised by skilled East African labour. With only two German scientists being present constantly at the large-scale excavations, the entire endeavour would not have been possible without the great number of skilled East African porters, excavators, and fossil preparators. Although the 'scientific dinomania' around 1900 was certainly also part of the colonial globality at that time, the omnipresent dependency on skilled East African labour at the Tendaguru reveals that this third case study was more profoundly shaped by East African preconditions compared to the two other case studies. Although physical violence also played its role in labour relations at the Tendaguru, it was almost negligible compared to the force exerted at the railway or in Kilossa. With many East African excavators even migrating long distances voluntarily for work at the Tendaguru, and the general significance of their skill and ability for the palaeontological excavation works, the last case study functions almost as a counter-case completing the multifaceted prisms of work in German East Africa. Finally, and especially at the Tendaguru, the role of reproductive labour and domestic and care work is not only investigated by examining female labour, but also by examining the central role of the two German palaeontologists' personal East African servants, their so-called *boys* and chefs.

2 Global Labour History *in* the Indian Ocean

2.1 From the History of the Indian Ocean to a History *in* the Indian Ocean

> It is still worth taking the trouble to write histories of labor [. . .] that keep the entire world in mind, even when focussing on a specific region.
>
> Andreas Eckert. 'Area Studies and the Development of Global Labor History'. 2018.[1]

Compared to other seas, general historical research on the Indian Ocean is still scarce and no overarching scholarly consensus has yet been reached. Thus, the concept of the Indian Ocean remains porous and open to numerous interpretations and approaches. Nevertheless, one can identify central parameters that denote the characteristics and significance of the Indian Ocean. First, the Indian Ocean is the third largest of all global waters and has been crossed by various civilisations for over 5,000 years. It is therefore the world's ocean with the longest history of human (long-distance) voyages. Central for this mobility and thus also decisive for the ocean's economy were the monsoon winds. With the monsoon enabling long-distance travel and goods transportation, it also posed seasonal limitations to mobility. Without the seasonal winds, there was hardly the possibility of any longer voyages before steam power also equipped cargo ships with engines from the second half of the nineteenth century onwards. Using the monsoon, trading routes for luxuries and cargo existed from the Arabian Peninsula via the East African islands and the continent's coast to the Cape of Good Hope via India to southern China and to western Oceania. Regarding culture, the Indian Ocean facilitated the spread of Islam in these regions while the religion also intermingled with numerous local traditions. Despite the wide range of themes and research foci of many scholars, there is consensus about the fact that the characteristics and developments of the Indian Ocean Area were independent from other world regions for the majority of the past centuries and millennia. European traders and seafarers like the Portuguese from ca. 1500 onwards were only one minor player among many and more important others. These others remained dominant until ca. the middle of the nineteenth century when the Indian Ocean experienced slow but steady integration into the gradually globalising world economy.[2]

1 Eckert. 'Area Studies', p. 173.

2 Cf. Schnepel, Burkhard. 'Konnektivität in Bewegung: Der Indische Ozean als maritime Kontakt- und Austauschzone'. *Forschungsbericht – Max Planck Institut für ethnologische Forschung:* 2016. Web. https://www.eth.mpg.de/4393439/research_report_10998872?c=2923387 (6 June 2021). Cf. Nagel, Jürgen G. 'Schifffahrt auf dem Indischen Ozean im 19. Jahrhundert. Technologie und Wis-

https://doi.org/10.1515/9783111218090-002

Michael Pearson expresses this transformation of the entire Indian Ocean by describing the history of the area before ca. 1850 as history *of* the Indian Ocean. By the history *of* the Indian Ocean Pearson stresses the area's general independence from other world regions, which only slightly influenced the seas between Africa and Oceania. In contrast to this understanding, Pearson coined the concept of a history *in* the Indian Ocean. The history *in* the Indian Ocean stresses that the area was "profoundly influenced by wider matters coming from outside its geographical boundaries"[3] and highlights that the waters were increasingly dominated by Europe and North America from the middle of the nineteenth to the end of the twentieth century and onwards. Despite such profound influence from places outside the Indian Ocean from ca. 1850 onwards, many characteristics of the Indian Ocean remained resilient and were not entirely altered by the influence of the other world regions. In cultural terms, Islam played a central role in this respect. But economic aspects must be considered as well. Although steam ships ousted many old-established sailing cargo boats and the opening of the Suez Canal revolutionised long-distance trading routes from 1869 onwards, local sailing boat trading routes via *dhaus* (sailing boat) remained intact; and the technological evolution of the transport system even enabled new trading routes that required and or used these traditional sailing boats as well. Moreover, the latest European technology often drew a lot on local expertise and knowledge in navigation and communication. Approaching history *in* the Indian Ocean must therefore be somewhat relativised without rejecting this concept entirely. Although the Indian Ocean experienced gradual integration into a globalising world from the middle of the nineteenth century onwards, many of its genuine characteristics remained intact. Furthermore, old-established protagonists of the region also managed to adapt to the changing circumstances. For the present global history of labour, the concept of history *in* the Indian Ocean urges a focus also on local specifics, especially as far as the East African coast and its hinterland are concerned.[4] In partic-

---

sen in der Transportrevolution der Moderne'. 61–80. *Zeitschrift für Weltgeschichte,* Jahrgang 18, Heft 2. Berlin: 2017. Cf. Alpers, Edward A. *The Indian Ocean in World History.* Oxford: 2014, pp. 1–18. Cf. Vink, Markus P.M. 'The Ocean Studies and the 'new thalassology''. 41–62. *Journal of Global History,* 2. London: 2007. Web. *Cambridge.org.* doi:10.1017/S1740022807002033 (4 June 2019). Cf. Pearson, Michael. *The Indian Ocean.* London and New York: 2006, pp. 1–13. Cf. Gupta, Ashin das (Ed.). *India and the Indian Ocean World. Trade and Politics.* Oxford: 2004. Cf. Markovits, Claude. *The Global World of Indian Merchants, 1750–1947. Traders of Sind from Bukhara to Panama.* Cambridge: 2000. Cf. Alpers, Edward A. *East Africa and the Indian Ocean.* Princeton: 2009. Cf. Pearson, M.N. (Ed.). *The World of the Indian Ocean, 1500–1800. Studies in Economic, Social and Cultural History.* Burlington: 2005. Cf. Pearson. *The Indian Ocean,* pp. 9–12, 190–248.

3 Vink. 'Indian Ocean Studies', p. 57.

4 Cf. Pearson. *The Indian Ocean,* pp. 9–12, 190–248. Cf. Nagel. 'Schifffahrt', pp. 78–79.

ular, the area's climate remained crucial for all three places of work under investigation. Although colonial labour regimes altered labour relations mostly violently, they were not able to influence general conditions of the environment. Especially the steady rhythm between the dry and rainy season in East Africa conditioned by the monsoon winds was the strongest force that constituted any colonial labour regime. Although varying to a certain degree when compared to each other, the intensity of labour at the *Central Railway*, at the *Otto* plantation in Kilossa and at the Tendaguru Mountain decreased to a minimum during the rainy season. As heavy precipitation inhibited any railway, plantation or excavation works, most of the East African workers employed went back home and cultivated their own subsistence fields. During the dry season, in turn, workers generally returned to or arrived at their workplaces. Evoking thus the shift from colonial wage labour to subsistence farming, the climate of the Indian Ocean Area was fundamental to any place of work under investigation.

2.2 The Indian Ocean, East Africa and the History of (Un-)free Labour

> It would be difficult today to begin an analysis of the precolonial economy and its external connections without setting them in a global or comparative context.
>
> Hopkins, G.A. *An Economic History of West Africa*. Second Edition. 2020.[5]

Passing his study on the economic history of West Africa published in the 1970s in review, G.A. Hopkins' observations are also relevant for the analysis of the socio-economic environment of pre-colonial East Africa. Particularly regarding its history of (un-)free labour, i.e. slavery, the Indian Ocean has received recurring scholarly interest recently. Although slavery was the most widespread form of unfree labour well into the nineteenth century, scholars seldom included slave labour into the realm of (global) labour history.[6] Yet, in the history of the Indian Ocean Area, the

5 Hopkins, G.A. *An Economic History of West Africa*. Second Edition. New York: 2020, p. 19.
6 Cf. Madacho, Pedro et al. (Eds). *Pearls, People, and Power. Pearling the Indian Ocean Worlds.* Athens (Ohio): 2020. Cf. Seetah, Krish (Ed.). *Archaeology and the History in the Indian Ocean.* Athens (Ohio): 2018. Cf. McDow, Thomas F. *Buying Time. Debt and Mobility in the Western Indian Ocean.* Athens (Ohio): 2018. Cf. Soske, Jon. *Internal Frontiers. African Nationalism and the Indian Diaspora in Twentieth-Century South Africa.* Athens (Ohio): 2017. Cf. Hooper, Jane. *Feeding Globalization. Madagascar and the Provisioning Trade, 1600–1800.* Athens (Ohio): 2017. Cf. Stiles, Erin E. and Thompson, Katrina Daly (Eds.). *Gendered Lives in the Western Indian Ocean. Islam, Marriage, and Sexuality on the Swahili Coast.* Athens (Ohio): 2015. Cf. Allen, Richard B. *European Slave Trading in the Indian Ocean, 1500–1850.* Athens (Ohio): 2015. Cf. Campbell, Gwynn et al. (Eds.).

gradual replacement of slave labour and the slave trade by other varieties of trade and labour were central to the region's history throughout the period of interest. In East Africa, the Zanzibar Archipelago acquired a central role in slavery and the slave trade as well as in the overall socio-economy of the area. Especially, the archipelago's major Island Unguja with its capital Stone Town was a cultural centre and an economic trading hub. Not far from the East African mainland – today's Tanganyika – caravan routes starting at numerous coastal towns at the shores of the Indian Ocean, crossed vast lands, and reached as far as the Congo Basin. In particular, slaves and ivory came from the African interior to coastal towns like Bagamoyo from where enslaved men and women as well as precious elephant tusks were shipped via *dhaus* to Stone Town. Although a significant number of slaves remained on the archipelago, important trading routes also went through numerous East African coastal towns, stretching from as far as today's Somalia to today's southern Mozambique. Of course, close links existed also to the Indian subcontinent as it was the Ocean's centre, located halfway between the African continent and Oceania. Furthermore, there were also strong economic ties to the Arabian Peninsula and especially to today's Oman. Given these profound connections to distant regions, the East African mainland simultaneously experienced a very dynamic phase of economic change, integrating a great variety of different populations into larger economic networks characterised by "Zanzibar-based merchant capital".[7] This merchant capital was not marked by capitalist accumulation of monetary means but rather by 'social wealth' through the establishment of social ties by means of marriage within a network of mutual quasi-client relationships. As far as the East African mainland is concerned, the most important import goods were cotton and beads, whereas internally traded goods on the mainland were primarily bark-cloth, salt, copper and several other items. Yet, the connections between Zanzibar, the East African mainland and the Arabian Peninsula went beyond the economy and included significant political ties. With the Sultan of Oman also being the Sultan of Zanzibar, he acted as the protector not only of the naval trade at the East African shores of the Indian Ocean, but also along the caravan routes reaching into central Africa. With the import and export trade centring on Zanzibar, the Omani Sultan Seyyid Said even transferred his place of residence to Unguja's Stone Town in 1837. Although the Sultan certainly had political power on the Zanzibar Archipelago and in Oman, his might gradually diminished with increasing distance from his place of residence and was only scarcely felt on the mainland's hinterland. Having still significant influence

---

Women and Slavery, Volume One. Africa, the Indian Ocean World, and the Medieval North Atlantic. Athens (Ohio): 2007.

7 Koponen, Juhani. *People and Production in late precolonial Tanzania. History and Structures.* Helsinki: 1988, p. 383.

on the East African Swahili coast and along the caravan routes, his political power must nevertheless not be taken as territorial sovereignty. Especially further inland, and regarding his protection of the caravan routes, the Sultan's influence rested primarily on his personal ties to local 'big men' and thus had the characteristics of an interpersonal client system that must not be mistaken as clear-cut territorial rule.[8]

Over the nineteenth century, European influence in the Indian Ocean, on Zanzibar and its neighbouring mainland, intensified significantly. Although the Portuguese had been the most important European players in the ocean since the Early Modern period, British influence became dominant. The Anglo-Saxons not only slowly but surely controlled all strategically important ports as well as waterways, but also gradually established direct territorial rule, e.g. in today's Uganda and Kenya from the 1880s onwards. In 1890, they established a protectorate on Zanzibar as well. The major reason for the growing interest of Britain in the area was its loss of the North American colonies in the late eighteenth century. Restructuring their empire, the British subsequently concentrated their imperial aspirations on India. As they soon regarded India as their imperial 'jewel in the crown', the subcontinent became the empire's most important imperial possession after the suppression of the Indian rebellion against the East Indian Company in 1857.[9] Shortly afterwards, the British influence and focus on India became even stronger after the opening of the Suez Canal in 1869. Primarily financed by British and French capital, traversing this isthmus by the canal reduced travel time and transport costs profoundly. Especially after steam technology became more efficient than transportation via sailing boats also in respect to cargo shipment, the impact of the Suez Canal multiplied British trade to India from the last third of the nineteenth century onwards. Before these revolutions in international trade, transport and communication – postal delivery service speeded up via steamers, too – the defeat of the Netherlands and France, during and by the end of the Napoleonic Wars, had already facilitated British influence especially in the eastern Indian Ocean:

---

8 Cf. Deutsch, Jan-Georg. 'Inventing an East African Empire: The Zanzibar Delimitation Commission of 1885/86'. *Studien zur Geschichte des deutschen Kolonialismus in Afrika. Festschrift zum 60. Geburtstag von Peter Sebald.* 210–219. Eds. Peter Heine and Ulrich van der Heyden. Pfaffenweiler: 1995, pp. 210–211. Cf. Koponen. *People and Production,* pp. 383–389. Cf. Iliffe. *A Modern History,* pp. 6–87. Cf. Marsh, Zoe and Kingsnorth, G.W. *A History of East Africa. An Introductory Survey.* Cambridge: 1972, pp. 64–77. Cf. Kreye, Lars. *«Deutscher Wald» in Afrika. Koloniale Konflikte um regenerative Ressourcen, Tansania 1892–1916.* Göttingen: 2021, pp. 60–86.

9 Cf. Darwin, John. 'Imperialism in Decline? Tendencies in British Imperial Policy Between the Wars'. 657–679. *The Historical Journal,* vol. 23, no. 3. Cambridge: 1980, pp. 667–670. Cf. Darwin, John. *Das unvollendete Weltreich: Aufstieg und Niedergang des Britischen Empires, 1600–1997.* Frankfurt o. M.: 2013, pp. 135–208.

> At the end of the eighteenth century, with the defeat of the Netherlands by France in 1795, Great Britain seized upon this enforced alliance between its main European and Indian Ocean rivals to take Cape Town, Ceylon (today Sri Lanka), and Java and Melaka from the Dutch, and the Mascarene Islands of Bourbon (now La Réunion) and Ile de France (now Mauritius) from the French. Twenty years later, by 1815, the British controlled the Cape, Ceylon, Melaka, and Mauritius, while Bourbon was returned to France by the Treaty of Paris. Just a few years later, the unauthorized occupation of Singapore [. . .] in 1819 and its formal possession by the British in 1823 almost immediately reduced the economic significance of both Melaka and Dutch Jakarta. [. . .] Thus, two decades into the nineteenth century the basic framework of British domination in the eastern Indian Ocean was established, with the Dutch limited to Indonesia and the French an afterthought.[10]

With this dominance in the eastern part of the Indian Ocean, it is therefore not very surprising that British imperial influence gradually expanded along the African continent and on the Arabian Peninsula as well. Strategically important ports like Aden fell under British sovereignty from 1839 onwards, and when direct rule could not be established for the time being, Britain established strategic alliances and political as well as economic dependencies in the region. This was especially the case regarding British influence in Oman. As the Sultanate of Oman was closely linked to the Zanzibar Archipelago, the British Empire also slowly but surely dominated the entire region from the Red Sea to the Cape, which included numerous islands in the region and parts of the East African mainland, too. In fact, as the economy of East Africa with Zanzibar at its heart relied heavily on the slave trade, British policies mainly followed the directive to introduce what they called 'legitimate trade' and to oust trading in slaves accordingly. Apart from the slave trade, piracy too limited British power in Oman and on Zanzibar until the 1880s. Both hindered British economic expansion in the Indian Ocean and to their view thus had to be restricted severely. As Britain had banned the slave trade already in 1807, she could no longer actively participate in this business. Seeking alliances in these strivings, the British-Dutch Treaty of 1824 settled "imperial divisions of maritime space and colonial territory in maritime Southeast Asia [. . .]. The European powers agreed to eliminate slavery and destroy the markets where pirates sold their captives."[11] Both measures were intended to secure as well as facilitate 'legitimate trade' and thus serve commercial interests of the European powers. The British policies were partly successful as there had been a sharp decline of piracy and slave trading by the beginning of the twentieth century. Nevertheless, they were never completely abolished and both the slave trade and piracy in the entire Indian Ocean persisted to a certain extent. Of course, this

10 Alpers. *The Indian Ocean*, p. 99.
11 Alpers. *The Indian Ocean*, p. 102. Cf. Eckert. 'Capitalism and Labor', pp. 170–173.

holds also true for the area between the Arabian Peninsula, the Zanzibar Archipelago, its neighbouring East African islands and the continent's mainland. As bans alone were not enough to oust competition for her economic interests, Britain pursued other strategies. As especially the control of the Arabian Sea was a great challenge to the British, they sought an alliance with the rulers of Oman. Together with the Omanis, the British particularly targeted the Qawasim, who were notorious for their activities in what the British called the 'Pirate Coast', and who frequently attacked cargo ships at the Strait of Hormuz in the Persian Gulf. The Omanis on their part primarily challenged the Qawasim because the latter were allies of the Wahhabis residing in central Arabia. With the Wahhabis challenging Omani rule on the Arabian Peninsula, the Omanis joined forces with the British to weaken the allies of their direct opponents close to their heartland. This alliance with the strongest European imperial power ultimately turned out fatal to the Omanis, however, as the British took advantage of these Arab political rivalries in the Gulf. The ultimate outcome was a greatly increased economic and political dependency of the Sultanate of Oman and Zanzibar on Britain, leading to the establishment of a British Protectorate over Zanzibar as a result of the Anglo-German Agreement of 1890.[12]

In the meantime, growing British dominance along the East African coast and its hinterland fostered the position of India within the Indian Ocean. With India having had decisive trading links to East Africa for centuries, British influence in Zanzibar, Kenya and Uganda not only strengthened these trading links, but also altered the character of Indian migration to East Africa. Already before 1839, when the Omani Sultan Seyyid Said transferred his residence to Zanzibar, there had been a substantial number of Indian traders doing business in the Omani capital Muscat, as well as in Mombasa and on Zanzibar. With India becoming a British crown colony and with the Omani-British alliance against piracy and the slave trade in the western Indian Ocean, Indian commercial activities and Indian (labour) migration in the area benefited and increased profoundly. Usurping the Quawasim, the Omani-British cooperation encouraged Indian trade under the British flag and Indian merchants took the opportunity to enhance their commercial networks between their subcontinent and East Africa. Consequently, Indian settlement on Zanzibar, which had had a primarily seasonal character and strongly influenced by the monsoon seasons, became more permanent: Indians even occupied or financed offices that were representative for the British Empire. The British Consulate in

---

12 Cf. Alpers. *The Indian Ocean*, pp. 99–105. Cf. Pearson. *The Indian Ocean*, pp. 196–199. Cf. Allen. *European Slave Trading*. Cf. Campbell et al. (Eds.). *Women and Slavery*. Cf. Deutsch, Jan-Georg. *Emancipation without Abolition in German East Africa, c. 1884–1914*. Oxford: 2006, pp. 1–52.

Zanzibar's Stone Town was not only appointed, but also financed by the Bombay government and the *British India Steam Navigation Company*. The latter further established a regular steamer service between Bombay and Zanzibar and the British Indian Post Office on the archipelago, too. As a result of increased economic and political ties, the number of Indians living on Zanzibar rose from ca. 1,000 in 1840 to almost 6,000 in 1860. There, Indians with diverse backgrounds acquired the central role not only in long distance trade, but also in petty trading, retailing, and money lending. For example, any European planning an expedition starting at the Zanzibar Archipelago to the African mainland could not help but purchase his *safari*[13] equipment from an Indian businessman. This advancing Indian dominance in the western Indian Ocean is also reflected by the increasing importance of the Indian Rupee, which soon dominated Zanzibar and the East African mainland. Replacing the old-established Maria Theresa Taler as the most common trade coin in the region, the Rupee became not only the official colonial currency of British Zanzibar, Kenya and Uganda, but also of German East Africa. With the subsequent expansion of the British and German colonies from the East African shores to the interior, Indian merchants also first settled in coastal trading hubs such as Bagamoyo, Tanga, Dar es Salaam and Lindi and later followed the railway lines and started business in more remote places such as Tabora and Ujiji. In the realm of labour, Indian migration was further fostered by indentured labour schemes from the subcontinent, especially during the construction of the British *Uganda Railway*. As the British Empire had banned slavery and the slave trade, allegedly free forms of wage labour, such as contract or rather indentured labour spread in the spheres of British dominance, largely replacing other forms of unfree, i.e. the most widespread form of unpaid labour, slavery. But there was also widespread unorganised and voluntary migration devoid of legal constraints from India to East Africa and back throughout the entire colonial period in the Indian Ocean.[14]

For the majority of the nineteenth century, German enterprises and German states played a negligible role in both politics and the economy in the Indian Ocean. Single companies, for example, the trading enterprise *O'Swald & Co.* from Hamburg, started their economic activities centring on Zanzibar where they established branches in Unguja's Stone Town from the 1840s onwards. Overall, German companies were only one out of many insignificant European players in the region, not to mention an almost negligible German political influence there. With the ab-

13 Safari (Swahili) = journey. In colonial contexts rather expedition accompanied by a caravan.
14 Cf. Mangat. *A History of the Asians*, pp. 27–62. Cf. Voigt-Graf, Carmen. *Asian Communities in Tanzania: A Journey to Past and Present Times.* Hamburg: 1998, pp. 27–38, 100–110, 170–180. Cf. Bertz, Ned. *Diaspora and Nation in the Indian Ocean. Transnational Histories of Race and Urban Space in Tanzania.* Honolulu: 2015, pp. 13–30.

sence of the German nation state, which only became a reality after the foundation of the German *Kaiserreich* in 1870/1871, German influence in the Indian Ocean in general, and in East Africa in particular, remained very limited. This only changed in the middle of the 1880s, when Carl Peters, with his *Gesellschaft für deutsche Kolonisation,* and the *Deutsch Ostafrikanische Gesellgeschaft (DOAG),* urged not only for profound German colonial expansion in East Africa, but also scammed local rulers considerable territory and claimed it as a possession of the colonial chartered company. Although German Chancellor Bismarck did not regard the establishment of German colonies as a major political goal, still he agreed that the privately run chartered company *DOAG* should be granted colonial sovereignty over its conquered regions. Acknowledging the general consent on behalf of the *Reich,* Bismarck further declared these colonial territories conquered by the *DOAG* as a 'German Protectorate' (*Deutsches Schutzgebiet*) in 1885.[15] However, this indirect German colonisation, on the part of the chartered *DOAG,* fundamentally changed its character in the following five years and found its ultimate transformation resulting from the Anglo-German Agreement of 1890.

Fundamental for this binational European political agreement in 1890 was not only British expansionism in the Indian Ocean but also the *DOAG's* political and economic mismanagement. The German chartered company aimed at ousting Zanzibari dominance on the East African mainland and legitimised their policy primarily by the argument of ousting slavery and the slave trade in the region. While the German colonial administration would tolerate slavery throughout the entirety of German colonial rule nevertheless, the attempt to disempower the Arab-Swahili dominance in politics and the (slave) trade provoked local resistance, of course.[16] Trying to replace the powerful caravan traders with strong links to Zanzibar, as well as attempting to enforce colonial claims to power ruthlessly along the East African coast, German colonialism was resisted by the East African coastal population by force of arms. The resulting so-called 'Abushiri-Revolt' fundamentally challenged the *DOAG's* military capacities, and the company had to call upon the German government for military reinforcements. Devoid of any official German colonial military, the *Reich* hastily commissioned Hermann Wissmann to recruit mercenaries especially in the newly established British spheres of influence in Egypt and Sudan. Bloodily subduing the East African forces, the so-called *Wissmanntruppe* (Wiss-

---

15 Cf. Koponen. *Development,* pp. 45–86. Cf. Pearson. *The Indian Ocean,* pp. 190–191. Cf. Hausschild-Thiessen, Renate. *'O'Swald, William'. Hamburgische Biografie. Band 2.* 310–311. Eds. Franklin Kopitzsch and Dirk Brietzke. Hamburg: 2003. Cf. "Oswald & Co.". *Deutsches Koloniallexikon. Band II,* 1920, p. 691. Web. *University of Frankfurt o.M.* http://www.ub.bildarchiv-dkg.uni-frankfurt.de/Bildprojekt/Lexikon/Standardframeseite.php?suche=O%27Swald (9 July 2021).

16 Cf. Deutsch. *Emancipation.* Cf. Eckert. 'Capitalism and Labor', pp. 170–173.

mann-troops) slowly but surely conquered all strategically significant locations between 1888 and 1890. On the East African mainland, the German military victory thus created facts on the ground and underlined German claims to territorial rule in the region. On the diplomatic level, both the Germans and the British had pressured the Sultan of Zanzibar both non-violently and literally by gun boat diplomacy to accept the German seizures in what subsequently became the colony of German East Africa. With the British acceptance of considerable German colonial influence on the East African mainland, the *Reich* renounced its claims on the Zanzibar Archipelago. The archipelago thus became a British Protectorate after the Anglo-German Agreement in 1890 while the Germans fostered their rule on the mainland. As a quasi-compensation for giving up their colonial claims to the most important trading hub in the western Indian Ocean, the British granted the North Sea's Heligoland Archipelago and the Caprivi Strip connecting the colony German South West Africa to the Zambesi River to the *Reich*. Furthermore, indirect German colonisation in East Africa came to an end and the *Reich* took over all competences formerly obtained by the *DOAG*, with the latter remaining an important economic power throughout German colonial rule in the region, nevertheless. With this Anglo-German horse-trading in the western Indian Ocean, old-established political and economic ties between the Zanzibar Archipelago and the East African mainland suffered severely and led to profound economic disintegration of the region. This entailed an economic downturn in the newly established colony of German East Africa. With their colony now cut off from its natural trading centre Zanzibar, German colonial policy makers and economic protagonists of the region called especially for the construction of railways to make the newly established colony an economic success and a symbol for German international standing.[17] From its very beginning, any German railway in the East African colony was embedded in the western Indian Ocean and beyond, as it had profound links to the Arabian Peninsula both during planning stages and in the course of its construction.

---

17 Cf. Glassman, Jonathon. *Feasts and Riot. Revelry, Rebellion, and Popular Consciousness on the Swahili Coast, 1856–1888.* Portsmouth: 1995, pp. 177–270. Cf. Deutsch. 'Inventing', pp. 210–219. Cf. Ratliff, William G. "Heligoland-Zanzibar Treaty of 1890". *Historical Dictionary of European Imperialism.* 279–280. Ed. James S. Olson et al. Westport: 1991, pp. 279–280. Cf. Tetzlaff. *Koloniale Entwicklung,* pp. 72–100, 177–191, 287, 292–293. Cf. Hill. *Permanent Way. Kenya Uganda,* pp. 3–23. Cf. Dernburg. *Zielpunkte des deutschen Kolonialwesens. Zwei Vorträge.* Berlin: 1907, p. 35. Cf. Schinzinger. *Die Kolonien,* pp. 154–158.

2.3 East Africa and German *Weltpolitik*

Two incidents are both symptomatic and symbolic for German colonialism in East Africa: The Anglo-German Agreement of 1890 and the construction as well as opening of the Suez Canal ca. two decades earlier. With the Suez Canal revolutionising global trade, transport and communication, it became one of the most famous symbols of technological mastery achievement built in an age of progress. The Major perpetrators of this technological progress were primarily the western imperial powers. In global politics towards the end of the nineteenth century "control over the major transport routes eventually became an obsession of European geopolitics."[18] Besides gigantic artificial water ways like the Suez Canal, the establishment of telegraphy underwater and overland, the construction of cable cars, as well as the construction of railroads crossing whole nations and entire continents was integral to this mania centring on the erection of infrastructure throughout the world. Several assumptions were held as certainties by the colonising nations regarding the establishment of such infrastructure. First of all, advocates of infrastructure – ranging from geographers to economists and politicians – held the opening up of space and the exploitation of resources all around the globe as a necessity. Even leftist critiques first articulated by Marx assigned the opening of vast territories via colonial infrastructure as an unavoidable phase in human history. Furthermore, European imperialism profoundly changed its face in the nineteenth century. Especially until the 1850s, the religious-missionary approach to allegedly enlighten extra-European territories by means of Christianity increasingly receded into the background. It gave way to an ideology that centred on the spread of modern civilisation that had materialism and technology at its heart. As a consequence of such thinking, non-capitalist societies were increasingly denied their right to existence: it was believed that any population that did not follow this credo necessarily had to yield to the expanding forces. Central to this understanding was the idea that those nations who would not jump on the bandwagon of global expansionism would certainly fall behind and lose their chances to survive the race of the fittest. The global construction of infrastructure was thus not only perceived as the lifeblood of an expanding imperial body but also as the neuralgic point to hit a competing rival the hardest. In turn, this was also where one's own empire was most vulnerable. Technical supremacy was thus regarded as the yardstick that determined a nation's

18 Laak, Dirk van. '"Auf den Hochstraßen des Weltwirtschaftsverkehrs". Zur Ideologie der "Erschließung" im ausgehenden 19. und frühen 20. Jahrhundert'. 104–126. *Comparativ. Zeitschrift für Globalgeschichte und vergleichende Gesellschaftsforschung*, vol. 19, no. 5. Leipzig: 2009, p. 108. Cf. Beese. *Experten*, pp. 77–103.

level of civilisation. Lagging behind in this technological race threatened the right to one's own existence and stirred fears of an empire's decline.[19]

To win the imperial race of the fittest, the German geographers, economists and politicians generally identified three spheres for potential German imperial expansion by means of infrastructure: eastern Europe bordering the contemporary kingdom of Prussia aiming at the colonisation of Poland and Russia; middle- and South-East European territories along the Danube River with a potential ending in Constantinople or even Baghdad; and a third sphere further south via Italy to the African continent and the southern Pacific.[20] Before WWI, only the second and third potential spheres for German imperial expansion experienced the construction of large scale infrastructures such as railways. In this respect, the most famous German imperial infrastructure project found its realisation in the Ottoman Empire and went down in history as the *Bagdadbahn* (Berlin-Baghdad railway). The vision was a long-distance railway track connecting the *Reich's* capital Berlin via Istanbul to Baghdad in today's Iraq. Financed by the *Deutsche Bank* and built by the company of *Philipp Holzmann* from Frankfurt o.M., intense construction works started in the early 1890s, only finding their end decades later in 1940. Already in the earlier phases of construction, the works experienced various setbacks. Major interruptions occurred especially around 1908 with the agitation of *Les Jeunes Turcs* who pushed for reforms in the Ottoman Empire and during the war between the Sultan's realm and Italy around 1912. Later, the construction progress almost came to a standstill during WWI and WWII, of course. After its independence from Britain in 1932, the newly established state of Iraq nationalised the railway in the same year and finished the tracks between 1936 and 1940, when the railhead ultimately reached Baghdad. By then, the railway had lost its economic and political significance, however, and German influence in the region after WWII diminished almost entirely after the defeat of the NS-Regime. Of course, the *Bagdadbahn* was not built in a German colony as such. The Ottoman Empire remained politically independent despite German imperial agitation in the Ottoman territories. Nevertheless, Malte Furhmann described German geopo-

19 Cf. Wenzlhuemer, Roland. *Connecting the Nineteenth-Century World. The Telegraph and Globalization.* Cambridge: 2013. Cf. Laak. "'Auf den Hochstraßen'", pp. 104–124. Cf. Jahn, Nicola. *Der gute Draht zum Nachbarn. Die deutsch-niederländische Kooperation im Telegrafenwesen ihrer Kolonien und Interessenssphären im pazifischen Raum 1899–1936.* Münster: 2020, pp. 31–35, 291–307. Cf. Rösser, Michael. 'Die Firma Wilkins & Wiese in "Neu-Hornow". Ein Drahtseilakt zwischen Rhein/Ruhr, Weißer Elster und Ostafrika'. *Nordrhein-Westfalen und der Imperialismus.* 128–150. Eds. Marianne Bechhaus-Gerst et al. Berlin: 2022.

20 Cf. Laak. "'Auf den Hochstraßen'", pp. 118. Cf. Seemann, Martin. *Kolonialismus in der Heimat. Kolonialbewegung, Kolonialpolitik und Kolonialkultur in Bayern 1882–1943.* Berlin: 2011, pp. 281–305.

litical policies towards the Ottoman Empire in general, and the project of the *Bagdadbahn* in particular, as "semi-colonial"[21] throughout 'the long nineteenth century', as the *Reich* sought indirect political, military and economic benefits in the region. Indeed, the *Bagdadbahn* was intended to challenge French plans of a trans-Sahara railway and the projected English Cape-Cairo railway. To the imagination of its staunch supporters, the *Bagdadbahn* was thought to serve political and economic ends, just as the transcontinental railways had contributed to the rise of the USA and was similarly regarded as significant as the Trans-Siberian Railway that connected the European parts of Russia to China in the Far East. Of course, the *Reich* searched for sales markets for their produce as well. Moreover, the Germans sought cultural imperial influence in the Ottoman Empire just as it hoped to gain raw materials – especially cotton – from the vast lands along the railroad. At the same time, the *Bagdadbahn* also challenged the privileged British access to the Indian subcontinent via the Suez Canal. Thus, the construction of this railway also had the potential to alter the economic and geopolitical realities prevailing in the Indian Ocean. The same applies to other infrastructure like the *Hijaz Railraod* built between 1900 and 1908 in the Ottoman Empire on the Arabian Peninsula in the Indian Ocean, which also featured German influence.[22]

Although the *Hijaz Railway* was primarily built to facilitate Muslim pilgrimage to Mecca, it was certainly also a successful attempt by the Ottoman Sultan to centralise power in his vast and decentralised administrative realm. By fostering his rule in the Ottoman Empire, the Sultan also attempted to fend off especially French and English imperial aspirations in his territories, but also flanked this railway infrastructure with the establishment of other technological large-scale projects. Like the Europeans with their imperial infrastructure, the Ottoman Empire attempted to generate geopolitical influence on the African continent as well.

---

21 Fuhrmann, Malte. 'Deutschlands Abenteuer im Orient. Eine Geschichte semi-kolonialer Verstrickungen'. *Türkisch-Deutsche Beziehungen. Perspektiven aus Vergangenheit und Gegenwart.* 10–33. Eds. Claus Schönig et al. Berlin: 2012. Cf. Fuhrmann, Malte. 'Anatolia as a Site of German Colonial Desire and National Re-awakenings'. 117–150. *New Perspectives on Turkey,* no. 41. N.p.: 2009.

22 The *Hijaz Railroad* connected Syrian Damascus to Medina and found its terminus at the ca. 1,300-km-distant Muslim pilgrimage hotspot Mecca on the Arabian Peninsula. Financed by Muslim donations and particularly by the Ottoman Empire, its leading technicians and engineers were German, like Heinrich August Meißner Pascha, one of the senior engineers for the *Hijaz Railroad,* the *Bagdadbahn* and other railways in Southeast Europe cf. Laak, Dirk van. *Über alles in der Welt. Deutscher Imperialismus im 19. und 20. Jahrhundert.* Munich: 2005, pp. 92–95. Cf. Laak, Dirk van. *Imperiale Infrastruktur,* pp. 150–164. Cf. Fuhrmann, Malte. 'Die Bagdadbahn'. *Kein Platz an der Sonne. Erinnerungsorte der deutschen Kolonialgeschichte.* 190–207. Ed. Jürgen Zimmerer. Bonn: 2013. Cf. Pohl. *Philipp Holzmann,* pp. 97–108.

As Mostafa Minawi points out, the Ottomans established a telegraphy system that generally followed the *Hijaz Railway* but was primarily erected to gain imperial influence on the African continent. Analogically, the Ottoman Sultan had similar quasi-colonial ambitions in Libya, the Eastern Sahara, and the Central African kingdoms. Although the 'Ottoman scramble for Africa' ultimately failed, as the Sultan was ousted by his European competitors in his strivings, it shows that large scale infrastructure projects in the Ottoman Empire in general, and on the Arabian Peninsula in particular, had the potential to influence the conditions in the Indian Ocean Area and were thus an important background to colonial infrastructure in East Africa as well.[23] Imperial infrastructure projects like the *Bagdadbahn* must therefore be considered in relation to other large-scale railway building of the German *Reich* and its empire in the nineteenth century.

In the context of such imperial infrastructural projects on behalf of all empires of the nineteenth century, the abovementioned Anglo-German Agreement of 1890 was one of the first contracts that fell into the era of German *Weltpolitik* ('world politics'). The contract between Britain and the *Reich* was signed only a few weeks after *Kaiser* Wilhelm II had dismissed Chancellor Bismarck and appointed Leo von Caprivi as the latter's successor. The release of Bismarck marked a significant turning point in German foreign policies under the young and ambitious German *Kaiser*. It heralded the credo of German *Weltpolitik*:

> In short, Wilhelmine Weltpolitik was the German Empire's claim to play an ongoing significant role in international politics. Behind this was the basic assumption that the credo of Bismarckian 'saturation' was to be abandoned after the founding of the [Kaiserreich] in 1870/71 and that the empire was now no longer primarily concerned with preserving its newly acquired position on the European continent but was instead to pursue an expansive foreign policy.[24]

With imperial infrastructure regarded as one of the most significant tools to secure economic and political influence beyond the borders of the nation state, the *Reich* also intensified the planning and construction of large-scale railway projects, of course. The *Bagdadbahn* in the Ottoman Empire was only one of these projects. Especially from 1890 onwards, the *Reich*, internationally operating German companies, and also their financing banks increasingly expanded their fields

23 Cf. Minawi, Mostafa. *The Ottoman Scramble for Africa. Empire and Diplomacy in the Sahara and the Hijaz.* Stanford: 2016, pp. 99–146. Cf. Ochsenwald, William. *The Hijaz Railroad.* Charlottesville: 1980, pp. 25–58, 151–156.

24 Rösser, Michael. '"Den Seegedanken zu pflegen"? Hagener Krieger- und Marinevereine. Krieg und Gewalt in China und im Kolonialen Afrika'. *Fernes Hagen. Kolonialismus und Wir*. 14–29. Eds. Fabian Fechner and Barbara Schneider. Hagen: 2021, p. 17.

of activity to foreign countries all around the globe. Regarding banking, especially the *Deutsche Bank* took centre stage, whereas companies such as *Philipp Holzmann* from Frankfurt o.M., *Arthur Koppel & Co.* as well as *Lenz & Co.* from Berlin acquired contracts for the construction of (railway) infrastructure in the Americas, Asia, Asia Minor and colonial Africa. Railway component suppliers like *Krupp* from Essen or bridge building enterprises such as *MAN* from Bavaria or the company of *Gutehoffnungshütte* from Oberhausen were the larger players of numerous vendors of railway equipment who were involved in this construction of imperial infrastructure all around the world. Naturally, many of these globally expanding German companies operated also in German East Africa. Observing both their German partners and foreign competitors closely all around the globe, there was also intercontinental cooperation and exchange among them in respect to various imperial infrastructures. As far as German East Africa is concerned, the most important connections existed between the construction of the *Bagdadbahn* and the *Central Railway* in the German colony in the Indian Ocean. Both railways were not only financed by the *Deutsche Bank* but also constructed by *Philipp Holzmann.*[25]

2.4 German Colonial Policies *in* the Indian Ocean

> If in the past one colonised with means of destruction, today one can colonise with means of preservation, and this includes the missionary as well as the doctor, the railway as well as the machine, that is, advanced theoretical and applied science in all fields.
>
> German Colonial State Secretary Bernhard Dernburg. Berlin: 1907.[26]

In the context of *Weltpolitik*, German planning and construction of imperial infrastructure intensified after 1890 all around the world. With German policies, banks and construction companies designing and building railways in the Near

---

25 Cf. Rösser. 'Transimperiale Infrastruktur?'. Cf. Plumpe. *Deutsche Bank*, pp.79–164. Cf. Kleinöder. 'A Place in the Sun?'. Cf. Pohl. *Philipp Holzmann*, pp. 81–120. Cf. Bähr. *MAN*, pp. 201–230. Cf. Historisches Archiv der Firma Krupp (HA Krupp). N 13/7. Gustav Neumann. Baumeister in Tanganyika und Ruanda, WA 70/1471. Abkommen über Klemmplatten für Kolonial-Eisenbahnen zw. 27.10.09–05.03.12., WA 4/1771. Schienenliferung an die Eisenbahngesellschaft für Deutsch-Ostafrika (Usambara-Linie) 1894/96/97, WA 16 g/4.3/231. Bau einer Brücke über den Sanaga-Fluss bei Edea, Kamerun. Cf. Historisches Archiv der Deutschen Bank (HADB). S 1514 Ostafrikanische Eisenbahn, S. 1515 Ostafrikanische Eisenbahn, S 1516 Ostafrikanische Eisenbahngesellschaft Expedition 1903 Ausrüstung, S 1518 Ostafrikanische Eisenbahn. Verhandlungen Koppel. Cf. Historisches Archiv/Museum der MAN AG Augsburg. Erzeugnisse Werk Gustavsburg. 42. 352/a/3-2.

26 Dernburg. *Zielpunkte*, p. 9.

East, Asia and the Americas, infrastructures in the *Reich's* colonial territories, especially in Africa took centre stage, too. In fact, most of these projects on the African continent did not leave the planning stage and construction seldom started before ca. 1900. The first 1,000 km of railways took twelve and a half years of construction until the opening of operations.[27] Only after 1905/1906 did the construction process in the German colonies intensify and by 1913 more than 4,000 km had been built and were in use accordingly. In terms of infrastructure building, German East Africa was the early, yet very slow, bird. The very first German colonial railway was the *Usambara Railway* in the north of the colony. It was originally intended to connect the coastal port Tanga to the *Nyanza* ('Lake Victoria') in the colony's northwest but never reached the great African lake, but finally going only to the foot of Mount Kilimanjaro. The first part of the railway was finished quickly and opened as early as 1894. However, it was only fourteen km long, and the next interim destination Mombo (ca. 130 km), took eleven years to complete. In the German colony at the Indian Ocean, intense railway construction took off only between 1905 and 1906 when the construction of the *Central Railway* started in coastal Dar es Salaam and finally reached ca. 1,200-km-distant Kigoma on the shores of Lake Tanganyika in summer 1914. The railroad's opening celebrations were held only a few weeks before WWI started. Although the *Central Railway*'s construction progressed rapidly especially after 1907, it was only started with a huge delay as its planning had already begun in the early 1890s.[28]

The reasons for the delay were manifold. First, various protagonists of the colonial administration, the military and the economy, held conflicting views over the priorities of railway construction. Those favouring the immigration of German settlers to the colony supported the enhancement of the northern *Usambara Railway*, whereas others supported the construction of a central railway connecting coastal Dar es Salaam with Lake Tanganyika, arguing that the neighbouring British *Uganda Railway* was enough to open the north of the German colony. Influential officials like Governor Götzen (1900–1906), who attempted to intensify the cultivation of cotton especially in German East Africa's south in order to attain independence particularly from US American raw cotton, favoured a southern railway line to facilitate the production of this cash crop. Besides these conflicting views on where to best build a railway in German East Africa, the *Reichstag* often rejected the colonial budget and thus prevented any costly railway projects. The decisions of the German parliament additionally reflected the increasing scepticism towards German

27 Baltzer, Franz. *Die Kolonialbahnen mit besonderer Berücksichtigung Afrikas.* Berlin: 1916, p. 28.
28 Cf. Baltzer. *Die Kolonialbahnen*, pp. 27–29.

colonialism in German politics, economic circles and the public. By the early 1890s, the once widespread enthusiasm of German society in favour of colonial conquest had given way to general disappointment about the *Reich's* overseas territories. Various scandals about excessive colonial violence, general mismanagement of the chartered German colonial companies, largely absent economic benefits and the high costs of the first colonial wars in almost all overseas territories disillusioned almost the entire spectrum of German society. Hence, there was also hardly any love lost for costly large-scale colonial railway projects until the turn of the century.[29]

This widespread scepticism towards more committed colonial expansion and investments only changed in the course of even more intense colonial warfare. Severely challenging aspects of German colonial rule especially in Africa – particularly, German genocidal warfare against the Ovaherero and Nama in German South West Africa, and to a certain extent the Maji Maji War in German East Africa (1905–1908) – reawakened interest in German colonialism in the *Reich*. Thus, debate about German colonial policies in general, and colonial warfare in particular, dominated the general elections held in the *Reich* in 1907. With the resulting win of the pro-colonial parties in the elections, the German parliament supplemented large sums to the colonial budgets to finance the extraordinary costs needed for the colonial military to win the wars in the African colonies. Resulting from these wars and their broad media coverage during the elections, colonial scepticism receded into the background and gave way to a willingness to restructure the administration of the German colonies. Moreover, broader circles now agreed to invest in various political and economic colonial projects. Subsequently, the *Reich* restructured its colonial administration and created the Colonial Department in Berlin in 1907. In this context, the newly appointed Colonial State Secretary Bernhard Dernburg took centre stage. Pursuing an unorthodox style of politics and having an individual public appearance and manner of speaking, this trained banker with international experience soon acquired the reputation of a hands-on and pragmatic politician. Although observed with suspicion by those colonial policy makers who urged for large-scale German overseas settlements, Dernburg was generally regarded as the politician with the right strategies to settle the colonial chaos and to stir the economy of overseas territories, especially at the beginning of his political career. Drawing a lot on his pre-

29 Cf. Koponen. *Development*, pp. 45–86, 167–250. Cf. Tetzlaff. *Koloniale Entwicklung*, pp. 25–80. Cf. Conrad. *Deutsche Kolonialgeschichte*, pp. 22–37, 54–61. Cf. Habermas. *Skandal in Togo*. Cf. Baltzer. *Die Kolonialbahnen*, pp. 35–60. Cf. Kolonialpolitisches Aktionskomitee (Ed.). *Die Eisenbahnen Afrikas. Grundlagen und Gesichtspunkte für eine koloniale Eisenbahnpolitik in Afrika. Nach der gleichnamigen amtlichen Denkschrift*. Berlin: 1907, pp. 65–75, 150–156.

ceding professional experience in the USA, Dernburg's colonial policies centred on three major objectives. First, he urged a scientific colonialism, aiming to use all the modern technology of Germany in the early twentieth century for the opening and development of its overseas territories. Secondly and strongly related to that, colonial infrastructure and especially railways were deemed central to both stimulate economic activity and enhance the capacities of the colonial military. Thirdly, Dernburg intended the imperial infrastructure to both attract large scale German plantation enterprises and to facilitate local African economic activity. The longer Dernburg stayed in office, the more he regarded the colonised population as 'the most valuable asset' of the entire colony instead of regarding them as a hindrance to German colonial conquest. Rhetorically, this was a radical departure from previous opinions that blustered of the 'necessary evil' to extinguish the African races for the good of the German colonisers. Dernburg's approach has thus long been labelled the 'reformed colonial policies'. Although his four-year term of office between 1906 and 1910, as head of the *Reich's* Colonial Department, appears as a radically new approach to the German colonies, Dernburg's reforms had very limited effects on the spot, however. All in all, his 'reformed colonial policies' have generally been overrated by historical research. Although several laws supported by Dernburg intended to improve the living and working conditions of the colonised populations, the actual effects of these policies were marginal. In essence not much changed for those men and women working daily on German colonial plantations or at the railway.[30]

30 Cf. Becker, Frank. 'Die Hottentotten-Wahlen (1907)'. *Kein Platz an der Sonne. Erinnerungsorte der deutschen Kolonialgeschichte.* 177–190. Ed. Jürgen Zimmerer. Bonn: 2013. Cf. Utermark, Sören. *"Schwarzer Untertan vs. schwarzer Bruder". Bernhard Dernburgs Reformen in den Kolonien Deutsch-Ostafrika, Deutsch-Südwestafrika, Togo und Kamerun.* Unpublished Dissertation. N.P.: 2011. Web. *Universität Kassel.* https://kobra.uni-kassel.de/bitstream/handle/123456789/2012082441677/DissertationSoerenUtermark.pdf?sequence=5&isAllowed=y (21 July 2021), pp. 318–329. Cf. Schiefel, Werner. *Bernhard Dernburg. 1857–1937. Kolonialpolitiker und Bankier im wilhelminischen Deutschland.* Zürich: 1974, pp. 45–142. Cf. Rathenau, Walther. 'Erwägungen über die Erschlieszung [sic!] des Deutsch-Ostafrikanischen Schutzgebietes'. *Reflexionen.* 143–198. Ed. Walter Rathenau. Leipzig: 1908. Cf. Pfeil, Joachim. *Vorschläge zur praktischen Kolonisation in Ost-Afrika.* Berlin: 1890, p. 59. Cf. Iliffe. *Tanganyika under German Rule,* pp. 49–81, 166–200. Cf. Naranch, Bradly D. '"Colonized Body," "Oriental Machine": Debating Race, Railroads, and the Politics of Reconstruction in Germany and East Africa, 1906–1910'. 299–338. *Central European History,* vol. 33, no. 3. Cambridge: 2000. Web. *Jstor.* http://www.jstor.org/stable/4546983 (13 July 2018). Cf. Schröder. *Gesetzgebung und 'Arbeiterfrage',* pp. 380–382, 584–598. Cf. Zimmerer, Jürgen. 'Deutscher Rassenstaat in Afrika. Ordnung, Entwicklung und Segregation in "Deutsch-Südwest" (1884–1915)'. *Von Windhuk nach Auschwitz? Beiträge zum Verhältnis von Kolonialismus und Holocaust.* 120–139. Ed. Jürgen Zimmerer. Berlin: 2011, pp. 134–136, FN 34. Cf. Dernburg, Bernhard. *Koloniale Erziehung.* Munich: 1907, pp. 9–11. Cf. Koponen. *Development,* pp. 670–671.

Nevertheless, Dernburg succeeded in mobilising German capital for the colonies and in generating public support for his colonial policies. As Colonial State Secretary he certainly did his share in setting in motion large-scale investments in vast plantations, such as the *Otto* cotton plantation or the massive expansion of the railway networks. Besides the abovementioned geopolitical and economic strategies of infrastructure building, a desire for German autarky from decisive globally traded and manufactured raw materials was significant. In this respect, the most important crop was cotton as its global market price had profound influence on the profitability of the large German textile industry. As one of the largest industrial sectors in the country, the textile industry employed not only a great share of the German working classes, but it was also one decisive factor in the *Reich's* overall economic policies. Envisioning control over the entire supply chain of textile manufacturing from raw materials to clothing, Dernburg and colonial lobby groups such as the *Kolonialwirtschaftliche Komitee – KWK* (colonial economic committee), alongside other European colonial powers, urged for independence especially from the USA as the largest raw cotton producer in the world. By cultivating cotton in its own colonies, many German experts, politicians and entrepreneurs hoped not only to gain economic independence from the USA, but to overtake competing British textile producers as well.[31]

Apart from such well-received geopolitical and economic colonial visions, Dernburg further popularised German colonialism among the largest part of German society, as he also improved the reputation of German colonialism internationally. Besides modern technology and financial investments, any science serving the German colonial cause came in handy to raise the prestige of German imperialism and her colonies.[32] In this respect, the discipline of palaeontology played a significant part. Since the middle of the nineteenth century, the emerging scientific discipline of palaeontology – which was strongly related to zoology, botany, archaeology, ethnology and geology – had tried to explain the origin of man and the genesis of the earth's species, flora and fauna. From its very beginning, the young academic discipline had strong links not only to the scientific debate, but its re-

---

31 Cf. Dernburg. *Koloniale Lehrjahre. Vortrag Gehalten in Stuttgart am 23. January 1907*. Stuttgart et al.: 1907, pp. 9–14. Cf. Sunseri. *Vilimani*, pp. 1–25, 113–135. Cf. Beckert. *Empire of Cotton*. Cf. Riello. *Cotton*. Cf. Zimmerman. *Alabama in Africa*. Cf. Robins. *Cotton and Race*. Cf. Powell. *Losing the Thread*.

32 Cf. Methfessel, Christian. *Kontroverse Gewalt. Die imperiale Expansion in der englischen und deutschen Presse vor dem Ersten Weltkrieg*. Cologne et al.: 2018, pp. 296–300. Cf. Sunseri. *Vilimani*, pp. 1–25, 165–192. Cf. Bleifuß and Hergenröder. *Die "Otto-Plantage,"* pp. 14–26. Cf. Dernburg. *Zielpunkte*. Cf. Dernburg. *Koloniale Lehrjahre*. Cf. Dernburg. *Koloniale Erziehung*, pp. 13–16.

search results were also widely debated in public via the media. In the course of this widespread interest, palaeontological research results intertwined with larger political and societal themes and generally reflected the contemporary worldview of European societies. Of course, this included tropes of racism and "the colonial image of the non-European world".[33] Often, palaeontological finds and related dominant scientific or public opinions were instrumentalised to legitimise colonial rule, and to insinuate European civilisational advantage over peoples living in the Americas, Asia, Oceania, or Africa. Although palaeontological research results had genuinely been generated and debated transnationally, the nation (state) remained one of the most significant focal points for the academic discipline. Thus, nationalist and even jingoist attitudes were also widespread in the field of science. In this context, the nations entered a race about research on the most efficient machines, the biggest guns and the largest navy, and used their economic and technological skill to expand their imperial spheres of influence.[34] Despite the fact that research results of palaeontology can hardly be transformed into matters of technological progress, military might or economic profits, the science of fossils became a matter of intense national interest. Like German archaeological excavations of ancient Babylon in today's Iraq, around 1900, for instance, academic success of any research institute in the *Reich* in any field easily translated into national prestige. Thus, the field of palaeontology also became a matter of international standing for the German *Reich* around 1900. In the overall context of imperial competition, any nation having imperial ambitions sought to generate the most spectacular research results. Regarding palaeontology, especially dinosaur fossils provided for the most sensational material. As the huge size of many bones discovered was quickly associated with the alleged greatness of the nation which had conducted the petrified bones' excavation, a veritable 'dinomania' emerged around 1900. This great scientific and popular interest led to a race for the discovery of the largest and most spectacular prehistorical dinosaur bone among the European imperial nations and the USA. With the dinosaur fossils found at the Tendaguru mountain in the southeastern region of *Lindi* in German East Africa, only shortly after the Maji Maji War had devastated the area between 1905–1907, palaeontological excavations by German scientists in the German colony were the perfect opportunity to refurbish the blemished imperial prestige of the German *Reich*, after the wars in German South West Africa (1904–1907) and German East Africa (1905–1908). For the time being, these fossils from the German colony in the Indian Ocean proved to be the largest

33 Schweighöfer, Ellinor. *Vom Neandertal nach Afrika. Der Streit um den Ursprung der Menschheit im 19. und 20. Jahrhundert.* Göttingen: 2018, p. 9.
34 Cf. Schweighöfer. *Vom Neandertal*, pp. 7–26, 369–378.

in the world and led many contemporary Germans to believe that the *Reich*'s colonial ambitions really enhanced their motherland's greatness. In line with this perception, Germany had accordingly won a scientific battle especially against competing palaeontologists from Britain and the USA.[35] Yet, despite this widespread enthusiasm among German society resulting from the gigantic dinosaur bones from the Tendaguru in German East Africa, German colonial policy makers around Dernburg likewise regarded the construction of imperial infrastructure as the decisive tool that symbolised German civilisational advance. Of course, railways were also intended to enhance the economic success of the *Reich's* colonies by opening up the colonial territory and enabling the extraction of urgently needed raw materials like cotton. The construction of the *Central Railway* in German East Africa between ca. 1905 and 1916, and the labour conditions at the construction sites as well as the labour relationships of all protagonists involved in the building process are analysed in the following first case study of this global history of labour.

35 Cf. Steinecke, Ernst-Christian. 'Die Ausgrabung von Babylon. Wissenschaftsförderung im Deutschen Kaiserreich am Beispiel der Archäologie'. *Von Käfern, Märkten und Menschen. Kolonialismus und Wissen in der Moderne.* 285–296. Eds. Rebekka Habermas and Alexandra Przyrembel. Göttingen: 2013. Cf. Rieppel. *Assembling*, pp. 80–90. Cf. Nieuwland. *American Dinosaur*, pp. 3–48. Cf. Tamborini, Marco. 'Die Vermarktung der Tiefenzeit. Paläontologie im Umbruch'. *Dinosaurier Fragmente. Zur Geschichte der Tendaguru-Expedition und ihrer Objekte, 1906–2018.* 124–135. Eds. Ina Heumann et al. Göttingen: 2018. Cf. Mehtfessel. *Kontroverse Gewalt*, pp. 266–316.

3 The *Central Railway*

3.1 From *Laissez Faire* to Obscure Regulations

3.1.1 Supervising a Colonial Railway

> We hear only a fraction of what is going on in railway construction; but the little that is known is still so bad that we cannot and will not take responsibility for its continuation.
>
> MP Gustav Noske – Social Democrats (SPD) – *Reichstag:* 10 March 1914.[1]

Gustav Noske's pledge to reject the *Reich's* colonial budget in early March 1914 is certainly typical for the policies of the Social Democrats in imperial Germany. Although the SPD gradually abandoned their fundamental opposition towards any German colonial policies and imperialism, it was one of the very few parties in the *Reichstag* that criticised German colonial policies. Along with parts of the Catholic party, the *Zentrum,* the Social Democrats condemned excessive violence exerted against the colonised populations and attempted to resolve colonial scandals repeatedly. The primary means to this end was often to reject the colonial budget, which was decisive to finance any colonial projects overseas.[2] In this respect, Noske himself was the central figure of the Social Democrats and acted as the party's expert and spokesman regarding German colonial policies in the *Reichstag.* Although generally criticising German colonialism on behalf of his party, Noske was certainly part of the right wing of the SPD. In German history, this politician is primarily notorious as minister of defence in the early years of the Weimar Republic. Having bloodily put down uprisings of the labour movement in Berlin of 1919 and 1920 with the decisive aid of anti-democratic and right-wing paramilitaries, he went down in history as 'worker slaughterer' and 'bloodhound'. Regarding German colonialism, Noske counted as one

1 Noske, Gustav. '232. Sitzung. Dienstag, den 10. März 1914'. 7984–7993. *Verhandlungen des Reichstags. Bd. 294.1914.* Berlin: 1914. Web. http://www.reichstagsprotokolle.de/Blatt_k13_bsb00003390_00080.html (21 June 2018), p. 7991.

2 Cf. Melber, Henning. '". . . dass die Kultur der Neger gehoben werde!" – Kolonialdebatten im deutschen Reichstag'. *Kolonialmetropole Berlin. Eine Spurensuche.* 67–72. Eds. Ulrich van der Heyden and Joachim Zeller. Berlin: 2002, p. 71. Cf. Becker. 'Die Hottentotten-Wahlen (1907)', pp. 177–190. Cf. Bösch, Frank. 'Der Ankläger. Erzberger und die Kolonialpolitik im frühen 20. Jahrhundert'. *Matthias Erzberger. Ein Demokrat in Zeiten des Hasses.* 47–71. Eds. Haus der Geschichte Baden-Württemberg in Verbindung mit der Landeshauptstadt Stuttgart. Karlsruhe: 2013, pp. 50–54. Cf. Guettel, Jens-Uwe. 'The Myth of a Pro Colonialist SPD: German Social Democracy and Imperialism before World War I'. 452–484. *Central European History*, vol. 45, no. 3. Cambridge: 2012. Web. *Jstor.* https://www.jstor.org/stable/23270519?seq=1 (26 October 2020).

https://doi.org/10.1515/9783111218090-003

of the very few experts on the issue in his party. In general, he was uninterested in any theoretical debate on colonialism and took a very practical approach towards German colonial policies. Taking the existence of the *Reich's* overseas territories for granted, he rejected excesses of colonial violence but strongly advocated the idea of allegedly lifting the 'cultural level' of the colonised people by means of colonial domination. Above all, he advocated using the economic benefits from colonialism to uplift the working classes in Germany. To Noske, this was only possible by increased economic activity that would improve the standard of living of the local populations in Africa, but also especially the living conditions of the German people living in the *Reich*. Central to Noske's understanding of German colonialism was the construction of infrastructure, i.e. particularly railways, to 'develop' the colonial territories. As an advocate of imperial infrastructure, Noske had personally been in favour of passing the colonies budget to finance colonial railway construction since 1911. Only his party's resistance to supporting German colonial politics compelled Noske to speak against corresponding railway plans in the *Reichstag*, as he had repeated his support for colonial railway construction as late as February 1914.[3]

Hence, Gustav Noske's criticism against colonial railway construction in German East Africa has exactly to be seen in this light. With the completion of the *Central Railway*'s construction only a few kilometres away, the MPs debated future railway projects for the colony in March 1914. Reminding the *Reichstag* of forced and convict labour at the *Central Railway* and insufficient sanitary conditions and medical treatment for the workers, Noske and his party spoke against any further railway construction in German East Africa such as the planned *Ruanda Railway* in 1914. Implicitly, Noske also criticised the inadequate information management prevalent regarding the construction sites, stating that the German public, parliament, and the governmental policy makers only knew "a fraction" about the living and working conditions along the railroad. While the working conditions will be investigated in the following sections, Noske's criticism about the poor information supply concerning the construction of the *Central Railway* directs attention to the question of which records about the *Central Railway*'s construction were conveyed from the construction camps to the German *Reichstag* or rather the German public. Apart from general questions of historical source criticism discussed above, it is crucial to

3 Cf. Wette, Wolfgang. "Noske, Gustav". *Neue Deutsche Biographie*, 19, 1998, pp. 347–384. Web. https://www.deutsche-biographie.de/pnd118588761.html (1 July 2021). Cf. Schröder, Hans-Crhistoph. *Gustav Noske und die Kolonialpolitik des Deutschen Kaiserreiches*. Berlin and Bonn: 1979, pp. 7–41, 48–55. Cf. Noske, Gustav. *Kolonialpolitik und Sozialdemokratie*. Stuttgart: 1914, pp. 198–208. Cf. Noske, Gustav. 'Kolonialpolitik nach dem Kriege'. 481–488. *Die Neue Zeit. Wochenschrift der Deutschen Sozialdemokratie*. Vol. 1, no. 21. 22 February 1918. Cf. Noske, Gustav. *Wie ich wurde. Selbstbiographien volkstümlicher Persönlichkeiten*. Berlin: 1919, p. 27.

understand which information was available to whom and how it was conveyed (if ever) from the actual construction sites in German East Africa to the *Reichstag*, the German public and the *Reich's* administration. If information was not delivered from the German colony to the *Reich*, one must ask the questions of *why* and *how*.

Considering the patch-work character of the 'colonial state' in German East Africa, as also in other German colonies, it is not very surprising that the quality and amount of the information about the overseas territories were most of the time far from satisfying. This included any information available to *Reichstag* MPs in general,[4] but also for railway construction in German East Africa in particular. Poor information supply was acute especially during the initial years of construction between 1905 and 1908. When the initial 200 km from coastal Dar es Salaam to Morogoro were being built, the question of why only very little reliable information about railway construction left the German colony is comparably easy to answer: hardly any documents were ever produced by the German authorities. Besides general questions of historical conveyance, the major reason for this absence of documents is the absence of any administrative bodies that supervised the construction process. Especially in this period, the *OAEG* and its direct construction organ, the company *Philipp Holzmann*, enjoyed a high degree of freedom devoid of any clear regulations and any supervising authorities. Neither the *Reich* in Berlin nor the *Gouvernement* in Dar es Salaam had issued any specific regulations that could have directed the companies to any specific labour policies. Consequently, there were no governmental bodies to supervise construction either.[5] Instead, paragraph seven of the railway building contract between *Holzmann* and the governmental administrations delegated all aspects regarding labour to the construction company. Accordingly, the company had not only to recruit the necessary workforce, it also had to take care of the labourers' food and lodging, as well as the workers' healthcare. Of course, *Holzmann* was often supported by the colonial government in all of these aspects, but contractual arrangements made the building company accountable for almost all decisions related to the construction process and deprived the *Gouvernement* of any forms of supervision.[6] This *laissez faire* policy followed by the German (colonial) authori-

4 Cf. Pesek. *Koloniale Herrschaft*, pp. 190–265. Cf. Habermas. *Skandal in Togo*, pp. 32–41, 99–102.

5 Cf. Stadtarchiv Frankfurt. *Wirtschaftsarchiv*. Philipp Holzmann. W1/2 – 278/1. Holzmann in Afrika. *Bau der Mittellandbahn Daressalam-Kigoma von Baurat Ferdinand Grages*. Frankfurt a.M.: 4 June 1948, pp. 7–8. Cf. Allmaras, Franz. 'Ich baue 2000 km Eisenbahnen'. *Heiß war der Tag. Das Kolonialbuch für das junge Deutschland.* 35–55. Ed. Hans Ernst Pfeiffer. Leipzig: 1938, pp. 41–42.

6 Cf. Stadtarchiv Frankfurt. *Wirtschaftsarchiv*. Philipp Holzmann. W1/2–517. Verträge Morogoro-Tabora, Tabora-Kigoma, Umbau Daressalaam-Morogoro, Ruandabahn, "Vertrag über den Eisenbahnbau von Morogoro nach Tabora (1908)", p. 6 and cf. "Vertrag über die Umbauten der Stamm-

ties regarding railway construction in general and regarding labour and the workforce in particular changed only gradually and incomprehensively in the course of the entire construction period until 1914. It is therefore not very surprising that without administrative bodies, there was and is only scarce documented information available especially for the first years of construction between 1905 and 1907. With little information ever produced in situ, even less information about railway construction in German East Africa was conveyed to any parts of the world, including the *Reich* and the public debates in the *Reichstag*, of course.

With the German authorities establishing some railway construction regulations and labour recruitment laws from 1909 onwards, the information situation about labour at the *Central Railway* improved, but still left a lot to be desired. In the course of Dernburg's introduction of general colonial labour protection rights – the *Arbeiterverordnungen* (workers' ordinances) from 1909 onwards – also many aspects regarding labour at the *Central Railway*'s construction sites were subject to more legislation subsequently. Along with the introduction of labour commissioners, who were intended to check and control the colonial employers as well as to exert disciplining measures on the African workers, the colonial administration established a separate office to supervise railway construction work. The railway commissioner's office (*Eisenbahnkommissariat*) was established in early 1909 and its railway commissioner Meier, who lived in Dar es Salaam, was primarily responsible for anything related to land procurement for the railroad and railway police. Meier's staff comprised the construction supervision (*amtliche Bauaufsicht*), consisting of one senior civil servant (first Mr Popcke, then Mr Batzner) and staffed with five to seven German civil servants who observed construction works and labour conditions on the spot along the tracks of the *Central Railway*. This supervisory body was supported by the railway department (*Eisenbahnreferat)* run by Mr Rosien. In early August 1912, the railway commissioner's office was readjusted: two more railway commissioners were employed, and their tasks and duties were enlarged. After this reform, there were three railway commissioners (*Eisenbahnkommissare*) on duty in German East Africa. Like the very low number of four labour commissioners responsible for the observation of the labour legislation in the entire colony, the three railway commissioners oversaw a railway network that was almost 2,000 km long. After the reform of 1912, the railway commissioners had their offices in coastal Dar es Salaam, central Tabora and in northern Buiko. As the railway commissioner in Buiko was exclusively in charge of the northern *Usam-*

strecke Daressalam-Morogoro (1912)", p. 6. Cf. Eckhart G. Franz and Geissler, Peter (Eds.). *Das Deutsch-Ostafrika-Archiv. Inventar der Abteilung 'German Records' im Nationalarchiv der Vereinigten Republik Tansania, Dar es Salaam. Band I. Einleitung, Zentralverwaltung.* Marburg: 1973, pp. 27–28.

bara Railway (by 1914 ca. 400 km), there were de facto only two (!) railway commissioners for the entire *Central Railway*. The one in Dar es Salaam observed the modification of the home line Dar es Salaam – Morogoro (200 km), as the initially built track had proven to have several flaws and weaknesses and needed reconstruction. The other railway commissioner in Tabora observed anything related to construction works between Morogoro and Kigoma, which were more than 1,000 km away from each other. As usual in German colonial East Africa, the administration was certainly understaffed for its assigned task.[7]

All three railway commissioners were trained railway engineers who had been given the status of civil servants by the colonial administration. They were thus subordinate to the *Gouverneur* only, but superior to the construction supervisors (*Bauaufsicht*) and works supervisors (*Betriebsaufsicht*). All these three bodies (*Bauaufsicht, Betriebsaufsicht* and *Eisenbahnkommissare*) had the duty to supervise the privately owned and privately run railway construction companies as well as the operating companies. The major construction company *Philipp Holzmann* and the operating company, the *Ostafrikanische Eisenbahngesellschaft (OAEG),* were therefore officially under the supervision of the railway commissioners as the major institution of oversight. Under the railway commissioners served the construction supervision and the works supervision as minor departments responsible for the local levels of supervision.[8] The general duties of the two superior railway commissioners

7 There were some modifications over time and some railway commissioners were moved from one location to another, depending on the construction process. The overall number of railway commissioners did not change, however. Cf. Eckhart and Geissler. *Das Deutsch-Ostafrika Archiv. Band I*, pp. 27–30. Cf. Tanzania National Archives (TNA). G17/63. Monatliche Berichte der örtlichen Baubeamten über den Fortgang der Bauarbeiten an der Tanganyika-Eisenbahn Morogoro-Tabora. Bd. 1. 1908–1910, "Dr. Ritter an den Herrn Eisenbahn-Commissar Dar es Salaam, Kidete 17. Januar 1909, VIII Personal- und Arbeiterverhältnisse". Cf. TNA. G17/64. Monatliche Berichte der örtlichen Baubeamten über den Fortgang der Bauarbeiten an der Tanganyika-Eisenbahn Morogoro-Tabora. Bd. 2. 1910–1911, "Bauaufsicht Zentralbahn no 1301. Kidete, 19. Juni 1910, an den Herrn Eisenbahn Kommissar Daressalaam, VIII Personal- und Arbeiterverhältnisse". Cf. TNA. G17/81. [Personal- und Verwaltungsangelegenheiten der Tanganyika-Eisenbahn Morogoro-Tabora, vorwiegend allgem.] 1912–1914. For a general overview about labour legislation in German East Africa cf. Schröder. *Gesetzgebung und "Arbeiterfrage"*, pp. 380–383, 595–598. For more technical details but less focus on the conflicts between the colonial administration and *Holzmann* cf. Beese. *Experten*, pp. 112–126. For understaffing and lack of administration at the *Congo-Océan Railroad* cf. Daughton. *In the Forest of No Joy*, pp. 214–238, 305–306.

8 Cf. "Eisenbahnkommissar". *Deutsches Koloniallexikon*, 1920, Band I, p. 544. Web. *University of Frankfurt o.M.* http://www.ub.bildarchiv-dkg.uni-frankfurt.de/Bildprojekt/Lexikon/Standardframeseite.php?suche=Kommissar (26 October 2020). Cf. "Eisenbahnbehörden". *Deutsches Koloniallexikon*, 1920, Band I, p. 529. Web. *University of Frankfurt o.M.* http://www.ub.bildarchiv-dkg.uni-frankfurt.de/Bildprojekt/Lexikon/php/suche_db.php?suchname=Eisenbahnbeh%F6rden (26 October

of the *Central Railway* were predominantly paperwork. They had to maintain constant correspondence with the colonial *Gouvernement,* the construction companies (esp. *Holzmann*), and the operating company (*OAEG*) informing about anything related to the track's construction. The regulations obliged the commissioners to send monthly reports about the construction works and labour conditions along the central railroad to the *Gouvernement, Holzmann* and the *OAEG* in written and tabular format. In contrast to this constant correspondence between these three bodies, the colonial legislation prohibited any direct correspondence between the railway commissioners and the Colonial Office in Berlin. Hence, any information gathered along the railroad by the commissioners had to pass the *Gouverneur's* office in Dar es Salaam first, before it was allowed to be forwarded to the *Reich's* Colonial State Secretary in Berlin.[9] As major supervisory bodies, both the railway commissioners and the *Gouverneur* were able to act as decisive gatekeepers about any information conveyed about railway construction.

In 1909, the *Gouverneur* appointed governmental master builder (*Regierungsbaumeister*) Molfenter as the railway commissioner based in Dar es Salaam. From the colony's capital at the Indian Ocean, he had to supervise the reconstruction of the home line from coastal Dar es Salaam to Morogoro. Governmental master builder Batzner took office as second railway commissioner of the central line in Tabora in the same year. Located in Tabora at the mid-point of the railroad, Batzner supervised the construction works and labour conditions between Morogoro and the ca. 1,000 km distant ending point of the railway, Kigoma at Lake Tanganyika. According to their contract, besides their paperwork both Molfenter and Batzner had to "visit the construction sites as often as possible" to gather as much information as they could about the railway's progress and the workforce. To assist them in their tasks, both railway commissioners could employ some supervisory staff. This supervisory staff worked primarily at the local level and travelled along the railroad almost every day. The local supervisory staff (*Streckenaufsichtsbeamte*) were obliged to keep journals about their observations at any time. Based on their journals, the supervisory staff had to send standardised monthly reports to the railway commissioner in charge. The latter processed their findings

2020). Cf. "Eisenbahnaufsicht". *Deutsches Koloniallexikon,* 1920, Band I, p. 525. Web. *University of Frankfurt o.M.* http://www.ub.bildarchiv-dkg.uni-frankfurt.de/Bildprojekt/Lexikon/php/suche_db.php?suchname=Eisenbahnaufsicht (26 October 2020). Cf. "Eisenbahnbeamte". *Deutsches Koloniallexikon,* 1920, Band I, p. 528–529. Web. *University of Frankfurt o.M.* http://www.ub.bildarchiv-dkg.uni-frankfurt.de/Bildprojekt/Lexikon/php/suche_db.php?suchname=Eisenbahnbeamte (26 October 2020). For more technical details but less focus on the conflicts between the colonial administration and *Holzmann* cf. Beese. *Experten,* pp. 112–126.

9 Cf. TNA. G17/81, pp. 1–3 (J. No. 16401/XII.). Cf. Beese. *Experten,* pp. 112–126.

and fused them into his own reports, which were then sent to the *Gouvernement*, *Holzmann* and the *OAEG*. The standardised monthly reports of the supervisory staff had to report about ten major aspects of the construction process: earth works, bridge constructions and culverts, building constructions, sub- and superstructure, the general progress of construction, exceptional occurrences (e.g. train accidents), labour conditions (food and lodging of the workers and their (medical) treatment), inventory, the supervisory staff's individual cash department and forwarding correspondence about postal or cargo delivery. Finally, these reports explained which works had been carried out by the construction company itself (i.e. *Holzmann*) and which tasks had been delegated to the numerous sub-contractors who were indispensable for the construction of the *Central Railway*.[10]

As a result of the administrational reform of 1912, the number of documents produced by the railway administration multiplied significantly and many of these historical documents survive in the archives. Therefore, much more information is available about the labour conditions along the *Central Railway* from 1912 onwards compared to the preceding years. Yet, as comprehensive as these reports might appear at first glance, much information about the working conditions at the *Central Railway* was lost in the administrative processes and the forwarding of correspondence. Briefly, not all information gathered in German East Africa necessarily reached the *Reich's* government in Berlin, not to mention the MPs of the *Reichstag* nor the German public in general. Although the reports were generally sent regularly by the supervisory staff to the railway commissioners and subsequently forwarded to the *Gouvernement*, some information always got lost on its way. In general, this reflects the ambivalent character of modern bureaucracy established especially in the nineteenth century. This ambivalence finds its expression "in the simultaneity of a relatively narrow legal binding and a relatively large scope for interpretation of the law in the working on individual processes."[11] Besides this ambivalent character of the interpretation of law, the reasons for the leaky information supply were rooted in the realities of colonial rule in German East Africa. A first reason was illness. In particular, the few men of the local supervisory staff often suffered from diseases such as malaria, blackwater fever, typhoid or heatstroke. Contracting such diseases could lay a member of the supervisory staff low for weeks. As substitutes for the men on duty would have had to be recruited in Germany, immediate replacement was

10 Cf. TNA. G17/81, "Dienstanweisung für die Streckenaufsichtsbeamten bei Neubauten und Umbauten auf Schutzgebietsbahnen", pp. 1–5. For more technical details but less focus on the conflicts between the colonial administration and *Holzmann* cf. Beese. *Experten*, pp. 112–126.

11 Becker, Peter. 'Bürokratie'. *Docupedia-Zeitgeschichte*. 30 August 2016. Web. http://docupedia.de/zg/Becker_buerokratie_v1_de_2016 (12 October 2021).

hardly ever possible. If the diseases turned out fatal, sending a new man to East Africa took at least a month. As a result of sickness, the information supply about individual route sections was often interrupted and neither the railway commissioner nor the Governor nor anybody in Germany received sufficient information about the individual supervisor's route section. At times only a minority of the supervisory staff was healthy enough to work, which further limited information supply. In January 1910, for instance, only two out of five men of the construction supervision could work: one had contracted malaria and two, typhoid – one case lethal. In July of the same year, four out of eight men of the supervision suffered from similar serious diseases again and another death occurred.[12] Thus, at times when large parts of the construction supervision were laid low, no accurate information about the railway's construction process was available. Noske's claim quoted above is therefore at least partly justified. Besides sickness, there were also other reasons why the information sent to Berlin proved at times unsatisfactory indeed.

Other reasons for insufficient reports were interruptions or failures in (postal[13]) delivery or delays of other supervisory bodies on whose information a member of the paramount supervisory staff relied. Sometimes, the actual number of workers employed at the *Central Railway* could not be provided and you can doubt whether an exact number was ever conveyed. Examining all surviving reports of the railway commissioners and the construction supervision, it is clear that the railway commissioners complained repeatedly about incomplete reports by the supervisory staff. According to the regulations, the latter's monthly standardised reports had to provide

12 Cf. TNA. G17/63, "Bericht über den Arbeitsfortschritt an der Zentralbahn im Monat März 1909, 8. Personal und Arbeiterverhältnisse", "Monatsbericht für Dezember [1909], [. . .] Kidete, 17. Januar 1909 [sic! 1910], VIII. Personal- und Arbeiterverhältnisse". Cf. TNA. G17/158. Allgemeine [Angelegenheiten der] Tanganyika-Eisenbahn Morogoro-Tabora. Bd. 3. 1909–1911, "Hillenkamp an Eisenbahnkommissar 8. Februar 1910". Cf. TNA. G17/64, "J. No. 1621. Monatsbericht über den Stand der Arbeiten am Ende des Monats Juli [1910]. XI. Personal der Amtl. Bauaufsicht". Cf. TNA. G12/202. Bauberichte und -dispositionen der Tanganyika-Eisenbahn Tabora-Kigoma [sowie der projektierten Eisenbahn Tabora-Kagera-Fluß (Ruanda-Bahn)] 1911–1913. Bd. 1., "Bauarbeiten an der Ostfrikanischen Mittellandbahn. Bahnbau Tabora-Kigoma. Monatsbereicht April 1912, IX. Personal- und Arbeiterverhältnisse", "Bahnbauten an der Ostafrikanischen Mittellandbahn. Bahnbau Tabora-Kigoma. Monatsbereicht Mai 1912, IX. Personal- und Arbeiterverhältnisse", "Bauarbeiten an der Ostafrikanischen Mittellandbahn. Bahnbau Tabora-Kigoma. Monatsbericht Juni 1912, X. Personal- und Arbeiterverhältnisse". Cf. Beese. *Experten*, pp. 134–146.

13 For a general idea about the postal correspondence between (colonial) Africa and Europe and all its necessities, difficulties and flaws, especially before the advent of telegraphy cf. Prass, Reiner. 'Briefe aus Äthiopien und dem Sudan. Die Briefkommunikation zwischen europäischen Reisenden und dem Kartographen August Petermann in Gotha, 1854–1880'. *Verbindung halten. (Post)Kommunikation unter schwierigen Verhältnissen.* 87–109. Ed. René Smolarski et al. Göttingen: 2021, pp. 92–103.

information on ten major aspects of railway construction ranging from earth works to labour conditions, but recurrently failed to provide all the information as demanded. Throughout the entire construction period between 1905 and 1914, there are complaints in the sources that information on the workers' health was not noted down, or information about wages was missing, for example. Moreover, at times the construction company *Holzmann* themselves failed to report significant incidents such as work-related accidents or train derailings to the supervisory bodies.[14] In general, quarrels about competencies and failures related to anything in the construction process of the *Central Railway* were frequent between the *OAEG*, *Holzmann*, the *Gouvernement*, the railway commissioners and their construction supervision. Occasionally, it even seems that the responsible parties deliberately held back information reporting shortcomings of anything related to railway construction.

3.1.2 From Conflicts to Concealment?

> The Gouvernement, the Schutztruppe, the planters and, last but not least, the contractor constantly made great demands on the labour force of the natives, whose numbers and willingness to work were generally insufficient [. . .][.] When, in the course of the construction period, the Gouvernement appointed its own labour commissioners to protect the natives against exploitation by unscrupulous planters and [sub-]contractors, the labour question was hardly brought any closer to a solution; but the complaints about the difficulties that the labour commissioners put in the way of the [sub-]contractors increased.
>
> *Holzmann* Engineer Ferdinand Grages. Frankfurt o.M., 4 June 1948.[15]

Building a railway is a complex long-term undertaking with manifold challenges and obligations. From planning to completion, numerous demanding tasks must be carried out adequately by a great variety of individuals and administrative bodies involved. Controversies about where and how to build a railway best are integral to such an endeavour. This holds true for the *Central Railway* in German East Africa too, of course. Such controversies were prevalent not only during the planning stage, but also during the construction process. Conflicts between the *Gouvernement*, the railway commissioners and their local supervisory staff, *Holzmann*

14 Cf. TNA. G17/63, "VII E. I no. 534 27. Febr. 1909, 8. Personal und Arbeiterverhältnisse", "VIIIE. 7 no. 541/09, 1. März 1909", "An die Firma Holzmann Hier. Drslm 22/3 10.", "Daressalam, den 26. März 1910. An den Herrn Eisenbahnkommissar". Cf. TNA. G17/65. Monatliche Berichte der örtlichen Baubeamten über den Fortgang der Bauarbeiten an der Tanganyika-Eisenbahn Morogoro-Tabora. 1908–1912, "Eisenbahnkommissar no. 659 23. März 1909. An die amtliche Bauaufsicht der Zentralbahn", "Goweko. 6.5.12. An den Herrn Eisenbahnkommissar Tabora".

15 Stadtarchiv Frankfurt. W1/2 – 278/1. *Grages*, p. 4.

and the *OAEG* ranged from technical issues, such as the railway's general alignment, its gradients and the allotment of ditches and drains, to issues of competencies and responsibilities regarding all aspects of the construction process. Another example for conflicts occurred in the context of controlling the disease of 'sleeping sickness'. To erase potential breeding grounds of the sickness' host, the tsetse fly, between Tabora and Kigoma, the railway commissioner urged *Holzmann* to clear bushes and woods along the newly built track in the years 1912–1914. As *Holzmann* had carried out the clearing job, they wanted the *Gouvernement* to pay for the work accordingly. Governor Schnee rejected any payment, claiming that the building contract required *Holzmann* to pay for it. In the end, a compromise was reached, and the costs were split. But the dispute was only settled after two years when the railhead had reached its destination Kigoma in 1914.[16] Conflicts also arose in the context of exchanging information about labour conditions. Although the latest research on colonial railway construction suggests general harmonious and effective cooperation

16 Cf. TNA. G17/30. Berichte des Baubeamten Buchner [über den Fortgang der Arbeiten an der Tanganyika-Eisenbahn Morogoro-Tabora]. 1908–1910. Cf. TNA. G17/158, "Holzmann an den Herren Eisenbahnkommissar, 22.3.1910". Cf. TNA. G17/125. Schlafkrankheitsbekämpfung an der Tanganyika-Eisenbahn Tabora-Kigoma. 1912–1914. For research on sleeping sickness cf. Ehlers, Sarah. *Europa und die Schlafkrankheit. Koloniale Seuchenbekämpfung, europäische Identitäten und moderne Medizin 1890–1950.* Göttingen: 2019. Cf. Webel, Mari K. *The Politics of Disease Control. Sleeping Sickness in Eastern Africa, 1890–1920.* Athens (Ohio): 2019. Cf. Ehlers, Sarah. 'Medical Missions – Racial Visions: Fighting Sleeping Sickness in Colonial Africa in the Early Twentieth Century'. *Health and Difference. Rendering Human Variation in Colonial Engagements.* 91–110. Eds. Alexandra Widmer Veronika and Lipphardt. New York: 2016. Cf. Isobe, Hiroyuki. 'Eine rationale Kolonialpolitik? Die Bekämpfung der Schlafkrankheit im deutschen Schutzgebiet Ostafrika vor dem Ersten Weltkrieg'. *Peripulus 2001. Jahrbuch für Aussereuropäische Geschichte.* 115–132. Ed. Christoph Marx. Berlin: 2011. Cf. Webel, Mari. 'Ziba Politics and the German Sleeping Sickness Camp at Kigarama, Tanzania, 1907–1914'. 399–423. *The International Journal of African Historical Studies*, vol. 47, no. 3. Boston: 2014. Web. *Jstor.* https://www.jstor.org/stable/24393436 (1 June 2021). Cf. Eckart, Wolfgang U. 'The Colony as Laboratory: German Sleeping Sickness Campaigns in German East Africa and in Togo, 1900–1914'. *History and Philosophy of the Life Sciences*, vol. 24, no. 1. Napoli: 2002. Web. *Jstor.* https://www.jstor.org/stable/23332441 (1 June 2021). Cf. MacKenzie, John M. 'Experts and Amateurs: tsetse, nangana, and sleeping sickness in East and Central Africa'. *Imperialism and the Natural World.* 187–212. Ed. John M. MacKenzie. Manchester: 1990. Regarding railway construction, sleeping sickness features repeatedly in the sources. They deal overwhelmingly with construction regulations at railway stations, intended to prevent the spreading of the disease. When visiting the archives in Dar es Salaam, I did not focus on the connection between sleeping sickness and labour. Generally, only few references to the connections between labour and sleeping sickness were found and they appear insignificant compared to incidents of smallpox. Cf. G17/123. Arbeiterverhältnisse der Tanganyika-Eisenbahn Tabora-Kigoma. Bd. 1. 1912–1913. Cf. G12/164. Bauberichte und -dispositionen der Tanganyika-Eisenbahn. 1909–1915. Cf. TNA. G17/64.

between the various protagonists,[17] numerous and profound conflicts were prevalent throughout the entire construction process.

Generally, *Holzmann* divided the entire railway into several construction 'sections' (*Bausektion*), each in charge of the building of some kilometres of railway. Generally, a construction section consisted of two major bodies. The first body was directly operated and administrated by *Holzmann* and the second body consisted of numerous European sub-contractors, as *Holzmann* outsourced many of their construction tasks. The route sections directly run by *Holzmann* proper employed ca. ten to twenty Europeans as engineers, foremen or overseers, some Indian or African craftsmen (ca. 100 maximum) for more complex tasks such as bridge building and a few hundred African workers for the simpler tasks like earth works (ca. 100–300). According to the regulations, each route section had to report monthly the numbers and types of workers employed by both *Holzmann* and the sub-contractors to the construction supervisor in charge. The construction supervisors then processed the information gathered and forwarded it to their superior railway commissioner. At times and for reasons unknown, *Holzmann's* route sections refused to provide the data related to labour conditions, for example claiming in the final months of 1913 that they were no longer required to do so. Irritated by this behaviour, construction supervisor Fick complained to his superior railway commissioner in December 1913:

> Precise information about the personnel employed by the company and the [sub-]contractors as well as about the work performed could not be given in the construction report, as Section 11 refused to provide information in this regard, advising to turn to the Tabora Construction Directorate. The reason for this practice is all the less explicable, as it is evident from the files here[.] [S]everal previous sections and, as hitherto, also Building Section 11 [have] readily answered such enquiries to their full extent[. . .].[18]

Other route sections also refused to provide the demanded information, causing the railway commissioner to intervene.[19] On the commissioner's request, *Holzmann* construction director Hoffmann confirmed the interrupted information flow and justified this new policy, stating:

> We do not consider it permissible for our subordinate departments to provide your supervisors with information to the extent required by your supervisors, without any control on

17 Cf. Beese. *Experten*, pp. 120–126.

18 TNA. G17/121. Monatliche Berichte der örtlichen Baubeamten über den Fortgang der Bauarbeiten an der Tanganyika-Eisenbahn Tabora-Kigoma. Bd. 2 1913–1914, "Kigoma[?], den 3. Dezember 1913. [. . .] Monatsbericht [. . .] Dezember 1913".

19 TNA. G17/121, "Scheel an Eisenbahnkommissar Sima, den 6. XII.13", "Forchmann an Eisenbahnkommissar Bericht über den Stand der Bauarbeiten am 30. November auf der Strecke von km 340–388 [. . .] Mikesse 30. November 1913".

> our part, which is then used by your supervisors and by you for official reports. The documents for your monthly reports can be obtained from us as far as we are able and obliged to give them to you.[20]

Railway commissioner Molfenter accepted Hoffmann's new policy but insisted on his right to observe the construction process and the construction company. Probably suspecting concealment by *Holzmann,* the railway commissioner reminded all of his subordinate construction supervisors "to provide useful information for control purposes on the basis of [your] own investigations. [. . .] On this occasion, I would also like to point out that according to the construction contract, you are entitled to access the workplaces, workshops and infirmaries at any time for the purpose of supervision."[21] This was neither the first, nor the only occasion when *Holzmann* behaved rather uncooperatively regarding information about labour conditions at the *Central Railway*. This made it difficult for the railway commissioners to complete their reports, of course. The complaint of the railway commissioner sent to *Holzmann* in June 1912 illustrates these difficulties:

> I ask you repeatedly to send me the requested documents. The [. . .] Gouvernement has requested a detailed report. Furthermore, it seems necessary to deal with individual questions in more detail, especially with regard to the workers, the state of health and nutrition, in order to counter various attacks in the Reichstag (especially from the Social Democratic side). I therefore humbly request you to send me documents on the following points: State of health of the Europeans, deaths and their causes. Composition of the coloured people according to tribes. Suitability of the various tribes for work, duration of commitment, voluntary commitment, influence of work and regular diet on the health of the people. What were the people fed on and how was the food obtained? Illnesses, deaths, cause of death, care during illness. Who provided the sick service, where were the medical staff and hospital stationed? As I have to prepare the annual report soon, I would be grateful if you could send me the documents by 20 June [1912] at the latest.[22]

Not only the fact that the railway commissioner stressed his repeated requests to *Holzmann,* but also the fact that he gave such a detailed list of the information required reveals that he had been far from satisfied with the information policies of the construction company thus far. More importantly, the railway commissioner even refers to the pressure exerted by the *Reichstag* or rather the Social Democrats (SPD) on the colonial administration to provide adequate information.

---

20 TNA. G17/121, "Hoffmann an Eisenbahnkommissar I 249/35, Tabora, den 18. Dezember 1913".
21 TNA. G17/121, "Der Eisenbahnkommissar der Tanganjika-Bahn. No. 2298. Tabora, den 20. Dezember 1913. Herrn Aufsichtsbeamten [?]".
22 TNA. G17/118. Monatliche Berichte über den Fortgang der Bauarbeiten an der Tanganyika-Eisenbahn Tabora-Kigoma. Bd. 1. 1912–1913, "Eisenbahnkommissar an die Fa. Philipp Holzmann J. no. 772, Tabora, 11. Juni 1912".

The railway commissioner thus implicitly confirmed Noske's criticism about lacking information on the labour conditions along the *Central Railway*; and if the railway commissioner himself, who was resident in German East Africa, felt not informed enough about the African workforce in the colony, then the *Gouverneur*, the Colonial Department in Berlin, the *Reich's* government and the *Reichstag* were certainly all deprived of sufficient information about the prevalent labour conditions. Furthermore, recalling the decisive gatekeeper positions of the railway commissioners and the Governor entails that information policies were prone to manipulations and omissions. Effectively, it seems that the railway commissioners of German East Africa themselves sometimes used this opportunity to make reports fit their own interests.

There is a varying degree of comprehensiveness between the monthly reports issued by the construction supervision that sent their reports to the railway commissioners and those monthly reports issued by the railway commissioners, sent to the Governor and to Berlin. Generally, those issued by the railway commissioners were less detailed than those issued by the construction supervision. This is not very surprising as the commissioners' reports were more or less a summary or rather condensed version of all the reports issued by the ca. five men working for each construction supervision.[23] Yet, in at least at one incident, it seems that some delicate information provided by the construction supervision was omitted in the report issued by Tabora's railway commissioner himself. In the beginning of August 1910, construction supervisor Rosien had not only reported that a considerable number of his subordinate staff were unable to work, because they were seriously sick (see above), but also that the afflicting smallpox had spread near Kigwe in the region of *Ugogo*. Both in the village of Kigwe proper, and in the nearby construction camp of the Greek railway sub-contractor Grammatikos, a considerable number of people had contracted the disease; three of them had already died. As the smallpox had spread along various labour camps at the *Central Railway*, Rosien's subordinate construction supervisor Böre had taken all actions necessary and had informed both the district office in Kilimatinde

23 For reports issued by the railway commissioner and forwarded to the next higher levels of administration Cf. TNA. G17/63. Cf. TNA. G17/64. Cf. TNA G12/164. Cf. TNA. G17/118. Cf. TNA. G17/119. Monatliche Berichte über den Fortgang der Bauarbeiten an der Tanganyika-Eisenbahn Tabora-Kigoma. Bd. 3. 1914–1915. Compare them to the reports by the construction supervision cf. TNA. G17/65, TNA. G17/119, TNA. G17/120. Monatliche Berichte der örtlichen Baubeamten über den Fortgang der Bauarbeiten an der Tanganyika-Eisenbahn Tabora-Kigoma. Bd. 1. 1912–1913, TNA. G17/121, TNA. G17/122. Monatliche Berichte der örtlichen Baubeamten über den Fortgang der Bauarbeiten an der Tanganyika-Eisenbahn Tabora-Kigoma. Bd. 3. 1914–1916. Compare them also to the typed reports issued by the railway commission and forwarded to the *Gouvernement* and the Colonial Office cf. TNA. G12/202.

and the medical officer in charge immediately. Shortly afterwards, the entire population of Kigwe proper and the railway construction camp were vaccinated to immunise the people against smallpox. Yet, in contrast to the construction company's obligations, Böre had complained about *Holzmann,* reporting that "it must be particularly emphasised that although the construction section *was well informed,* not the slightest step was taken to prevent the disease."[24] That means that despite their better knowledge, the construction company *Holzmann* had done nothing to combat a disease that could have killed a significant number of their workers. The company's construction section had therefore deliberately violated paragraph seven of the construction contract obliging them to take care of their workers' physical integrity. Even more intriguing is the fact that Dar es Salaam's railway commissioner Molfenter discarded any delicate information about the smallpox incident conveyed in Rosien's report. Against his better knowledge, Molfenter only forwarded the following sentence to Berlin: "In Kigwe, smallpox was detected among the people [. . .] on 10 July. [omitted complaint about the construction section quoted above]. The necessary measures were taken by the Kilimatinde district office."[25] Summing up, the handwritten report by the local construction supervision containing delicate information was issued 6 August, 1910 by Rosien and reached the railway commissioner's office in Dar es Salaam on 15 August. There, railway commissioner Molfenter processed or rather censored the report and forwarded the shortened and typed version to the *OAEG's* office on 24 August. At the office of the *OAEG,* it was read three days later and probably forwarded to Berlin devoid of any information concerning *Holzmann's* violation of paragraph seven as it lacked any delicate information about the smallpox incident. Moreover, Molfenter's typed and censored report lacked any information about the contraction of diseases and the resulting sick leave of the four men of the construction supervision. Molfenter had censored this information, too.[26]

In the following month, Molfenter held back controversial information again. Throughout August 1910, at least nine train accidents occurred, and construction supervisor Rosien reported all of them to railway commissioner Molfenter. These accidents were either derailings or train collisions resulting from deficient wagons, or improperly built tracks. Sometimes they were also the result of carelessness in

---

24 TNA. G17/64, "J. no. 1621. Monatsbericht über den Stand der Arbeiten am Ende des Monats Juli [1910]. X. Allgemeines".

25 TNA. G17/64, "J. no. 1621. Monatsbericht über den Stand der Arbeiten am Ende des Monats Juli [1910]. X. Allgemeines".

26 Cf. TNA. G17/64, "J. no. 1621. Monatsbericht über den Stand der Arbeiten am Ende des Monats Juli [1910]".

the daily construction business as one accident had occurred because rocks, which had fallen off a train, had not been removed from the tracks. At least three of these accidents left behind a total number of five people "seriously injured" and six "slightly injured". About "two [. . .] accidents [. . .] more information [was] unavailable, because [. . .] as everywhere, the reporting of the supervisor Tönjes ha[d] completely failed. Not the slightest official information about any of the accidents was given to the official construction supervision by the construction company."[27] As in the smallpox incident, railway commissioner Molfenter omitted this entire cited passage in his report. Thus, neither the Governor in Dar es Salaam, nor the Colonial Department in Berlin was ever able to receive any information about the sick supervisory staff or about the train accidents. One month later, when at least three other train accidents had occurred, nothing had changed for the better as construction supervisor Rosien noted: "Accidents are still not reported to the official construction supervision."[28] Again, Molfenter dismissed this information from his own subordinate construction supervision. Some months later, in February 1911, Rosien reported to Molfenter that the European staff of Dodoma's railway workshop had taken up a strike as they were unsatisfied with their working conditions and salaries. Once again, this information did not leave the railway commissioner's office in Dar es Salaam, leaving his superiors uninformed.[29]

As if not enough, in the summer of 1912, the local construction supervision generally criticised the lack of hygienic conditions in the workers' housing and urged *Holzmann* and the sub-contractors to find a remedy for the grievances. On behalf of the construction supervision, the medical officer thus delivered a detailed handout to *Holzmann* giving precise instructions about the required workers' houses' allotment, the spatial distance in between and the erection of decent and sufficient lavatories in the construction camps to avoid general untidiness and the spread of diseases among the workers. However, railway commissioner Batzner merely stated in his report to the *OEAG*, the Governor and the Colonial Department in Berlin: "The construction company [i.e. *Holzmann*] has issued precise instructions to its [sub-]contractors regarding the construction and keeping

---

27 TNA. G17/64, "Rosien an Eisenbahnkommissar Daressalaam, No. 1575. Dodoma 6. September 1910, Bericht über den Stand der Arbeiten beim Bau der Zentralbahn gegen Ende des Monats August 1910, X. Allgemeines".

28 TNA G17/64, "Rosien an Eisenbahnkommissar Daressalam, No. 1653. Dodoma 3 Oktober 1910, X. Allgemeines".

29 Cf. TNA G17/64, "Rosien an Eisenbahnkommissar Daressalaam, no. 1864. Dodoma 3. February 1911, VIII. u. IX. Personal- und Arbeiterverhältnisse".

clean of the workers' camps."[30] It is telling of the inefficiency of the construction supervision that *Holzmann* followed the regulations half-heartedly at best. After his subsequent inspection tour to all construction camps from km 235 to the railhead (ca. fifteen camps) in November 1912, construction supervisor Kanert assessed: "The order issued by the company [i.e. *Holzmann*] regarding the building of the construction camps is not in the hands of all the [sub-]contractors and is only considered as a formality."[31] Whether this information about the lax implementations of workers' housing regulations was ever censored by the railway commissioner is hard to say. Similarly, it is difficult to assess why the documented censorship proven above and issued by the major railway supervisory bodies occurred at all. Two reasons appear plausible, however.

First of all, in the middle of August 1910, *Gouverneur* Rechenberg had an inspection tour along the newly built railway track between Dar es Salaam and central Dodoma[32] (ca. 450 km). Railway commissioner Molfenter might thus have wanted to avoid any unpleasant further investigations on behalf of the Governor himself, which could have resulted in a negative image of all bodies of the railway commissioners. Moreover, it seems likely that the railway commissioner sought to prevent any negative information from reaching broader circles. Supposedly such broader circles must have been the German public and the *Reichstag*, i.e. the comparatively anti-colonial MPs of the Social Democrats, leading to the second probable reason. At this point in time, in summer 1910, plans for the extension of the *Central Railway* from Tabora to Kigoma were already being made, while the *Reichstag* only approved its funding more than one year later in late December 1911. Simultaneously, railway construction in German East Africa faced imperial competition from other colonial powers. By the time the funds were granted for the ultimate part of the German colonial railway in East Africa to reach Lake Tanganyika from the east, the Belgians had already been building their *Lukuga Railway* connecting Lake Tanganyika to the Congo basin for half a year. With the Belgian *Lukuga Railway* targeting the same waters from the west in the neighbouring Congo colony as the German *Central Railway* did from the east, this imperial race for the fastest completion of colonial railroads to Lake Tanganyika might have urged Molfenter not to deliver any information that might have fuelled heated *Reichstag* debates about the *Central Railway*'s funding.

---

30 TNA. G12/202, "Bauarbeiten an der Ostafrikansichen mittellandbahn Bahnbau Tabora-Kigoma (Restarbeiten Morogoro-Tabora) Monatsbereicht August 1912, X. Personal- und Arbeiterverhältnisse".

31 TNA. G 17/120, "Bericht der Lagerbesichtigungen der Strecke km 235 + 00 – Bauspitze während der Zeit vom 14–16. Nov. 1912". Cf. TNA. G12/202, p. 103.

32 Cf. TNA G17/64, "Rosien an Eisenbahnkommissar Daressalaam, no. 1575. Dodoma 6. September 1910, Bericht über den Stand der Arbeiten [. . .] August 1910, X. Allgemeines".

Public outcries about badly treated African workers or other abuses, as had occurred in the debates about colonial warfare in German East Africa and German South West Africa between 1904 and 1908, certainly had the potential to harm rapid railway construction. As experience had shown, colonial scandals and colonial violence could indeed cause especially the Social Democrats and parts of the Catholic *Zentrum* to reject or suspend colonial budgets. Moreover, the general elections were only ca. one year ahead in summer 1910, and the previous elections of 1907 were largely characterised by fierce debates about the atrocities of German colonialism.[33] Hence, concealing colonial failures in the course of railway construction in the wake of renewed pro-funding campaigns in the *Reichstag* and simultaneously carrying out planning work in German East Africa for an extended track might have appeared opportune to the railway commissioners in August 1910. To prevent any delays in railway construction, they apparently obstructed delicate information.

There are of course also many other possible reasons why railway commissioner Molfenter concealed the smallpox incident, for example. But investigating this aspect even more thoroughly is rather pointless for the research question of this investigation. What remains from the analysis of the railway commissioner's censorship is twofold however: First, the construction supervision of the *Central Railway* was often not reliable, due to understaffing or because of conflicts with the construction company *Holzmann*, who in their own interests, repeatedly refused to provide comprehensive information about labour at the *Central Railway*. Secondly, even if there was significant information provided, the smallpox incident shows that failures regarding anything related to railway construction and labour might not be processed adequately by the supervising bodies. These shortcomings in railway supervision multiplied when a third party was added to the conflict-laden relationship between the governmental supervising bodies and the construction company *Holzmann*. As *Holzmann* outsourced the vast majority of railway construction to sub-contractors, information flows about working conditions from the building sites suffered even more. Analogically, responsibilities and accountabilities regarding labour and working conditions were generally spurned by all parties involved in the construction process.

33 Cf. Baltzer. *Die Kolonialbahnen*, pp. 50–52, 243–245. Cf. TNA. G12/188. [Durchführung der politischen, wirtschaftlichen und technischen Erkundungen und] Vorbereitungen [für den Bau der] Eisenbahn Tabora-Tanganyika-See. Bd. 1. 1910–1911. Cf. "Das Deutsch-Belgische Wettrennen zum Tanganikasee". *DOAZ*, XIV, no. 88. Daressalam: 2 November 1912. Cf. Methfessel. *Kontroverse Gewalt*, pp. 266–350. Cf. Becker. 'Die Hottentotten-Wahlen', pp. 177–190. Cf. Habermas. *Skandal in Togo*, pp. 77–109, 231–266.

3.2 Sub-contractors at the *Central Railway*

3.2.1 Outsourcing Responsibilities

> In the meantime, I had learned that there was a lot of money to be made in the railway embankment construction work that was being carried out at the time. [. . .] [I was] assigned 60 people as a favour by an acquaintance who was employed by the railway construction company Holzmann & Co [. . .]. I had the task of building a stretch of railway embankment for myself without remuneration [. . .]. Of course, I was largely supported and advised in this activity by the engineers and technicians. [. . .] I negotiated with the construction director Grages.
>
> Heinrich Langkopp. *22 Jahre im Innern Afrikas.* Gnötzheim: 1929.[34]

Outsourcing most of the construction work of the *Central Railway* to numerous sub-contractors was nothing new in German East Africa when ground breaking took place in Dar es Salaam in February 1905. The construction of the previously built *Usambara Railway* – initially planned to connect the Indian Ocean to the *Nyanza* ('Lake Victoria') in the northern part of the colony – followed a similar approach at times. With its first ca. forty km built under the umbrella of the *Deutsch Ostafrikanische Gesellschaft (DOAG)* between 1896 and 1899, the *Usambara Railway* had to be nationalised due to insufficient funding. Afterwards, "the idea of continuing the railway to Lake Victoria [. . .] receded into the background. First, the construction up to Korogwe [ca. eighty km] was awarded in different lottery tickets to individual [sub-]contractors and the preliminary work for the railway up to Mombo [ca. 130 km] was completed."[35] Further construction experienced several standstills. Finally, the Berlin company *Lenz & Co.* took over both the entire construction work and the railway's operation and extended the line as far as Moshi near Mount Kilimanjaro (ca. 400 km) by 1911.[36] As especially the operation of both the *Usambara Railway* and the *Central Railway* followed similar regulations from at least 1909 onwards,[37] it is not very surprising that the principle of outsourcing construction work as practised at the *Usambara Railway* was also applied to the *Central Railway*. In contrast to the *Usambara Railway*, which experienced only one phase of construction outsourced to sub-contractors, almost the entire construction

---

34 Langkopp, Heinrich. *22 Jahre im Innern Afrikas. Was ich erstrebte, erlebte, erlitt.* Gnötzheim b. Würzburg: 1929, p. 43.

35 Baltzer. *Die Kolonialbahnen*, p. 35.

36 Cf. Baltzer. *Die Kolonialbahnen*, pp. 35–38.

37 Cf. TNA. G12/167. Allgemeine [Angelegenheiten der] Tanganyika-Eisenbahn. 1908–1912, p. 91.

works of the much larger *Central Railway* was outsourced to sub-contractors from the ground breaking in Dar es Salaam in 1905 until the railroad's completion in 1914.

Only a fraction of the construction of the *Central Railway* was carried out by the construction company *Philipp Holzman* themselves. Browsing through the tabular reports of the railway commissioners illustrates the disproportion between the work done by *Holzmann* proper and their numerous sub-contractors. As there were no governmental bodies observing railway construction between 1905 and 1907, and both the *Holzmann* company archives as well as the files held about colonial railway construction in the predecessor institution of the German *Bundesarchiv* were seriously destroyed during WWII, only administration documents between December 1908 and summer 1914 survive in the Tanzanian National Archives, providing information about labour at the *Central Railway*. Generally, the total number of railway workers fluctuated significantly. It ranged from a few hundred during the rainy season to over 15,000 in the dry season, when the workmen and -women were not busy cultivating their fields at their homes. Besides this general observation, the tabular reports reveal another interesting trend. From late December 1908 to ca. September 1910, the workers directly employed by *Holzmann* outnumbered those outsourced to railway sub-contractors. Especially during 1909, *Holzmann* employed twice as many workers as all sub-contractors taken together did. At one point, Holzmann even employed two-thirds of the entire workforce: for example, in July 1909 the entire workforce was 14,183 of whom *Holzmann* had hired 10,381, leaving only the much smaller share of 3,802 workers for the sub-contractors. In the course of the year 1910 the numbers gradually converged. From April 1910 onwards, the ratio of workers employed directly by *Holzmann* was only one-third higher compared to those working for the railway sub-contractors. During the second half of 1910, the numbers were almost equal, like in July 1910 when the count was 7,585 for *Holzmann* proper and 6,950 for the sub-contractors. In September of the same year, the number of workers hired by sub-contractors outnumbered those hired by *Holzmann* for the first time by ca. 100. This started a trend that remained intact until the very end of railway construction in 1914. Although some rare exceptions occurred, from April 1911 onwards the sub-contractors always employed at least twice as many workers as *Holzmann* proper did, while the ratio was two to one most of the time. In summer 1912, the discrepancy peaked, when all sub-contractors taken together employed ca. 10,000 workers while *Holzmann* proper had hired ca. 1,000 only. In 1914, the very last year of the actual construction works, the numbers converged again, showing an almost equal share of workers between *Holzmann* proper and the sub-contractors working at the *Central Railway*.[38]

Holzmann's own procedures for hiring sub-contractors seem to have been far from clearly regulated. This opened the floodgates to several forms of arbitrariness in the context of labour recruitment. Starting with the initial earthworks in 1905, the construction company divided the future railway into several route sections, which were each up to forty km long. Similar to the allocation practice of the *Usambara Railway* some years before, prospective sub-contractors of the *Central Railway* could apply for a lottery that would grant employment to the designated contractor for one route section, if luck was on his side.[39] Besides this, less regulated ways to seek employment were also possible, as revealed by Langkopp's example quoted above. When searching for a job at the construction site, the sub-contractor Heinrich Langkopp himself did not apply for any lottery but was accepted in a rather unorthodox way. According to his own accounts, one of his acquaintances at the time responsible for building an individual route section had a surplus of sixty workers and transferred them to Langkopp simply as a favour. Allegedly without any payment, Langkopp and his (probably African) workforce then built one section of railroad embankment. With the help of *Holzmann* engineers and technicians, he acquired enough skills to apply for another contract for a further route section only six weeks later – this time for payment, however. Now cocksure in his skill and ability, he subsequently went to *Philipp Holzmann's* headquarters, called upon *Holzmann's* top-ranking government building officer Ferdinand Grages, and asked for further employment. Grages declined, claiming that the soil conditions for the earthworks currently under construction were too burdensome: in his view, Langkopp would not make any profit in such circumstances. However, if soil conditions improved, Langkopp could reapply whenever he wished.[40] In the meantime, less profitable railway construction work was primarily being done by Greek sub-contractors. Only sometime later, Langkopp, who had come to the construction sites of the *Central Railway* in German East Africa after several employments as a mercenary in South Africa and as a retail employee and journalist in Dar es Salaam, became a self-reliant labour recruiter and cattle raiser based in the central *Iringa* region.[41] Langkopp's autobiography about his work at the *Central Railway* is one of the very few remaining sources about sub-contractors and labour in the ini-

38 Cf. TNA. G17/63. Cf. TNA. G17/118. Cf. TNA. G17/119.

39 Cf. "Von Unserer Bahn". *DOAZ*, VII, no. 23. Daressalam: 10 June 1905. This route section lottery apparently existed throughout the construction process. Cf. TNA. G12/202, p. 163.

40 Cf. Langkopp. *22 Jahre*, pp. 43–47.

41 Cf. Rösser. 'Transimperiale Infrastruktur?'. Cf. Aas and Sippel. *Koloniale Konflikte*, pp. 21–29, 131–142.

tial years of railway construction between 1905 and 1907, because there are hardly any administrative files for this period. Langkopp's memories point to the arbitrariness by which *Holzmann* delegated their own accountabilities to the lower – or rather outsourced – levels of construction work.

As paragraphs five to seven of the construction contract between *Holzmann* and the colonial authorities delegated all accountabilities regarding labour to the construction company, soon the question arose whether *Holzmann* themselves or their numerous sub-contractors were specifically accountable for the many responsibilities connected to labour at the *Central Railway*. According to the construction contract, the duties of *Holzmann* ranged from the recruitment of the workforce to the provision of the workers' food, lodging and healthcare. Of course, *Holzmann* was often supported by the colonial government in all these aspects to facilitate quick railway construction, but the legal regulations made the building company accountable for almost everything related to the building process.[42] Yet, throughout the entire construction process, *Holzmann* attempted repeatedly to pass any responsibility related to the workforce on to their sub-contractors – or rather – to outsource their own responsibilities. As demonstrated above, the supervisory powers of the railway commissioners and their subordinate construction supervisors were insufficient throughout the construction process. Given the fact that their power to observe the work of *Holzmann's* staff alone was limited, this suggests that their ability to keep an overview of the work of the numerous railway sub-contractors was even lower. Moreover, *Holzmann*, as the sub-contractor's superior construction body, generally refrained from exerting pressure on their sub-contractors if the railway commissioners criticised that the outsourced contractors did not obey the regulations of the construction contract and working conditions that it demanded. Rather, *Holzmann* either concealed many of the sub-contractors' deficiencies or claimed not to be responsible for the outsourced construction staff at all.

Generally, *Holzmann* enjoyed a great leap of faith on the part of the colonial government regarding the conclusion of contracts with their sub-contractors. All

42 Cf. Stadtarchiv Frankfurt. W1/2–517, "Vertrag über den Eisenbahnbau von Morogoro nach Tabora" (1908), p. 6 and "Vertrag über die Umbauten der Stammstrecke Daressalam-Morogoro" (1912), p. 6. Cf. TNA. G12/167, pp. 1–90. Cf. TNA G12/164, p. 4. HADB. S 1521. Konsortium Ostafrikanische Eisenbahn, "Bauvertrag Daressalaam-Morogoro". HADB. S 1522. Konsortium Ostafrikanische Eisenbahn, "Vertrag über den Bau der Eisenbahn von Morogoro nach Tabora". HADB. S 1525. Konsortium Ostafrikanische Eisenbahn. Tabora-Kigoma, "Vertrag über den Bau der Eisenbahn von Tabora nach Kigoma und der Hafen- und Zollanlagen in Kigoma". HADB. S 1523. Konsortium Ostafrikanische Eisenbahn. Stichbahn Ruanda, "Vertrag über den Bau der Eisenbahn von Tabora nach dem Kagera (Ruandabahn)".

parties involved were aware of this fact. When in summer 1912 a well-remunerated proposed contract between *Holzmann* and their sub-contractor, the Greek Scutari,[43] endowed with the extraordinary sum of six million marks (!), aroused the jealousy of especially German sub-contractors, *Gouverneur* Heinrich Schnee was very clear on the issue. Writing to the Colonial State Secretary in Berlin, he stated: "The wording of the colonial railway construction contracts is such that extensive reliance on the construction company is the prerequisite. With regard to the correct and appropriate use of funds [. . .] the construction company has almost unlimited freedom."[44] Generally, the sub-contractors paid less to their workers than did *Holzmann* proper for the same task of work. This was of course in line with the overall interest of *Holzmann* and the *Gouvernement* who both wanted railway construction to be as cheap as possible.[45] Regardless of the financial issues, the leap of faith towards *Holzmann* was not justified as far as ensuring the payment of (decent) wages to the railway workers was concerned. Neither did the sub-contractors care about decent food and lodging, as demanded by paragraphs five to seven of the construction contract. In either case, *Holzmann* took the view that they could not be held responsible for any violation of the construction contract on the part of their sub-contractors. For instance, at the end of 1913 a conflict emerged between *Holzmann* and a German resident of Pugu near Dar es Salaam, Walter Grund. Grund had worked as a sub-contractor at the reconstruction of the line between Dar es Salaam and Morogoro in 1913 when considerable disagreement about his achievements occurred. Grund himself claimed that *Holzmann* had not delivered any payment to him, leaving him unable to pay his workers. Regardless of which party, *Holzmann* or Grund, was in the right – Grund even opened a legal case – *Holzmann's* reaction towards the issue is remarkable.[46] When Grund petitioned to various colonial authorities about his problems with paying his workers, the railway commissioner in charge confronted *Holzmann* with Grund's accusation. In a corresponding letter, the colonial official urged the company to find a remedy, explicitly referring to paragraph seven, subsection six

43 Like some other sub-contractors, Scutari had been directly employed by *Holzmann* as an engineer before he worked as sub-contractor. Cf. Beese. *Experten*, pp. 114.

44 TNA. G12/202, p. 155.

45 Cf. TNA. G17/63, "Bericht über den Arbeitsfortschritt an der Zentralbahn im Monat März 1909. 8. Personal- und Arbeiterverhältnisse".

46 Cf. Railway Museum Nairobi (RMN). German Tanganyika Files (GTF). Row 1. Shelf 10. Umbau Daressalaam-Morogoro. Akt. VIII. Bd.1. Gesundheits- und Arbeiterverhältnisse, "An das Kaiserliche Eisenbahnkommissariat, J. no. 3181 [?], Daressalam 20.01.14", "An Herrn Grund. Pugu. 3200. 23. Januar 14", "Grund An das Kaiserliche Gouvernement Daressalam. Pugu, den 23. Januar 1914.", "Reinconcept. 3283. Beschwerde Grund wegen Holzmann & Cie. 6. Mai 1914", "Rechtsanwalt Dr. Hoffmann an den Herrn Eisenbahnkommissar Daressalam. Daressalam, den 11. Febr. 1914".

of the construction contract,[47] which demanded that "the Contractor [i.e. *Holzmann*] shall pay particular attention to the welfare and proper payment and treatment of workers, taking into account the relevant provisions in force in the protected area at the time."[48] Yet, on behalf of *Holzmann*, building official engineer Rehfeldt declined, claiming that *Holzmann* were not liable for any of their sub-contractors' workers:

> We note first of all that Mr Grund is an independent entrepreneur whose obligations towards his indigenous workers we cannot cover, if only for legal reasons. The workers can [. . .] if [. . .] the wages due to them are not paid, have the credit balance of the debtor seized by the authority authorised to represent their claims.[49]

In other words, *Holzmann* held themselves not responsible for any acts of their sub-contractor and advised the damaged party of African workers to appeal to the colonial courts for their rights. As colonial legislation structurally disadvantaged anybody of African descent for racist reasons,[50] the construction company's view was very convenient for themselves, indeed. In practice, African workers going to court to enforce payment of wages had little chance of winning their cases.

Holzmann confirmed this stark attitude on other occasions. Throughout the years 1912 and 1914, both the railway commissioner and the Governor admonished the company to provide for adequate medical treatment of the railway workers and to ensure decent housing in the construction camps. In the view of the governmental officials, *Holzmann* had additionally neglected their duties regarding the spread of smallpox in several construction camps. *Holzmann* denied any responsibility and claimed not to have the means necessary to completely isolate any construction camp having smallpox and argued that the *Gouvernement* was responsible for such affairs. Moreover, the company blamed the colonial administration for a lack of vaccines and protested a new bill, which obliged *Holzmann* to establish several medicine cabinets along the newly built track to ensure the availability of medical treatment for the railway workers. Acting Governor Methner could not help the impression "that these statements [were] dictated by

47 Cf. RMN. GTF. R1. S10, "Abschrift. J. no. 3184. Der Eisenbahnkommissar an die Fa. Philipp Holzmann & Cie. Daressalaam, den 21. Januar 1914".

48 Stadtarchiv Frankfurt. W1/2-517, "Vertrag über den Umbau der Stammstrecke Daressalaam-Morogoro", p. 6.

49 RMN. GTF. R1. S10, "Holzmann an den Eisenbahnkommissar, J. no. 3200 zu J. no. 3184, Daresssalam, den 21. Januar 1914".

50 Cf. Schaper. *Koloniale Verhandlungen*, pp. 67–85. Cf. Nuzzo, Luigi. 'Kolonialrecht'. *Europäische Geschichte Online (EGO).* Ed. Institut für Europäische Geschichte (IEG), Mainz 2011-07-14. Web. http://www.ieg-ego.eu/nuzzol-2011-de URN: urn:nbn:de:0159-2011051270 (14 January 2020).

the company's desire to transfer to the administration part of the tasks that fall to the company's health service according to their contract".[51] Moreover, once again, *Holzmann* argued that if any deficiencies had occurred that had violated the workers' well-being, these had occurred in the camps of the sub-contractors and not in the camps operated directly by the construction company. As *Holzmann* claimed not to be liable for their sub-contractors' failures, the construction company were allegedly not the ones to blame.[52] In line with the railway commissioner and the governmental medical officer, *Gouverneur* Schnee dismissed these arguments, explicitly referring to the construction contract once again. Accordingly, he insisted on the introduction of medicine cabinets:

> This decision does not in any way affect your obligation under § 7 number 6 of the construction contract to provide free medical treatment for all workers employed on the railway construction. It does not need to be explained that you cannot release yourself from this obligation by handing over part of the work to sub-contractors who employ their own workers. [. . .] Having said all this, even if the position that the workers of your self-employed contractors cannot be considered as your employees is maintained, there are several ways that you can fulfil the discussed fulfilment of the construction contract provision with regard to all workers employed in railway construction. The fulfilment of the obligation imposed on you by the final clause of §7 of the construction contract[, i.e., to vaccinate all workers,] must be adhered to under all circumstances.[53]

This tension between *Holzmann* and the colonial administration, ongoing until the very end of railway construction in 1914, reveals that *Holzmann's* outsourcing of most of the *Central Railway*'s route sections not only entailed conflicts; it also made the supervision of the labour camps time consuming, inefficient and unnecessarily complex. *Holzmann's* attempts to fend off any liabilities for the deeds of their sub-contractors certainly influenced the living and working conditions for the many thousands of men and women who constructed the railroad. Yet, to make things even more complex, many of *Holzmann's* sub-contractors themselves outsourced several tasks to their own sub-sub-contractors.

---

51 TNA. G17/123, "Kaiserlicher Gouverneur von Deutsch-Ostafrika. J. no. 20273/12. V. Daressalam, den 23. August 1912, no. 1392. An den Herrn Eisenbahnkommissar in Tabora.".

52 CF. TNA. G17/123. Cf. TNA. G17/124. Arbeiterverhältnisse der Tanganyika-Eisenbahn Tabora-Kigoma. Bd. 2. 1913–1915. Enthält vorwiegend: Gesundheitsdienst., "Holzmann an den Eisenbahnkommissar. I/247/33. Auf Ihr Schreiben [. . .] J. no. 1859. Tabora, den 24 Oktober 1913", "Holzmann an den Herrn Eisenbahnkommissar. Malagarassi 12[?]X. 1913 [?]", "Revision der Arbeiterlager der Strecke Tabora-Kigoma", pp. 1–7.

53 TNA. G17/124, "Abschrift. 31394/13. II. J. Daressalam, den 13. Januar 1914". Cf. HADB. S 1525, "Vertrag über den Bau der Eisenbahn von Tabora nach Kigoma und der Hafen- und Zollanlagen in Kigoma", p. 7.

3.2.2 Sub-contractors, Sub-sub-contractors and Labour Recruiters

> All contractors in the supervisory section are subcontractors of the company Mutopoulus & Co.
>
> Construction Official Haken to Railway Commissioner. Kigoma, 1 October 1913.[54]

There were at least three levels of contractors responsible for the construction of the *Central Railway*. At the top of the hierarchy was *Holzmann*, of course. They had won the official contract on behalf of the *Reich* and thus of the colonial administration and carried out their construction work under the umbrella of the *OAEG*. As the largest body responsible for construction, they disposed many of their construction tasks and responsibilities to sub-contractors. In turn, these sub-contractors outsourced several of their tasks to sub-sub-contractors themselves. Given the difficulties of railway construction supervision resulting from the very first level of outsourcing, it is only logical that the longer the chains of outsourcing, the more difficult the supervision became. In this respect, overseeing the work of *Holzmann* was the easiest job for the governmental supervising bodies, as the large German company with numerous projects around the world had not only headquarters in Germany's Frankfurt o.M; they also had branches in German East Africa's capital Dar es Salaam and around the midpoint of the *Central Railway* in the town of Tabora, from which they administered the sectional construction of the railway. Hence, the colonial administration, i.e. the railway commissioners and their supervisory staff, could easily reach a contact person of *Holzmann* if necessary. In major railway hubs like Tabora or Dar es Salaam, correspondence was even possible via telegram as installing the infrastructure necessary for telegraphy was integral to the construction of the railway.[55] Supervising the sub-contractors was more challenging. They erected their construction camps often only temporarily and moved to another construction site as soon as their task had been completed. At these rather remote places, there was neither telegraphy of course, nor could they be contacted as easily as the staff of *Holzmann's* proper. With *Holzmann* constantly denying any responsibilities for their

54 TNA. G17/121, "J. no. 1761. Monatsbericht für Bauaufssichtsstrecke der Tanganyikabahn von km 388 bis Kigoma für Monat September 1913, Kigoma, den 1. Oktober 1913".
55 Cf. Wenlzhuemer. *Connecting*, pp. 97–134, 211–261. Cf. TNA. G17/120, "7.8.1912. J. no. 1071. Bericht über den Stand der Bauarbeiten der Strecke Tabora-kigoma von km 0 + 000 – 46 + 000 am 31. Juli 1912. 9. Personal- und Arbeiterverhältnisse", "Ussoke, am 31. August 1912. Baubericht der Sektion 2 für Monat August 1912. X. Personal- und Arbeiterverhältnisse", "30.9.12. Baubericht für Monat September. Stand der Bauarbeiten in Sektion 3 (km 93–135). X. Personal- und Arbeiterverhältnisse". Cf. TNA. G17/123, "Abschrift Bi III.155. Philipp Holzmann & Cie. Lit. D. no. 21/6. Frankfurt a/M, den 13. Januar 1913. An den Herrn Staatssekretär des Kolonialamtes Berlin", p. 2.

sub-contractors, enforcing labour policies along the construction sites of the *Central Railway* proved very demanding for the supervising bodies. As soon as sub-contractors themselves outsourced tasks or entire route sections to their own sub-sub-contractors, enforcing labour protection rights became almost impossible.

The sub-contractors' own outsourcing was widespread during the *Central Railway*'s construction. The quote above from supervisor Haken refers to one of the financially strongest sub-contractors entrusted with constructing large sections of the railway: the Greek sub-contractor Mutopoulus. Haken supervised the railway section from km 388 to Kigoma, and he notes in his report to the commissioner that almost this entire section of fifty-kilometres-length was being built by Mutopoulus' sub-sub-contractors. Accordingly, Haken reported that fifteen Europeans were working as Mutopoulus' sub-sub-contractors, employing a total number of 785 railway workers. That was more than twice as many as *Holzmann* proper employed along the same route section. The latter amounted to only four Europeans with 290 workers. Interpreting these numbers, almost two-thirds of the supervised track was outsourced to sub-sub-contractors, all of whom had been hired by one single sub-contractor, the Greek Mutopoulus. This must have been a normal occurrence, as Haken did not characterise this fact as extraordinary in his report. In addition, other files too confirm that numerous sub-contractors of *Holzmann* outsourced their tasks to their own sub-sub-contractors.[56] The sources about the abovementioned *causa* Scutari in several passages clearly imply that sub-sub-contractors working for sub-contractors was nothing unusual during the *Central Railway*'s construction. Sometimes, sub-contractors even attempted to outsource route sections to themselves. Apparently, Scutari, for example, seems to have planned to outsource his six million marks route section contract not only to other sub-sub-contractors, but also to himself in 1912.[57] Whether his attempt was successful is not clearly conveyed by the sources. Yet, the available sources and Scutari's attempt to outsource his own route section to himself illustrate how obscure and complicated the entire process of outsourcing at the *Central Railway* was – and so was its supervision.

Such entanglements of outsourcing were prone to entail the (re-)employment of dubious (sub-)sub-contractors who had actually been suspended from railway construction, because they had violated colonial labour protection rights and therefore clearly abused African workers. Especially when *Holzmann* had difficulties in

56 Cf. TNA. G17/121, "J. no. 1761. Monatsbericht für Bauaufssichtsstrecke der Tanganyikabahn von km 388 bis Kigoma für Monat September 1913, Kigoma, den 1. Oktober 1913, X. Personal- und Arbeiterverhältnisse".

57 Cf. TNA. G12/202, pp. 147–174.

obtaining enough workers needed for rapid railway construction, the company was ready to ignore sanctions issued against (sub-)sub-contractors previously. In June and July 1913 at least sixteen of *Holzmann's* sub-contractors were accused by both the supervisory bodies (railway commissioner and construction supervision) and African workers themselves of several violations. According to the allegations made, the workers were either deprived of their wages, or compelled to remain at the work site after their actual contracts had ended. Many sub-contractors were thus accused of fraud, coercion, and unlawful detention. Among them was also the sub-contractor duo Sclavos & Patzimas, who were officially warned by the colonial authorities and *Holzmann* that they would be prosecuted if they kept on violating labour laws. Most seriously, Patzimas was accused of having threatened his workers with a firearm to assert his interests.[58] Besides the mentioned accusations, Patzimas did neither waste a thought on housing his workers well. In July 1913, when on inspection tour, the medical officer in charge reported to the *Gouvernement* about the living conditions in the construction camps and stressed Patzima's noncompliance:

> The regulations for the construction of the camps have been followed everywhere, and it must be acknowledged that the current construction of the huts represents a significant progress compared to the earlier ones, with very few exceptions, insofar as the huts are built solidly and appropriately, offering protection from cold and rain. The camps of the contractor Xekalos at construction kilometre 281 and especially that of the contractor Patzimas at km. 304, who did not at all comply with the requests and instructions to the existing camp regulations, are a salient exception. The official of the track supervision in charge had informed him about the existing camp regulations and requested to comply with them repeatedly.[59]

Yet, it seems that next to nothing would change Patzima's behaviour and the construction section finally decided not to deliver any more workers to the subcontractor. Yet, once again illustrating the obstructive character of outsourcing at the railway, *Holzmann's* director Hoffmann reported to the railway commissioner some weeks later in September 1913:

58 Cf. TNA. G17/123, "Abschirft. 226/1 Sima, den 8. Juli 1913 Bauabteiltung II. Elias an die Herren Philipp Holzmann Tabora.", "937 I/240/30. II/226/1. Philipp Holzmann an den Eisenbahnkommissar. Tabora, den 19. Juli 1913", "783. Konzept. 10. Mai 1913. An die Firma Philipp Holzmann & Cie. Tabora. Betrifft übelbeleumundete Unternehmer im Anschluss an mein Schreiben J. no. 612 vom 18. April 1913", "Philipp Holzmann. J. no. I. 238/3. Tabora, den 8. Mai 1913. Den Herrn Eisenbahnkommissar", "Mitteilung von dem Kaiserlichen Bezirksamt an Eisenbahnkommissariat der Mittellandbahn. Tabora. J. no. 444. z. Zt. Kurrukurru, den 29. Mai 1913 [angefügte Liste über derjenigen 16 Sub-Unternehmer die beschuldigt wurden; attached list of 16 accused subcontractors]".

59 TNA. G17/123, "Bahnarzt. J. no. 258. Tabora, d. 31. Juli 1913 an den kaiserlichen Gouverneur Daressalam".

> To the [. . .] letter of the 4th of this month, no. 1498, we humbly reply that according to the notifications of the Construction Section II, no further workers have been transferred to the [sub-]contractors Sclavos & Patzimas after the termination of their current contracts. On the other hand, the aforementioned are employed as [sub-]sub-contractors by the construction company [sub-contractor] Scutari, which we do not wish to prohibit for the sake of the existing labour shortage. We have also repeatedly warned the [sub-]contractors and hope that the grievances that have occurred will not be repeated.[60]

In other words: *Holzmann* regarded some scolding without real consequences as a proper and adequate response to challenge a great variety of violations against labour protection rights ranging from fraud to unlawful detention connected to the use of firearms. The case of Patzimas is particularly telling, as he had been accused of incompetence and overt violence as early as November 1906, i.e. already six years before these other complaints were made. In this very early period of railway construction, *Holzmann* had already dismissed Patzimas and his companion from the construction site on their very first engagement, as they had failed to finish their works at the track as demanded by their contract. Confronted with these allegations, Patzimas' companion accepted the dismissal, whereas Patzimas himself incited his workmen to fight with knives against this decision. Consequently, *Holzmann's* construction director Grages brought a case against Patzimas and complained against him at the Governor's office; yet it did not hinder *Holzmann* from reemploying him in 1912 and even keeping him employed – despite renewed and similar allegations – in 1913.[61]

Apart from the dubious character of outsourcing route sections to (sub-)sub-contractors, one significant aspect of railway construction has not been considered yet. This is the issue of labour recruitment: the procurement of the predominantly African workers necessary to make the infrastructure become a reality. Again, the autobiography of the German railway sub-contractor and labour recruiter Heinrich Langkopp gives an example of how labour recruitment worked especially in the first years of railway construction between 1905 and 1907. In these initial years, the ratio between outsourced route sections (sub-contractors) and those route sections built directly by *Holzmann* was exceptional. In contrast to the construction period after 1909, two-thirds of the number of workers were directly employed by the German construction company and only one-third of track was outsourced to sub-contractors. While this ratio reversed itself from ca.

---

60 TNA. G17/124, "I. 245/23. II. 23/5. Philipp Holzmann an den Herrn Eisenbahn – Kommissar Tabora. Eingang 23.09.13, no. 1677. Tabora, den 22. September 1913".

61 Cf. TNA. G12/82. Bau der Eisenbahn Daressalaam-Morogoro Bd. 2. 1905, "Philipp Holzmann an Kaiserlichen Gouverneur. Daressalam, den 14. November 1906". Whether Patzimas was ever sued is not conveyed by the sources; the file TNA. G12/82 is severely damaged.

Figure 1: English: "H. Langkopp, Iringa G(erman) E(ast) A(frica). On-sale-return. Forwarding agent. Recruitment of plantation workers, porters. Purchase and sale of cattle, etc".
Source: *DOAZ* XII, No. 97.
Daressalam: 07 December 1910.

1909 onwards, *Holzmann* generally did not often recruit workers themselves. First of all, throughout the entire process of railway construction between 1905 and 1916, *Holzmann* received great support from the colonial administration, which supplied the construction company with 'tax workers'. These were men and women resident in the colony who were sent to the railway to work off their tax debt that had previously been imposed on them by the colonial administration. Secondly, as the initial years of railway construction coincided with the Maji Maji War (1905–1908), the *Gouvernement* even sent POWs as convict workers directly to *Holzmann* to facilitate railway construction. Thirdly, if the workers provided by the colonial administration were not enough, *Holzmann* turned to freelance labour recruiters, who roamed and often raided several regions of the colony to obtain the required workers.[62] For this service, *Holzmann* paid the freelancers a monthly salary, their expenses and a fixed sum per delivered railway worker. About his wage bargaining with construction officer Ferdinand Grages (of *Holzmann*), Langkopp stated:

> Since he [Grages] knew that I was good with the blacks, he suggested that I recruit black workers for the railway construction work at a salary of Mk. 400 and free lodging as well as a bonus of Mk. 2 per capita. [. . .] I first moved to Iringa and found extensive support for my recruitment from the head of station there, Captain Nigmann. [. . .] Nigmann [. . .] showed the greatest interest in a possible acceleration of the railway construction, as this would

62 Cf. Rösser. *Transimperiale Infrastruktur*, pp. 277–284. Cf. Sunseri. "Dispersing", pp. 561–567. Cf. Koponen. *Development*, pp. 396–415.

> open up the country most quickly. I recruited many hundreds of workers there in a short time and moved on to Mahenge.[63]

Symptomatic for the entire process of railway construction is the fact that labour recruiters often outsourced their work to quasi labour sub-recruiters. For labour recruiters, this was a strategy to not get their own hands dirty, but to comfortably pursue the profitable business of labour recruitment. Describing his outsourcing in labour recruitment Langkopp explained:

> I bought [. . .] writing paper in large quantities, made small pieces of paper and wrote on them: ["]Recruited by Langkopp["] [. . .]. Now I picked [. . .] a dozen smart blacks and sent them [. . .] into the district. They had to go to the black local chiefs [. . .] and tell them that the railway construction was to be promoted with the greatest speed at the request of the government and that workers were needed for this. This work was government work [. . .]. The thing worked out. [. . .] One day the first troop of 80 men appeared.[64]

As revealed by Figure 1 – an advertisement published by the *DOAZ* – Langkopp not only recruited railway workers but also plantation labourers and porters. Moreover, he was certainly not the only labour recruiter who purported to give himself authority by distributing slips of papers to various sub-labour recruiters. There are also documented cases of labour recruiters equally faking official permissions to make their recruitment appear as sanctioned by the colonial administration.[65] In general, labour recruitment was as dubious as the railway sub-contractor business. Additionally, labour recruitment often entailed the raiding of villages for workers, fraud, physical force, as well as false promises about payment or working and living conditions at the work site. As the colonial administration had introduced at least some regulations by 1913 to regulate so-called 'wild recruitment' across the colony, some recruiters lost their permission to carry out their job, including the abovementioned Heinrich Langkopp.[66] Sometimes, colonial courts opened cases and even punished the most serious cases. In 1913, the colonial administration produced a list of thirty-six labour recruiters, who had officially been suspended from the recruitment business. Of those thirty-four men, thirteen were German, twelve were Greek, one was Austrian, and six East African. As the file is severely damaged, information on two labour recruiters is not conveyed. Nevertheless, besides revealing that labour re-

---

63 Langkopp. *22 Jahre*, p. 44.

64 Langkopp. *22. Jahre*, p. 45.

65 CF. TNA. G21/412. Ermittelungssache gegen den Arbeiteranwerber Michael Georgiades, Mkalama, Bez. Kondoa-Irangi, wegen Betruges, Körperverletzung, Freiheitsberaubung und Nötigung. 1911–1912, pp. 2–7.

66 Cf. Aas and Sippel. *Koloniale Konflikte*, pp. 65–78. For labour recruitment at the *Congo-Océan Railroad* cf. Daughton. *In the Forest of No Joy*, pp. 70–113.

cruiters were predominantly German or Greek, the list shows that men originating from East Africa were also involved in this business.[67]

Although suspending these thirty-six men officially from labour recruitment, the colonial administration knew very well in advance that any regulations regarding labour protection would be ineffective in most cases of recruitment. Discussing several initiatives to regulate labour recruitment in a confidential letter to the Colonial Department issued in 1911, Governor Rechenberg was very clear in this respect. Once again, outsourcing was the major difficulty: "It is true that the approved recruiters then send coloured or black sub-recruiters into the country again, and that these people are not very monitorable, alone even the 'trustworthy European worker recruiters' of the northern planters cannot do without such sub-recruiters."[68] In other words: any legislation issued to hedge the excesses of outsourced labour recruitment would always prove unenforceable. If you wished sufficient labour supply, you could never do without labour sub-recruiters. Briefly, the colonial authorities conceded victory to the grievances of labour recruitment if insufficient labour supply would threaten significant flagship projects like railway construction.

Yet another important aspect of labour and railway construction has still to be considered. Labour recruitment and the work as railway sub-contractor were closely intertwined with each other. This was especially the case when railway sub-contractors built the majority of the route sections at the expense of *Holzmann* from ca. 1909 onwards. Of course, *Holzmann* proper still received workers from the colonial administration and hired freelance labour recruiters themselves if in need of workers for the route sections under their direct command.[69] But the longer the *Central Railway* was being built, the more labour recruitment became integral to the tasks of a potential railway sub-contractor. On top of the task of guiding the construction works of an individual route section of the *Central Railway*, any of *Holzmann's* sub-contractors had to recruit their workers before they could start track building. To be precise, the recruitment of a sufficient number of workers was the most fundamental pre-condition for being accepted as railway

67 Cf. TNA. G1/95. Verstöße gegen die Arbeiterwerbeverordnung (Personenverzeichnis) [1913]. Cf. Rösser. 'Transimperiale Infrastruktur?', pp. 277–284. Cf. Sunseri. "Dispersing", pp. 561–567.

68 RMN. GTF. R3. S48. Diverse Vertraulich, "Abschrift Rechenberg an das Reichs-Kolonialamt Berlin, Betr. Arbeiterverhältnisse, K no. 222, Daressalam 11, February 1911".

69 Cf. RMN. GTF. R1. S10, "An den Herrn Gouverneur in Daressalam, Drsl. 19.Oktober. 1912", "Gouverneur Schnee an Bezirksämter Daressalam, Bagamojo, Morogoro. Daressalam, den 12. November 1912", "Deutsch Ostafrikanische Gesellschaft an Eisenbahnkommissar Molfenter. Tabora 19. February 1913", "Philipp Holzmann an den Herrn Eisenbahnkommissar. Daressalam, den 21. September 1913", "Abschrift. Philipp Holzmann [Rehfeldt] an das Bezirksamt Bagamoyo. Auf [Telegram] des Bezirksamtes Bagamoyo an Holzmann vom 23. Juli", "Kaiserliches Bezirksamt Bagamoyo an den Herrn Eisenbahnkommissar. J. Dr. 2273/13. Bagamoyo, den 4. Oktober 1913".

sub-contractor in the first place. Depending on the sub-contractor's financial capacities and his individual abilities to keep an already recruited workforce, the number of the so-called worker base (*Arbeiterstamm)* of each individual sub-contractor varied greatly. Based on the monthly reports of the construction supervision and the railway commissioners, each sub-contractor needed at least a group ca. twenty workers to be allotted with one task of a route section. As far as revealed by the files, the number of workmen and women could rise to an exceptional 1,000. But the numbers seldomly exceeded a worker base of 200–300 men and women. Interestingly, the type of construction work had very limited influence (if any) on the number of workers. The number of workers employed for earth works, e.g. varied from ca. thirty to over 500, just as did the number of workers employed for pre-extension works, gravel hammering or other tasks.[70] Self-evidently, those sub-contractors having the largest workforce generally obtained the largest, most lucrative and most responsible jobs and were also preferred by *Holzmann*.[71] Summing up, anybody who planned to construct an outsourced section of *Holzmann's* railway business had to recruit the workforce necessary before they could even apply. In turn, this means that the occupation as a railway sub-contractor required a prior occupation as a labour recruiter. Indeed, most of the railway sub-contractors pursued labour recruitment, but also and/or simultaneously turned to freelance labour recruiters if they needed more workers.

Although the construction of the *Central Railway* in German East Africa took place in a German colony, was financed by a German bank and was carried out by a German construction company, only a fraction of those really constructing the *Central Railway* were German. Most Germans held only the top positions of the construction business, such as construction director or engineer. Apart from that, Germans were significantly outnumbered by many other people of different origins. Besides the largest group of the East African workforce, which numbered up to 20,000 men and women, there was also a large number of Indians employed as craftsmen. Besides the group of Germans, there were also many other different European nationalities working at the *Central Railway* in German East Africa as sub-contractors. They came from all directions of Europe and from the American

70 Cf. monthly reports about the progress of railway construction between 1912–1913. Esp. subsections 8 – 10 named "Personal und Arbeiterverhältnisse". Cf. TNA. G17/120. Cf. TNA. G17/118. Cf. TNA. G17/123, "Phillipp Holzmann an Eisenbahnkommissar. Tabora, 11. April 1913. Tabelle II".

71 Cf. TNA. G17/123, "Mittellandbahn 616 concept. Tabora, 16. April 1913. 792. 1107. 1.) Auf den Erlass no. 4837/XII vom 10. III. 1913. Betrifft deutsche und griechische Unternehmer", p. 3. Cf. TNA. G12/176. [Verursachung von Betriebs-] Unregelmäßigkeiten beim Bau und Betrieb der Tanganyika-Eisenbahn [durch Unfälle und Betriebsstörungen sowie Beschwerde des Bauunternehmers C. Berger [. . .]. 1913–1916, pp. 10–16.

continent. Yet, by far the largest European group employed as railway sub-contractors was Greek.[72] The following section deals with their migration to German East Africa in general and their role as railway sub-contractors and labour recruiters in the colony. Moreover, the chapter sheds light on their conflict-laden existence as white subalterns in the colonial society.

3.3 Entangling Employments: (South-East) European Railway Sub-contractors

3.3.1 The Greeks in (East) Africa

A large part of the modern history of Greece is a history of emigration. At the same time, South-East Europe experienced those phenomena typical of the era of imperialism from the 1870s onwards. With a globalising economy between 1870 and 1914, the rise of nationalism, and the increased competition between the imperial powers, the South-East European societies experienced profound upheavals. While industrialisation was slower in the South-East than in Central Europe, the imperial competition of the global superpowers of the time was even more prominent. In the context of the so-called 'scramble for Africa' and increased colonial expansion in Asia, South-East Europe also became a target for quasi-colonial aspirations. With the decline of the Ottoman Empire, especially Russia and Austria-Hungary sought to expand their influence in South-East Europe at the expense of the Ottomans. At the same time, after the Great Eastern Crisis (*Balkankrise* or *Orientalische Krise)* of 1875–78 had ended, various South-East European nationalist movements pushed further for independence. Conflicts always smouldered and flared up repeatedly, culminating in the Balkan Wars (1912/1913) and the assassination of the Austrian successor to the throne, which triggered WWI in summer 1914. This context preceding WWI certainly had negative effects on the South-East European economy that had already been struggling to sustain the ongoing population growth of the 'long nineteenth century'. Together with political instability, lacking opportunities in life was the major reason why especially young men left their homes and sought better working and living conditions overseas. This included a large number of Greeks, particularly from the 1880s onwards and reaching a peak between 1900 and 1914. While most of these Greek emigrants

72 Cf. Rösser. 'Transimperiale Infrastruktur?', 277–284. Cf. Rösser. '"*Shenzi Ulaya*"'. Cf. Sunseri. "Dispersing", 561–575.

headed for the USA, some also went to various colonies in Africa, including German East Africa.[73]

In the German colony at the Indian Ocean, the Greeks were the most important group of Southern European settlers, with a considerable number of Italians having the second rank. Most of the Greeks had migrated to German East Africa via Egypt, where there had been a large Greek diaspora since the middle of the nineteenth century. Most of those Greeks had come to Egypt to plant and manufacture cotton there. With the American Civil War (1861–65) inducing a global shortage in raw cotton production, the cultivation of cotton promised a lucrative business along the Nile for the Greeks. In addition, during German colonial rule in East Africa, many Greeks of the diaspora from Egypt migrated especially to the northern region at Mount Meru to plant coffee there from the 1890s onwards. Although the Greek settlers were generally more successful than their fellow German planters, German colonial discourse regarded them as second-rate whites or rather as 'quasi-Orientals' who would lower the white men's prestige in the colony.[74] In fact, there is much more to say about the Greeks in German East Africa: they were not only a significant minority in the German colony as such. Their migration to and from German East Africa illustrates thus far neglected facets of the 'colonial globality' around East Africa of 1900 in which the diaspora of many peoples entered a new phase in many parts of the world.[75] Moreover, the Greeks resident in German East Africa often worked as labour recruiters and sub-contractors for the construction of the *Central*

73 Cf. Calic. *Südosteuropa*, pp. 344–423. Cf. Brunnbauer and Buchenau. *Geschichte Südosteuropas*, pp. 108–206. Cf. Kaloudis. *Modern Greece*, pp. 41–108. Cf. Gallant. *Modern Greece*, pp. 1–2, 16–24, 157. Cf. Frangos. *Greeks in Michigan*, pp. 7–19. Unavailable for German libraries and at the book market at the time of publishing cf. Chaldeos, Antonis. *The Greek Community in Tanzania.* Athens: 2019. Cf. Rösser. '"*Shenzi Ulaya*"'.

74 Cf. Söldenwagner. *Spaces*, pp. 58–60. Cf. Boonen, Sofie and Lagate, Johan. 'A City Constructed by *'des gens d'ailleurs'*. Urban Development and Migration Policies in Colonial Lubumbashi, 1910–1930'. *From Railway Juncture to Portal of Globalization: Making Globalization Work in African and South Asian Railway Towns.* 51–69. Ed. Geert Castrick. *Comparativ*, 25, Heft 3. Leipzig: 2015, pp. 51–64. For a short passage illustrating an individual case between a German military officer and a Greek merchant in German East Africa's Ruanda cf. Wegmann, Heiko. *Vom Kolonialkrieg in Deutsch-Ostafrika zur Kolonialbewegung in Freiburg. Der Offizier und badische Veteranenführer Max Knecht (1874–1954).* Freiburg i.Br.: 2019, pp. 223–225. Cf. Röser. '"*Shenzi Ulaya*"'. Cf. Papakyriacou, Marios. *Formulation and definitions of the Greek national ideology in colonial Egypt (1856–1919).* Unpublished Dissertation. Freie Universität Berlin: 2014. Web. *Freie Universität Berlin.*https://refubium.fu-berlin.de/bitstream/handle/fub188/3114/Dissertation_Papakyriacou_Marios_12_2014.pdf?sequence=1&isAllowed=y (12 October 2021), pp. 51–73.

75 Cf. Cohen, Robin. *Global Diasporas. An Introduction.* London and New York: 2008, pp. 141–158, 159–177. Cf. Kokot, Waltraud. 'Themen der Forschung'. *Peripulus. Jahrbuch für Außereuropäische Geschichte.* 1–10. Ed. Christoph Marx. 14. Jahrgang. Münster: 2004. Cf. Bertz. *Diaspora and the Na-*

Railway and were therefore decisive actors that shaped the labour relations at the railroad's construction sites and at many other endeavours like plantations.

There are two major reasons why it is actually very difficult to delineate the history of the Greek diaspora in (East) Africa, which still numbers approximately 100,000 people today over the whole African continent. First of all, there are only very few studies on Greek history that go decisively beyond the national history of Greece. Secondly, today's State of Greece is not identical with that of the nineteenth century. Only a minor part that comprises the country of Greece today was an independent country back then. Large parts of today's Greece were still part of the Ottoman Empire and the Ottoman Empire as such hosted a large Greek minority in the 'long nineteenth century'. Although Ottoman Greeks were a visible and comparably homogenous group within the Ottoman Empire, it is difficult to trace Greek people in the colonial archives as they were often labelled as Ottomans, Ottoman citizens or Levantines despite their Greek descent.[76] In German East Africa, sometimes the German colonial administration themselves could not decide whether they regarded an individual as Greek or Turkish.

One example documented by German colonial courts in East Africa is telling in its recording of the personal data of Michael Georgiades. Georgiades, who was from the island of Rhodes, had migrated to German East Africa by 1906 and worked

---

tion. Cf. Korma, Lena. 'The Historiography of the Greek Diaspora and migration in the twentieth century'. 47–73. *Historien*, 16. Web. http://dx.doi.org/10.12681/historein.8778. (22 January 2021).

76 Cf. Dalachanis, Angelos. *The Greek Exodus From Egypt. Diaspora Politics and Emigration, 1937–1962.* New York: 2017, pp. 1–7. Cf. Clogg, Richard. 'The Greek Diaspora: the Historical Context'. *The Greek Diaspora in the Twentieth Century.* 1–24. Ed. Richard Clogg. Basingstoke: 2001. Cf. Tziovas (Ed.). *Greek Diaspora.* Cf. Tziovas, Dimitris (Ed.). *Greece and the Balkans. Identities, Perceptions and Cultural Encounters Since the Enlightenment.* Ashgate: 2003. Cf. Korma. 'The historiography of the Greek Diaspora', pp. 47–73. Cf. Bruneau, Michel. 'Hellénisme et diaspora grecque. De la Méditerranée orientale à la dimension mondiale.' 33–58. *CEMOTI*, no. 30, n.p.: 2000. Web. https://doi.org/10.3406/cemot.2000.1550https://www.persee.fr/doc/cemot_0764-9878_2000_num_30_1_1550 (28 March 2018), pp. 47–48. Cf. Tamis, Anastasis Myrodis. *Greeks in the far Orient.* Thessaloniki: 2011. Cf. Chaldeos. *The Greek Community.* A post WWI biography of the Greek Tsafendas and his family background gives fascinating insights into the Greek diaspora (in Africa). Cf. Woerden, Henk van. *Der Bastard. Die Geschichte des Mannes, der den südafrikanischen Premier ermordete.* Berlin: 2002, pp. 11–71. Cf. Adams, Zuleiga. *Demitrios Tsafendas: Race, Madness and the Archive. A dissertation submitted for the degree of Doctor of Philosophy in History. University of the Western Cape, December 2011.* Web. https://etd.uwc.ac.za/xmlui/bitstream/handle/11394/2912/Adams_PHD_2011.pdf?sequence=1&isAllowed=y (9 December 2019). Cf. Dousemetzis, Dimitri. *The Man who killed Apartheid. The Life of Dimitri Tsafendas.* Johannesburg: 2019. Cf. Harlaftis, Gelina. 'Mapping the Greek Maritime Diaspora from the Early Eighteenth to the Late Twentieth Centuries'. *Diaspora Entrepreneurial Networks.* 147–172. Eds. Ina Baghdiantz et al. Oxford and New York: 2005. Cf. Gallant. *Modern Greece,* pp. 55–82, 299–318. Cf. Kaloudis. *Modern Greece,* pp. 41–108, 175–204. Cf. Papakyriacou. *Formulation and definitions*, pp. 9–29, 51–73.

as a cattle trader and labour recruiter seeking railway workers first around the northern towns of Tanga and Singida, then near the colony's capital Dar es Salaam. Georgiades, who had been already sentenced twice by the colonial courts and had received one year in prison for manslaughter – he had shot dead an East African village elder, who had refused to sell cattle to him – and was indicted for fraud in September 1911. In this latter case, he had allegedly recruited workers without official permission. As one witness reported at court, Georgiades had also made false promises and not paid the recruited workers: neither their *posho* nor their recruitment rewards.[77] Apart from these incidents illustrating some of the realities of labour recruitment and the colonial judicial system, the court files of Georgiades reveal another important aspect of the society of German East Africa: namely the fact that German colonial authorities were not able to clearly judge Georgiades' nationality. In recording the nationality and background of Michael Georgiades, the court official noted: "State: Turkey or Greece [. . .] Native country: Turkey?".[78] The obvious confusion about Georgiades' motherland clearly demonstrates that the colonial archive is not necessarily able to give reliable information regarding the background of individual Southern Europeans. Hence, assessing any file featuring Greek or Turkish sounding names or statements of corresponding nationalities is therefore always a comparatively tricky affair. Not to mention that the colonial archives barely reveal the motivations of individual (South-East) Europeans, explaining why, when, and how these people exactly migrated to the German colony.[79] Keeping these difficulties in mind, there are also well documented cases revealing why many Greeks came to German East Africa after 1900. Indeed, a large number of them migrated to the German colony because they intended to find employment as sub-contractors at *Holzmann's Central Railway*.

77 *Posho* = daily food allowance. Cf. TNA. G21/412, pp. 1–29.

78 TNA. G21/412, p. 37. Cf. Minawi. *The Ottoman Scramble*, pp. 2, 82.

79 The 'Orient Büro' (Orient Office) of the *Deutsche Bank* having files of the personnel of the *Bagdadbahn* and its *Anatolische Eisenbahngesellschaft* (Anatolian Railway Company) has a list of contractors and employees. Many Greek names (among others) are labelled with Ottoman or Turkish citizenship. Cf. HADB. P8049. Anatolische Eisenbahngesellschaft. Diverse Listen ihrer Angestellten, pp. 2–11. Cf. also TNA. G21/373. Ermittelungssache gegen den Aufseher Christo Antonio, Goweko, Bez. Tabora, wegen Vergehens gegen die Arbeiteranwerbeordnung. 1911–1912, pp. 6–5. For assessing colonial archives cf. Stoler. *Along the archival grain* 2009. Cf. Stoler. 'Colonial Archives', pp. 83–109. Cf. Büschel. 'Das Schweigen'.

3.3.2 From *Bagdad* to Dar es Salaam: Engineers and Greek Sub-contractors

> The rumour of a planned huge railway construction in East Africa had found its way to the Greeks living in the Near and Middle East [. . .]. Many entrepreneurs and those who wanted to become such [sub-]contractors one day were attracted by the country. As our company had just finished the first section of the Bagdadbahn by the end of 1904, many employees of this former railway construction site were enrolled for the new works in German East Africa.
>
> *Holzmann's* Construction Officer Ferdinand Grages, Frankfurt o.M.: 1948.[80]

In view of historian Philippa Söldenwagner's claim that most of the Southern Europeans arrived between 1908 and 1914 not directly from Greece, but via Egypt,[81] particularly colonial railway construction in German East Africa seems to have facilitated Greek immigration via *Philipp Holzmann's* global company networks. With the company's various railway construction projects in Europe, in the Americas and in Asia (Minor), indeed the most significant connection between all these infrastructure projects was that between the construction of the *Central Railway* in German East Africa and the *Bagdadbahn* in the Middle East. In this respect, there are not only the memories of *Holzmann's* building officer Ferdinand Grages that document this fact; in addition, reports of the *Deutsch Ostafrikanische Zeitung* (*DOAZ*) and the files held at the archives of the *Deutsche Bank* confirm the connections of the East African railway to the *Bagdadbahn*. Examining these sources, numerous entanglements between the two prestigious infrastructure projects existed from planning stage to the execution of construction work at various levels.[82] Already at the planning stage, the construction consortium around the *Deutsche Bank* stressed the importance of employing "experienced engineers with knowledge of the tropics, who also have general knowledge of overseas conditions."[83] As there were only few companies and engineers in Germany obtaining such skill and knowledge, *Holzmann* was one of the very few

80 Stadtarchiv Frankfurt. W1/2 – 278/1. Grages, p. 3.

81 Cf. Söldenwagner. *Spaces*, p. 58.

82 Cf. Richter, Otto. 'Holzmann in Asien. Die Anatolische und die Bagdadbahn'. *Philipp Holzmann Aktiengesellschaft im Wandel von Hundert Jahren. 1849–1949*. 249–273. Ed. Hans Meyer-Heinrich. Frankfurt o.M.: 1949, p. 249–264. Cf. Rösser. 'Transimperiale Infrastruktur?'. According to the Blog of the Greek Historian Antonis Chaldeos, some Greek sub-contractors working at the central railway in German East Africa came also from the Horn of Africa, where they had been busy in constructing railroads as well. Cf. Chaldeos, Antonis. 'Τρίτη, 28 Μαΐου 2019. The Greek Constructors of the Railway in Tanzania'. *Greeks of Africa*. Web. http://greeksofafrica.blogspot.com/2019/05/. (11 September 2019). Cf. Gillman, Clement. 'A Short History of the Tanganyika Railways'. 14–56. *Tanganyika Notes and Records*, no. 13. Dar es Salaam: 1942, pp. 24–29. Cf. Hill. *Permanent Way. Vol. II*, pp. 85–88.

83 HADB. S 1518, "Arthur Koppel an Deutsche Bank, Berlin 15. April 1901, Anlage", p. 5.

companies to turn to. Having built the first sections of the most prestigious German imperial railway, the *Bagdadbahn*, *Holzmann* employed and knew many of those German engineers with 'knowledge of overseas conditions' and it is therefore no coincidence that engineers who had previously worked in Asia Minor went to German East Africa to construct another prestigious German imperial railway there and vice versa.

Exploring the track layout of the *Central Railway* from Dar es Salaam to Morogoro in 1903, all three senior engineers involved had worked at large scale infrastructure construction sites overseas before coming to the German colony. Mr Kröber had previously constructed a railway in southern Brazil for *Holzmann's* competitor, the company *Arthur Koppel* from Berlin. His two other colleagues – the German engineer Riese, who would organise the expedition to German East Africa, and the Austrian engineer Auner – had both worked for *Holzmann* for some years already, either exploring the layout or leading the construction work for significant parts of the *Bagdadbahn*. As Auner had fallen ill soon after his arrival to German East Africa in summer 1903, he was replaced by *Holzmann* engineer Mavgorodato. As Mavgorodato was at the time working at a construction site of the *Bagdadbahn*, he arrived in December 1903 to reinforce the decimated team.[84] In the years to come, when the railway had moved from planning to the construction stage, Mavgorodato and his *Holzmann* colleague Petersen travelled between East Africa and the Ottoman Empire and vice versa, occupied with various tasks of railway construction either on behalf of the *Central Railway* or on behalf of the *Bagdadbahn* – but always on behalf of *Holzmann*, of course. The sources confirm the travelling of another senior engineer, Mr Deininger, between the *Central Railway* and the *Bagdadbahn*, further showing the significant links between the two prestigious infrastructure projects.[85]

Yet, interrelationships between senior *Holzmann* engineers in German East Africa and Asia Minor are only one side of the coin. The most significant connection between the *Bagdadbahn* and the *Central Railway* arises from Greek sub-contractors: They had worked for *Holzmann's* railway in Asia Minor first and then deliberately travelled for railway construction to German East Africa. Generally, Greek sub-contractors at the *Central Railway* by far outnumbered both German engineers and German sub-contractors. Moreover, Construction Officer Grages (quoted above) is accurate in stating that Greek sub-contractors migrated deliberately from railway construction employment in Asia Minor to railway construction in German East Africa.

---

84 Cf. HADB. S 1515, "Arthur Gwinner [Deutsche Bank] an Gouverneur Graf von Götzen, Dar es Salaam, 02. Juli. 1903", pp. 1–5.

85 Cf. Hill. *Permanent Way. Vol. II*, p. 101. For an engineer preferring East Africa over Asia Minor cf. HA Krupp N 13/7, pp. 100–101. For engineering personnel in general cf. Beese. *Experten*.

On their part, the company of *Holzmann* also facilitated this movement. As the sources are relatively silent on the details of this Greek migration, various sources must be considered on the issue. First of all, there is the *DOAZ*. As the German settlers' organ of the colony, the newspaper attempted to reflect and promote the German emigrants' interests in the first place. As any non-German migration to German East Africa was generally regarded with suspicion by the newspaper, it closely observed Greek migration to the colony. Taking the published articles lamenting Greek migration to German East Africa as an indicator of peaks in actual Greek immigration to the German colony, it has to be stressed that the peaks in press coverage concorded with the onset of the construction of new route sections of the *Central Railway*. Whenever construction work at the *Central Railway* intensified, the number of articles published by the *DOAZ* about Greeks in the colony peaked as well.

With the start of the actual construction work in January 1905, the colony experienced a major influx of Greek people, who seem to have spent some time in Dar es Salaam just after their arrival.[86] When the home line from Dar es Salaam to Morogoro had been fulfilled in 1907, actual construction work resumed in late 1908. Once again, the *DOAZ* published numerous articles on the so-called 'Greek Question' (*Griechenfrage*) and its relationship to railway construction.[87] According to the *DOAZ*, there were only six German *Holzmann* employees responsible for the construction of individual route sections between 1907 and 1912.[88] By early 1912 the railhead had reached central Tabora, which became one of the most important railway hubs in the entire colony. With the *DOAZ* giving details about the European population in Tabora, it becomes clear that especially Greeks remained indispensable for *Holzmann* to fulfil the building task of the *Central Railway* throughout the entire construction period. According to the *DOAZ*, in January 1912, Tabora counted 433 European inhabitants (390 male). Of those, 202 were Greek. They were listed as (railway sub-) contractors (sixty), craftsmen (seventy), or traders (twenty-five). They were either employed as railway sub-contractors by *Holzmann* or profited indirectly as traders from the new railway as it generally stirred economic activity. Confirming that not every migrant was able to make a living off the construction of the *Cen-*

---

86 Cf. "Eine Ernste Gefahr für unser Prestige". *DOAZ*, VII, no. 12. Daressalam: 25 March 1905. Cf. "Aus der Kolonie". *DOAZ*, VII, no. 13. Daressalam: 01 January 1905.

87 Cf. Dr. H. Krauß. "Über die Gesundheitsverhältnisse in Deutsch-Ostafrika". *DOAZ*, X, no. 94. Daressalam: 05 December 1908. Cf. "Streifzüge in Ostafrika". *DOAZ*, XI, no. 19. Daressalam: 10 March 1909. Cf. "Zur Griechenfrage". *DOAZ*, XI, no. 42. Daressalam: 25 March 1905.

88 Cf. "Deutsche Unternehmer für den Bahnbau Tabora-Tanganika". *DOAZ*, XIV, no. 8. Daressalam: 27 January 1912.

tral Railway, forty-one Greeks were also listed as unemployed.[89] This general impression provided by the colonial newspaper especially during the first half of the railway construction period is confirmed by the sources produced by the railway supervisory bodies from 1911 onwards.

Accordingly, railway construction was not only primarily carried out by subcontractors at the expense of *Holzmann* proper: it was overwhelmingly carried out by Greek sub-contractors who had primarily migrated from the *Bagdadbahn* to the railway construction sites in German East Africa. Not only *Holzmann*, but also most of the colonial administration regarded Greek railway sub-constructors as the most reliable and most able men to fulfil the construction of the large-scale infrastructure in the German colony. They had been the first group who had taken up outsourced railway construction in German East Africa and remained the most numerous national group of sub-contractors until the completion of the *Central Railway* in 1914. Only very few of these Greek sub-contractors had been resident in German East Africa before the advent of the *Central Railway* and the vast majority had come to the German colony exactly for the purpose of railway construction. Generally, they planned to leave East Africa for their homeland as soon as they had earned enough money and/or completed their contracts with *Holzmann*. In August 1912, according to information provided by the company, *Holzmann* employed a total number of fifty-eight sub-contractors responsible for the construction of individual route sections between the central town Tabora and the 235-kms distant station of Malagarassi. Of those, fourty-seven men (eighty-eight percent) were non-Germans and only eleven men (twelve percent) were German. According to the information provided by the German sub-contractor Berger, of those forty-seven non-German sub-contractors "45 were Greek and Turkish subjects", along with only "7 citizens of the German *Reich* [*Reichsdeutsche*]".[90] The other two non-Germans were the Italian sub-contractors Eredi and Natalicio. Whether the difference of four Germans comprises either ethnic Germans having previously lived overseas, e.g. in Latin America, or ethnic Germans of Austrian citizenship is not clear in this file. Other files confirm that there were some Austrians and some Germans who had lived overseas before, who were now employed as engineers at the *Central Railway* and who were regarded as ethnic German by *Holzmann* and the colonial authorities. It is therefore very likely that some of the listed Germans without residence in the *Reich* proper had also been hired as sub-contractors by *Holz-*

89 Cf. "Aus unserer Kolonie". *DOAZ*, XIV, no. 96. Daressalam: 30 November 1912. Cf. "Die wirtschaftlichen Verhältnisse des Bezirks Tabora im Jahre 1911". *DOAZ*, XIV, no. 92. Daressalam: 16 November 1912. Cf. Rösser. 'Transimperiale Infrastruktur', pp. 277–84.
90 TNA. G12/176, p. 3.

mann. Yet, neither the given ratio nor the numbers provided reflect the overall share of work adequately.[91]

As a matter of fact, the overall contribution of Greek sub-contractors to railway construction was much higher than the contribution of German sub-contractors. The major reasons are that Greek sub-contractors generally had more workers at their disposal, had better financial means, and were regarded as more competent than German sub-contractors by *Holzmann*. For all these reasons, Greek sub-contractors generally received route sections larger than those of the German sub-contractors.[92] In fact, comparing German to non-German sub-contractors is too simple, as one sub-contractor responsible for one individual route section generally employed several European overseers or other auxiliary staff. These European men assisting in railway construction were not necessarily of the same nationality as the actual sub-contractors. The following section gives more details of the composition of these sub-contractor teams and of all the different European nationalities working at the construction sites of the *Central Railway* in German East Africa.

3.3.3 Blurring National Borders: Diverse European Sub-contractor Teams

> Of the 147 contractually employed civil servants and craftsmen, 85% are Reich Germans and 15% are foreigners, whose nationality is distributed almost equally among England, Austria, Hungary, Italy, Sweden, Denmark, Switzerland, Turkey, the United States of North America, Argentina and Chile. Most of these are engineers who received their technical education at German universities or civil servants who can look back on a long career in the company's service.
>
> *Holzmann* to *Deutsch Ostafrikanische Zeitung*, 11 October 1910.[93]

The construction of the *Central Railway* in German East Africa was to a great extent an international affair indeed. Besides the global pursuit for imperial railways and the strong connections between the German imperial *Bagdadbahn* in the Ottoman Empire and the *Central Railway* in German East Africa, there were also links to other various parts of the world. Regarding their own staff directly employed, i.e. not hired as sub-contractors, these are revealed first of all by the

91 Cf. TNA. G12/176, pp. 2–16. Cf. TNA. G17/64, "Monatsbericht über den Stand der Arbeiten beim Bau der Zentralbahn Ende September 1910. VIII und IX. Personal- und Arbeiterverhältnisse". Cf. TNA. G17/158, "Philipp Holzmann an die DOAZ Daressalam, den 11 October 1910".

92 Cf. TNA. G12/176, pp. 2–16. Cf. TNA. G17/64, "Monatsbericht über den Stand der Arbeiten beim Bau der Zentralbahn Ende September 1910. VIII und IX. Personal- und Arbeiterverhältnisse". Cf. TNA. G17/158, "Philipp Holzmann an die DOAZ Daressalam, den 11 October 1910".

93 TNA. G17/158, "Holzmann an Deutsch Ostafrikanische Zeitung. Daressalam, den 11 October 1910".

nationalities of the engineers directly employed by *Holzmann* quoted above. Despite many Germans, at least six other European nationalities were mentioned alongside engineers from the Americas and Turkey.

Secondly, there were not only Greek sub-contractors at the *Central Railway*'s construction sites, but also many other nationalities. Apart from the senior employees like engineers, *Holzmann* had, by their own account, another "55 civil servants, craftsmen and supervisors employed on a daily wage in German East Africa [of whom] 60% were *Reichsdeutsche* [citizens of the German *Reich*] and 40% foreigners".[94] Thirdly, the numerous sub-contractors working at the *Central Railway* themselves employed other Europeans for auxiliary tasks. The latter worked as overseers or foremen and came from a variety of European countries. Generally, each sub-contractor employed at least one European foreman who observed the manual work performed by the African staff. The number of European overseers per sub-contractor varied according to the number of African workers the sub-contractor employed as well as the sub-contractor's individual preference. Normally, the larger the workforce, the more overseers were employed by a sub-contractor. In general, it was not necessarily the case that German sub-contractors would exclusively employ German overseers. Neither would Greek sub-contractors exclusively hire Greek overseers. This is reflected by the list of sub-contractors and their overseers at the route sections between Tabora and Kigoma in 1913. In this route section, there were thirty-eight European sub-contractors working at that time. Although there was a trend to nationally homogenous sub-contractor teams, there were more diverse sub-contractor teams at the same time. Of the thirty-eight teams, there were five teams of mixed nationalities. Of those, the Greek sub-contractor Grammatikos employed one German and two Greek overseers; the German sub-contractor Behrens employed one German, one Italian, and two Greek overseers; and the Greek large-scale sub-contractor Scutari employed four 'foreigners' whose nationalities we do not know. This observation is especially important as there were not only Greeks and Germans working as sub-contractors or overseers at the *Central Railway*'s construction sites, but many other nationalities as well. Besides the Italians mentioned already, there were also Albanians, Romanians, French, Swiss, English and others. Needless to say, also Swahili or rather East Africans could become overseers or even sub-contractors.[95] Yet, single nationalities

94 TNA. G17/158, "Holzmann an Deutsch Ostafrikanische Zeitung. Daressalam, den 11 October 1910".

95 Cf. TNA. G17/123, "Philipp Holzmann. Entg. 534, 501, 472. An Eisenbahnkommissar Tabora. Tabora, 11. April 1913. Tabelle II". Cf. Oxford. Bodleian Library. Gillman Diaries. Mss. Afr. S. 1175/1,2_1, no. 9, pp. 1–3. Cf. TNA. G21/262. Ermittlungssache gegen Aufseher der Firma Philipp Holzmann & Cie., Frederic Sainsburg, Kondoa, Bez. Morogoro wegen fahrlässiger Tötung seines Dien-

were not only transcended by mixed railway construction teams; several individual engineers and sub-contractors too had backgrounds that transcended one nationality, or had lived in many different parts of the world. The biographies of *Holzmann* railway engineer Clement Gillman and the sub-contractor John Zavellas illustrate this fact.

3.3.4 Transcending Nationalities at the *Central Railway*: The Cases of John Zavellas and Clement Gillman

> I was appointed associate judge of the imperial district court in Tabora in September 1911 and participated in my first session instantly. In this trial Zavellas, a Greek sub-contractor, was sentenced to two and a half months imprisonment because of unlawful detention. These responsibilities are very difficult for me.
>
> *Holzmann* engineer Clement Gillman, November 1911.[96]

Greek railway sub-contractors did not exclusively reach East Africa coming from the *Bagdadbahn* or Egypt. As the personal details of some court files reveal, there were cases of Greek sub-contractors and labour recruiters who had previously been in South Africa or the USA[97] before coming to the German colony. In the course of the 'long nineteenth century' many young – and especially male – Greeks emigrated to seek a better life overseas, because the South-Eastern European economy could hardly sustain the contemporary population growth of their motherland.[98] Besides trying to make a living as petty traders or tobacco planters and cigarette manufacturers, many Greeks migrating to South Africa sought employment as sub-contractors at the Cape Railways between 1905 and 1909, or the railroads in Transvaal between 1910 and 1913. Like the German railway sub-contractor Langkopp, many Greeks also fought in the Second South African War on either side: while

ers Amdallah [durch eine diesem zugänglich gemachten Pistole]. 1909, pp. 1–5. Cf. TNA. G21/361. Ermittelungssache gegen den Aufseher Henry Parsons, Itigi, Bez. Dodoma [wegen Verursachung einer Schlägerei zwischen seien Arbeitern und denen der Beamten der OAEG Eredi und Kurbjeweit]. 1911, pp. 24–30.

96 Gillman Diaries. Mss. Afr. S. 1175/1,2_2, no. 13, pp. 43–44.

97 There is also a case of a Muslim Goanese who had migrated from Brazil to German East Africa cf. TNA. G23/40. Strafsache gegen den Goanesen Castro de Lobo, Muhesa, Bez. Tanga, wegen Unterschlagung [von Prämien zur Arbeiteranwerbung] 1914, pp. 1a, 19–20.

98 Cf. Brunnbauer and Buchenau. *Geschichte Südosteuropas*, pp. 108–200. Cf. Calic. *Südosteuropa*, pp. 344–423.

Greeks from the southwestern part of the Cape colony tended to join the British, those living in Transvaal joined the forces of the Boers.[99] This reflected the tendency of the Greek diaspora in African colonies to support the ruling colonial power, which guaranteed their presence in the foreign territory.[100]

Besides this general information about the Greek diaspora in African colonies, there are court files that document the biographies of two Greek men in particular who worked as sub-contractors at the *Central Railway* in German East Africa. Neither of them had been to Egypt, nor to the Ottoman Empire before coming to the German colony at the Indian Ocean. The first one is Georges Kayakos. Whether Kayakos had left South Africa because of the Boers' defeat after 1902, like Lankopp did, or whether he had finished working on the Transvaal Railroad before coming to German East Africa is not entirely clear. His court file of 1915 only reveals that he had previously lived in the Transvaal region, was ca. forty-two years of age, Christian orthodox and contemporarily recruited workers for the German military during WWI. In any case, the biography of his fellow Greek railway sub-contractor, John Zavellas, extends even beyond Asia Minor and the African continent. Before coming to German East Africa, Zavellas had initially emigrated to the State of New York in the USA. His court file does not reveal much about his life in the USA, unfortunately. It only says that he had left Greece around the age of fifteen with the surname 'Gerakos', and was taken care of by an older Greek immigrant living in the USA named Zavellas. As Gerakos was quasi adopted by the elder Zavellas, the teenage immigrant therefore also took his protector's surname and became John Zavellas. After having lived in North America for some years, John Zavellas left the USA around 1900 and migrated to German East Africa where he first worked at a rubber, and later at a sisal, plantation. By 1911 at the latest, Zavellas had finally become one of *Central Railway*'s numerous Greek sub-contractors and produced gravel for the track bed at a quarry, alongside another Greek colleague. Accused of violating labour protection rights, Zavellas was brought before *Holzmann* engineer and associate judge Clement Gillman at court in September 1911.[101]

99 Cf. Mantzaris, E.A. 'The Greeks in South Africa'. *The Greek Diaspora in the Twentieth Century.* 120–136. Ed. Richard Clogg. Basingstoke: 2001, pp. 120–123. Cf. Mantzaris, E.A. 'Greek Workers in South Africa. The Case of the Railway Workers and Cigarette-makers. 1905–1914'. 49–63. *Journal of the Hellenic Diaspora,* vol. XIV, no. 3 & 4. N.P.: Fall/Winter: 1987, pp. 49–53. Cf. TNA. G21/645. Ermittelungssache gegen den Unternehmer George Koyakos, Kilossa, Bez. Morogoro, wegen Vergehens gegen die Arbeiteranwerbeverodnung [vom 5.2.1913]. 1915, pp. 2–3.

100 Regarding Mozambique and South Africa cf. Dousemetzis. *The Man who killed Apartheid,* pp. 34–72, 140–173.

101 Cf. TNA. G27/27. Strafsache gegen den Unternehmer John Zavellas, Tabora, wegen Anstiftung [mehrerer Aufseher zur Freiheitsberaubung]. 1911, pp. 13–15. Cf. TNA. G27/73. Strafsache gegen den Unternehmer John Zavellas, Kilossa, Bez. Morogoro, wegen Vergehens gegen die Arbeiterver-

As far as Gillman is concerned, the case against Zavellas was not his only trial as an associate judge and the fact that senior *Holzmann* employees of Central-European origin were also incorporated in the judicial system of German East Africa clearly shows that the separation of power in the colony was insufficient. Yet, analogically to Zavellas background, Gillman's biography reveals how individual biographies of men working at the central railroad in German East Africa transcended mere nationalities. Clement Gillman was the son of an Anglo-Swiss father (Fritz) and a German mother (Margarethe von Petzholdt), who, as the daughter of a German Professor for agricultural technology at the Tsarist University of Dorpat (today's Tartu), grew up in Estonia, which belonged to the Russian Empire at that time. Educated as a geologist and engineer in Freiberg (Saxony), Fritz Gillman moved to Spain to work at his father's silver-mines in Granada from 1867 onwards. Only a few months before Fritz left for Southern Europe, the couple had first met in Dresden, where the well-educated cosmopolitan Margarethe completed her education. It would be another thirteen years until Fritz and Margarethe got married in Freiburg im Breisgau in 1881, where Margarethe's father had chosen to live after his retirement. Immediately afterwards, the newly married couple moved to Madrid, where their son Clement Gillman was born on 26 November 1882 into a 'patchwork family', as Margarethe had already had two children from a previous marriage.[102]

Predominantly raised at his maternal grandparents' home in Freiburg from 1884 onwards, Clement entered a five-year engineering course of study at the Swiss Federal Institute of Technology (*ETH*) in Zurich in October 1900. While studying, Clement not only learned the art of engineering, but also extensively travelled Switzerland and Germany. In Zurich he became a close friend of Paul Rieppel, the son of Anton von Rieppel, who was then head of the *MAN* Company and it is noteworthy that *MAN's* engineers would later construct railway bridges not only in German East Africa, but also in other German colonies.[103] It was Paul Rieppel, whose business relationships to German engineering companies were facilitated by his father who made Clement's post-study job-hunting successful; Paul knew one of the chief directors of Frankfurt's *Philipp Holzmann* company personally and brokered Clement a job there. After spending only a few months at *Holz-*

---

ordnung [vom 5.2.1912 – Nichtführung von Lohnlisten] und Führung eines unrichtigen Namens. 1914–1915, pp. 4–10, 39–42. Cf. Rösser. 'Transimperiale Infrastruktur?', pp. 277–284.

102 Cf. Hoyle, B.S. 'Clement Gillman, 1882–1946: Biographical Notes on a Pioneer East African Geographer'. 1–16. *East African Review,* no. 3, n.p.: April 1965, p. 1. Cf. Hoyle. *Gillman*, pp. 33–44.

103 Cf. Historisches Archiv/Museum der MAN AG Augsburg. 42, 352/a/3-2. Cf. Stadtarchiv Frankfurt. W1/2 – 278/1. *Erinnerungen an den ersten Bahnbau in Ostafrika von Baurat Wilhelm Imm,* p. 19.

mann's headquarters in Frankfurt, Clement Gillman left for German East Africa in September 1905 as an assistant engineer of the colony's *Central Railway*, on which construction had been started only seven months earlier by *Holzmann*.[104]

Although having been decisively involved in German colonial railway construction in East Africa between 1905 and 1914, Gillman's 'cosmopolitan' background scarcely fitted the jingoistic atmosphere before, but especially during WWI. As an Anglo-German engineer, and since 1908 married to an ethnic German woman called Eva Kerber, who was actually born and raised in St. Petersburg, Russia,[105] Gillman and his family were first put on leave between September 1914 and May 1916 by the German colonial authorities after WWI had started in August 1914. The reason was that, to the taste of the German administration, Clement was judged as 'too English' and his wife not 'German enough' to be completely trusted. As fierce fighting increased on East African soil between German, British and Belgian forces, Gillman was then also made a POW and consequently interned in a concentration camp in Tabora between May 1916 and September 1916 by the German colonial authorities. The allied forces slowly but surely gained the upper hand in German East Africa, and the Gillmans were released as soon as the allied forces had invaded Tabora. They were still regarded with suspicion, however. Now it was the other way around with the British authorities: as Clement had previously worked for a German company (i.e. *Holzmann*) and was practically raised in Germany, the British did not immediately regard him as a reliable British subject. Analogically, Eva was widely regarded as being predominantly 'German'. Hence, it took another year to overcome these nationalist hurdles until the British acknowledged Gillman's useful engineering experience gathered in East Africa, and he was first made railway officer of the British colonial military and shortly afterwards promoted to chief engineer during the last years of WWI. While his first tasks were to rebuild railway sections and bridges that had been destroyed by the German forces during their retreat, he later continued working for the British Mandate authorities in what was by then called 'Tanganyika Territory' after the Treaty of Versailles. He continued to work and live in East Africa until his death in October 1946.[106] During his entire professional life, Clement Gillman

104 Cf. Hoyle. 'Biographical Notes', pp. 1–3. Cf. Hoyle. *Gillman*, pp. 45–56.

105 A highly educated woman, who had also studied in Zurich, where they met. She also had a very cosmopolitan background, having been born and raised in Russia's St. Petersburg to a wealthy German family with high-ranking business relations; among others, Eva's father, Eduard Kerber, acted as representative of the *Krupp* consortium, which coincidentally also provided the iron bars of the German colonial central railway in East Africa. Vgl. Hoyle. *Gillman*, p. 53. Cf. Kilian, Dieter E. *Kai-Uwe von Hassel und seine Familie. Zwischen Ostsee und Ostafrika. Militär biographisches-Mosaik*. Norderstedt: 2013, p. 98.

106 Cf. Hoyle. 'Biographical Notes', pp. 3–9. Cf. Hoyle. *Gillman*, pp. 108–370.

kept his diary assiduously and published scientific articles on various subjects from engineering to geography. The result is an almost unmanageable number of documents ranging from diaries, scientific notes and correspondence to articles produced over forty years that also shed light on labour relationships in his own construction camp. Gillman, as a senior railway engineer, lived a comparatively luxurious life in the German colony. He received not only decent salaries, but compared to the numerous European sub-contractors, he was also privileged in the colonial society, as demonstrated by his involvement in the colonial judiciary system. In contrast, railway sub-contractors like John Zavellas often lived insecure itinerant lives, not only affecting their standard of living, but also their societal standing.

3.3.5 Struggling Along the Railroad: Making a Living as a Railway Sub-contractor

> 'We are all broke!' shouted the chairman. [. . .] 'Broke. That's what we are indeed!' echoed the second. [. . .] The third one, an older gentleman, nodded three times conformingly with a friendly smile. Then, he took a sip of whisky-soda silently.[107]
>
> Zimmermann, Adolf. *Mit Dernburg nach Ostafrika*. Berlin: 1908.

That is how the journalist Adolf Zimmermann, who accompanied State Secretary Bernhard Dernburg to German East Africa in 1907, recalls his meeting with "the united German Civil Population of Sadani"[108] in his travel report. As this scene of "German sociability in distant German-Wild-East"[109] illustrates, being a settler in the East African colony was very far from the *Herrenmenschentum*, which many European migrants had probably anticipated before leaving their country of origin. On the contrary, their life was often marked by scarcity and many even struggled to sustain their own subsistence farming. Hence, a large number of them kept wandering around the colony, seeking more profitable employments or an extra income besides their farming estate. Lacking success in any undertaking, some were even expelled, because the colonial administration would not tolerate white people in need of the benevolence of the African population to survive as this would challenge the racial hierarchy in the colony.[110] Many of these individuals probably rejoiced when hearing that the building company *Philipp Holzmann* had started actual construction of the *Central Railway* in January 1905. The rail-

107 Zimmermann, Adolf. *Mit Dernburg nach Ostafrika*. Berlin: 1908, p. 118.
108 Zimmermann. *Mit Dernburg*, p. 118.
109 Zimmermann. *Mit Dernburg*, p. 118.
110 Cf. Söldenwagner. *Spaces*, p. 166–177.

road promised not only a spur to macro-economic activity, but also direct employment opportunities. Yet, recalling the population statistics of the railway hub Tabora published by the *DOAZ* in 1912, despite railway construction and its economic impulse, the unemployment rate among the European population of the town was high. Forty-one out of 433 Europeans were out of work: an unemployment rate of about ten percent. Even if someone found a job at the railway as a sub-contractor, the standard of living of many European sub-contractors seems to have remained low throughout the entire construction process.

When Edwin Hennig, one of the leading palaeontologists working for the Tendaguru Expedition in German East Africa's southeast, visited the *Central Railway* for geographical investigations close to the newly built track on 14 February 1910, he described the poor living conditions of railway sub-contractors in his diary:

> I met the two Europeans [. . .] at the station of Kidugallo who are expanding the quarry here[.] They seem to struggle along quite miserably and their only wish is to be able to return [home] quite soon. They asked me to stay for lunch. Not to my delight, because their grass house [. . .] was overrun by cobwebs a[nd] [. . .] the dining room right next to the kitchen (from where a female voice was to be heard and which also seems to serve for sleeping), was miserably small and greasy. All around there was hardly any footpath to be found leading through the grass.[111]

Although Hennig uses the word 'Europeans', his diary does not reveal the nationalities of the two men working for the railway. But having processed the palaeontologist's diary it must be stressed that his German acquaintances are generally remembered by name, while railway sub-contractors who were from Southern Europe remained usually anonymous. With Hennig only very reluctantly accepting the invitation of these two 'miserably struggling' sub-contractors for lunch in their shabby hut, the palaeontologist's statement reveals not only that it was hard for railway sub-contractors to make a living in German East Africa. Of course, there were also very successful large scale sub-contractors of South-East European descent, such as the already mentioned Greek Scutari. But Scutari had not only been in the service of *Holzmann* for many years, he seems to have also been of a wealthy family. This did not apply to all sub-contractors, as Hennig's diary entry shows. Moreover, it also reveals that class and standard of living were central to the status a European would acquire in the East African colonial society. But mate-

---

111 Universitätsarchiv Tübingen (UAT). 407/80. Nachlass Hennig (1882–1977). Tagebuch, Teil 1, p. 131.

rial wealth was not the only indicator of class in the society of German East Africa. Standard of living intermingled with concepts of race and the *whiteness* of any European: especially when South-East Europeans or rather Greeks were concerned.

3.4 White Subaltern Railway Men and Precarious Whites

3.4.1 White Subalterns Versus Precarious Whites

> [. . .] [A]nthropologists have taken the dichotomy of the colonizer and the colonized as a given, rather than as a historically shifting pair of social categories that needs to be explained. Certainly, this is not to suggest that anthropologists have not attended to the ambiguity and manipulation of racial categorization. [. . .] But this interest has rarely been coupled with a focus on European communities, or the powerful cultural idioms of domination in which they invest.
>
> Laura Ann Stoler. 'Rethinking Colonial Categories'. Ann Arbor: 1992.[112]

Stoler's research on the colonial community in Sumatra is almost thirty years old. Nevertheless, she is certainly right, as racist colonial discourses could indeed target population groups that one might not have expected. Indeed, European peoples could also become subject to racist and prejudiced colonial discourses analogical to those faced by African workers, Indian craftsmen, and Chinese coolies in German East Africa.[113] These discourses materialised especially when a people or an individual did not meet the characteristics of an ideal-typical coloniser at the turn of the nineteenth century, who was male, of upper or at least middle-class origin and most importantly from Central Europe. In this respect, Harald Fischer-Tiné, in particular, has examined for British colonial India how British lower-class colonists could lose their superior status when their material means and way of life, did not concord with the ideal image of a white (male) middle-upper-class European coloniser with an almost pious character. Especially when Europeans originated from the working class, lacked financial or other material means, showed deviant behaviour or had an affinity to drink, the superior status of the white men in the colony was severely challenged. The same mechanisms applied to European women, who would face even more severe discrimination if they were occupied as sex workers, or to so-called 'Eurasian' people of a mixed European-Indian background. Moreover, a European would lose his or her *white* prestige if he or she abandoned a

112 Stoler, Laura Ann. 'Rethinking Colonial Categories: European Communities and the Boundaries of Rule'. *Colonialism and Culture.* 319–352. Ed. Nicolas B. Dirks. Ann Arbor: 1992, p. 321.
113 Cf. Yekani. "'Inder und Chinesen'", pp. 209–225.

rather unspecified, but generally bourgeois European way of life and shared the habits or aspects of daily life with the colonised indigenous people. Despite their still superior legal status, British colonisers in India who did not fit the colonial discourse of white supremacy would be seen as 'low and licentious Europeans' who were ranked as 'second-rate whites' by the colonial discourse. This phenomenon, which Fischer-Tiné rather provocatively called 'white subalternity', does not mean that overarching mechanisms of colonial racism that ranked 'black' or 'coloured' people lower than 'whites' were no longer relevant. Borrowing approaches from American social sciences and gender studies, Fischer-Tiné is convinced that social inequality is not a fixed, one-dimensional phenomenon, but rather an ever-evolving

> 'multi-dimensional process that is constantly adapting to the different contexts in which it is embedded. This process is organised upon multiple intersecting hierarchies of race, ethnicity, class, gender, sexuality, nativity and other hegemonic systems, which pervade the status, lived experiences, and collective dynamics of both marginalised and empowered groups.'[114]

While stressing that each case of 'white-subalternity' depended highly on the context and individual circumstances, Fischer-Tiné is convinced "there were arresting parallels in the discursive strategies of exclusion used for white subalterns on the one hand and the colonized population on the other".[115] 'White subalternity' was such a pressing issue in British colonial India as it posed a serious threat to the ideology of colonialism and the practices of colonial rule: with destitute whites living on the breadline, sharing their daily lives with the indigenous population or taking up manual, unskilled and poorly paid jobs, the line between coloniser and the colonised blurred. From the perspective of any colonial administration, not only in India but also in other colonies, any phenomenon that posed a threat to the colonial ideology had to be avoided. That is why in almost all colonial empires, so-called mixed-race marriages between coloniser and the colonised were made increasingly difficult or even forbidden, and destitute or delinquent 'white subalterns' were hidden away from the public or even deported to their countries of origin.

Fischer-Tiné's research results regarding British colonial India are significant for the discursive mechanisms for 'white subaltern' Europeans in German East Africa as well. As 'white subalterns' challenged the ideal-typical colonial hierarchies of white European superiors and coloured-African inferiors, any Europeans who did not meet the standards of the colony were regarded with suspicion by the colonial authorities. In the case of the settler community in German East

114 Walter Allen and Angie Y. Chung. '"Your Blues Ain't like my Blues": Race, Ethnicity and Social Inequality in America'. *Contemporary Sociology*, 29, no. 6. 2000, p. 799. Qutd. in Fischer-Tiné. *'Low and Licentious'*, p. 17.

115 Fischer-Tiné. *'Low and Licentious'* p. 22, cf. pp. 1–23.

Africa, Philippa Söldenwagner observes that some white settlers were even pressured to leave the colony by the authorities as they were accused of undermining white prestige by becoming impoverished or by mixing too closely with the African population. While many (German) settlers in need were supported either by missions, the colonial government or the welfare lottery, especially European settlers who were not genuinely so-called *Reichsdeutsche* were regarded as 'second rate whites'. This was particularly true for some Boer families who had come to German East Africa after the Second South African War (1899–1902) and some German Russian families who had been invited by the colonial authorities to leave Russia for the German colony in the course of a German missionary initiative around 1905. Initially welcomed by the government, which was contemporarily trying to attract more German settlers to the colony, the Boers soon realised that economic opportunities were low in the German colony, and they were subsequently increasingly concerned that they were not regarded as 'white enough' – either by the authorities or by their fellow European settlers. Similarly, attracting German Russians to the colony raised criticism from their fellow German settlers, as they were not regarded as proper *Reichsdeutsche.* Furthermore, they held a comparatively low socio-economic status and were accused of living a life on the breadline in the German colony. For example, when some German Russians were found wandering pennilessly around the northern town of Tanga, they were accused of being a threat to white prestige, and six families were even expelled from the colony and deported to Hamburg.[116]

Historian Minu Haschemi Yekani generally agrees with the findings of Söldenwagner and Fischer-Tiné, but avoids the terminology of 'white subalternity': Although the discriminatory mechanisms directed against 'white subalterns' and the colonised population were similar in the colonies, she highlights the fact that in contrast to the colonised subalterns, 'white subalterns' had the opportunity to restore their racial prestige and their blemished *whiteness.* As soon as 'white subalterns' would return to their motherland, they would again become part of a *white* society that dominated the Global South through their empires and colonies, claims Yekani. In contrast to the 'white subalterns', the colonised would always remain subaltern. First of all, because of their skin colour, which the colonial discourse rated as inferior. Secondly, because colonial law really treated or rather made them inferior, and thirdly because colonised subalterns were generally not able to return to a society that dominated the rest of the world and

116 Cf. Söldenwagner. *Spaces*, pp. 58–70, 166–170. Cf. Methner, Wilhelm. *Unter drei Gouverneuren. 16 Jahre Dienst in deutschen Tropen.* Breslau: 1938, pp. 180–185. Cf. Dernburg, Bernhard. *Südwestafrikanische Eindrücke. Industrielle Fortschritte in den Kolonien. Zwei Vorträge.* Berlin: 1909, p. 11.

could thus not re-establish their socio-economic rank by means of migrating back to their motherland. That is why Yekani rejects the term 'white subalternity' and opts for the term white precariousness instead. White precariousness therefore describes that the *whiteness* of a Central-European could on the one hand indeed be challenged in German East Africa when it did not fit the ideal of a middle-class European way of life. But white precariousness also meant on the other hand that *whiteness* could be restored as soon as social circumstances altered and/or the standard of living of a precarious white improved. While the first aspect of white precariousness is quasi-analogous to the experience of the colonised subaltern, the second way was barred to the colonised people who would always remain subaltern according to the racist discourse.[117]

Yekani's criticism is certainly significant and contributes to a better understanding of racist discourses in a colony such as German East Africa. There are two limitations to Yekani's observations, however. The first limitation arises from the fact that class and material means also mattered in all societies in Europe. Of course, someone who had lived as a precarious white in German East Africa could return to the German *Reich* and live his or her life in a society of a European colonial power again. It is however doubtful if the living conditions of any precarious white would automatically improve when he or she returned penniless from Africa to his or her home. Someone who had been deported from a German colony due to his or her low standard of living and his or her struggling to survive might not attain a higher socio-economic status than that of a pauper or factory worker back in Europe; and the living and working conditions of the working classes in Germany around 1900 were very low and precarious indeed. On an individual level, the restoration of an individual's *whiteness* by returning to his or her motherland need not necessarily have paid off in a literal sense although he or she was structurally privileged as far as global standards apply, i.e. that a precarious white could then live a life in one of the imperial powers that dominated eighty percent of the world.[118] Secondly, it has to be stressed that Yekani's concept of white precariousness does not apply to all supposedly white Europeans, but exclusively to white Central Europeans. Yekani quite rightly observes that Southern Europeans, especially Greeks, did not fit into the concept of

117 Cf. Yekani. *Koloniale Arbeit*, pp. 197–276.

118 For a comparison between the labour rights of colonised Africans and those of (factory) workers in the German *Reich* cf. Schröder. *Gesetzgebung und "Arbeiterfrage"*, pp. 102–105, 161–163, 374–382, 594–598, 606–614. Cf. Kocka, Jürgen. *Arbeitsverhältnisse und Arbeiterexistenzen. Grundlagen der Klassenbildung im 19. Jahrhundert.* Bonn: 1990, pp. 507–525. Cf. Schmidt, Jürgen. *Arbeiter in der Moderne. Arbeitsbedingungen, Lebenswelten, Organisationen.* Frankfurt o.M.: 2015, pp. 33–68, 79–103.

white precariousness, because only Central Europeans were able to restore their *whiteness* when returning to their countries of origin. In contrast, Southern Europeans were still ranked inferior according to the hegemonic colonial discourse that elevated a Central European, middle-class way of life, and judged Greeks and Southern Europeans as 'half-Orientals' and 'semi-civilised'. As even the Greek officer Achmed Fahim Effendi and the Armenian Mihram Effendi of the German colonial military in German East Africa were subsumed in historical sources as 'black' *Askari* despite their European origin, this argument is fundamentally supported.[119] In fact, Yekani treats this aspect only as a sideshow and does not investigate further on the issue.[120] Yet, the role of Southern Europeans and especially Greeks is of central importance as far as labour at the construction sites of the *Central Railway* in particular, and labour recruitment in German East Africa in general, are concerned.

3.4.2 Discourses Against South(-East) European Sub-contractors

> The difference of climate is in any case the main cause [. . .], for it determines both the physical development of the individual and consequently his material labour power [. . .], as well as his general mental qualities, the national character. [. . .] This is especially true of the northerners, who as a rule remain able to work in the tropics for only a few years and then either leave the country or gradually perish. Southern Europeans do much better, they are more resistant and have fewer needs [. . .] and their adaptability to tropical customs and traditions is very significant.
>
> Senior Railway Engineer of Rio de Janeiro Dr. R.A. Hehl. Berlin: 1902.[121]

There were only few experts of overseas railway construction in Germany and only three German companies capable of fulfilling such projects. Besides *Holzmann*, there were Berlin's *Lenz & Co.* and *Arthur Koppel*. Consequently, those German experts who had been in countries outside Europe for railway construction had a strong voice among their colleagues. Apparently, Dr R.A. Hehl was one of these more experienced experts. Before publishing his book, senior engineer Hehl had built railways in "tropical and sub-tropical" Brazil for many years. Based on his experience, he felt entitled to provide guidance for railway engineers working not only in Latin America, but also in Africa as he viewed Brazil as having "great

119 Askari = African soldier/mercenary in service of the German colonial military. Cf. Michels, Stefanie. *Schwarze deutsche Kolonialsoldaten. Mehrdeutige Repräsentationsräume und früher Kosmopolitismus in Afrika*. Bielefeld: 2009, pp. 13–18.

120 Cf. Yekani. *Koloniale Arbeit*, pp. 212, 255, 267. Cf. Rösser. "'*Shenzi Ulaya*'".

121 Hehl, R.A. *Eisenbahnen in den Tropen. Spurweiten, Bau und Betrieb*. Berlin: 1902, pp. 1–2.

similarities with the similarly situated countries in the African continent."[122] When exploring the future track layout for the *Central Railway* in German East Africa in 1903, it seems that the engineers sent on behalf of the consortium of the *Deutsche Bank* were indeed aware of Hehl's ideas. His book *Eisenbahnen in den Tropen* (Railways in the Tropics) ranked first on the planning engineers' list of resources to be consulted.[123] In this work, Hehl gave not only advice on the technical aspects of railway construction 'in the tropics' – such as track gauge, high rise structures or the calculation of operating costs – he also provided his thoughts on labour. In line with the zeitgeist, Hehl's ideas about labour in the 'tropics' intermingled with contemporary discourses of race, class, climate and national identity that melded significantly with ideological or quasi-religious concepts of work. As revealed by the excerpt from his book cited at the beginning of this section, Hehl's ideas further intermingled with discourses about South(-East) Europeans and their work at railway construction sites in places that Hehl perceived as 'the tropics'. In essence, to Hehl, these tropical places were any railway construction sites in overseas or colonial territories.[124]

Racist discourses analogising the culture of African peoples to Southern Europeans were widespread in Germany and other European Empires. They ranked 'second-rate whites' or rather white subalterns below Central Europeans. Writing the official report on his joint inspection tour to German East Africa in 1908 with Bernhard Dernburg, the Colonial State Secretary's economic advisor Walther Rathenau, the Weimar Republic's later Foreign Minister, held the following view on labour in the colonies:

> Assuming [. . .] that the Negro is not used to work is simply wrong. If he, having lived under different climatic, historical, and racial conditions, shirks continuous work pursued day after day just like some Southern Europeans love to do; if he prefers one kind of work over

122 Hehl. *Eisenbahnen*, p. III.
123 Cf. HADB. S 1516, "Seydel's Technische Buchhandlung".
124 Cf. Hehl. *Eisenbahnen*, pp. III–V, 1–20, 229–241. Cf. Yekani. *Koloniale Arbeit*, pp. 265–276. Cf. Yekani. "'Inder und Chinesen'". Cf. Axster, Felix and Lelle, Nikolas. '«Deutsche Arbeit». Kritische Perspektiven auf ein ideologisches Selbstbild. Zur Einführung'. *«Deutsche Arbeit». Kritische Perspektiven auf ein ideologisches Selbstbild*. 7–36. Eds. Felix Axster and Nikolas Lelle. Göttingen: 2018. Cf. Konitzer, Werner. "Rasse' und 'Arbeit' als dichte Begriffe'. *«Deutsche Arbeit». Kritische Perspektiven auf ein ideologisches Selbstbild*. 76–87. Eds. Felix Axster and Nikolas Lelle. Göttingen: 2018. Cf. Axter, Felix. 'Arbeit an der 'Erziehung zu Arbeit'. Oder: die Figur des guten deutschen Kolonisators'. *«Deutsche Arbeit». Kritische Perspektiven auf ein ideologisches Selbstbild*. 226–251. Eds. Felix Axster and Nikolas Lelle. Göttingen: 2018. Cf. Conrad. *Globalisation*, pp. 275–379. Cf. Rösser. "'*Shenzi Ulaya*'". Details regarding discourses separating *white* from *black* but disregarding nuances in between colonisers and colonised, and also neglecting Hehl and Yekani cf. Beese. *Experten*, pp. 126–160.

> the other, there is still no reason to bereave him of his right to self-determination under the label of 'education'. If the negro had the qualities of a European, we had actually no right to colonise his land.[125]

Rejecting overt physical violence to force the African population to colonial labour, Rathenau's statement is in line with Dernburg's colonial policies after 1907. Although these colonial policies were termed 'reformed' after the devastating effects of the Maji Maji War, they nevertheless justified European colonial rule in Africa particularly based on the perception that the local population had to be 'educated' to work properly. More importantly, equating the presumed character of African people to that of Southern Europeans, Rathenau's statement implies the claim that Southern Europeans would not have the same capabilities of work as Central Europeans would. In turn, such claims suppose that Southern Europeans as white subalterns also had to be 'educated to work' and were racially inferior to Central Europeans.[126]

Rathenau's view was not only shared by Colonial State Secretary Bernhard Dernburg himself, but also by the German senior engineers of *Philipp Holzmann*. Having this discriminatory opinion not only implied the feeling of Central European superiority, however. It also implied the view that Southern Europeans were particularly qualified for colonial railway construction. On the part of the German engineers such as Hehl and *Holzmann's* Ferdinand Grages, especially the image of Greek railway subcontractors oscillated between white subalternity and Greek special suitability for railway construction in German East Africa. Grages was of the following opinion:

> It must be stressed that numerous Greeks registered as petty-[sub-]contractors and fulfilled minor tasks. Some of them failed because of lacking knowledge or because of lacking [financial] means. Others however – primarily due to their self-interest and due to material matters – remained true to the company until the very end. They have proved themselves as formidable [sub-]contractors. Some have become rich men or very successful planters in the end. Their success is rooted also in their frugality, their adaptability, and their great skill to familiarize quickly with the natives' customs and practices.[127]

---

125 Rathenau. 'Erwägungen', p. 163, my emphasis.

126 For similar discourses against Southern Europeans, esp. Italians, cf. Guglielmo, Thomas A. *White on Arrival. Italians, Race, Color, and Power in Chicago, 1890–1945.* Oxford: 2003, pp. 59–92, 146–176. Assessing similar anti-(southern) European discourse (among others) by means of Marxist and gender approaches in southern Rhodesia after WWI. Cf. Ginsburgh, Nicola. *Class, Work and Whiteness: Race and Settler Colonialism in Southern Rhodesia, 1919–1979.* Manchester: 2020, pp. 1–32, 133–224, 257–263. Cf. Rösser. '"*Shenzi Ulaya*"'. Cf. Papakyriacou. *Formulation and definitions*, pp. 51–73. Daughton mentions such discourses but only treats them as a sideshow. Cf. Daughton. *In the Forest of No Joy*, pp. 156–161, 289–291.

127 Stadtarchiv Frankfurt. W1/2 – 278/1. *Grages*, pp 3–4. Cf. Dernburg. *Südwestafrikanische Eindrücke*, p. 58.

Although perceived as helpful deputy colonisers by the *Holzmann* engineer Grages, the alleged Greek 'frugality and adaptability' and their 'familiarization with the natives' customs and practices' in German East Africa was also intermingled with overt racism and classism.[128] Particularly during times of Greek migration, the *DOAZ* published articles that lamented about the Southern Europeans' coming to the colony.

With the start of the actual construction work in January 1905, the colony experienced a major influx of Greek people.[129] Drawing on classist and racist discourses, the *DOAZ* immediately coined them "Tramps" and "Bassermann's figures of Oriental descent", who "rush to [German East Africa to] try their luck at the railway construction site".[130] The newspaper's very next edition demanded the reintroduction of registration laws to enable the government to expel destitute people in general, but particularly the "international proletariat", who had come to the German colony because of work opportunities in the railway.[131] Only two weeks later, another article lamented another thirty work-seeking Greeks who had just arrived in the colonial capital, while a further 150 were waiting in Zanzibar for the next ship to ferry them over. This time however, not only the mere issue of migration was the perceived problem, but also especially the fact that the Greek migrants allegedly did not seek to settle permanently in German East Africa but planned to stay for one to two years only, and then return to Asia Minor as soon as their contracts with the railway had ended. As a result, they would extract economic means from the German colony when returning home with their earnings. Whenever the *Reich's* government made decisions to grant additional funds necessary to continue railway construction towards Lake Tanganyika, the publication of articles featuring anti-Greek discourses peaked in the *DOAZ*. Most articles were published around 1909 and 1912, when the *Reichstag* had decided to build the track from Morogoro to Tabora first and then from Tabora to the railroad's ultimate terminus at Kigoma in the west of the colony.[132]

---

128 Cf. Papakyriacou. *Formulation and definitions*, pp. 51–73.

129 Cf. "Eine Ernste Gefahr". *DOAZ,* VII, no. 12.

130 "Eine Ernste Gefahr". *DOAZ,* VII, no. 12. "Bassermann's Figure" = "Bassermansche Gestalten": suspicious, questionable Individuals. Term coined by Friedrich Bassermann at the proceedings of the *Paulskirchenverfassung* 1848 in Frankfurt to describe Berlin's population, which was apparently heavily affected by poverty. Cf. Angermann, Erich. "Bassermann, Friedrich Daniel". *Deutsche Biographie.* 1, 1953, S. 624–625. Web. https://www.deutsche-biographie.de/sfz35199.html#ndbcontent. (22 December 2017).

131 "Aus der Kolonie". *DOAZ,* VII, no. 13.

132 Cf. "Gewissenlose Berichterstattung". *DOAZ,* IX, no. 60. Daressalam: 19 October 1907. Cf. "Zur Griechenfrage". *DOAZ,* XI, no. 42. Cf. "Aus unserer Kolonie. Die weiße Bevölkerung Deutsch- Ostafrikas". *DOAZ,* XII, no. 28. Daressalam: 08 April 1911. Cf. "Deutsche Unternehmer für den Bahnbau

Anti-Greek discourses were also prominent in *Reichstag* debates. Generally, MPs of the SPD and some members of the Catholic *Zentrum* were the only ones mouthing criticism about German colonial policies and labour and the treatment of African workers.[133] This also applied to railway construction in German East Africa. Yet, although the SPD were generally critical about such matters, their MP Gustav Noske particularly blamed Greek sub-contractors for the majority of the grievances at the railroad. In the general debate on the colonies' budget in 1914 that also decided on the funding of the construction of the so-called *Ruandabahn* – another track to be built intending to connect the recently built *Central Railway* to the northern part of German East Africa Ruanda – Noske did not mince his words:

> Attempting to lower the construction costs, the Holzmann Company [. . .] does not do the construction work itself; it rather employs a large number of sub-contractors. Of those, at least some are of dubious value. Some are Greeks of the very worst kind. They cheat the workers out of their wages, occasionally the entire amount. [. . .] It is certain that the Greeks do not care a damn about the labour laws [. . .] which have been enacted and those men in charge of supervision either don't notice everything or don't want to notice everything.[134]

Certainly, Noske blamed *Holzmann* for cutting costs at the expense of decent treatment of the African workforce by outsourcing route sections to cheaper sub-contractors. In general, the Social Democrat held these cost savings primarily responsible for the mistreatment of the workmen and women along the *Central Railway*. Indeed, sub-contractors paid less than *Holzmann* for the same working tasks. Yet, Noske further criticised that the supervisory bodies turned a blind eye to the issue and did not interfere decidedly enough. However, Noske particularly blamed Greek sub-contractors and accused them especially of being worse than other Europeans responsible for outsourced route sections. He even went so far as to call one Greek sub-contractor a "beast of a Greek" and accused especially the South-East Europeans of disregarding the labour protection rights issued by the colonial administration.[135] Although Greek sub-contractors certainly abused African workers, blaming South-East Europeans for most of the labour grievances at the *Central Railway* rather reflects German discourses discriminating white subalterns in the colonies. Yet, examining unpublished archival sources reveals

---

Tabora-Tanganika". *DOAZ*, XIV, no. 8. Cf. "Aus unserer Kolonie". *DOAZ*, XIV, no. 96. Cf. "Die wirtschaftlichen Verhältnisse des Bezirks Tabora im Jahre 1911". *DOAZ*, XIV, no. 92.

133 Cf. Habermas. *Skandal in Togo*, pp. 29–54. Cf. Guettel. 'The Myth', pp. 452–484. Cf. Bösch. 'Der Ankläger', pp. 47–71. Cf. Schröder. *Gustav Noske*, pp. 40–55.

134 Noske. '232. Sitzung ', p. 7991.

135 Noske. '232. Sitzung', p. 7992, cf. pp. 7991–7993.

that also German and other European sub-contractors were at least on a par with their Greek colleagues as far as the violation of labour legislation is concerned.

3.5 "All Treat the Workers Equally Bad": (South-East) European Sub-contractors and the African Workforce

3.5.1 The Complaint of the German Sub-contractor Berger

> The foreign contractors are preferred by the company Ph. Holzmann & Co, in every way when awarding construction contracts, without a German contractor first being asked to submit a bid [. . .]. [. . .] So far, individual German contractors have had to be content with small objects [. . .]. Larger works have always been entrusted to Greeks. The undersigned do not wish to bring the firm of Ph. Holzmann & Co into disrepute with the Imperial High Colonial Office, nor do they wish to oust foreigners from the work, they only demand preferential treatment, but least of all equal treatment in the awarding of building contracts to foreigners.
>
> German sub-contractor Berger to Colonial State Secretary Wilhelm Solf, 1 August 1912.[136]

On 1 August 1912, the German sub-contractor C. Berger, who had formerly been directly employed by *Holzmann* as assisting constructor, took the opportunity of addressing colonial State Secretary Wilhelm Solf personally via letter. Solf had just started his tour of inspection to the German colonies in Africa and visited the *Central Railway* in German East Africa. Alongside five other German sub-contractors – Heinrich Herling, Hans Haugg, Kurt Pfau, I. Hering and Mr Behrens – Berger bitterly complained about the allocation of new route sections, claiming that the *Holzmann* company would not privilege German sub-contractors as promised, but preferably hired Greeks instead. Berger not only complained about the large number of Greeks working at the *Central Railway* as such; he particularly resented the fact that, because *Holzmann* preferred Greek sub-contractors, German entrepreneurs had no chance of obtaining similar contracts and consequently had to take up work as sub-sub-contractors under a Greek boss. Besides the fact that such procedures turned the dominant discursive colonial hierarchy upside down, Berger appears to have been angry at *Holzmann* because he had recently been rejected to build the upper construction as sub-contractor of a route section, although he claimed to be not only more qualified than his Greek competitor, but also significantly cheaper: with Berger being a "former technical official" of *Holzmann's* he

136 Cf. TNA. G17/123, "Abschrift B. III. 3283. Berger an Staatssekretär Solf, Tabora 1. August 1912".

had allegedly offered to build one kilometre of railway upper construction for 350 Rps. instead of 400 Rps. like the competing Greek "entrepreneur who calls himself a businessman".[137]

Apparently, Berger and his German colleagues received considerate attention not only from the German colonial press, but also from senior colonial officials. Previous to Berger's letter to Solf, the *DOAZ* published an article titled "German entrepreneurs for the railway construction Tabora-Tanganyika" on 17 January 1912, which featured quite the same arguments as Berger did in his letter of complaint. As a reaction to this newspaper article, *Holzmann* felt the urge to have an official response published in the *DOAZ* only ten days later, on 27 January 1912. Rejecting all allegations made and justifying their staff management, *Holzmann* stated in this article that whenever a suitable German candidate was at hand he would "receive preference over any non-German".[138] More importantly, after this public debate, Berger's letter even reached colonial State Secretary Wilhelm Solf half a year later. Indeed, Solf must have taken the allegations against *Holzmann's* alleged Greek preference seriously. How else would you explain that Berger's letter found its way to the acting Governor Methner in Dar es Salaam by the end of 1912, who subsequently urged the local railway commissioner, who supervised any issue related to labour at the *Central Railway*, to investigate on the issue both immediately and confidentially? No sooner said than done, *Holzmann* was ordered to report to the colonial authority about the state of affairs and elaborate on how many Germans and foreigners were currently employed by the company, what kind of contracts they had, how much money they earned, and if there were any differences between the price levels of the German sub-contractors and their Greek colleagues.[139] Accordingly, *Holzmann* reported to State Secretary Solf directly and gave details about their European personnel then working at the route section between Tabora and Malagarassi: in total, fifty-eight European sub-contractors worked at this 235-km long part of the *Central Railway*. Of those, forty-seven were "foreigners", while only eleven were German citizens. Admitting the predominance of non-Germans, *Holzmann* justified their staff policies, stating that a sub-contractor's productivity and reliability were the primary criteria that decided whether a sub-contractor was hired or not. In this respect, the Greeks were simply superior competitors compared to their German counterparts. According to *Holzmann's* government building

137 TNA. G17/123, "Abschrift B. III. 3283. Berger an Staatssekretär Solf, Tabora 1. August 1912". Cf. TNA. G12/176.

138 Cf. "Deutsche Unternehmer für den Bahnbau Tabora-Tanganyika". *DOAZ*, XIV, no. 8.

139 Cf. TNA. G17/123, "Abschrit B. III. 3410 und Abschrift Bi III.155 Philipp Holzmann & Co. L. Rse. Frankfurt a/M An den Herrn Staatssekretär des Reichs-Kolonialamts Exzellenz Berlin, Vertraulich 3 April 1913. An die Firma Pihlipp Holzmann & Cie. Gmbh. Tabora". Cf. TNA. G12/176.

official Ferdinand Grages, the Greeks' productivity was higher because they had generally succeeded in creating a larger stock of African workers, who went along with the sub-contractor from one construction site to the next. As recruiting a sufficient number of workers was very challenging throughout the entire construction process of the *Central Railway* and also very costly, it was only natural for *Holzmann* to grant those sub-contractors with a larger workforce more labour-intensive and therefore generally bigger commissions, regardless of their nationality. Finally, Grages assured Solf that there were no pay gaps between German and non-German sub-contractors as payment was dependent on the type of work and its complexity.[140]

Besides these aspects of productivity and reliability in general, what busied the colonial administration, adjunct and in combination with this investigation, was the question whether German or Greek sub-contractors would be better equipped for work in a tropical colony such as German East Africa. Another concern was the question of which group of sub-contractors would treat the African workers better. Apart from *Holzmann's* Ferdinand Grages and State Secretary Solf, this investigation would plague several government officials from the highest to the lowest levels of rank as well as the construction company *Holzmann* for many months to come: the Governor, the district officers, the railway commissioners, the government inspector and the construction supervisors of the local route sections produced, circulated and discussed reports on the conditions of the labour camps, and legal proceedings and court rulings against sub-contractors and labour recruiters of any nationality. The ultimate outcome of this large investigation was mixed, if not even contradictory.

3.5.2 Large-Scale Investigations and an (Un-)surprising Outcome

> According to our observations, the German pieceworker is considerably inferior to the Greek pieceworker in his frugality, in his ability to get, treat and keep workers, in his sobriety, diligence, ability to adapt to the climate and business sense; the business successes of the Greeks can be attributed to these undoubted abilities.

> *Holzmann* Construction Officer Grages to Colonial State Secretary Wilhelm Solf, 13 January 1913[141]

140 Cf. TNA. G17/123, "Abschrift Bi III.155 Philipp Holzmann & Cie. Frankfurt a/M, den 13. Januar 1913. An den Herrn Staatssekretär des Kolonialamtes Berlin". Cf. TNA. G12/176.

141 TNA. G17/123, "Abschrift Bi III. 155. An den Herrn Staatssekretär des Kolonialamtes Berlin. Frankfurt a.M., den 13. Januar 1913".

Personally, Ferdinand Grages believed there were a variety of reasons why the Greeks were more successful in the sub-contractor business at the *Central Railway* than their German counterparts. On the one hand, Grages confirmed the widespread discourses about Southern Europeans working in a colonial environment. In this respect, Grages attributed the Greek sub-contractors' success to their "frugality", their "ability to adapt to the climate" and their alleged cunning business acumen. On the other hand, Grages' statement also irritates and contradicts these contemporary discourses against the Greeks as white subalterns. Despite reproducing the image of the Greek *shenzi ulaya,*[142] Grages highlights the South-Eastern European sub-contractors' rationality, soberness and especially their diligence, which enabled their success at the *Central Railway* in German East Africa. This is striking as such character traits were generally reserved to describe the essence of the German 'work ethos' that was very prominent in the 'long nineteenth century' and beyond.[143]

Similar contradictions can be seen in the conclusions by colonial government officials and *Holzmann* in the course of investigating several law proceedings and court rulings against German and Greek (sub-)contractors who had violated labour protection rights. Juxtaposing those findings with reports about the sanitary conditions at the labour camps of German and Greek sub-contractors, as well as reports by the Moravian railway mission, reveals that the reality was often more complex than the discourse. While the Moravian missionaries generally praised *Holzmann* proper for treating their workers well, the Moravian missionary Löbner resented the Greek railway sub-contractors:

> The workers here and generally everybody directly employed by Holzmann & Co. do not suffer. It is strictly observed that no overseer mistreats anybody and that everybody receives only work in accordance to his strength and ability. They [the workers] receive their Posho either as money, flour or rice, according to their preference. If somebody is sick, he is sent to

---

142 Even with a high level of prosperity and distinct cultural capital, Greeks were considered "half-Orientals" in the context of the German-colonial discourse of East Africa, as expressed by the Anglo-German railway engineer Clement Gillman. This term was not uncommon to vilify Greeks living in the German colony. The former Governor of German East Africa, Eduard von Liebert (1896–1901), explicitly called the Greeks *shenzi ulaya*. The term *shenzi ulaya* derives from Swahili, which is widely spoken in East Africa. *Ulaya* can be translated as "Europe". *Shenzi* was initially a discriminatory term used by the Muslim coastal population of East Africa to refer to the non-Muslim people in the East African hinterland. Thus, *shenzi ulaya* can be translated mutatis mutandis as 'uncivilised European', and so the concept of *shenzi ulaya* can be understood as the German colonial version of the 'white negro' for East Africa. Cf. Rösser. *'Shenzi Ulaya'*.

143 Cf. Axster and Lelle. 'Deutsche Arbeit', pp. 7–36. Cf. Thiel, Jens. *"Menschenbassin Belgien". Anwerbung, Deportation und Zwangsarbeit im Ersten Weltkrieg.* Essen: 2007, pp. 89–97. Cf. Papakyriacou. *Formulation and definitions*, pp. 51–73. Cf. Conrad. *Globalisation*, pp. 334–379.

> the hospital immediately. The treatment on behalf of the Greek sub-contractors is different, of course. Superficially it seems to be alright, indeed. If you manage to look behind the scenes, you will change your opinion. Just one example to illustrate how these Greeks act in order to veil their iniquities. The district officer or a Gentlemen of the official construction supervision travels around the labour camps [. . .]. At once a messenger is sent from one Greek camp to another, reporting that somebody is expected. Just as fast as this message arrives, the alerted gathers his people and promises them a lot of pombe, if they will only say that they have a good life at his place. If they won't, he will threaten them with various punishments.[144]

It is difficult to judge whether Löbner's observations are trustworthy. A closer view on the Moravians' mission in German East Africa and their connections to railway construction has revealed that the Moravians concorded with discourses against white subalterns and were therefore generally prejudiced against Greeks in the colony, too.[145] Moreover, the Moravians were also dependent on *Holzmann's* funding to finance their missionary work in German East Africa. Consequently, conflicts of interests between their own funding and their opinion about Greek sub-contractors are not unlikely. Interestingly, the local supervisors of the colonial railway commissioner held a different view. In stark contrast to the Moravian missionary Löbner, the construction supervisor reported to his superior railway commissioner when inspecting the construction of the route section between km 289 and km 381:

> I take the view that the Greek contractors treat the workers better [and] do not demand the same amount of work [as the Germans do]. The construction of the houses in the labour camps of contractors like Mutopoulus, Lukas and Gerinimakis etc. is far better than that of the German contractors. [. . .] The labour camps of the German contractors are generally cleaner, built in a more symmetrical manner while they are also more spacious compared to those of the Greek contractors. Exceptions were the camps of contractors Mutopoulus and Lukas, which are [. . .] very good.[146]

In other words: the investigations revealed a plethora of contradictions, and except for nuances and individual differences there were no decisive differences in how German or Greek railway sub-contractors treated and housed their African workers. It is therefore not surprising that Tabora's railway commissioner, who received and processed similar reports of several route construction supervisors monthly,[147] ultimately came to the obvious conclusion regarding the quality of

144 Unitätsarchiv Herrnhut (UAH). MD 1532. Missionsdirektion Unyamwezi. Briefwechsel mit dem Superintendenten u. Vorsteher 1909–1911, "Briefwechsel [. . .] J.N. 356. Löbner to Henning Sikonge, d. 29.3.11.", n.p.

145 Cf. Rösser. "'*Shenzi Ulaya*"'.

146 TNA. G17/123, "Sia, den 27. März 1913. Auf Vefügung J. no. 472 vom 17. März 1913 [. . .] Eing. Eisenbahnkommissar. 29.III.13. J. no. 534".

147 E.g. cf. TNA. G17/124.

housing: "On average any labour camp was as bad as the other"[148] no matter if German or Greek; but further:

> The treatment of the [Africans] by the German [sub-]contractors leaves a lot to be desired. The good Greek [sub-]contractors like Grammatikas, Mutopolos etc. treat their people definitely better. On the whole, it has to be noted further that the treatment of the workers on behalf of the [sub-]contractors is generally very bad. Mistreatments, wage evasions, Posho reductions and withholding wages after the end of an employment occur frequently. But such grievances are committed by both Germans and Greeks; at all times more often by Greeks than by Germans, however. There are several legal proceedings pending in this regard at the imperial district court in Tabora at the moment.[149]

It is not clear whether the railway commissioner considered the overall ratio of German and Greek sub-contractors working at the *Central Railway* when claiming that Greeks were committing more grievances than the Germans. Recalling that the final 400 km of the entire railway between central Tabora and Kigoma at Lake Tanganyika was divided into thirty-eight route sections in April 1913 and that each route section was outsourced to at least one sub-contractor, it must be mentioned that of these thirty-eight sub-contractors, twenty-six were Greek, ten German and two Italian.[150] Given the fact that Greek sub-contractors by far outnumbered their German counterparts, it would not have been very surprising that there were more accusations made against the Southern Europeans as far as absolute numbers are concerned: just because there were simply more Greeks working at the *Central Railway* than Germans. Another list produced by *Holzmann* between May and June 1913 supports this argument. It lists sixteen European sub-contractors, sub-sub-contractors and overseers who had violated labour protection rights to such an extent that their employment had apparently become unbearable; all on the list had not paid their workers their wages and half of them were also accused of bodily harm and/or unlawful detention. Of those sixteen, four were German, while the others were Greek. The numerical composition of this list would quite fit the overall German-Greek ratio of sub-contractors at

148 TNA. G17/123, "Mittellandbahn 616 concept. Tabora, 16. April 1913. 792, 1107 1.) Auf den Erlass no. 4837/XII vom 10. III. 1913. Betrifft deutsche und griechische Unternehmer. An den Herrn Kaiserlichen Gouverneur", p. 7.

149 TNA. G17/123, "Mittellandbahn 616 concept. Tabora, 16. April 1913. 792, 1107", p. 6.

150 Cf. TNA. G17/123, "Philipp Holzmann. Entg. 534, 501, 472. An Eisenbahnkommissar Tabora. Tabora, 11. April 1913. Tabelle II".

the *Central Railway* and therefore relativise any allegations made against the Greeks solely based on absolute numbers.[151]

Despite these findings, it is quite remarkable that the railway commissioner stated in the very same report of April 1914, quoted immediately above, that the German sub-contractors were discriminated against in favour of their Southern European colleagues. Apparently, the railway commissioner and his subordinate route section supervisors turned at least one blind eye to grievances committed by the German sub-contractors. At the same time, they prosecuted Greek entrepreneurs more consequentially for comparable offences than German sub-contractors: "In case of poor labour performance or bad treatment of the workers, the sub-contractors are withdrawn from work. If Germans are concerned, we attempt to sit back and watch whenever possible, while we intervene immediately regarding ordinary [sic!] Greek entrepreneurs."[152] In this respect, MP Gustav Noske (SPD) was quite right in saying that those in charge of supervision did indeed often knowingly ignore the violation of labour protection rights. In contrast to the predominant anti-Greek discourse that Noske also reproduced in the *Reichstag* however, it was not the Southern European sub-contractors that were privileged before colonial prosecution, but their German colleagues.

To make matters a bit more complicated, it must be stressed that the clear distinction between Greeks and Germans was actually not entirely applicable recalling the general process of outsourcing construction work at the *Central Railway*: a German sub-contractor could allocate (sometimes the files feature the word 'sell' for this process) his route section to a Greek sub-sub-contractor or the other way around. Thereby the line between Greek sub-contractors and Germans was decisively blurred. Moreover, each sub-contractor employed at least one European overseer who observed the manual work performed by the African staff. As the number of the European overseers per sub-contractor varied according to the number of African workers he employed as well as the sub-contractor's preferences, it was not necessarily the case that German sub-contractors would only employ German overseers. Neither would Greek sub-contractors exclusively hire Greek over-

151 Cf. One was probably Italian. The list, unfortunately, does not feature the nationality of the Europeans, but sometimes other documents in the same folder state the nationality of an individual. Moreover, the name enables to distinguish between a German and Greek sub-contractor, albeit someone with a Greek sounding name might exceptionally have had German citizenship. Cf. TNA. G17/123, "Mitteilung von dem Kaiserlichen Bezirksamt In Eisenbahnkommissaritat der Mittellandbahn. Tabora. J. no. 444. z. zt. Kurrukurru, den 29. Mai 1913. Beiliegende Liste und Mitteilungen".

152 TNA. G17/123, "Mittellandbahn 616 concept. Tabora, 16. April 1913. 792, 1107", p. 8.

seers. Moreover, as there were not only Greeks and Germans working as sub-contractors or overseers at the *Central Railway*'s construction sites, but many other (European) nationalities and East Africans like Swahili, the idea of clearly differentiating between 'Greek' and 'German' sub-contractors is generally absurd.[153]

Regardless of the multinational reality of the construction sites, colonial discourses also devalued the work done by those other than Germans and simultaneously overestimated the work performance of German protagonists. As several studies on German global and colonial history have shown in recent years, the period around 1900 was decisive in shaping the trope and myth of buzzwords such as 'German work' or 'Made in Germany'. This myth of German work superiority can be regarded as the other side of the coin of anti-Greek colonial discourses as far as the context of labour and work at the *Central Railway* are concerned. Nineteenth century discourses about 'German work' revolved around a big variety of issues that included Social Darwinism, work and gender, religion, nationality, communism and the class struggle as well as globalisation and economic growth. What matters most for the analysis of labour at the *Central Railway* in German East Africa is first and foremost that the nineteenth century experienced a discourse that allocated each nationality a specific work ethic and way of work. In Germany, of central concern was not what kind of work a German performed, but how. Accordingly, Germans and work had a special relationship, and a German did not only work for profit, i.e. to make a living, but a German worked because he or she regarded it as an end in itself. Work even acquired a quasi-sacred character in these discourses in Germany and German work ethics were *per se* regarded as the primary commodity of export that should conquer the world. Whenever 'German work' was challenged, not only economic profit was at stake, but also quasi-religious feelings and the German claim to (colonial) power.[154] The predominance of Greek white subaltern labour at one of the most prestigious German colonial infrastructure projects thus challenged German colonial claims, no matter how successful or productive German labour really was.

153 Cf. TNA. G17/123, "Philipp Holzmann. Entg. 534, 501, 472. An Eisenbahnkommissar Tabora. Tabora, 11. April 1913. Tabelle II". Cf. Gillman Diaries. Mss. Afr. S. 1175/1,2_1, no. 9, pp. 1–3. Cf. TNA G21/262. Cf. TNA. G21/361.

154 Cf. Conrad. *Globalisation*, pp. 338–379. Cf. Yekani. *Koloniale Arbeit*, pp. 265–276. Cf. Axster, Felix. 'Arbeit an der "Erziehung zur Arbeit"', pp. 226–251. Cf. Achinger, Christine. 'Deutsche Arbeit und die Poetisierung der Moderne'. *«Deutsche Arbeit». Kritische Perspektiven auf ein ideologisches Selbstbild.* 252–284. Eds. Felix Axster and Nicolas Lelle. Göttingen: 2018, pp. 252–284. Cf. Groß, Lothar. *Anmerkungen zu 'Made in Germany'. Deutschlands Wirtschaftsgeschichte von der Industrialisierung bis heute.* BoD (Books on Demand). N.P.: 2019. pp. 2–11. Cf. Campbell, Joan. *Joy in Work, German Work. The National Debate, 1800–1945.* Princeton: 1989, pp. 178–311, 376–385.

Remarkably, any report about the work performance of sub-contractors ranks German sub-contractor accomplishments below those of other (South) Europeans, the Greeks in particular: "It must unfortunately be expressed that the German contractors are generally not as productive as the Greek contractors."[155] The railway authorities were well aware of the reasons for that, apart from discourses that saw Greeks as 'white negroes' or allegedly closer to the African race. Accordingly, the Greeks had more financial means, and better knowledge of Swahili, which enabled them to communicate (more efficiently) with most of their workers and helped them establish and maintain contact with them. Their language skills also helped them recruit better-skilled workers, and maintain a larger workforce. With a better-qualified and larger staff, Greek sub-contractors were awarded larger building contracts. On top of that, the Greeks had been in the railway construction business since the very beginning of construction in 1905 and some had even already built parts of the *Bagdadbahn* before coming to East Africa. According to the railway commissioner, the majority of German sub-contractors had entered the business comparatively late, from the railway station of Saranda onwards – a place ca. 130 km west of Dodoma – and therefore roughly five years later (around 1909) than the Greeks had. Given *Holzmann's* own pursuit of profit and the administration's desire to keep the construction funds' budget in order, it is therefore not very surprising that the railway commissioner concluded that "business interests always matter most. The question of nationality ranks second."[156] Only if the first premise was not threatened, the second premise was observed: in which case, German sub-contractors were then given preference over their Greek colleagues, because *Holzmann* did indeed fear allegations of violating the discourse of 'German work' in East Africa.

There was another reason why *Holzmann* would only choose its German sub-contractors in anticipatory obedience so long as business interests were not threatened. The construction company had also had the experience that the Greek sub-contractors – apart from violating labour protection rights – had seldomly raised issues, which *Holzmann* had to explain or justify publicly. In contrast to this loyalty, the German sub-contractors were prone to complain about their employment. Indeed, it was the German sub-contractor Berger who had initiated the letter of complaint that preoccupied not only the German colonial public via the *DOAZ*; through State Secretary Wilhelm Solf, it had also reached the highest levels of the German colonial administration in Berlin, and maybe even Noske's anti-Greek statement in the *Reichstag* was inspired by Berger's letter of complaint as it was also debated in

155 TNA. G17/123, "Mittellandbahn 616, concept. Tabora, 16. April 1913. 792, 1107", p. 5.
156 TNA. G17/123, "Mittellandbahn 616 concept, Tabora, 16. April 1913. 792, 1107", p. 10.

the media. Be that as it may, according to the files under investigation, Berger had no reason to complain, but acted out of his own (business) interest and his general tendency to file petitions to the colonial administrations in German East Africa and Berlin. Of course, apart from his letter of complaint, the files do not directly reflect Berger's own accounts and both the railway commissioner's and *Holzmann's* assessments of Berger's work must be met with some reservations. But both of the latter's records agree about Berger's constant poor performance. For example, *Holzmann's* Government Building Official, Ferdinand Grages, had known Berger for many years. Before coming to East Africa, Berger had worked in Europe as a construction assistant for several of *Holzmann's* projects, but only achieved low results. Not only his general "skills" as an assistant, but also his work "performance had been in inversed ratio to his constant petitions for salary increase", complained Grages. Only Berger's "urgent pleading" and his not further specified "unfortunate family background" had been the reasons why he was hired as sub-contractor – not only at the very beginning of constructing the *Central Railway*, but also for a second time after his initial contract had ended in 1908. As Grages was very satisfied with the work of the four other German sub-contractors who had filed the petition, he was convinced that Berger had persuaded his colleagues to join his complaints in order to eke out better salaries and future contracts.[157] There are several telegrams and letters issued either by the local route section supervisors or the railway commissioner accusing Berger of various violations of labour protection rights typical for most sub-contractors. The offences ranged from cheating the workers of their wages and insufficient food supplies to poor housing. According to the reports, in Berger's labour camps – the "worst of all" – the workers had been living in small tents for months instead of adequate mud or grass houses, while simple sanitary facilities were either missing or inadequate. When criticised for the poor sanitary conditions by *Holzmann's* route section engineer Winkelmann, Berger had allegedly replied: "I am not here to build privies, but to make money!"[158] Whether Berger really made this statement is difficult to assess as the documents had circulated many administrative levels. In any case, thanks to Berger's complaints, both *Holzmann* and the colonial administration in German East Africa had to justify their policies before the public and the Colonial State Secretary in Berlin.

157 TNA. G17/123, "Abschrift Bi III.155 Philipp Holzmann & Cie. Lit. D. no. 21/6. Frankfurt a/M, den 13. Januar 1913. An den Herrn Staatssekretär des Kolonialamtes Berlin", p. 2.

158 TNA. G17/123, "Mittellandbahn 616 concept, Tabora, 16. April 1913. 792, 1107", p. 7, cf. pp. 8–9. Cf. TNA. G17/123, "Abschrift. Niederschrift über die Lagerbesichtigungen in der Zeit vom 26–29. März 1912". Cf. TNA. G17/123, "530. Concept. 5. April 1913. An den Aufsichtsbeamten Herrn ~~Baldamus~~ Kanert km ~~196~~ 247". Cf. TNA. G17/123, 781, 788, 530, "Conept. 608, 706. 5. April 1913 S.h. Herrn Distriktkommissar Werner, Guruguru".

On the whole, the question of Berger's individual's character and work performance is only secondary. What matters most in regard to Berger's petition is that it illustrates the complexity of the *situation coloniale* at the construction sites of the *Central Railway*. This colonial complexity reveals that, at a large-scale place of work, not only the two well-known poles of coloniser versus the colonised were negotiated; there were also entanglements and disputes concerning discourses of 'German work' as well as discourses of 'white subalternity' and Southern European or rather Greek white subalterns. Moreover, Berger's case reveals that (personal) business interests mingled very well with such discourses, were used to seek individual advantage and could set entire administrations and the German (colonial) press in motion. Hence, the case of Berger's petition shows that discourses had real effects on labour relationships in German East Africa and were not simply existent in a vacuum.[159] On top of this, questions about class, *whiteness,* white subalternity, white-precariousness as well as railway construction skills were also relevant. Their importance will be further revealed in the following sections.

3.6 Economies of Skill? Craftsmen and Office Clerks at the *Central Railway*

3.6.1 From Chinese 'Coolies' to Indian (Indentured) Labour

> Dernburg thought the German East African Central Railway in analogy to the Uganda Railway [. . .]. Like at any other colonial railway, the labour recruitment problem was the major difficulty. The Uganda Railway Company had solved the question by importing tens of thousands of Indian coolies. This comfortable way was barred to the construction company from Frankfurt. The labour force had to be recruited in [German East Africa].[160]
>
> Tetzlaff, Rainer. *Koloniale Entwicklung und Ausbeutung*. Berlin: 1970.

India and Indian people have had a significant impact on the history of the Indian Ocean Area and East Africa since the eighth century. Today, the Indian minority is

159 It seems indeed that the ratio of German sub-contractors increased throughout the building progress. Clement Gilliman, a *Holzmann* engineer working in German East Africa for the entire construction period and beyond, regretted that less-qualified Germans increasingly replaced foreign sub-contractors. Cf. Gillman Diaries. Mss. Afr. S. 1175/1,2_2, no. 13, pp. 69–70.
160 Tetzlaff. *Koloniale Entwicklung*, p. 88.

still an important population group in East Africa. Throughout the nineteenth century and within the networks of the British Empire in an increasingly globalising world, the exchange between India and East Africa intensified. Using the British imperial networks,[161] Indian 'imperial citizenship' was also fundamentally characterised by long-distance migration particularly within the British domains.[162] Also for major imperial infrastructural building projects of the nineteenth century, such as the *Uganda Railway* in British East Africa, Indian labour was of major importance. Indeed, over 30,000 Indian indentured labourers were recruited from India to work at the railway's construction sites between 1895 and 1901.[163]

As the *Uganda Railway* served as a role model for any railway construction in German East Africa in various ways,[164] it is very surprising that Indian (indentured) labour at the *Central Railway*'s construction sites has received little attention in German colonial historiography. This is even more so, given prominent contemporary German utterances about the importance of Indian labour by people who had visited both the British and the German East African colonies. The journalist Adolf Zimmermann, who accompanied Bernhard Dernburg to East Africa in 1907, regarded the appallingly high mortality rate of Indian workers (ca. thirty percent)[165] at the construction sites of the *Uganda Railway* as a necessary

161 For an example of how 'white subalterns' were able to use such British imperial networks cf. Crosbie, Barry. *Irish Imperial Networks. Migration, Social Communication and Exchange in Nineteenth-Century India.* Cambridge: 2012.

162 Metcalf, Thomas R. *Imperial Connections. India and the Indian Ocean Arena. 1860–1920.* Berkeley et al.: 2007, p. 3. Cf. 46–67.

163 Cf. Elkins, Caroline. *Imperial Reckoning. The Untold Story of Britain's Gulag in Kenya.* New York: 2005, p. 2. Cf. Metcalf. *Imperial Connections*, pp. 165–203. Cf. research project by Aselmeyer, Norman. *The Shadow Line. Railway and Society in Colonial East Africa, ca. 1890–1914 (Provisional Title).* Web. https://www.uni-bremen.de/institut-fuer-geschichtswissenschaft/personen/a-z/aselmeyer-norman (19 September 2021). Cf. Hill. *Permanent Way. Kenya and Uganda,* pp. 141–246. Cf. Mangat. *A History of the Asians*, pp. 27–62.

164 Cf. "Lernen wir von der Ugandabahn". *DOAZ,* VII, no. 1. Daressalam: 07 January 1905. Cf. Zimmermann. *Mit Dernburg*, p. 39–49. Cf. Allmaras, Franz. 'Ich baue 2000 km', p. 41. Cf. "Aus unserer Kolonie. Offizielle Eröffnung der Mittellandbahn bis Tabora". *DOAZ,* XIV, no. 61. Daressalam: 31 July 1912. Cf. Hill. *Permanent Way. Vol. II*, pp. 70, 79–82. Cf. Gillman. 'A Short History', pp. 14–15.

165 Cf. Elkins. *Imperial Reckoning,* p. 2. High death tolls were integral to (almost) all colonial infrastructure projects. At the Congo-Ocean Railroad, at least between 15,000–23,000 workers died – one of the highest absolute numbers of deaths at an infrastructural construction site known in history. Cf. Daughton. *In the Forest of No Joy.* In 13 years of construction, Daughton gives the annual death rate of 15–20%, but considers it much higher, cf. pp. 8, 189, 275. According to Tetzlaff, the death rate of the workers at the central railway ranged from 25% for singular worker cohorts to 1.7%, on average, a year; he relies largely on published sources after WWI and newspaper articles. Cf. Tetzlaff. *Koloniale Entwicklung,* pp. 88–89. Conducting a random sample

by-product of 'cultural and technological progress': "As on the Suez Canal, so on the Uganda Railway [. . .] thousands and thousands of those who built it rest. [. . .] They had to die so that the great cultural work could be built. Would anyone want to miss the canal or the railway for the sake of the human lives they claimed?"[166] Also senior men of *Philipp Holzmann* like Riese and Ritter warned their local building director Grages, working in Dar es Salaam, that their construction company and German prestige could lose face if the construction progress of the German colonial railway in East Africa remained slower than that in neighbouring British East Africa:

> Should our construction progress lag behind that achieved in the construction of the Uganda Railway, we would be exposed to derogatory criticism that would be detrimental not only to us but also to the reputation of German technology in general. Every possible means must therefore be sought to speed up construction progress. [. . .] 1) The procurement of numerous workers. [. . .][167]

While contemporaries like Zimmermann and even *Holzmann* drew a link between the enormous role of Indian labour in the *Uganda Railway* and any similar construction aspirations in German East Africa, established German historical studies on German East Africa either ignore or – like Tetzlaff – even deny any Indian involvement at the *Central Railway*'s construction sites in the neighbouring German colony.[168] Others only treat Indian labour at the *Central Railway* as a sideshow.

Writing a history of the East African railways according to a British imperial self-image in the late 1950s, M.F. Hill mentions Indian labour briefly. His study published by the *East African Railways and Harbours* in Nairobi 1957 notes that Sikhs and Punjabis were involved in railway construction in German East Africa.[169] Yet, earlier publications about the history of the *Central Railway* in German East Africa too had confirmed the involvement of Indians indeed. The Anglo-German *Holzmann e*ngineer Clement Gillman, who had been employed as a railway engineer during German colonial times and after WWI also for the British authorities during

---

for the year of 1908, I used the tabular monthly reports of railway construction at the central railway. It lists the workers employed, the sick and the dead. For the year of 1908, the average mortality rate was below 1%; the average rate of reporting sick ca. 10%. There were however higher death rates for individual worker cohorts, e.g. in Ugogo. Cf. TNA. G17/63.

166 Zimmermann. *Mit Dernburg*, pp. 51–52. Cf. Allmaras. 'Ich baue 2000 km ', p. 51.

167 TNA. G12/164, p. 2.

168 Cf. Tetzlaff. *Koloniale Entwicklung*, p. 88.

169 Cf. Hill. *Permanent Way. Vol. II*, p. 96. Cf. Gillman. 'A Short History', p. 27.

the British Mandate of Tanganyika Territory, stated in an article published in 1942 that "chiefly in the accountancy and clerical branches [. . .] 226 [. . .] Asiatics" were employed by the "railway company" in 1913, while 118 were European and 3,420 African.[170] Moreover, Indian labour at German colonial railway construction sites seems not to have been a new occurrence in 1905 when the construction of the *Central Railway* started. Investigating Swahili poetry as a historical source, the Historian J.A.S. Casco states that some Indians were – amongst other forms of punishments – forced to perform punitive labour at the construction site of the *Usambara Railway*, because they had allegedly sponsored an anti-colonial war, led by the caravan trader Hassan bin Omari Makunganya, against German authorities between 1894 and 1895 in the southern region of *Kilwa*.[171] Shortly before the advent of WWI, the traffic manager of the *Usambara Railway* reported to the Imperial German Government that at least twenty-five Indian artisans and officials were employed by the northern railway. Moreover, there had been plans by German colonial officials to recruit Indian 'coolies', who had come to British East Africa to construct the *Uganda Railway*, for the construction of the *Usambara Railway* around 1900. In fact, the plan never materialised.[172] Whether *Holzmann* regarded Indian involvement at the *Usambara Railway* as a kind of 'role model' for its own *Central Railway* cannot be answered in detail here.[173] Nevertheless, there must have been some connections between Indian labour, the *Uganda Railway* in British East Africa and the larger infrastructural project in German East Africa – the *Central Railway*.

On 28 November 1910, the administrative board of the *OAEG* met in a conference room of the *Deutsche Bank* and discussed the report of the governmental building master Mr. Habich, who had visited East Africa in the summer of 1910. Habich had travelled to both British East Africa and German East Africa to gather information about the British *Uganda Railway* in general and to inspect the home

---

170 Cf. Gillman. 'A Short History', pp. 31–32.

171 Cf. Casco, José Arturo Saavedra. *Utenzi, War Poems, and the German Colonial Conquest of East Africa. Swahili Poetry as a Historical Source.* Trenton and Asmara: 2007, pp. 220–226. There is one application letter, maybe issued by an Indian, as he describes himself as "British-Subject". His name "Wazirali" does not indicate an Indian background clearly. Cf. TNA. G51/1. [Angelegenheiten der] Usambara-Eisenbahn. Bd., 2. 1899–1902, p. 92.

172 Cf. Hill. *Permanent Way. Vol. II*, pp. 66, 69–70, 77.

173 According to Sunseri, many Wanyamwezi had already worked at the *Usambara Railway* and the *Uganda Railway* before working at the central railway. If their number was considerable is another question as there were up to 10–15 years between the construction of the individual railways. Cf. Sunseri. *Vilimani*, p. 168. Apparently, there were very few engineers who had first constructed the *Usambara Railway* and then worked at the central railway. Hill gives the singular example of the Dutch engineer Leon Kooyker who had walked to German East Africa from South Africa by 1908. Cf. Hill. *Permanent Way. Vol. II*, p. 74.

line of the *Central Railway* between Dar es Salaam and Morogoro as well as to examine the progress of harbour construction in Dar es Salaam. Regarding labour, Habich stated: "There is a shortage of coloured foremen; an attempt to attract Indian foremen from British East Africa or India has failed because of the Indian government's measures."[174] Yet, roughly one year later, the situation appears to have changed, as the *Indian Voice of British East Africa, Uganda and Zanzibar* reported in September 1911. This Indian community newspaper published in Nairobi mentioned labour migration from the *Uganda Railway* in British East Africa to the *Central Railway* in German East Africa that had started in September 1911 at the latest. Indian railway employees apparently moved from British East Africa to the neighbouring German colony deliberately to work at the *Central Railway*'s construction sites: It "is said that some railway employees [sic] at the coast [of British East Africa] have left for German East Africa being induced by good offers from the German railways".[175] Hence, recruitment of Indian (indentured) labour might not have been exclusively an overseas business. Instead, Indian labour migration regarding the construction of the *Central Railway* in German East Africa – whether indentured or not – was probably also an intercolonial phenomenon taking place between British and German colonies in East Africa, at the least. Moreover, as patchy as the available information might be, it proves that Indians were involved in the construction of the *Central Railway* in German East Africa from the very beginning in 1905 until the very end in 1914.

In this respect, it seems that Indians were primarily employed as skilled workers, either as craftsmen for *Holzmann* right at the construction sites or as clerks for the *OAEG's* offices. As far as the recruitment of skilled craftsmen is concerned, hiring indentured labourers from abroad seems to have been a significant option to obtain the workforce necessary throughout the entire construction process. As there was a serious labour shortage during the construction process on various occasions, the colonial administration and the construction companies tried to obtain indentured labourers from farther distant places of the Indian Ocean Area, either from Southeast Asia, China, or indeed India. With many of the 'labour exporting' countries under British domination having had very negative

174 TNA. G12/167, p. 129.

175 "Notes of the Week". *The Indian Voice of British East Africa, Uganda and Zanzibar*. Nairobi: 6 September 1911, p. 8. Web. *African Newspapers*. http://public.maximus.newsbank.com//images/L00000005/cache/pdf/bitonal_tiff_g4/13D0F5BDA3FEA150_13D0F21E098FF7B0.pdf (24 January 2018).

experiences with the German colony in East Africa during the 1890s, due to the mistreatment of Southeast Asian workers on German plantations there, the corresponding authorities shunned any further agreements with the Germans, however.[176] Thus, especially the skilled labour of craftsmen was in high demand. To ease this shortage at the railway construction sites around 1906, *Holzmann* sought 500–2,000 Chinese 'coolies', who would work for them particularly as craftsmen.[177] In the end no Chinese workers came to German East Africa, however. With the few existing sources giving conflicting reasons for this, it is not clear whether contemporary racially biased anti-Chinese sentiments about the 'Yellow Peril', prominent in Germany and throughout the world at the turn of the century, were responsible for the ultimate failure of Chinese labour migration to German East Africa, or whether there were specific reasons to be found in the colony.[178] While the

---

176 Cf. Koponen. *Development*, pp. 338–339. Recently cf. Yekani. *Koloniale Arbeit*, pp. 41–114. Cf. TNA. G8/58. [Klärung allgemeiner Fragen hinsichtlich der] Anwerbung von Indern [als Handwerker und Gärtner für das Gouvernement von Deutsch-Ostafrika mit Hilfe des deutschen Generalkonsulates in Kalkutta]. Cf. TNA. G8/59. Anwerbung und Ansiedlung von Indern [Singhalesen und Eingeborenen]. Bd. 1. Cf. TNA. G8/60. Anwerbung und Ansiedlung von Indern [Singhalesen und Eingeborenen]. Bd. 2. Cf. TNA. G8/61. Anwerbung und Ansiedlung von Indern [Singhalesen und Eingeborenen]. Bd. 3. Cf. TNA. G1/16. [Beziehungen zu den] deutschen konsularischen Vertretungen in Arabien und Ostindien [Aden, Bombay, Calcutta, Batavia, Mahé].

177 Cf. Koponen. *Development*, pp. 338–339. Cf. "Aus der Kolonie. Einfuhr von Chinesen". *DOAZ*, VIII, no. 7. Daressalam: 17 February 1906. Cf. "Aus der Kolonie. Chinesen-Einfuhr". *DOAZ*, VIII, no. 19. Daressalam: 12 March 1906. The *DOAZ* was lukewarm on the issue of Chinese workers, because of the experiences of 1890. The 'coolies' were allegedly very expensive, demanding and not effective. Also, racist stereotypes warned of the immigration of the 'yellow peril'. Drastic measures of control were proposed cf. "Chinesische Arbeiter". *DOAZ*, VIII, no. 20. Daressalam: 19 May 1906. Cf. "Aus der Kolonie. 500 Chinesen kommen". *DOAZ*, VIII, no. 33. Daressalam: 18 August 1906. Cf. Bundesarchiv (BArch). R1001/116. Einsatz fremder Arbeiter, v.a. von Chinesen, p. 92, "Nation und Welt – Beilage der Deutschen Nationalzeitung. Berlin 28. März 1906". Cf. BArch. R1001/116, p. 122, "Wandres an das kaiserliche Deutsche Konsulat Swatau, 30. September 1906". Cf. Yekani. *Koloniale Arbeit*, p. 71. Yekani also quotes BArch R1001/116, p. 122. She is wrong in stating that the 'coolies' were wanted for the *Usambara Railway*. In contrast to *Holzmann's* central railway, the northern *Usambara Railway* was not built by *Holzmann*, but by Berlin's company, *Lenz & Co.* In 1906, there was no further construction work in Usambara at all. Cf. "Eisenbahnen". *Deutsches Koloniallexikon*, 1920, Band II, p. 529. Web. *University of Frankfurt o.M.* http://www.ub.bildarchiv-dkg.uni-frankfurt.de/Bildprojekt/Lexikon/Standardframeseite.php?suche=eisenbahn (26 November 2019). Yekani further states that the contract between *Holzmann's* Wandres and a Chinese, Smith Siu Wu, would have been signed by both parties. During my research, I could only find the draft of a contract between Wandres and the Chinese smith Lai ah Sing, which was not signed. Cf. Yekani. *Koloniale Arbeit*, pp. 72 Fn. Cf. BArch. R1001/116, p. 125.

178 Cf. Conrad. *Globalisation*, pp. 25, 203–274. Cf. Yekani. '"Inder und Chinesen"'. Rather a history of technology, Cf. Diogo, Maria Paula and Laak, Dirk van. *Europeans Globalizing. Mapping, Exploiting, Exchanging*. New York: 2016, pp.171–200. For the issue of indentured labour and colonial

DOAZ blamed the Chinese government for having cancelled the agreement at the last instant,[179] *Holzmann* engineer Grages had a different view:

> There was such a need for workers in the first year of construction that the construction site management was urged to seek for foreign aid. As soon as the Gouvernement had hesitatingly agreed to import several thousand Chinese coolies, the Deutsche Bank contacted a middleman living in China. The negotiations were not followed through however, because the construction site management shunned the huge responsibility of importing the coolies. That was primarily because they feared [. . .] the unwelcoming impact of Chinese customs and practices on the [African population].[180]

Given the patchy source material, one can only speculate why no Chinese workers eventually came to German East Africa. If *Holzmann* refrained from the deal with China themselves, the top managers might have feared a colonial scandal abroad in the event that the Chinese workers were treated improperly by *Holzmann* or by one of their many sub-contractors. It is also possible that *Holzmann's* or the *Gouvernement's* decision stemmed from the prominent anti-Chinese discourse that was widespread around the globe in the 'long nineteenth century' and which had increased in the aftermath of the Russo-Japanese War of 1905. As Chinese labour had, inter alia, been central to the construction of the transcontinental railways in the USA from the mid-nineteenth century onwards and corresponding immigration from China remained subject to xenophobic and racist attitudes targeting especially migrants from China, US-anti-Chinese discourses might have played a role as well. After all, the first legislation to restrict immigration to the United States – the Chinese Exclusion Act of the 1882 – had just been renewed in 1902 and was now made permanent. Hence, these events in the USA might have had an influence on German colonial discourses about migration policies as well.[181] Grages himself does not explicitly mention the corresponding highly topical issue of the 'Yellow Peril' or the outcome of the Russo-Japanese War, but it is important to note that the so-

---

racial hierarchy in German South West Africa and beyond cf. Lindner, Ulrike. 'Indentured Labour in Sub-Saharan Africa (1880–1918): Circulation of Concepts between Imperial Powers'. 59–82. Eds. Sabine Damir-Geilsdorf et al. Bielefeld: 2016. For the British East and South African case cf. "We Hear". *The Indian Voice of British East Africa.* Nairobi: 10/05/1911. Web. *African Newspapers.* http://public.maximus.newsbank.com//images/L00000007/cache/pdf/bitonal_tiff_g4/13D0F59812493A88_13CF57D782C56578.pdf (24 January 2018).

179 Cf. "Aus der Kolonie. Vorläufig keine Chinesen". *DOAZ,* VIII, no. 35. Daressalam: 01 September 1906.

180 Stadtarchiv Frankfurt. W1/2 – 278/1. *Grages,* pp. 4.

181 Cf. Chin, Gabriel J. and Yoon, Diana. "Chinese Exclusion Act of 1882". *Encyclopedia.com,* 29 May 2018. Web. https://www.encyclopedia.com/history/united-states-and-canada/us-history/chinese-exclusion-act (1 June 2023). Cf. Chang, Gordon H. et al. (Eds.). *The Chinese and the Iron Road. Building the Transcontinental Railraod.* Stanford: 2019.

called 'Yellow Peril' was not exclusively linked to China, but also mingled with Japan. With Japan as the first Asian country to force a military stalemate against the significant European power Russia in 1905, "the unwelcoming impact of Chinese practices" could mean that potential 'coolies' from the Far East should not import ideas of non-European sovereignty or human equality to a German colony or challenge the colonial racial order.[182] With large Russian battleships anchoring in the harbour of Dar es Salaam in 1905 when on their way to Asia, the Russo-Japanese War was indeed a topical issue in German East Africa and still remembered decades later.[183] Furthermore, as the *Deutsche Bank* was also an important player within the syndicate financing the 400 km long German colonial *Shantung Railway* in China between 1899 and 1904, negative experiences from this East Asian infrastructural project might have played an important role as well. The planned *Shantung Railway* had provoked militant resistance among the local Chinese population, who feared the loss of their land crossed through by the railway and resented the intrusion of any western imperial power in general. As the rural Chinese population not only killed five Germans working for the railway company and even allied with the *Yìhétuán* movement (the so-called 'Boxer War' from 1899 to 1901), the alleged "unwelcoming impact of Chinese customs" cited by the construction site management might trace back to this background in the Far East.[184]

182 Cf. Diogo and Laak. *Europeans*, pp. 181–200. Cf. Akira Iriye. 'Japan's drive to great-power status'. *The Cambridge History of Japan. Volume 5. The Nineteenth Century.* 721–782. Ed. Marius B. Jansen. Cambridge: 1989, pp. 770–782. Cf. Nish, Ian. *The Origins of the Russo-Japanese War*, London: 1985, pp. 15–17, 238–257. Cf. Jones, David. 'Military Observers, Eurocentrism and World War Zero'. *The Russo-Japanese War in Global Perspective. World War Zero. Volume II.* 135–179. Eds. David Wolf et al. Leiden: 2007, pp. 135–175. Cf. Sachiko, Hirakawa. 'Portsmouth Denied: The Chinese Attempt to Attend'. *The Russo-Japanese War in Global Perspective. World War Zero. Volume II.* 531–550. Eds. David Wolf et al. Leiden: 2007, pp. 531–550. Cf. Jacob, Frank. *The Russo-Japanese War and its Shaping of the Twentieth Century.* London: 2018, pp. 1–73, 145–148.

183 Cf. Gillman, Clement. 'Dar es Salaam 1860–1940: A Story of Growth and Change'. 1–23. *Tanganyika Notes and Records,* no. 20. Dar es Salaam: 1945, p. 6.

184 Cf. Wendels, Claudia. *Die Schantung-Eisenbahn. Das Interesse der Finanzwelt an der deutschen Bahnlinie in Ostchina.* Siegburg: 2012, pp. 26–80. Cf. "Shantung-Eisenbahn". *Deutsches Kolonial-Lexikon, 1920, Band III,* p. 259. Web. *University of Frankfurt o.M.* Web. http://www.ub.bildarchiv-dkg.uni-frankfurt.de/Bildprojekt/Lexikon/Standardframeseite.php?suche=shantung (22 October 2020). Cf. Laiqing, Yang. 'Die Ereignisse von Gaomi und der Widerstand der Bevölkerung gegen den deutschen Eisenbahnbau'. *Kolonialkrieg in China. Die Niederschlagung der Boxerbewegung 1900–01.* 49–58. Eds. Mechthild Leutner and Klaus Mühlhahn. Berlin: 2007. Cf. Rösser. 'Den "Seegedanken zu pflegen"?', pp. 34–49. For a general introduction to indentured labour and corresponding anti-Chinese sentiments, cf. Hoefte, Roesemarijn. 'Indentured Labour'. *Handbook The Global History of Work.* 363–376. *Eds.* Karin Hofmeester and Marcel van der Linden. Berlin and Boston: 2018, pp. 371–373. For Chinese indentured labour in French colonial railway building in Africa after WWI cf. Daughton. *In the Forest of No Joy*, pp. 174–180.

Sharing the generally negative sentiment towards China, the *DOAZ* linked the issue of Chinese coolies to African convict workers during the Maji Maji War. It seems that the *DOAZ* believed Chinese skilled workers were not needed, because the Maji Maji convict workers would substitute the need for coolies:

> We would congratulate the railway company if it succeeded to manage railway construction without the import of Chinese workers. At the beginning of this week, another 413 convict workers from Kilwa have arrived in Dar es Salaam on board of the steamer 'König'. They are supposed to find employment at the railway here.[185]

Previous and succeeding volumes of the colonial newspaper issue further reports about Maji Maji convicts forced to work at the *Central Railway*, but do not clarify to what extent convict workers could really make up for the lack of skilled labour, which was so desperately needed by *Holzmann*. It appears that the newspaper tended not to differentiate between skilled and unskilled labour and subsumed the need for skilled labour under the omnipresent 'labour question' and therefore preferred simple answers for rather complicated questions.[186] Be this as it may, the lack of craftsmen must have been solved by other means. In fact, senior *Holzmann* engineers do report of a significant number of Indian workers – especially craftsmen – who indeed worked at the German railway. *Holzmann's* Ferdinand Grages stated:

> The rumour of a planned huge railway construction in East Africa had found its way to the Greeks, Indians, and other peoples from the Near and the Middle East. [. . .] Indians were initially employed as craftsmen. [. . .] They were primarily employed as carpenters, cabinet makers, metalworkers, and smiths.[187]

Senior engineer Walter Rehfeldt, who came to German East Africa in 1908, also confirms Grages' claim about the employment of Indians and stresses Indian migration to East Africa throughout the entire construction process of the *Central*

185 "Strafarbeiter aus Kilwa für die Bahn". *DOAZ,* VIII, no. 37. Daressalam: 15 September 1906.
186 Cf. "Strafarbeiter für den Bahnbau". *DOAZ,* VIII, no. 40. Daressalam: 6 October 1906. Cf. "Thätigkeit des Arbeiterkommissariats" and "500 Chinesen kommen". *DOAZ,* VIII, no. 33. Cf. "Einfuhrzölle und Arbeiterfrage" and "Über den Fortgang der Arbeiten an der Eisenbahn Dar es Salaam – Morogoro". *DOAZ,* VIII, no. 27. Daressalam: 07 July 1906. Cf. "Aus der Kolonie. Bedingungen des Gouvernements für die Gestellung von Zwangsarbeitern" and "Verschiffung von Arbeitern für die Nordbezirke". *DOAZ,* VIII, no. 23. Daressalam: 6 October 1906. Cf. "Wie wir von gut unterrichteter Seite erfahren". *DOAZ,* VIII, no. 4. Daressalam: 27 January 1906. Reichart also quotes some of the *DOAZ's* articles. At least one reference is wrong, however. Cf. Reichart. *Gari,* p. 49.
187 Stadtarchiv Frankfurt. W1/2 – 278/1. *Grages*, p. 3 and 7.

Railway: "During the initial years, the skilled engineering workers available were exclusively Indians, who constantly poured into the land leaving their overpopulated home country behind. Their increase in number was far from being a pleasant growth to the East African population."[188] In any case, it is very likely that *Holzmann* finally turned to Indians, because no Chinese skilled workers arrived in German East Africa in the end. Other – more practical – reasons might have played a role as well. Not only had Indians had long-established links to East Africa also in terms of indentured labour, but they seem to have regarded (German) East Africa as a potential country of immigration themselves.[189] Examining British archives, J.S. Mangat confirms the patchy research results taken from the German archives. He stressed that although no official schemes of indentured labour were allowed to be established in German East Africa, this did not apply to voluntary migration of Indians. He is thus convinced that especially skilled Indian (petty) traders, craftsmen, and clerks left India for German East Africa. While the (petty) traders established business at ports such as Dar es Salaam and later along the *Central Railway*, Indian craftsmen and office clerks mostly sought work at the *Central Railway* up until WWI.[190]

In any case, Rehfeldt's disrespectful comment about his Indian craftsmen allegedly having negative effects on the local African population points to one major discourse prominent in colonial German East Africa. Analysing this discourse might prove helpful in explaining the role of Indian labour there. Generally, the Indian population of East Africa experienced various prejudices. They were often regarded as cunning businessmen who cheated the 'African wards' and who also destroyed the businesses of hard-working German settlers by lowering the wage levels and engaging in unfair money lending. Indeed, the so-called 'Indian Question' flared up repeatedly in colonial publications. Regarding the articles in the *DOAZ*, it is important to notice that the publication of anti-Indian propaganda by the colonial newspaper always peaked shortly after the *Reichstag* had voted in favour of financing a new route section of the *Central Railway*. Whenever *Philipp Holzmann* prepared for new construction work, the colonial

188 Stadtarchiv Frankfurt. W1/2 – 278/1. *Von unserem Leben und von unserer Arbeit in Ost-Afrika von Dipl. Ing. Walter Rehfeldt*, p. 13. Cf. Müllendorf, Prosper. *Ost-Afrika im Aufstieg.* Essen: 1910, p. 109.

189 Reasons for Indian migration in the Indian Ocean Area were manifold, and indentured labour was just one aspect of that. For the British East African/Kenyan case cf. Aiyar, Sana. *Indians in Kenya. The Politics of Diaspora.* Cambridge: 2015, pp. 2–9, 22–69. Also dealing with the British East African context cf. Herzig, Pascale. *South Asians in Kenya: Gender, Generation and Changing Identities in Diaspora.* Münster: 2006, pp. 7–20. Cf. Gillman. 'Dar es Salaam', pp. 1–4, 12.

190 Cf. Mangat. *A History of the Asians*, pp. 30–33, 38, 45, 46–51, 58, 67–69, 72–77, 83–84, 93–95.

newspaper lamented the high influx of Indian people to the colony just as it did regarding Greek immigration.[191] In contrast to Greek migration, the involvement of Indian labour in the construction process of the *Central Railway* is hardly ever made explicit, however. The articles call Indian migration a "cancer"[192] to the German colony or complain about an Indian monopoly in petty trading and money lending.[193] While the Southern Europeans were undoubtedly involved in the construction works, this holds also true for their Asian counterparts, albeit scattered and often inconclusive evidence.

All in all, the sources about Indian labour in German East Africa consulted so far do not provide a clear picture. This applies especially for questioning *when* Indians were employed. Whereas both senior *Holzmann* engineers Grages and Rehfeldt claim that Indian craftsmen, who had initially been involved in constructing the *Central Railway*, were slowly but surely replaced by recently educated

191 Regarding the beginning of the construction work in 1905 cf. "Der wirtschaftliche Aufschwung im Bezirk Muansa und die Inder-Einwanderung". *DOAZ*, VII, no. 1. Daressalam: 07 January 1905. Cf. "Sind die Europäer in den Tropen in wirtschaftlicher Beziehung dauernd den Indern überlegen?". *DOAZ*, VII, no. 17. Daressalam: 29 May 1905. Cf. "Die Inder-Überschwemmung Deutsch-Ostafrikas". *DOAZ*, VII, no. 18. Daressalam: 29 April 1905. Cf. "Zur Abwehr der Indergefahr". *DOAZ*, VII, no. 22. Daressalam: 03 June 1905. Another article laments Indian migration and calls the Indians 'coolies', but does not refer directly to any involvement in railway construction cf. "Was ich auf meiner Reise von Dar es Salaam nach Kilossa sah". *DOAZ*, VII, no. 28. Daressalam: 15 July 1905. Cf. "Indische Völkerwanderung nach Deutsch-Ostafrika". *DOAZ*, VII, no. 43. Daressalam: 28 October 1905. For the route section that followed from 1908/09 onwards, recurring increased Indian migration is noted. One author even complains about Indian migration to central German East Africa, because the new railway would make it easier for the Indian people to spread their petty-trading and money lending businesses. No connections are however made to Indian craftsmen working at the central railway. Cf. "Zur Inderfrage". *DOAZ*, X, no. 36. Daressalam: 16 May 1908. Other articles blame Governor Rechenberg and his good relationships with Indians for the new influx. Cf. "Eine indische Kraftprobe". *DOAZ*, X, no. 99. Daressalam: 24 December 1908. Cf. "Samassa über die Inderfrage". *DOAZ*, XI, no. 61. Daressalam: 04 August 1909. Cf. "Ein Deutscher Kaufmann über die Inderfrage". *DOAZ*, XI, no. 62. Daressalam: 07 August 1909. For the last route section from Tabora to Kigoma from 1911/12 onwards cf. "Aus unserer Kolonie. Die Inder in Deutsch-Ostafrika". *DOAZ*, XIII, no. 22. Daressalam: 18 March 1911. Allegedly, there were very few African craftsmen, and almost only Indian craftsmen were available cf. "Morogoro. Ungesunde Lohnverhältnisse". *DOAZ*, XIII, no. 65. Daressalam: 16 August 1911. For a report claiming Indian migration resulted in famines in India as the newly arrived Indians would control all petty-trade along the central railway. Cf. "Die Zunahme der Einwanderung unbemittelter Inder". *DOAZ*, XIII, no. 72. Daressalam: 09 September 1911. Cf. Gillman. 'Dar es Salaam', p. 2.

192 "Soll Deutsch-Ostafrika eine deutsche Kolonie werden oder eine Hamburg-indische Domäne bleiben? 5. Die Inderfrage und die Behandlung der Farbigen". *DOAZ*, VII, no. 31. Daressalam: 05 August 1905.

193 Cf. "Samassa über die Inderfrage". *DOAZ*, XI, no. 61.

African skilled workers – primarily people like the Swahili, Wasaramu, Waluguru and later also the Wanjamwezi[194] – an article by colonial geographer and secretary of the district office in Dar es Salaam, Dr Franz Oskar Karstedt, as well as the article by *Holzmann* engineer Clement Gillman cited above contradict *Holzmann's* sources. Both Karstedt and Gillman confirm the involvement of Indian craftsmen at the construction site of the *Central Railway* as late as 1913. Karstedt even highlights the outstanding role of Indian craftsmen for the entire colonial economy in general. He explicitly characterises the employer-employee relationship between the railway construction company and the Indian craftsmen as "contract workers in indentured labour".[195] Such an employment relationship might then have implied systematic recruitment by *Holzmann* and corresponding proceedings in India. Apart from the question whether there was systematic recruitment of Indian indentured labour despite its official ban, other sources confirm that Indian labour was involved in the building until the very end of the construction process of the *Central Railway* in German East Africa, including forms of indentured labour.[196]

With the colonial administration of railway construction especially expanding after ca. 1908, the railway supervisors and commissioners report about Indian (skilled) labour at the construction sites of the *Central Railway* repeatedly. Yet, there is no evidence answering the question whether these Indians were recruited by schemes of indentured labour or whether they had come to German East Africa for work at the railway differently. The regular administrative reports note Indians, Banians and Goanese working at the construction sites. They were particularly employed at the railway's workshop, as locksmiths, as station masters, as train drivers, as typists or even as sub-contractors responsible for the erection of the workforce's housing or pre-extension works. Especially as craftsmen, they earned decent wages of up to 100 Rupees a month. The monthly report

---

194 Cf. Stadtarchiv Frankfurt. W1/2 – 278/1. *Rehfeldt*, p. 13. Cf. Stadtarchiv Frankfurt. W1/2 – 278/1. *Grages*, p. 3 and 7. Cf. Reichart. *Gari*, p. 67.

195 In contrast to the Indians, the African craftsmen would not work independently and would need constant supervision. Cf. Karstedt, F.O. Dr. "Beiträge zur Inderfrage in Deutsch-Ostafrika IV. (Schluß)". *DOAZ*, XV, no. 79. Daressalam: 01 October 1913. For Indians as indentured labourers cf. Karstedt, F.O. Dr. "Beiträge zur Inderfrage in Deutsch-Ostafrika I". *DOAZ*, XV, no. 76. Daressalam: 20 September 1913.

196 Cf. Karstedt, F.O., Dr. "Beiträge zur Inderfrage in Deutsch-Ostafrika I". *DOAZ*, XV, no. 76. Cf. Gillman, Clement. 'Vom Bau der ostafrikanischen Mittellandbahn'. 160–166. *Schweizerische Bauzeitung*, 61/62, no. 12. Zürich: 1913. Web. *ETH-Bibliothek*. http://doi.org/10.5169/seals-30784 (08 February 2018.), p. 163. Cf. Gillman, Clement. 'Vom Bau der ostafrikanischen Mittellandbahn'. 176–179. *Schweizerische Bauzeitung*, 61/62, no. 13. Zürich: 1913. Web. *ETH-Bibliothek*. http://doi.org/10.5169/seals-30786 (08 February 2018.), p. 178.

of November 1912, for example, contains information about pay gaps between Indians and Banians compared to Goanese. Whereas Indians and Banians earned 2.5 to 4.0 Rupees a day, Goanese made 3.25 to 4.5 Rupees in the same period.[197]

Regarding the year of 1913 – and to a lesser extent also the year 1914 – evidence taken from the Railway Museum in Nairobi proves a significant presence of Indians working for the *OAEG* either at the railway itself or at the flotilla based in Dar es Salaam. The railway and the previously governmental flotilla stood under the administration of the *OAEG* from 1913 onwards, which received payroll records listing Indian employees from this year onwards.[198] Other rather patchy sources were issued by local medical services (*Sanitätsdienststellen)* along the railroad, located e.g. in Tabora or Morogoro, which either reported of Indian or "coloured" (*Farbige)* employees who had received medical treatment, or reported about the health of Indian employees working as station masters for the *OAEG*.[199] In addition, several bills issued by the *Sewa Hadji Hospital* and sent to the *OAEG* survive in the archives for the entire year of 1913 and the first half of 1914. The *Sewa Hadji Hospital*, built in 1897 and extended in 1899, was named after the Muslim Indian merchant and philanthropist, who was born in East Africa's Bagamoyo in 1851 and died in 1897 in Zanzibar. Sewa Hadji had traded several goods on behalf of the Sultan of Zanzibar and equipped numerous (European) caravans until the end of the 1890s. Having become a rich man, he had supported sick men and women for several years and donated the stately sum of almost 13,000 Rupees to the German colonial administration to enable the construction of a hospital, which would treat any person regardless of their origin or race. During the German

---

197 Cf. TNA. G17/120, "Baubericht der Bausektion 2,3 und 4 der Neubaustrecke Tabora-Kigoma für den Monat Januar 1913, X. Personal und Arbeiterverhältnisse". Cf. TNA. G12/167, "Ostafrikanische Eisenbahngesellschaft Berlin. Betriebsleitung Daressalam. J. no. 849 P. Daressalam, den 19. April 1911". Cf. TNA. G12/164, pp. 121, 232, cf. "Monatsbericht August 1911". Cf. TNA. G17/63, "Monatsbericht über den Stand der Vorarbeiten an der Zentralbahn Ende August 1909". Cf. TNA. G17/ 122, "J. no. 485. Bericht über den Stand der Arbeiten im Hafen Kigoma Endpunkt der Tanganjikabahn für den Monat Juni 1915, X. Personal & Arbeiter". Cf. TNA. G17/120, "Lulanguru, den 30. IV. 12, J. no. 861. Monatsbericht [. . .] Juni 1912, 8. Arbeiterverhältnisse". Cf. TNA. G17/118, "Bauarbeiten an der Ostafrikanischen Mittellandbahn. Bahnbau Tabora-Kigoma, Restarbeiten Morogoro-Tabora, Monatsbereich November 1912, XI. Lohn- und Verpflegungsverhältnisse".

198 Cf. Eckhart and Geissler. *Das Deutsch-Ostafrika Archiv*, pp. 27–28.

199 Cf. RMN. GTF. R3. S8. 157. Lohnauszahlungen, "Betr. Werkmeisterei Dodoma", "Direktor der DOAEG an Herrn Betriebswerkmeister Horn, Dodoma. Daressalam, den 20. Januar 1914". Cf. RMN. GTF. R1. S9. Sanitätsdienststellen, "Rechnung der Sanitätsdienststelle Dodoma, 27. Dezember 1915", "Rechnung der Sanitätsdienststelle Tabora, 1. Dez. 1915", "Rechnung der Sanitätsdienststelle Dodoma, 3. Juli 1915". Cf. RMN. GTF. R3. S5. 1.1.13. [no title], "An die Deutsch Ostafrikanische Eisenbahngesellschaft bezüglich des Gesundheitszustandes des Stationsvorstehers von Kilossa, Inders Hassan Ali, Morogoro, den 9. März. 1913".

colonial period, the *Sewa Hadji Hospital* was known as *Eingeborenenkrankenhaus* (hospital for the indigenous) in Dar es Salaam and thus primarily treated those who counted as 'indigenous' or rather as non-European in German East Africa.[200]

The hospital bills held in the archives of the Railway Museum Nairobi list the names and origin of the people treated and therefore provide details of individual illnesses as well as the costs of treatment. All of those listed in the *Sewa Hadji Hospital's* monthly bills were employed by the *OAEG* either working at the railway or at the company's flotilla. The majority of those treated in the hospital were of East African origin, but Indians ranked second. Although many of those listed in the monthly bills were treated repeatedly, i.e. were listed not only in one month but reappeared in others, the surviving sources, as patchy as they may be, indicate a decisive number of Indians employed by the *OEAG*. Interestingly, it seems that the number of Indians employed by the *OAEG's* flotilla surpasses the number of Indians employed for the railway. According to the *Sewa Hadji* bills featuring those men employed by the flotilla, between thirty percent and fifty percent were of Indian descent. Of those bills issued by the *Sewa Hadji Hospital* which featured men employed at the railway only five percent to ten percent were of Indian descent; also a few Banians, one Turk, two Goans, a few Arabs, a Sudanese, a Swahili, one person from Madagascar and one Chinese person are mentioned.[201] Of course, these files have only very limited validity in several ways. First of all, you cannot deduce the overall ratio of nationalities employed by the *OAEG* from the bills issued by the *Sewa Hadji Hospital*. People of Indian descent might have suffered from tropical diseases to a greater extent than their East African colleagues because they might not have adapted well to the East African climate. Secondly, many names are mentioned more than once and chronically, and thus seriously ill men in need of long-term treatment may distort the overall statistical value. Thirdly, given the realities of the racist colonial rule, Indians, who were ranked above Africans in German colonial discourses, might have had easier access to medical treatment in a hospital run by the colonial administration. Finally, only the bills for the entire year of 1913 and a few months of 1914 are given and there are no sources at all listing the backgrounds of all the

---

200 Cf. Eckart, Wolfgang U. *Medizin und Kolonialimperialismus. Deutschland 1884–1945.* Paderborn et. al: 1997, pp. 316–317, 336. Cf. "Krankenhäuser". *Deutsches Kolonial-Lexikon*, 1920, Band II, S. 372. Web. *University of Frankfurt o.M.* http://www.ub.bildarchiv-dkg.uni-frankfurt.de/Bildprojekt/Lexikon/Standardframeseite.php?suche=Sewa (14 October 2020). Cf. Hasse, Rolf. 'Das Testament des Sewa Hadji'. Ed. *Mitteilungsblatt des Traditionsverbandes ehemaliger Schutz- und Überseetruppen*, no. 90, 1/2004, pp. 43–53.

201 Cf. RMN. GTF. R2. S10. I_6, 1913/14. Sewa Hadji Hospital, Rechnung. Cf. RMN. GTF. R3. S10. 2. Sewa Hadji Hospital. Rechnung.

workers employed at the *Central Railway*. Hence, nothing can be said about the overall ratio of nationalities employed by the *OAEG* in general. Yet, as patchy as these sources might be, the medical bills prove the presence of numerous Indians employed by the *OAEG* at both the flotilla and the *Central Railway*, at the least.

Although nothing reliable can be said about the overall exact numbers of Indians employed by the *OAEG*, their role must have been significant as the *OAEG* even planned to erect over ten houses in Dar es Salaam to accommodate their Indian employees. In May 1914, *OAEG's* manager Hillenkamp argued that his company would always need several regular members of staff either for the operation of the colonial railway service as such, or for always recurring repair works along the railroad. As company housing was built whenever there was no suitable accommodation available by comparable railway operating companies back home in Germany, the *OAEG* was likewise required to provide suitable housing in German East Africa. In accordance with colonial housing policies that allotted each 'race' to a specific residential area, the Indian employees of the *OAEG* were required to live exclusively in an Indian quarter, and married and single Indians were separated from one another.[202] As WWI interrupted any plans of the *OAEG*, this building scheme never materialised, however. Yet, these documents about the *OAEG* company housing policies and plans, combined with the *Sewa Hadji Hospital* bills and other documents, at least prove that Indians were involved in railway construction and maintenance from the very beginnings of the construction of the *Central Railway* until the eve of WWI.

As also revealed by Figure 2, Indian labour appears to have been skilled labour most of the time. The probably staged photography depicts a group of men fixing a railway bridge using apparently modern technology. The headgear, such as turban or fez distinguishes three non-European men from three other European men who wear sun-helmets. The latter, who are probably German railway engineers, apparently supervise the riveting work of supposedly Indian craftsmen who wear turbans and another skilled worker who – according to the headgear – may originate also from India or the Middle East (Ottoman Empire or even Greece).

Other evidence further supports this argument. It seems that the colonial government tried to issue immigration legislation attempting to reduce Indian migration to German East Africa, starting from the end of 1912.[203] It apparently lacked effectiveness. Whether bypassing the immigration legislation was rooted merely in Indian agency, or if the colonial administration maybe even tolerated the circumvention of

202 Cf. TNA. G8/146. [Angelegenheiten der] Ostafrikanische Eisenbahngesellschaft (1913-)1916. Bd. 3., pp. 6–8.

203 Cf. "Anwendung der Einwanderungsverordnung auf Farbige". *DOAZ*, XIV, no. 90. Daressalam: 09 November 1912. Cf. Karstedt, O.F. Dr. "Beiträge zur Inderfrage in Deutsch-Ostafrika II. (Fortsetzung)". *DOAZ*, XV, no. 77. Daressalam: 24 September 1913.

Figure 2: Indian craftsmen riveting bridge parts using modern machinery at the Malagarassi-Bridge 1912–13.
Source: BBWA. U5/03/17, Nr. 177. Bildarchiv der Philipp Holzmann AG / Hauptverband der Deutschen Bauindustrie e.V. im Berlin-Brandenburgischen Wirtschaftsarchiv.

the laws – because rapid railway construction required further Indian craftsmen – must remain mere speculation for now.[204] In any case, Indian labour at the construction of the *Central Railway* in German East Africa was indeed an important aspect throughout the entire construction process. As far as the files can tell, the involvement of Indian labour in the construction of the *Central Railway* was manifold. It ranged from indentured labour to apparently voluntary labour migration from neighbouring British East Africa and India to German East Africa. Moreover, Indians primarily worked as skilled craftsmen at the construction sites or as office clerks for *Holzmann* or the *OEAG.* These employments were of high rank compared to the tasks of an ordinary railway worker, whose tasks were shovelling and carrying most of the time. Consequently, skilled (Indian) workers received higher wages than ordi-

204 Cf. "Lokales. Personenschmuggel". *DOAZ*, XV, no. 94. Daressalam: 22 November 1913.

nary workers. This comparatively high standing of skilled Indian labour also found its way into colonial discourses on Indian labour in German East Africa and was also reflected in publications of the Indian community newspaper *The Indian Voice of British East Africa, Uganda and Zanzibar.*

3.6.2 Discourses About Indian Labour and Indian Labour Protest

Regarding the overall issue of labour in the (German) colonial context, much has been written about the colonial ideology of 'educating the Negro to work' or about forced labour practices in German colonies in general. African resistance against (forced) labour was often labelled as mere laziness and 'educating' the local population to work was seen as the 'white man's burden' in the colonial context. Accordingly, the colonial discourse also regarded the enduring African (passive) resistance against corporal punishment as part of their 'indolent character traits' that also legitimised racially discriminatory laws, which disadvantaged Africans and advantaged Europeans.[205] With respect to the involvement of Indian labour at the railway construction site, it must be stressed that so-called 'coloured' people were subject to 'indigenous' legislation in German East Africa. They were however exempt from corporal punishments such as strokes and enchained imprisonment for violations of labour legislation.[206] Although Indians were not regarded as equals by the European colonisers, they were also not entirely subsumed under the same colonial discourse as the population of African descent. While the so-called 'labour question' and the necessity of forced labour practices to deal with African resistance against labour were constantly debated in the *DOAZ*,[207] the same newspaper reported about Indian means of labour resistance and collective action differently. As reported by the *DOAZ* as early as 1906, Indian craftsmen employed by the flotilla's workshop run by the *OAEG* went collectively on "strike", because a European employee had committed a physical assault on

205 Cf. Conrad. *Globalisation*, pp. 77–143. Cf. Sippel. '"Wie erzieht man"', pp. 311–333.
206 Cf. Schröder, Martin. *Prügelstrafe und Züchtigungsrecht in den deutschen Schutzgebieten Schwarzafrikas*. Münster: 1997, pp. 25–34.
207 E.g. Cf. "Arbeitserziehung und Arbeitszwang". *DOAZ*, VIII, no. 22. Daressalam: 02 June 1906. Cf. "Aus unserer Kolonie. Von den Arbeitskarten im Bezirk Wilhelmstal". *DOAZ*, XII, no. 79. Daressalam: 05 October 1910. Cf. "Berliner Telegramme. Ein Wechsel in der Haltung der kaiserlichen Regierung zur Frage der staatlichen Arbeiteranwerbung?". *DOAZ*, XV, no. 72. Daressalam: 09 September 1913. Cf. "Gouvernementsrat (4. Verhandlungstag)". *DOAZ*, XVI, no. 55. Daressalam: 6 October 1906.

one of their Indian colleagues. In protest, the workers originating from the subcontinent refused to work and urged the *Gouvernement* and the flotilla to punish the European employee. Their petition apparently met with success, probably because the colonial authorities were dependent on the skilled Indian workers.[208] Another incident occurred in October 1909, when craftsmen employed by *Philipp Holzmann* went on strike because they were neither satisfied with their salaries, nor with their working hours.[209] Although it is in this case not clear whether the strike was initiated by employees of African or Indian descent, another comparable incident occurred in August 1913. This time the population groups involved were identified as Indian and Goan. Roughly sixty-six craftsmen demanded their daily coffee-break in the morning, which had been reduced by the *OAEG* to only fifteen min. Feelings ran so high that the antagonists even instigated a physical fight. As the Indian craftsmen, and their alleged Goanese ringleaders, were subject to 'indigenous law', the result was thirty Rupees fine for breach of contract.[210] It remains however remarkable that publications such as the *DOAZ*, which usually endorsed colonial discourses, labelled the labour dispute of the Indian workers as a *strike* instead of calling it 'idleness', 'indolence' or 'laziness' as the colonial discourse would normally have it regarding African workers. Generally, the term 'strike' was exclusively used to describe the resistance of workers employed by major industrial factories in Europe, and hardly ever in the colonial context. As skilled workers remained scarce throughout the entire German colonial period and especially at the railway construction sites, the use of this terminology may illustrate the railway companies' strong dependency on Indian employees and the relatively high prestige of their skilled labour.

As Indian involvement in railway construction in East Africa was important regarding skilled labour, and decisive in the British case (*Uganda Railway*), one must also consider sources illustrating the Indian perspectives on the issue. Although there was certainly some forced and indentured labour involved, Indian labour migration in the Indian Ocean Area was at times also the result of genuine Indian initiative. This reflects the fact that such Indian labour migration was not necessarily a one-way street from India to East Africa. It also entailed the opportunity to leave East Africa again for India and to come back again another time. Of course, such migratory practice was often impossible regarding 'coolie' la-

208 "Aus Dar es Salaam und Umgebung. Ein Streikversuch der indischen Flotillen Handwerker". *DOAZ*, VIII, no. 2. Daressalam: 13 January 1906.
209 Cf. "Aus unserer Kolonie. Morogoro. Streik". *DOAZ*, XI, no. 85. Daressalam: 27 October 1909.
210 Cf. "Lokales. Streik bei der Ostafrikanischen Eisenbahngesellschaft". *DOAG*, XV, no. 70. Daressalam: 30 August 1913.

bour,[211] but it is worth noting that Indians of a relatively high social status at the railways, such as craftsmen or office clerks, apparently had the opportunity to leave their country for East Africa, work for a railway employer and return to the subcontinent as soon as their contract had been fulfilled. The reasons for returning to India might have been profoundly individual, as a poem by an Indian railway clerk published by the *Indian Voice* in April 1911 illustrates:

To Africa.

By a disgusted Indian Clerk on retiring from the Service of the Railway.

Satan's own Pandemonium thou art,
Africa! Thy barren wastes, nature's worst part,
Thy scorching fields and thy waterless tracts,
Can never be improved by Human arts;
Fittest thou art for the arch Demon's home,
And thy trackless wilds for wild brutes to roam,
Heaven never made thee for pure human seat,
Attempts for that thy climate must defeat;
Let England pour on thee her boundless gold,
Let Germany exert her powers untold,
Let France attempt to help thee with her light,
Let Italy serve thee with her fallen might.
Nothing, sure, can make thee a country good,
Thy poisonous soil can produce no human food,
Say what avails thee of thy central lakes,
What avails thee what course old Nilus takes;
Their joint actions cannot a vast region feed,
Nor thy clime fit to rear a manly breed,
As thou art, thou must always be, a waste
A home for monkey, Darwin's human beast;
Nature, to show, how bad a place could be,
Heaved thee up from the bottom of the sea,
She has placed thee beneath the burning line,
A death dealing torrid sun is always thine;
Thy sea-board, hot and moist, thy centre hot,
Fever or sunstroke is thy children's lot,
By chance at times, escape them both, one may
To be, to lion, or dysentery a prey;
Jigars and cancers, thy peculiar trait,
Maladies which all must dread, low or great,
Heroes and Kings from old Amon's son,

---

211 Cf. Yekani. *Koloniale Arbeit*, pp. 44–71. Cf. Tappe, Oliver and Lindner, Ulrike. 'Introduction: Global Variants of Bonded Labour'. *Bonded Labour. Global and Comparative Perspectives (18th – 21st Century)*. 9–34. Eds. Sabine Damir-Geilsdorf et al. Bielefeld: 2016.

Down to the modern and great Correi[?]an;
Who sought to conquer countries for their fame,
And to leave behind them, a lasting name,
All rightly considered thee unfit to yield,
To human exertion a worthy field,
All ages shunned thee for thy infernal mould,
And shunned shalt then be but where Pharaoh's Ruled,
Now for thy arid sands let Germans fight,
And the English exert their latent might;
But I must surely leave and see thee no more,
As soon as my three years penance is o'er,
In my native home I should rather be,
A beggar, than get here a Monarchy.[212]

Apart from exemplifying the fact that Indians employed by East African railway companies in high ranks had opinions of their own about their work and their reasons for migrating within the Indian Ocean, the poem of 'a disgusted Indian clerk' illustrates various other aspects of research interest. Although *The Indian Voice's* general editorial policy followed a rather cosmopolitan approach intended to be "the hope of all who suffer", it nevertheless also (re)produced ideologies of colonial racial hierarchies.[213] "Africa [. . .] acted as a boundary from which Indians measured their status [. . .] and Indians were deemed more developed and [. . .] more civilized than the 'African native'."[214] Accordingly, the poem's author compared Africa to John Milton's Capital of Satan and his Peers characterised by the corresponding barren environment (cf. 1–7).[215] In addition, the people of African descent were described as animal-like "beasts" or "monkeys" (20), which implied Indian superiority in turn. Thereby, the author confirmed the contemporary colonial hierarchy, which attempted to assign the lowest ranks to people of African descent. In fact, the author then foiled this very colonial hierarchy, which ranked European people first, by doubting the ability of the colonising powers to 'develop' the African continent (cf. 10–20, 40–41). As all European efforts in Africa were in vain, the author preferred a superior way and chose to return to his mother country of

---

212 "To Africa. By a Disgusted Indian Clerk on Retiring from the Service of the Railway". *The Indian Voice of British East Africa, Uganda and Zanzibar.* Nairobi: 19 April 1911. Web. *African Newspapers.* http://public.maximus.newsbank.com//images/L00000007/cache/pdf/bitonal_tiff_g4/13D0F5904120B628_13CF496663BB9D10.pdf (24 January 2018), p. 6.

213 Cf. Nasar, Saima. '*The Indian Voice:* Connecting Self-Representation and Identity Formulation in Diaspora'. 99–124. *History in Africa,* Volume 40. Cambridge: 2013. Web. https://www.cambridge.org/core/terms.https://doi.org/10.1017/hia.2013.10 (26 January 2018), pp. 119–122.

214 Nasar. '*The Indian Voice*', p. 121.

215 Cf. Milton, John. *Das Verlorene Paradies.* Altenmünster: 2016, pp. 20–22.

India (cf. 43–45), which he regarded as the best country in the world. Moreover, the author regarded his employment as a clerk at an East African railway as "penance" (43) and could not wait for his three-year-long obligation to come to an end. "Disgusted" by his job, he left East Africa never to be seen again (cf. 44–45), illustrating most importantly that skilled labour such as being a railway clerk opened up a degree of freedom when employed in colonial businesses.[216] Whatever hardships the author might have experienced while on duty in (probably British) East Africa, nevertheless, he held a rather privileged position compared to other employees who were charged with the physically very demanding construction work on the building site. Apparently, expertise was an important means to eke out advantages when working at the *Central Railway* in German East Africa. This applies not only for skilled Indian craftsmen and office clerks, but also for East Africans who obtained an expertise urgently wanted at the *Central Railway*'s construction sites.

3.7 (Un-)wanted Workers: Contesting Skilled African Labour at the *Central Railway*

3.7.1 Moravians Fighting Railway Modernity? Between Colonial Cooperation and Competition

> We rejoice with you at the tremendous cultural work of the railway's completion until Tabora for the time being. It is a proud work of German energy and efficiency which will extraordinarily facilitate our colonial tasks in German East Africa. Our very remote and hardly accessible missionary stations will also enjoy the blessings of the railway's construction.
>
> Moravian Missionary Director Henning to *Philipp Holzmann*, 15 August 1910.[217]

As far as the files of the Moravian Mission to East Africa can tell, the idea for a railway mission to the *Central Railway* in German East Africa developed out of connections within the 'colonial globality' taking place around the year 1900. In early 1905, members of the Moravian Mission Board travelled to German East Africa for an inspection tour of their missionary stations in the colony. While on board the steamer that took them to East Africa, the Moravians met an ethnic German who was born in Transylvania (today's Romania). It turned out that the Transylvanian was an engineer, who had recently been transferred from a railway construction site in Asia Minor to Ger-

---

216 Cf. Gunn. *Outsourcing*, pp. 10–15.

217 UAH. MD 1560. Verschiedenes. 3. Briefwechsel mit Verschiedenen 1909–1915, "Henning Missionsdirektion der evangelischen Brüder Unität Herrnhut an die Herren Philipp Holzmann & Cie. GmbH. 15. August 1912", p. 2.

man East Africa by his employer *Philipp Holzmann*. Apparently, an invigorating conversation between the Moravian Mission Board and the railway engineer developed and thus contributed to the Board's idea to set up a railway mission in German East Africa targeting the African men and women working and living in the construction camps along the track. As there was no other railway construction work in Asia Minor by *Holzmann* except for the *Bagdadbahn* at that time, it is obvious that the *Bagdadbahn* was not only significant for providing experienced Southern European sub-contractors for the East African *Central Railway*. Indeed, the construction of the *Bagdadbahn* appears to have further stimulated thoughts about a railway mission to German East Africa on the part of the Moravians. In addition to this Middle Eastern dimension, other Moravian missions to Africa were influential for the railway mission in German East Africa, too. With the Moravians having had a positive experience with railway missions to South African railways, the prospect of founding a railway mission to the *Central Railway* in German East Africa appeared equally promising.[218]

Rebekka Habermas and Richard Hölzl argue that missions and missionaries were decisive actors in globalising processes just like other comparatively well-researched actors of globalisation of the nineteenth century. Despite the widespread disregard of missions and missionaries in the field of global history, the two historians stress that, when analysed as "new mission history", not only European missionaries, but also their locally recruited translators, catechumen, porters, employees and teachers employed at mission schools made up for an "entangled mission history" and a "global history of the religious".[219] Given Habermas and Hölzl's characterisation of nineteenth-century missionaries as central protagonists of global history, the Moravian Mission is no exception, of course. This is particularly valid considering the fact that the history of the Moravian Mission from the 1720s until the 1850s has already been researched thoroughly and that the Moravians have been characterised as a "global community"[220] accordingly. Having had mission communities particularly in many European countries and across the Atlantic since the early modern period, the global character of the Moravian Mission holds true also for the nineteenth century.[221] It is therefore not very surprising that the personnel manage-

---

218 Cf. UAH. MD 1560, "Missionsdirektion der evangelischen Brüder Unität Herrnhut an die Herren Philipp Holzmann & Cie. GmbH. 03. Dec. 1909", pp. 1–3.

219 Habermas, Rebekka and Hölzl, Richard. 'Mission global – Religiöse Akteure und globale Verflechtung seit dem 19. Jahrhundert'. *Mission Global. Eine Verflechtungsgeschichte seit dem 19. Jahrhundert.* 10–28. Eds. Rebekka Habermas and Richard Hölzl. Cologne et al.: 2014, p. 27.

220 Mettele, Gisela. *Weltbürgertum oder Gottesreich. Die Herrnhuter Brüdergemeinschaft als globale Gemeinschaft 1727–1854*. Göttingen: 2009.

221 Cf. Mettele. *Weltbürgertum*, pp. 9–32. The Moravians were, of course, not acting in vacuum. Particularly, their relationship with the evolving modern nation sates and nationalism of the

ment of the Moravian railway mission to the *Central Railway* in German East Africa also illustrates its embeddedness in the 'colonial globality' that transcended the boundaries of the German *Reich* and German colonies. With Nis Gaarde and Mads Löbner becoming the most important figures of the Moravian railway mission in German East Africa, two (ethnic) Danes reported regularly to the Moravian Mission Board in Herrnhut (Germany) about their work along the railroad being built in East Africa by *Philipp Holzmann*.[222]

In fact, besides the overseas connections between the Moravian railway mission and Asia Minor and South Africa, it seems that the mission also had roots in Central Europe. The new technological means of transport and communication of the nineteenth century fundamentally transformed European societies and labour markets. Central to this development was the expanding railway network that enabled and accelerated the connections between political and economic centres and the hinterlands. The construction of railways entailed not only new forms of labour migration and labour recruitment in German colonies, but it had also repercussions in the German *Reich* proper. The transformation of German society, economy and the labour market not only meant new forms of employment and a booming economy, it entailed also social disruptions and opened up new forms of exploitation and abuse in the labour market. Transient and migrant workers arriving in economic centres via train seeking jobs in factories or as servants particularly were targeted by untrustworthy middlemen right upon their arrival at a town's railway station. Especially young single women became victims of economic exploitation or were even coerced into sex work. Tackling such social evils, female activists founded associations to support young single women as soon as they arrived at railway stations. The first German associations emerged in 1882 following the example set by the Swiss female middle-class Protestant movement called *Freundinnen junger Mädchen* ('Friends of Young Girls'), which had been founded in 1872. The major area of activity of such associations was to provide affordable housing for the young female workers and help them establish contact with trustworthy employers. Before Protestant and Catholic associations started joint ecumenical

19th century also influenced the Moravians. A closer investigation on this issue is unfortunately beyond the scope of this study.

222 Especially for Gaarde, the question of citizenship and nationality is comparatively complex: he was born in Northern-Schleswig, which was annexed by Prussia in the 1860s. Gaarde was, however, born into the Danish Protestant community of Hjartbro. Cf. UAH. MD 767. Personalakten Mission. Gaarde, Nis Hansen. Cf. UAH. MD 893. Personalakten Mission. Löbner, Mads Hansen. Cf. UAH. MD 1530. Missionsdirektion Unyamwezi. Jahresberichte der Provinz 1906–1940, "Bericht für die Missionsdirektion London, J.N. 3/9, 3. Dezember 1920". Cf. UAH. MD 1532, "Löbner an Hoffmann, 10. Feburar 1910".

work in the field in 1910, several Christian associations of both denominations alongside Jewish movements offered their assistance independently. By 1912 there were ca. ninety *Bahnhofsmissionen* (railway (station) missions) all around the German *Reich*, which slowly but surely expanded their field of activity and offered help to any kind of traveller in need, no matter if male or female. In 2021, the German *Bahnhofsmission* celebrated its 125th anniversary and is still present at many major railway stations in Germany.[223]

Almost simultaneously to the joint ecumenical action in the *Reich* in 1910, the Moravian Protestant Mission in German East Africa initiated their railway mission, which targeted the local African population living nearby the *Central Railway* in general, but especially the migrant workers who had recently arrived at the construction camps in the German colony. With the workers migrating to the construction sites often without their families and subsequently living in a strange environment, the Moravian railway mission regarded the migrant workers as particularly prone to becoming victims of the temptations of modernity, which the newly built railroad allegedly entailed. Consequently, and in addition to their longer-established ordinary missions, the central board of the Moravian Mission decided to set up a special railway mission to counter, by the strength of Christianity, the perceived vices of alcohol, sex work and the religion of Islam. Unfortunately, the sources do not reveal whether there was any direct connection between the establishment of the *Bahnhofsmissionen* in the German *Reich* and the Moravian Mission to the *Central Railway* in German East Africa. But the fact that the joint ecumenical work in Germany was started almost at the very same moment as the Moravian railway mission in German East Africa suggests that the mission's board may have been inspired by the developments in Europe and thought it wise to fight the dark sides of 'modernity' also in the German colony in East Africa. According to the correspondence between the Moravian Mission Board and *Philipp Holzmann*, the idea to set up a railway mission in East Africa had been a long-held wish of the Moravians in 1909 and was part of the contemporary zeitgeist anyways. At home in Germany, but also in other European countries, especially Protestant missions targeted 'lost souls' particularly among the

---

223 Cf. Reusch, Wolfgang. *Bahnhofsmission in Deutschland 1897–1987. Sozialwissenschaftliche Analyse einer diakonisch-charitativen Einrichtung im sozialen Wandel.* Frankfurt o.M. et al: 1988, pp. 17–65. Cf. Nikles, Bruno W. *Soziale Hilfe am Bahnhof. Zur Geschichte der Bahnhofsmission in Deutschland (1894.1960).* Freiburg i. Br.: 1994, pp. 11–14, 17–227. Cf. Schröder, Iris. *Arbeiten für eine bessere Welt. Frauenbewegung und Sozialreform 1890–1914.* Frankfurt o.M. and New York: 2001, pp. 185–221. Cf. Hürlimann, Esther et al. *Das Fräulein vom Bahnhof. Der Verein Freundinnen junger Mädchen in der Schweiz.* Zürich: 2021. Cf. Bahnhofsmission Deutschland e.V. '125 Jahre Bahnhofsmission'. *www.bahnhofsmission.de.* Web. https://www.bahnhofsmission.de/index.php?id=15 (05 August 2021).

working classes in the slums of European metropoles, while they simultaneously attempted to baptise and thereby allegedly 'civilise' as many peoples as possible in various colonies around the globe. In any event, quite often at least a mental or rather rhetorical link was established between 'darkest Africa' and the 'godless populations' in Europe.[224] Hence, a link between railway missions to stations in European towns and cities and the railway mission to the *Central Railway* in German East Africa appears very plausible.

While the *Bahnhofsmissionen* in the German *Reich* sought interdenominational cooperation, things were different in colonial East Africa. The Moravians did not unite their efforts with the Catholic missions in German East Africa. Quite the contrary, Catholic missionaries were seen as competitors for 'heathen souls'.[225] Marking out the mission territories was therefore central to both denominations throughout German colonial rule but also required a certain amount of cooperation and agreement. All the Christian missions to German East Africa resented Islam – the most widespread monotheistic religion in East Africa for centuries – which was simultaneously gaining ground along the *Central Railway*. Christian missionaries complained that the policies pursued by the colonial administration would even foster Islam in East Africa at the expense of their efforts in the German colony instead of facilitating the European 'civilising mission'. The missions had thus always been critical about the colonial administration's preference of literate Muslims and/or Swahili – who had valued and produced poetry and literature as a means to praise Islam and to transmit their history of East Africa long before the dominance of the European powers[226] – as *Akida, Jumbe, Liwali, Askari*,[227] or as teachers at governmental schools as well as interpreters or clerks for the colonial administration. By hiring predomi-

224 Cf. UAH. MD 1560. "Missionsdirektion der evangelischen Brüder Unität Herrnhut an die Herren Philipp Holzmann & Cie. GmbH. 03. Dec. 1909", pp. 1–3. For a link between the Bethel Mission in Germany and East Africa cf. Conrad. *Globalisation*, pp. 77–143. For a link between the slums of London and the Empire by means of the Salvation Army cf. Fischer-Tiné. *'Low and Licentious'*, pp. 324–369. For an analysis between religious and middle class thought in terms of the religious civilising missions, cf. Dejung. 'From Global Civilizing Missions', pp. 251–272.

225 Cf. Reichart. *Gari*, pp. 24–41. For a general overview of Christian missions of all confessions and their perspective on East Africa as a promising field for mission work esp. regarding Islam cf. BArch R1001/846. Evangelische Brüder-Unität Herrnhut, pp. 129–134. For the Catholic Benedictines in (German) East Africa cf. Hölzl, Richard. *Gläubige Imperialisten. Katholische Mission in Deutschland und Ostafrika (1830–1960).* Frankfurt o.M.: 2021.

226 Cf. Casco. *Utenzi*, pp. 1–142.

227 *Akida (*Swahili) = indigenous administrator in service of the Germans on the local level, *Jumbe* (Swahili) = village elder/representative, *Liwali* (Swahili) = indigenous administrator in service of the Germans on a regional level, *Askari* (Swahili) = African mercenary/soldier in service of the German colonial forces.

nantly literate and educated Muslims for the high-ranking occupations in German East Africa, African Christian converts and mission pupils, as well as the prestige of Christianity would fall behind, complained the Christian missions. The missionaries' reservations towards Islam even increased with the construction of the *Central Railway*. Their major fear was the following: As the rails followed the pre-colonial caravan routes, which had been dominated by Muslim traders for decades, the new means of transportation along these old routes would accelerate the spread of Islam and therefore make the mission's work even more difficult. Consequently, not only the Moravian Mission, but also the Catholics and other Protestant missions, like the Berlin Mission, targeted the hotspots along the railway: while the Moravians focussed on the region of central *Unyamwezi*, the Berlin Mission operated between Dar es Salaam and Kilossa. Between Mpapwa and Kilossa the Church Missionary Society attempted to missionise the railway workers.[228]

With Tabora experiencing a revival as a traffic hub in the course the advent of the railway, this central town of German East Africa became one of the Missions' bones of contention. The major reason why the Moravians ultimately focussed on hot spots such as Tabora was the fact that they could not sustain a long-lived railway mission in German East Africa. The actual Moravian Mission to the railway indeed ended as early as 1912 after only two years, because of ongoing difficulties regarding funding, but particularly due to a lack of suitable missionaries skilled to do the job. On top of this, several agreements with *Holzmann* limited the missionaries' activities to Sundays or the few hours in the evening after the

228 Cf. Yekani. *Koloniale Arbeit,* pp. 150–196. Cf. Reichart. *Gari,* pp. 58–76, 102–105. Cf. Sippel, Harald. 'Mission und Gewalt in Deutsch-Ostafrika. Das Verhältnis zwischen Mission und Kolonialverwaltung'. *Mission und Gewalt. Der Umgang christlicher Mission mit Gewalt und die Ausbreitung des Christentums in Afrika und Asien in der Zeit von 1792 bis 1918/19.* 525–538. Eds. Ulrich van der Heyden and Jürgen Becher. Stuttgart: 2000. pp. 525–536. Cf. Pawliková-Vilhanová, Viera. 'Crescent or Cross? Islam and Christian Missions in Nineteenth-Century East and Central Africa'. *Mission und Gewalt. Der Umgang christlicher Mission mit Gewalt und die Ausbreitung des Christentums in Afrika und Asien in der Zeit von 1792 bis 1918/19.* 79–96. Eds. Ulrich van der Heyden and Jürgen Becher. Stuttgart: 2000, pp. 79–95. Cf. Pesek, Michael. 'Kreuz oder Halbmond. Die deutsche Kolonialpolitik zwischen Pragmatismus und Paranoia in Deutsch-Ostafrika 1908–1914'. *Mission und Gewalt. Der Umgang christlicher Mission mit Gewalt und die Ausbreitung des Christentums in Afrika und Asien in der Zeit von 1792 bis 1918/19.* 97–111. Eds. Ulrich van der Heyden and Jürgen Becher. Stuttgart: 2000, pp. 97–110. Cf. UAH. "Bericht des Missions Departments an die Generalsynode 1899", pp. 10–13. Cf. UAH. "Bericht der Missionsdirektion an die Generalsynode 1909", pp. 64–69. Cf. UAH. FI. A2. 35. "Bericht der Missionsdirektion an die Generalsynode 1914", pp. 66–75. Cf. UAH. MD 1542. Missionsdirektion Unyamwesi. Stationsberichte Usoke 1906–1914, "Jahresbericht der Station Usoke 1913".

railway workers had returned home from the construction sites to their camps. These limited time slots for actual missionary work made the missionary's activities rather sporadic, largely unsuccessful and therefore very frustrating. Another problem was that the railhead itself kept moving further west in the course of construction and workers who had listened to the Moravians' preaching at one place, then moved on with the railhead.[229] Moreover, the missionaries faced staunch competition from Muslim teachers along the railroad, who often challenged the Christian religion successfully. Some Africans who had visited the Moravians once were – according to the files of the mission – socially excluded and returned to their non-Christian fellows. As a local report described: "We Christians are simply half *shenzi*, who worship several Gods and who believe in a crucified saviour (what a folly – upuuzi!) and who do not know God's commandments or do at least not adhere to them",[230] wrote missionary Löbner to the Mission Board in 1913. Although this was written after the actual abandonment of the railway mission by Löbner in 1913, the railway missionary Gaarde reported regularly about similar events during his duty along the railway between 1910 and 1912, illustrating the comparatively low prestige of the Christian religion in central German East Africa.[231] Moreover, the strict views of the Protestant missionaries that condemned polygamy, alcohol consumption and the itinerant lifestyle of seasonal workers either made the Christian converts or Africans living in the missionary environment ultimately abandon the Moravians – or the Moravians themselves excluded the 'sinners'.[232] As a consequence, the Mission board finally felt that they could hardly ever reach a steady flock to missionise and stopped the

---

229 Cf. UAH. MD 1532. "J. N. 87, Löbner an Henning, 4. November 1911". Cf. UAH. MD 1543. Prov.: Missionsdirektion Pert.: Unyamwesi/Tansania Stationsberichte. Bahnmission (Berichte u. Briefwechsel). 1910–1912., "Bericht über den Anfang der Bahnmission (von Oktober bis Ende Dezember 1910)", p. 1.

230 UAH. MD 1544. Berichte der Missionsstation Tabora, "Bericht der Missionsstation Tabora 01. April – 30. Juni 1913", p. 2.

231 Cf. UAH. MD 1543, "Bericht über den Anfang der Bahnmission (Oktober – Ende 1910)", pp. 2–4, "Bericht über die Bahnmission 1. Januar – 31. März 1911", pp. 7–8, "Bericht über die Bahnmission. 1. April – 30. Juni 1911", "Bericht über die Bahnmission (1. Jan. – 31. März 1912)".

232 Cf. UAH. MD 1537. Prov. Missionsdirektion. Stationsberichte. Ipole 1909–1916, "Jahresbericht Ipole 1914", p. 3. Cf. UAH. MD 1539. Missionsdirektion Pert. Unyamwesi. Stationsberichte Kitunda 1909–1918, "Jahresbericht der Station Kitunda 1912", pp. 1–6. Cf. UAH. MD 1541. Missionsdirektion. Unyamwesi. Stationsberichte Urambo 1909–1916, "Bericht der Sation Kilimani Urambo vom Jahre 1909", "Vierteljahresbericht aus Urambo vom 1.IV. – 30.VI.1912", "Vierteljahresbericht von Urambo 1. Juli – 30. September 1912", "Jahresbericht der Station Usoke 1913.", "Erster Vielteljahresbericht 1914 der Station Usoke".

railway mission in favour of traditional forms of missionary work in German East Africa.

Facing these obstacles, the Moravians thus decided to concentrate on Tabora and established a constant mission centre in this central town. From this revived transport hub, the Moravians sought to tackle their most important goals: challenge Islam, consolidate their shortcomings in personnel, missionise the railway workers part-time and become more influential than their Catholic competitors. While the Moravians could comparably easily reach an agreement with other Protestant missions and consolidated their individual sphere of missionary influence,[233] the most important aspect was marking out the spheres of influence against the Catholic mission. Corresponding conflicts were often symbolised by real-estate ownership and the question which denomination would be allotted which area in town. Initially in fear of conflict with the Catholic White Fathers in Tabora, the Moravians shunned any closer discussions. But with the Moravians finally realising that the railway mission could not be sustained and Tabora as such had to be targeted instead, they established closer contacts to the Catholic mission in German East Africa and to the *Gouvernement* to settle the issue by marking out clear-cut spheres of influence. Although not enthusiastic about the Moravian plan to settle permanently in Tabora, the Catholics were aware that they "could not hinder"[234] the Protestants from purchasing real estate in Tabora. As soon as the district commissioner and the *Gouvernement* approved of the Moravians' plan to purchase a plot in Tabora, missionary Löbner was able to move into a stone house in the heart of the railway hub. From there, Löbner himself, alongside former railway missionary Gaarde, attempted to continue their mission to the African railway men and women part-time only, because the construction company *Holzmann* would not allow them to preach to the railway workers while at work. Gaarde and Löbner thus dedicated most of their time to the Moravian mission schools in Tabora, health work, the study of African languages or the erection of churches. As well, they hoped to challenge Islam, of course.[235]

Yet, reaching an agreement with the colonial administration and the Catholic mission were not the only preconditions for the Moravian Mission to the *Central Railway* in German East Africa. What mattered most for the Moravians to genuinely initiate their railway mission was to be on good terms with the railway construction company *Philipp Holzmann*. Generally, the Moravians needed the company's permission to preach to the railway (wo)men working and living along the railroad's con-

233 Cf. UAH MD 1543, "Bericht über den Anfang der Bahmission. Okt-Dez 1910", n.p.
234 UAH. MD 1532, "J.N. 82 Löbner an Henning 10.11.1911".
235 Cf. UAH. MD 1532, "J. N. 87 Löbner an Henning 4. November 1911", "J.N. 82 Löbner an Henning 10.11.1911". Cf. BArch R1001/846, p. 172a, pp. 52–53.

struction sites. Moreover, establishing a mission along the railway also required the construction company's financial assistance to become a reality. As the Moravian Mission financed its endeavours in large part through private donations,[236] constant fundraising was an existential problem for the Moravian board. Hence, as soon as the plan to start a railway mission along the *Central Railway* in German East Africa materialised, Moravian missionary Director Henning turned to the financially strongest company of German East Africa, *Philipp Holzmann,* to fund the railway mission. The monthly wages of the railway missionaries were especially needed, but housing and transportation too required financial means. Having received the Moravian request, *Holzmann's* government building official Riese responded positively and promised 1,000 Marks annually as initial financial assistance for the first two years to help establish the mission. On top, *Holzmann* agreed to assist the missionaries with building their accommodations along the *Central Railway* and granted travel and freight transportation free of charge to any member of the Moravian Mission. Although these financial means granted by *Holzmann's* Riese did not entirely meet the request of the Moravian Henning – who conducted the negotiations on behalf of the Mission's board – and who had asked for 3,000 Marks annually for missionary salaries alone – the railway mission to the new track in German East Africa was only enabled with *Holzmann's* support indeed. Yet, in return for their financial aid, *Holzmann* applied several terms and conditions the Moravians had to observe. First and foremost, the railway mission was strictly not allowed to interfere with the labour supply of the construction company. Indeed, Riese could not be misunderstood in this regard as he wrote to the mission board:

> Complying with your request, we must ask you for your best support regarding our efforts to win and maintain a steady and competent number of good and skilled workers for our endeavour. The extraordinarily high costs for labour recruitment that we now have to pay for each worker obliges us to this request. The loss of any worker, which might be the result of your own efforts, would mean a not unsubstantial financial sacrifice for us.[237]

In other words, *Holzmann's* representative Riese feared increased competition for workers once the railway mission was established. As any mission also required workers, Riese's reservations about competition for African labour were not unjustified. Yet, it appears that *Holzmann* supported the railway mission not

---

236 Donations by church members or wealthy donors. On top, each mission station was also an economic undertaking and had to produce goods that would co-finance the local mission stations. Cf. Arnold. *Steuer und Lohnarbeit*, pp. 23, 231–232. Cf. Hüsgen, Jan. 'Die Herrnhuter Brüdergemeinde als globales Unternehmen'. 13–27. *Zeitschrift für Weltgeschichte,* Jahrgang 14, Heft 1. Berlin: 2013.

237 UAH. MD 1560, "Philipp Holzmann to Moravian Missionary Board (C.O. Henning). J. no. 1045. Frankfurt o.M. 15 December 1909".

for nothing. Rather, the construction company wanted the Moravians to actively support rapid railway construction in return for their (financial) services, as a letter by *Holzmann's* construction officer Hoffman to Moravian missionary Löbner shows. In that letter, Hoffman generally consented with the idea of supporting the railway mission to *Unyamwezi* financially and immaterially, provided that the Moravians would urge the local population to take up railway construction work and treat the matter "discreetly" in general, and further: "We assume that you will not prevent the Vanyamwezi [sic!] people, who have been our best workers so far, to join us for work. We rather hope that you will draw their attention to the benefits of working at the railway."[238] Hence, by investing financial means in the railway mission, the representatives of *Holzmann* sought to turn the tables and to transform the Moravian missionaries from potential competitors for labour into labour recruiters providing the railway constructing company with a skilled and reliable workforce.

In fact, the Moravians had their own agenda regarding the railway mission in German East Africa and did not want to be pocketed in the sense of legwork for *Holzmann*. While the Moravians pledged to generally support railway construction, they shunned fully flung cooperation regarding labour recruitment:

> As I had already ensured you in my letter dating from the 14th of June last year, we will never interfere in labour, but will only urge the people to duty and loyalty; I would like to repeat that for you and I hope, that you will have the experience that those people under our influence will not be of the lowest kind of workers; in this respect you can surely count on our indirect cooperation. I suspect that you will also understand that we will not be able to agree with direct cooperation, e.g., as labour recruiter etc. [sic!], because we must still prefer sedentism and quiet family life for our people. I only mention that to avoid any possible misunderstandings and I am sure that you will not misunderstand my remarks. You can always count on us as an indirect employee [. . .] and we trust in you, as you can always trust in us.[239]

In this respect, the Moravians went along with general policies of 'educating' the African population to work but protected their own missionary agenda at the same time. Of course, this was not entirely to the taste of the construction company and cooled down the mutual relationship between the mission and *Holzmann*. Overall, the Moravian's standpoint did not prevent cooperation with *Holzmann*, but examining the sources of the Moravians, you can notice *Holzmann's* diminishing support. Generally, *Holzmann* kept their principal promises, such as building a house for the railway missionary and transporting him along the railway. But regarding

238 Löbner quotes *Holzmann's* Hoffmann in a letter to Henning. UAH. MD 1532, "J.N.982. Löbner to Henning 01.Nov. 1909". Cf. UAH. MD 1532, "J.N. 622".
239 UAH. MD 1532, "J.N. 334, Abschirft. Löbner an Hoffman. Usoke, den 10. February 1910".

less clearly regulated agreements, the construction company revealed its increasing reservations towards the Moravian railway mission. When railway missionary Gaarde met Building official Ferdinand Grages in Dar es Salaam in autumn 1910 right after his arrival in German East Africa, Grages showed himself very "amiable", but simultaneously explained that he was "sceptical towards the whole affair" of the railway mission. On behalf of *Holzmann*, Grages only paid 375 Rupees of the entire promised missionary's salary (1,000 Rps.) while promising to deliver the rest a few months later "as long as [*Holzmann*] would be still willing to do so".[240] In contrast to Löbner's hopes, the relationship between the Moravians and *Holzmann* was not entirely characterised by mutual trust or support and Gaarde only received transportation free of charge between Dodoma and the railhead (ca. fifty km) but not between Dar es Salaam and Dodoma (ca. 450 km). On top, Gaarde only received transportation free of charge for himself and still had to pay high tariffs for his cargo along the entire track. Moreover, Gaarde's simple housing was still not finished by 3 January 1911, showing that *Holzmann's* support for the Moravians was far from overambitious.[241] Rather, it seems that *Holzmann* put the Moravians under scrutiny for the time being and had no premature praises for the railway mission. The construction company appears to have only supported the railway mission as long as the Moravians would not interfere with their top priority of rapid railway construction and was ready to pull back their support if they felt it necessary.

While both the Moravians and *Holzmann* tried primarily to foster their own major objectives and often held differing views, they also cooperated in many ways. Engineers and other railway personnel regularly visited not only several Moravian missionary stations, but they finally also paid for and erected the missionaries' simple housing along the railway and a mission stone house in Tabora after 1912. When the missionaries approached labour camps of *Holzmann* engineers or any sub-contractors, they were generally welcomed and supported in their mission work. In turn, railway missionary Gaarde limited his devotion to the labour force to the few evening hours after the end of work or to Sundays when there was generally no railway construction work going on. Essentially, the Moravians kept their promise and did indeed not interfere with *Holzmann's* top priorities regarding labour supply.[242] Remarkably, *Holzmann's* engineers also sent their *boys* or other East African personnel to the Moravian railway mission or the mission school in

---

240 UAH. MD 1532, "J.N. 19", p. 5.

241 Cf. UAH. MD. 1532, "J.N. 30", p. 5, "J. N. 356".

242 Cf. UAH. MD 1543, "Bericht über den Anfang der Bahnmission. Oktober bis Ende Dezember 1910.", pp. 2–3. Cf. UAH. MD 1543, "J.N. 338. Bericht über die Bahnmission 1. Januar – 31. März 1911", pp. 5–6. Cf. UAH. MD 1543. "Bericht über die Bahnmission z.Z. Tabora 1.Juli – 30. Sept. 1911",

Tabora for training in a European form of education. Even Clement Gillman, the Anglo-German engineer working for *Holzmann* at the *Central Railway*, who stated in his diary that "one does not notice any effect of the Christian mission to the railway workers", judged Gaarde as an unexpectedly "very nice and humble man". Just as Gaarde proved to be a "welcomed and amiable companion" to Gillman, likewise "Superintendent Löbner" was regarded by the Anglo-German as "very peaceful".[243] It seems that Gaarde too valued Gillman as a person and, although the latter was generally sceptical towards the railway mission, Gillman even sent his personal water carrier, named *Songaleli*, to the mission schools of the Moravians, for training. In this regard, the name of Gillman's water carrier – *Songaleli* – is telltale. In actual fact, not only Gillman employed somebody named *Songaleli*, but the Moravians mention numerous *wasongaleli* ('wa' = plural) employed by *Holzmann* to construct the *Central Railway* in the sources under investigation. In fact, the Swahili word *wasongaleli*[244] means 'those who are installing the rails', and this points to a very important dimension regarding the interrelationship among labour, the Moravian Mission, *Holzmann* and the African agency.[245] Despite contrary contemporary statements stipulated by so-called 'colonial experts' in numerous publications in Germany, former (railway) mission pupils were in high demand as educated workforce at the railway constructing company. Potentially skilled East African workers were significantly sought after by *Philipp Holzmann* not only for the manual task of railway construction, but also for maintaining and operating the newly built railroad. In turn, these skilled East African workers knew very well how to exploit their comparatively strong position in the labour market to find relatively privileged positions in the colonial society. Like Gillman's *Songaleli* – who had probably managed to rise from being a low skilled manual railway worker who literally 'installed the rails' to being the personal servant of one of *Holzmann's* engineers – it appears that many Moravian Christian converts or mission pupils used their newly acquired skills in mission schools wisely, within the disadvantaging colonial labour market.

---

p. 1. Cf. UAH. MD 1542, "Vierteljahresbericht der Station Usoke II. Quartal 1912", n.p. Cf. UAH. MD 1542, "Jahresbericht der Station Usoke 1913", n.p.

243 Gillman Diaries. Mss. Afr. S. 1175/1,2_2, no. 13, p. 40.

244 Swahili Kusonga = (here) install; Swahili leli = reli i.e., rail.

245 Cf. UAH. MD 1543, "Bericht über die Bahnmission (1. Jan. – 31. März 1912)", n.p. Cf. UAH. MD 1543, "Bericht über die Bahnmission. 1. April – 30. Juni 1911", n.p. Cf. UAH. MD 1544, "Bericht der Missionsstation Tabora vom 9. Mai bis 30. Sept. 1912", n.p. Cf. UAH. MD 1544. "Jahresbericht der Missionsstation Tabora für 1912", n.p. Cf. UAH. MD 1544, "Bericht der Missionsstation Tabora 1. April – 30. Juni 1913", p. 2.

3.7.2 (Un-)wanted Workers at the *Central Railway*

> Especially young people who know how to read and write are wanted and in demand as writer, telephone boy etc. At the moment, there are four young Christians from the Usoke community at the railway, and one catechumen as the youngest. Among the first mentioned is even the leper Petelo [. . .]. Who knows, if he will come back one day. Stefan, Musanizi and Jakob are employed as scribe and telephonboy respectively. You can only rejoice that their industriousness and their school education pays-off for them now. Let us hope that they will also have the inner strength to withstand the many dangers and temptations. They need many intercessions.
>
> Report of the Moravian missionary Station Ussoke. July-September 1913.[246]

As a Protestant mission to Africa, the Moravian railway mission was of course not an economic endeavour as such. Economic issues only ranked second. What mattered most to any mission was the number of 'heathen souls' they could convert. Any other efforts such as in education, labour or science were only a means to this end. 'Educating' the local population to work was only properly accomplished if the Christian convert would ultimately take up work and pursue a lifestyle that was agreeable to God and therefore devoid of vices such as alcohol consumption or pursuing worldly things such as money, fame or lust.[247] Yet, as particularly historians of Africa have pointed out, especially the offsprings of the African elite went to (mission) schools in order to equip themselves with the whole arsenal of western education. Realising that the European colonisers had become a power factor that had to be reckoned with, their major goal was to improve their position of power within the political economy of (East) Africa.[248] Moreover, as far as (the Moravian) files can tell, in the context of labour, a great number of the East

246 UAH. MD 1542, "Bericht der Station Ussoke vom Juli bis Sept. 1913", n.p.

247 For the trope of 'educating the colonised to work' cf. Conrad. *Globalisation*, pp. 77–143. Cf. Yekani. *Koloniale Arbeit*, pp. 121–135. Cf. Koponen. *Development*, pp. 355–359.

248 Cf. Lawrence, Benjamin, N. et al. 'Introduction: African Intermediaries and the "Bargain" of Collaboration'. *Intermediaries, Interpreters, and Clerks. African Employees in the Making of Colonial Africa.* 3–36. Eds. Benjamin N. Lawrence et al. Wisconsin: 2006, pp. 3–36. Cf. Klein, Martin. 'African Participation in Colonial Rule: The Role of Clerks, Interpreters and other Intermediaries'. *Intermediaries, Interpreters, and Clerks. African Employees in the Making of Colonial Africa.* 273–288. Eds. Benjamin N. Lawrence et al. Wisconsin: 2006, pp. 273–277. Cf. Jézéquel, Jean-Hervé. '"Collecting Customary Law": Educated Africans, Ethnographic Writings, and Colonial Justice in French West Africa'. *Intermediaries, Interpreters, and Clerks. African Employees in the Making of Colonial Africa.* 139–158. Eds. Benjamin N. Lawrence et al. Wisconsin: 2006, pp. 150–155. For an East African example cf. Iliffe, John. 'The Spokesman. Martin Kayamba'. *Modern Tanzanians. A Volume of Biographies.* 66–94. Ed. John Iliffe. Dar es Salaam: 1973, pp. 66–75.

African people that the mission had regarded as future devout Christians would also individually use the newly acquired skills often learned at the mission schools for their own purposes and often contrarily to the missionaries' intentions. In this respect, people like Dr Karl Oetker, who had worked as head of the *Central Railway*'s medical service between 1905 and 1907, were certainly wrong in claiming that "nobody [wants] to employ the mission pupils, because they are generally lazier, more unreliable, more dishonest and more insubordinate than the other negroes".[249] Taking the perspective of a skilled East African railway worker, they were well aware of their skills or rather their 'human capital'. Consequently, skilled literate men preferred those jobs fitting their profile and rejected manual labour, as railway missionary Gaarde reports:

> Elia from Sikonge [arrived] here to look for work, I was able to get him a job in the local section office. His work mostly consisted of carrying letters to the officials and [sub-]contractors in the section. This occupation suited him very much. However, when he had to push trollies a few times, he was less pleased and urgently wanted to be relieved of this work because it was too heavy for him. I was supposed to help him. But as he was big and strong and also well paid, his request did not seem justified to me. Brother Löbner [. . .] also rebuked him and admonished him not to bring shame upon himself and us. On the second day we learned that he had nevertheless left secretly. [. . .] A few days later, Joshua Maganga came from Sikonge to look for work here as well. Because of the experience I had just had, I had little pleasure in recommending him. He has now taken the place from which Elia left.[250]

Even Oetker's former employer *Philipp Holzmann* had proven to seek the Moravians' assistance to recruit the workforce necessary for railway construction and had attempted to turn the Moravians from missionaries into labour recruiters (see above). In contrast to Oetker's claim, it seems that *Holzmann* and their senior engineers like Clement Gillman happily employed former missionary pupils, not least because of their missionary school education. Ironically, although any Christian convert or former mission pupil migrating for work to the *Central Railway* was a potential 'lost soul' to the Moravians, the missionaries themselves wanted their converts to do their best when working at the construction sites: "The Lord provide for counterevidence challenging the common phrase widespread among numerous Europeans that 'all Christians are slackers and scoundrels'."[251] This wish might have arisen out of the pressure exerted by colonial players like *Holzmann*, who insisted on the priority of railway construction over missionary work.

249 Oetker, Karl früher Leiter des Gesundheitsdienstes beim Bahnbau Daressalam-Morogoro (Ostafrika). *Die Neger-Seele und die Deutschen in Afrika. Ein Kampf gegen Missionen, Sittlichkeits-Fanatismus und Bürokratie vom Standpunkt moderner Psychologie.* Munich: 1907, p. 24.
250 UAH. MD 1543, "Bericht über die Bahnmission (1. Jan. – 31. März 1912)", n.p.
251 UAH. MD 1543, "Bericht über die Bahnmission (1. Jan. – 31. März 1912)", n.p.

But one may also assume that the Moravians attempted to do their best to become 'proper colonisers' themselves. Nevertheless, numerous Moravian missionaries lamented regularly about their mission school pupils leaving the catchment area of a missionary station in order to take up work at the *Central Railway*.

In fact, not all of the people leaving the catchment area of various Moravian missionary stations left for skilled work or because of their school education took better positions at the *Central Railway*. Many of them were simply *wasongaleli* – those who install the rail – and performed simpler, but physically very demanding tasks like shovelling soil at the construction sites. In any case, anybody leaving for work at the *Central Railway* was perceived as a loss for the Moravians. Just like the religion of Islam threatened to allegedly take away their flock, railway work and the life at the construction camps offered many temptations that contradicted Moravian ideals. Just as in the case regarding the *Bahnhofsmissionen* in Europe, the Moravians attempted to save people from modernity and 'modern' licentious vices such as drink, an itinerant lifestyle and a promiscuous sex life. On top of this, worldly strivings, such as earning money only for its own sake, were also regarded as dangerous. This was especially the case when earning money was combined with an itinerant lifestyle like labour migration to the *Central Railway*. Such a mobile lifestyle contradicted the Moravian ideal of sedentary families living and working together close to their homes. In contrast, labour migration had long been common in *Unyamwezi* where many men regularly left their homes for seasonal work as porters or plantation workers at the coast or to sell their products at trading hubs like Tabora. In this respect, taking up railway work or seeking the newly establishing sales markets along the railway line appears to have merely been an adaptation of the (pre-colonial) Wanyamwezi tradition of labour migration.[252] It is therefore not surprising that every missionary station reported about numerous, generally rather young, predominantly men but also women leaving the corresponding Moravian mission region for work at the railway. The official annual report of the Moravian Mission stated in 1912 for the region of *Unyamwezi*:[253]

252 Cf. UAH. MD 1541, "Vierteljahresbericht aus Urambo vom 1. IV. – 30.IV.1912", "Vierteljahresbericht von Urambo. 1. Juli – 30. September 1912". Cf. Gottberg. *Unyamwesi*, pp. 51–92. Cf. Koponen. *People and Production*, pp. 81–125, 360–391. Cf. Rockel, Stephen. *Carriers of Culture. Labor on the Road in Nineteenth-Century East Africa*. Portsmouth: 2006, pp. 229–236. Cf. Greiner, Andreas. 'Permanente Krisen. Opposition, Kooperation und Konkurrenz ostafrikanischer Träger in europäischen Expeditionen'. *Der Träger. Zu einer 'tragenden' Figur der Kolonialgeschichte*. 181–204. Eds. Sonja Malzner and Anne D. Peiter. Bielefeld: 2018, pp. 181–187. Cf. Reichart. *Gari*, pp. 58–72, 89–93.

253 Cf. UAH. MD 1537, "Jahresbericht Ipole des Jahres 1914", pp. 4–5, "Vierteljahresbericht von Ipole [?] – 30. September 1915 (Abschrift)", p. 2.

> The year of 1912 means the beginning of a new era for the Mission's area. The Central Railway's construction sites had reached Tabora by February 26th. [. . .] Labour, i.e., the opportunity to earn more money than ever before, and to enjoy this money more than ever before, was the idea that captured a world which had been suddenly touched by civilisation. At once, everything was different than before. The quiet missionary stations were also touched by these waves of the new era. [. . .] The people appeared to have been captured by the only thought of making money. Many left the station secretly.[254]

In general, many reports of local missionary stations confirmed the statement of this official report published in 1912.[255] Particularly skilled workers, who had studied at mission schools and/or knew how to read and write, were happily employed by *Holzmann* or the *OAEG*. In June 1913, Neu Langenburg's District Officer Stier informed the *OAEG* that "people who can read and write often come here and ask for proof of work opportunities as *Kerani* [here: office clerk] and the like" and enquired "whether there is any use for such applicants in the establishment there and to where they may be sent".[256] In the course of the *Central Railway*'s construction, *Holzmann* increasingly replaced skilled Indians with educated East Africans – in the roles of "acolyte, telephone operator, office boy, track mail carrier, stoker, brakeman, track worker and assistant for the European craftsmen",[257] as remembered by *Holzman's* building officer Ferdinand Grages. Thus, the *OAEG* Operation Director's answer to District Officer Stier in summer 1913 does not come as a surprise: although "Indians, Arabs and Baluchis [. . .]"[258] also remained potential employees for the railways, the company was "ready to hire any native who can write. Above all, [they] lack[ed] natives who can read, write and speak German." Therefore, the *OAEG* asked "to send these people equipped with an identity card to our centre in Tabora"[259] where they would receive employment immediately.

In this respect, it is striking that skilled workers were in such high demand that *Holzmann* even employed a seriously ill man like the abovementioned leper Petelo to meet their labour needs. Former mission school pupils of other denominations were quickly employed as skilled workers at the *Central Railway* as well.

254 BArch R1001/846, pp. 172a, p. 150.

255 Cf. UAH. MD 1530, "Jahresbericht 1908", n.p. Cf. UAH. MD 1539, "Bericht von der Station Kidunda 1. Juni-30. Sept. 1912", p. 7. Cf. UAH. MD 1539, "Jahresbericht der Station Kitunda 1912", pp. 1, 6.

256 RMN. GTF. R3. S8. Direktion. Behörden. Betriebsdirektion, "J. no. 2004/1913. Kaiserliches Bezirksamt Neu Langenburg".

257 Stadtarchiv Frankfurt. W1/2 – 278/1. *Grages*, p. 7.

258 RMN. GTF. R3. S8, "an das Kaiserliche Gouvernement, 7.2.14, 2690/14 II.B.".

259 RMN. GTF. R3. S8, "An das Kaiserliche Bezirksamt Neu-Langenburg von Betriebs Direktor DOAEG, 14. v. Mts. 2004/13".

This applies not only to the Moravians' Catholic competitors in German East Africa, but to many other former mission pupils not only from within the German colony, but also from the neighbouring colonies. While many skilled workers employed at the *Central Railway* had been educated by the Benedictines in coastal Dar es Salaam or near to central *Iringa* (probably the missionary station in Tosamaganga), many Moravian missions report about East African Catholic and Protestant converts who had come to the railway in the German colony as craftsmen from Uganda or as far as Livingstone in British Rhodesia.[260] In this respect, the statement of *Holzmann's* building official Ferdinand Grages about the gradual replacement of Indian craftsmen working at the *Central Railway* by African employees has to be modified to a certain extent: not only German colonial (missionary) school education provided the skilled African workers needed at the *Central Railway*, but also skilled workers from the neighbouring colonies came to work at the railroad's construction sites in German East Africa. Moreover, the migration of (skilled) East African Christian converts and mission pupils was not limited to the German colony. Quite the contrary: some files report that Moravian mission pupils also left the Moravian missions in German East Africa for the Congo, Rhodesia or British Nyassaland.[261]

Sometimes the Moravians were even themselves the beneficiaries of the African skilled workers' expertise despite their fear of 'railway modernity'. Having received European training, e.g. as craftsmen at the Moravian schools, the former mission pupils had not only enhanced their local knowledge by western school education, but they also broadened their skills in various kinds of construction at the labour camps of the *Central Railway*. To the surprise of the European Moravian missionaries, if coming back to the missionary stations, some former railway workers also applied their recently acquired expertise in the catchment areas of the mission:

> The helpers of the outposts have built a dead straight road from the school to the missionary station through their pupils without any impulse on our behalf. [. . .] Our helpers of the outposts also proposed road construction. That is also why a straight road has emerged from here to Ipembe. People who had been acolytes at the railway pegged them.[262]

Unfortunately, the files do not provide the actual reasons why the Moravian helpers took the initiative themselves to construct roads in close cooperation with retur-

260 Cf. UAH. MD 1543, "Bericht über den Anfang der Bahnmission (Oktober bis Ende Dezember 1910)", p. 4, "Jahresbericht über die Bahnmission 1. Jan – 31. Dez. 1911", n.p. Cf. Reichart. *Gari*, p. 48.
261 Cf. UAH. MD 1544, "Bericht der Missionsstation Tabora 1. April – 30. Juni 1912", pp. 1–2.
262 UAH. MD 1539, "Jahresbericht der Station Kitunda 1912", pp. 6–7.

nees from the railway. It is however certain that many East Africans in touch with the Moravians used their skill and contacts wisely to eke out advantages in the racist colonial environment and often led lives that did not necessarily fit the ideals of the Moravians.[263] With the Moravians disapproving anybody who pursued worldly things such as striving for money as such, an excessive lifestyle that included feasts, alcohol consumption and extramarital sexuality, the labour camps at the *Central Railway* – sometimes peopled by several hundred men and women – were seen as a threat to the missionary work of the Moravians. In contrast to the Christian ideals, all these so-called immoral things were common parts of daily life in any larger labour camp in German East Africa not only at the *Central Railway*, but also at large scale plantations, for example. Needless to say, also most of the Moravian mission school pupils spent their wages earned at the railway construction sites according to their own wishes – and as a matter of fact these preferences often contradicted the commandments of the Moravians.[264]

In any case, working at the *Central Railway* was not necessarily a merely 'voluntary' affair for most of the Moravian missionary pupils or those people who lived in the catchment areas of a missionary station. Among other reasons, paying colonial taxes was a decisive incentive for many East Africans to prefer railway work over many other forms of employment.[265] Attempting to meet the demanded amount of taxes as quickly as possible, East African 'taxpayers' tended to

---

263 For African strategies to cope with German colonial agitation and the introduction of the railways in general cf. Sunseri. '"Dispersing"'.

264 Sunseri. *Vilimani*, pp. 136–164. Cf. Reichart. *Gari*, pp. 42–72. Cf. UAH. MD 1544, "Jahresbericht der Missionsstation Tabora für 1912", n.p. UAH. MD 1537, "Jahresbericht Ipole des Jahres 1914 (Abschrift)", p. 3, "Vierteljahresbericht Ipole, 17. 6.[?] – 30. September 1915 (Abschrift)", p. 2. Cf. UAH. MD 1539, "Bericht der Station Kidunda 1. Juni – 30. Sept. 1912", n.p. Cf. UAH. MD 1541, "Vierteljahresbericht aus Urambo vom 1.IV. – 30. VI.1912", n.p., "Vierteljahresbericht von Urambo. 1. Juli – 30. September 1912", n.p. Cf. UAH. MD 1542, "Jahresbericht der Station Usoke 1913", n.p., "Erster Vierteljahresbereicht 1914 der Station Usoke", n.p. Cf. UAH. MD 1530. Jahresbericht der Provinz Sikonge 1906–1940, "Jahresbericht 1908", n.p. Cf. UAH. MD 1547–1533. Stationsbriefwechsel versch. Stationen. 3. Kitunda, "Bruder Jonathan and Bruder Hartmann. Mpapua Mai 30 1908", n.p.

265 For a general assessment of why East Africans – especially Wanyamwezi – preferred railway work over other colonial employments like plantation work cf. Iliffe. *A Modern History*, pp. 137, 157–158, 161. Koponen denies the voluntary character of railway work, claiming that tax work was, in effect, also a form of forced labour cf. Koponen. *Development*, pp. 410–413. Cf. Reichart. *Gari*, pp. 47–57. Also cf. Sunseri. *Vilimani*, pp. 165–193. Cf. Sunseri. '"Dispersing"', pp. 558–583. An assessment of the issue by District Commissioner Sperling of Mpapua cf. BArch. R155F 81413 Pos., "Jahresbericht für das Bezirksamt Mpapua für das Berichtsjahr 1908/1909", pp. 15–18. Cf. Rösser, Michael. *Forced Labour in 'German East Africa'. Between 'Colonial Amnesia' and Structural Similarities to WWI in Europe*. Regensburg: 2015. (unpublished *Zulassungsarbeit* (thesis)), p. 41.

prefer those employers paying the highest salaries, of course. Consequently, the Moravian Mission as an employer often found itself in wage competition with *Holzmann* and repeatedly lost out in this race in various regions,[266] but particularly in *Unyamwezi*, as an annual report of the mission post Urambo illustrates:

> It is painful; it is discouraging! [. . .] [I thought] it was perhaps possible to keep the people if we were able to offer them work. As the rainy season had been so bad and as famine was to be feared, we provided for work. But what happened? Many went to the coast or to the railway all the same.[267]

Yet, sometimes also *Holzmann* themselves could not compete with better wages offered elsewhere for skilled labour. Records show that some left railway work for employment at an Indian's construction site, as the Indian employer paid the high wages of "1 Rp. a day".[268] But the East African 'taxpayers' in the catchment area of the Moravian missionary stations did not limit their strategies to obtain higher wages to voting by foot. When employed at the missionary stations they also sought to meet their demands by withdrawing their labour, as an internal letter correspondence between the mission posts reveal: "They [the East African mission pupils] refused to come back to work after yesterday's wage payment. They held the view that they had received too little."[269] Despite such disagreements, many East Africans living and working in the catchment area of the Moravian missionary stations also used the Protestant missions as strongholds to protect themselves against raids by the colonial administration and labour recruiters who quasi-kidnapped workers for various construction tasks at the *Central Railway*.

3.7.3 Moravian Missionary Stations and Labour Recruiters: Refuge or Training Ground?

> [. . .] There is no legal limit to what the government can or cannot demand. Direct taxes don't mean much. But no black person [. . .] can be sure that he will not be called upon to

266 Cf. Arnold. *Steuer und Lohnarbeit*, pp. 181–210.

267 UAH. MD 1541, "A. Seibt Kilimani-Urambo, 14 January 1910. Annual Report of the mission station Urambo of the year 1909". Cf. UAH. MD 1541, "Vierteljahresbericht von Urambo 1. Juli – 30. September 1912", n.p. Cf. UAH. MD 1557. Missionsdirektion Unyamwesi. Schriftwechsel mit dem Kaiserlichen Gouverneur und dem Kaiserlichen Bezirksamt in Tabora 1900–1927, "Löbner an das Kaiserliche Bezirksamt Tabora, Sikonke, den 20. Juni 1910, J.N. 745", n.p., "Antwort des Bezirksamtes. V. Gross an Löbner. Tabora, den 22. Juni 1910", n.p.

268 UAH. MD 1532, "J.N. 79 Empf. 23. Nov. Bent. 14. Dez Z.z. Usoke, d. 14 Oktober 1911.".

269 UAH. MD 1547–1533, "J.N.: 563. 27. Konferenz. 10. Dezember 1909", n.p.

> do some drudgery for which he receives nothing, and this indirect tax makes everything insecure for them. Maybe they have to cut wood for the boma or build or carry loads. The boma sends to some king: Get us some 100 men [. . .]. The king then sends his men out and at night they surround some villages and lead the men away bound to their work. They don't go voluntarily as there is no pay for them, and when the king's men come during the day, they hide. But what should the king do, he has to deliver the people. Can one be surprised then if the men emigrate, no! [. . .] The government has protected the blacks against labour recruiters and planters, but has forgotten to protect [the people from] the government itself. [. . .] [W]hen the men are gone, they take the women. [. . .] We lack a law that gives a certain limit to what can be demanded by the government. [. . .] And in the same way, the government would have to pay its workers. [. . .]
>
> Moravian Missionary Löbner to Mission Board. Usoke, 3 January 1910.[270]

Löbner characterises tax work by highlighting coercion, corporal punishments, (absent) colonial wages, the process of labour recruitment, colonial governance and the role of the chiefs. Further, he also illustrates African workers' agency, their means to resistance and their demands for better working conditions. All these aspects are highly relevant for the relationship between the Moravian missionary stations and the people living in their catchment areas. Like many other regions, the Moravian missionary stations and their surrounding areas were targets for both governmental *Askari* searching for tax workers and also for labour recruiters seeking future railway or plantation workers.[271] Despite the fact that especially skilled mission pupils appear to have actively sought employment at the railway construction sites, e.g. as craftsmen or office workers, a large number of people living in the surroundings of the Moravians sought and found refuge at the missionary posts when threatened by coercion to work. Whether those seeking refuge at the missions were predominantly unskilled and comparatively poor men and women, as Captain Styx for the military station of Iringa, suggests is not entirely clear, but plausible.[272] In any case, East African men and women used the Moravian mission posts to escape either coerced governmental or railway work.

Regarding unpaid and coerced work for the colonial government, the local population not only resisted by fleeing to hidden or distant places, but they also made use of the special status of the missions in the colonial society. Having ar-

270 UAH. MD 1532, "Löbner to Henning, Usoke d. 3 Januar 1910". *Boma* (Swahii) = lit. fortress/here: German colonial stronghold and/or centre of administration.
271 e.g. district reports and files of the region of Unyamwezi, Uhehe, Ungoni. BArch. R155F/81406 Neg. Jahresberichte 1908. Ssongea, Tabora, Mahenge. Cf. BArch. R155F/81414 Pos. Jahresberichte 1908. Mpapua, Morogoro, Muansa u. Shirati.
272 Cf. BArch. R155F/81414 Pos. Jahresberichte Iringa, p. 42.

rived decades before the colonial state, the missions originally obtained executive and judiciary functions on their estates. The German colonial administration only gradually assumed these legal competencies, declaring the East African territory as *'Schutzgebiet'* in 1885 and taking further steps in the aftermath of the 1890 Anglo-German Agreement. However, the missions openly challenged the administration's competencies at least until 1911, and if disagreements occurred, influential lobbies often backed the Protestant missions in the colonial metropole. If a Protestant mission originated from another country, Berlin often feared international conflicts with other European powers; if Catholic, the *Reich* feared the Vatican might intervene.[273] As a result, the colonial administration had to respect a certain amount of missionary autonomy and the local East African populations understood how to use this missionary autonomy to their own advantage. As Löbner points out in his statement about labour recruitment, local African authorities acting on behalf of the German colonial administration – such as Chiefs, *Jumbes* or Sultans – were often pressured to deliver up their villagers to work for the colonial government. With the *Gouvernement* having declared services such as *boma* building or road construction to be 'public works' as early as 1896, it demanded this work without any pay.[274] Naturally, the local population tended to evade any forced labour measures. According to the legislation of German East Africa, people residing on Moravian real estate – and that of other missions – were exempt from 'public works'. It is therefore not surprising that many people targeted for governmental forced labour resisted and sought refuge at Moravian missionary stations:

> It is a pleasing sign [. . .] that many people have recently requested to settle on our station ground. Once, the influx was so high that I had to cancel. The Sultan had great difficulty to keep his people for road construction, indeed; many had fled him. Many of those runaways asked for accommodation on our land. It was instantly clear what they wanted. According to all legislations, once on our land, they would be exempt from any work for the Sultan. When called to work, one was even so eager that he straight away demolished the house

---

273 Cf. Sippel. 'Mission und Gewalt', pp. 528–534.

274 For the Mwanza region cf. Itandala, Buludu. 'African Response to German Colonialism in East Africa: The Case of Ussukuma, 1890–1918'. 3–29. *Ufahamu. A Journal of African Studies*, no. 20, 1. UCLA: 1 January 1992. Web. https://escholarship.org/uc/item/7nh0x2p1 (21 November 2019), pp. 8–24. Cf. Oxford. Bodleian Library. Micr. Afr. 446. Service in German East Africa & Germany Foreign Office 1902–1933. Extracts Gunzert, pp. 41–45. Cf. Rösser, Michael. 'Juristisches Seminar. Theodor von Gunzert'. *Koloniale-spuren-heidelberg.de.* Web. http://www.koloniale-spuren-heidelberg.de/juristisches-seminar-theodor-gunzert/#1478787905103-829876ab-548d761b-259b8d7e-2b64 (5 December 2017). Regarding the Moravians cf. UAH. MD 1557, "Löbner an das Kaiserliche Bezirksamt Tabora. Sikonge, den 20. Juni 1910. J.N. 745". Cf. BArch. R155F/81414 Pos., "Jahresbericht Iringa", pp. 4–5.

> which he had just built the year before and asked me to erect another on the mission ground. (By the way, this road construction was ordered by the Gouvernement; the Sultans had the order to provide for the people and to supervise the work.)[275]

But the local populations surrounding the Moravian missionary posts could not only avoid coerced governmental work by using the relative autonomy of the missions; occasionally, the mission also offered a place of retreat when labour recruiters targeting potential workers for the *Central Railway* raided the areas.[276] Sometimes even the protection of the Moravians did not deter unscrupulous labour recruiters, as the Moravian Hartmann in Kitunda stated: "Once a Greek even took the people [. . .] by force out of their villages on the mission ground at night. We resisted and mostly set the people free. Back then, mistreatments occurred every day."[277] As it was difficult for labour recruiters to exert violence on potential workers in the Moravian sphere of influence, they increasingly replaced the stick by the carrot. Instead of physical coercion, they thus attempted to win the potential workers' hearts by extravagant promises, extra payments, *pombe* evenings and feasts including the provision of concubines on the eve of departure to the railway construction sites.[278] In fact, although many East African men and women fled to Moravian missionary stations to evade any form of coerced labour, it is far too simple to regard the Moravian missionary posts as merely places of refuge for the local African population. Moreover, the missionaries themselves may not only be regarded as the advocates or protectors of the local population against (violent) labour recruiters *per se*. As with most aspects regarding the global history of labour, the case of the Moravians and their relationship to labour recruiters and potential workers was much more complex.

275 UAH. MD 1541, "Vierteljahresbericht von Urambo vom 1. Juli – 30. September 1912", n.p. For a governmental confirmation of the legislations cf. UAH. MD 1557, "Kaiserliches Bezirksamt and Löbner. J. No. 1264. Tabora, den 9. Juli 1908".

276 Occasionally, the Moravians also sued violent labour recruiters. Cf. UAH. MD 1542, "Vierteljahresbericht von Usoke Januar – März 1910", n.p. Cf. UAH MD 1532, "Löbner an Henning. J.N. 533. Usoke, 16. März 1910", pp. 3–4. Cf. UAH. MD 1557, "Kaiserliches Bezirksamt an Löbner. J. no. 1264. Tabora, den 9. Juli 1908", n.p. Cf. UAH. MD 1530. Jahresberichte der Provinz Sikonge 1906–1940, "Jahresbereicht 1908", n.p.

277 UAH. MD 1547–1533, "Hartmann an Löbner. J.N. 650. Kitunda-Kiwere, d. 21.IV.10.", n.p. There were even incidents when missionaries threatened labour recruiters or chiefs by the use of firearms. Cf. UAH. MD 1532, "J.N. 658 Empf. 24.VI.10 Beant. 27.VII.10. Sikonge, 5. Mai 1910".

278 Cf. UAH. MD 1547–1533, "Hartmann an Löbner. J.n. 650. Kitunda-Kiwere, d. 21.IV.10.", n.p. Cf. UAH. MD 1540. Missionsdirektion Unyamwesi/Tansania. Stationsberichte 4. Sikonge. 1909–1917, "Jahresbericht von Sikonge-Ngulu 1913", n.p. Cf. UAH. MD 1547–1533, "Hartmann an Henning. J. N. 650. Kitunda-Kiwere, d. 21.IV.10", n.p. Cf. UAH. MD 1542, "Bericht der Station Usoke vom Juli bis Sept. 1913", n.p.

Although generally regarded as a nuisance by the missionaries, at times the Moravians tolerated the presence of labour recruiters on their grounds and sometimes also cooperated with them when they visited their posts, like in the case of Usoke in 1912: "We had a lot of guests recently. They were mostly engineers, who are working at the railway. [. . .] A Greek, I have forgotten his name, was also [?] welcomed [?]."[279] One Moravian missionary, like a certain Brother Richter, was even employed directly by *Holzmann* and once used his position to support the Moravians by delivering porters needed for the railway mission.[280] Moreover, the sources report about former East African mission school pupils who became labour recruiters themselves and even resided on the territory of the Moravians in Urambo: "Labour recruiters have plied their dreadful trade here again, unfortunately. Two had been trained here or rather in Kitunda, a certain Makweja and a certain Julemo. And the first type resides on our property. Again, many have fallen victim to their pretentions [and left for work at the *Central Railway*]."[281] Whether 'victims of their pretentions' or of overt physical violence, or even in the case of voluntary labour migration to the *Central Railway*, Africans still decisively shaped their workplaces in the colonial environment – always trying to accomplish their own preferences.

3.8 Labour and Everyday Life at the *Central Railway*'s Construction Sites

3.8.1 The Colonial Order of a Construction Camp

Taking a closer look on the construction of the *Central Railway*, it must be stressed that there was no such thing as one single construction site. In fact, there were several construction sites. As up to 200 km of track were at times simultaneously under construction, many construction camps were scattered along the line. Their populations varied from a few hundred to 5,000. Except for the camps of the senior engineers and civil servants – who lived in the central building or traffic hubs like Tabora and therefore had their own casino, hospital and other leisure facilities – ordinary engineers like the abovementioned Clement Gillman

279 Cf. UAH. MD 1547–1533, "Hartmann and Henning. J.N. 650. Kitunda-Kiwere, d. 21.IV.10", n.p. UAH. MD 1542, "Vierteljahresbericht der Sation Usoke II. Quartal 1912", n.p.

280 Cf. UAH. MD 1543, "Bericht über den Anfang der Bahnmission (Oktober bis Ende Dezember 1910)", p. 2.

281 UAH. MD 1541, "Vierteljahresbericht von Urambo vom 1. Januar – 31. März 1910.", n.p. Cf. UAH. MD 1544, "Bericht der Missionsstation Tabora vom 9. Mai bis 30. Sept. 1912", n.p.

or sub-contractors ranking below lived a rather lonely camp life as far as interaction with other Europeans was concerned. They established themselves close to their workers, living in temporary accommodation like tents or mud houses and were responsible for the construction of an individual railroad section, the latter being ca. ten km long.[282] Despite the comparatively small size of each construction camp, their topography appears to have resembled that of larger colonial settlements: at least as long as Clement Gillman's sketches and descriptions of his construction camp can be regarded as representative examples. According to the ideal image of all European colonial powers, any colonial settlement should reflect the prevailing racial hierarchy in the colony: the *white* European colonisers would not only occupy the most privileged spots, but they would also move into the most prestigious houses made of the most prestigious construction materials, ideally stone. The second rank areas and housing were reserved for Arabs, Indians or Eurasians whereas the local African population were allotted the outskirts of any colonial settlement and intended to live in simple mud or grass houses.[283] Although a railway engineer's life away on a job lacked the luxuries of major colonial cities, the detailed sketches and descriptions in Clement Gillman's diary about his first construction camps, at railway km thirty-nine and km forty-five, illustrate that the Anglo-German engineer did indeed attempt to reflect the colonial hierarchy in his small temporary settlements too. Whether Gillman did this consciously or unconsciously is not clear as the engineer gives no explicit information about this in his diary. Remarkably, the racial allotment of his construction camp erected in 1905 coincides with his research on Dar es Salaam's racial topography during the British colonial period in 1945.[284] Moreover, Gillman's construction camp architecture contributes to a better understanding of everyday life at a construction camp of the *Central Railway*.

Having received an order by his *Holzmann* superiors to move from km thirty-nine forward to km forty-five early in the morning on 9 November 1905, Gillman spotted a suitable place for his new camp immediately. While six of his workmen were left at this very spot to erect the first storage sheds needed, Gillman himself went the few kilometres back to the railhead in order to fetch construction material for the railway, and his future camp, of course. Finally arriving at km forty-

---

282 Cf. Reichart. *Gari*, pp. 42–43. Cf. Gillman Diaries. Mss. Afr. S. 1175/1,2_1, no. 9, pp. 4–6, 8–10.

283 Cf. Müllendorff. *Ost-Afrika*, pp. 77–88. Cf. Gillman Diaries, Mss. Afr. S. 1175/1,2_1 no. II, pp. 76–79. Cf. Seifert, Annika and Moon, Karen (Eds.). *Dar es Salaam. A History of Urban Space and Architecture*. DARCH, Dar Centre for Architectural Heritage. Dar es Salaam: 2017, pp. 27–74. Cf. Boonen and Lagate. 'A City', pp. 51–69. Cf. Stoyke. 'Suche'. For segregation when on train or travel cf. Beese. *Experten*, pp. 207–222.

284 Cf. Gillman. 'Dar es Salaam', pp. 15–19.

five, with 200 men who had physically carried all this material, the first task for his African workmen was to clear the place from bush to have an open space of twenty-five metre around what would be the engineer's hut in the very middle of the camp. This privileged position in the middle of the camp was further enhanced by a mango tree right next to Gillman's hut, protecting him from the tropical sun. In his direct neighbourhood were settled is personal servants, who would make his camp life agreeable: the *boys'* hut and the kitchen as well as provisions like a henhouse or a mule stable were only a few metres away from the engineer's domicile and arranged parallelly to his building. Shortly after the initial erection of the camp, the European sphere was enhanced by an extra bathing hut and a W.C. for the engineer. Moreover, an *Askari* who served primarily for Gillman's personal protection resided close to the engineer whenever the latter felt his authority threatened. In addition, the *Askari* executed corporal punishments imposed on workers and further functioned as deterrence for the entire workforce against slackening the reins of work discipline. If no *Askari* was present, Gillman dealt out corporal punishments himself. A small path led away from

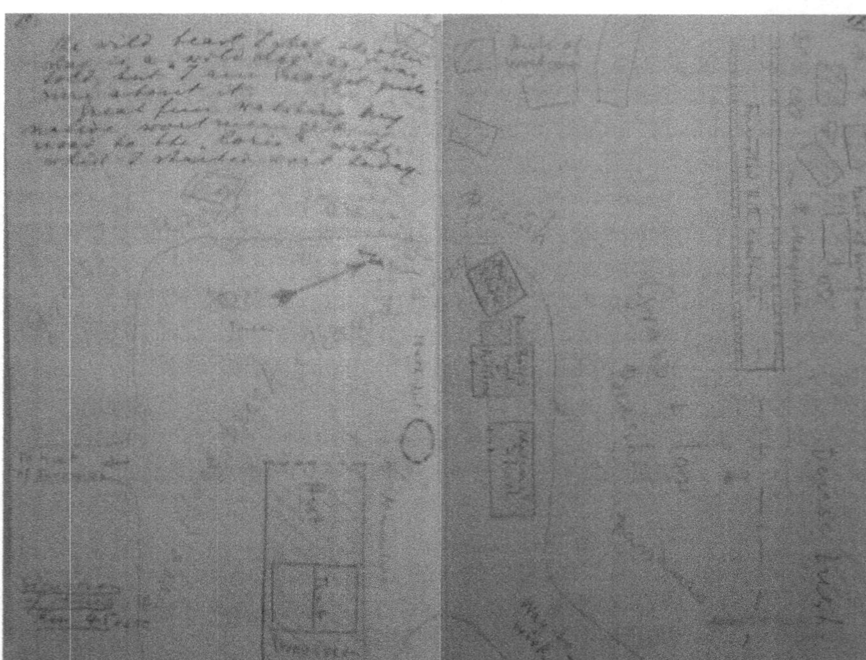

Figure 3: Gillman's sketch of his construction camp at km 45, Nov. 1905.
Source: Oxford, Bodleian Libraries, Gillman Diaries, MSS. Afr. S. 1175/ 1,2_1, no. 9, pp. 16–17.

Figure 4: English: "Grass huts of railway workers, no. 458".
Source: BBWA U5/03/17, Nr. 181, Bildarchiv der Philipp Holzmann AG / Hauptverband der Deutschen Bauindustrie e.V. im Berlin-Brandenburgischen Wirtschaftsarchiv.

Gillman's dwelling and went southwards to "the hut of [the] foreman", an Italian, who appears to have had a colleague from Montenegro living nearby.[285] This is where the sphere for Europeans-only ended, and another began.

The cleared rectangular enclave of symmetrically arranged simple buildings was surrounded by banana plants and "grass and low bush", which separated the European area from the accommodations for the ca. 200 African workers. Erected rather haphazardly compared to the European camp area, the latter lived in simple grass huts right next to the current construction works of "finished R[ail] R[oad] cuttings", "mango trees" as well as "dense bush". Finally, Gillman's sketch only reports of African "work*men*" (my italics), not mentioning the presence of any (African) women.[286] In analogy to the 'double geography' of Gillman's diary writing and the research results about the topography of colonial towns, the arrangement of Gillman's construction camp at the *Central Railway* reflected the colonisers' needs to structure a colonial territory according to racial hierarchies intended for

285 Cf. Gillman Diaries. Mss. Afr. S. 1175/1,2_1, no. 9, pp. 6–17, 24–25, 52–53, 62–64, 70.
286 Gillman Diaries. Mss. Afr. S. 1175/1,2_1, no. 9, pp. 14–17, cf. pp. 6–17, 52–53, 62–64, 70.

the entire society of German East Africa. *White*, middle-class and Middle Europeans held the privileged position centring the entire construction camp. In their direct environment were private servants doing the care work necessary for the Europeans' daily needs and well-being and therefore the sustenance of their engineering work. Southern Europeans, like Gillman's Italian foreman, occupied the next best position in the camp, but still apart from *white* colonial elites characterising them as white subalterns. Separated from this symmetrically ordered European sphere by the extensions of wild nature and close to the 'wild and uncivilised' "dense bush" lived the African workers. In this respect, the position of their housing in the construction camp reflected the colonisers' view of Africans as being an 'uncivilised' and 'wild' people. Moreover, with the African workmen living right next to the actual construction site of the railway, their housing position further reflects which role the colonisers intended to assign the colonised African population. The Africans were merely regarded and valued as workers whose major purpose was to make the colonial endeavour profitable for the German colonisers.[287]

Working at the *Central Railway* was similarly intended to follow the ideal typical image of 'modern' work, which followed the principles of an industrialised and efficient work ethos. Germans writing and publishing about these construction sites generally emphasised their 'proper' organisation and regulation, of both housing and labour. When engineers like Gillman had completed the necessary paper and survey work, the track was subsequently pegged and ready for the preparatory works preceding actual construction. Ferdinand Grages describes works like those underway at the time when Gillman sketched the scene of his construction camp: "I remember clearly [. . .] how [. . .] the future track was driven in its entire width through steppe, bushes, and forests and how grass, bushes and forests were burnt down, trunks cut down and how the trunks' roots were removed through cauterisation." Afterwards, a big variety of construction work had to be done. As soon as the work train had reached the railhead, the workers had to carry the construction material to its destination first before other tasks followed:

> I [remember], how the work trains unloaded at the railhead, how the sleepers were laid on the planum and how the rails were fixed and adjusted there. I [remember] how the workers undid the soil with their pickaxes, shovelled it into raffia baskets, carried it to the installation location on their shoulders, dumped it on the dams and hammered it on them if necessary. [. . .] At rocky sections, I [remember] how the workers crush stone, how they carry it to the planum later in order to plug the track. [. . .] Further, I [remember] how [they] erected [. . .] scaffolds for bridges and passages and how the workers dragged over stones, concrete,

287 Cf. Methner. *Unter drei*, pp. 338–339.

> sand and water; I [remember] how the masonry grew steadily and how iron beams were installed and set in concrete.[288]

As detailed as Grages' picture-book description of one of the *Central Railway*'s construction sites might appear at first glance, it not only excludes numerous details of the construction work, but also the genuine perspective of the African workers and the overall circumstances of living and working at the *Central Railway*'s construction sites in German East Africa. These are examined in the following section.

3.8.2 Labour and Coercion at the Construction Sites

> [My father] said, he worked with them [the Germans] when they were laying the central train coming to Mwanza here. He worked with them, but it was only two weeks. [. . .] He carried all these things [. . .]. He carried the iron bars. He said it was a very strong work. [. . .] The German did not want to have some time to smoke. There was no things like that. [. . .] He was working for little payment. You know how they were doing, they were coming and they were taking people without asking them. The very young and strong people. They were taken to work. [. . .] When it was work, it was time for work. [. . .]. They were forced. The chief can gather some strong persons [. . .]. During those time the Chief was like a God. If you were caught by the Chief you cannot resist. No. You go. So, the German came to take them from the Chief. [. . .] So, they were going without knowing where they are going to. [. . .] There were other people who tried to escape and run away. When they were caught, they were given strokes. This was the punishment. Twenty strokes and then you do not escape again and go away.[289]
>
> Reverend John*. Mwanza, 8 September 2016.

In 2016, John*, an Anglican Reverend and Tanzanian resident born in 1944, recalled the memories of his father, who worked at the *Central Railway*'s extension to Ruanda at the end of the German colonial period. Although oral history sources have various shortcomings and John*'s utterances are 'second-hand' information only, they touch upon significant aspects of labour at the *Central Railway*'s construction site. John* not only mentions the various types of colonial labour and their duration, but also illustrates coercion, corporal punishments, (low) colonial wages, the process of labour recruitment, colonial governance and the role of the chiefs. Further, he also illustrates African workers' agency, their means of resis-

---

288 Grages, Ferdinand. 'Holzmann in Afrika'. *Philipp Holzmann Aktiengesellschaft im Wandel von Hundert Jahren. 1849–1949.* 285–298. Ed. Hans Meyer-Heinrich. Frankfurt o.M.: 1949, p. 296.

289 Interview with Reverend John*. Mwanza: 08/09/16, 1:14:20 – 1:20:41. * = name changed due to privacy reasons.

tance and their demands for better working conditions. Of course, labour was the most important aspect which structured the daily experience of the workers. Although Clement Gillman's sketch of a labour camp and Ferdinand Grages' memories quoted in the previous section give an initial idea about how a construction camp might have looked, and which types of work were performed there, they are nevertheless only the genuine perspectives of two individual colonisers and reflect their ideal typical image of what daily life at a *Central Railway*'s construction camp should look like. Investigating further on the issue, it becomes clear that these perspectives veil as many aspects as they initially reveal.

Although Grages mentions many tasks of skilled construction work, for instance, the special issue of skilled labour and the important role of Indian and African craftsmen do not appear clearly in his documents. Gillman's sketch does similarly neither feature craftsmen nor their presence at the construction camp. Recalling the many difficulties of obtaining enough craftsmen through either 'coolie recruitment' from China, indentured labour and labour migration of Indian craftsmen and the employment of skilled East African Moravian mission pupils helps elucidate the diversified and many facets of labour at the *Central Railway*'s construction camp. Although Gillman does not include Indian craftsmen in his construction camp sketch, he recorded their presence and importance as skilled workers already in the first months of his work in East Africa:

> I have now got several Indian carpenters, who work on daily wages + I am very satisfied with them. They are intelligent + diligent + know their trade + are altogether different from those lazy fellows I had before + still have who have got their contract with monthly wages, last certainly made a very big mistake. These daily workmen get also 3 Rps. per day but their work is worth that money.[290]

These wage levels for skilled Indian labour reported by Gillman correspond to the wage levels generally of craftsmen at the *Central Railway*. They fluctuated between 1.5 and 2.5 rupees per day for East African *fundis* (masters) and 2.5 to 4.5 Rupees a day for Indian, Banian and Goanese craftsmen.[291]

Apart from skilled labour, simpler forms of manual labour such as shovelling soil, carrying and fixing iron bars or sleepers as well as cutting and carrying rocks were the most common types of work. As already illustrated in the chapter

---

290 Gillman Diaries. Mss. Afr. S. 1175/1,2_1, no. II., p. 66. Cf. Gillman Diaries. Mss. Afr. S. 1175/1,2_1, no. 9, p. 41.
291 Cf. Reichart. *Gari*, pp. 66.

about the Moravian Mission's connection to railway construction, despite voluntary migration to the railway construction site of predominantly skilled workers, many East Africans rejected working at the railway and sought refuge at the Moravian missionary stations to escape labour recruiters, for example. As far as the Moravian files could tell, those rejecting labour at the railway were generally those who had to perform the simple, unskilled, repetitive, and physically demanding construction tasks. The question in-how-far these comparatively unskilled railway workers were subject to coercion is as old as the historiography investigating on the issue and remains significant today.[292]

Whereas studies mostly originating from the 1970s had already stressed African preference for railway work over plantation labour due to higher wages, better living conditions and less supervision,[293] especially Thaddeus Sunseri and Reichart-Burikukiye confirmed these early findings decades later, when investigating the Moravian files and therefore also especially for the region of *Unyamwezi* where the railway was constructed between 1908 and 1912. As seasonal male absence from home had been integral to the economy of the Wanyamwezi since pre-colonial times because they used to work as caravan porters, railway labour was regarded as an extension of their former caravan wage labour occupation. Moreover, Sunseri and Reichart-Burikukuye are convinced that coercion to take up labour at the railway construction was an almost negligible aspect as labour conditions would have improved significantly from 1908 onwards.[294] In stark contrast, Koponen denies the voluntary character of railway work. He is convinced of a certain amount of force being prevalent throughout the entire building process. The only difference from other cases was that colonial officials and the construction companies in German East Africa refrained from any measures that would result in another anti-colonial war, such as the Maji Maji War, after 1908.[295] Taking a closer look at the source material used by the most important historians – John Iliffe, Rainer Tetzlaff, Thaddeus Sunseri, and Juhani Koponen – reveals an ambiguous picture. Whereas the studies of the 1970s primarily examine documents produced between 1908 and 1910, Koponen quotes sources originating between 1911 and 1914. Hence, a sufficient labour supply in the immediate years after the Maji Maji War might have been the

292 Cf. Cooper. 'The Labour Question', pp. 624–625. Cf. Fall, Babacar and Roberts, Richard L. 'Forced Labour'. *General Labour History of Africa. Workers, Employers and Governments, 20th–21st Centuries*. 77–118. Eds. Stefano Bellucci and Andreas Eckert. Exeter: 2019, pp. 77–118.
293 Cf. Iliffe. *A Modern History*, pp. 157–185, p. 161. Cf. Tetzlaff. *Koloniale Entwicklung*, pp. 88–89.
294 Cf. Sunseri. 'Labour Migration', pp. 581–586, 597–598. Cf. Sunseri. '"Dispersing"', pp. 558–565. Cf. Sunseri. *Vilimani*, pp. 167–171. Cf. Reichart. *Gari*, pp. 48–61. Cf. Rockel. *Carriers of Culture*.
295 Cf. Koponen. *Development*, pp. 410–413.

result of the widespread famine, induced by colonial 'scorched-earth' policies during and after battles.[296] People deprived of food might have readily taken up colonial employment just for the sake of survival. Moreover, with every kilometre, the *Central Railway* stirred colonial economic activity, which had experienced a significant slump in the beginning of formal colonial rule, and therefore also increased the labour demand for all working places in the colony (cf. Sections 5.2 and 5.3).[297] Hence, it might be the case that forced labour policies were more intense between 1911 and 1914 than between 1908 and 1910, because of increased competition for African labour when the economy experienced an upturn. This interpretation runs counter to Sunseri's and Reichart-Burikukiye's argument that coercion to work was negligible in the later years of railway construction. But Sunseri might be too optimistic in stating that after 1908 working conditions had improved so much that forcible measures appear to have been an insignificant aspect.[298] Files held in both the Tanzanian National Archives and the Railway Museum Nairobi, which were not consulted in the aforementioned studies, confirm this suggestion. For example, in February 1909, *Holzmann's* construction director Grages pressured the Governor:

> According to a telegraphic report from our preparatory work department in Mpapua, the work of the study brigades is being hampered by a severe shortage of workers, as the Wagogo have so far only been able to work with difficulty and in very insufficient numbers. The intervention of the district office would probably be able to remedy this situation without difficulty. We therefore take the liberty of suggesting to Your Excellency that the Mpapua district office should intervene in a suitable manner with the Wagogos in order to induce them to accept work in sufficient numbers.[299]

Governor Rechenberg complied with *Holzmann's* request, issuing a telegram to the district office only shortly after the request of the construction company recommending to use especially defaulting taxpayers for the task and simultaneously exert pressure on the local Wagogo population, but to refrain from any

---

296 Cf. Wimmelbücker, Ludger. 'Verbrannte Erde. Zu den Bevölkerungsverlusten als Folge des Maji-Maji Krieges'. *Der Maji-Maji Krieg in Deutsch-Ostafrika. 1905–1907.* 87–99. Eds. Felicitas Becker and Jigal Beez. Berlin: 2005, pp. 87–97. Cf. Becker, Felicitas. 'Sudden Disaster and Slow Change: Maji-Maji and the Long-Term History of Southeast Tanzania'. *Maji Maji. Lifting the Fog of War.* 295–322. Eds. James Giblin and Jamie Monson. Leiden: 2010, pp. 295–305.

297 Cf. Tetzlaff. *Koloniale Entwicklung,* pp. 84–92, 93–100, 176, 191, 293.

298 Cf. Sunseri. *Vilimani,* pp. 167–171. I have presented the gist of this argument already in my *Zulassungsarbeit* (thesis). Cf. Rösser. *Forced Labour,* pp. 41–44.

299 TNA. G17/66. Arbeiterverhältnisse der Tanganyika-Eisenbahn Morogoro-Tabora. 1909–1911, "Abschrift! Phllipp Holzmann & Co. Gesellschaft mit beschränkter Haftung Bahnbau Morogoro-Tabora Daressalam, den 9. February 1909". Cf. Reichart. *Gari,* pp. 50–52.

measures that could result in an militant uprising.[300] The local track supervisor in Kikombo confirmed the content of this correspondence, explaining to his superior railway commissioner only a few days later: "It is self-evident that the authorities must continue to support the extensive construction works of the railway by all means except direct coercion. But it must be said that this has always been done by the local [district office] as a proactive measure [. . .]."[301] This support comprised not only verbal pressure on the local population in general, and on defaulting taxpayers who had to work around one month at the railway in particular, but it also meant that the district office equipped *Holzmann* engineers like Mr Lodes with a number of armed *Askaris.* With military support, representatives of the construction company went to several villages and demanded workers. The construction supervisor also commented that this was not a singular event as it was obvious that this procedure necessitated a certain degree of force. Between 1909 and 1910, representatives of the construction company attempted to coerce the local population living near the newly built track to construction work. First and foremost, they targeted the Wagogo, whose homeland the railroad had started to cross. Looking for a workforce that lived in the direct neighbourhood of the construction sites saved *Holzmann* a good deal of money because they could avoid the per capita fee for workers recruited from more distant places. Although some of the *Holzmann* engineers tended to lack any moderation when making use of their military support provided by the district office, the track supervisors initially refrained from active intervention and decided to remain "neutral on the issue", only giving "off duty" reports of violence. One supervisor "confidentially" took the view that the "matter shall therefore only be dealt with here in a reporting manner in order to keep the railway commissioner informed of all events [. . .]."[302] In other words, all official bodies were well aware that coercion and physical violence occurred to lower construction costs when constructing the railway in the central region of *Ugogo.* Additionally, all governmental bodies tolerated these measures as long as no new war against German colonial rule was provoked. Several reports by construction supervisors and the railway commissioner complained that, especially, the Wagogo resented railway work and often deserted. Even though there was famine in March 1910, "nevertheless, the Wagogo [were]

300 Cf. TNA. G17/66, "Governeur Rechenberg an Bezirksamt Mpapua 9/7 via telegram".

301 TNA. G17/66, "Bauaufsicht an den Herrn Eisenbahnkommiser. Kikombo, 16.02.09", p. 74.

302 TNA. G17/66, "Bauaufsicht an den Herrn Eisenbahnkommissar. Kikombo, 16.02.09", p. 75, cf. pp. 69–75. Regarding the duration of tax labour cf. Reichart. *Gari*, pp. 50–52.

hardly to be persuaded to do wage labour" and they kept on running away from the workplace, at least until 1912.[303]

Yet, coercion did not only target the Wagogo and these practices did not occur only in 1909 but endured at least until 1913. When reconstructing the default home line between Dar es Salaam and Morogoro between 1912 and 1913, the terminology regarding forced labour practices used by *Holzmann*, the *Gouverneur* and the railway commissioner was strikingly similar. Again, equipped with armed *Askari* to enforce labour recruitment, Governor Schnee urged the District Officers of Dar es Salaam, Bagamoyo and Morogoro:

> The railway commissioner of the Central Railway and the chief engineer of the Dar es Salaam-Morogoro railway line have made appearances here to support the recruitment of workers as far as possible. As the early completion of the reconstruction is in the interest of the administration, I request the district office to occasionally draw the attention of the people there to this work.[304]

Despite the resulting efforts of the district offices, labour scarcity prevailed for several more months and *Holzmann* complained accordingly. When the district office of Bagamoyo finally sent a total number of 900 men, 600 for railway construction work proper, and 300 more for tree cutting, the construction company remained unsatisfied. Many workers had fled the workforce immediately, leaving *Holzmann* with only 350 workers, whereas at least 700 were needed. Denying any responsibility for the escape of the men and women, and blaming the supplying district office for insufficient labour supply, *Holzmann* warned that now, devoid of sufficient workers, railway construction would become slower. They further stressed that as the construction company now had to seek for workers themselves, the overall costs for construction would increase. Bagamoyo's district office rejected the allegations and blamed *Holzmann* for the workers' escape. The men and women had fled the workplace as on-site conditions had been unbearable: of the 600 men, forty-four had died and seventy-six had returned home seriously ill. No wonder the workers fled: inadequate food as well as poor working

303 TNA. G17/63, "J. no. 436. Monatsbericht über den Stand der Arbeiten an der Zentralbahn für März 1910. VI. Verpflegung und Lohnverhältnisse", cf. "VIII Personal und Arbeiterverhältnisse". Cf. TNA. G17/64, "Monatsbericht über den Stand der Arbeiten an der Zentralbahn Ende April 1910. XIII. Personal und Arbeiterverhältnisse". Cf. TNA. G17/118, "Eisenbahn-Bautaetigkeit Mittellandbahn", p. 4. Cf. Reichart. *Gari*, pp. 50–52.

304 RMN. GTF. R1. S10, "Abschrift J. no. 25526. Schnee an Bez. Amt Daressalam, Bagamoyo, Morogoro. Daressalam, 12. Nov. 1912", cf. "J. no. 20461. X. Auf J. no. 2281. I. E. vom 21.11.10.", "Telegram Buchner an Eisenbahnkommissar. Eisenbahnkommissar Eing. 25.1.11. J. no. 127.", "J. no. 309. Conzept. Drslm, 19. Oktober 12. An den Herrn Gouverneur in Daressalam.", "DOAEG an Eisenbahnkommissar Molfenter. Tabora, 19. February 1913".

and housing conditions were causing the spread of lethal diseases. Moreover, the employer would have treated the workers ruthlessly, in general, and in case of illness, even worse. In addition, pieceworkers were urged to work eleven hours a day and *Holzmann's* sub-contractors, Giese and Haase, had withheld the workers' wages. Of course, both the *OAEG* and *Holzmann* denied the allegations. In the end, all parties involved were left unsatisfied and *Holzmann* finally claimed to have recruited enough workers themselves by November 1913, cancelling their request for workers provided by the colonial administration.[305] Nevertheless, complaints about improper treatment of the workers persisted beyond the construction of the *Central Railway* proper. When the initial works of the *Ruanda Railway*, intended to connect *Central Railway*'s Tabora with the most northern part of the colony, were started by *Holzmann* in 1914, reports about unruly subcontractors and abuses of the workers continued. Once again, Governor Schnee insisted on paragraph seven of the construction contract that demanded decent food and lodging for the workers and a closer supervision of the sub-contractors to meet the colonial labour laws. Such incidents finally only ceased with the combat operations of WWI in German East Africa; by 1916, all railway construction work on behalf of German colonialism ended in East Africa.[306]

Having reassessed the files of the Moravians in the previous section, and examining sources not consulted by other historians, a multifaceted picture emerges. First of all, whether work was skilled or not had significant influence on the degree of violence and coercion exerted on the workers. Moravian missionary pupils, equipped with education and skills, tended to work rather voluntarily as craftsmen or employees at the *Central Railway* and some former mission pupils even became labour recruiters themselves. At the same time, many of those targeted as simple manual workers for the railway or similar governmental building tasks, rejected

305 Cf. RMN. GTF. R1. S10., "J. no. 957. Haase an Eisenbahnkommissar. Mbaruku, 13. April 13", "An den Herrn Gouverneur in Daressalam. Arbeiterverhältnisse beim Umbau der Stammstrecke. 19. Juni 1913.", "Holzmann an den Herrn Eisenbahnkommissar der Tanganyikabahn. Daressalam, den 21. September 1913", "Abschrift. Philipp Holzmann & Cie. Das Bezirksamt drahtete uns am 23. Juli auf Anfrage", "Kaiserliches Bezirksamt Bagamoyo an den Herrn Eisenbahnkommissar der Tanganyikabahn. Bagamoyo, den 4. Oktober 1913", "Ostafrikanische Eisenbahngesellschaft an den Herrn Eisenbahnkommissar. 15. Oktober 1913.", "Philipp Holzmann an den Herrn Eisenbahnkommissar. Zu J. no. 1797. Daressalam, 17. Oktober 1913", "Kaiserlicher Bezirksamtmann gez. Eggebrecht An die Firma Philipp Holzmann. Daressalam, den 16. Oktober", "Holzmann an den Herrn Eisenbahnkommissar. Daressalam, den 15. November 1913". Cf. RMN. R3. S5. 154. [no title], "Arbeitermangel bei Umbau von Stammstrecke". Cf. RMN. GTF. R4. S3. 98. Gouvernementskrankenhaus, Institut für Seuchenbekämpfung, Sewa Haji Hospital, Sanitätsdienststellen, Behörden, "Abschrift. J. no. 5594. Daressalam, den 28. September 1913".

306 Cf. TNA. G17/153. Arbeiterverhältnisse der Ruanda-Eisenbahn. 1914.

any governmental work and sought refuge at Moravian missionary stations. The large-scale investigations by the colonial authorities about living and working conditions at the camps of the Greek and other European sub-contractors show that living and working conditions indeed left a lot to be desired, even until the very end of construction work.

Summing up, neither any source material nor various secondary literature on the issue provide for an unambiguous picture of forced and coerced labour at the railway's construction sites, especially regarding *when* coercion was most prevalent. As generally the case for any colonial labour relationship, it seems that the degree of coercion oscillated between the two poles of overt physical violence and more indirect forms of coercion such as food scarcity or the imposition of taxes, or 'reminders' and 'urgings' by the district offices. In any case, the issue seems to be best addressed differently. The question is not whether coercion was imposed on the African workforce. Coercion and physical violence were certainly integral to any labour relationship at the *Central Railway*'s construction sites. But much more important than this fact is the question whether each type of worker was subjected to the same degree of violence. Skilled workers who had been Moravian missionary pupils, for example appear to have been less subject to coercion and physical violence, and even voluntarily took up work with *Holzmann*. The same holds true for some unskilled workers of *Unyamwesi* who left the catchment areas of the Moravian Mission somewhat voluntarily for either better wages or new experience. On the other hand, many people especially in *Ugogo*, *Bagamoyo* and in *Unyamwesi*, rejected work at the railway and, therefore, sought either refuge at the missionary stations, or fled to more distant places or deserted the worksite itself. Hence, it appears that in very general terms, the less skilled the workers were, the more they were subjected to coercion. In turn, the more skilled a worker was, the less force he or she faced. Whether skilled or unskilled, recruited voluntarily or by force, the African workers' agency to influence daily living and working conditions in the construction camps endured. This holds true also for female workers, who are addressed in the section following the next.

3.8.3 Labour and Everyday Life at the Construction Camps

Labour and work expectations as well as regulations were certainly integral to everyday life at any construction camp of the *Central Railway*. Yet, what regulated any labour at the *Central Railway* most was nature. First of all, during the rainy season, hardly any work was done in any construction camp. Most of the construction works were thus done during the dry season.[307] Secondly, given the natural light conditions of East Africa and the absence of electricity at the construction sites, an ordinary day of work could theoretically last from sunrise to sunset, that is from ca. six a.m. to six p.m. On average, each worker was occupied with one specific task for ten hours a day. In fact, there was generally no obligation to fulfil a fixed amount of ten hours work daily. At least after 1908, there was rather a system of flexitime imposed that demanded a certain amount of piecework to be met by an individual worker:

> Regarding the earth works the employer expected the daily piecework performance of a normally hard-working and ordinary skilled worker working for ca. 10 h; depending on the qualities of the soil that was ca. 1 cubic metre of earth movement. You were able to observe that out of fifty workers, ca. 6 fulfilled their workload at around 11 a.m., ca. 20 at around 2 p.m., 16 around 3 p.m. and the rest at around 4 p.m. A worker only seldomly met the workload of two days on one single day; but you could regularly meet people, who, after they had started one task in the late afternoon and had finished this task in the morning to follow at 8 a.m., would start a new task only at the third day. They then rather preferred to rest the whole day. Given this freedom, to come to and leave from work as it pleased them, many workers preferred such piecework to temporary employment.[308]

With this mode of work, railway workers could earn eight to twenty-one Rupees a month according to their work-performance, *posho* and the daily food allowance included. According to Reichart-Burikukiye, who processed the *Deutsche Kolonialblatt* issued by the colonial administration, not only the workers, but also the construction company and the colonial administration preferred piecework. For the latter, piecework saved a lot of money because it required fewer expensive (European) overseers. Furthermore, piecework led to higher and more regular work performance, having a self-disciplining effect on the workforce. Hence, it was believed that such freedom at the workplace would be the right tool to 'educate' the Africans at the railway to work. But given the absence of clear rules, especially in the beginning of railway construction when there was practically no labour legislation at all, it was also open to abuse. This occurred especially when time was pressured or during colonial warfare like the Maji Maji War. The *OAEG* openly reported about their cooperation with the colonial authorities regarding the Maji Maji convict workers in 1906 and reaffirmed their demand for labour supply simultaneously:

> The uprising in German East Africa [. . .] prevented us from keeping a sufficient stock of permanent workers. With the people recruited in Muansa and Tabora, we had about 5500

307 Cf. Section 3.2. For a personal account provided by Gillman's self-narratives about the difficulties of railway construction during *masika* cf. Gillman Diaries. Mss. Afr. S. 1175/1,2_1, no. 9_1, pp. 70–80.
308 *Deutsches Kolonialblatt* 1911, p. 709. Qutd. in Reichart. *Gari*, pp. 61–62.

> workers available at the beginning of the year under review. New influxes would have been necessary for our needs. Instead, however, [. . .] a reduction soon occurred again. [. . .] The question of workers was a constant concern for our construction management [. . .]. Thankfully, the governorate provided us with support by transferring 800 punishment workers in October, when some of the others left the workplaces to cultivate their fields.[309]

For the same year of railway construction, the Anglo-German engineer, Gillman, gives more information about the convict workers' (health) conditions when arriving at the railway. He noted in his diary on 18 August 1906:

> My endless shortage of labour is momentarily solved by 150 convict workers. They participated in the rising behind Morogoro and expiate their six months long punishment at the railway construction. Naturally, the work requires to let them live devoid of their chains. They are keeping themselves well. They are horribly stupid and weak and not used to any work at all, however. 1/3 [cubic meter] m^3 is the maximum daily workload in ten hours. Many are afflicted with scabies. Now, in the for the natives cold season, also a lot of pneumonia. One of the workers has recently died, causing the escape of 120 and leaving me embarrassed. Let's see how it is going to be with the convicts. The superstructure must not be stopped and will not be stopped. I have to insert some night shifts for the provisional bridges' insertion every now and then.[310]

Whereas, it is not entirely clear in this statement whether the nightshifts applied to Gillman only or also included his workforce, nightshifts did indeed occur if the light conditions permitted doing so and if leading engineers like Gillman thought it necessary:

> 2.XII. [1906]
> This morning, after my people had been occupied from yesterday morning 6 a.m. until today's morning 6. a.m. with tracklaying, i.e., working with heavy iron materials with only three hours of rest, they walked the 1 ½ kms back to the camp dancing and singing. Even though they had complained a lot about tiredness between 1 and 3 o'clock in the morning and were very listless. – As far as I am concerned, I enjoyed the full moon night and especially the European-fresh morning (between 4 and 6); it helped me to overcome all the stresses and strains.[311]

Besides showing that nightshifts did occur despite the workers' protests, reassessing this statement also reveals that an entire workday lasted longer than the actual time of work. It often also included at least a thirty-minute walk from the camp to the construction site and work had to be done despite the workers' complaints of exhaustion. Of course, workers also influenced their working and living conditions. For instance, Gillman himself noted in his diary that his workers were

309 "Die Ostafrikanische Eisenbahngesellschaft". *DOAZ*, IX, no. 28. Daressalam, 29 July 1907.
310 Gillman Diaries. Mss. Afr. S. 1175/1,2_1, no. 10, p. 12.
311 Gillman Diaries. Mss. Afr. S. 1175/1,2_1, no. 10, p. 24.

"very peculiar about doing no work on Sundays", and it was indeed the rule that there was at least one day of rest per week.[312] As far as Gillman's accounts are concerned, he nevertheless urged his workers sometimes to work on Sunday as well, but was generally able to "persuade [. . .] only a few".[313] Yet, *Holzmann* engineers like Gillman, assisted by European foremen as overseers, were not always able to impose their will when facing a workforce of up to 300 people, despite their self-image as "mwana mkuba" or the "great master".[314] Generally, Sundays remained free of work and if the weather was cool or exceptionally rainy, the work(wo)men generally succeeded in staying at home in the camp or even deserted from the workplace.[315] Moreover, 'blue Mondays' also occurred frequently: after a *pombe* evening or similar feasts; the workers were often reluctant to work after the night of partying and succeeded in their demand to rest.[316] Gillman notes as well:

> Last night [Sunday], the [Africans] had received two poshos, for yesterday + today. But however, they [ate] them both + about 150 of them therefore were unable to work or do anything today, lying about half dead + holding their stomachs. When we tried to make them move out in the morning to Daressalam to bring up some railway material, some of them left the camp [and] have not returned yet. It is very difficult to manage these men [. . .].[317]

When confronted with European methods and tools of manual labour like capstans, shovels or wheelbarrows, the African workers insisted upon their own methods to do the work, often to the bewilderment of the European spectators. As already mentioned above, singing was integral to these workers, not only to keep the work rhythm, but also to establish and maintain a particular identity and community spirit among those who had come to the *Central Railway*'s construction sites or other workplaces such as plantations from all over East Africa. It was further not uncommon that a song text included open criticism against colonialism or colonial labour conditions.[318] When Gillman arrived in East Africa in autumn 1905, he was immediately confronted with gangs of enchained convict (female) workers in the streets of Tanga and Dar es Salaam escorted by an *Askari*.

---

312 Gillman Diaries. Mss. Afr. S. 1175/1,2_1, no. 9, p. 22, cf. p. 12. Cf. Reichart. *Gari*, pp. 58–67, cf. Sunseri. *Vilimani*, pp. 167–171.

313 Gillman Diaries. Mss. Afr. S. 1175/1,2_1, no. 9, p. 12.

314 Gillman Diaries. Mss. Afr. S. 1175/1,2_1, no. 9, p. 10.

315 Cf. Gillman Diaries. Mss. Afr. S. 1175/1,2_1, no. 9, pp. 57, 84.

316 Cf. Reichart. *Gari*, pp. 58–67. Cf. Sunseri. *Vilimani*, pp. 165–171.

317 Gillman Diaries. Mss. Afr. S. 1175/1,2_1, no. 9, p. 12.

318 Cf. Sunseri. *Vilimani*, p. 152. Cf. Gunderson, Frank. *Sukuma Labor Songs. 'We never Sleep, we dream of Farming'*. Leiden: 2010, pp. 112–225, 453–455. Cf. Gillman Diaries. Mss. Afr. S. 1175/1,2_1, no. 8, p. 73.

As he watched "[n]atives on a gangspill [sic] pulling up a lighter on the shores [of Dar es Salaam] [. . .] they kept singing a monotonous tune always repeating itself[:] 'Kuwa nina njaa, njaa, njaa' ('I am hungry, hungry, hungry')".[319] But also, when introduced to tasks involving shovels or wheelbarrows, the workers asserted their own *Eigen-Sinn*[320] [self-will] and stubbornly imposed their own methods. Gillman used to complain regularly in his diary:

> A [sub-]contractor imports wheelbarrows. The people then fill them and want to carry them on their heads. Working with wheelbarrows had to be abandoned. Infinite difficulties to teach those people, who have come to work recently, the use of shovels + pickaxes. [. . .] The earthworks are done most quickly if you allow the people to keep working according to their own traditional way. That means, they fill the loosened soil in the unavoidable Hickapos (baskets) and carry them, even if only for a few steps and at a very slow pace. – Watching this requires the highest amount of patience. Of course, I am talking here about the hinterland peoples, who are not used to earthworks. – The peoples from the coast a[nd] the Wanyamwesis a[nd] similar peoples who have been working for years, can, if they want, do the earthwork fairly well.[321]

Other *Holzmann* engineers like Walter Rehfeldt confirmed the insistence of African workers to carry baskets instead of using wheelbarrows throughout the entire construction process.[322] Apart from the fact that Gillman's perspective on the way of African labour performance was well rooted in his own perception to regard Africa as 'backwards' or 'uncivilised', the tone of the engineer's statement clearly illustrates his annoyance and reluctant resignation about his ultimate defeat against his workers. Like it or not, Gillman had to accept that European methods of railway construction would be adapted to local realities by his African work(wo)men.

But the pace and style of manual labour were not the only things the African workers could exact from European engineers like Gillman. From the very beginning of their employment, the workers sought individual and collective advantages. Both Reichart-Burikukiye and Sunseri have shown that many workers who came to work at the construction sites of the railway, rather voluntarily, followed the old established rhythms of being employed as seasonal porters or plantation workers. Those coming voluntarily for work to the railway would usually stay only half a year and return afterwards to their homes. Of course, they could face despotism and coercion,

319 Gillman Diaries. Mss. Afr. S. 1175/1,2_1, no. 8, p. 71, cf. pp. 56, 68–70.
320 Cf. Lüdtke, Alf. *Eigen-Sinn. Fabrikalltag, Arbeitererfahrungen und Politik vom Kaiserreich bis in den Faschismus.* Hamburg: 1993, pp. 120–160, 351–442. Cf. Auslander. 'Accommodation, Resistance, and *Eigensinn*', pp. 205–217.
321 Gillman Diaries. Mss. Afr. S. 1175/1,2_1, no. 9, pp. 29–30. Cf. Gillman Diaries. Mss. Afr. S. 1175/1,2_1, no. 8, p. 74.
322 Cf. Stadtarchiv Frankfurt. W1/2 – 278/1. *Rehfeldt* p. 10.

but potential workers learned from their experiences. If they had experienced mistreatment by an individual labour recruiter, sub-contractor or railway engineer, or if the latter had bad reputations, they would shun further employment accordingly and tell their fellow African workers to follow only those men who would treat them comparatively well. Thus, before leaving for the construction site, the type of work was agreed upon, preventing bad surprises. If mistreated *en route* to the construction site, workers would simply run away or move to a different employer. As a sufficient number of workers was constantly in demand and many labour recruiters competed with each other in one region, workers could choose another employer if offered better pay or other provisions. Moreover, experienced workers often went to a workplace on their own and checked the environment and the labour conditions there, refraining from taking up work with a cruel or poorly organised sub-contractor or engineer.[323] Yet, the workers' bargaining power did not stop at the construction site. Besides what was already shown regarding work pace, working hours and food provisions by examining Gillman's diary entries, there were further means to enhance one's wages apart from railway construction work.

Certainly, *ngomas*[324] were integral to the life at the construction camp and they were celebrated by the workmen/women for their own sake. They often included the consumption of *pombe*[325] and took place frequently at the railway construction sites. *Pombe* was sanctioned by the colonial authorities and the construction firm, as both shared the view that the availability of alcohol would make the workforce accept longer working contracts. In addition, the joint consumption of alcohol enabled the workmen/women to establish a distinct railway subculture that merged the different backgrounds of the ethnically diverse workforce and that often also circumvented the control of the colonial elites.[326] From performances of *ngoma* at *pombe* evenings or similar feasts, the workforce also succeeded in making some extra money in their quasi 'free-time':

> Tonight a big 'goma' (dance) of the Wanamesi [sic!] people. About 100 of them in front of my tent dancing + howling + making their noise on a big drum + a kind of bow, with an empty coconut attached to it to serve as resonances. Dances of the women very elegant [. . .]. Huge fires light up the night + it was a fine picture to see these [. . .] mostly tall men + women dancing. It was nearly 11 pm. When I stopped them + gave them their backshish [Arabic:

323 Cf. Reichart. *Gari*, pp. 51–58.
324 Ngoma (Swahili) = drum, here: feast/party including dance and song performance.
325 Pombe (Swahili) = locally produced alcohol.
326 Cf. Sunseri. "'Dispersing'", pp. 568–569. Cf. Reichart. *Gari*, pp. 44–46. Cf. Gillman Diaries. Mss. Afr. S. 1175/1,2_1, no. 9, pp. 28, 65–67.

> tip] – a few handsfull of coppercoins – they cheered me + went to sleep, [and] [. . .] seemed quite happy + content.[327]

Similarly, when Gillman watched a blood brotherhood ceremony of two of his female labour camp dwellers, the engineer had to pay "copious amounts of 'backshish' [. . .] of course" to both the "participants a[nd] [other] spectators".[328] Moreover, having the self-image of an 'educated man', Gillman was not content with only being an engineer in East Africa. Instead, he took up a variety of intellectual free-time occupations, such as geography, botany, philosophy, and ethnography.[329] In turn, it seems that the African workers were not ignorant of the passions of the Anglo-German engineer and used the emerging market at the construction camps to sell supposedly 'authentic ethnographic objects' to enhance their wages:

> 1st December 05. This morning in the [sub-]contractors camp. One of the [. . .] workmen showed me 3 figures he had cut out of ebony wood of which I purchased two paying 1 Rp. for each. [. . .] However rough the carving is done it speaks of a good deal of artistic feeling + more of a good deal of observing power of the man who has made them + who as far as I could make out, comes from somewhere near Victoria-Nyanza lake. [. . .] These little 'bits of art' [. . .] gave me much pleasure.[330]

On another occasion, Gillman purchased two "turtles carved of wood [and a] walking stick with two carved figures on the top made by one of the wanawesi [sic!] men[.] For the last [Gillman] paid 1.50 Rp."[331] This is a fairly high price, as an unskilled worker received between five and twenty-one Rps. a month, depending on his individual piecework performance. Given the demanded hut tax of three Rps a year, one woodcarver was able to earn the entire colonial tax by selling ca. two pieces of art – clearly illustrating the fact that the *Central Railway*'s workers in German East Africa were also able to use the colonial arts market for their own benefit.[332]

---

327 Gillman Diaries. Mss. Afr. S. 1175/1,2_1, no. 9, p. 43.

328 Gillman Diaries. Mss. Afr. S. 1175/1,2_1, no. 9, p. 4.

329 Cf. Hoyle. *Gillman*, pp. 374–401.

330 Gillman Diaries. Mss. Afr. S. 1175/1,2_1, no. 9, p. 31.

331 Gillman Diaries. Mss. Afr. S. 1175/1,2_1, no. 9, p. 43.

332 Thanks to Annika Dörner (University of Erfurt) for providing me with this literature dealing with the art market in Africa, in general. Cf. Schildkrout, Enid and Keim, Curtis A. 'Objects and Agendas: re-collecting the Congo'. *The Scramble for Art in Africa.* 1–36. Ed. Enid Schildkrout and Curtis A. Keim. Cambridge: 1998. Cf. Fabian, Johannes. 'Appendix: On the Ethnography and Economies of Collecting from Leo Frobenius' Nochmals zu den Bakubavölkern'. *The Scramble for Art in Africa.* 101–108. Ed. Enid Schildkrout and Curtis A. Keim. Cambridge: 1998. Talking about wages, skilled workers like carpenters could earn between 3 and 5 Rps. a day, that is, many times the wages of an unskilled worker. It has already been stressed that in the beginning of railway

Besides these examples of African agency and opportunity to influence the labour process and the working and living conditions at the railway, desertion has already been mentioned as one strategy to deal with conditions that were not satisfactory. The individual factors that could make labour at the *Central Railway* unbearable varied from unsatisfactory housing, food, mal-treatment, weather, poor health conditions, lacking motivation or fear of warfare. Gillman reports of several occasions when hundreds of his workers left him, never to be seen again: in December 1905, the reason was too rainy weather; on another occasion in January 1906 "they did not like to stay".[333] In fact, desertion was not the only form of labour protest. It also occurred that workers challenged the racist hierarchy of Gillman's construction camp. In November 1905, three workmen "in a rebellious mood went for one of my 2 white *Aufseher* [overseer] [. . .], as these two *Aufseher* don't know how to treat the black [and] therefore the authority of us white was in danger to go lost."[334] In January 1906, after a *pombe* night with heavy drinking, a gang of Wanyamwezi workers challenged the racist order of the construction camp and transgressed the boundary to the European zone. Without Gillman's noticing, because he was asleep, they even "unlocked the outer door of [his] hut, [. . .] open[ed] the tent" and stole one "sack of rize [sic] [. . .], lots of fruit, 2 towels [and] [Gillman's] strap for sharpening razors." This incident caused him to call the construction company *Holzmann* and ask for protection, with the result that an "*Askari* arrived [and Gillman] now slep[t] under military protection". This *Askari* further had the right to corporally punish those workers not willing to comply with the amount of work to be done or to sentence those who transgressed the construction camp's order.[335] If no *Askari* was present, like in the incident in November 1905, Gillman wielded the *kiboko*[336] himself: "[. . .] I fetched the 3 niggers in front of all the rest [and] whipped them with the effect that they [and] all the others went to work with great ambition [and] that at least my authority was

---

construction, skilled work was often done by Indians. In addition, Reichart stresses that a lot of Arabs and Swahili were also employed as craftsmen at the railway construction site. Yet, as already mentioned above, particularly, Indian skilled labour was increasingly replaced by African skilled labour during railway construction, but it seems that Africans were already employed in higher positions during the initial years of construction. Cf. Reichart. *Gari*, pp. 66–68. Confirming Reichart's finding that these Africans originated often from the coast, Gillman reports about one of his foremen being a "Msaram". Msaram = *Mzaramu* people, originating from the East African coast esp. from Bagamoyo, Rufiji and Dar es Salaam. Gillman Diaries. Mss. Afr. S. 1175/1,2_1, no. 9, p. 19.

333 Gillman Diaries. Mss. Afr. S. 1175/1,2_1, no. 9, p. 62, cf. p. 57.

334 Gillman Diaries. Mss. Afr. S. 1175/1,2_1, no. 9, p. 25.

335 Gillman Diaries. Mss. Afr. S. 1175/1,2_1, no. 9, pp. 67–68.

336 Kiboko (Swahili) = lit. hippo, here: whip made from Hippo skin (leather).

well safet [sic].” Although Gillman regarded this “as a very nasty experience [. . .] for an educated man [. . .]”[337] he continued this practice at least until 1913, if his authority or the ambitious work performance seemed to be threatened and no *Askari* was at his disposal for dealing out corporal punishments.[338] Hence, coercion and physical violence were certainly integral in any labour relationship at the *Central Railway*, but the degree varied. Not only was the question whether the work was skilled or unskilled important. The circumstances of the actual setting were significant. All workers were able to exert some agency to enhance their wages or living and working conditions, and some even transgressed racist hierarchies to protest mistreatment and colonial command. The same holds also true for female workers, whose role is somewhat more difficult to assess, because they are often not explicitly addressed in the sources. Clement Gillman’s diaries feature a lot of passages where women are mentioned at the railway construction camps and therefore shed light on the issue.

3.9 Female Labour and Sex Work

3.9.1 Female Labour

The special role of women at the *Central Railway*’s construction site has its origins in conditions already existing before the actual construction work and before being recruited for working at the railroad. It is rooted in the overall agricultural economy prevalent in East Africa in the German colonial period. Criticising how the historiography of labour migration and plantation labour in East Africa had been shaped predominantly by South African scholars until the mid-1990s, Thaddeus Sunseri urged a focus on East African economic parameters, which were decisively different from those of its South African counterpart. He concentrates on the agency of the African workers and their mostly successful means of influencing their living and working conditions at various places of work. He argues that the South African model of the ‘kraal economy’ is not applicable to East Africa under German colonial rule, due to the latter’s preservation of a migratory agricultural economy and the absence of a large mining industry.[339] Sunseri generates his findings by analysing the impact and the process of railway construction in the central region of *Unyamwezi* where the railway line was being built between ca. 1907–1912. In Sunseri’s

337 Gillman Diaries. Mss. Afr. S. 1175/1,2_1, no. 9, pp. 25–26.
338 Cf. Gillman Diaries. Mss. Afr. S. 1175/1,2_2, no. 14, p. 77.
339 Cf. Sunseri. ‘Labour Migration’, pp. 581–586, 597–598.

view, the African agency in the context of labour is best illustrated by the failure of German colonial policies in the region applied after the Maji Maji War (ca. 1905–1908). Accordingly, colonial economic policies after ca. 1907 shifted from the 'plantation imperative' to small-scale indigenous cash crop production. Instead of large-scale plantations run by European companies, export products would now be produced independently by African households. The colonisers' task was then to facilitate means of production and transportation, particularly by providing the necessary infrastructure, that is, especially railways. Judged as a well-peopled area and therefore promising for economic cash crop production based on African small-scale planting, *Unyamwezi* was considered crucial to make the *Central Railway* an (economic) success. The African reaction towards these colonial 'development schemes' proved the policies false, however. Sunseri argues that both men and women preferred working at the construction site of the *Central Railway* to plantation labour due to higher wages, better working conditions and less supervision, which led to increased African migration to the railroad. The production of cash crops at home was thus neglected and reduced the amount of potential cash crops that could be transported and/or exported via railway. Consequently, one major income source to the future railway failed and thwarted the colonisers' vision of a very profitable railway.[340]

Sunseri's general critique holds true for the socio-economic-historical gender analysis, first developed in South Africa and later applied to East Africa. The role of women was distinct in German East Africa and not comparable to South Africa, due to the nature of capital penetration, the participation of peasants shaping the colonial economy and the comparative weakness of the white settler community.[341] In German East Africa, seasonal male absence from home had been integral to the economy of the Wanyamwezi since pre-colonial times, as they used to work as caravan porters. Whereas, male railway labour was soon integrated into this tradition of seasonal migratory labour, migratory female labour was a rather new phenomenon, although a certain amount of women were certainly also present in pre-colonial caravans for various forms of occupations. Nevertheless, there was a significant shift in male migratory labour regarding their occupations in pre-colonial caravans, for example, and railway labour. While men had previously brought the majority of their wages received from porterage back home, many male railway workers spent a fair share of their wages at the *Central Railway*'s labour camps. As these labour camps were often inhabited by thousands of workers, the camps offered several opportunities to consume their wages. Moreover, many men re-

340 Cf. Sunseri. '"Dispersing"', pp. 558–565.
341 Cf. Sunseri. 'Labour Migration', pp. 581–586, 597–598.

mained remarkably longer at the construction sites and a significant number would never return to their homes. Compensating for these income losses, and simply taking advantage of new income opportunities, many women, although to a lesser extent than men, also left for the construction sites of the railway for performing (lighter) construction work, beer brewing, or as sex workers. As both genders left their homes, the few remaining (mainly elderly and female) people in the villages could not sustain the former Wanyamwezi economy anymore, which relied on the seasonal return of men. Hence, especially, women retreated to more sparsely populated areas, off the central routes in less-accessible regions, where they were able to pursue a subsistence economy that could be run with less labour, that is, without the presence of their men. The result was not only a vastly depopulated region of *Unyamwezi* that promised fewer economic opportunities and would not sustain the economic fantasies of colonial policy makers. It also meant that sub-contractors or labour recruiters had more difficulties to find female workers, who had fled to areas that were less known and less accessible to European intruders.[342] Yet, there were certainly also women who came (for work) to the construction camps of the *Central Railway* on their own initiative.

As Rockel pointed out "[c]aravan women [. . .] were the first female migrant laborers in East Africa".[343] Thus, female labour at the *Central Railway* may also be regarded as an extension of the tradition of migratory caravan labour, especially as far as the Wanyamwezi are concerned. Like in pre-colonial labour relations in caravans, the reasons why women came to work at the construction sites were as manifold as their occupations therein. It oscillated between the poles of free and unfree labour, reproductive, wage and self-employed labour. In the first place, wives often accompanied their husbands migrating to the *Central Railway*. Many of these women were then responsible for the household's reproductive work. But many women arrived independently. They not only performed construction work, but also sold locally produced alcohol or worked as *vakapela*.[344] While the issue of sex work is dealt with in the following section, the sources produced by the colonial administration seldomly refer to female workers explicitly. Although Reichart-Burikukiye is convinced that manual railroad construction by women was "very likely", especially in the first years

342 Cf. Rockel. *Carriers of Culture*, pp. 117–130. Cf. Sunseri. '"Dispersing"', pp. 566–578. Cf. Sunseri. *Vilimani*, pp. 51–71.

343 Rockel. *Carriers of Culture*, p. 117, cf. 117–130.

344 Term used especially in region of *Unyamwezi* meaning "prostitute" or "sex worker" cf. Reichart. *Gari*, p. 71.

of construction, she admits that there is "hardly any evidence for it".[345] Once again, Gillman's diary proves as a precious substitute on the issue, as (African) women feature regularly in his personal documents, especially before Gillman's wife Eva and their young children joined him in East Africa after 1909.[346] Having arrived in Dar es Salaam in Autumn 1905, Gillman already observed that women not only did lighter construction work, but were "employed frequently for carrying stones or sand at house-building [and] harbor work [in Dar es Salaam]. They carr[ied] [. . .] fairly sized stone[s] or a basket with 2 shovels full of sand on their heads [. . .]."[347] As *Holzmann* not only built the *Central Railway* but also Dar es Salaam's harbour, the railway station, its custom house, a hotel and many other buildings in the capital, it is very likely that the construction company also employed women for heavy manual work for the *Central Railway*'s construction.[348] This is even more likely, as other European colonial powers did indeed employ women for the construction of infrastructure.[349]

Regarding the overall ratio of female workers at the *Central Railway*'s construction sites, it seems to be the case that between one-third and one-half of the overall labour camp population must have been female. This is not only the case because many wives accompanied their working husbands to the construction sites, being then responsible for the so-called 'reproductive work' that greatly facilitated if not enabled their husbands to take up work at the railway. Female labour migration to the railway was also mentioned by many Moravian missionaries, and Gillman's diary provides a specific gender ratio for one gang of newly arriving workers in December 1905: "The arrival of 120 fresh workmen with about 50 females of the [. . .] Wanamesi [sic] brought some change. They are busy putting up their camp quite close to mine."[350] Of course, Gillman's note reports only about one singular event, but it nevertheless proves that a significant part of the labour camp population and the workforce at the *Central Railway* were female indeed. In terms of wages, over the course of the construction period, the gender pay gap seems to have increased. Whereas, Reichart-Burikukiye indicates that women even earned more

345 Reichart. *Gari*, p. 68.

346 Cf. Gillman Diaries. Mss. Afr. S. 1175/1,2_1, no. 8, pp. 56, 70, 72, 79. Cf. Gillman Diaries. Mss. Afr. S. 1175/1,2_1, no. 9, pp. 29, 34–35, 43, 45, 60, 65–67. Cf. Gillman Diaries. Mss. Afr. S. 1175/1,2_1, no. 10, pp. 4–5, 10, 17, 32–33.

347 Gillman Diaries. Mss. Afr. S. 1175/1,2_1, no. 8, p. 72.

348 Cf. Gillman Diaries. Mss. Afr. S. 1175/1,2_1, no. 8, p. 72. Cf. Stadtarchiv Frankfurt. W1/2 – 278/1. *Grages*, pp. 6–8. Cf. Stadtarchiv Frankfurt. W1/2 – 278/1. *Imm*, p. 19. Cf. Gillman. 'Dar es Salaam', pp. 1–23.

349 Cf. Akurang-Parry. 'Colonial Forced Labor'. For a general assessment of female labour in (colonial) Africa cf. Dennis. 'Women in African Labour History', pp. 125–140. Cf. Coquery-Vidrovitch, Catherine. *African Women. A Modern History*. New York: 1997.

350 Gillman Diaries. Mss. Afr. S. 1175/1,2_1, no. 9, p. 37.

(!) money than men in the initial years of construction, this trend reversed in the years to follow. By 1907, women received only eighty per cent of the men's wages and by 1911, the pay gap had increased to fifty per cent. The reasons for this reversal are not entirely clear. Reichart-Burikukiye suggests that with an increasing availability of workers in the course of the construction process, the wages of women working at the railway decreased because *Holzmann* preferred male work. With decreasing wages, women sought other sources of income at the railway. Besides petty trade and sex work, the most profitable business was apparently beer brewing: it provided the workforce with beverages at *ngomas* and *pombe* evenings and was therefore crucial for maintaining a constant number of (male) workers. For the employer *Holzmann*, the availability of alcohol was central for rapid railway construction: with the presence of wives and other women as well as the availability of alcohol and other goods of consumption like cotton, cloth and tobacco, the male workers would accept longer working contracts and were more likely to sign up for a succeeding contract.[351] Besides these (wage labour) occupations at the labour camp, women could also receive *backshish* for their dance performances alongside their fellow male dancers from engineers like Gillman (cf. above).

Apart from railway construction and reproductive work, other aspects of female presence at the construction camp were significant. For railway engineers like Gillman, who valued education very much, learning Swahili appeared to be an important tool for doing their job properly. That of course does not mean that all Europeans coming to German East Africa would learn the local language, rather the contrary. But for Gillman it was "the first thing [. . .] to learn the language as soon as possible [. . .]"[352] and especially his *boys*' wives appear to have played a significant role in Gillman's learning. The engineer met with his *boys*' wives, particularly after railway construction work had ended in the evenings and when everybody was back in the camp. Then, especially, Gillman practiced Swahili: he once comments in his diary that he "spent half [an] hour joking away with [his] boy[']s wife, a real beauty" and realised that his "Suaheli is getting on quite well [and] [. . .] [he] underst[oo]d most [of what] they sa[id]."[353] Although this is not the only passage of Gillman's diary revealing affection and a certain degree of sexual desire for Indian or African women, there is no passage reporting explicitly that Gillman had any sexual relationship with any (African) women

---

351 Cf. Reichart. *Gari*, pp. 58–72. Cf. Sunseri. *Vilimani*, pp. 165–178.

352 Gillman Diaries. Mss. Afr. S. 1175/1,2_1, no. 8, p. 10.

353 Gillman Diaries. Mss. Afr. S. 1175/1,2_1, no. 9, p. 34, cf. pp. 29, 45.

living in the construction camp or another place. Nevertheless, sex and sex work played a crucial role regarding railway construction. Just as in the case of alcohol, the availability of sex encouraged the male workers to stay longer at the railway construction sites. Hence, apart from wives doing the so-called 'reproductive work' or working as beer brewers, sex work at the *Central Railway* was not only sanctioned by the construction company, but generally significant for rapid railway construction.

3.9.2 Sex(,) Work and Sexualised Violence

> Those Puellae who came from Dar es Salaam to the track were sick for the large part. They had mostly known that themselves and fled the hospital treatment, they would have faced in Dar es Salaam. That is why many of those employed at the track became sick, mostly because of gonorrhoea and soft chancre. Taking the hygienic view, it was therefore not to be condemned if the individual kept one black girl during his stay in Africa.[354]
>
> Dr Krauß. Railway Doctor of the *Holzmann* Company. *DOAZ*, 24 October 1908.

In general, the *vakapela* living and working at the railway's construction sites were sanctioned most of the time. They were welcomed by the colonial authorities and the representatives of the construction company, as the presence of women was regarded as necessary to attract sufficient male migratory workers to the construction sites. Only a minority of the workmen were accompanied by their wives and families, and many workers had indeed sex with prostitutes (but also with 'non-professionals' who were not married to them) – one aspect that inclined male workers to stay longer at the railway construction site. Hence, sex work and sex workers were integral to the overall construction progress of the *Central Railway* in German East Africa.[355] Of course, also European men working as engineers or sub-contractors at the railway had a demand for sex work. Generally, discourses about colonial Africa claimed that living in the colonies affected the sexuality of both European sexes. Yet, male Europeans outnumbered female Europeans in German East Africa by seven to one and, therefore, charged the colonial society with a male-dominated demand for sex. In any case, contemporary beliefs about male sexuality in the colonies were not absolutely clear-cut. On the one hand, it was argued that the colony's climate and the 'lax' sexual morals of

354 Krauß, Dr. Ehemals Bahnbauarzt der Firma Holzmann & Cie. "Der Gesundheitsdienst beim Bahnbau Daressalaam – Morogoro". *DOAZ*, X, no. 82. Daressalam: 24 October 1908, p. 5.

355 Cf. Sunseri. *Vilimani*, pp. 171–185. Cf. Reichart. *Gari*, pp. 66–72. Cf. Sunseri. '"Dispersing"', pp. 567–569.

the African population heightened European male sexuality. Following this view, European men were not to supress their drives, as that could seriously harm their nervous systems or make them turn to homosexual relationships or masturbation instead. According to the zeitgeist, both had to be avoided. On the other hand, the discourse warned that European men living in the colonial environment could lose their ability to resist the attractiveness of indigenous women, thereby contributing to the colonies' alleged degenerative effect on the European race when it came to inter-racial sexual relationships.[356]

In general, sexual access of European men to African women occurred in three ways. Although sexualised violence must not be confused with consensual sexual intercourse, it has to be mentioned in the context of sex work that rape of African women by European men was common in the colonies. Rape was considered part of the 'colonial frontier', as it bolstered the image of hegemonic colonial masculinity, and was thus certainly also present at the *Central Railway*'s construction sites, although there are only few sources documenting this fact. Secondly, concubinage, and to a lesser extent also marriage, occurred frequently in the colonies. But colonial legislation in Africa tended to forbid these forms of relationships, especially with increasing numbers of European settlers. This holds particularly true for Afro-European marriages. As German citizenship law made the child of a German father automatically a German citizen, the colonial authorities feared any offspring with a potential German African ancestry as such lineage challenged the ideal typical order of any colonial society that generally sought to separate African from European. With legislation making Afro-European marriages increasingly difficult and complicating legal forms of concubinage, prostitution was thus the most widespread form of African-European sexual interaction. Generally speaking, prostitution was neither legally nor socially disdained among the European population in the colonies. The reason for this was predominantly that, at least – to the colonial view – the relationship did not become formal, thus preventing any legal, financial or other demands of potential German-African children. Moreover, African prostitutes could be legally and socially marginalised, analogically to the situation in the European countries, providing the colonial administration with several (legal) means to have control over sex work and sexual intercourse between European men and African women.[357]

356 Cf. Walther, Daniel J. *Sex and Control. Venereal Disease, Colonial Physicians, and Indigenous Agency in German Colonialism, 1884–1914.* New York: 2015, pp. 24–30.

357 Cf. Walther. *Sex and Control*, pp. 35–46. For a contemporary view on European male sexuality in German East Africa by a railway doctor employed by *Holzmann* between 1905–1907 cf. Oetker. *Die Negerseele*, pp. 29–36. Cf. Daughton. *In the Forest of No Joy*, pp. 129–130, 151–152, 169–170, 281.

Given the statement of the former *Holzmann* railway doctor quoted above, Europeans employed at the *Central Railway* did indeed buy sex offered by the *vakapela* resident at the construction camps. Quoting missionary files, Reichart-Burikukiye confirms this finding. Accordingly, the railway missionary of the Moravians, Gaarde, reported about his first visits to the *Central Railway*: "It has occurred on several occasions that some have asked me, if I had come to search for a 'Bibi' (woman). They unfortunately know from experience that it is a profitable business to supply the white Bwana (Sir) with one of their beauties."[358] Besides Gillman confirming by one diary entry that Gaarde visited the *Central Railway* some months later in September 1911,[359] the diaries of the Anglo-German do not provide any details whether Gillman himself bought sex while working as an engineer at the *Central Railway* or whether his colleagues did. In any case, Gillman's sexual desire does occasionally shine through his diary entries. Although no information is given about him having sex with (African) women in the construction camp or anywhere else in German East Africa, it appears that he bought sex when he was still in Europe. When on his first passage from Europe to East Africa in autumn 1905, he visited the archaeological excavations of the Roman city of Pompeii near Naples, which had been destroyed by a volcanic eruption in the first century. In Pompeii, Gillman had also the chance to visit the ruins of an antique brothel and reported in his diary on the same evening:

> By kindness of the managers and by aid of several tips managed to get into the little collection of paintings found in the Pompeii-whore-houses. Very interesting, though very dirty. Saw a series of utensils [. . .] in the shape of male genitalien [sic!]. Remarkable that only the male genitals are used for this purpose and <u>no</u> female. Before going on board visited a dark Italian girl, at 6 o'clock. 7 went on board.[360]

Although maybe premeditatively focused on sexual issues by his visit to the Pompeii 'whore-houses', the 'dark Italian girl' was very likely a sex worker – an assumption perhaps confirmed by the rather short duration of the visit. Similar entries about Gillman as a sex worker's client do not exist in the diaries, but the general issue of sex is mentioned on other occasions. As soon as Gillman sets foot on East African soil, he exoticises and sexualises the physical appearance of African and Indian women on several occasions. More telling, perhaps, is when Gillman notes down the price levels of several items needed for the construction of the *Central Railway*, as well as food and medicine: also the wages of workmen,

---

358 UAH. MD 1543, Bericht über die Bahnmission z.Z. Manyoini bei Kilimatinde, 1. Januar-31. März 1911. Qtd. in: Reichart. *Gari*, p. 46.
359 Cf. Gillman Diaries. Mss. Afr. S. 1175/1,2_2, no. 13, pp. 40–42.
360 Gillman Diaries. Mss. Afr. S. 1175/1,2_1_no. 8, p. 7.

personal servants ('*boy*') and a *bibi* (concubine) are recorded. With fifteen Rupees per month, a *bibi* would receive at least the same salary as a *boy* or cook (ten to fifteen Rupees per month).[361] Hence, one cannot say without doubt if the *bibi* meant by Gillman would be employed only as cook, for example, or as a personal servant in charge of the engineer's household or as a concubine. In addition, in modern Swahili, *bibi* translates also simply into 'lady', 'madam' or 'grandmother', without any distinct sexual meaning. Nevertheless, *bibi* generally described a female concubine or a sex worker (during the colonial period) as well. The statements of the railway missionary, Gaarde, and other sources suggest this too.[362]

Whereas it is not clear whether Gillman had a concubine at the construction camp and whether he bought sex there must remain in speculation, his diary shows that the wife of one of his *boys* must have caught Gillman's fancy. When at his first construction camp in December 1905, it seems that he attempted at least to flirt with her – an offer that was distinctly rejected, however.

> I spent an other [sic!] half hour joking away with my boy's wife, a real beauty [. . .]. I notice here that these muhammedan wives are very faithful + that nothing can make them be unfaithful to her husbands, at least as long as he treats them well. I also noticed that these "ladies" think very little of their "fallen sisters" in D[ar es Salaam]. + won't have anything to do with them.[363]

Here, the wife of Gillman's *boy* not only illustrates her own sexual self-determination as a woman, but she also underlines her societal status. Describing sex workers as 'fallen sisters', her statement, as noted down by Gillman, also illustrates the societal marginalisation of the *vakapela* in German East Africa, which gradually increased towards the end of formal German colonial rule.[364] As far as the sources are concerned, there is not – and cannot be – an unfiltered female voice to be found in Gillman's diary. Generally, remarks about his relationship to African and Indian women become less frequent and almost nonexistent from ca. 1907 onwards. The reason is probably Gillman's marriage to Eva Kerber in 1908 during his first holiday in Europe. Shortly after the wedding, Eva joined Gillman in the colony and a few months later, their first son was born. With their son still being a toddler, the entire family lived together in German East Africa, partly in construction camps but also in proper buildings in colonial towns such as Tabora.[365]

---

361 Cf. Gillman Diaries. Mss. Afr. S. 1175/1,2_1_no. 8, pp. 54–57, 61, 74.

362 Cf. Walther. *Sex and Control*, p. 27. Cf. TNA. G 21/403. Ermittelungssache gegen Unbekannt [wegen angeblicher Freiheitsberaubung, begangen an einer eingeborenen Prostituierten]. 1912.

363 Gillman Diaries. Mss. Afr. S. 1175/1,2_1_no. 8, pp. 34–35. Cf. pp. 29–30.

364 Cf. Sunseri. *Vilimani*, pp. 178–186.

365 Eva's role is decisive in terms of (domestic care) work. For the wedding and married life until the 1920s Cf. Holye. *Gillman*, pp. 84–170.

The disappearance of references to sex in Gillman's diaries does of course not mean that also sex work vanished from the *Central Railway*'s construction sites. Assessing other sources and studies, it must be stressed that sex work remained integral until the very end of formal German colonial rule in East Africa and was one central aspect of the global history of labour in East Africa, too. Dr Karl Oetker, who was employed by *Holzmann* between 1905–07 as railway doctor, almost boasted retrospectively that he had "treated at least 46 fresh cases of Europeans having venereal diseases" during his "relatively short stay" in Africa and thus put forward the opinion by his colleague Dr Krauß, quoted above, that concubinage should be preferred to sex work, as this form of 'coloniser-monogamy' would prevent the spread of venereal diseases.[366] Yet, the favouring of concubinage at the expense of sex work does not mean that concubinage between a European man and an African woman was necessarily free of coercion. Generally, the line between concubinage, sex work and rape at the *Central Railway*'s construction sites was very thin indeed. Often, Europeans in German colonies targeted especially underage females because they held the view that having intercourse with sexually inexperienced girls would reduce the probability of contracting venereal diseases.[367] In this respect, one individual court proceeding against a Greek sub-contractor, illustrates the many facets and entanglements of labour, (sex) work and sexualised violence at the *Central Railway*'s construction sites.

Between December 1911 and March 1912, the district court of Tabora handled a case against a twenty-four-year-old Cretan Greek Orthodox Christian railway sub-contractor, Emmanuel Jeronimakis, who was working for the German engineer Giese at km 592 of the *Central Railway*. The Greek was accused of having had sex with a minor East African female, called Adaa. Adaa had accompanied her older brother Degera from Ussandawa near Dodoma to the construction camps of the *Central Railway*. It seems that Degera was unmarried because it was Adaa's task to do the housework for her brother when he was occupied constructing the railway during the daytime. With Adaa accompanying her brother to the construction camp, she genuinely enabled his employment at the construction site, as she sustained his working capabilities with her devotion to domestic work. Although the defendant Jeronimakis had already had an older East African concubine, named Tinde, for some time, the Greek wanted Adaa to become his second *bibi*. Trying to convince Adaa to become his concubine, Jeronimakiks offered her consumption goods such as soap and cloth as well as forty Rps. In fact, Adaa firmly rejected the sub-contractor's approach and literally threw the objects offered to her in Jeronimakis' face. Furious, the Greek sub-contractor did not refrain from his plan, carried out

366 Oetker. *Die Negerseele*, p. 33, cf. pp. 29–36.
367 Cf. Walther. *Sex and Control*, pp. 24–52.

similar assaults and ultimately kidnapped Adaa's brother Degera and threatened to whip both Degera and Adaa with his *kiboko*. Threatened by violence and facing her brother in custody, Adaa finally joined Jeronimakis and became his second *bibi* involuntarily. Those witnesses heard in court, who were not directly employed by Jeronimakis, like his cook or *boy* and who were not of European descent, reported that Adaa had been much too young for any sexual relationship and had suffered throughout her entire forced concubinage with Jeronimakis. These witnesses further reported that after one preceding unsuccessful attempt, Adaa committed suicide as she had probably not seen any other way to escape her bondage with the Greek sub-contractor. Even though almost all witnesses at court testified that Jeronimakis had coerced Adaa into concubinage, Adaa's death as such was not part of the prosecution against the Greek sub-contractor. The only thing pending before the court was the question whether Jeronimakis had had sex with a minor female person and not the question whether he had driven her into suicide. The investigation found that it could not unambiguously ascertain whether Adaa was underaged or not, even when questioning nine witnesses. All the European witnesses and those employed by Jeronimakis judged Adaa to have been fifteen or sixteen years of age and therefore physically mature enough for sexual intercourse. In contrast, the non-European witnesses and those not employed by Jeronimakis claimed predominantly the opposite, saying that Adaa had still been a child and therefore judged any sexual relationship of Adaa as illegitimate. Attempting to clarify the issue, the court sought to exhume the dead body and question Adaa's parents about her date of birth. Whereas the German physician assistant Schreier concluded after the examination of the dead body that Adaa must have been seven or eight years of age only, the questioning of Adaa's father found that she had been sixteen years of age. Given such conflicting views, the court found that it was not able to judge Adaa's age unequivocally and ultimately ruled that Jeronimakis had to pay 100 Rps. indemnity to Adaa's father for his loss.[368]

Thus, it seems that Europeans working at the *Central Railway* could rather easily get away with serious sexual offences and assaults without any significant consequence. In this respect, Adaa's individual case is probably only the tip of the iceberg, as a 'sexual frontier' was part of the mindset of colonial conquest and only a minority of incidents was ever heard at court.[369] At the least, Adaa's case shows that rape, concubinage and sex work are difficult to differentiate in the

368 Cf. TNA. G27/53. Strafsache gegen den Unternehmer Emanuel Jeronimakis, km 592 der Tanganyika-Eisenbahn, wegen Verführung [der angeblich minderjährigen Adaa und Verschuldung ihres Selbstmordes]. 1911–1912, pp. 1–14, 20–50.

369 For several legal proceedings due to sexual offences cf. TNA. G21/403. Cf. TNA. G21/680. Strafsache gegen den Landwirt Leopold Hierl, Dabaga bei Iringa [aufgrund einer Strafanzeige des Haupt-

colonial context. As far as the global history of labour is concerned, Adaa's case demonstrates the multifaceted entanglements of labour at the *Central Railway*'s construction sites. Adaa came to the railway site to enable and support her brother's work there, just as many other women accompanied men to the railway for this reason. Her experience of sexualised violence and coerced concubinage – by a European who already had another concubine – proves that such practices were widespread at the *Central Railway*, and illustrates the thin line between colonial sex work and rape as part of the 'colonial frontier'. In Adaa's case, it seems her only means of resisting that frontier was the extreme of suicide.

manns Tom v. Prince] wegen Unzucht [mit der minderjährigen Eingeborenen Mdene]. 1899–1900. Cf. TNA. G21/210. Strafsache gegen den ehemaligen Kanzleigehilfen, Heinrich Klemp, Morogoro, wegen Sittlichkeitsverbrechen [an der Tochter des gefangenen Sultans Masudi aus Tabora]. 1908–1911. Cf. G21/271. Ermittelungssache gegen den Zollhilfsbeamten Kurt Robscheit, Daressalaam, wegen Notzucht an der Binti Nasoro. 1909–1910. Cf. TNA. G21/686. Strafsache gegen den italienischen Unternehmer Marras Salvatore, km 412 der Tanganyika-Eisenbahn, wegen versuchter Notzucht und Mißhandlung [der Fatuma]. 1910–1911. Cf. TNA. G21/347. Ermittelungssache gegen den Polizeiwachtmeister Lindner, Daressalaam, wegen Vergewaltigung [der Mwatonya binti Hanyange] 1911. Cf. TNA. G21/428. Ermittelungssache gegen den Gouvernements-Büroassistenten Thurmann Bezirksnebenstelle Kibata, Bez. Kilwa, wegen Notzucht [an der Frau seines Kochs Thumi sowie der Frau des Polizeiwachtmeisters Littmann, Kilwa]. 1912. Cf. TNA. G21/592. Strafsache gegen den Unternehmer Max Miersen, Daressalaam, wegen Versuchter Notzucht [an der Geliebten eines Askaris der 18. Feldkompanie, Habiba binti Mkondo]. 1915–1916. Cf. TNA. G21/644. Ermittelungssache gegen den Stadtkassenbeamten Fernandes Persi, Daressalaam, wegen versuchter Notzucht [an der Andikalo binti Baruti]. 1915.

4 "The Machine" Defeats an Engine: The *Otto* Plantation in Kilossa

4.1 There Is Something Rotten in the State of the 'Empire of Cotton'

> [The Empire of] Cotton [. . .] brought seeming opposites together [. . .]: slavery and free labor, states and markets, colonialism and free trade, industrialisation and deindustrialisation [as well as] plantation and factory, slavery and wage labor, colonizers and colonized, railroads and steamships – in short, [. . .] a global network of land, labor, transport, manufacture and sale.
>
> Sven Beckert. *Empire of Cotton*. 2014.[1]

Analysing the history of cotton, the "nineteenth century chief global commodity", in his *New History of Global Capitalism*, Sven Beckert observes that cotton was first cultivated and manufactured over 1,000 years ago. Ever since, the production of cotton textiles had been the most important industry in Asia, South America and Africa. In contrast, the role of cotton was negligible in Europe, where sheep wool and linen were the major fabrics and where textiles made from cotton remained a scarce luxury item for centuries. From 1600 onwards, the production of cotton and its global circulation was significantly altered by violent European economic agitation, which was termed 'war capitalism' by the historian Sven Beckert: independent networks of cotton production and distribution all over the world were integrated by European military agitation, thus amalgamating Asian textile manufacturing with European capital and American raw material production. Slavery was at the heart of this system of 'war capitalism' as Indian textiles were the currency to buy slaves in West Africa, who were deported to the Americas subsequently. With these deported slaves working on cotton plantations all over the Americas, the widespread resource scarcity in cotton textile production in Europe was slowly but surely overcome, which enabled as well as fuelled the 'industrial revolution' in the northern hemisphere. As the invested European capital was hedged by guarantees on raw material supplies like cotton or by mortgages on slaves, the initially multipolar global network of cotton and textile production was turned into a unipolar network centering on the British trading hub of Liverpool and the textile producing region of Lancashire.[2]

---

1 Beckert. *Empire of Cotton*, pp. xix–xx.

2 Cf. Beckert. *Empire of Cotton*, pp. 3–28. Cf. Rösser, Michael et al. 'Baumwolle, die Firma Joh. Anton Lucius aus Erfurt und der koloniale Kapitalismus'. 9–12. *Heimat Thüringen*, 27. Jahrgang,

https://doi.org/10.1515/9783111218090-004

By the beginning of the nineteenth century, textile factories had become the backbone of the entirety of western European industry and therefore, also of the national income. For example, in 1830s Britain every sixth worker was employed by the textile industry where he or she processed cotton that had been grown on slave plantations, especially those in the US southern states. By increasing the industrialisation and mechanisation of textile production in Europe, 'war capitalism', marked by slavery and industrial capitalism and characterised by large-scale investments, mutually reinforced each other, leading to a steady rise in global economic activity until the American Civil War between 1861 and 1865. The American Civil War disrupted this early global economic system as it challenged the core and central economic element of the global production of cotton: slavery. The resulting first world-wide economic resource crisis left thousands of workers in Europe unemployed. This so-called 'cotton famine' engraved itself into the memory of all Europeans involved in cotton processing, and made businessmen and state dignitaries alike aware of their dependency on cheap raw materials that had predominantly originated from slave plantations in the US South. With the 'Reconstruction Era' ending slavery in the South of the USA after the Civil War, old-established forms of slave labour gave way to other exploitative forms of work such as sharecropping. This mode of cotton cultivation secured the supply of raw cotton on the one hand but posed other challenges to the textile industry on the other. As the price level of raw cotton would never return to antebellum levels, textile production became more costly, and industrial capitalism thus sought new alliances to produce cheap raw materials for the sake of a flourishing European textile industry. This new ally of industrial capitalism was the modern European nation states that had emerged in the course of the 'industrial revolution' and now provided industrial production with an efficient bureaucracy to lower production costs once again. The new bureaucratic tools such as a sophisticated legal system and a reliable bureaucracy was enabled by and centred on a formal colonisation that had been typical for the last third of the 'long nineteenth century'. Instead of the privately run colonising enterprises, the modern nation state now sought to expand its administrative system to its overseas territories and attempted to rule these territories accordingly. Flooding the markets of the Global South with European industrial textiles led to a wave of deindustrialisation in Asia and Africa and radically rearranged the Global South's agriculture. There, millions of people abandoned old-established occupations such as hand spinning and hand weaving, and Euro-

Heft 1. Weimar: 2020, pp. 9–12. Cf. Rösser, Michael. 'Knotenpunkte des Kolonialen'. *Vorstudie 'Kolonialistisches Denken und Kolonialkultur in Stuttgart'.* Ed. Stadtarchiv Stuttgart. Stuttgart: 19 July 2021. Web. https://archiv0711.hypotheses.org/files/2021/07/Stadtarchiv_Stuttgart_Kolonialistisches-Denken-Stuttgart.pdf (10 September 2021), pp. 11–12, 25–26.

pean trading houses replaced old-established sales networks, formerly dominated by local merchants. Meanwhile, the European imperial states pushed for cotton monocultures in their overseas territories, which were increasingly incorporated into formal colonial administrations. The German *Reich* and her colony, German East Africa, also played their part within this 'empire of cotton' at the turn of the nineteenth to the twentieth century.[3]

In fact, Beckert's master narrative of western 'war capitalism' slowly but surely ousting the cotton production of the Global South needs some historical adjustment. Regarding the 'big picture' of the history of globalisation, Beckert's master narrative is certainly correct.[4] But with Jonathan E. Robins having demonstrated that the 'empire of cotton' also witnessed 'failed states' within its realm, it must be stressed that the history of the Global North as the dominator of global cotton and textile production also includes histories that do not entirely fit Beckert's master narrative. Although the general trend in the global history of cotton proves Beckert right in the long run, Robins' study about the failure of the British Cotton Growing Association (BCGA) in British colonial Africa, for example, proves that individual cotton production schemes did not necessarily confirm the narrative of the steady rise of the 'empire of cotton'. As in the case of the BCGA, which sought to boost African colonial cotton production for the profits of the British Empire, many individual cotton production schemes, or individual enterprises like cotton plantations, failed or had very limited economic success.[5] This holds true not only for the BCGA, but also for German East Africa and the history of the textile producing company of *Otto*, which established a cotton plantation in the town of Kilossa in 1907. Formal colonisation and an alliance between the imperial state and cotton producing companies *à la* Beckert serves as a significant historical background for the history of the *Otto* plantation in Kilossa as well. But as the cotton production of the *Otto* plantation failed comprehensively, the entrepreneurial history of *Otto* and German cotton colonialism rather points to Robins' findings. With Beckert providing the grand narrative of global capitalism and Robins showing an individual case of a failed colonial cotton production scheme,

3 Cf. Beckert. *Empire of Cotton*, pp. 29–378. Cf. Rösser. 'Baumwolle', pp. 9–12.

4 For another study explaining the rise of the western world as the major cotton supplier besides that of Beckert (and others) centring particularly on the fall of India at the expense of the west cf. Riello. *Cotton*.

5 Cf. Robins. *Cotton and Race*, pp. 1–29, 72–115. Cf. Pepijn Brandon: Review on: *Robins, Jonathan E.: Cotton and Race Across the Atlantic. Britain, Africa, and America, 1900–1920*. Martlesham. Web. *Connections. A Journal for Historians and Area Specialists*. 29 September 2019. www.connections.clio-online.net/publicationreview/id/reb-26130 (21 October 2019). Cf. Dernburg. *Südwestafrikanische Eindrücke*, pp. 60–61.

the two studies are complementary. Their combination shows, on the one hand, the 'empire of cotton' was on the rise globally, while on the other hand, this rise was not linear and all encompassing but also took various forms of dead ends and diversions.

In any case, both studies neglect the perspective of the many individuals who peopled the 'empire of cotton' and both lack a detailed analysis of the phenomenon of labour. That is why this case study seeks to focus on the protagonists of the history of global cotton production and their agency, relationships, contradictions and conflicts in the context of labour in German East Africa. This is especially important because influential research about the global history of cotton has "given little space to labour"[6], so far. Only the historian of Africa Thaddeus Sunseri stressed comparatively early that the German colonial "*Arbeiterfrage* and the *Baumwollfrage* – the labour question and the cotton question – [were] the two most pressing issues in the political economy of German East Africa."[7] Accordingly, he investigated the agency of East Africans when growing and harvesting the cash crop cotton on colonial plantations and on their own petty farms in German East Africa. As his work was published before the rise of the global history approach, it is therefore limited in its scope. Even though Sunseri's research results in general, and about the *Otto* plantation in Kilossa in particular, are very precious for the present study, he nevertheless fails to notice the broader dimensions of the history of cotton and (German) colonialism at the turn of the nineteenth century. Sunseri therefore misses the entanglements of the history of cotton, German colonialism and the global history of labour as they go far beyond East Africa and Germany. Besides the German *Reich*, German East Africa, and the local history of Unterboihingen, this study encompasses many regions of the world: especially German colonies such as Togo, but also the US American South, southwest India, as well as the British colonial Nigeria and Uganda. Hence, this global labour history reinvestigates the history of the *Otto* cotton plantation in Kilossa, and the relationships of the individual protagonists involved in the context of labour at this enterprise.

6 Riello. *Cotton*, p. 11.
7 Sunseri. *Vilimani*, pp. 2–3.

4.2 Cotton Between Alabama, Africa, India and Unterboihingen

> We can learn extraordinarily much from our neighbours about the introduction of suitable cultivation to our colonies. [. . .] Questions about cultivation suitable for the production of textiles matters most in Württemberg and I have been told that people are fairly surprised that only a very small amount of [German colonial] cotton is in our market..
>
> State Secretary Bernhard Dernburg. Speech in Stuttgart, 23 January 1907.[8]

The cultivation of cotton was one of the most important issues discussed in the course of German colonialism. Like the other European imperial powers, the German *Kaiserreich*, as a relatively recent colonial Empire, also sought cheap raw materials for its significant textile industry that employed a large share of the entire national workforce. Simultaneously, the southwestern German textile company *Otto*, from Unterboihingen near Stuttgart, wanted to emancipate itself from British and US American cotton imports. The complementary interests of the German *Reich* and the Swabian textile company thus intersected in the colony of German East Africa at the southwestern town of Kilossa located in the *Kilwa* district. As the German *Reich* was the third largest producer of cotton yarn and the second largest textile exporter in the world, by the turn of the nineteenth century, ideas to increase raw cotton production were central to German colonial policies. Throughout this century, the high fluctuation of raw cotton prices in general as well as major political crises like the Napoleonic Continental System (1806–1813) and the American Civil War (1861–1865), repeatedly posed major challenges to the German textile industry. To provide the significant German textile industry, which employed one-tenth of the entire German industrial working class, with a stable amount of raw cotton at reasonable prices had thus become one of the major long-term goals of many German textile companies. At the same time, it had also been a matter of national interest for the *Reich* and its individual member states. The idea to produce cotton in territories controlled by Germany gained renewed momentum at the beginning of the twentieth century. The idea to become a significant raw cotton producer was also inspired by many influential Germans who had lived and worked in the USA and who later became central to German colonial cotton policies in Africa. Besides German textile companies and senior German colonial representatives, the idea to produce German colonial cotton to overcome global fluctuations of raw cotton prices and the dependency on the USA as the major producer of this raw material was further pushed by German lobby associations. These groups demanded colonial expansion, fostering the self-controlled pro-

8 Dernburg. *Koloniale Lehrjahre*, pp. 12–13.

duction of raw cotton in these overseas territories. The most important association in terms of German colonial cultivation was the colonial economic committee (*Kolonialwirtschaftliches Komitee – KWK*), founded by the Nuremberg businessman Karl Supf. It supported the idea of German cotton autarky through increased colonial production in her territories overseas. Since its foundation in 1896, the *KWK* had lobbied both the *Reich's* administration and German textile businesses to pursue this goal accordingly. Indeed, many colonial cotton schemes – in Togo and other German colonies in Africa – bore the *KWK's* handwriting.[9]

In this respect, Andrew Zimmermann has first revealed the global connections between the *KWK*, the economies of cotton in the US American South, German colonialism in West Africa's Togo, and German domestic policies and its territories in East Prussia. In the same speech quoted above, Bernhard Dernburg expressed his admiration for post-Reconstruction US American cotton cultivation, as he regarded it as a 'role model' for corresponding German policies in her colonial territories. Besides German East Africa, he noticed "keen interest" especially in "West Africa" in the textile manufacturing "circles of Stuttgart"[10], not only deriving from the century-long tradition of West African indigenous cotton cultivation, but also from the well-known joint project of the German *KWK* and Booker T. Washington's Tuskegee colleges in the USA. German colonialism, the US American cotton cultivation and the conservative ideas of the Afro-American civil rights leader Washington intersected first in German colonial Togo in 1900. There, German colonial policy makers attempted a more systematic and sustained approach to stir the economy of colonial Togo, intending to make cotton the number one cash crop in the colony. German governmental officials and the *KWK* took a look across the Atlantic in search of inspiring methods of cultivation that would promote the planting of cotton in Togo. America's way of cultivating cotton in its southern states, in cooperation with Washington's Tuskegee colleges, appeared promising to the members of the *KWK* and the German colonial administration:

> The German interest in the Tuskegee graduates was rooted in the conviction that race relations in the American South might offer a model for Germany's African colonies. German bureaucrats and social scientists [around Max Weber] were particularly taken with Booker T. Washington, [. . .] who had [. . .] his conception of natural hierarchies of race. Washing-

---

9 Cf. Beckert. *Empire of Cotton*, pp. 3–378. Cf. Haller, Lea. Review on Beckert, Sven*: King Cotton. Eine Geschichte des globalen Kapitalismus. München: 2014. H-Soz-Kult.* 29 January 2015. Web. www.hsozkult.de/publicationreview/id/rezbuecher-23097. (16 July 2019). Cf. TECHNOSEUM – Landesmuseum für Technik und Arbeit in Mannheim (LTA). 871.1-otto-233. Chronik, pp. 69–71. Cf. Demhardt, Imre Josef. *Deutsche Kolonialgesellschaft. 1888–1918. Ein Beitrag zur Organisationsgeschichte der deutschen Kolonialbewegung*. Wiesbaden: 2002, pp. 70–71.
10 Dernburg. *Koloniale Lehrjahre*, p. 9, cf. pp. 4, 11, 13.

> ton assumed that there would be a need – after the abolition of slavery – first to 'educate' the African Americans in a Christian life, manual labor, and small-scale farming, so that gradually over time they might acquire the status of full citizens. His conservative views on social and racial relations were well aligned with the European imperialist understanding of control and segregation. [. . .] Washington for his part supported imperialism, for he regarded Africa as backward and in need of a civilizing mission – and he was convinced that the Germans were particularly well suited for the task.[11]

It therefore appeared only logical, for both the *KWK* and Washington, to send Afro-American Tuskegee graduates from the American south to German colonial Togo, as German scholars in the emerging subject of sociology had insinuated a similarity between Togo's colonial economy and the US America's 'New South'. As pious Afro-(American) Christians 'properly educated' in the manual skills of small-scale cotton cultivation, the Tuskegee graduates' task as experts in the cultivation of cotton was to pass their knowledge on to the African inhabitants of Togo. It was hoped that the global transfer of knowledge by black Americans to black Africans would ultimately lead to a flourishing Togolese colonial economy, with cotton as its major cash-crop. When arriving in Togo, the Afro-American Tuskegee experts James Calloway, John Winfrey Robinson, Allan Burks and Shepard Harris attempted to avoid the mistakes made in the US American south and rejected the German colonisers' idea to push for cotton monocultures in the colony. Instead, the Tuskegee experts recommended the "joint development of cotton and food crops [for individual subsistence] in 'harmonious ways'".[12] They thus rejected the increasing coercion exercised by German colonial officials and planters towards the local population in Togo. But all in vain: Calloway, Robinson, Burks and Harris' appeals were increasingly ignored by the German colonial administration that finally imposed their policies, against the advice of the Tuskegee representatives. Ignoring the deficiencies of US-cotton production, and transplanting a defective scheme from Alabama to a German colony soon proved to be as disastrous as the previous German colonial policies in Togo. One major reason for this failure was the fact that the German colonial policies of cotton cultivation in Togo met the fierce resistance of the Ewe people, who were the dominant ethnic group in Togo's south, who fiercely opposed urgings to change the division of labour among the sexes, for example. Likewise, they rejected labour recruitment practices and the so-called 'education for work' approach, not to mention the imposed labour conditions on German colonial cotton plantations – often characterised by corporal punishment and policies of forced labour.[13]

11 Conrad, Sebastian. *What is*, p. 138.
12 Beckert. *Empire of Cotton*, p. 373.
13 Cf. Conrad. *What is*, pp. 137–139. Cf. Zimmerman. *Alabama in Africa*, pp. 112–172, 237–250.

The German *Reich* was not alone in its failed colonial cotton schemes: likewise, British colonialists, associated with the British Cotton Growing Association (BCGA), also failed in Nigeria and Uganda almost simultaneously. Although not a quasi-state-sponsored association like the German *KWK*, but rather a privately run 'semi-philanthropic' endeavour, the BCGA regarded the 'Alabama in Africa' approach as a role model to follow in British colonies as well. It is therefore not very surprising that their approach also failed because of local African resistance and ignorance towards the economic realities of British colonies in Africa.[14] Yet, experimental cotton schemes were not only pursued in Togo, Nigeria or Uganda, they were also integral to colonial policies in German East Africa. Again, US American cotton cultivation served as a corresponding role model and influenced the policies of significant representatives of the German (colonial) administration.

4.3 German Colonial State Dignitaries and Their Admiration for US Cotton Policies

> Cotton is in the foreground of interest. [. . .] The extraordinary demand of the home country on the one hand [. . .], and on the other hand the concern which has been carried into domestic circles by price manipulations in the main producing country, the United States, have made the supply of cotton a burning question. [. . .] [W]e may today speak of well-founded expectations that we will succeed in covering a very considerable percentage of our imports of raw textiles from our own colonies within a foreseeable period of time.
>
> Bernhard Dernburg. Public Speech in Dresden, 17 January 1909.[15]

Stakeholders in the German cotton trade, financial institutions and textile producers in places such as Bremen, Hamburg, Frankfurt o.M. or Barmen had strong ties to US raw cotton production throughout the nineteenth century.[16] When Germany had finally become a colonising nation in the 1880s, US American cotton production remained a focal point for top-ranking German colonial officials. In German East Africa it was Gustaf Adolf Götzen, Governor from 1900 to 1906, who first decidedly pushed for expansive colonial cotton policies. He thus intended to enhance the production of cotton in German East Africa by urging the local African population into the cultivation of this crop. Having worked as German Military Attaché in Washington D.C. between 1896 and 1898, Götzen's experience in

14 Cf. Robins. *Cotton and Race*, pp. 116–164.

15 Dernburg. *Südwestafrikanische Eindrücke*, pp. 56–57.

16 Cf. Gaul, Patrick. *Ideale und Interessen. Die mitteleuropäische Wirtschaft im Amerikanischen Bürgerkrieg*. Stuttgart: 2021, pp. 15–32, 291–296.

the USA seems to have influenced his (economic) policies in German East Africa significantly. When Governor of German East Africa, Götzen's cotton plans were probably further fuelled by the Empire Cotton Exhibition organised by the BCGA in London in 1904, the *Landwirtschaftliche Ausstellung* (agricultural exhibition) in Zanzibar of 1905 and the Louisiana Purchase Exhibition of St. Louis in 1904 (St. Louis World's Fair), where cotton from German East Africa won a gold medal for its quality.[17]

Given this background and having lived in the USA, Götzen's subsequent colonial policies as Governor of German East Africa thus centred on the idea of boosting German colonial cotton production. By increasing taxes, fostering railway construction and introducing *Kommunalschamben*[18] to the colony, Götzen attempted to increase the cultivation of cotton there. The *Kommunalschamben* required every man of a particular village who was not employed at a European estate to work twenty-four days a year on such fields. The profits would be distributed among the *Akida* or *Jumbe*, and the village and its population. However, payment was only delivered months later, once the produce had been shipped to and sold in Europe. Sometimes, the African planters did not receive any payment at all and therefore resented the *Kommunalshamben*.[19] Whereas Götzen's taxation policies and the cotton *Kommunalshamben* had become notorious as being the major reasons behind the Maji Maji War (1905–1908), the Governor's unsuccessful lobbying for the so-called *Südbahn* (southern railway) or *Nyassa Railway* is less known:[20] Götzen intended this railway to give the colony's south an economic boost by providing the infrastructure necessary for increased agricultural, that is primarily cotton, production and transportation. Attempting to

17 Cf. Robins. *Cotton and Race*, pp. 60–61. Cf. Kolonialwirtschaftliches Komitee e.V. (Ed.). *Wirtschaftsatlas der deutschen Kolonien.* Berlin: 1906, n.p. cf. instead 'Ergebnisse' and 'deutschkoloniale Ausstellungen im Auslande'. Cf. German Imperial Commissioner (Ed.). *Official Catalogue of the Exhibition of the German Empire. International Exposition St. Louis 1904.* Berlin: n.Y, p. 488. Regarding world fairs and international exhibitions cf. Geppert, Alexander C.T. 'Weltausstellungen'. *EGO – Europäische Geschichte Online.* Web. http://ieg-ego.eu/de/threads/crossroads/wissensraeume/alexander-c-t-geppert-weltausstellungen (29 June 2020). Cf. Schröder, Iris. *Das Wissen von der ganzen Welt. Globale Geographien und räumliche Ordnungen Afrikas und Europas 1790–1870.* Paderborn: 2011, pp. 6–8, 51.

18 *Kommunalshamben* = 'community field' cf. Klein-Arendt, Reinhard. 'Ein Land wird gewaltsam in Besitz genommen. Die Kolonie Deutsch-Ostafrika'. *Der Maji-Maji-Krieg in Deutsch-Ostafrika 1905–1907.* 28–48. Eds. Felicitas Becker and Jigal Beez. Berlin: 2005, pp. 46–48. Cf. Gründer. *Geschichte*, p. 158.

19 Cf. Klein-Arendt. 'Ein Land', pp. 46–48. Cf. Gründer. *Geschichte*, p. 158.

20 Where to build colonial railways first was contemporarily hotly debated in German politics and among experts. Cf. section 3.1. Cf. Beese. *Experten*, pp. 77–104.

stir economic activity particularly in the southern half of the German colony, Götzen's view in favour of a colonial railway traversing the colony's south at the expense of a *Central Railway* must indeed be regarded in this light.[21] Although Götzen's railway plans never materialised, his cotton policy was nevertheless one major reason for the outbreak of the Maji Maji War against German colonial rule and its cotton policies in East Africa. Alongside the war against the Ovaherero and Nama (1904–1907) in German South West Africa, the Maji Maji War and the German general elections of 1907 increased the awareness and interest of both the German public and the German industry in the colonies and their economic potentials. Of course, the German textile industry was very interested in the considerations about the German colonies' potential to produce cotton. Thus, the issue remained at the heart of German policies towards colonial (East) Africa, despite – or even because of – the very costly colonial wars.[22]

Analogical to the project in Togo, Götzen and other German colonial officials also sought US American expertise and the support of the *KWK* to boost cotton cultivation in German East Africa.[23] The *KWK* thus hired a German-Texan cotton expert team in 1904 to transfer their knowledge about American cotton cultivation to the Mpanganya cotton school located near the Rufiji River in German East Africa. The Mpanganya cotton school was founded by the *KWK* to promote cotton cultivation among the local East African population, primarily in the period preceding the Maji Maji War. The German Texan cotton expert team was "headed by the German-American cotton farmer and former County Commissioner in Texas J.H.G. Becker. He [was] assisted by a cotton farmer, H.J. Wiebusch, also from Texas, as an agricultural assistant, and Karl Sasse, a master machinist with a background in cotton machinery." Especially in the Rufiyi area, "the German-American cotton expert F.A. Holzmann, who had previously been in charge of an experimental and teaching station in Texas in the service of the American government, was chosen. Among other things, a cotton school for the training of cotton instructors [was] established in this area." Furthermore, "Imperial Deputy Consul

21 Cf. Wegmann. *Vom Kolonialkrieg*, pp. 278–280. Cf. Götzen, Gustav Adolf. *Deutsch-Ostafrika im Aufstand 1905/06*. Berlin: 1909, pp. 18–20, 80–83. Cf. Wilhelm, Friedrich. 'Götzen, Adolf Graf von'. *Neue Deutsche Biographie*, 6, 1964, pp. 593–594. Web. https://www.deutsche-biographie.de/pnd11907253X.html#ndbcontent (21 October 2019). Cf. HADB. S 1514, pp. 141–159. Cf. Fuchs, Paul. *Die wirtschaftlichen Erkundungen einer ostafrikanischen Südbahn*. Berlin: 1905.

22 Cf. Giblin and Monson (Eds.). *Maji Maji. Lifting the Fog of War*. Cf. Becker, Felicitas and Beez, Jigal (Eds.). *Der Maji-Maji Krieg in Deutsch-Ostafrika 1905–1907*. Berlin: 2005. Cf. Becker. 'Die Hottentotten-Wahlen', pp. 177–189.

23 At the same time, similar strategies were also pursued by the British in Nigeria, Sudan, and Uganda. Cf. Robins. *Cotton and Race*, pp. 72–164.

Scheidt in Galveston [made] a point of engaging cotton experts. [. . .] [T]he Imperial Consulate ha[d] also taken over the protection of German farmers to be sent to the Agricultural and Mechanical College of Texas."[24] The abovementioned Wiebusch later also became the director of the Mpanganya cotton school. As constant cross-references to Togo's cotton schemes were not only made in the specialist journal *Der Tropenpflanzer,* but also at other occasions by representatives of the *KWK,* it is obvious that something similar to the Togo-Tuskegee peasant cotton system was believed to be promising not only for West Africa, but also for East Africa. Yet, there were also differences to be found between German colonial Togo and Mpanganya: Instead of recruiting Afro-American Tuskegee graduates for East Africa, German-Texan cotton experts were employed to educate "'intelligent'" East African "'natives', literate in Swahili", in Mpanganya for the task. They were sent to the surrounding areas of the *Rufiji* district to teach the 'proper way' to cultivate cotton to the local African populations. Mpanganya was thereby not the only institution established to educate local Swahili cotton experts, but it was the only agricultural school that existed over a longer period. From ca. 1904 onwards, that is prior to the Maji Maji War and until the end of the German colonial rule in East Africa after WWI, there were ca. five institutions like Mpanganya. Before taking up work in Kilossa, the *Otto* company's boss, Heinrich Otto, and his local plantation manager in Kilossa Ranga Kaundinya visited such experimental cotton plantations run by the KWK in early 1907. These cotton schools remained an important focal point and resource of knowledge for *Otto's* cotton cultivation until WWI: for instance, in summer 1913, Fritz Otto – one of the leading men of the family business – visited not only the *Otto* plantation itself but also institutions strongly related to and very similar to Mpanganya cotton school. Among these was the Miombo governmental agricultural research centre, which was intended to boost, particularly, cotton cultivation in German East Africa.[25]

24 Supf, Karl. 'Deutsch-koloniale Baumwoll-Unternehmnungen 1903/1904'. 411–417. Ed. Kolonialwirtschaftliches Komitee. *Der Tropenfplanzer. Zeitschrift für Tropische Landwirtschaft,* no. 8, August 1904, pp. 414–416.

25 Sunseri. *Vilimani,* p. 119. Cf. Stadtmuseum Wendlingen am Neckar. Konrad Steinert's private document collection, "Tagebuch von der Reise nach Kilossa. 26.6. – 18.9.1913 von Fritz Otto, Abschrift", p. 22. Cf. Kaundinya. *Erinnerungen,* pp. 18–20. Cf. Demhardt. *Deutsche Kolonialgesellschaft,* pp. 70–71. Paasche reports that Mr. Wiebusch was head of the school for cotton cultivation. Cf. Paasche, Hans. "'Der Aufstand" und "Gefechte am Rufiyi" aus: "Im Morgenhlicht. Kriegs-, Jagd- und Reise-Erlebnisse in Ostafrika"'. *Hans Paasche. Das Verlorene Paradies. Ansichten vom Lenbensweg eines Kolonialoffiziers zum Pazifisten und Revolutionär.* 48–86. Eds. P. Werner Lange und Helga Paasche. Berlin 2008, p. 51. Cf. Paasche, Hermann. *Deutsch-Ostafrika. Wirtschaftliche Studien.* Hamburg: 1913, pp. 111–113, 340–358. Cf. Supf. 'Deutsch-koloniale Baumwoll-Unternehmnungen 1903/1904'., pp. 412–417. Cf. Supf, Karl. 'Deutsch-koloniale Baumwoll-

In fact, it was not only Götzen's cotton policies before the Maji Maji War between 1905 and 1908 that were embedded in this context. German colonial cotton policies in East Africa, also after the Maji Maji War, bore a significant US American background. These post-war cotton policies were developed by Bernhard Dernburg, who took office as Colonial State Secretary in the Foreign Ministry in 1906, and who became head of the Colonial Department from 1907 onwards. Dernburg, himself a trained banker, had spent his formative years in the USA. In total, Dernburg visited the United States seven times and kept up strong relationships with the country throughout his entire life. As early as the 1890s, he had spent a substantial part of his training as a banker and as an investor in New York. Furthermore, he had contributed to the organisation and functioning of the German exhibition at the World's Fair, taking place in Chicago in 1893, of which Friedrich Dernburg, Bernhard's father, was a member of the German commission responsible for the German exhibition at the fair. In Chicago Friedreich Dernburg was, furthermore, the German press representative, and reported about the World's Fair repeatedly. Apart from these close connections, Bernhard Dernburg was employed by *Ladenburg & Thalmann & Co.* in this period. This bank was strongly associated with the influential German banking dynasty of the *Bankhaus S. Bleichröder* that had numerous investments in North America during Bernhard Dernburg's initial stays in the USA. Furthermore, the future German Colonial State Secretary had established close ties with the German American railroad magnate Henry Villard (Heinrich Hilgard), who as a senior figure of numerous major American railways (e.g. *Northern Pacific Railroad*) had channelled major investments of leading German banks into US American railway construction and was to inspire Dernburg's colonial railway policies in Africa in the future.[26]

Other people Dernburg had met in the USA would also become important men in the colonial administration of German colonies in Africa. Freiherr Bruno von Schuckmann, for instance, whom Dernburg had met in the USA in the 1890s, was later even appointed Governor of German South West Africa in 1907 by Dernburg.

Unternehmungen Bericht IV (Herbst 1904)'. 615–621. Ed. Kolonialwirtschaftliches Komitee. *Der Tropenpflanzer. Zeitschrift für Tropische Landwirtschaft*, no. 11, November 1904, pp. 615–621. Cf. Delegated Representatives of Master Cotton Spinners' and Manufacturer's Association. *Official Report of the Proceedings of the First International Congress.* Manchester: 1904, pp. 20–24. Cf. Schanz, Moritz. 'Der koloniale Baumwollanbau und Deutschland'. 160–172. Ed. Internationaler Verband der Spinner und Webervereinigungen. *Offizieller Bericht des Achten Internationalen Kongresses der Baumwoll-Industrie.* Manchester et al: 1911, pp. 167–171. Cf. Dernburg. *Zielpunkte*, pp. 5–21. Cf. Naranch. 'Colonised Body'.

26 Cf. Schiefel. *Bernhard Dernburg*, pp. 17–24. Cf. Dernburg, Friedrich. *Aus der weißen Stadt. Spaziergänge in der Chicagoer Weltausstellung und weitere Fahrten.* Berlin: 1893, pp. 1–8, 31–38, 101–109.

Given his close ties and admiration for both Schuckmann, Villard, and the latter’s railway empire, it is therefore not very surprising that Dernburg regarded railway construction as the most decisive tool of any colonial economy. Yet, Governor of German East Africa, Albrecht von Rechenberg (1906–1912), also exerted significant influence on the Colonial State Secretary as far as the economy of the colony was concerned. Rechenberg emphasised the incorporation of small-scale African cash-crop production into the colonial economy. Having observed how the *Uganda Railway* had improved the sales and transport opportunities of East African farmers in British East Africa, Rechenberg was convinced that railways would boost the economy in the neighbouring German colony, too. Dernburg agreed and it seems that, to him, not only were Rechenberg’s arguments decisive, but so also was the fact that he regarded the US economy as a role model for any successful politics and a thriving economy. To Bernhard Dernburg’s father, there was no doubt that for “the way a patriotic man does his duty to the fatherland, [his son Bernhard] had in mind the American statesmen as masters”.[27] As railways had been the backbone of the US westward expansion, Dernburg’s colonial policies centred on railways analogically. Not only in German East Africa, but also in German South West Africa, railway construction was thus reinforced as a priority after Dernburg had taken office in the *Reich’s* colonial department from 1907 onwards. Besides railways, the US production of cotton was a subject of Dernburg’s admiration as well: to study the southern Afro-American cotton economy more closely, Dernburg visited Texas in 1909 only shortly after his inspection tours to German East Africa, German South West Africa and South Africa, between 1907 and 1908. This was certainly no coincidence as Texas was the largest raw cotton exporting region in the world at that time.[28] Clearly, it appears that the combination of US raw cotton production and US railway infrastructure must have made a lasting impression, not only on Governor

---

27 Dernburg, Friedrich. ‘Aus Bernhard Dernburg’s Werdegang’. 402–407. *Koloniale Rundschau. Monatsschrift für die Interessen unserer Schutzgebiete und ihrer Bewohner,* no. 7, Berlin: July 1910, p. 406.

28 Cf. Rösser. *Forced Labour,* pp. 22–24. Cf. Iliffe. *Tanganyika under German Rule,* pp. 71–80. Cf. Schiefel. *Bernhard Dernburg.*, pp. 17–24, 30–62, 66–80, 90–100. Cf. Dernburg, Bernhard. *Baumwollfragen. Vortrag, gehalten auf Veranlassung des Deutschen Handelstages am 14. April 1910.* Berlin: 1910, pp. 2–5, 9–10. Cf. Jöhlinger, Otto. ‘Bernhard Dernburg. Ein kaufmännischer Minister’. *Der Kaufmann und das Leben. Beiblatt zur Zeitschrift für Handelswissenschaft und Handelspraxis.* 1–13. Eds. Arthur Schröter and Heinz Rühl. Leipzig und Kassel, no. 5. Mai 1911, pp. 1–4, 6–8, 11–13. Cf. Schumacher, Martin. “Hilgard, Heinrich”. *Neue Deutsche Biographie,* 9, 1972, p. 139. Web. https://www.deutsche-biographie.de/pnd119068605.html#ndbcontent (05 February 2020). Cf. “Schuckmann, v.”. *Deutsches Koloniallexikon,* 1920, Band II, p. 306. Web. *University of Frankfurt o.M.* http://www.ub.bildarchiv-dkg.uni-frankfurt.de/Bildprojekt/Lexikon/Standardframeseite.php (05 February 2020). Cf. “Eisenbahnen”. *Deutsches Koloniallexikon.*

Götzen but also on Colonial State Secretary Bernhard Dernburg. Both men had had significant experiences in the USA and pushed for corresponding policies, equally stressing cotton and railroads in German East Africa and in other colonies of the *Reich.* Dernburg's statement made to the southwestern German textile producers quoted above must be seen precisely in this context. His corresponding policies can be differentiated into two major phases: Before the end of the Maji Maji War, that is between ca. 1906 and 1908, Dernburg laid his emphasis on the support of large-scale cotton plantations like *Otto's* that intended to cultivate large-scale cotton monocultures, with modern steam machines. Afterwards, the Colonial State Secretary switched and focussed on small-scale peasant cotton cultivation, centring on African farmers. Simultaneously, he decreased his support for capital-intensive European monoculture plantations. Delivering his election speech in Stuttgart in 1907 on his proposed colonial policies, Dernburg was still supporting large-scale cotton plantations for East Africa. On this occasion, he addressed various high-ranking representatives of the German textile industry in an attempt to encourage investment in the cultivation of cotton in German colonies in Africa. His request met with interest indeed, as various corresponding endeavours were started afterwards by several German textile companies. Amongst others, one of the companies taking up the colonial quest for cotton was the German textile company *Otto.* This enterprise, based in the Swabian town of Unterboihingen near Stuttgart, had been founded in 1816, and began to plan a cotton plantation in German East Africa, right after Dernburg's speech in 1907.[29]

4.4 The *Otto* Company: From Unterboihingen via America to East Africa

> Dernburg [. . .] came to Stuttgart during a series of lectures in winter 06/07 and gave a lecture to the entire Württemberg industry [. . .] on the expansion of the colonies and the opportunities offered there [. . .] in which a large part of the Württemberg cotton industry took part. Dernburg had mainly recommended German East Africa [. . .] for the cultivation of cotton. Experiments initiated there had been successful. More details can be found in the 1906 Economic Atlas of the Kolonialwirtschaftliche Komitee in Berlin.
>
> Company Chronicles of *Otto* in Unterboihingen by Fritz Otto. Compiled 1937–1943.[30]

The *Otto* company's history encompasses the regions of southwest as well as northern Germany, Britain, the USA and colonial Africa. Before the company's

29 Cf. Sunseri. *Vilimani*, pp. 2–17. Cf. Bleifuß and Hergenröder. *Die "Otto-Plantage"*, pp. 14–26.
30 LTA. 871.1-otto-233. Chronik, p. 69.

global expansion, its actual foundation around 1813 was only made possible by Napoleon's Continental System, which kept cheap British cotton textiles away from Europe's mainland markets. As a result, German textile entrepreneurs like *Otto* were able to produce competitive textiles for the first time. However, as soon as peace was settled, as a consequence of the Congress of Vienna in 1815, all German textile companies faced recurrent competition as British products entered the markets of mainland Europe.[31] The *Otto* company thus turned to British methods of industrial textile production. Simultaneously, *Otto* distanced itself increasingly from economic links to Switzerland, which previously had been the traditional textile trading partner of southwestern German textiles companies. Given the increasingly unipolar system of global cotton and textile production centring around the southern US American states and Great Britain from 1815 onwards, the leading figures of the *Otto* company attempted to incorporate Anglo-Saxon expertise that would slowly but surely supplant their older business relationships with Switzerland's Basel. Almost all senior figures of the *Otto* company as well as their most important employees were thus sent to the USA or Great Britain to get acquainted with the cotton business at the very heart of the 'empire of cotton'. Especially in the wake of the political and economic crises like the German Revolution of 1848 and the strengthening movement of Social Democracy in Germany in the second half of the nineteenth century, *Otto* was worried about its business in Germany and was ready to expand to overseas territories. Even emigration from its motherland to the USA was considered for the sake of the family business: "I.F. Otto was very anxious about such proceedings [the German Revolution and Social Democracy] [. . .] and it gave him little cause for optimism regarding Germany's future. This led partly to his decision to send his third son Robert as a colonizer to America for the younger generation."[32]

Besides the UK and the US as the focal points of their business, German textile centres like Barmen (today's Wuppertal) were the most preferred educational institutions for the important men of the *Otto* company. Another destination for gathering expertise in cotton and textiles was the German northern city of Bremen with its cotton exchange founded in 1872. Likewise, Bremen's cotton trading harbour was also an important educational institution for most of the members of the *Otto* company throughout the 'long nineteenth century'. Most leading men of *Otto* would receive training in Barmen and Bremen before they were allowed to take up any significant post in the family business. Afterwards, they often stayed several

31 Cf. Bleifuß and Hergenröder. *Die "Otto-Plantage"*, pp. 9–14. Cf. Beckert. *Empire of Cotton*, pp. 157–158, 167.

32 LTA. 871.1-otto-233. Chronik, p. 11. For interconnections between the US American Civil War and the (German) revolution(s) of 1848 cf. Gaul. *Ideale und Interessen*, pp. 33–58.

months or even several years in global cotton centres like New Orleans in the US American South or in England's Liverpool. Their grand tour of cotton went primarily through the company networks of the partnered and through the Engels family's also related textile corporation, *Pferdmenges-Pryer & Co.*[33] It seems that the *Otto* company particularly valued their US contacts throughout the 'long nineteenth century'. For example, Georg Schurz, nephew of the famous German American '48er revolutionary' Carl Schurz, was a long-serving personal secretary of the company's owner Heinrich Otto between ca. 1900 and 1913. Precisely in this period, *Otto* started its plantation in German East Africa's Kilossa. Moreover, Georg Schurz himself would even be sent to the German colony on the Indian Ocean to manage the bookkeeping of the cotton enterprise from 1910 onwards. According to the files consulted, he apparently remained in German East Africa until WWI, became a British POW and died in custody in early 1918.[34]

---

33 LTA. 871.1-otto-233. Chronik, pp. 11, 15–16, 21, 25, 57,60, 69, 79, 107, 114. Probably run by the textile entrepreneur, Wilhelm Albert Pferdmenges. Pferdmenges' son Robert, a banker, became an important figure for Konrad Adenauer's first governments in the newly established Federal Republic of Germany in the 1950s and 1960s. As Adenauer's close friend, he was the Chancellor's senior economic advisor. Besides economics and banking, Robert was well-known for his Protestant faith. Furthermore, he was a member of the supervisory board of numerous leading German banks and industrial companies, ranging from the heavy industries to textile producers. In 1930, when Britain annexed the Mandate Tanganyika Territory to British East Africa, Robert Pferdmenges – alongside many pro-colonial associations and leading German industrialists like Carl Duisberg – signed a petition that demanded the restitution of East Africa to the German *Reich* publicly. Cf. Teichmann, Gabriele. "Pferdmenges, Robert". *Neue Deutsche Biographie,* 20, 2001, pp. 331–332. Web. https://www.deutsche-biographie.de/pnd118791729.html#ndbcontent (18 July 2019). Cf. Bach, Christine. "Pferdmenges, Robert". *Konrad Adenauer Stiftung.* Web. https://www.kas.de/web/geschichte-der-cdu/personen/biogramm-detail/-/content/robert-pferdmenges-v1 (18 July 2019). Cf. Treue, Wilhelm. 'Das Porträt. Robert Pferdmenges (1880–1962)'. 188–210. *Geschichte im Westen.* N.P.: 1990, no. 2, pp. 188–205. Web. http://www.brauweiler-kreis.de/wp-content/uploads/GiW/GiW1990_2/GiW_1990_2_TREUE_PFERDMENGES.pdf. (18 July 2019). Cf. Koloniale Reichsarbeitsgemeinschaft Berlin – Afrikahaus. *Protest der deutschen Wirtschaft gegen den Raub von Deutsch-Ostafrika.* Berlin: 1930, p. 24. Cf. N.A. 'Pferdmenges: Geld aus dem Fenster'. *Der Spiegel,* 5/1954, 27 January 1954. Web. https://www.spiegel.de/spiegel/print/d-28955044.html (02 July 2020). For the Bremen cotton exchange cf. Bärwald, Annika. 'Bremer Baumwollträume. Bremer Wirtschaftsinteressen und das Streben nach Rohstoffautarkie im kolonialen Togo'. 1–30. *Bonjour Geschichte. Bremer online Journal,* no. 5, 2017, pp. 1–11. For the significance of US raw cotton produced by slaves for the German textile industries and financial centres and trading hubs before the foundation of the German *Reich* cf. Gaul. *Ideale und Interessen,* pp. 33–242.

34 Cf. LTA. 871.1-otto-233. Chronik, p. 74. Cf. Kaundinya, *Erinnerungen,* p. 103. Carl Schurz actively participated in the democratic 1848 March Revolution in Baden (southwest Germany) and subsequently emigrated to France, Switzerland, Britain and finally to the USA. There, he first worked as a lawyer and author. Later, he became Minister of Domestic Affairs in the USA as a member of the Republican Party under President Rutherford B. Hayes. Cf. Nagel, Daniel. *Von republikani-*

Keeping the Togolese and British colonial dimensions in mind, the case of the *Otto* plantation in German East Africa's Kilossa had some similarities to the 'Alabama in Africa' project. In the first place, similarities between German East Africa and Togo are to be found in the colonisers' conviction that the so-called 'modern' or 'scientific' means of colonisation were key for any successful colonial endeavour. When starting the cotton plantation near Kilossa, the *Otto* company had been decisively influenced by Bernhard Dernburg's promotion of 'reformed' and 'modern' colonial policies, particularly right after his assumption of office. With the colonial warfare in German South West Africa (1904–1907) and German East Africa (1905–1908) causing criticism amongst sections of the German public, Dernburg rejected Götzen's policies as outdated and irrational, and attempted to pursue colonial policies that would instead 'preserve' and not 'destroy' the most important economic asset of the German colonies. To Dernburg, the most important economic asset was the local African population, who should be 'educated to work' and produce especially cash-crops for global markets.[35] Another similarity between Togo and German East Africa is the fact that colonial officials in both cases sought US American expertise and the support of the *KWK* to boost cotton cultivation – a strategy also pursued by the British in Nigeria, Sudan and Uganda.[36] In the East African colony, the *KWK* thus hired a German-Texan cotton expert team that would transfer their knowledge about cotton from America to institutions like the Mpanganya cotton school located near the Rufiji River in German East Africa in 1904.

It was not only the attempted transfer of knowledge about cotton cultivation from the South of the US to the German colony in East Africa that was similar to the case in Togo. The Mpanganya cotton scheme, intended to promote the cultivation of cotton among the local population, also met fierce African resistance in German East Africa. The colonisers' demand to grow cotton as a monoculture contradicted the traditional inter-cropping cultivation methods in East Africa, which mixed the cotton crop with corn cultivation, for instance. Inter-cropping cultivation was done on purpose and for a good reason, as famines could be avoided if the cotton crop failed in a season or when low cotton prices prevented making a living by exclusively selling cotton. In analogy to Togo and the British cases in

schen Deutschen zu deutsch-amerikanischen Republikanern. Ein Beitrag zum Identitätswandel der deutschen Achtundvierziger in den Vereinigten Staaten 1850–1861. St. Ingbert: 2012. Cf. Gaul. *Ideale und Interessen,* pp. 55, 113–115, 159–161. Cf. LTA. 871.1-otto-199. Vergleichsregelung zwischen Fa. Otto und dem deutschen Reich. Letter by the Otto company to the Verband der württembergischen Kolonialdeutschen (association of south west colonial Germans), Unterboihingen, 19 April 1919.

35 Cf. Dernburg. *Koloniale Lehrjahre.* Cf. Esp. Dernburg. *Zielpunkte,* pp. 5–9.

36 Cf. Robins. *Cotton and Race,* pp. 72–164.

colonial Africa, the local population also resented recruitment by force, penal labour and the general colonial intrusion into their social environment that was characteristic of Governor Götzen's economic cotton policies until 1906. This is also why the peasant cotton scheme encouraged by the *KWK* and the colonial administration, and subsequent similar programmes, would neither become very successful nor popular amongst the local population during European colonialism in East Africa and beyond.[37]

But there were also differences between Togo and German East Africa as far as the company of *Otto* and its plantation in Kilossa is concerned. *Otto's* approach differed also from that of the Mpanganya cotton school in German East Africa. First of all, the gist of Dernburg's 'reformed' colonial policies was not only about the application of allegedly improved 'modern' and 'scientific' cotton cultivation like Tuskegee's, as a means to improve German colonial cotton production. At the heart of Dernburg's policies were also the promotion of the latest technologies. As Dernburg highlighted the importance of modern infrastructure, railways in particular, technology and machinery for the colonial economy were also central to his colonial policies. This focus on modern technology and machinery, fused with another difference between cotton plantations in German colonial Togo and East Africa, right after Dernburg became the most influential German policy maker: the matter of scale. Especially in the very beginning of his career as Colonial State Secretary in the first phase of his cotton policies, Dernburg promoted large-scale plantations like *Otto*'s, and discouraged Tuskegee-like peasant cotton cultivation programmes under the direct control of the colonial government. Certainly, Dernburg readjusted his policies after his official tour to German East Africa in 1908 and highlighted small-scale cash-crop production by individual East African farmers at the expense of large-scale cotton monocultures. But when Dernburg and *Otto* first met in 1907, the Colonial State Secretary still emphasised his desire for gigantic monocultural cotton plantations. Of course, such vast plantations had to be organised differently than individual cash-crop production by East African small-scale farmers. With an increasing area under cultivation, manual labour had to be replaced with industrialised means of agricultural production. Hand in hand with Dernburg's vision of large-scale plantations went thus the use of the most modern steam technology of the industrial age. In this respect, Dernburg's approach agreed with *Otto's* company tradition. Having always applied the latest technology to their factories back home in Germany, the vision of vast cotton

---

37 Cf. Sunseri. *Vilimani*, pp. 119–127. Cf. "Mpanganya". *Deutsches Koloniallexikon*, 1920, Band II, S. 595. *University of Frankfurt o.M.* http://www.ub.bildarchiv-dkg.uni-frankfurt.de/Bildprojekt/Lexikon/Standardframeseite.php (18 June 2019). Cf. Demhardt. *Deutsche Kolonialgesellschaft*, pp. 70–71.

fields in Kilossa worked with steam engines appeared not only promising to the State Secretary but also to the *Otto* textile company. Like Dernburg, *Otto's* leading men expected much from the anticipated construction of the *Central Railway* as well as from the use of steam locomobiles and steam ploughs.[38] This was even more the case for senior family like Fritz Otto, with the abovementioned economic atlas issued by the *KWK* in 1906 advertised the usage of modern steam ploughs made by the company *Fowler & Co.*, with its German branch in Magdeburg, for colonial cotton cultivation. Moreover, the atlas already projected the *Central Railway* to pass nearby Kilossa, where – according to the economic atlas, too – soil conditions promised rich cotton harvests in the future. Indeed, the steam ploughs made by *Fowler & Co.* were ultimately used by both the *KWK's* cotton plantation in Saadani and by *Otto* in Kilossa.[39]

In the end, another important difference between *Otto's* cotton cultivation and the case in Togo must be stressed regarding the phenomenon of labour at the *Otto* plantation in Kilossa: although the *Otto* company had traditionally also had strong links to American and British cotton cultivators and textile companies, no connection either to the Tuskegee colleges or Texas was ever established between Unterboihingen and Kilossa. Instead, the most significant connection beyond the German *Reich*, German East Africa and Swabia would not be to the USA's south but India. This fundamental connection between the textile company of *Otto*, German East Africa and India is predominantly revealed by the family background, biography and employment of Ranga Kaundinya as manager of the *Otto* plantation in Kilossa.[40]

38 Cf. Dernburg. *Zielpunkte*, pp. 5–21. Cf. Naranch. 'Colonized Body', pp. 299–338. Cf. Sunseri. *Vilimani*, pp. 136–159 Cf. Iliffe. *A Modern History*, pp. 144–147. Cf. Kaundinya. *Erinnerungen*, pp. 18–20. Cf. Dernburg. *Südwestafrikanische Eindrücke*, pp. 56–58.

39 Cf. LTA. 871.1-otto-233. Chronik, p. 69. Cf. Kolonialwirtschaftliches Komitee e.V. (Ed.). *Wirtschaftsatlas*, pp. no. 7–8, cf. Appendix (*Anhang*) advertisement of steam ploughs produced by John Fowler in Magdeburg & co. and 'Kolonialmaschienenbau Theodor Wilkens'. Cf. "Aus unserer Kolonie. X. Kilossa". *DOAZ*, X, no. 63. Daressalam: 19 August 1908.

40 For connections between the *KWK* and India cf. Berkhout, A.H. 'Ziele, Resultate und Zukunft der Indischen Forstwirtschaft'. 303–313. *Der Tropenpflanzer. Zeitschrift für Tropische Landwirtschaft.* 13. Jahrgang, no. 7. Berlin, July 1909. Cf. Roeder, Georg. 'Aus Indiens Kolonial-Technik'. 403–428. *Der Tropenpflanzer. Zeitschrift für Tropische Landwirtschaft.* 13. Jahrgang, no. 9. Berlin, July 1909. Cf. Tholens, R. 'Zum Baumwollbau in Ägypten'. 567–573. *Der Tropenpflanzer. Zeitschrift für Tropische Landwirtschaft.* 13. Jahrgang, no. 7. Berlin, July 1909. Cf. Schanz, Moritz. 'Die Negerfrage in Nordamerika'. 573–585. Ed. Kolonial-Wirtschaftliches Komitee. Beiheft zum 'Tropenpflanzer', Jahrgang XIII, no. 3, March 1909. Cf. Kolonial-Wirtschaftliches Komitee. 'Unsere Kolonialwirtschaft in ihrer Bedeutung für Industrie und Arbeiterschaft'. 45–56. Beiheft zum 'Tropenpflanzer', Jahrgang XIII, no. 3, March 1909. Cf. Kolonial-Wirtschaftliches Komitee (Ed.). *Unsere Kolonialwirtschaft in ihrer Bedeutung für Industrie und Arbeiterschaft.* Berlin: 1909, pp. 9–16.

4.4.1 From Conversion to Plantation and Beyond: The Kaundinya Family and the *Otto* Company

> [. . .] [T]he Family is also an economic entity while the company appears to be a social entity that is highly influenced by traditions and emotions. [. . .] [I]t was precisely this combination of family and entrepreneurial sphere that paved the way for a family firm [. . .].[41]
>
> Christof Dejung. *Commodity Trading, Globalization and the Colonial World.* New York: 2018.

Despite *Otto's* connection to the Anglo-Saxon cotton world, its most significant connection beyond the German *Reich,* German East Africa and Unterboihingen was to India. India's cotton cultivation within the 'empire of cotton' was also an area of general interest for the *KWK.*[42] However, the most important connections between the *Otto* company, German East Africa and India are notably revealed in the biography of Ranga Kaundinya. As plantation manager, he became the central figure of *Otto's* plantation in German East Africa's Kilossa. His life and work were decisively embedded within the global Pietist networks of the *Otto* company, which remained loyal to the plantation manager despite profound setbacks in Kilossa. Ranga Kaundinya was born in India, raised in Swabia and Basel (Switzerland), and later worked in India and in German East Africa. Although Sunseri mentions Ranga Kaundinya's Indo-German background and his central role in the *Otto* plantation, he disregards the history of the Kaundinya family, which goes beyond the period of formal German colonial rule.[43] In fact, the history of the Kaundinya family links the period of formal German colonialism (1884–1919) to the more inconspicuous facets of Germans involved in European colonialism before the Berlin Conference of 1884 and after the Treaty of Versailles in 1919. It also links the local history of the town of Unterboihingen and the story of the *Otto* company as an economic heavyweight to the global and colonial economy of the 'empire of cotton'. Moreover, the history of the Kaundinya family further

41 Dejung. *Commodity Trading,* p. 135.

42 Cf. Berkhout, A.H. 'Ziele, Resultate', pp. 303–313. Cf. Roeder. 'Aus Indiens Kolonial-Technik', pp. 403–428. Cf. Tholens. 'Zum Baumwollbau in Ägypten', pp. 567–573. Cf. Schanz. 'Die Negerfrage in Nordamerika', pp. 573–585. Cf. Kolonial-Wirtschaftliches Komitee. 'Unsere Kolonialwirtschaft', pp. 45–56.

43 Cf. Sunseri. *Vilimani,* p. 151. Cf. Kaundinya. *Erinnerungen.* Ranga Kaundinya's Indian background receives little attention also in Bleifuß and Hergenröder. *Die "Otto-Plantage",* pp. 37–39, 61–62. Sven Beckert dedicates only a minor remark on Kaundinya's background and also does not mention his name. Cf. Beckert. *Empire of Cotton,* p. 377. For general remarks about the postcolonial dimensions of German history cf. Zimmerer, Jürgen. 'Kolonialismus und kollektive Identität: Erinnerungsorte deutscher Kolonialgeschichte'. *Kein Platz an der Sonne. Erinnerungsorte der deutschen Kolonialgeschichte.* 9–40. Ed. Jürgen Zimmerer. Bonn: 2013.

highlights the significance of this (Pietist) mission and the company's networks to German colonialism.

The southwest German region of Swabia or rather the Kingdom of *Württemberg* cannot be analysed historically with regard to colonialism without taking into account Pietism and its worldwide connection with Christian missions overseas. Likewise, the *Otto* company cannot be thought of without their Pietist company or rather their family networks. Similarly, the Basel Mission from neighbouring Switzerland, which was active in the colonies of various European colonial powers, cannot be thought of without considering the Swabian area around *Württemberg's* capital Stuttgart. After all, since the foundation of the Basel Mission in 1815, more than half of all its missionaries were born in Swabia and "all inspectors and most theological teachers [were] from *Württemberg*[.] [S]econdly, over half of the trained missionaries came from the Swabian region". In addition, one of the very first Basel missions was established in southwest India, reflecting the Kaundinya family's involvement with Christianity, Swabia and the *Otto* company.[44]

It does not come as a surprise that the Kaundinya family's historical interconnections with India, Switzerland, Unterboihingen and Germany can be traced to the beginning of the nineteenth century. In fact, its history was decisively connected to the beginnings of the Basel Mission to India. Ranga Kaundinya's father, Hermann Anandrao Kaundinya, was born in Mangalore, southwestern India, in 1825 to a Brahmin family. As Hermann Anandrao's father worked for the British colonial high court as a lawyer and therefore had good connections with the British administration, Anandrao Kaundinya attended an English language missionary school in Mangalore from 1840 onwards. At this mission school, he first met Basel Missionaries who would become central for his future life. It was particularly Kaundinya's close friendship with the Missionary Hermann Mögling that ultimately led to Hermann Anandrao's baptism. Still a young man, Hermann Anandrao Kaundinya converted to Protestantism in 1844 and as his baptism was carried out by Mögling himself, Kaundinya adopted his godfather's first name 'Hermann'. As Kaundinya appeared a promising convert to Mögling, Kaundinya was ultimately accepted as a student at the Basel Missionary School in Switzerland in 1846. There, Herrmann Anandrao Kaundinya graduated as the first – and for a long time also the only – Indian-born Christian missionary in 1851. Returning to India only a few weeks after his graduation in Basel, he remained in India until his death in February 1893. There, he became one of the most important figures of the Basel Mission to India, teaching at

44 Konrad. *Missionsbräute*, p. 465, cf. 465–467. Cf. Gleixner, Ulrike. *Pietismus und Bürgertum. Eine historische Anthropologie der Frömmigkeit*. Göttingen: 2005, pp. 13–25. Cf. Rösser. 'Knotenpunkte des Kolonialen', pp. 11–12, 39–42.

several missionary schools, working as an itinerant preacher and founding the Christian community of Anandapur in the district of Kodagu. To finance the settlement of Anandapur and to meet his own expenses, Kaundinya started rice and coffee plantations. As his plantations never became a very profitable business, his budget was constantly strained and therefore did not allow him to travel outside India. Andandrao Kaundinya therefore never returned to Europe, except on one occasion for his own wedding.[45]

Like in many other Pietist societies, Basel missionaries did not choose their wives on their own. Instead, the board of the Basel Mission sorted requests of women who sought to marry a missionary and approved a wedding if both parties agreed. Regarding Kaundinya's marriage, it was again his close relationship to Hermann Mögling that played the decisive role, as Mögling's wife arranged Kaundinya's marriage to the German Marie Reinhardt from Swabia. The wedding of Hermann Anandrao and Marie took place in 1860 and right after their marriage, Hermann Anandrao and Marie Kaundinya travelled to India in the service of the Basel Mission and they stayed there together for over thirty years. Only after her husband's death in 1893 would Marie Kaundinya finally leave India. She subsequently lived near Stuttgart, until her death in 1919, close to the home of one of her and Hermann Anandrao's sons.[46]

In total, Marie and Hermann Anandrao had eleven children who were born between 1861 and 1883. All of them spent most of their childhoods and teenage lives far away from their parents, either in Germany, Switzerland or in Britain. In Europe, the Indo-German children went to school or pursued other kinds of training. Keeping their children in Europe was a common procedure for Pietist missionaries in the nineteenth and early twentieth centuries. For this purpose, the Basel

45 Cf. Frenz, Albrecht. *Freiheit hat Gesicht. Anandapur – eine Begegnung zwischen Kodagu und Baden Württemberg.* Stuttgart: 2003, pp. 41–56. Cf. Becker, Judith. *Conversio im Wandel. Basler Missionare zwischen Europa und Südindien und die Ausbildung einer Kontaktreligiösität, 1834–1860.* Göttingen: 2015, pp. 13–18, 663–682. Cf. Stadtmuseum Wendlingen am Neckar. Konrad Steinert's private document collection, "Zum Stammbaum von Kaundinya".

46 Marie Reinhardt was Kaundinya's second wife. With his first wife, Lakshmi, he shared a household for a very long time. Lakshmi herself, and her family, were not ready to accept Hermann Anandrao's conversion to the Christian faith for a long time. Lakshmi died a short period after their reconciliation. Cf. Kaundinya, H.A. *Die Lebensgeschichte des in Mangalur bekehrten Brahminen Hermann Anandraja Kaundinja.* Basel: 1854, pp. 17–23. Also quoted by Frenz and Becker. Cf. Frenz. *Freiheit*, pp. 50–52. Cf. Konrad. *Missionsbräute*, pp. 30–32, 45–46, 56–78, 87–88, 469–470. Cf. Stadtmuseum Wendlingen. Steinert's collection, "Zum Stammbaum von Kaundinya". Cf. Becker. *Conversio*, pp. 15, 51, 150, 163, 542, 581, 609, 648, 655–666. For a general introduction to the history of Pietism and the bourgeoisie in the southwest German Kingdom of Württemberg cf. Gleixner. *Pietismus und Bürgertum*, pp. 13–28, 392–408.

Mission even maintained a special children's home to board the missionaries' sons and daughters in Basel. To protect their children from the influences of the 'outer world', as the missionaries would call it, the Pietist community in Europe educated the Kaundinya children with corresponding Christian ideals; although a common practice for all the children of Pietist missionaries, the case of the Kaundinyas was also special. Despite being regarded as "converted 100 per cent", Hermann Anandrao Kaundinya, the first Indian Christian missionary of the Basel Mission, met with reservations in Switzerland as his fellow but European Basel missionaries sometimes doubted his devotion to Christianity. Likewise, the Kaundinyas children also had "sort of a special status as 'half-Indians'", although most of them spent a considerable part of their childhood and youth in the mission's children's home in Basel.[47] Besides staying in Basel, first-born Ananda Kaundinya (1861–1914) and second-born Ranga Kaundinya (1863–1919) – later manager of the *Otto* plantation in Kilossa – also spent some of their teenage years in Esslingen am Neckar near Stuttgart, which was not far from Unterboihingen and where the head office of the textile company of *Otto* was located. In Esslingen, they were taken care of by Hermann Mögling and his family, the abovementioned close friend of Herman Kaundinya, who had retired from (missionary) work in 1869 and lived in southwest Germany until his death in 1881.[48] Later generations of the Kaundinyas would also be raised in the southwest German region around or in the city of Stuttgart. Among them was Ananda Kaundinya's son, Otto Günther Kaundinya (1900–1940), who would later become the first star of handball – a sport that had become very popular in Germany in the first half of the twentieth century.[49]

It was probably during his stay as a teenager and young adult in southwest German Esslingen am Neckar when second-born Ranga Kaundinya first met members of the *Otto* company. According to the company chronicles written between 1937 and 1943, Ranga had done an apprenticeship in nearby Nürtingen around 1885 at the tree nursery of Emanuel Otto. Emmanuel Otto was the grandchild of the founder of the *Otto* textile company in Unterboihingen, which was started in 1816.

---

47 Konrad. *Missionsbräute*, p. 338.

48 Cf. Konrad. *Missionsbräute*, pp. 329–340. Cf. Stadtmuseum Wendlingen. Steinert's collection, "Zum Stammbaum von Kaundinya". Cf. Stadtmuseum Wendlingen am Neckar. Konrad Steinert's private document collection, "Ranga Reinhardt Rao Kaundinya (1863–1919). Leiter der Otto-Pflanzung Kilossa (1907–1916)", "Zum Stammbaum von Kaundinya". Cf. Ledderhose, Karl Friedrich. "Mögling, Hermann Friedrich". *Allgemeine Deutsche Biographie, 22*, 1885, pp. 47–52, Web. *Neue Deutsche Biographie*. https://www.deutsche-biographie.de/pnd119490633.html#adbcontent (20 June 2019).

49 Cf. Eggers, Erik. 'Porträt. Otto Kaundinya – der erste Star des Handballs'. *Handball. Eine deutsche Domäne*. 73–76. Ed. Erik Eggers. Göttingen: 2007, pp. 73–76.

After his apprenticeship at this tree nursery in Nürtingen and school education in Basel, Ranga Kaundinya travelled to India and lived with his parents for some time. In Anandapur, the Christian village his father had founded, he was involved in his father's coffee plantation and received further (unspecified) training in agricultural business. When Ranga Kaundinya returned to Germany as a "plantation owner"[50] in 1894, he came there to marry the German Thekla Sophie Faisst in Stuttgart through the Basel Mission networks. Shortly afterwards, the recently married couple returned to India and started a cotton plantation in India, probably in a town named Ferok in southwest India.[51] Unfortunately, there is no further information about their lives or their business in India to be found in the sources under investigation.[52]

Furthermore, the sources also fail to provide a clear picture of the reasons why Ranga Kaundinya ultimately became the manager of the *Otto* plantation in German East Africa's Kilossa in 1907. According to his own autobiographical accounts, Ranga had sold his own cotton plantation in India after twenty-three years of business, in early 1907, and was simply looking for a new challenge. With the *Otto* company offering him the opportunity to become "the manager of a large business in the midst of the wild jungle" and to start such a "pioneering business [. . .] from scratch", an allegedly long-cherished dream had become a reality.[53] In contrast, the company chronicles of the *Otto* company paint a less rosy picture: After losing all his fortune in the course of a banking crisis in spring 1907, Ranga sent a letter of application to the *Otto* textile company, as he had known the family since his apprenticeship at Emmanuel Otto's tree nursery back in 1885. Apparently, Kaundinya had read about *Otto's* plan to take up cotton cultivation in German East Africa in a newspaper article and offered his services as an experienced cotton planter accordingly.[54] Known by senior company members since the apprenticeship in his youth, Ranga Kaundinya was accepted as a future

50 Stadtmuseum Wendlingen. Steintert's collection, "Ranga Reinhardt Rao Kaundinya (1863–1919)".

51 LTA. 871.1-otto-233. Chronik, p. 72.

52 Cf. Maybe, some insights will be provided in the future by the contemporary research project about migrant children of the nineteenth century, conducted by Sandra Maß. It features the Kaundinya family. Cf. her website at the University of Bochum. https://www.ruhr-uni-bochum.de/transhistory/ueberuns/prof/index.html.de (15 October 2019). Cf. private mail correspondence with Sandra Maß 26 September 2019. Recently published cf. Maß, Sandra. 'Constructing global missionary families: Absence, memory, and belonging before World War I'. 340–361. *Journal of Modern European History*, Vol. 19, 3. N.P.: 2021. Web. https://journals.sagepub.com/doi/pdf/10.1177/16118944211019933. (03 March 2022).

53 Kaundinya. *Erinnerungen*, p. 22.

54 Cf. Stadtmuseum Wendlingen. Steintert's collection, "Ranga Reinhardt Rao Kaundinya (1863–1919)". Cf. LTA. 871.1-otto-233. Chronik, pp. 30–31, 70–73. Cf. Konrad. *Missionsbräute*, pp. 338–340.

manager of *Otto's* plantation near Kilossa immediately. Shortly after his letter of application was read by senior members of the company, Kaundinya received a telegram ordering him to "take the next steamer to Dar es Salaam for a meeting with [the company's owner] Heinrich Otto", who was currently on his way to German East Africa. Accompanied by Colonial State Secretary Bernhard Dernburg, and the famous German palaeontologist Eberhard Fraas as geological advisor, Heinrich Otto intended to inspect suitable land for future cotton cultivation in the German colony and therefore wanted to talk to his future plantation manager Kaundinya on the same occasion.[55]

Recalling the history of the Kaundinya family and the rapid decision of the *Otto* company to start a cotton business in German East Africa, the evidence suggests that *Otto's* company chronicles are more plausible than Kaundinya's autobiography. It is more likely that Kaundinya was searching for new employment as he had just turned bankrupt with his unprofitable plantations in India. The speedy meeting of Heinrich Otto and Kaundinya in German East Africa further supports this argument. As the company of *Otto* must have been in urgent need of an experienced plantation manager, they were ready to employ Kaundinya as the first who came along. Not much more than four months had passed since senior figures of the Otto family had listened closely to Dernburg's speech in Stuttgart at the end of January 1907 (see above), and Heinrich Otto and Bernhard Dernburg's joint journey to German East Africa in May of the same year. It appears that the *Otto* company started its colonial cotton business very hastily, and Ranga Kaundinya's application letter arrived to Unterboihingen just at the right moment. The textile company had not had a lot of experience running colonial business in Africa and was therefore lacking the trained staff for such an endeavour. In analogy to the Togolese case, where the German colonial administration hired cotton experts from Booker T. Washington's Tuskegee colleges in the US to boost the colonial cotton production in West Africa, "[e]xpertise was in high demand"[56] in German East Africa. *Otto* had found this supposed expertise in India. In the overall context of the 'empire of cotton', Kaundinya probably appeared as the perfect candidate for a colonial business in East Africa as his personal profile combined the colonial discourse about 'fitness for service in the tropics', with the ideal of a European school education in line with Christian values, and professional experience at coffee and cotton plantations in India. India, which had been the centre of global cotton cultivation and manufacturing before the subsequent

55 LTA. 871.1-otto-233. Chronik, p. 72, cf. pp. 70–74. Cf. Kaundinya. *Erinnerungen*, pp. 18–25. Cf. Bleifuß and Hergenröder. *Die "Otto-Plantage"*, pp. 21–26. Cf. Sunseri. *Vilimani*, pp. 2–18, 136–138. Cf. Maier. *African Dinosaurs*, pp. 1–3, 6–26.

56 Beckert. *Empire of Cotton*, p. 362.

global 'European domination', had traded cotton and textiles with East Africa for centuries and was still well-known for this industry.[57] Although at that moment on the decline,[58] this reputation of India being a sub-continent of decent cotton production complemented Kaundinya's biography as an Indian planter and his corresponding family background. Kaundinya's positive impression was probably reinforced as he had married the German Thekla Faisst of a good family, originating from nearby Ludwigsburg and Stuttgart. Finally, Ranga Kaundinya had already worked for a member of the Otto family and was thus not unknown to the most important contacts of the Swabian Pietist textile producer.[59]

Anticipating the difficulties of the *Otto* plantation in Kilossa throughout its entire existence, the hasty planning as well as the company's lack of experience and Kaundinya's previous poor performance as a plantation manager must have had significant influence on the ultimate failure of *Otto's* endeavour in German East Africa. Although he had probably been as unsuccessful as his father as a plantation manager in India, Ranga Kaundinya's failure in Kilossa was not only the result of his lacking skills and fortune; it was also a result of German East Africa's societal atmosphere that disadvantaged and discriminated against him as a so-called 'half-caste-man'.

4.4.2 *Otto's* Pietist Textile Networks and Ranga Kaundinya's Employment in Kilossa

Besides constant investment in the latest technology, another significant characteristic of the *Otto* Company and the family behind it was its Protestant Christian faith. With southwestern German Unterboihingen being primarily inhabited by Roman Catholics, the Otto family consciously lived in the Protestant diaspora and sought to maintain as well as support their Pietist denomination. They sent their own sons for further education in the textile business to other entrepreneurs who pursued their faith consciously: Robert Otto, born in 1849, for example, did his apprenticeship at the company *C.F. Klein-Schlatter* in Barmen, a hotspot of the

57 Beckert. *Empire of Cotton*, pp. 18–28, 312–340.

58 Cf. Robins. *Cotton and Race*, pp. 77–79, 180.

59 Cf. LTA. 871.1-otto-233. Chronik, pp. 71–72. Cf. Stadtmuseum Wendlingen. Steintert's collection, "Ranga Reinhardt Rao Kaundinya (1863–1919)". Belifuß and Hergenröder summarise Kaundinya's application and employment but do not compare the sources critically. Cf. Bleifuß and Hergenröder. *Die "Otto-Plantage"* p. 61. Kaundinya himself sustains the discourse about the 'fitness for the tropics' and recommends living an ascetic life, strongly reducing the consumption of meat, tobacco, alcohol and to strictly limit sexual intercourse. Cf. Kaundinya. *Erinnerungen*, p. 96. Cf. Dejung. *Commodity Trading*, pp. 56–79.

German textile industry. His stay in Barmen served several purposes. Besides fostering a friendly relationship to this company, the Ottos were convinced that "the religious attitudes of the owners of the company, *F.W. Röhrig und C.F. Klein*, entirely resembled those of the Otto family" and they would send young Robert Otto back to southwestern Germany not only equipped with skills and knowledge about the textile business, but also "internally strengthened" in his faith. This was also the reason why Robert was neither the first nor the last member of several *Otto* generations who would receive their training for these very purposes in Barmen.[60] Apart from maintaining such Pietist entrepreneurial networks, in Unterboihingen itself, the family organised and actively participated in Bible studies and financed several institutions to support the Protestant faith, such as a Protestant church and a school for Protestant children.[61] As Pietist entrepreneurs, the Ottos probably had friendly relations with other Pietist circles, like the Basel Mission. It is thus very likely that the shared Protestant faith between Kaundinya and *Otto* was an important part of Ranga Kaundinya's first working experience with *Otto*, as an apprentice at Emmanuel Otto's tree nursery in 1885. Considering the ongoing support for their faith at home and strong links to other Pietist textile company owners like *Röhrig and Klein*[62] as well as the abovementioned *Pferdmenges, Pryer & Co.*, it is very likely that the Otto family was also sympathetic to the Pietist Basel Mission overseas and therefore also towards the Kaundinya family, whose children were educated and brought up nearby Unterboihingen. In a nutshell: hiring Ranga Kaundinya for the cotton plantation in Kilossa as its manager was not only a matter of perceived skill and experience, but equally – if not primarily – a matter of faith. To the leading men of the Pietist *Otto* Company, Kaundinya appeared to be a devout Indo-German Christian, and he continued to be employed and trusted by *Otto*, despite the eventual poor economic performance of the company's plantation in Kilossa.

---

60 LTA. 871.1-otto-233. Chronik, pp. 7, 21, 57. Cf. Hergenröder, Gerhard. *Wendlingen am Neckar. Auf dem Weg zu einer Stadt. Die Geschichte von Wendlingen, Unterboihingen und Bodelshofen.* Wendlingen am Neckar: 1992, pp. 251–261, 291–298, 312, 378.

61 Cf. LTA. 871.1-otto-233. Chronik, pp. 28,36, 51, 54–55.

62 Carl Friedrich Klein was the son of a vicar in nearby Nördlingen (southwest Germany). Born in 1803 in Württemberg, he became involved in the cotton business first in Augsburg and then in Munich. He later founded his own business in Barmen after his arrival there in 1828. His wife Christine Schlatter was from St. Gallen (Switzerland), a Protestant town surrounded by a Catholic countryside. Analogically to the Otto family, the couple also financed and supported Protestant schools and youth associations. Cf. Schreiner, Hanna. 'Carl Friedrich Klein und Christine Klein'. 56–61. *Wuppertaler Biographien*, 5. Wuppertal: 1965. Cf. Klein, Jochen. *"In Unruh und Arbeit". C.F. Klein-Schlatter. 150 Jahre Weberei. 1828–1979.* Ratingen: 2001, pp. 1–63.

Yet, such a comparatively supportive environment, characterised by a shared religion, does not automatically mean that Protestant Christians of German Indian descent did not face prejudices and racist discrimination. Quite the contrary: many members of the Kaundinya family experienced reservations even in Pietist circles, but especially beyond. As far as the sources can tell, most Kaundinyas faced discrimination throughout their lives. Although Hermann Anandrao Kaundinya proved himself a devout Christian missionary in India and was a close friend of German missionaries like Hermann Mögling, he had to fight for equal status as a missionary on several occasions. Many of his fellow missionaries of European descent as well as Basel's mission board occasionally doubted Hermann Anandrao Kaundinya's equal status as a missionary and disregarded his judgements or opinions on various issues.[63] But Hermann Anandrao was not the only Kaundinya who experienced discrimination in his life. Like his father, Hermann Anandrao's firstborn son, Ananda Kaundinya, faced obstacles when starting his career as well. Seeking employment as a government official in India, Ananda's application was rejected as the British colonial government of India did not want to employ so-called 'Eurasians'.[64] Despite his experience and education in Germany, Switzerland, India and (probably) Great Britain, and his Christian denomination, Ananda Kaundinya, therefore, had to take up employment as an overseer of a saltworks in India,[65] because the British colonial authorities did not regard him as equal to a British citizen. Apparently, it took many years until Ananda Kaundinya ultimately became a British government official and it seems that he later worked in the British Indian public sector until the beginning of 1914.[66] Other family members experienced similar discrimination, as the analysis of the files reporting on Ranga Kaundinya's work as a plantation manager in German East Africa's Kilossa illustrate.

Although produced in 1936 during the period of National Socialism in Germany, *Otto's* company chronicles – celebrating 120 years of its existence – do not utter one negative word about Ranga Kaundinya's work in Kilossa. This fact is par-

63 Cf. Becker. *Conversio*, pp. 28–30, p. 682. Cf. Frenz. *Freiheit*, pp. 40–56.

64 Konrad. *Missionsbräute*, p. 338.

65 Cf. Ebay Offer by second-hand bookshop *Tucholsklavier* (Theodor Schmidt, Berlin). 'Handball-Nationaltrainer OTTO KAUNDINYA: 3 Briefe von 1913 (u.a. über Zukunft)'. 04 August 2018. Web. https://www.ebay.de/itm/Handball-Nationaltrainer-OTTO-KAUNDINYA-3-Briefe-von-1913-u-a-uber-Zukunft/302442788301?hash=item466afeb5cd:g:tCwAAOSwa4FZsCPW (19 July 2019).

66 Cf. Konrad. *Missionsbräute*, pp. 337–339. Cf. Eggers. 'Porträt Otto Kaundinya', p. 73. Cf. Ebay Offer by second-hand bookshop *Tucholsklavier* (Theodor Schmidt, Berlin). '36 dt. Briefe (188 S.) von 1902 aus INDIEN //Ananda H. & Helene KAUNDINYA'. 21 June 2018. Web. https://www.ebay.de/itm/36-dt-Briefe-188-S-von-1902-aus-INDIEN-Ananda-H-Helene-KAUNDINYA-/152825391361 (19 July 2019).

ticularly important as the chronicles do occasionally reveal the zeitgeist of the NS-Regime: they portray Bernhard Dernburg's Jewish family background disrespectfully, for instance. One would thus have anticipated corresponding discriminatory remarks about Ranga Kaundinya's Indo-German descent and negative remarks about his unsuccessful work in Kilossa twenty years before the company chronicles were produced, too.[67] Besides the shared Pietist faith of the Kaundinyas and *Otto* that might have served as a 'spiritual tie', preventing a negative image about their cooperation in the sources, another aspect has to be considered when reading the company chronicles. With the company chronicles being written from the middle of the 1930s onwards, their positive portrayal of Ranga Kaundinya also may have been influenced by his ties to someone else: namely Ranga's nephew, Otto Günther Kaundinya, who was a very famous person in the 1930s. As mentioned above, Otto Kaundinya was the first handball star in the history of the sport. Handball had become one of the most popular sports in Germany since the early 1900s and Otto Kaundinya was not only the best handball player in the world in the 1920s and 1930s, but he later also became an influential trainer, sports functionary, and theoretician of handball. Considered as a legend at the beginning of the 1930s, Otto Kaundinya also trained the German Olympic handball team, which subsequently won the Olympic Games in Berlin in 1936 – an event loaded with National Socialist propaganda. In general, Otto Kaundinya was considered as "politically reliable"[68] by the Nazis, and even published pamphlets featuring racist political considerations about the sport of handball, in line with the 'racial thinking' of National Socialism.[69] While Otto Kaundinya's contemporary fame might have been one reason why the *Otto* Company's chronicles are sympathetic towards his uncle, Ranga Kaundinya, other sources chronologically closer to the actual events still illustrate discrimination against Ranga. This is particularly the case for the files produced by the German colonial administration, which are held in Tanzania's National Archives today. This discrimination faced by the Kaundinya family because of their Indian background, experienced in both German and British colonial environments, is particularly important as it influenced Ranga Kaundinya's work in Kilossa significantly.

---

67 Cf. LTA. 871.1-otto-233. Chronik, pp. 69, 87. Cf. LTA. 871.1-otto-229. [Firmenjubiläum am 12. November 1936].

68 Eggers. 'Porträt Otto Kaundinya', p. 75.

69 Eggers. 'Porträt Otto Kaundinya', pp. 73–75. Cf. Eggers, Erik. 'Handball im Nationalsozialismus'. *Handball. Eine deutsche Domäne.* 63–92. Ed. Erik Eggers. Göttingen: 2007, pp. 63–90. Cf. Kaundinya, Otto. *Die sportliche Leistung. Ihre biologischen, rassischen und pädagogischen Voraussetzungen.* Leipzig: 1936. Cf. Kaundinya, Otto. *Das Handballspiel. Technik, Taktik, Spielregeln, Training.* 1. & 2. Edition. Leipzig 1935 and 1941.

Although obtaining a prestigious job position as *Otto's* plantation manager, he was discriminated against by both the German colonial administration and other Germans living in the colony. His attributed position in the colonial society as a white subaltern certainly influenced his work performance at the cotton plantation negatively.

4.5 Managing a Plantation in a German Colony

> It is however inexcusable that Otto had made a half-caste-man the leading figure of the endeavour. Although he had proved himself incompetent as a manager throughout his employment, Otto kept him in this position despite numerous warnings.
>
> Governor Rechenberg to the German Colonial Department. Dar es Salaam, 1 October 1910.[70]

Ranga Kaundinya worked and lived as a white subaltern in German East Africa. Congruent with the racist colonial environment there, several files suggest that Ranga's colleagues, the German colonial lobby and the colonial administration were prejudiced against him as a person and judged his work performance accordingly. As revealed by the quotation above, Ranga Kaundinya's family background was judged to be one of the major reasons why *Otto's* plantation in Kilossa experienced mismanagement. The source quoted above, in which Governor Rechenberg called Kaundinya an 'incompetent half-caste man', was a reaction towards an article published by the *Kölnische Zeitung* on 28 October 1910. In this German newspaper's article, Heinrich Otto, the company's head, admitted the shortcomings of his plantation in Kilossa but blamed the colonial administration for the difficulties.[71] Investigating the issue of whether the accusations against the colonial administration in the newspaper were justified, the Governor of German East Africa produced a corresponding report about the plantation and sent it to the German Colonial Office in Berlin in October 1910. The report listed not only the shortcomings of *Otto's* company managers in Germany but also the mistakes of its personnel in Kilossa. Although acknowledging Kaundinya's industriousness and eagerness when first arriving at the *Otto* plantation in Kilossa in 1907, besides disparaging his ancestry, Rechenberg also doubted Ranga Kaundinya's work experience: "K[aundinya] had never planted any cotton before coming to Kilossa.

---

70 This statement is crossed out in the original document and replaced by milder terminology of similar content. TNA. G8/894. [Angelegenheiten der Pflanzung des] Kommerzienrates Heinrich Otto [Kilossa, Bez. Morogoro]. Bd. 1, p. 111.
71 Cf. TNA. G8/894, pp. 121, 136–138.

Hence, he had absolutely no experience in this field."[72] On top of Rechenberg's doubts about Kaundinya's self-portrayal as an experienced plantation manager, the publicly appointed agricultural expert of the *Gouvernment*, Dr Paul Vageler, who examined the *Otto* plantation and the soil conditions surrounding it, also criticised Kaundinya's "low expertise" in a confidential report to the Governor in Dar es Salaam in 1909.[73]

According to the sources, in addition to Kaundinya's unsatisfactory family background, it was his lack of experience as cotton plantation manager that had led to a number of serious mistakes. First of all, Kaundinya was held responsible that the contracts of the first African workers recruited had ended too early and no substitutes had been hired in time. The result was a shortage of hands and the plantation had therefore come to a standstill shortly after its foundation. Furthermore, the work processes were organised deficiently: allocating the workers to the plantation's numerous sites of operation was allegedly done randomly and the workers therefore had to move constantly around the plantation. The result was that work was not done fast enough, as the workers spent many hours walking from one end of the vast plantation to the other every day. Moreover, the construction of both the houses of the European staff as well as the grass huts of the African workforce had not been supervised properly and they either collapsed or turned out to be built at the wrong locations. Hence, the accommodations had to be rebuilt from scratch periodically and cost the *Otto* Company a fortune. Similar mistakes had been made regarding the construction of costly roads and drinking fountains. The latter were so far away from the houses of the European personnel's settlement that up to thirty African workers, who had actually been employed for cotton cultivation, daily had to carry drinking water and water for domestic use half an hour uphill, as the *white* personnel wanted to have a constant water supply at their disposal. One of the major cost-intensive calamities resulted from deficient personnel management. Besides himself as plantation manager and a newly recruited German commercial manager, Kaundinya had employed ten to eighteen other Europeans, who worked primarily as overseers of the African workforce.[74] These European overseers, sometimes even younger

72 TNA. G8/894, p. 118. Cf. also p. 113.

73 TNA. G8/894, p. 84. Cf. "Vageler". *Deutsches Koloniallexikon*, 1920, Band III, S. 598. Web. *University of Frankfurt o.M.* http://www.ub.bildarchiv-dkg.uni-frankfurt.de/Bildprojekt/Lexikon/Standardframeseite.php?suche=Vageler (23 July 2019).

74 After WWI, the Otto Company listed twelve former employees besides Kaundinya and Schurz, the commercial manager. Cf. LTA. 871.1-otto-199. Letter by the Otto company to the Verband der württembergischen Kolonialdeutschen (association of southwest colonial Germans), Unterbohingen, 19 April 1919. Otto's company chronicles report about 11 Europeans working for Otto

than twenty-two years, received 300 Rp. a month (1 Rupee = 1.33 German Marks), roughly twenty-five times the wages of an African worker. As they were each responsible for the supervision of only twenty African workers or twenty-five hectares under cultivation, the *Otto* plantation was overstaffed and lost a lot of money on wages. According to the judgement of the Governor, six European employees would have been enough to do the job, meaning that Kaundinya could have saved up to two-thirds of his overall European personnel expenses.[75] More importantly, these European employees were, according to the Governor's report, recruited without considering their individual biographies and therefore regarded as "low-quality material", whose activities quickly earned the *Otto* plantation the reputation of being a "gangster colony", soon enough.[76] Besides, the *Gouvernement's* report sent to the German Colonial Department, published reports by the *KWK* about the *Otto* plantation also complained that "some of the [eleven] European employees [. . .], ha[d] often not met [. . .] the expectations; a fact which has primarily to be attributed to the consumption of alcohol."[77]

Despite their dubious character, these 'gangster' employees, primarily of German descent, challenged the authority of Ranga Kaundinya as a plantation man-

in July 1909 Cf. LTA. 871.1-otto-233. Chronik, p. 83. Kaundinya mentions one Greek overseer working for him and also 10–12 other Europeans working for Otto's plantation Kilossa besides himself and Schurz. Cf. Kaundinya. *Erinnerungen*, pp. 72, 142. In a petition filed by Kaundinya on behalf of the Otto plantation ca. in February 1909 and signed by eight other enterprises in the Kilossa district, urging the colonial administration to employ a doctor for the Kilossa district, Kaundinya lists 15 European employees at his plantation. Cf. TNA. G5/38. Bemühungen um Entsendung eines Stationsarztes nach Kilossa (Petition der ansässigen Europäer), pp. 1–4. Clement Gillman, who worked as a route section engineer in Kilossa for some time, met Kaundinya and his wife and also visited the plantation himself. He even mentions up to 28 Europeans working at the Otto plantation in January 1910, attributing the large number of three European managers and 28 assistants as the major reason for the plantation's failure. Cf. Gillman Diaries. Mss. Afr. S. 1175/1,2_2. June 1908 bis September 1913, no. 13, pp. 10–13. Given the conflicting numbers, the average of these numbers has to be presumed. Moreover, the *DOAZ* reported in May 1909 that Indians and Goans would have been employed as plantation assistants. Cf. "Aus unserer Kolonie. Kilossa". *DOAZ*, XI, no. 37. Daressalam: 12 May 1909.

75 Cf. TNA. G8/894, pp. 112–118, 137. The engineer Grüninger employed by the Otto plantation, who was primarily responsible for the irrigation in Kilossa, rejected the Governor's and *DKG's* allegations in a letter to the Governor in 1911. In fact, he only addresses his alleged personal shortcomings in detail. Grüninger's responsibilities are not part of this paragraph, however. Besides the article of the *Kölnische Zeitung*, there are no documents revealing the company's opinion on the issue. Cf. TNA. G8/904 [Angelegenheiten der Pflanzung des] Kommerzienrates Heinrich Otto [Kilossa, Bez. Morogoro]. Bd. 2., pp. 9–12. Cf. Kaundinya. *Erinnerungen*, p. 97.

76 TNA. G8/894, p. 119.

77 Supf, Karl. 'Deutsch-Koloniale Baumwoll-Unternehmungen. Bericht XI (Frühjahr 1909)'. 161–162. Ed. Kolonial-Wirtschaftliches Komitee. Beiheft zum "Tropenpflanzer", Jahrg. XIII, no. 5,

ager constantly. Although the *whiteness* of *Otto's* European employees appears to have been of 'precarious' character, as they were judged as 'gangsters' or 'low-quality material' by the colonial administration, they still felt entitled to challenge Kaundinya's status as plantation manager, because he had "Indian blood in his veins".[78] This racist colonial environment certainly made Kaundinya's work in Kilossa a difficult endeavour. This fact is also confirmed by other sources. Besides the files of the Tanzanian National Archives, the chronicles of the *Otto* Company report that Kaundinya faced various obstacles because of his ancestry as well. Accordingly, despite "his competence and his experience in the tropics", Kaundinya had, as "half-Indian, [. . .] difficulties to assert himself against the German employees under his authority as well as against the [colonial] government".[79] According to the chronicles of the *Otto* Company, it was the constant discrimination of the colonial society in German East Africa, which disturbed Kaundinya's work significantly. Occupied by fighting against the disadvantaging environment, Kaundinya was in effect not able to manage the plantation's bookkeeping properly and was subsequently restricted in his responsibilities. He was thus degraded to the post of agricultural manager of the plantation only, while the board of the *Otto* Company sent two German accountants to Kilossa to take charge of the financial affairs. One of them, Mr Sandleben, had been in Dar es Salaam previously, but had failed to check Kilossa's accounts properly as he had relied on mail and telegraphy only. The plantation's financial distress and conflicts with the colonial government must have been severe indeed, as the boss of the family business, Heinrich Otto, even sent his personal secretary, Georg Schurz, all the way to East Africa to restore the budget's order after the results of the initial planting seasons had turned out to be a significant financial loss. While Georg Schurz, the nephew of the famous German American '48er revolutionary', Carl Schurz, seemed to quickly assume authority over his precarious white German 'gangster' employees, and organised the further expansion of the plantation's buildings properly, it was Heinrich Otto's partner, Fritz Engels, in place of Kaundinya, who would negotiate successfully with the colonial government for further land leases for the plantation in Kilossa. In the face of Kaundinya's problems as a white subaltern plantation manager, expansion was considered to be the only way to make the cotton fields profitable.[80]

May 1909. Cf. TNA. G8/894, p. 112. Kaundinya himself explained that the European plantation assistants had "difficulties" getting acquainted with the workload and the climate. They used to complain a lot, particularly in the beginning. Cf. Kaundinya. *Erinnerungen*, pp. 97–98.

78 TNA. G8/894, p. 119.

79 LTA. 871.1-otto-233. Chronik, p. 84.

80 Cf. LTA. 871.1-otto-233. Chronik, pp. 84–85, 89–91, 94–95.

Although the files under investigation feature racist discriminatory remarks against Kaundinya indeed, some criticism against his work performance was certainly justified. It was not only the fact that Kaundinya could not assert himself against the colonial administration in German East Africa that delayed the expansion of the land under cultivation at *Otto's* plantation, the *Gouvernement* repeatedly noted that Kaundinya had neither provided the territory's maps nor the land survey reports needed for further land leases on several occasions. As far as the correspondence between the colonial administration and Heinrich Otto can be reconstructed, Heinrich Otto must have been well aware of this fact and the resulting delays for almost one year. Otto remained nevertheless loyal to Kaundinya – at least as far as the field of agricultural management is concerned – although Kaundinya's difficulties in Kilossa appear to have endured at least until summer 1913.[81]

Ranga Kaundinya himself reports nothing about his life as a white subaltern in German East Africa. Although discrimination against people who were not perceived as German – or rather considered as non-central European men not belonging to the middle and upper classes – was common in all German colonies in legal and societal terms, Kaundinya himself does not mention any incident of such discrimination himself. Although all other sources consulted in this chapter clearly show that there were at least some reservations towards his ancestry, Kaundinya's autobiography published in 1918 is generally silent on the issue. Regarding the strained financial situation of the *Otto* plantation around 1910 and the company's decision to withdraw any financial authority from him, Kaundinya succinctly mentions in his autobiography that because of the "multifaceted tasks" and the ever-increasing bureaucracy, it "had turned out impossible to manage the always increasing paper-work".[82] Hence, an extra hand exclusively in charge of bookkeeping was required, and subsequently also employed. Even more important in terms of racial discrimination is the fact that Kaundinya describes himself as a "decent and respectable middle-European"[83] in his autobiography, repeatedly. Although his entire family had experienced racist discrimination in various colonial environments and for two generations at least, not only in German East Africa but also in India, Britain and Switzerland, his autobiography remains silent on both racism and any personal experiences of discrimination. What is more, as a 'decent and respectable middle European', Kaundinya even portrays himself in his autobiography as a plantation manager who had done his part to 'educate the uncivilised African people to work'. As 'education to work' was one of the major

81 Cf. TNA. G8/894, pp. 5–54. Cf. Stadmuseum Wendlingen. Steinert's document collection, "Tagebuch Fritz Otto", p. 22.

82 Kaundinya. *Erinnerungen*, pp. 103, 142.

83 Kaundinya. *Erinnerungen*, pp. 96, 142.

necessities of every 'civilised' European nation, Kaundinya therefore promoted the importance of further expansion by the German *Reich* and glorified the topos of 'German work'.[84]

It is impossible to identify Ranga Kaundinya's real intentions behind his autobiographical accounts. The reader is thus left to speculate on the reason why he publicly praised German colonialism and concealed the racism he had experienced himself. Some reasons may derive from an interest in future occupation in the German colonial plantation business, or an attempt to raise his autobiography's sales figures among the German readership. It is however also plausible to assume that Ranga Kaundinya regarded himself as a 'proper' middle-class German citizen who simply wanted to share his plantation experience with the German target audience. Despite all the discrimination against him, he might have perceived himself, nevertheless as a full member of German society with work experience in the colony of German East Africa. Legitimising his own employment in Kilossa and maybe seeking future colonial employments, he might have strategically supported Germany's 'civilising mission' overseas as well. Needless to say, given his family background, his German wife and close connections to southwest Germany as well as his past employment in a German colony, he probably felt more at home in Germany than in Britain or India, anyway. In this respect, the date of publication of Kaundinya's autobiography is significant as well. Published in Leipzig in 1918, Ranga Kaundinya must have started his book during WWI. With wars generally hardening attitudes and his brother working as a British colonial state official in India simultaneously, Kaundinya might have felt the urge to take Germany's side publicly to protect himself and his family from German jingoist hostilities. As an Indo-German, who had already experienced racism by German (colonial) societies, he might have attempted to fend off any allegations accusing him of support for the British Empire. This last argument is reinforced by the fact that Kaundinya's autobiography about his life in German East Africa was not his only publication during WWI. In 1916, using the pen name Ganga-rao Brahmputr,[85] he published a pamphlet about India's role during WWI,

84 Cf. Kaundinya. *Erinnerungen*, pp. 7–17, 30–42, 70–73, 96–111, 142–143.

85 With thanks to the sociologist, Juhi Tyagi, who used to work at the Max-Weber-Centre of the University of Erfurt, Germany. She made me aware of the fact that Ganga and Brahmaputra are two rivers that flow from the west and east of the Himalayan range before meeting. While Ganga is the sacred river for the Hindus, of course, the Brahmaputra flows through China, India and Bangladesh. Perhaps, Kaundinya might be trying to suggest some synchronicity regarding his Hindu-German background. Rao is a Hindu upper caste surname. To Juhi Tyagi, the three names suggest sacredness, power and extensiveness. Moreover, 'Ganga-Rao' refers to his own biography and upbringing in missionary circles in southern India, Switzerland, and Germany. The time spans of his

and India's suggested role in global politics after the war. In this pamphlet, Kaundinya explains to the interested German reader why the huge and powerful country of India had become an English colony and why there was no significant anti-British agitation there. Taking a decidedly pro-German standpoint in this book, Kaundinya alias Ganga-rao suggests that the Indian population would pursue a subtle evolution instead of a rapid revolution, which would ultimately throw off the yoke of the British colonisers. Apparently, Kaundinya also toured throughout Germany and delivered corresponding speeches on the issue until the end of 1920, when he finally died. To strengthen Germany's global position, Kaundinya alias Ganga-rao recommended a close German relationship with an independent India of the future. As one of the benefits of independence, Germany and India should seek a strong alliance to create a new *Indogermania*, stretching from the North Sea via the Balkans and the Persian Gulf all the way to India. To his mind, the resulting *Indogermania* would ultimately prevent global conflicts and guarantee world peace – and ensure that Kaundinya as an Indo-German could live a peaceful life within German society, with less discrimination.[86] In this respect, Kaundinya aka Ganga Rao largely echoed many voices heard, especially in the last third of WWI. With the increasing importance of Erich Ludendorff, among others, and his and other geopolitical plans to expand the *Reich* massively into Eurasia, Kaundinya's final writings reveal the societal atmosphere of WWI, illustrating how widespread such ideas were in German society also amongst white subalterns like Kaundinya at that time.[87]

Be that as it may, it is impossible to pinpoint the genuine intentions of Ranga Kaundinya's autobiography and his other writings. Nevertheless, his biography as well as his book about his work in German East Africa do certainly illustrate that the *Otto* plantation in Kilossa has to be regarded as a contested place of labour. At this contested place of labour, the areas of conflict were not only to be found in Kaundinya's relationship to his European employees, the German colonial ad-

stays at the different places equal those of Ranga Kaundinya. This means that Ganga-Rao and Kaundinya are certainly one and the same person. Cf. Brahmputr. *Indien*, pp. 9–10.

86 Cf. Brahmputr. *Indien*, pp. 3–11, 45–50, 60–63. Cf. LTA. 871.1-otto-233. Chronik, pp. 132–133.

87 Cf. Nebelin, Manfred. *Ludendorff. Diktator im Ersten Weltkrieg.* Munich: 2011, pp. 173–216, 283–400. Cf. Murphy, David T. *The Heroic Earth. Geopolitical Thought in Weimar Germany, 1918–1933.* Kent (Ohio) and London: 1997, pp. 1–24. Cf. Tooze, Adam. *The Deluge. The Great War and the Remaking of the Global Order. 1916–1931.* London et al.: 2014, pp. 33–172. The *MAN* railway engineer working in China, Dr. Gerdung, also urged Ludendorff, *Krupp* and *MAN* to expand massively into Eurasia via railway construction cf. HA Krupp WA 4/2589. Cf. Rösser, Micheal. 'Von Afrika nach Eurasien? Deutsche Unternehmen zwischen kolonialem Eisenbahnbau und geopolitischer Planungsphantasie während des Ersten Weltkriegs'. 183–204. *Vierteljahrschrift für Sozial und Wirtschaftsgeschichte (VSWG)*, vol. 110, no. 2. Stuttgart: 2023. doi.org/10.25162/vswg-2023-0005.

ministration, the board of the *Otto* Company and the African workforce. Other areas of conflict were also to be found between the *Otto* Company, the colonial administration and the railway construction company, *Philipp Holzmann*. Setting aside Kaundinya's unclear publication intentions, what remains clear is the fact that the failure of the *Otto* plantation in Kilossa was not only Ranga Kaundinya's fault. The ultimate failure of *Otto* in Kilossa was also the result of general management errors by the leading figures of the *Otto* Company, their inexperience in the cultivation of colonial cotton and its disadvantageous behaviour towards the German colonial government.

4.6 Venture Capital, Modern Technology and Comprehensive Failure

> To those who [. . .] wish to set up their own plantations [. . .] it must be said that, as a rule, this involves not inconsiderable assets, which must be managed sparingly, since it can be expected that, for several years, money will have to be spent until the plantation becomes profitable, and since failure is often to be expected in the first few years as a result of ignorance, the necessary reserves must be available.
>
> Ranga Kaundinya. *Erinnerungen aus meinem Pflanzerjahren*. Leipzig: 1918.[88]

After its foundation in the early nineteenth century, the *Otto* Company had always been a forerunner in the implementation of modern means of technology in their production in the German-speaking areas. Besides decent training of the leading family members at home in Swabia and in northern Germany, Britain, and the USA, implementation of the latest technologies available for textile production was also always central. Just like in other quickly industrialising areas of the 'empire of cotton' the success of *Otto's* textile business and the resulting wealth in the region of Swabia enabled and stirred other industries in the course of the nineteenth century.[89] With increasing economic success and the resulting political influence, the relationship between the *Otto* Company and the monarchs and governments of *Württemberg* and the German *Reich* changed its character over time. In the beginning of the nineteenth century, by advocating Anglo-Saxon machinery, the company challenged the policies of the King of *Württemberg*, who regarded English-style industrialisation with scepticism and favoured the agricultural sector instead. In the long run, *Otto's* approach proved successful, however: By the end of the

88 Kaundinya. *Erinnerungen*, p. 8.

89 Cf. Beckert. *Empire of* Cotton, pp. 83–174. Cf. Hergenröder. *Wendlingen*, pp. 291–298.

nineteenth century, the *Otto* Company had become the leading textile manufacturer in southwestern Germany and could even compete with other leading German companies originating primarily from Saxony and Bavaria.[90]

When industrial capitalism sought an alliance with the recently established modern nation states in the 'empire of cotton', the *Otto* Company's relationship to the German government changed as well. As one of the largest employers and one of the strongest regional players in the textile business, the Otto family sought to establish and cultivate good relationships with German governments at all levels. Whenever the German *Kaiser* or the King of *Württemberg*, who had, like many members of the royal family, himself become a member of the colonial lobby organisation *Deutsche Kolonialgesellschaft (DKG)* since 1899,[91] visited the region around Unterboihingen, leading figures of the *Otto* company would dine with the dignitaries and discuss the latest policies behind closed doors. Likewise, leading men of the company, such as Heinrich Otto, were prominent members of influential German lobby associations – such as the *Verein Deutscher Industrieller* (Association of German Industrialists), *Verein süddeutscher Baumwoll-Industrieller* (Association of South German Cotton Industrialists), the *Hansa-Bund* or the *Deutscher Flottenverein* (German Navy League) – which either fostered the interests of large-scale companies or promoted German *Weltpolitik* (world politics). Likewise, the German governments also embraced significant economic players like *Otto*, as cotton imports and German textile production had become both a matter of national (economic) interest and a matter of national prestige by the end of the nineteenth century.[92] It is therefore no coincidence that close connections between the *Otto* Company, the Colonial Office in Berlin and the *Gouvernement* in Dar es Salaam were equally important when the *Otto* Company attempted to expand their business overseas to German East Africa. Besides shared economic interests between the German *Reich* and the textile producer, *Otto* regarded their expansion to German East Africa also as a contribution to the German *Reich's* international standing. Kaundinya, too, called his occupation in Kilossa a "satisfaction of patriotic duty" – a view shared by the board of the *Otto* Company, whose media-friendly company strategy included announcements in German newspapers about the progress of the plantation in Kil-

90 Cf. Bleifuß and Hergenröder. *Die "Otto-Plantage"* pp. 9–20. Cf. Hergenröder. *Wendlingen*, pp. 248–261, 291–298. Cf. LTA. 871.1-otto-233. Chronik, pp. 44, 47, 55, 57, 61, 66.

91 Cf. Deutsche Kolonialgesellschaft Abteilung Stuttgart. *Mitgliederverzeichnis 1899.* Stuttgart: 1899, p. 1. Cf. Deutsche Kolonialgesellschaft Abteilung Stuttgart. *Kurzer Rückblick auf die Tätigkeit der deutschen Kolonialgesellschaft und des kolonialwirtschaftlichen Komitees seit seiner Gründung 1881 u. 1896.* Stuttgart: 1912, pp. 19–20.

92 Cf. Beckert. *Empire of Cotton*, pp. 312–378. Cf. LTA. 871.1-otto-233. Chronik, pp. 20, 25, 31, 35–36, 45, 62, 86–87, 161, 164.

ossa. In German East Africa, too, the *DOAZ* reported repeatedly about *Otto's* large-scale plantation as well.[93]

Apart from the cotton plantation in Kilossa, the *Otto* Company had two other affiliated enterprises in German East Africa. Principally, Fritz Otto, alongside his partner Fritz Engels, and other southern German textile entrepreneurs, became involved in a smaller cotton plantation and founded the *Baumwollpflanzungs-Gesellschaft Kilwa G.m.b.H.* – the Kilwa Cotton Plantation Limited – in the southern coastal region near Kilwa in German East Africa. This region had already been made famous for the cultivation of cotton. Moreover, a regular steamship service between Kilwa and Dar es Salaam provided cheap and fast transport facilities to the *Otto* Company. Even more promising for the cultivation of cotton appeared the northern region around Mwanza near Lake Victoria where the other *Otto* business had started before the plantation in Kilossa. This largest lake in Africa – the size of Ireland or the contemporary Kingdom of Bavaria – had been connected to the Indian Ocean by the *Uganda Railway* in British East Africa since the 1890s. Given this good connection to a railway, the *Otto* Company founded a subsidiary transport enterprise to reach the British colonial railway, from the company's very beginning. To cross the huge Lake Victoria, Heinrich Otto thus bought an old *Alster* river steamer from Hamburg, sent it to East Africa and remodelled it into a cotton transport ship, intended to take cotton from German East Africa to neighbouring British East Africa in the future. Heinrich Otto's resulting *Victoria-Nyanza-Dampfschiffahrts-Gesellschaft m.b.H.* – Victoria-Nyanza-Steamship Corporation Limited – was joined by his brother Fritz Otto, their partner Fritz Engels and finally Albert Schwarz, who owned a banking business in Stuttgart. The manager of the *Victoria-Nyanza-Dampfschiffahrts-Gesellschaft* was Carl Jungblut, who had worked in German East and German South West Africa before. Although partly successful in a side business of rice plantations around Mwanza, both the *Victoria-Nyanza-Gesellschaft* as well as *Otto's* plantation near Kilwa cast long shadows into the future of other business run by *Otto* in German East Africa. Like the *Otto* plantation in Kilossa some years later, neither the *Baumwollpflanzungs-Gesellschaft Kilwa G.m.b.H.* nor the *Victoria-Nyanza-Dampfschiffahrts-Gesellschaft m. b.H.* ever turned into profitable businesses, and Jungblut and the *Otto* Company had long lasting legal disputes over responsibilities and mismanagement as far as the *Victoria-Nyanza-Gesellschaft* was concerned.[94] Moreover, the transportation of the *Alster*

93 Kaundinya. *Erinnerungen*, p. 21, pp. 18–22. Cf. LTA. 871.1-otto-233. Chronik, pp. 69–75. Cf. editions of the *DOAZ*, IX, no. 48; X, no. 53; X, no. 63; X, no. 88; X, no. 70; XI, no. 9; XI, no. 37 XI, no. 20; XII, no. 18; XII, no. 39; XII, no. 78; XII, no. 11; XIV, no. 69.

94 Cf. LTA. 871.1-otto-233. Chronik, pp. 70–72. Cf. Bleifuß and Hergenröder. *Die "Otto-Plantage"*, pp. 44–50. Cf. LTA. 871.1-otto-195. Deutsche Nyanza-Schiffahrtsgesellschaft. Cf. LTA. 871.1-otto-197. Geschäftskorrespondenz über die Baumwoll-Pflanzungsgesellschaft "Kilwa" im ehemaligen

steamer to Mwanza turned out to be more difficult than expected. It left Europe for East Africa on the same day as Heinrich Otto left for German East Africa alongside Dernburg in 1907. The ship should have been transported via the British *Uganda Railway* from Mombassa's port to *Nyanza* ('Lake Victoria'), but experienced several setbacks on its journey. The railway company at first rejected its transportation because of the *Alster* steamer's huge weight, and it took *Otto* an official request to the British Colonial Office to ultimately transport the steamer to Port Florence.[95]

The problems related to the *Victoria-Nyanza-Dampfschiffahrts-Gesellschaft m.b.H.* were the result of *Otto's* management errors and their lacking experience in colonial business. For their initial colonial enterprises, senior board members of the *Otto* company decided to start businesses in *Kilwa* and at *Nyanza* ('Lake Victoria') on their own. They thus had no official support from the German colonial authorities. For Kilossa, the situation was different however: the colonial administration, especially Governor Rechenberg, would strongly advise *Otto's* board members to abandon the company's plan to cultivate cotton in the northern Mwanza region and to start their business ca. 700 km south in Kilossa instead. Officially, the colonial administration urged cotton plantation further south as it judged the soil quality in the northern Mwanza region as poor and regarded the regional climate unsatisfactory for cotton cultivation. Instead, they favoured southern Kilossa for several reasons: with the colony's north already having a comparatively high number of colonial plantations, it was hard to find any workers there and, above all, the small *Alster* river steamship of the *Victoria-Nyanza-Schiffahrtsgesellschaft* could not manage the heavy swell of the *Nyanza*, frustrating the attempt to reliably connect with the *Uganda Railway* in British East Africa. Hence, transporting raw cotton from Mwanza via *Nyanza* to Europe for further manufacturing turned out to be almost impossible for *Otto* because they had underestimated the naval challenges of *Nyzana*. In contrast to the deficient transport facilities in the colony's north, starting the plantation near Kilossa promised to solve such infrastructural deficiencies, because the expected arrival of the *Central Railway* to Kilossa guaranteed cheap and fast transportation of cotton to Europe in the future. Besides the anticipated arrival of the railway, there was already a telegraph and telephone line as well as a road that connected Kilossa to coastal Dar es Salaam. Moreover, a military station provided security in a region that had seen severe fighting recently in the Maji Maji War. As proper infrastructure had always been an important concern for the *Otto* company in all their businesses back home in southwest Germany – they had always built their factories close to the latest rail-

Deutsch-Ostafrika. Cf. Kaundinya. *Erinnerungen*, pp. 20–22, 25–27, 37–40. Cf. Jungblut, Carl. *Vierzig Jahre Afrika. 1900–1940.* Berlin: 1941, pp. 14–18, 41–69. Cf. Ettlich, Guido. *Konsul Schwarz. Bankier, Bürger & Bahá'í in Stuttgart und Bad Mergentheim.* Berlin: 2019, pp. 328–343.

95 Cf. LTA. 871.1-otto-233. Chronik, pp. 72–75.

way lines and sometimes even also built rails, canals or minor bridges themselves if they promised to facilitate their own business – Governor Rechenberg ultimately convinced *Otto* to start the cotton plantation in Kilossa rather than in the colony's northern region.[96]

Whereas the focus on proper infrastructure was one of the strengths of the *Otto* textile enterprise in Germany, their overseas business policies regarding infrastructure were mindless. Analogically to the *Victoria-Nyanza-Schiffahrts Gesellschaft*, the *Otto* plantation's success seems to have suffered from overhasty management decisions, particularly in the field of infrastructure. As a result, the leading company figures had several disputes about these issues with the colonial government and the railway building company *Philipp Holzman* right up until the end of the formal German colonial rule in East Africa. In contrast to this view, historians of local history, Bleifuß and Hergenröder, have called the *Otto* plantation in Kilossa a 'visionary' endeavour that primarily failed because the German colonial authorities in Dar es Salaam and Berlin were not supportive enough towards the textile manufacturers from Unterboihingen.[97] In fact, more comprehensive studies have already shown that the colonial authorities generally treated the *Otto* plantation benevolently. This view was even shared by Heinrich Otto himself in a letter to the Governor in 1910.[98] In this respect, a closer investigation of the sources reveals that some company decisions appear incomprehensible and suggests that the planning and management of the *Otto* plantation was anything but visionary. It rather seems that *Otto's* board was in good company with many other colonial enterprises that simply started their businesses without any proper consideration of fundamental parameters. Ignorant of essential preconditions required for a profitable plantation, such as good soil conditions, infrastructure capacities, or labour supply, they naively assumed that the latest modern agricultural technology would automatically provide for successful colonial cotton economies of scale. Moreover, they appear to have been convinced that cotton was the 'black man's crop', thinking that the local African population would happily embrace European large-scale cotton schemes without any hesitation.[99] Soon, the opposite turned out to be true. Yet, the leaders of the colonial businesses kept clinging stubbornly to their ill-considered assumptions for years.

---

96 Cf. LTA. 871.1-otto-233. Chronik, pp. 70–72. Cf. Bleifuß and Hergenröder. *Die "Otto-Plantage"*, pp. 44–50. Cf. Hergenröder. *Wendlingen*, pp. 269–272. 291–299. Cf. LTA. 871.1-otto-233. Chronik, pp. 38, 44–45, 47, 51–57, 61, 66. Cf. Dejung. *Commodity Trading*, pp. 51–56.

97 Cf. Bleifuß and Hergenröder. *Die "Otto-Plantage"*, pp. 44–46, 51–54, 69–71.

98 Cf. Koponen. *Development*, pp. 292–293, 408–409. Cf. Sunseri. *Vilimani*, pp. 151–156. Cf. TNA. G8/894, p. 116.

99 Cf. Robins. *Cotton and Race*, pp. 74–81. Cf. Rösser. 'Baumwolle', pp. 9–12.

4.7 Puffing Engines: The Steam Ploughs' Odyssey to Kilossa

The *Otto* Company committed two far-reaching management failures in regard to infrastructure in German East Africa. Just as the *Victoria-Nyanza-Schiffahrts Gesellschaft* had sent the wrong type of ship from Germany to Africa, leading men of *Otto* could not delay themselves until the *Central Railway* arrived in Kilossa. Both decisions ultimately led to great financial losses. Moreover, the previous transportation problems of the *Alster* steamer across British East Africa via the *Uganda Railway* proved to be not the last occasion on which the *Otto* company had difficulties regarding the transportation of heavy machinery via rail and, in general. Although the extension of the railway to Kilossa had been a key element in the company's decision to place its plantation site in the southern part of the colony, whether the railway really existed or not did in effect not matter to the *Otto* Company's decisions. It seems that *Otto* attempted to solve any problem related to the cotton plantation in Kilossa either merely by money or by blind faith in technology, or both.

Symptomatic and symbolic for this reliance on exuberant investment and the naïve belief in modern machinery was the export of two steam ploughs and a steam locomobile to German East Africa's Kilossa. While the locomobile was intended to generate power needed for raw material processing machinery like a cotton gin, both steam ploughs were intended to maximise cotton yields primarily in two respects: First of all, the ploughs should speed up the turning of the soil while simultaneously curbing labour costs. With mechanised digging, fewer workers would be required for this work stage and a large amount of labour costs would be saved. Secondly, using modern machinery would enable the plantation owners to cultivate vast areas of land that would consequently further lower the overall production costs. However, the company had no experience in transporting heavy steam machinery through the African countryside at all. As Kilossa had not been connected to the *Central Railway* yet, the machinery's transportation posed a big challenge. The *Otto* Company had furthermore neither investigated if steam ploughs were at all suitable for the soil in Kilossa, nor had the company sufficiently investigated the exact traffic and transport facilities in the German colony. The only thing the company appears to have known was the fact that it was roughly 350 km from Dar es Salaam's port to Kilossa, and that the *Central Railway* had just reached the district capital Morogoro. From there, it was still around 100 km from the railhead to *Otto's* intended destination of Kilossa. Even if the railway had been finished entirely and if Kilossa had thus been connected to modern infrastructure, the steam plough's whole transportation via rail would have been easier, but would still have borne enough challenges. Already between Dar es Salaam and Morogoro, the transportation of the heavy machinery via rail caused problems. Only when the ploughs arrived in Dar es Salaam, did *Otto* first realise that the *OAEG* had no waggons at their disposal that could manage the ploughs' large size. Moreover, many of the structures of the railway's bridges and tunnels were too small for the heavy machinery and had to be modified accordingly to prevent any damage to either the railway or the machines or both. As a result, it took the railway company months to do away with the major obstacles, causing *Otto* to keep their ploughs in Dar es Salaam for several months from 18 August 1908 onwards. Although railway tunnels were enlarged and the capacity of the railway bridges enhanced, the machinery was still too big and the machines had to be dismantled, put into boxes, and finally loaded onto the railway waggons. Despite all these complications, the first 200 km of transport to Morogoro was comparatively easy as the railway was ready for use on this route. Yet, other major obstacles remained: only small trails connected Morogoro to the 100 km distant Kilossa and it was obvious that it was impossible that human porterage could transport the heavy machinery on this last stretch. One plough worth 80,000 marks weighed sixty-one tons in total, while the heaviest individual parts, the steam boilers, weighed six tons each.[100] With an average human porter being able to carry a load of thirty kg over long distance, it would have required over 2,000 porters to lift just one steam boiler. Such an undertaking was simply impossible and there remained only two options: either wait for the *Central Railway* to arrive in Kilossa for further railway transport or reassemble the individual parts of each steam plough in Morogoro, fire their engines and send them the last 100 km using their own power. For whatever reason, *Otto's* leading men chose the second option.

Sending the steam ploughs to Kilossa using their own power appears incomprehensible. Given the fact that the approval of the railway extension to the colony's central town of Dodoma had already been passed by the *Reichstag* in the beginning of 1908 and Kilossa would fairly soon receive its railway connection, there was no sound reason to send the ploughs there earlier. This is even more so as the *Gouvernement* had explicitly warned *Otto* not to take such risks, precisely because of the poor transport facilities. Instead, the colonial administration had strongly recommended avoiding any premature action, but all in vain. Having already considered driving the ploughs the entire way from Dar es Salaam to Kilossa before the machinery's arrival to East Africa, *Otto* was clearly too impatient to wait another year for the railway to arrive in Kilossa by the end of 1909. Heinrich Otto thus ordered his European engineers to reassemble the individual parts of the steam ploughs in Morogoro and drive them to Kilossa. Meanwhile, various prepara-

100 Cf. "X. Kilossa. Dampfpflüge". *DOAZ,* X., no. 63. Daressalam: 19 August 1908.

tions remained essential before the ploughs' odyssey to Kilossa could begin: As the small caravan path's marking trenches along the colony's woods were too small, aisles wide enough for the heavy machinery had to be cut through large parts of the East African forests. Remaining tree stumps had to be removed and uneven passages had to be levelled out to let the ploughs pass. Furthermore, as the steam engines required constant power supply to move forward, their drivers had to gather firewood and fresh water every second kilometre. To avoid fuel shortages, caches of both water and firewood had to be readied before the beginning of the trek, of course. Finally, there were several rivers to cross, requiring the erection of minor dams or improvised bridges that would sustain extremely heavy loads. Although all necessary preparations eventually appeared to have been taken, unexpected incidents could not be avoided entirely. As illustrated by figure 5 on one occasion, one plough even sank in the Mukondoa River. Fortunately for the *Otto* enterprise, plantation manager Ranga Kaundinya succeeded in rescuing the machine. This saved the company a huge sum of money.[101]

Besides other comparatively minor difficulties on the way, the decision to drive the ploughs to Kilossa using their own power cost the *Otto* Company a good deal of money in general. Furthermore, it led to conflicts with the colonial government and the railway constructing company *Philipp Holzmann*. Whenever possible, the plough trek avoided clearing its way through the African bush and tried to use the sparsely existing infrastructure of German East Africa. Therefore, the ploughs primarily drove on simple caravan routes or roads built either by the colonial administration or *Holzmann*, if possible. Yet, at the same time, these tracks were also fundamental to the colonial administration officials and the railway construction company. Both urgently needed them to transport building material for the railroad's construction sites and objected to the ploughs' passing through for the following reasons: As the caravan routes were made primarily for human porterage, they could not sustain *Otto's* heavy machinery and the steam ploughs simply destroyed the roads when travelling on them. With the sixty-one-ton heavy ploughs devastating the existing infrastructure, the *Otto* Company therefore provoked a quarrel with the railway construction company and local colonial government officials. On 25 October 1908, when realising the destruction of his road, Morogoro's district commissioner sent a telegram to the Governor urging Kaundinya's trek to stop. Only when *Otto's* employee, Sandleben, guaranteed that his company would pay for the necessary repairs of the caravan routes did the steam ploughs receive

101 Cf. "Eisenbahnen". *Deutsches Kolonial-Lexikon*. Cf. "Kilossa". *DOAZ*, X, no. 65. Daressalam: 26 August 1908. Cf. "Kilossa". *DOAZ*, X., no. 90. Daressalam: 21 November 1908. Cf. Sunseri. *Vilimani*, pp. 151–156. Cf. LTA. 871.1-otto-233. Chronik, pp. 80–81. Cf. Kaundinya. *Erinnerungen*, pp. 85–98. Cf. TNA. G8/894, pp. 77, 106.

permission to move forward. When, only a few days later, the railway constructing company *Holzmann* realised that the repair works necessary to make the simple roads passable again would take longer than expected, they increasingly resented the ploughs' moving on. Even worse for the railway company, repairing the damaged roads themselves not only tied up *Holzmann's* lorries, but also consumed important building material like concrete that was urgently needed for railway construction. For the sake of rapid railway construction, the ploughs had to be halted. Hence, only four days after the district commissioner's telegram of complaint from Morogoro to Dar es Salaam, *Holzmann's* government building official Allmaras also protested and likewise sent a telegram to the Governor, urging that Kaundinya's trek stop. Allmaras, who was responsible for the rapid progress of the railway, demanded the interruption of the ploughs' journey and urged *Otto* to wait for the completion of the railway instead. Again, Governor Rechenberg stopped the trek for some days. Yet, *Otto* was determined to resume their quest and leaned on the good relationship between the company's owner Heinrich Otto and State Secretary Bernhard Dernburg. After many unsuccessful telegrams and pleadings by *Otto* to the Colonial Office in Berlin, Dernburg finally ordered Governor Rechenberg on 6 November 1908, via telegram, to let the trek pass. On their part, *Otto* promised to pay for *Holzmann's* repair works once again. Finally, the district commissioner of Morogoro also bowed to the order and the ploughs started moving again on 10 November. They ultimately arrived in Kilossa one month later in December 1908.[102]

It is doubtful whether *Otto's* transportation effort was worth it. At 35,000 Rps. (ca. 46,000 marks), the entire endeavour cost the *Otto* company more than half of a brand-new steam plough. In addition, the journey on the rough 'roads' certainly did not improve the quality of the heavy machinery either. Even worse, when the steam ploughs finally reached Kilossa on 3 December 1908, the rainy season was about to start. As the ploughs were too heavy for the cultivation of wet soil, sinking into the soaked ground, their use had to be postponed to the end of April 1909, when the rainy season would slowly come to an end. In any case, the usage of the ploughs remained unsatisfactory and never provided any advantage in terms of cotton cultivation at all. Proving disastrous for the profitability of the cotton plantation in Kilossa, the steam ploughs dug too deeply into the soil and unearthed layers of the ground that were unfertile for the cotton crop. Briefly, the steam ploughs ruined the fields, lowered the cotton yields, and did not make manual plantation labour redundant. It

---

102 Cf. TNA. G8/894, pp. 42–48. Cf. LTA. 871.1-otto-233. Chronik, pp. 80–81. Cf. Kaundinya. *Erinnerungen*, pp. 85–98. Cf. Sunseri. *Vilimani*, pp. 151–156.

Figure 5: Steam Plough Sunk in Mukondoa River.
Source: Stadtmuseum Wendlingen am Neckar. Diashow Kilossa 1907–1916. 20 Min. 151 Bilder mit Musik.

is said that Heinrich Otto even attempted to sell both steam ploughs to other planters because they were of no use to his plantation in German East Africa at all.[103]

As the company's chronicles report, *Otto's* investments in East Africa were burdensome indeed:

> The large new ventures of the year 07 naturally required more capital than we had available from current income, especially as [. . .] no income could be expected from Kilossa [. . . .] in the first few years. The open bank credit of M 685,000 (Stahl & Federer, W. Bankanstalt, Stuttgart and Deutsche Bank Frankfurt each M 200,00 [. . .]) which we have had at our disposal since then had now mostly been fully utilised to finance our cotton purchases. [We were also] forced to increase our long-term debts.[104]

103 Cf. LTA. 871.1-otto-233. Chronik, pp. 80–81. Cf. Kaundinya. *Erinnerungen*, pp. 85–98. Cf. TNA. G8/894, pp. 77, 106, 110. There were also other companies sharing the fate of *Otto*. Like *Otto*, the *Leipziger Baumwollspinnerei* in Bagamoyo tried to sell their useless steam ploughs, while the Mgohori cotton plantation in the Rufiji district attempted to sell their plough equipped with a combustion engine. Cf. Sunseri. *Vilimani*, pp. 12, 18. Cf. Rösser. 'Baumwolle', pp. 10–11.
104 LTA. 871.1-otto-233. Chronik, p. 78.

Whether the *Deutsche Bank* also had direct investments in any of *Otto's* other businesses or even in Kilossa is not conveyed in the sources, but worthwhile to investigate, given the financial institution's involvement in the *Central Railway*, the *Bagdadbahn* and the Tendaguru Expedition. In any case, to compensate for the financial losses caused by the steam ploughs and their transportation, *Otto's* board turned to other business strategies to make the cotton plantation in Kilossa profitable. As the modern machinery had not yielded any cost advantages in cotton production, the company tried to lower its average costs by expansion. By September 1908, that is even before the actual arrival of the steam ploughs at Kilossa, Heinrich Otto had already sent a letter to the *Gouvernement* in Dar es Salaam demanding further land leases to expand the *Otto* plantation dramatically. By his own accounts, Heinrich Otto had already invested over one million Marks in the plantation and sought returns on his investments, of course. Excluding the significant funds needed for the erection of the houses for the Europeans, a warehouse and a cotton ginnery, *Otto's* investment so far had been spent merely on machinery, the shipping of the ploughs from Europe and materials for an anticipated irrigation system. Facing the exploding costs of his endeavour in German East Africa, *Otto* urged the Governor to grant him 25,000 ha of land to make his plantation ultimately profitable.[105] Given the fact that the entire amount of cultivated land (cotton, sisal, and other crops) on the *Otto* plantation counted ca. 1,400 ha by 1913, this demand was nothing but excessive. As all the cotton-producing European plantations in German East Africa taken together cultivated only 6,400 ha in 1913 (!), *Otto* was demanding the quadruple for only this one plantation. Of course, not all land was used for cotton, but also for housing, foodstuffs, and other cash crops, but the discrepancy of the dimensions speaks for itself.[106] The *Gouvernement* and the district commissioner reacted correspondingly and remained lukewarm on the issue. Cordially but determinedly, Governor Rechenberg wrote to the representatives of the *Otto* plantation in May 1909 discouraging Otto's request: "I would like [you] [. . .] to allow me the comment [. . .] that it [. . .] seems impossible, even for the best founded enterprise, to cultivate and work an area as big as 25,000 ha."[107] Several fruitless negotiations about further land purchases followed, but given the *Gouvernement's* general attitude of benevolence towards *Otto,* the colonial administration finally agreed to lease 15,000 ha of land for a very decent price. Leasing, rather than selling, the land to *Otto* was the largest concession possible. Selling the land would have been hardly justifiable to

105 Cf. TNA. G8/894, pp. 38, 61–62.
106 Cf. Bleifuß and Hergenröder. *Die "Otto-Plantage"*, pp. 69–71, 90. Kaundinya. *Erinnerungen*, pp. 120–144.
107 TNA. G8/894, p. 73.

smaller settler enterprises and the German public that had always resented the colonial administration's advantaging of large-scale businesses. Furthermore, Rechenberg had generally become more sceptical towards *Otto* as the latter appeared to be losing its interest in planting cotton in Kilossa at all. At this point in time, *Otto* seemed to be attempting to cover its financial losses by real estate speculation in East Africa. To prevent *Otto* from starting such a speculative real estate business, Rechenberg insisted on land lease, which was the most common format for real estate business in German East Africa. Frustrated by his unsuccessful undertaking in Kilossa, and also being criticised publicly by the *Kölnische Zeitung* in an article on 16 October 1910 for his mindless business endeavours in East Africa, *Otto* apparently tried to exert his influence within the inner circles of the German textile-producing industrialists in the *Reich* to discourage them all from further cotton investments in German East Africa.[108]

With *Otto* finally turning to the public and blaming the colonial administration for his lack of success, Governor Rechenberg lost his patience and attempted to confront *Otto* sharply as a draft of a letter reveals:

> It is not true that we intend to minimize the amount of Europeans migrating to the country and any success of any corporation is warmly welcomed by the Gouvernement. ~~But it would not be any loss to the colony, if those [companies] returned back home soon, who spend their money purposelessly and aimlessly, who are unsatisfied with the prevailing regulations and who constantly cause massive amounts of work by filing petitions devoid of any substantial reasons repeatedly.~~[109]

It is not clear which content the final letter of Governor Rechenberg to *Otto* contained. But this draft of the letter, (probably) written in 1910 clearly shows that Rechenberg's patience was wearing thin. The Governor was simply fed up with *Otto's* stubbornness, as well as its constant and recurring demands for further concessions. It is not entirely clear how the negotiations between Rechenberg and *Otto* were finally settled, but as far as the sources reveal, further negotiations between the colonial administration and the *Otto* plantation were less strained. The textile firm appears to have realised that their previous business policies in Kilossa had really been unsatisfactory. Without any proper experience in colonial business and without any knowledge about the soil and water conditions necessary for cotton cultivation in German East Africa, the *Otto* company had not only failed in Kilossa, but also at its other two colonial enterprises at *Nyanza* and in *Kilwa*. Facing the disaster caused by the introduction of the steam ploughs in Kilossa, *Otto* turned from large-scale cultivation using heavy modern machinery to a

108 Cf. TNA. G8/894, pp. 84–143. Cf. Kaundinya. *Erinnerungen*, p. 62.
109 TNA. G8/894, p. 137.

style of agriculture that centred the human labour of the African population – just like any other successful planter in the German colony.[110] Of course, the necessity to keep employing African workers had significant influence on the labour relationships between representatives of the *Otto* Company of Unterboihingen, its European personnel and the African workers and their families on the spot.

4.8 White Subalterns, Precarious Whites and African Labour at the Cotton Plantation

4.8.1 The Beginnings of Labour in Kilossa

> 'Mais, monsieur le directeur [. . .] aux Indes vous aviez des hommes, des hommes très intelligents; mais ceux-ci, ils sont des singes, monsieur, ils sont des singes, des bêtes, des singes, des bêtes[!]'
>
> Greek Plantation Assistant Kosmetos to Ranga Kaundinya ca. 1907.[111]

Otto's labour policies were not well adapted to the East African environment. Having successfully manoeuvred between their workers' policies, the agitation of trade unions, increasing German governmental social security policies, demands of social democracy and their own business strategies back home in Germany,[112] *Otto* had difficulties adapting to the colonial business environment. Recruiting, maintaining and managing a reliable and efficient workforce well in an overseas territory were aspects the *Otto* company was barely acquainted with, or had never cared much about, before starting the business in German East Africa. Whereas Governor Rechenberg regarded Kilossa's plantation manager Ranga Kaundinya as inexperienced and incompetent (cf. above), the *Otto* company valued their employee's experience as a plantation manager 'in the tropics' and his Pietist faith. In fact, there was no such simple thing as 'the tropics' even though colonial discourses might suggest otherwise. Even Kaundinya himself stressed in his own autobiography that he had to get acquainted with the German East African environment and its inhabitants first. To him, there was hardly any similarity between India and the German colony: "The most important and most valuable

110 Cf. TNA. G8/904. Cf. Sunseri. *Vilimani*, pp. 148–159.

111 Translated into English: "But sir, Mr Manager, in India, you have human beings, very intelligent human beings; but these here, they are apes, sir, they are apes, they are beasts, they are apes, they are beasts!" Kaundinya. *Erinnerungen*, p. 72.

112 Cf. Hergenröder. *Wendlingen*, pp. 291–297, 299–310, 312–318. Cf. LTA. 871.1-otto-233. Chronik, pp. 20, 25–27, 41, 62, 65–68, 98.

discovery was that, despite twenty-three years of experience as a tropical planter, I had to completely retrain myself in many respects in Africa, because these conditions could not be compared with India."[113] In contrast to the *Otto* Company and many officials of the colonial administration, Kaundinya did indeed observe a difference between southern India and German East Africa. In his autobiography, Kaundinya explicitly warned his readers that the life of a planter in German East Africa was far from a bountiful *Herrenmenschentum* that promised quick riches. Instead, starting a plantation entailed a life full of privation for most aspiring colonialists. Hence, before starting work in Kilossa, Kaundinya himself went to the central districts of Bagamoyo and Saadani to observe the usage of steam ploughs at an experimental plantation run by the *KWK.* Of particular importance was to get an idea about the "labour relations [. . .], on the position which the German East African government took on this important question, the treatment of negroes, the clearing of African forests, the wage relations, the establishment of labour recruitment and their catering etc.". At Saadani, Kaundinya also enticed a "Greek plantation assistant" to join *Otto's* plantation in Kilossa, who had previously worked as a "trainee" at a Greek plantation in the central district.[114] With some other Greeks of the Egyptian diaspora owning smaller plantations also in the *Lindi* district, for example, whether this Greek plantation assistant was the abovementioned Kosmetos, who in the end worked many years at the *Otto* plantation, is not clear. In any case, all these efforts show that Kaundinya at least tried to include some kind of 'East African expertise' at the new planation in Kilossa. Kaundinya himself also tried to acquire some relevant knowledge, including basic Swahili language skills, which he started to learn right after his arrival in Dar es Salaam before he took up working in Kilossa. Yet, he regarded learning this language as "very hard" in the beginning, which certainly inhibited his ability to communicate with his African workers in Kilossa.[115]

In contrast to plantation manager Kaundinya, the leading men of the *Otto* Company did not consider the local conditions relevant for their overseas investments. Besides general mismanagement, one of the reasons why the budget of *Otto's* plantation in Kilossa was strained was the high wages for the many Europeans employed. As indicated above, half the number, or approximately six Europeans, would have been enough to run the entire plantation more profitably. Although Kaundinya probably had significant influence on the question of whom

113 Kaundinya. *Erinnerungen*, p. 42, cf. pp. 7–8, 17.

114 Kaundinya. *Erinnerungen*, p. 42.

115 Kaundinya. *Erinnerungen*, p. 35, cf. pp. 25–37, 44, 68–73. Cf. Dernburg. *Südwestafrikanische Eindrücke*, pp. 58.

to employ, he certainly must have acted in accordance with the attitudes of his bosses when hiring many more Europeans than necessary at the cotton plantation in Kilossa. Despite Kaundinya's background, it appears that *whiteness*[116] and European descent were the most important qualifications for prospective employees at the *Otto* plantation. Reflecting primarily the German settler community's sentiment, just as in the case of railway construction, the work of Germans was glorified. The *DOAZ* praised *Otto's* human resource management in East Africa in September 1907 as patriotic: "Manager [of the plantation] is Mr Kaundinya [. . .] [and in] the course of the entire endeavour no foreigners shall be hired, but only Germans will be employed."[117] Besides the fact that the *DOAZ's* report was simply wrong – given Kaundinya's Indian background and the fact that Kaundinya also employed the Greek assistant Kosmetos[118] at *Otto's* cotton plantation – the policy to employ primarily Germans proved unsatisfactory.

Especially, the selection of the European personnel further illustrates the mindlessness of the entire colonial business in Kilossa in several ways. First of all, if *Otto* had employed African overseers instead of numerous Europeans, the textile company would have saved a fortune: Africans would not only have received a fraction of the Europeans' wages, but they would also have had sufficient language skills and genuinely known the East African environment to the necessary degree. Both aspects would have been helpful to obtaining a reliable workforce for the cotton plantation. Despite these simple facts, there is no evidence that *Otto* had ever given any thought to any staffing choices when starting their plantation. Instead, *Otto* simply had the naïve belief that European colonisers were superior employees than Africans. Reflecting these naïve assumptions, *Otto* even had the lofty plan to send "100–150 [German] farmer and weaver families to settle in the surroundings" of the plantation in Kilossa.[119] Although this plan never materialised, and there is no further archival evidence that could tell whether *Otto* was serious on the issue, it shows that the *Otto* Company was also

---

116 Regarding the concept of *whiteness* in a colonial environment cf. Natermann, Diana Miryong. *Pursuing Whiteness in the Colonies. Private memories from the Congo Free State and German East Africa (1884–1914).* Münster and New York: 2018, pp. 11–41, 217–230. Cf. Rösser, Michael. Review on 'Natermann, Diana Miryong: Pursuing Whiteness in the Colonies. Private Memories from the Congo Free State and German East Africa (1884–1914)'. Münster: 2018. *H-Soz-Kult.* 15 March 2019. Web. www.hsozkult.de/publicationreview/id/rezbuecher-30169 (26 July 2019).

117 "Aus der Kolonie. Die Riesenplantage bei Kilossa". *DOAZ,* IX, no. 48. Daressalam: 07 September 1907. Cf. Bleifuß and Hergenröder. *Die "Otto-Plantage",* pp. 61–65, 69–72.

118 Cf. Kaundinya. *Erinnerungen,* p. 72. Cf. Stadmuseum Wendlingen, "Tagebuch Fritz Otto", p. 17.

119 "Aus der Kolonie. Die Riesenplantage bei Kilossa". *DOAZ,* IX, no. 48. Cf. Bleifuß and Hergenröder. *Die "Otto-Plantage",* pp. 61–65, 69–72.

ill-prepared regarding the recruitment of labour in German East Africa. When *Otto's* thoughts about the German weavers' emigration were published by the *DOAZ*, the company was still occupied with sending their steam ploughs to German East Africa. As this modern machinery was intended to replace human workers at the cotton plantation by the mechanisation of plantation labour, *Otto* apparently devoted no deeper considerations to the employment of (African) workers. Yet, the latter were indispensable to clear the land and to plant as well as harvest the cotton cash crop.

Despite such mindlessness regarding the recruitment of workers, labour supply was not a problem in the first dry season when Kaundinya was able to hire 150 men quickly. Unfortunately, there is not much information available about these workers' backgrounds. Examining the sources, it is not entirely clear how Kaundinya succeeded in recruiting these first 150 workers, necessary to clear the land intended for cotton cultivation. In his autobiography, Kaundinya only explains that these initial workers had previously worked for *Holzmann* sub-contractors at the railway construction sites between 1905 and 1907 and that Kaundinya succeeded in taking these men on for his own purposes.[120] As historians have repeatedly suggested that East Africans preferred railway labour to plantation labour, it appears that Kaundinya was simply able to take advantage of the interrupted railway construction process between 1907 and 1909. With the completion of the railway home line between coastal Dar es Salaam and inland Morogoro in 1907, at this moment in time, the German *Reichstag* had not decided if it would pass further financial means for the *Central Railway*'s extension further west. Hence, actual construction work stopped and was only resumed in the dry season in the beginning of 1909. During this interruption of railway construction between 1907 and 1909, workers initially occupied at the railroad were indeed available to be employed by Kaundinya at the *Otto* plantation. Instead of competition for workers between *Holzmann* and the *Otto* plantation, there might have even been cooperation between the two colonial employers between 1907 and 1909 as far as the labour supply was concerned. After *Holzmann* had stopped railway construction in 1907, the construction company might have urged their sub-contractors to deliver their workers to the *Otto* plantation. Yet, whether the workers had been previously hired by freelance labour recruiters for railway construction or whether they were instead provided by the colonial administration is difficult to assess. This question is especially relevant because some of the railway workers between 1905 and 1907 were Maji Maji POWs forced to work at the railway construction sites, about whom only limited traces are left in the archives. Although sources are particularly scarce regarding

120 Cf. Kaundinya. *Erinnerungen*, pp. 43.

labour at the *Central Railway* between 1905 and 1907, the few existing documents indicate that a significant number of these initial railway workers were recruited by force, and there were also a considerable number of war convicts being punished for having fought the colonial government during the Maji Maji War.[121]

Given this background, there may have been another reason why Kaundinya might have had to initially employ former railway convict workers or other forced labourers for the plantation in Kilossa. The devastating effects of the Maji Maji War remained relevant for his labour policies in the initial two years. As the region around Kilossa had been destroyed by the German colonial military's 'scorched earth' policies during that war, the local population was generally hostile towards any new colonising intruders. The people living in the area were thus reluctant to take up any work at *Otto's* new cotton plantation. This was even more so as the colonial administration's rigid determination to plant cotton had been one of the major reasons why the Maji Maji War had in fact started. In evidence of this, upon arriving in Kilossa for the first time, Kaundinya's porters attempted to run away after the local population told them about their experiences during and after the war. It took the German Indian plantation manager, several incentives like immediate and extra pay to persuade his African employees to stay in Kilossa and start the plantation in the first place.[122]

In any case, in order to obtain workers for the cotton plantation, the *Otto* Company was prepared to use not only the carrot, but also the stick. For instance, the company's boss Heinrich Otto pressured the colonial administration to enforce the supply of workers in a letter to the colonial office in February 1908, even if he avoided the word 'force' itself when mentioning the problems of labour supply.[123] But such views did not only exist in faraway Unterboihingen, but also on the spot in Kilossa. There, corporal punishments were as ordinary as at similar colonial enterprises. Public whippings or enchained imprisonments were "small scenes that occurred several times a week" in Kilossa, as Fritz Otto noted in his diary when visiting the family-owned plantation in Kilossa in 1913.[124] Kaundinya himself also did not refrain from the use of force regarding labour. Only when he first arrived in Kilossa did he refrain from violence as it "was not diplomatic to

121 Cf. Koponen. *Development,* pp. 398–400. Cf. Gillman Diaries. Mss. Afr. S. 1175/1,2_1, no. 10, pp. 11–12. Cf. Koponen. *Development,* pp. 398–400. Cf. Allmaras. 'Ich baue 2000 km', pp. 42–44. Cf. Wegmann. *Vom Kolonialkrieg,* p. 169.

122 Cf. Kaundinya. *Erinnerungen,* pp. 60–62. For agency and bargaining power of porters in German East Africa cf. Greiner. 'Permanente Krisen', pp. 187–200.

123 Cf. Bleifuß and Hergenröder. *Die "Otto-Plantage",* pp. 40–43, 60–64. Cf. Wegmann. *Vom Kolonialkrieg,* pp. 112–184. Cf. TNA. G8/894, p. 9.

124 Stadtmuseum Wendlingen, "Tagebuch Fritz Otto", p. 18.

take coercive measures right from the beginning".[125] Initially, he hoped to establish friendly relationships with the local population in the course of establishing the plantation in Kilossa. Despite such comparatively benevolent labour policies, Kaundinya was generally not satisfied with the work performance of the first African workers he succeeded to employ and complained about it correspondingly. Comparing the East African workers' allegedly low performance with the experiences he had supposedly had with Indian 'coolies' in Asia, Kaundinya scolded his Greek plantation assistant Kosmetos for having failed to accomplish the demanded workload, together with his cohort of African workers. Confronted with such allegations, Kosmetos rejected any personal criticism and blamed the African workers instead: "But sir, Mr Manager, [. . .] in India you have human beings, very intelligent human beings; but these here, they are apes, sir, they are apes, they are beasts, they are apes, they are beasts [!]"[126] Recalling that Greeks in German East Africa were vilified as 'half Orientals' by German colonialists in East Africa, this utterance appears grotesque, especially because Kosmetos uttered it wholeheartedly to Kaundinya of all people, who had faced anti-Indian discrimination himself. Besides illustrating remarkable confluences of racist colonial discourses, Kosmetos' statement nevertheless points to the much more important question of the role of African workers at the *Otto* plantation in Kilossa, and their perspectives on the issue. The African workmen and -women were not only indispensable for *Otto's* plantation in Kilossa, they also managed to subvert and resist colonial labour policies and eked out advantages in the context of the high demand for workers by many colonial businesses. They further enhanced their standing when proving to be skilled and experienced cotton planters.

4.8.2 Obtaining and Organising the 'Living Machine'

African labour was always central in Kilossa. By the time *Otto's* plantation fields had been cleared and the soil was ready for cotton cultivation by the beginning of 1909, the *Reichstag* had already approved the funds to extend the *Central Railway* from Morogoro to central Tabora. As the first sections of the route passed through the Kilossa region, the railway's construction sites absorbed all the workers available there. Thus, almost no worker was to be found for Kaundinya. It therefore must be stressed that *Otto's* impatience not only made the transportation of the steam ploughs very costly, but it was also very bad timing as far as the recruit-

---

125 Kaundinya. *Erinnerungen*, p. 61.
126 Kaundinya. *Erinnerungen*, p. 72.

ment of African workers was concerned. By the time Kaundinya had actually started cultivation after the arrival of the steam ploughs in the dry season of 1910, the railhead had finally reached the area around Kilossa and the *Otto* plantation suddenly found itself in competition for workers with the railway constructing company *Philipp Holzmann.* Even worse, the steam ploughs intended to save the costs of a significant number of workers did not live up to *Otto's* expectations. Quite the contrary: as the steam engines had to be constantly fuelled with water and firewood, the machinery even created more labour demand. Instead of saving labour, the ploughs needed a larger number of workers: many workers were busied collecting water and cutting trees for the firewood needed to generate steam to keep the engines running. Instead of saving labour, the usage of the steam ploughs required five to six times more labour than needed for the old-established hoe agriculture devoid of the latest technology. Besides their costly transportation and the fact that the ploughs ruined the soil, the great effort necessary for their maintenance was the final blow for most modern machinery at *Otto's* plantation in Kilossa. "Within a few years Otto realized that he was just as dependent on African labor as any other plantation in the colony [. . .]."[127] As a result, Kaundinya turned to hiring migrant workers who had been recruited by freelance labour recruiters, primarily in the central regions around *Iringa.* Apparently, hiring workers from *Iringa* was not enough in the following years and turning to workers originating from the even more distant district of *Tabora* became necessary. For the subsequent recruitments, "several [labour] recruiters were constantly on their way"[128] to procure enough workers for planting cotton in Kilossa. Modern machinery was thus replaced by African manual labour at the cotton plantation in Kilossa.[129] What Kaundinya termed the 'living machine' would slowly but surely completely replace the steam engine by 1912. For cultivation, Kaundinya divided the vast cotton fields into smaller sectors, with each sector amounting to an area of ten meters squared. Then, the 'living machine' worked these squares systematically (cf. figure 6):[130]

> Using African overseers for every cadre of twenty-five workers, rows of workers were bound together with rope or chain to poke seed holes in regular, straight rows [. . .]. Behind a lead row of men, a row of women deposited cotton or grain seed. Overseers attempted to regulate worker motions through call-and-response singing.[131]

---

127 Sunseri. *Vilimani,* p. 153. Cf. Kaundinya. *Erinnerungen,* p. 102.
128 LTA. 871.1-otto-233. Chronik, p. 83.
129 Cf. Kaundinya. *Erinnerungen,* pp. 102–113. Bleifuß and Hergenröder. *Die "Otto-Plantage",* p. 64.
130 Cf. Kaundinya. *Erinnerungen,* p. 105.
131 Sunseri. *Vilimani,* pp. 153–154; Sunseri quotes Kaundinya. *Erinnerungen,* p. 107. Cf. Sunseri. *Vilimani,* pp. 150–154. Cf. Kaundinya. *Erinnerungen,* pp. 104–112.

This 'living machine' was part of an overall strategy that many colonial plantations pursued. In terms of labour, the 'living machine' had defeated the steam engines at *Otto's* technically equipped plantation in Kilossa.

As 'modern' colonisers[132] devoid of useful modern machinery, it was felt that at least the African labour force should follow a daily routine that resembled the rhythm of an industrial factory. After the failure of the steam ploughs at the cotton plantation in Kilossa, the organisation of African labour there was done differently compared to the *Central Railway* and the Tendaguru Expedition. Whereas piece work dominated the *Central Railway*'s construction sites, workers at the Tendaguru had a fixed number of daily work hours from morning to the afternoon. In Kilossa, the plantation management combined the two systems and fused the 'labour card system' with elements of piece work. The labour card system, which was originally termed the *Wilhelmstal* labour card system, was first introduced in the colony's northern districts where many European planters had settled. Its legal prerequisite was Governor Götzen's *Verordnung, betreffend der Heranziehung der Eingeborenen zu öffentlichen Arbeiten* (regulation concerning the attraction of the natives to public work), issued on 1 April 1905. This law effectively required the African population to construct, repair, and clean public roads without any payment.[133] The labour card, created in the mountainous *Usambara* area in the west of Tanga named *Wilhelmstal* (today's Lushoto), aimed at providing sufficient workers, particularly for large-scale plantations, but also for mission plantations and for small-scale settler agriculture. The significance of the latter was increasingly important as migration statistics show a comparably high influx of European settlers to German East Africa from the turn of the century onwards. When most of them settled in the cooler climate of the mountainous regions of the country, where many missions and most plantations were also located, competition for workers increased. Consequently, the former strategies of (forced) labour supply by pressuring African leaders to provide workers collapsed in 1905. As a solution, Protestant Bethel missionaries proposed the introduction of a labour card system, and Governor Götzen approved it. Every man, except those who were working for the colonial administration, had to obtain a labour card containing thirty squares. These squares symbolised thirty days of work, which were filled according to the number of days worked for European employers. These could be plantations, missions or settlers. Salaries were set around the average wages and the thirty working days had to be fulfilled within four months. If not completed by that time, or refused entirely,

132 Cf. Kundrus, Birthe. *Moderne Imperialisten. Das Kaiserreich im Spiegel seiner Kolonien.* Cologne et al: 2003, pp. 281–294.

133 Cf. Klein-Arendt. 'Ein Land wird', p. 47. Cf. Tetzlaff. *Koloniale Entwicklung*, p. 86. Cf. Koponen. *Development*, pp. 401–402. Cf. Sippel. '"Wie erzieht man"', p. 327.

the card holder could be sent to public works where they received less or no payment at all. After Götzen's introduction, Governor Rechenberg and State Secretary Dernburg also agreed on the usage of the labour card system in 1907 as it provided several advantages. First of all, labour was supplied by indirect means of force, which freed the local authorities from constantly using direct means of coercion. In turn, the African workers could choose their employer themselves and accordingly shunned those notorious for treating workers most violently. Evidence cannot clarify if the labour card system was limited to the densely settled area of northern *Wilhelmstal*. Believing that it was economically unsuitable for the regions without a considerable number of German settlers, Rechenberg and Dernburg might have intended to keep it within *Wilhelmstal*, but remaining documents suggest that very similar labour card systems were introduced in many of the northern districts. Even though documents cannot entirely prove area-wide use in the north, at least in the northern district of Kilimanjaro in 1913, a "colonial investigator [. . .] did not meet a single *Chagga* man without a labour card [. . .]"[134] and various forms of the labour card system had spread from *Wilhelmstal* southwards into the central districts of Bagamoyo and Morogoro from 1910 onwards. Whether it was intended, willy-nilly tolerated or introduced to other districts without the colonial authority's consent due to a lack of administrative means of control, must remain uncertain.[135]

In any case, for those located in the Morogoro district, a labour card system was indeed introduced. As Kilossa was located in this district, it was also in use at the *Otto* cotton plantation. Thus, an ideal typical workday using this system had the following characteristics: Workers and their families would be woken up early in the morning by drums and were called to work. Subsequently, they had to line up and their so-called 'labour cards' were checked. The system in Kilossa was very similar to that used in the northern region of *Wilhelmstal:* Each labour card had thirty squares, each indicating one day of labour. As soon as a worker had completed one day of labour, one box was checked. After the card's completion, the worker would receive his or her payment at a central pay dock. Work was scheduled roughly from sunrise to sunset, working ten hours on average, lunch break excluded; so much for the theory. In practice, workers often simply refused to come to work daily, and it was typical for a worker to take several months for the completion of one thirty-day labour card. Moreover, workers often decided unilaterally when a six-months-contract had ended and wanted to

134 Koponen. *Development*, p. 404.

135 Cf. Koponen. *Development*, pp. 400–407. The passage about the labour card system was already used in my *Zulassungsarbeit*. Cf. Rösser. *Forced Labour*, pp. 37–39.

leave Kilossa after a week or two, instead of six months. Resistance towards the industrialised work regime occurred also on the job: During a workday, workers attempted to extend their breaks, did not return to work after lunch break or left the workplace immediately as soon as the *ngoma* rang out calling for closing time, without returning their hoes and other tools to the magazine. The engine of the 'living machine' also sputtered frequently as Africans working in Kilossa sometimes acquired key positions in the labour process and transformed the intended factory-like work into a mode of work that followed their own principles: "[. . .][W]ork rhythms were under the control of African singers. [. . .] [And] workers broke ranks and 'hoed back and forth in all directions,'" thereby breaking the intended industrialised labour discipline.[136]

To break resistance and *Eigen-Sinn*, Kaundinya tried to fuse the labour card system with piece work and set up a very bureaucratic combination of both labour regimes. Consequently, Kaundinya's labour policies required the supervision of numerous overseers:

> We decided to work for ten hours a day, if possible on daily tasks: i.e. every morning the supervising assistant or head of department determined the amount of work that had to be done. Those who worked diligently were finished earlier and allowed to go home. [. . .] This system entailed that in each department the Europeans in charge of supervising the staff had to stay with the department from the start until the end [. . .]. [. . .] When a worker has finished his day's work [. . .], he brings his card to the head of department, who checks it himself [. . .] and then enters his initials on the card. Only then is the card fully valid for the day. After everyone has finished their task, a note with a short report on the workers under his supervision, indicating the type of work, number of workers and amount of piece work, is written out and handed in at the office. In the evenings after work is finished, all the [European overseers] usually gather here to report [. . .] and to discuss with the management the disposition for the next day.[137]

If the workload was not met as required, Kaundinya chose from several punishments. He threatened the workers, demanded extra work in the evening, or denied their payment or the food ration – *posho* – after work.[138] The necessity to establish such a sophisticated and bureaucratic system of labour control already indicates that enforcing the colonial labour regime in Kilossa proved to be very difficult for plantation manager Kaundinya. These difficulties to establish, maintain and impose such a comprehensively controlled work system – in line with European standards of 'modern' factory-like work rhythms – on the African workers appears to be the major reason

136 Sunseri. *Vilimani,* pp. 153–154; Sunseri quotes Kaundinya. *Erinnerungen,* p. 107. Cf. Sunseri. *Vilimani,* pp. 150–154. Cf. Kaundinya. *Erinnerungen,* pp. 104–112.
137 Kaundinya. *Erinnerungen,* pp. 94, 100.
138 Cf. Kaundinya. *Erinnerungen,* pp. 72–73, 94, 119.

why Kaundinya had to employ so many Europeans. Without constant European supervision, the workforce followed their own ideas about labour and once again proved *Otto's* assumptions about labour in East Africa wrong. In the end, not only the inefficient steam ploughs cost *Otto* a lot of money, but also the high number of Europeans required to enforce labour discipline was very costly, and contributed to the plantation's economic failure. All in all, the imagined dominance by means of modern work discipline was rather the fantasy of the colonisers and not the reality at the plantation in Kilossa. Finally, Kaundinya also tried to enforce colonial command in another manner: Just as at the labour camps at the *Central Railway*'s construction sites and at the palaeontological excavation camp at the Tendaguru Mountain, the *Otto* plantation management intended to establish a colonial topography as far as the residential areas of Europeans and Africans were concerned. Although attempting to separate black from white and to supervise the workforce residences at the plantation more comprehensively, nevertheless, the residential areas of the workers, that is the labour camps, bore many opportunities to challenge colonial rule at *Otto's* plantation as well.

4.9 Contesting Labour at the Workers' Camp

4.9.1 The Labour Camp in Kilossa

> The Indian, Arab and Negro neighbourhoods [in Dar es Salaam], which form special districts on their own, are of particular interest to the foreigner. I found the Negro neighbourhoods to be particularly curious. I knew Indians and Arabs sufficiently from India.
>
> Ranga Kaundinya. *Erinnerungen aus meinen Pflanzerjahren*. Leipzig: 1918.[139]

Kaundinya's utterance about the colony's capital is intriguing. Having stressed that Kaundinya had the self-image of being a 'decent' central European of middle-class origin indeed, his comment about Dar es Salaam's topography appears to be somewhat inverted. Kaundinya is certainly correct in observing that the colonial capital's different neighbourhoods were curious to most Europeans coming to German East Africa for the first time. Kaundinya, too, found Dar es Salaam's different quarters fascinating indeed, albeit with some restrictions: The only quarter that mattered to him was that of the East African, which Kaudinya described in his autobiography in detail.[140] In contrast, despite having lived for over twenty years in India, both the Indian and the Arabic quarters were of no interest to

139 Kaundinya. *Erinnerungen*, p. 30.
140 Cf. Kaundinya. *Erinnerungen*, pp. 30–34.

Figure 6: Planting cotton in Kilossa.
Source: Stadtmuseum Wendlingen am Neckar. Diashow Kilossa 1907–1916. 20. Min. 151 Bilder mit Musik.

him. This indifference to the Indian and Arab quarters is precisely the difference between Kaundinya's descriptions about German colonial Dar es Salaam and similar descriptions by other European people devoid of a bi-ethnic background. Contrary to his perpetuated public self-image as Central European, his Indian family background appears to have mattered to him. Obviously, it was a relevant horizon of experience to him at least. Although Kaundinya rarely mentioned this explicitly, he did call India his homeland once in his autobiography.[141] Despite this rare show of appreciation for one of his motherlands, as far as the labour camps in Kilossa are concerned, Kaundinya attempted to reproduce the topography of colonial command. Thus, the topography of the labour camps in Kilossa was in line with his dominant self-image that classified himself into the European sphere. Overall, the face of the *Otto* cotton plantation in Kilossa changed significantly between 1907 and 1914. Besides the ever-expanding fields under cultivation, the changes applied to the housing facilities as well. The living and working area were surrounded by the foothills of the Uluguru Mountains in the east and the Udzungwa Mountains in the west. In the beginning of the plantation, both the accommodation of the European staff and the houses of the African workers lay next to

141 Cf. Kaundinya. *Erinnerungen*, p. 23.

the cotton fields in the plains of Kilossa, near the banks of the Mukondoa River. From the very start, plantation manager Kaundinya separated the quarters of the African workers from himself and the other European personnel. In line with the colonial topographies of major colonial settlements and comparatively small labour camps like those at the *Central Railway*, Kaundinya ordered his European employees to settle centrally and close together when arriving in Kilossa in the beginning: "we Europeans [sic!]" (per Kaundinya) lived in a "small guest house" provided by the local colonial district officer. As this guest house was not big enough, there were also tents located right next to the local governmental *boma* "until temporary dwellings, grass houses and corrugated iron barracks were built for us".[142] The African workers, too, lived in simple grass huts in the beginnings of the *Otto* plantation, but separated from the Europeans (cf. figure 7). According to their habits from home, the East African workers erected either rectangular or round huts on a cleared field using bundled branches for the structures and afterwards covered their roofs with grass. In such houses, four to six people or rather one to two worker families lived during their employment in Kilossa. For both parties, European and African, this accommodation was used until the end of the first rainy season. Afterwards, new housing was built for each group as the initial settlement in the lowlands turned out to be an unhealthy area. Located close to the Mukondoa River, the humid environment with its swamps and ponds was the perfect breeding ground for mosquitos. It therefore led to a high infection rate of malaria and other diseases among all people at the *Otto* plantation:

> Soon, however, we had the bad experience that the lowlands were unhealthy because of many swamps and ponds. Our European supervisors and black workers were often down with malaria and dysentery. So, we decided to clear [. . .] a narrow strip of land up the mountain, where more advantageous housing was available for the workers' village, the farmyard and even higher for the officials' housing.[143]

The situation must have been severe indeed, as not only were the European staff unable to work due to their sickness, but also numerous African workers, supposedly better accustomed to the climate, needed to rest because of their diseases.

As this loss of working hours was not only a health concern but also a big monetary loss to the already strained financial situation of the plantation, something had to be changed urgently. Kaundinya therefore decided to relocate all settlements onto a nearby mountain to distance the African workforce and the

142 Kaundinya. *Erinnerungen*, p. 65.
143 Kaundinya. *Erinnerungen*, p. 75.

Figure 7: First workers' camp in Kilossa.
Source: Stadtmuseum Wendlingen am Neckar. Diashow Kilossa 1907–1916. 20 Min. 151 Bilder mit Musik.

European personnel from the malaria-prone areas. Once again, the newly erected labour camp was modelled around the ideal typical colonial topography. Although everybody involved in the plantation moved upwards, the Europeans took the highest located accommodation, separated from the other buildings. On the next lower level, the buildings frequented by Europeans and Africans alike such as the market hall, the slaughterhouse, the warehouse and the farmyard were located. These were followed by the African workers' village on the lowest level. This design privileged the Europeans as they received the most spacious, airy, and therefore, the supposedly healthiest locations for their settlements, whereas the Africans had to settle at a comparatively 'lower' and, therefore, unhealthier level. This hierarchy was also reflected in the consideration of medical services. Kaundinya had urged Undersecretary of State of the Colonial Department Friedrich Lindequist and Governor Rechenberg to employ a doctor for the Kilossa district when the two officials visited the *Otto* plantation on 15 January 1909. To strengthen his appeal, Kaundinya even filed a petition on behalf of the *Otto* plantation management ca. in February 1909, which was also signed by eight other companies of the Kilossa district, *inter alia* also *Philipp Holzmann*. The sources do not reveal whether his appeal was heard by the colonial administration, but the petition shows that Kaundinya was primarily, if not exclusively, concerned about professional medical treatment for his "15 European" employees at the Kilossa plantation; the necessity to provide professional medical care for the African workers was never mentioned in the petition.[144]

The architecture of the newly erected houses further reflected the lower status attributed to the African workers. The African workers continued to dwell in houses made of bundled wood, clay and grass roofs while the European staff houses were improved constantly. Over time, even stone houses, equipped with solid roofs, were built for them.[145] Moreover, the allotment of the African village reflected Kaundinya's approach to enforce a topography intended to put colonial command into architectural practice:

> In the new workers' village, paths and spaces for the individual houses were marked out with measurements and guidelines. Soon the settlement got a decent appearance, not without some misery for the negroes, who had no sense of order and direction at all and preferred to build houses in the middle of the road, preferably of the size and height of doghouses instead of decent living quarters.[146]

Apparently, the African workforce had their own views regarding their settlement and did not care much about Kaundinya's topographical plans. Furthermore, living separately from the European sphere also allowed the African workers and their families several freedoms that helped in evading colonial command. Overall, social life in the workers' residences tended to subvert 'modern' colonial labour discipline, instead of reinforcing comprehensive control.

Around *Otto's* plantation in Kilossa, migrant workers and workers originating from the Kilossa region settled either alone or with their families, and thereby created worker villages. According to *Otto's* files, on average, between 500 and 1,000 male workers settled permanently in the direct environs of the plantation before WWI. Together with their families, a village of up to ca. 2,000 inhabitants emerged. Of course, the actual number of the population fluctuated as it was decisively influenced by economic activity. Moreover, like at the *Central Railway* or at the Tendaguru, the climate of the Indian Ocean Area was crucial to the labour conditions in German East Africa. Whether it was the rainy or dry season strongly influenced the number of workers present in Kilossa. Given the provided numbers of men working in Kilossa, and an unknown number of children living in

---

144 TNA. G5/38, appendix, cf. pp. 1–4. Friedrich Lindequist became Bernhard Dernburg's successor as Colonial State Secretary from 1910 onwards. He resigned by the end of 1911. Cf. Gründer, Horst. "Lindequist, Friedrich von". *Neue Deutsche Biographie,* 14, 1985, p. 601. Web. https://www.deutsche-biographie.de/pnd117025259.html#ndbcontent (08 July 2020).

145 Cf. Kaundinya. *Erinnerungen,* pp. 63–67, 75–76. Cf. Stadtmuseum Wendlingen, "Tagebuch Fritz Otto", pp. 14–21.

146 Kaundinya. *Erinnerungen,* pp. 75–76.

the labour camp of the *Otto* plantation, one can assume that up to one-third of the inhabitants were female. Enabling their husbands or partners to take up wage labour at the *Otto* plantation, the women were generally occupied with care work, such as cooking, childcare, and the collection of firewood. Apart from these, fetching water needed for the workforce's survival and the irrigation of fields was incumbent on the women (as well as a few men). This duty also included ensuring large amounts of water for the running of the steam engines in the two ploughs and the locomobile. Yet, women were also involved in (cotton) seed planting as part of the 'living machine' for up to eight to ten hours a day: as the men hoed, the women followed, putting seeds into the furrows and covering them with soil.[147]

Analogically to the railway construction sites, but on a smaller scale, the *Otto's* labour village also attracted other people from the surrounding villages who were not directly involved in plantation labour. Petty traders supplied the workmen and workwomen with foodstuffs, clothing and other items of daily use. At the same time, especially single women, sold locally brewed beer or worked as sex workers. With the constant arrivals and departures of many people every day, the labour camp in Kilossa could not be controlled comprehensively by the plantation management. Often, it followed the rules of the East Africans living there for most of the time:

> The ongoing interaction between workers and local villages was a double-edged sword for planters. While plantation social life attracted workers, many planters complained that ngomas and pombe drinking subverted labor discipline. After a ngoma with heavy drinking, workers might not show up for work for several days, whiling away the time in neighboring villages. Villages furthermore offered refuge to contract breakers, since planters did not have a good sense of their workers' identities.[148]

On top of this, these workers' settlements were not only a refuge for 'contract breakers', they also appeared as an untapped source of labour to (European) freelance labour recruiters or employees of other plantations. There, they could lure *Otto's* workers away to other enterprises – especially when such recruiters knew the environment, its workers, and the workers' preferences well, a plantation like *Otto's* in Kilossa was the perfect target for recruitment.

---

147 Cf. TNA. G8/904, p. 33. Cf. Kaundinya. *Erinnerungen*, pp. 45, 46–66, 90, 103, 106, 135.
148 Sunseri. *Vilimani*, p. 155.

4.9.2 Skilled Plantation Labour Wanted: The Legal Case Against Walter Grund

> The trained worker hacks 1600–2400 square meters in six hours, i.e., 267–400 square meters per hour, the untrained 200–400 square meters in 10 h, i.e., 20–40 square meters per hour. The performance of the former is thus ten times that of the latter, the wage difference at most 25 percent. A well-trained worker is therefore not only often worth ten times the performance of newcomers, but also serves as a role model and proof that higher performance can be achieved.
>
> Ranga Kaundinya. *Erinnerungen aus meinen Pflanzerjahren*. Leipzig: 1918.[149]

Planting cotton is no simple form of agriculture. It took Kaundinya a considerable effort of time to train workers who had never worked on a plantation before. Keeping qualified and skilled workers the longest time possible at a plantation was thus one of the top priorities to make any plantation a profitable business, as Kaundinya explains above. Undoubtedly, other planters knew about this fact as well. They were thus ready to compete at all costs for skilled African plantation workers. In this respect, the local historian Bleifuß is certainly wrong when he states that there was no competition about African labour for *Otto* in Kilossa.[150] Besides the competition of the railway constructing *Holzmann* Company in the second dry season after the foundation of the *Otto* plantation, other planters also attempted to lure away workers from Kilossa. In this respect, many African workers were happy to leave *Otto's* plantation as they had experienced harsh treatment by at least some of *Otto's* German employees. A well-documented case is the criminal proceeding against the German planter Walter Grund from Pugu near Dar es Salaam. The case opened in February 1914 and sheds light on the general characteristics of labour at *Otto's* plantation in Kilossa, the African workers' agency and relationship with the European employees, as well as competition for labour at *Otto's* plantation. According to the file, the authorities accused Grund of violating the *Anwerbe-* and *Arbeiterverordnung* (recruitment and workers ordinance) when hiring workers who were contemporarily employed by *Otto* in Kilossa.[151]

The German Walter Grund was born in Tilsit in East Prussia on 17 September 1879, and had probably arrived in German East Africa around 1900. When *Otto* started its plantation in Kilossa, he was one of the first Europeans Kaundinya had employed. The files report that Grund left *Otto's* plantation in Kilossa after some years in 1911 and subsequently worked as railway sub-contractor between Dar es Salaam and Morogoro (cf. 3.2). When prosecuted by the German colonial

149 Kaundinya. *Erinnerungen*, pp. 110–111, cf. p. 116.
150 Cf. Bleifuß and Hergenröder. *Die "Otto-Plantage"*, p. 64.
151 Cf. TNA. G21/545. Strafsache gegen den Pflanzungsassistenten Walter Grund, Pugu, Bez. Daressalaam, wegen Vergehens gegen die Arbeiter- und Anwerbeverordnung [vom 5.2.1913.] 1914.

authorities in 1914, Grund was working as a planter and entrepreneur in Pugu, close to Dar es Salaam. Nevertheless, Grund used to travel the 300 kilometres from Pugu to Kilossa occasionally to purchase cattle there. When visiting Kilossa, he also used to pay his former colleagues at *Otto's* plantation a visit and spend some time with them. As far as the court files reveal, Grund also used these visits to Kilossa to seek hands for his own plantation. Occasionally, some workers would leave Kilossa, joining Grund to go to his plantation in Pugu instead. As Grund apparently also hired some workers who were already employed by *Otto* at the time, the plantation management around Kaundinya increasingly resented Grund's visits and his labour recruitment. When three African workers attempted to leave the *Otto* plantation for Grund's in Pugu, despite their valid contracts with *Otto*, Kilossa's plantation management opened a case against him.[152]

As a German colonial planter, Grund certainly had the intention to recruit as many workers as possible for his own business. It is however wrong to assume that the labour poaching occurred exclusively because of Grund's initiative. In this particular legal case, it was rather the initiative of the three plantation workers – Wagodi, Malikwisha[153] and Kapanda – who had come from northern *Ussukuma* and central *Unyamwezi* to work at the *Otto* plantation in Kilossa and who attempted to leave it for good. The major reason for these Wassukuma and Wanyamwezi men to abandon Kilossa was the bad labour conditions they faced at the *Otto* plantation. The three East Africans had already worked for years in Kilossa. According to their labour cards, Kapanda and Malikwisha had started working there in August/September 1911. Wagodi must have even been one of the very first migrant workers in Kilossa, as he had been there since April 1909, when *Otto* was in competition for workers with the railway construction company *Holzmann*. All three, Kapanda, Malikwisha and Wagodi, had been allocated to the labour section of the German plantation assistant, Paul Wörz, who supervised them with the help of two African *Wanyamparas*, Kapembe and Nusu Rupia.[154] In 1914, *Otto's* German overseer Wörz was still a young man, who had just started working for *Otto* two or three years before. As far as the files can tell, Wörz had planned to leave East Africa for Germany by autumn 1914, but WWI ultimately ruined his

152 Cf. TNA. G21/545, pp. 1–5, 22.

153 Malikwisha is certainly a nickname, the worker had given to himself. The name consists of the two Swahiilian Words, *mali* = property/wealth and *kwisha* = has ceased/has come to an end; i.e. Malikwisha probably took up working at the Otto plantation due to financial distress or an emergency.

154 Analogically to the nickname Malikwisha (s.a.), Nusu Rupia is also very likely a nickname. Nusu = half and Rupia = the currency of German East Africa. Hence, the meaning is "half a Rupee". This name may indicate Nusu Rupia's demand for decent wages or the minimum wage he would demand. *Wanyampara* = overseer (here).

plans as the war stranded him in the colony. Before WWI, while employed in Kilossa, Wörz was on good terms with the leading European men of the plantation such as Schurz and was valued as a competent member of staff accordingly.[155]

Apparently however, Paul Wörz was less popular among the African workers. According to their court testimonials, the three East African workers who had been working for years at the *Otto* plantation had already attempted to leave their employment repeatedly. The reason why they had not been successful was Paul Wörz. Wagodi stated that Paul Wörz had forced him to stay at *Otto's* plantation in Kilossa:

> I have completed 23 labour cards at the Otto plantation. As I wanted to return home, I demanded my dismissal. Mr Wörz, assistant at the Otto plantation, refused to dismiss me. He said I should go home by the time he would leave for Europe. I had asked for my dismissal three times, but in vain. I only took the 24th labour card as I did not dare to resist Mr Wörz. One day, I saw Mr Grund in Kilossa and together with Malikwisha and Kapanda, I went to him. I had known him from former times, because he had also been at the Otto plantation in Kilossa once. Mr Grund asked me, whether I had completed my kipande [labour card]. I replied that I had completed 23 cards and that the 24th had been forced (kwa nguvu) [by force] on me against my will. [. . .]. He [Grund] asked me whether I had ruhusa [permission to leave the plantation] [and] I said 'no'; whenever we had asked for ruhusa, Mr Wörz would make matata [problems; difficulties]. Mr Grund then said that he would employ me.

Further reasons for Wagodi to leave Kilossa in order to work at Grund's plantation in Pugu were that Wagodi had "already worked under Grund" and regarded him as a decent employer, and that his "mother had already been living in Pugu for a long time".[156] Four other African witnesses and Grund himself confirmed at court that it was a common practice at the *Otto* plantation to refuse the workers their dismissal. One worker testified that Wörz had withheld his wages to keep him at the plantation. Among the four witnesses was also Maganya, who said that he was once beaten when he asked Wörz for his dismissal on another occasion and was detained at the plantation in Kilossa when he attempted to complain at the governmental *boma:* "I demanded *ruhusa* from Mr. Wörz, but was not given permission to leave, and was slapped in the face by Mr. Wörz. I wanted to sue Mr. Wörz at the *boma* in Kilossa but was prevented by him by force."[157] Wörz himself was not questioned during the entire proceedings, but his German superior and

155 Cf. TNA. G21/545, pp. 1–5. Cf. LTA-871.1-otto-202. Schriftwechsel über die Planung einer Pflanzung in Deutsch-Ostafrika. 1926–1928, pp. 20–23.
156 TNA. G21/545, pp. 6, 16.
157 TNA. G21/545, p. 17.

Kaundinya's co-plantation manager Schurz denied the charges against his European colleague, of course.[158]

Apart from the incident and the legal case as such, the file provides further information about labour in Kilossa. It reveals its contested characteristics at the *Otto* plantation, and the relevant protagonists involved. As far as the file can tell, it was not Grund alone who had lured away workers from the cotton plantation in Kilossa repeatedly. Apparently, in this very case, but also on previous occasions, he was assisted by his *boy* Meli, a Myamwezi from Tabora, who was also questioned in the legal proceedings. At court, Meli testified:

> I accompanied Mr. Grund to Kilossa where he was buying up cattle. There, three workers from the Otto plantation came to my master and asked for work. Mr Grund asked them if they had finished their cards, to which they replied that they had finished some cards, but Mr Wörz had refused to dismiss them. The next day the three people went with us to Pugu. They spent the night with me in the kitchen house of the hotel.[159]

Interestingly, before becoming Walter Grund's personal servant[160] as a *boy,* Meli had himself been an ordinary cotton worker at the Otto plantation in Kilossa. He had apparently left Kilossa and subsequently joined Grund's plantation in Pugu. Whether Meli had initially worked as an ordinary worker at Grund's plantation there for some time or whether he had become Grund's *boy* immediately after leaving Kilossa, is not provided by the sources. Yet, having been employed as an ordinary plantation worker by *Otto* first, it seems that Meli quickly assumed larger responsibilities in Pugu as he was not only Grund's second *boy* but also his personal de facto labour recruiter. At least *Otto's* co-plantation manager Schurz accused Meli of having come to *Otto's* plantation on several occasions to lure away workers to Pugu. Confirming Meli's role, Schurz reported at court:

> Grund used to work on the Otto plantation and of course knows our long-serving and good workers. His boy Meli is also a former worker of the Otto plantations. He [Meli] has [. . .] come to the Otto plantation camp several times and has [tried] to persuade mainly long-serving, good workers to join Grund against promises of particularly high wages. In some cases he succeeded; the people concerned first worked off their cards, then asked for dismissal and then went to Grund in the end.[161]

Although the court was not able to conclude that Meli was occupied as Grund's labour recruiter in this case but also in general as "an order on his part could not

158 Cf. TNA. G21/545, pp. 6–9, 15–25.

159 TNA. G21/545, pp. 6–7.

160 The role of personal servants in German East Africa is made more explicit in the chapter about the Tendaguru Expedition.

161 TNA. G21/545, p. 8, cf. pp. 8–10, 16, 20.

be established",[162] it seems that the court largely accepted Schurz's statement. Accordingly, it believed Schurz' allegation that the *boy* Meli had previously come to Kilossa for labour recruitment. Unfortunately, this question must remain uncertain as there is neither more information available about Meli's life nor information about his work at Grund's plantation in Pugu as a *boy* or as his labour recruiter. Yet, Meli's case hints at the central role of personal servants such as *boys* who often obtained influential positions in German East Africa. In this respect, Meli's occupation at Walter Grund's business foreshadows the central role of personal servants at the Tendaguru Expedition that will be dealt with in the chapter to follow. Moreover, this case against Walter Grund reveals that particularly skilled labour was in high demand. Like at the *Central Railway*, skilled plantation labour was also essential to the cultivation of cotton and other colonial cash crops.

As far as Paul Wörz's employment as an overseer of the Otto plantation is concerned, the court file under investigation does not provide much more information. As the legal proceedings did not target Wörz's treatment against his employees as such, the questions about corporal punishments or denying the workers their dismissal did not matter much to the court official's ultimate judgment. Relevant was only whether Grund had violated the *Anwerbe-* and *Arbeiterverordnung* that prohibited anybody of one district the recruitment of workers in another district. This violated colonial law, especially if those recruited workers were currently employed by somebody else. As Schurz confirmed that Grund had repeatedly lured away workers from Kilossa to employ them at his own plantation in Pugu, and all the African workers who testified and most of the other witnesses had also confirmed this fact, the court sentenced Walter Grund to a fine of twenty Rupees. This comparatively mild penalty derived from the fact that Wagodi, Malikwisha and Kapanda had left the *Otto* plantation on their own accords and had themselves offered their service to Grund. Indeed, two other aspects also contributed to the judge's mild sentence. First, the judge acknowledged that the workers wanted to leave Kilossa in order to live closer to their families. Secondly, the court also considered that Wagodi, Malikwisha and Kapanda had left the *Otto* plantation because of maltreatment and because they had been refused dismissal. In this respect, although Schurz had denied the allegations against his employee, Wörz, the colonial court indirectly confirmed Wörz's violent behaviour against the African employees by its decision.[163] As Paul Wörz did not get the chance to speak in the files for this case, his motivation or thoughts on the issue must remain obscure. Other docu-

162 TNA. G21/545, p. 20.
163 Cf. TNA. G21/545, pp. 23–25.

ments nevertheless shed some light on his character, his precarious life during and after WWI, and the *Otto* Company's opinion about their plantation assistant and his treatment of the workforce.

4.9.3 Precarious White Labour in Kilossa and Colonial East Africa

> In the German homeland, the life and work of the planters is often judged quite incorrectly. Many a young striker believes in golden mountains and is tempted by the hope of easily attainable wealth to leave home and try his luck outside, and then experiences severe disappointments.
>
> Ranga Kaundinya. *Erinnerungen aus meinen Pflanzerjahren.* Leipzig: 1918.[164]

Moving to a colony did not automatically entail abundance. Indeed, by falling into a poor standard of living, the prestige of *white* people could be severely blemished. Recalling both (Greek) sub-contractors at the *Central Railway* and Ranga Kaundinya's contested standing as a plantation manager at *Otto's* cotton plantation in Kilossa, it has to be stressed that *whiteness* was especially challenged in German East Africa if a *white* person had no exclusive Central European ancestry or if he or she had no middle- or upper-class background. If he or she thus lacked the financial means to provide for a middle-class existence, even a German citizen was threatened with expulsion from the colony. This was also the reason why many of the early European employees at Kilossa were regarded as 'gangsters' by the *KWK* and the colonial administration, as they had become notorious, primarily because of their extreme drinking habits. As Paul Wörz took up work in Kilossa from ca. 1911 onwards, it is not entirely clear if he was one of those 'gangsters' at the *Otto* plantation. As Kaundinya's standing as plantation manager remained challenged all throughout his occupation in German East Africa, it is very likely that Paul Wörz had indeed been one of those European overseers employed at the *Otto* plantation in Kilossa who had discriminated against Ranga Kaundinya because of his Indo-German ancestry. In any case, Wörz later experienced for himself how his status as a *white* person could be threatened as his lifestyle acquired an increasingly precarious character.

In the first place, the colonial courts opened a legal case against Paul Wörz. Besides the allegations made against him by the East African witnesses during the legal proceedings against Walter Grund, Paul Wörz was separately prosecuted in another manner by the district court of Dar es Salaam. He was accused of having

---

164 Kaundinya. *Erinnerungen*, p. 7.

mistreated the farmer Georg Buzello, who lived close to the *Otto* plantation.[165] The sentence must have been rather mild, as correspondence kept in *Otto's* company archives reveals that Paul Wörz was released from their employment and conscripted as early as August 1914. Subsequently, WWI had a profound influence on his life. Wörz first fought for the German colonial army led by Lettow-Vorbeck in German East Africa, until the end of 1917 at least. By February 1918, Wörz had become a British POW and was detained, together with four of his former European colleagues from Kilossa, in Egyptian Maadi, near Cairo. It appears that Wörz returned to Germany together with his four fellow detainees by the end of 1918 and lived in Stuttgart at first. He later moved to the nearby town of Ulm. After his return to Germany, it seems that he nursed a plan to return to East Africa as soon as possible, although German citizens were denied entry to what had become, by 1922, Tanganyika Territory, a mandate under British administration after WWI. Consequently, his former existence in German colonial East Africa had abruptly come to an end and his return to the British Mandate was very unlikely in the first years after the war. In fact, immigration restrictions for German citizens as well as investment restriction for German companies eager to invest in the colonies softened again in the mid-1920s. Wörz, thus applied for the role of a cotton plantation manager at *Heinrich G. Oppermann K.G. Import-Export* at the end of 1925. This Hamburg-based company, which had primarily traded with Angola's *Loanda* region, now attempted to expand its business to East Africa and tried to purchase 8,000 ha of land in the former German colony. When *Oppermann* asked the *Otto* Company for a reference regarding Wörz's work performance in Kilossa, *Otto's* company board replied: "we can highly recommend Mr Wörz to your new endeavour. [. . .] We may say that, during his employment, he was one of the most capable assistants. He was also very competent in treating the negroes correctly".[166] Whether this assessment of Wörz's employment as plantation overseer either reflects the company board's ignorance towards the realities at the *Otto*

---

165 Cf. TNA. G21/89. Strafsache gegen den Pflanzungsassistenten Paul Wörz, Kilossa, Bez. Morogoro, wegen Mißhandlung des Landwirtes Georg Buzello. 1914–1915. Cf. Eckhart, Franz G. and Geissler, Peter (Eds.). *The United Republic of Tanzania. National Archive of Tanzania. Guide to the German Records. Vol. II. Prepared by National Archives of Tanzania and Archivschule Marburg – Insitut für Archivwissenschaft. Second Edition.* Dar es Salaam and Marburg: 1984, p. 468. When visiting the Tanzania National Archives between August and November 2018, the file could not be found.

166 LTA-871.1-otto-202. Schriftwechsel, p. 20. Cf. LTA-871.1-otto-202. Schriftwechsel, pp. 20–23. Cf. LTA-871-otto-198. 8 Schreiben mit Kriegsnachrichten aus Kilossa, Ostafrika. 1915–1918. Cf. LTA-871-Otto-199. Vergleichsregelung. Cf. Clasen, Sönke. *Die Angehörigen der Kaiserlichen Schutztruppe für Deutsch-Ostafrika zur Zeit des Ersten Weltkriegs. Ein biographisches Verzeichnis.* Norderstedt: 2021, p. 364.

plantation or acknowledges the widespread violence on German colonial cotton plantations is not clear. Moreover, it is also uncertain whether Wörz or *Oppermann* succeeded in their plans, as the files consulted do not reveal whether Wörz was hired or not, or whether *Opperman* did indeed expand its business to East Africa at all. The remaining files do however tell the story of a precarious white man, who struggled to restart his colonial life in a former German colony but failed to succeed for many more years to come. By the late 1920s, Wörz had started several short-lived colonial businesses. For financial support, he and other former colleagues of the plantation in Kilossa had turned several times to *Otto* seeking assistance. Despite these attempts, his life remained torn between Germany and East Africa for many years.[167] In fact, by 1936, it seems that Wörz had finally succeeded in taking his wife to Tanganyika Territory as the *Deutsches Kolonial- und Handelsadressbuch* lists him as a "married" cotton planter living in Ngerengere, a town located at the *Central Railway* line.[168] Afterwards, his traces disappear in the archives consulted.[169]

As far as the company of *Otto* itself is concerned, its board generally refrained from renewed colonial business after WWI, even though such endeavours were considered repeatedly.[170] In any case, *Otto* was not unsympathetic towards its former employees like Paul Wörz, or towards other former German colonialists throughout the 1920s and 1930s or towards German colonialism. Heinrich Otto generally answered the letters of his former Kilossa employees, provided them with several references as well as established and kept close contact with them. Moreover, the company became a member of revisionist German colonial societies like the *Kolonialer Zentralverband e.V.* or the *Deutsche Kolonialgesellschaft (DKG).* In summer 1928, the company *Otto* participated in the German colonial exhibition

---

167 Cf. LTA-871.1-otto-202. Schriftwechsel, pp. 22–23. Cf. LTA-871.1-otto-202. Chronik, p. 18. Cf. LTA-871-Otto-199. Vergleichsregelung. Cf. LTA-871-otto-203. Kriegsentschädigung für Kolonialbesitz. 1926–1934, Letter Wörz to Otto Kidete, 10 August 1927 and letter Wörz to Otto Kidete, 15 November 1927.

168 Marcus, August and Kolonialwirtschaftliches Komitee (Eds.). *Kolonial Handels- und Adreßbuch. Mandatsgebiete in Afrika. 1936. 19. Jahrgang.* Berlin: 1936, p. 313.

169 Marcus. *Kolonial Handels- und Adreßbuch,* p. 285, cf. p. 276. Cf. *Handbuch der deutschen Aktien-Gesellschaften: ein Hand- und Nachschlagebuch für Bankiers, Industrielle, Kapitalisten, Behörden etc.* Berlin and Leipzig: 1943, p. 5218. Cf. *Report by His Britannic Majesty's Government on the Mandated Territory of Tanganyika for the Year 1960. London: 1960,* p. 105. Cf. Authaler, Caroline. *Deutsche Plantagen in Britisch-Kamerun. Internationale Normen und lokale Realitäten 1925 bis 1940.* Cologne: 2018. For the longevity of colonial thought in Germany after WWI. Cf. Schilling, Britta. *Postcolonial Germany. Memoirs of Empire in a Decolonized Nation.* Oxford: 2014, pp. 13–40, 68–89, 157–194.

170 Cf. LTA. 871.1-otto-233. Chronik, p. 157.

held in Stuttgart, which attracted ca. 200,000 visitors. In this context, numerous voices spoke of reclaiming the previously owned colonies and *Otto* proudly presented the history of their cotton plantation in Kilossa.[171] On top of this, *Otto* also financed colonial revisionist political rallies and donated money to former German colonialists whom they had not necessarily known in person.[172] Among them was the previously mentioned farmer, railway sub-contractor, and labour recruiter Heinrich Langkopp, who had lost his colonial existence as a result of WWI, just like Wörz. After Langkopp had worked for *Holzmann* and established himself as an independent cattle trader and farmer in the *Iringa* region, he became a soldier of the *posse comitatus* of the German colonial forces during WWI. Like Wörz, he was captured by the British, became a POW and finally returned to Germany after imprisonment in Egypt. Returning almost penniless to the Republic of Weimar from his pugnacious life in colonial East Africa, Langkopp faced tough times. After his return to Europe, he tried unsuccessfully to receive compensation for his lost property in German East Africa from the German *Reichsentschädigungsamt*.[173] After eight years of unsuccessful attempts and a life on the poverty line, not in East Africa but in Germany, he went with his gun to the governmental buildings in Berlin and fired several shots in the auditorium of the building. As a result, Langkopp was taken into custody and indicted with having attempted an assassination. The incident reached a wider public in Germany and stirred general sympathy towards Langkopp's biography. It also found its way to the *Otto* Company. Together with many other fellow Germans, Fritz Otto participated in a donation appeal issued by the *Kolonialer Zentralverband e.V.*, which organised rallies advocating in favour of Langkopp's case, and paid Langkopp's lawyer for his work on the case as well. For both purposes, Fritz Otto was ready to pay 100 Marks each.[174]

---

171 Cf. Kolonialausstellung Stuttgart 1928. *Amtlicher Ausstellungsführer*. Stuttgart: 1928, pp. 7, 12, 41–56. Cf. Rösser. 'Knotenpunkte des Kolonialen', pp. 126–128.

172 Cf. Nöhre, Joachim. *Das Selbstverständnis der Weimarer Kolonialbewegung im Spiegel Ihrer Zeitschrift.* Münster: 1998, pp. 142–144. Cf. LTA-871-otto-203. Kriegsentschädigung. Cf. LTA-871-Otto-202. Schriftwechsel, Cf. LTA-871-otto-204. Korrespondenz Karl Oskar Kübel, Deutsche Kolonialgesellschaft, Cannstadt. 1928–1936.

173 Cf. Hainbuch, Dirk. *Das Reichsministerium für Wiederaufbau 1919–1924. Die Abwicklung des Ersten Weltkrieges: Reparationen, Kriegsschäden, Beseitigung, Opferentschädigung und der Wiederaufbau der deutschen Handelsflotte.* Frankfurt o.M.: 2016.

174 Cf. Langkopp. *22. Jahre*, pp. 3–4, 119–122. Cf. Aas and Sippel. *Koloniale Konflikte*, pp. 79–138. Various unnumbered and often undated newspaper articles, e.g. by the *Montag Morgen* or *Tägliche Rundschau* reporting about Langkopp's trial. Furthermore, correspondence between Fritz Otto and Dr. N. Hansen, head of the *Kolonialer Zentralverband*. All dated – as far as provided – from January to August 1928. Cf. LTA-871-otto-203. Kriegsentschädigung. Whether Fritz Otto or

In fact, *Otto's* support for Langkopp links the case study of the *Central Railway* to the history of the *Otto* plantation in Kilossa. Moreover, the third case study of the present research into the global history of labour – the palaeontological excavations at the Tendaguru Mountain in the *Lindi* district – is also linked to the *Otto* plantation. When the textile company's head, Heinrich Otto, first visited German East Africa in 1907, State Secretary Bernhard Dernburg was not his only company. The famous German palaeontologist Eberhard Fraas had joined them as a geological advisor, examining the soil quality in the northern regions around Mwanza and investigating whether *Otto* could expect coal or other valuable deposits ready to exploit in German East Africa. Heinrich Otto and Fraas were both born in the areas around or in Stuttgart and had known each other for many years. Moreover, both were close to German Protestant circles and therefore trusted each other. Yet, as soon as Fraas had finished his job with *Otto*, he was urgently called to the colony's south: An East African employee of the German Bernhard W. Sattler's *Lindi Schürfgesellschaft* had found "something curious in the African bush".[175] It seemed that gigantic dinosaur fossils had been discovered. As the only professional palaeontologist then present in German East Africa, Eberhard Fraas hurried several hundred kilometres south from Mwanza to the *Lindi* district. There he confirmed the palaeontological sensation: the initial bones were indeed dinosaur fossils. Subsequently, the Tendaguru Expedition would become the largest paleontological excavation the world had seen so far.[176]

the entire company generally played a significant role in any of Weimar's numerous revisionist colonial associations is beyond the scope of this study, but certainly worthwhile to investigate.

175 Maier. *African Dinosaurs*, p. 1, cf. pp. 3, 6–26. Cf. Quenstedt, Werner. "Fraas, Eberhard". *Neue Deutsche Biographie*, 5, 1961, pp. 307–308. Web. https://daten.digitale-sammlungen.de/0001/bsb00016321/images/index.html?id=00016321&groesser=&fip= eayaqrsqrseayaenfsdrfsdrxsxdsydenxs&no = 3&seite = 323 (6 July 2020).

176 Cf. Stoecker, Holger. 'Maji-Maji-Krieg und Mineralien. Zur Vorgeschichte der Ausgrabung von Dinosaurier-Fossilien am Tendaguru in Deutsch-Ostafrika'. *Dinosaurier Fragmente. Zur Geschichte der Tendaguru-Expedition und ihrer Objekte 1906–2008*. 25–38. Eds. Ina Heumann et al. Göttingen: 2018, pp. 35–37. Cf. Kaundinya. *Erinnerungen*, pp. 20–22.

5 Bones of Contention? The Tendaguru Expedition

5.1 'Dinomania' and Palaeontological Excavations Around 1900

> At the end of the first rainy season [. . .] we could [. . .] admire Halley's Comet [. . .]. The impression on the population was not great. We had been preparing the more sensible among our people for half a year [. . .]. With wise caution the Gouvernment had also announced the coming event everywhere and reassuringly pointed out that no famine or lack of clothes would result. Such familiarity with the mysterious can only serve to enhance the reputation of the Gouvernment, and forethought is better than hindsight.[. . .] When I asked one of our overseers whether people in his home village [. . .] would have been afraid [. . .], he gave me this delicious answer: 'No, it was forbidden (!), and we had not even known before the government decree that people had to be afraid of it.'
>
> Edwin Hennig. *Am Tendaguru*. Stuttgart: 1912.[1]

Halley's Comet is probably one of the most spectacular celestial phenomena that can be clearly and remarkably seen by the naked eye. Travelling in its orbit, it comes close to the planet Earth every seventy-five to seventy-six years, and it has been observed and studied by humankind since antiquity. During the heyday of European colonialism, it appeared in the sky between 10 April 1910 and 20 April 1910 even more amazingly than usual as it came closer to Earth than in many previous cycles. This time, Earth would even pass through the tail of the comet, and this evoked widespread hysteria amongst the colonising societies of Europe. This hysteria was characterised by apocalyptic prophecies, claiming – among other disaster scenarios – that the gases of the comet's tail would poison all living creatures on Earth. Despite some sensible reassurances that no life was in danger, 'doomsday' scientists and one of the first popular mass media hypes fuelled a widespread feeling of fear at *the fin du siècle*. Among other strategies, people panic-bought the latest military equipment such as gas masks to protect themselves from the allegedly harmful gases of the comet's tail. In the end, nothing happened to humanity despite all the hysteria and massive media coverage, especially in the rapidly industrialising European and North American mass media societies.[2]

1 Hennig. *Am Tendaguru*, pp. 96–97.

2 Cf. Fried, Johannes. *Dies Irae. Eine Geschichte des Weltuntergangs*. Munich: 2016, pp. 199–202. Cf. Froböse, Rolf. *Der Halleysche Komet*. Thun: 1985, pp. 1–46. Cf. Harpur, Brian. *Halleys Komet. Das offizielle Buch der 'Halley's Comet Society'*. Frankfurt o.M.: 1985, pp. 47–90, 141–164.

https://doi.org/10.1515/9783111218090-005

At the palaeontological excavations at the Tendaguru Mountain in German East Africa, the panic related to Halley's Comet was somewhat absurd. Under the supervision of the two German palaeontologists, Edwin Hennig and Werner Janensch, up to 800 East Africans exposed the most spectacular dinosaur fossils known to humankind so far. Relatedly, according to the most plausible theory, it was indeed a comet's impact on the Earth that had led to the dinosaurs' extinction millions of years before the beginnings of German colonialism in East Africa. In this sense, a phenomenon similar to Halley's Comet – though with the big difference that it actually killed living beings on planet Earth – had indeed been the most decisive precondition that enabled something like the Tendaguru Expedition to happen in the first place. Yet, there was more to fear from humankind itself than from the toxic gases in the tail of Halley's Comet: in a matter of only a few years, soldiers in WWI would be required to wear respiratory masks to protect themselves from the recently developed weapons of chemical warfare.

The Tendaguru palaeontological expedition, organised and carried out by the forerunner of today's Museum for Natural History in Berlin between 1907 and 1913, would soon prove to become the largest and most successful dinosaur excavations so far known in human history. Indeed, the sheer scale of the find is not the only reason why the expedition is a historical phenomenon worth studying. For our purposes, it is rather the Tendaguru Expedition's embeddedness in the history of the 'colonial globality' taking place around 1900 that makes it a fascinating field of research, particularly as far as the global history of labour is concerned. As illustrated by Edwin Hennig's comments above, taken from his report on the Tendaguru Expedition published in 1912, the return of Halley's Comet entailed not only massive media coverage in Europe but was also a matter of anticipation and debate in the colonies of various European powers.[3] As revealed by Hennig's statement, some concern about Halley's Comet also found their way to the German colonial administration in East Africa. Consequently, the *Gouvernement* issued several announcements assuring the local population that the comet was no omen for anything, and urged people to keep the colony at peace. It was feared that the local population would take the comet as a kind of heavenly signal to rebel against German colonial rule once again. To prevent any anti-colonial warfare, the colonial administration, therefore, never got tired of repeating that Halley's Comet was an ordinary occurrence and tried to use the appearance of the comet for its own benefits accordingly. By demonstrating the ability to fore-

3 There are some files suggesting that the appearance of Halley's Comet in 1910 may have contributed to the Chinese Xinhai Revolution, ending the over 2,000-year-old Chinese Empire cf. Hutson, James. *Chinese Life in the Tibetan Foothills.* Shanghai: 1921, p. 207.

cast such a celestial event, the colonial administration hoped to boost its own prestige among the East African population as a kind of powerful fortune teller and, thereby, reinforce German colonial rule.[4] Yet, this strategy of the *Gouvernement* seems to not have had the intended effect: By stating that his fellow villagers 'would not have even known that there was any reason to fear' any celestial object, Hennig's East African overseer challenged the alleged soberness of European civilisation, whose societies had indeed – and in contrast to the East African people – experienced widespread hysteria because of the advent of Halley's Comet in the skies above Europe. Moreover, the provocative statement of the overseer challenged German colonial rule openly by ridiculing excessive colonial laws that would allegedly even forbid unavoidable human feelings such as fear. This shows not only the self-confidence of one of Hennig's leading employees, but also points to the overall significance of the East African workforce for the Tendaguru Expedition. Furthermore, in the attempts to reassure the East African population by explaining the normality of Halley's Comet, the German colonial administration revealed its prevailing alert towards potential anti-colonial wars in German East Africa. As the last skirmishes of the Maji Maji War had just faded in 1908, only one year before the beginnings of the Tendaguru Expedition in April 1909, it is not surprising that the colonial administration appears to have been nervous indeed. Even more so, as the palaeontological excavations took place in the *Lindi* district, which had been severely affected by warfare. The population of the *Lindi* district experienced widespread famine because of the war, and the local population was primarily the potential workforce available for the Tendaguru Expedition: these two post-war circumstances were decisive in the background as far as the labour supply for the palaeontological excavations was concerned.

Finally, the widespread hysteria about Halley's Comet took off in Europe thanks to the emerging mass media in European and American societies. Likewise, German mass media helped popularise Edwin Hennig's report about the discovery of dinosaur fossils in East Africa – *Am Tendaguru*, published in 1912 right after his return to Germany. A valuable historical source, the report's popularity reflects the fact that sciences like palaeontology were deeply embedded in popular culture and could reach a wide public indeed. Furthermore, the publicity about Tendaguru

4 Documents intending to inform the colonial population in Swahili cf. "Nyota wa Mkia". *Kiongozi. Habari kwa Watu Wote Wa Deutsch-Ostafrika*, no. 58. Tanga: March 1910. Cf. Geheimes Staatsarchiv Stiftung Preußischer Kulturbesitz (GehStArch). GehStArch. VI. HA. Nachlass Heinrich Schnee no. 72. Bekanntmachungen und Verordnungen in Suaheli und lateinischer Umschrift. Bezirksämter Wilhelmstahl, Bagamoyo, Tanga, Lindi 1906–1912. "Elani no. 17, Lindi 10th February 1910". Cf. "Vermischte Nachrichten. Der Stammbaum des Kometen". *DOAZ*, XII, no. 20. Daressalam: 12 March 1910. Cf. "Unser Wissen von den Kometenschweifen". *DOAZ*, XII, no. 17. Daressalam: 02 March 1910.

helped to popularise German colonialism among the masses, which encouraged funding urgently needed for scientific endeavours.[5] For example, a letter of March 1911 from Carl Hagenbeck (a German zoological entrepreneur) to Prof. Dr Wilhelm Branca – director of Berlin's Geological and Palaeontological Institute and of Berlin University's Museum – about funding the third tranche of the Tendaguru Expedition is telling:

> After all, these excavations are a major national undertaking. We Germans must in no way be inferior to the Americans. But these people are very lucky that their rich people [. . .] are contributing financially to these excavations. [. . .] [S]ince I am a well-known personality among the rich of Germany, I will [. . .] write directly to many different people, [. . .] in order to raise the funds, [. . .] we [. . .] need. My only wish with this undertaking [. . .] is that you will allow me [. . .] to have [. . .] plaster models made [. . .] by my artist [. . .] of complete skeletons. As you probably know, I have exhibited [. . .] a large number of prehistoric animals of the American fauna here in my zoo.[6]

The historian, Ilja Nieuwland, describes the intense interest in palaeontology in European and American societies during the heyday of western imperialism as 'dinomania'. Especially in the urban centres of industrialised societies, the beginnings of consumerism and free-time leisure activities had been growing since the 1850s. First in Britain, later also in the other European countries and America, free-time activities had become not only part of middle-class culture, but also part of working-class culture. Integral to these free-time activities were the phenomena of popular culture such as zoos or the so-called ethnological exhibitions (*Völkerschauen)* that attempted to display animals and peoples from all parts of the world in the major cities of Europe and America. Particularly, the *Vökerschauen* conveyed the fiction of allegedly 'primitive' peoples, whose only reason for existence seemed to be colonisation by western countries and, in this way, they supported and legitimised colonial conquest. Yet, those *Völkerschauen* were far from the realities of the people displayed. Instead, the ethnological exhibitions merely served and strengthened western expectations and discourses about white racial supremacy and global domination. The German Carl Hagenbeck, born in Hamburg, was one of the businessmen who most successfully exploited the desires of the recently emerged consumer societies to reaffirm the alleged superiority of their civilisations. Indeed, Hagenbeck became a rich man by gathering wild animals all over the world and

---

5 Cf. Hennig. *Am Tendaguru.* For the historical context and genesis of travel writing from the late eighteenth to the late nineteenth and early twentieth centuries cf. Schröder. *Das Wissen,* pp. 113–198. Cf. Keighren, Innes M. et al. *Travels into Print. Exploration, Writing, and Publishing with John Murray, 1773–1859.* Chicago and London: 2015, pp. 1–33, 209–226.

6 Museum für Naturkunde (MfN). Historische Bild und Schriftgutsammlungen (HBSB). Tendaguru Expedition 7.3. Finanzierung, p. 101.

selling his trophies to various zoos, where they would be displayed as singular attractions or as additions to exhibitions of allegedly 'uncivilised' human beings.[7] It seems surprising only at the first glance that a man like Carl Hagenbeck, who catered to the demands of the masses with his (human) zoos, contacted a man of science like the university professor, Wilhelm Branca. In fact, the line between the perpetrators of 'dinomania' and men of science was very thin indeed. Especially in the first decades of the discipline, palaeontology and the public circus-like display of the 'terrible reptiles' could hardly be distinguished from each other. Moreover,

> [a]n important element in the early portrayal of dinosaurs had always been their size – and frequently little else. From the early days after their discovery, they represented brute, dumb force and were in a way representative of the uncontrollable forces of nature – not entirely different from the way in which the savage wildlife of Africa or many unknown peoples were perceived.[8]

Only from the 1890s onwards did palaeontology emerge as a serious, comparatively well-defined scientific discipline that borrowed significantly from subjects such as geology, geography and biology. Hence, not only the roots of their disciplines had a common background but Branca's profession and Hagenbeck's business also overlapped in some significant ways in the year 1911: both, (human) zoos and public institutions like museums had recently developed out of the masses' demand for leisure activities. The widespread 'dinomania' of European and American societies at the *fin du siècle* was indeed an integral part of the emerging consumer and free-time societies that also included educational institutions like museums. In addition, the zeitgeist was obsessed and fascinated by hugeness, which mingled smoothly with the concepts of imperialism and colonialism. Large size was equated with modernity, progress and importance. As any western nation wanted to be regarded as the most powerful, all colonial powers were in competition regarding prestige objects and achievements like having the largest navy, the most impressive architecture, the largest exhibition and weapons of the greatest firepower. Size mattered indeed and dinosaurs were, there-

7 Cf. Rieppel. *Assembling*, pp. 1–13. Cf. Nieuwland. *American Dinosaur*, pp. 21–48. Cf. Mohr, Erna. "Hagenbeck, Carl". *Neue Deutsche Biographie*, 7, 1966, pp. 487–488. Web. https://www.deutsche-biographie.de/pnd118700502.html#ndbcontent (26 February 2020). Cf. Hagenbeck, Carl. *Von Tieren und Menschen.* Web. *Zeno.org.* http://www.zeno.org/Naturwissenschaften/M/Hagenbeck,+*Carl/Von+Tieren+und+Menschen* (26 February 2020), Chapters 2, 3, and 5. Cf. Dittrich, Carl and Rieke-Müller, Annelore. *Carl Hagenbeck (1844–1913): Tierhandel und Schaustellungen im Deutschen Kaiserreich.* Berlin et al.: 1998, pp. 13–143, 144–172, 234–260. Cf. Thode-Arora, Hilke. 'Hagenbeck: Tierpark und Völkerschau'. *Kein Platz an der Sonne. Erinnerungsorte deutscher Kolonialgeschichte.* 244–256. Ed. Jürgen Zimmerer. Bonn: 2013, pp. 244–255.
8 Nieuwland. *American Dinosaur*, p. 33.

fore, the perfect display item for the period preceding WWI to represent the power of proud colonial empires like the German *Reich*. Thus, the Tendaguru Expedition to German East Africa was not only a matter of German national interest but also a matter of prestige for German science.[9]

Size therefore translated well into cultural and economic capital for Berlin's natural museum and the Tendaguru Expedition. Before the fossils were discovered in German East Africa, the bones of the *dipolodocus carnegii* – named after the US industrialist Andrew Carnegie, (one of those 'rich people' that Hagenbeck referenced) who financed dinosaur excavation in America – were known as the largest in the world. With the Tendaguru bones proving to be even bigger than the American fossils, Berlin's Museum of Natural History experienced a sharp rise in its scientific reputation, its number of visitors and its financial means. Large lower leg and upper arm dinosaur fossils were deliberately chosen for display in Berlin after their discovery in German East Africa, to boost the Tendaguru Expedition both materially and immaterially. Remarkably, displaying the largest bones found during the initial excavations even provided enough money to finance the third and last German expedition to the Tendaguru after 1911. In turn, with the Germans now in possession of the largest dinosaur fossils in the world, the *Reich* had surpassed not only Britain, France and Belgium, but also the USA in the competition for the largest fossils in the world.[10]

9 Cf. Nieuwland. *American Dinosaur*, pp. 3–48. Cf. Rieppel. *Assembling*, pp. 1–42. Cf. Schweighöfer. *Vom Neandertal*, pp. 7–20, 369–378. For the German Tendaguru Expedition cf. Maier. *African Dinosaurs*, pp. 13–22. Cf. Mogge, Winfried. '"Im deutschen Boden Afrikas". Wilhelm Branca, die Tendaguru-Expedition und die Kolonialpolitik'. *Deutsch-Ostafrika. Dynamiken Europäischer Kulturkontakte und Erfahrungshorizonte im kolonialen Raum.* 125–144. Eds. Stefan Noack et al.: Berlin et al.: 2019, pp. 133–139, 142–144. Cf. Kretschmann, Carsten. 'Noch ein Nationaldenkmal? Die Deutsche Tendaguru Expedition 1909–1913'. *Inszenierte Wissenschaft. Zur Popularisierung von Wissen im 19. Jahrhundert.* 191–212. Ed. Stefanie Samida. Bielefeld: 2011. Cf. Vennen, Mareike. 'Auf Dinosaurierjagd. Wissenschaft, Museum und Unterhaltungsindustrie'. *Dinosaurier Fragmente. Zur Geschichte der Tendaguru-Expedition und ihrer Objekte 1906–2008.* 208–231. Eds. Ina Heumann et al. Göttingen: 2018, pp. 218–222. For a general introduction to Empires, the media and the popularisation and globalisation of knowledge and science cf. Przyrembel, Alexandra. 'Empire, Medien und die Globalisierung von Wissen im 19. Jahrhundert. Einführung'. *Von Käfern, Märkten und Menschen. Kolonialismus und Wissen in der Moderne.* 197–220. Eds. Rebekka Habermas and Alexandra Przyrembel. Göttingen: 2013. For (free-time) consumerism particularly among the working classes in the German speaking countries cf. Bänziger. *Die Moderne als Erlebnis*, pp. 201–326.

10 Cf. Vennen, Mareike. 'Wer hat den Größten? Zur Verwertung und Verteilung der ersten Tendaguru-Exponate'. *Dinosaurier Fragmente. Zur Geschichte der Tendaguru-Expedition und ihrer Objekte. 1906–2018.* 136–165. Eds. Ina Heumann et al. Göttingen: 2018. Cf. Hennig. *Gewesene Welten*, pp. 20–22.

Funding has always been decisive for any field of science. Searching for financial means for the Tendaguru Expedition, Hagenbeck's proposal to contact his rich German acquaintances to donate to the palaeontological excavations illustrates this fact. In contrast to many of the American excavations at the Tendaguru, there was neither any single German tycoon, like Andrew Carnegie, who would sponsor the entire excavation by himself, nor any German governmental institution that agreed to wholly finance the expedition. Given the patchwork character of the nineteenth-century German funding institutions, mixed financing was the only way. Ultimately, there were many people and institutions donating to the prestigious German scientific endeavour. Yet, despite this insecure financial situation, the initiators of the funding campaign explicitly refrained from asking the average citizen for donations. In line with the tradition of *the Gesellschaft Naturforschender Freunde zu Berlin* (Berlin Society for Friends of Natural Science), the two members of this association and initiators of the Tendaguru funding committee – Branca and the pathologist David Paul von Hansemann – intentionally approached only an exclusive circle of people consisting of representatives of German politics, business, science, the higher nobility and colonial dignitaries, relying solely on them to join the funding committee. Despite the widespread 'dinomania' of the masses, the leading figures agreed that the gigantic bones should remain a matter of prestige for not only the entire nation and Berlin's science circles, but also for their German society. Hence, all the donors of the Tendaguru Expedition shared a similar background: they were almost exclusively male, loyal to the *Kaiser,* German nationals, aristocratic and very wealthy or members of the academic elite. Moreover, Branca and Hansemann succeeded in convincing Johann Albrecht zu Mecklenburg[11] to become the representative patron of the Tendaguru funding committee, further stressing the prestigious character of the palaeontological excavations by crowning the endeavour with a vibrant and well-known personality in colonial and public circles. The Duke zu Mecklenburg had already supported many colonial endeavours both financially and idealistically, and as the long-standing chairman of the *Deutsche Kolonialgesellschaft* (1885–1920), he was predestined to act as the honorary president of the Tendaguru funding committee.[12] To win the hearts of the remaining German na-

---

11 Cf. Diebold, Jan. *Hochadel und Kolonialismus im 20. Jahrhundert. Die imperiale Biographie des 'Afrika Herzogs' Adolf Friedrich zu Mecklenburg.* Vienna et al.: 2019, pp. 79–130.

12 For the historical background of this founding tradition, especially concerning the members of British, French and German scientific associations cf. Schröder. *Das Wissen,* pp. 35–68. For the history of the *Gesellschaft Naturforschender Freunde* cf. Heesen, Anke te. 'Vom naturgeschichtlichen Investor zum Staatsdienst. Sammler und Sammlungen der Gesellschaft Naturforschender Freunde zu Berlin um 1800'. *Sammeln als Wissen. Das Sammeln und seine wissenschaftliche Be-*

tionalistic upper-class target group, the committee further showed anticipatory obedience towards anti-Semitic resentments and strategically avoided attracting the support of German Jews who lived their religion publicly. At the same time, the funding committee still received funds from German Jews who were willing to support the excavation at the Tendaguru. In particular, they accepted donations from German Jews who were rather distanced from their backgrounds, like Colonial State Secretary Bernhard Dernburg,[13] who could thus appear as a benefactor publicly.[14]

The lion's share of the complete funding sum of 231,607.45 marks was collected in the initial years between 1909 and 1911, when 183,607.45 marks were donated. One-sixth of the complete sum was derived from scientific societies like the *Gesellschaft Naturforschender Freunde zu Berlin,* founded as early as 1773[15] – where Branca was an influential member – or foundations that sponsored scientific projects like the *Alexander von Humboldt Stiftung für Naturforschung und Reisen* (Alexander von Humboldt Foundation). Given their societal and economic power in the *Reich,* it is especially surprising that companies in the German heavy industries were rather reserved towards the Tendaguru project and many refrained from donations. Other companies like the *Deutsch-Ostafrika-Linie (DOAL)* or *Maggi* supported the expedition indirectly. The *DOAL* granted a discount on their transport rates for all dinosaur fossils transported from East Africa to Germany, while *Maggi* equipped the Tendaguru Expedition with preserved foods throughout the entire excavation works. Among these few German industrial tycoons, only the family members of economic heavyweights such as *Krupp, Siemens* and *Röchling* were ready to donate significant sums. Indeed, the largest share of the final sum was donated by wealthy upper-class people loyal to the *Kaiser* and the German *Reich*: in addition to these donors, there were banking families, publishers in Leipzig, government officials, doctors in Berlin, members of the nobility, merchants and wealthy private

deutung. 62–84. Eds. Anke te Heesen and E.C. Spary. Göttingen: 2002. Exemplary for the funding of scientific expeditions during the *Kaiserreich* cf. Steinecke. 'Die Ausgrabung von Babylon', pp. 285–296. For a general overview cf. Vogel, Jakob. 'Public-private partnership. Das koloniale Wissen und seine Ressourcen im langen 19. Jahrhundert. Einführung'. *Von Käfern, Märkten und Menschen. Kolonialismus und Wissen in der Moderne.* 261–284. Eds. Rebekka Habermas and Alexandra Przyrembel. Göttingen: 2013.

13 Cf. Schiefel. *Bernhard Dernburg,* pp. 11–16. For a Jewish perspective on Dernburg cf. Bartmuss, Hartmut. *Bernhard Dernburg. Kolonialpolitiker der Kaiserzeit.* Berlin: 2014.

14 Cf. Stoecker, Holger. 'Über Spenden und Sponsoren. Zur Finanzierung der "Deutschen Tendaguru Expedition"'. *Dinosaurier Fragmente. Zur Geschichte der Tendaguru-Expedition und ihrer Objekte. 1906–2018.* 79–93. Eds. Ina Heumann et al. Göttingen: 2018. Cf. Mogge. *Wilhelm Branco,* pp. 133–162, 199–222, 271–294.

15 Cf. Schröder. *Das Wissen,* p.36.

scholars or professors. Given the significance of the *Deutsche Bank* (probably for both the *Otto* Plantation in Kilossa and) for the construction of the *Central Railway*, it deserves to be stressed that Arthur von Gwinner, director of the *Deutsche Bank*, was one of the major donors to the Tendaguru Expedition. Moreover, Gwinner not only supported the palaeontologists by private donations, but he also used his position as head of the leading German bank for the same purpose, as he established and managed the bank account administrating the Tendaguru donations.[16]

Like Hagenbeck, Gwinner promised Branca and Hansemann to advertise for donations to the Tendaguru Expedition among his rich friends and acquaintances. And like Branca and Hansemann, Gwinner was aware of the necessity to act strategically to make funding a success:

> If it is your wish to concentrate the funds at Deutsche Bank, you only need [. . .], expediently through me, to open an account at our Deposit Office. The account could be opened in your name with the addition "Tendaguru-Account" and you would then be entitled [. . .] to collect the necessary contributions from the account. [. . .] The bank would not charge a commission. But I repeat, it seems to me to be more convenient if you wait at least another month and then ask for the transfer [. . .] by a printed [. . .] circular of the secretary. After all, there could be this or that person, especially among those who, from experience, are most likely to donate for public purposes, who is so petty as to want to give nothing or less when the money is being collected at Deutsche Bank. If you prefer to collect the money elsewhere, the Deutsche Bank will of course resign. My intention is solely to serve the cause and not to make a small advertisement for the Deutsche Bank, which can do without one.[17]

The director of one of the most significant German banks was therefore not only financing German colonial endeavours that would promise lucrative profits like the *Central Railway* or the *Otto* Company. Gwinner also generally supported colonial projects, ideally if they promised to boost the (scientific) prestige of the German *Reich*. As the *Deutsche Bank* was on good terms with the railway constructing companies in German East Africa, it also thought to share valuable experiences gained at the railway with the Tendaguru Expedition. Preparing for the fossil excavations, the men in charge wondered how the petrified bones could be transported best from the Tendaguru Mountain to the coast. One idea was to use motor vehicles or rather, early lorries. *Holzmann* had tried to use this new technology for the transportation of railway building materials, and Gwinner recommended that Branca contact *Holzmann's* headquarters in Dar es Salaam to enquire about the issue and to purchase a lorry for the transport of the palaeontological materials.[18]

---

16 Cf. Stoecker. 'Über Spenden und Sponsoren'. Cf. Mogge. *Wilhelm Branco*, pp. 133–162, 199–222. 271–294.

17 MfN. HBSB. 7.3, pp. 28–29.

18 Cf. MfN. HBSB. Tendaguru Expedition 1.3. Vorbereitungen, pp. 36–37.

Yet, as the early lorries built by Mercedes-Benz (so-called *Gaggenau Wagen)* had not been able to withstand the exposure to the East African traffic conditions, Branca's idea to use lorries for transportation would not become a reality.[19] Instead, the Tendaguru Expedition had to rely on human porterage and African labour. Both remained decisive for the palaeontological endeavour from the very beginning to the end. From the start of the excavations in 1909 until their end in 1913, the few Europeans at the Tendaguru would rely significantly not only on manual African labour, but also on East African expertise related to all kinds of excavation works.

5.2 Discovering Bones in the War-Ridden Area of *Lindi*

> Since my birth I have never seen such scarcity. I have seen famine but not one causing people to die. But in this famine, many are dying, some are unable to do any work at all, they have no strength, their food consists of insects from the woods which they dig up and cook and eat. [. . .] Many have died through eating these things from the woods and wild fruits.
>
> Agnes Sapuli to Rev. C.C. Child, from Mwiti, 28 February 1907[20]

Recent research has shown that the reasons, course, and outcome of the Maji Maji War against German colonial rule were not uniform. Although the people of the southern half of the colony were united in their case for overthrowing German rule, the immediate causes that led to ultimately deciding to take up arms against the colonisers varied from region to region.[21] In any case, the overall consequences for the areas affected by the war were devastating: up to one-third of the entire (civil) population died – not because of warfare as such, but predominantly because the German military pursued a 'scorched earth' strategy to defeat the African forces after they had taken up guerrilla tactics.[22] The German troops either confiscated foodstuffs and used them for themselves, or burnt down African provisions as well as crop-producing fields and countless villages. Governor Götzen stated in his official report of 1909:

> As in all wars against uncivilized peoples [. . .], in the present case, too, the planned destruction of the hostile population's property and possessions was indispensable. The destruction

---

19 Cf. Stadtarchiv Frankfurt. W1/2 – 278/1. *Rehfeldt*, pp. 2–3. Cf. TNA. G 17/63, "VII E. I No. 534, 27. Febr. 1909".

20 Agnes Sapuli To Rev. C.C. Child, from Mwiti, 28.02.1907, UMCA A/5. Qutd. in: Iliffe and Gwassa. *Records of the Maji Maji Rising*, p. 27. Also qutd. in: Seeberg, Martin. *Der Maji Maji Krieg gegen die deutsche Kolonialherrschaft*. Berlin: 1989, p. 81. Cf. Rösser. *Forced Labour*, p. 34.

21 Cf. Giblin and Monson (Eds.) *Maji Maji. Lifting the Fog of War*.

22 Cf. Wimmelbücker. 'Verbrannte Erde'.

> of economic values, such as the burning of villages and food stocks, may seem barbaric to those far away. On the other hand, if you consider [. . .] [that] such an action was the only way to force the opponent into submission, then one will arrive at a milder understanding of this 'dira necessitas'.[23]

The outcome was widespread famine, as described by Agnes Sapuli in 1907. This famine killed the majority of the overall war victims. Even worse, after the last skirmishes had come to an end by 1908, the rainy season in the year to follow failed and kept the provision of foodstuffs at a minimum, at best. The populations resident and, therefore, also most affected in the southeastern district of *Lindi* were the Wayao, the Wamuera, the Wamakua and the Wangoni, who maintained complex interactions, rivalries and interdependencies with each other. In the district of *Lindi*, especially the cultures of the Wamakua and Wamuera societies were overwhelmingly organised in a decentralised manner. Without any paramount chief, they had no central authority and each of their small villages was generally organised on its own account. This societal structure provided the inhabitants with a high degree of flexibility and enabled them to escape the designs of the German colonial administration repeatedly. They hid in the bush or moved to less-accessible areas and managed to remain comparatively untouched by German colonial rule before the war. Yet, despite this relative isolation, the people of the *Lindi* district also had several direct experiences with representatives of the German colonial administration or German companies. Just like in other areas of German East Africa, colonial humiliation and abuse was not welcomed in the *Lindi* district. As a result, the population of the southeastern district took up arms against colonial taxation and corporal punishments, as well as forced and/or low-paid labour and porterage ordered by the colonial authorities or German planters up to 1905. As most of the Germans living in the district resided along the coast, north and south of the district's capital of *Lindi*, the Maji Maji War started not at the coast where colonial power was concentrated. Instead, it started in the district's hinterland. In the course of the war, as in other parts of the colony, the German military put down the African resistances brutally and the *Lindi* district faced severe famine after the war from 1907 onwards. Another consequence was also a severe loss of its population.[24] When visiting the neighbouring district of

23 Götzen. *Deutsch-Ostafrika*, pp. 247–248. Also qutd. in: Seeberg. *Der Maji Maji Krieg*, p. 80.

24 Cf. Libaba, P.M. 'The Maji Maji Rising in the Lindi District'. Maji Maji Research Project no. 7/68/2/1. Gwassa, G.C.K. and Iliffe, John (Eds.). *Records of the Maji Maji Rising*. Dar es Salaam: 1968, pp. 1–12. Cf. Aas. *Koloniale Entwicklung*, pp. 28–63, 88–97.

Kilwa in summer 1913, Fritz Otto of the *Otto* plantation still "saw many traces of the uprising of 1905"[25] and the consequences for the entire southern half of the colony were severe for many years to come.[26]

For the German cotton, rubber and sisal plantations and other companies in the district, the war turned out to be a disaster. As many plantations were destroyed in the war, they had to be restarted from scratch. Moreover, the death of so many people living in the war-ridden area entailed the loss of potential workers for German plantations or other colonial enterprises. When Eberhard Fraas, the famous palaeontologist from Stuttgart, inspected the fossils in 1907, he too reported on the war's fatal consequences around the major fossil discovery locations. Before coming to the Tendaguru, Fraas had been in the north of the colony, near *Nyanza* ('Lake Victoria'), as a geological advisor for the German textile entrepreneur Heinrich Otto, who sought to establish a cotton plantation there (cf. Chapter 4). After the German engineer Bernhard Sattler had sent a report about the fossil discovery locations to the *Reich*, Fraas travelled from one of the most northern districts of German East Africa to the southern districts to confirm the palaeontological sensation with his well-trained eye.[27]

Remarkably, the actual reason why Sattler had come to the Tendaguru Mountain was also rooted in the consequences of the Maji Maji War. As already mentioned, the war included the destruction of several German colonial businesses in East Africa, and one of the suffering German enterprises was the *Lindi Schürfgesellschaft* (Lindi Mining Company), which had employed Bernhard Wilhelm Sattler. Sattler was not only the company's most important figure on the ground, but he also played a significant part in the beginnings of the Tendaguru Expedition. After the war, Sattler's business and his *Lindi Schürfgesellschaft* was nevertheless close to bankruptcy because of severe war damage. The only way to save the *Lindi Schürfgesellschaft* appeared to be expanding the company's field of activities. Sattler thus decided to expand the enterprise's catchment area and search for raw materials such as mica in Lindi's hinterland, ca. 100 km away from the former headquarters of the mining company. When searching for minerals, one of his African employees directed his attention to something very different from any raw material: something which appeared to be a gigantic bone of some animal. This incident would go down in history as the initial discovery of the Tenda-

25 Stadtmuseum Wendlingen am Neckar, "Tagebuch Fritz Otto", p. 29.

26 Cf. Becker, Felicitas. 'Südost-Tansania nach dem Maji-Maji-Krieg. Unterentwicklung als Kriegsfolge?'. *Der Maji-Maji-Krieg in Deutsch-Ostfafrika 1905–1907.* 184–195. Eds. Felicitas Becker and Jigal Beez. Berlin: 2005. Cf. Becker. 'Sudden Disaster', pp. 295–320.

27 Cf. Stoecker. 'Maji-Maji-Krieg und Mineralien', pp. 25–33.

guru Expedition – an incident that was intrinsically linked to the history of the Maji Maji War and its fatal social and economic consequences.[28]

5.3 Labour and the Potential Workforce of the Tendaguru Expedition in the *Lindi* District

> In addition to the measures applied against famine so far [. . .], two further measures could be considered: Calling the able-bodied starving people to work on plantations and forcibly transferring the starving population to the areas spared by the uprising. I immediately considered the first means, and since the first attempts were unsuccessful – when asked if they wanted to work, some people said that they preferred to die of hunger – I was not afraid to let the Akidas exert gentle pressure here and there. [. . .] Only as many people are called to plantation work as to not harm the tilling of the indigenous' shambas [fields].
>
> Acting District Officer of Lindi, Mr ten Brink, to the Governor. Lindi, 8 March 1907.[29]

German colonial labour policies, in the context of the Maji Maji War, were generally merciless. By 'the measures applied against he famine so far', Acting District Officer of *Lindi*, Mr ten Brink, meant that the colonial authorities were willing to provide foodstuffs only to those people who were willing to work for the colonial government or German enterprises such as plantations. This statement shows four things: first of all, it reveals that the local colonial authorities around District Officer ten Brink were still willing to let the population die of starvation after the German colonial military had induced the rampaging famine by applying the 'scorched earth' policies to the populations of *Lindi*. Secondly, it shows that ten Brink was still ready to force emaciated people to work, just like other colonial officials had done before him. During famines, not induced by the colonial authorities, and when the colony was officially not at war, food relief had been regarded as a handy indirect incentive to force the people to work in the 1890s and around 1900, not only by senior colonial officials, but also by missions.[30] Thirdly, it shows that the local population was exclusively valued as a potential workforce by people like *Lindi*'s District Officer ten Brink. In the fourth place, ten Brink's statement makes clear that even the cruellest

28 Cf. Stoecker. 'Maji-Maji-Krieg und Mineralien', pp. 25–33. Cf. Tetzlaff. *Koloniale Entwicklung*, pp. 259–262. Cf. Maier. *African Dinosaurs*, pp. 8–11. Cf. UAT. 407/2,1. Nachlass Hennig (1882–1977). Brief-Tagebuch an die Familie, Teil 1, p. 82.

29 TNA. G4/75. [Bestellung der Mitglieder und Sitzungsprotokolle des] Bezirksrates der Kommune Lindi, p. 18.

30 Cf. Koponen. *Development*, p. 346. Cf. Bald, Detlef. *Deutsch-Ostafrika. Eine Studie über Verwaltung, Wirtschaft und Interessensgruppen.* Munich: 1970, pp. 69–70. Cf. Dernburg. *Südwestafrikanische Eindrücke*, p. 37–38.

war strategies could not break the resistance of the local populations against German colonial rule entirely, as many of them chose starving to death instead of working for the coloniser, even if the war had almost come to an end. This fact is particularly important for the analysis of labour and labour relationships at the palaeontological excavation site of the Tendaguru, which started only one year after the last skirmishes of the Maji Maji War had ended. This situation in the *Lindi* region must be regarded as the most important background for the German palaeontologists, Edwin Hennig and Werner Janensch, who would rely on up to 800 African workers for their scientific excavation between 1909 and 1911.

At the onset of the Tendaguru Expedition, the war's fatal consequences were still prevalent in the minds of the local population, who had not only endured the war itself, but continued to struggle with its aftermath. When the European party of the contemporary Tendaguru Expedition arrived at Lindi's port in early April 1909, they camped for one night outside the town, with 160 African men and women who would carry their provisions and material from the coastal district capital to the ca. eighty km distant Tendaguru Mountain. At dusk and during the night, they were joined by the ca. twenty-five European men and women who lived in Lindi, and a farewell party began. Amongst the 160 Africans, Wangoni, Wayao and Wamuera people were present, who all performed their war and "national dances"[31] to the European and African audience. Clearly audible, also to the unaccustomed ears of the palaeontologist Edwin Hennig, who had just arrived in German East Africa for the first time and did not know any Swahili or other East African languages yet, was the war cry 'Maji Maji', which had permeated the air during the preceding years of anticolonial warfare between 1905 and 1908. Apart from the war cry as such, the European parts of the audiences, who did not understand any African languages, also fairly understood that the dances and singing recounted the events of the past struggle and its historical importance and fatal consequences for the local populations. Although the major acts of war in the *Lindi* district had ceased by January 1906 and the area was declared as 'pacified' by the colonial military[32] during the entire duration of the Tendaguru Excavation, the consequences of the Maji Maji War flared up occasionally in Hennig's diary, illustrating its enduring importance. On his very first day in Lindi, 7 May 1909, Hennig also noticed "many enchained prisoners",[33] who were probably convicts who had been detained during the Maji Maji War. Moreover, when the party left for the Tendaguru Mountain the next morning, they encountered several remnants of the war such as "the skulls of killed insurgents on

31 Hennig. *Am Tendaguru*, p. 16, cf. 12–19.
32 Cf. Maier. *African Dinosaurs*, p. 10.
33 UAT. 407/80, p. 5, cf. pp. 5–7.

stakes" and an old military *boma* near the Noto-Plateau, where the caravan even camped the second night on their way to the future excavation site.[34] Although the last prisoners of the Maji Maji War were released by the end of 1911, on the granting of amnesty in recognition of the *Kaiser's* birthday, the atmosphere still appeared strained in some areas, according to Hennig's impressions. When in *Kilwa* in May 1911, Hennig noted he "would put the Kilwa district in a position to rebel at any moment" as he and his fellow fossil excavators had encountered passive but staunch resistance to any European intruder, and to his African company and their palaeontological work, near a place called Makangaga.[35] Given the widely noticeable consequences of the Maji Maji War, such as the remarkable population loss, the fairly recent resistance of the local populations against labour for German companies even in the face of death and the Tendaguru Expedition's dependency on a local workforce, the question arises of how workers could be recruited for the palaeontological endeavour at all.

Although Ohl, Stoecker and Vennen had considered labour and work at the Tendaguru Expedition primarily using image sources and by investigating the work of East African overseers and preparators,[36] they overlooked examining the phenomenon of labour at the Tendaguru in the overall context of labour supply in the *Lindi* district. None of them therefore consulted Norbert Aas' instructive study about the society and economy of the *Lindi* district during the German colonial period, which gives an excellent overview about the labour supply of the district by investigating the plantations in the areas surrounding the Tendaguru. Examining the similarities and differences between the labour supply at the German plantations in the *Lindi* district and that at the Tendaguru Expedition, Aas' study provides the necessary background to answer the questions of why potential workers took up work at the Tendaguru, or why they did not. According to Aas, all European enterprises that focussed primarily on the production of cash crops such as cotton, sisal and rubber, or exceptionally, on the extraction of raw materials, were concentrated on the coast. Like the abovementioned Sattler, all of them attempted to expand to the district's hinterland only exceptionally during the German colonial

34 MfN. HBSB. 9.2. Expeditionsdokumentation Tagebuch Janensch, p. 10. Cf. UAT. 407/2,1, pp. 99–104, 108–112. Cf. Maier. *African Dinosaurs*, pp. 9–10, 25, 38. For an analysis of East African poetry processing the Maji Maji War cf. Casco. *Utenzi*, pp. 239–280.

35 UAT. 407/81. Nachlass Hennig (1882–1977). Tagebuch, Teil 2, p. 135. Cf. UAT. 407/82. Nachlass Hennig (1882–1977). Tagebuch, Teil 3, p. 3. Cf. UAT. 407/2,2. Nachlass Hennig (1882–1977). Brief-Tagebuch an die Familie, Teil 2, p. 483. Cf. Maier. *African Dinosaurs*, pp. 38, 55.

36 Cf. Vennen. 'Arbeitsbilder – Bilderarbeit', pp. 56–77. Cf. Ohl, Michael and Stoecker, Holger. 'Taxonomien am Tendaguru. Wie die Berliner Saurier ihre Namen bekamen'. *Dinosaurier Fragmente. Zur Geschichte der Tendaguru-Expedition und ihrer Objekte 1906–2008*. 232–252. Eds. Ina Heumann et al. Göttingen: 2018.

rule. According to Aas, the source material is scarce for every single enterprise as the files of privately owned companies that existed in German East Africa have been almost entirely destroyed. If there are any sources at all, they are comprised mostly of officially published company documents such as annual reports, while governmental files contain some information about these enterprises too. Overall, there were two types of colonial companies in the *Lindi* district that depended on East African workers. The first group was companies that were privately owned by individual European, that is predominantly German and some English and Italian, settlers trying their luck in the German colony. Of those small-scale enterprises, Aas counts fourteen for the entire district between the 1890s and 1914. Unfortunately, the sources available document barely anything else than their mere existence. For the second group of colonial enterprises, more information is available as they were much larger and run as well as owned cooperatively. Primarily, by means of annually published business reports and other publications, Aas provides insight into the business of five larger companies operating in the *Lindi* district: the *Pflanzung Ngambo/Kitunda* (founded in 1895) and the *Plantagengesellschaft Südküste* (founded in 1906), run by Karl Perrot; *Die Ostafrika-Kompagnie* (founded in 1906), with its directorate's most prominent member being Walter von St. Paul-Illaire, a former member of the *Schutztruppe* and already a colonial entrepreneur in the northern districts of German East Africa; the *Plantagengesellschaft Kilwa-Südland*, primarily founded by Dr Schäffer and Carl Peter's associate Joachim Graf Pfeil as well as the President of the *Reichstag* Prof. Paasche and the Principal of Stuttgart's Technical University Prof. Moritz Fünfstück in 1907; and last but not least, *Die Lindi-Kilindi-Gesellschaft mbH*, founded and run by the former District Officer of *Lindi*, Ewerbeck, in 1908, who employed a German called Linder as manager. Despite the better documentation of the cooperatively owned plantations, the sources remain nevertheless extremely patchy. Aas thus cannot give any information about their profitability, for example, but he can nevertheless determine one central research result: The longer the companies existed, the more their management personnel and their business interests converged. "In the end" concludes Aas, during the last few years preceding WWI, "all companies were run by the same people in Berlin"[37] who were somehow related to the *Deutsch-Ostafrikanische-Gesellschaft* (*DOAG*).

For example, Arthur von Osterroth-Schönberg was not only Chairman of the board of the *Lindi-Handels- und Plantagengesellschaft*, but also member of the administrative board of the *DOAG*. Paul Fuchs, who featured prominently in the foundation of the *Otto* plantation in Kilossa and in the general introduction of cotton to German East Africa, was not only general secretary of the *KWK* but also a member

37 Aas. *Koloniale Entwicklung*, p. 131. Cf. Bald. *Deutsch-Ostafrika*, pp. 114–116.

of the board of the *Südküste* and CEO of the *Lindi-Kilindi-Gesellschaft.* Walter von St. Paul Illaire was not only a member of the board of the *Ostafrika-Kompagnie,* but also a member of the advisory board of the *Südküste.* J.J. Warnholtz was both a member of the board of the *DOAG* and deputy director of the advisory board of the *Lindi Kilindi Handels- und Plantagengesellschaft.* The interconnections between the businesses were therefore significant indeed and Aas is further convinced that the *DOAG* had its hand in many of the companies listed above, and must also have played the decisive role in trading with *Lindi*'s local population.[38] Moreover, both the *DOAG* and the *Lindi Kilindi Handels- und Plantagengesellschaft* held large shares of the *Lindi-Schürfgesellschaft,* which employed Bernhard Sattler, who would later be declared as the person who had discovered the initial dinosaur bones near the Tendaguru Mountain.[39]

With the *DOAG* as the junction of nearly all relevant businesses in the *Lindi* district, it is therefore hardly surprising that the *DOAG* played a central role in the logistics of the Tendaguru Expedition as well. In the course of the palaeontological excavations, any provisions and equipment shipped from Germany to East Africa and finally transported to the Tendaguru Mountain were administered via the company networks of the *DOAG.* The same applies to the transport movement in the other direction. Any dinosaur fossils found at the Tendaguru were stored in a building of the *DOAG,* close to the port of Lindi, before they were ultimately shipped to the harbours of Germany. As far as the Tendaguru Expedition is concerned, the *DOAG* provided all these services tax-free and also forwarded Janensch's and Hennig's mail. The *DOAG* further provided telegraph service between the German palaeontologists and Berlin, telephone services for the German crew of the Tendaguru Expedition within German East Africa, and also housed the German palaeontologists, at no cost, at their facilities. Moreover, the *DOAG* procured porters who would transport the dinosaur fossils from the Tendaguru to the coast.[40] Finally, the *DOAG* sent both Sattler and one of his *DOAG* colleagues, Mr Besser, to the palaeontological excavation site, where they assisted Janensch and Hennig, especially in the first weeks after the palaeontologists' arrival to East Africa in April 1909. Both Sattler and Besser would prove indispensable for the Tendaguru Expedition as they

38 Cf. Aas. *Koloniale Entwicklung,* pp. 101–133.

39 Cf. Stoecker. 'Maji-Maji-Krieg und Mineralien', pp. 26–27, 30–32.

40 Cf. MfN. HBSB. Tendaguru Expedition 2.2. Transport. Cf. MfN. HBSB. Tendgaguru Expedition 2.3. Transport/Ausrüstung (Afrika 1910–1912). Cf. MfN. HBSB. Tendaguru Expedition 3.1. Versorgung/Alltag. Cf. MfN. HBSB. Tendaguru Expedition 4.3. Versorgung/Alltag (Jagd). Cf. MfN. HBSB. Tendaguru Expedition 4.5. Versorgung/Alltag. Cf. MfN. HBSB. Tendaguru Expedition 7.4. Finanzierung. Cf. UAT. 407/80, p. 93. Cf. Maier. *African Dinosaurs,* pp. 19, 24, 43, 45, 57, 75, 77. Cf. Vennen. 'Arbeitsbilder', p. 72. Cf. Vennen. 'Auf Dinosaurierjagd', p. 211.

introduced the two German palaeontologists, who had never visited a (German) colony before, to the East African colonial realities. Finally, Janensch and Hennig met many of the *DOAG's* men mentioned above, either at the Tendaguru or when they visited them in the colony's north. Hennig and Janensch met St. Paul-Illaire there during the first rainy season in Tanga. Of particular note, when visiting the colony's north, the *Lindi-Kilindi Gesellschaft's* manager, Linder, even recruited workers for the Tendaguru Expedition.[41]

Despite their close interconnections and their strong relationship to the Tendaguru Expedition, the overall economic importance of *Lindi*'s enterprises was very low compared with those of the northern half of the colony. In 1914, there were roughly 700 plantations in German East Africa. With nineteen small- and large-scale plantations, of which many were short lived, only a fraction was to be found in *Lindi*. This is also reflected in the number of Europeans living in the *Lindi* district and in the nearby town of Mikindani. With 151 Europeans – 140 Germans – living in these southeastern areas, the European population of *Lindi* had found its peak in the years immediately before WWI. Comparing these numbers to the overall number of 5,336 Europeans living in the entire colony in 1913 – one-fourth of them in the northern districts near Mount Kilimanjaro – illustrates that the impact of the plantation economy for *Lindi* indeed had its limits. This is further shown by juxtaposing these numbers to those of the African population residing in the area: In 1905, the colonial authorities estimated the local African population at 255,469, and the total number of Goans, Arabs and Indians at 431.[42] Of course, this low number of European plantations and European inhabitants in *Lindi* also entailed that the district's nineteen privately owned businesses had comparatively little impact on the overall socio-economic environment of the *Lindi* area. Being largely dependent on the manpower of individual owners, the viability of the fourteen small-scale plantations was immediately endangered in the event of owner illness. This was very often the case. In this respect, the larger companies had several advantages compared to their smaller competitors, especially regarding financial and human resources. Although the larger companies expanded significantly from 1906 onwards, their rise in economic activity came to a standstill as early as 1912. The number of workers available to the few colonial businesses in *Lindi* simply could not sustain the companies' demand. Consequently, all of the enterprises lamented the recurring 'labour calamity' during the last few years of German colonial rule in East Africa between 1912 and 1914.[43]

---

41 Cf. Maier. *African Dinosaurs,* pp. 20, 33, 52. Cf. MfN. HBSB. Tendaguru Expedition 5.1. Korrespondenzen von Janensch und Hennig, pp. 14–15, 18.

42 Cf. Aas. *Koloniale Entwicklung,* p. 93. Cf. Gründer. *Geschichte,* p. 166.

43 Cf. Aas. *Koloniale Entwicklung,* pp. 130–133.

Examining the sources of the five larger companies, Aas observes a sufficient labour supply – meaning a surplus of potential workers – in the final year of the Maji Maji War in 1907, and for some years afterwards. Those seeking work at colonial enterprises in the aftermath of the war appear to have been primarily women, who sought employment out of pure necessity because their husbands had died during or shortly after the war. Now on their own and facing destroyed food provisions and burnt down fields, the women sought survival by working for colonial companies. None of the five larger companies had great difficulty recruiting the workforce necessary until ca. 1911 and did not need to recruit workers from other districts in this period. The situation changed dramatically in 1912, however, when all the companies under investigation complained about the lack of supply of labour and constantly rising wages. As a result, all of them seem to have pressured the colonial authorities to exert force on the local populations to make them work at the plantations. Apparently, the planters succeeded in their concentrated lobbying, as by 1914 the 'labour calamity' had been solved without raising any taxes. Regarding plantation work as such, work discipline and harsh punishments for not meeting the demands of colonial plantation owners were of course common in colonial labour processes, and in the *Lindi* district as well. Yet, believing that all African workers came to work only by indirect or direct force is as wrong as believing that all colonial labour was easy work where physical violence and humiliation were not an integral part. Indeed, Aas finds that the great majority of the *Lindi* population was generally not willing to work for colonial enterprises. In fact, interviewing local elders in 1980s *Lindi*, Aas found two further reasons, besides pure necessity, why the population might choose to work voluntarily for German colonial companies, although they were well aware of the realities of colonial labour: One was giving them the ability to pay (cash) taxes, and the other was the ability to buy simple consumer goods, such as clothing. Given the presented source material and its numerical estimates, it is striking to ascertain that the few colonial enterprises of the *Lindi* district were only able to recruit a maximum number of workers of 5,323 in 1911, while there were at least 360,500 people living in the area under investigation at that time. According to Aas, there are three major reasons for this. First of all, plantation labour was generally very hard, and it was always very difficult to win workers for such employment. As illustrated by the comments of the Acting District Officer ten Brink quoted above, potential workers resisted working for the plantations even when faced with starvation. Of course, rather indirect means of force, such as taxing the population, often did not necessarily lead to a work supply that would sustain the colonial businesses in *Lindi*. In cases where the plantations succeeded in their labour recruitment, the planters of the district valued especially the work of the Wayao and the Wangoni. According to the colonial discourse, they were judged as intelligent and hardworking and when facing a shortage of labour, the latter were often even recruited from the neighbouring district of *Songea* where the majority of the Wagoni lived. By contrast, the Wamakonde and the Wamuera were numerically insignificant as workers for *Lindi*'s plantation economy, although they were the majority of the peoples living in the district. According to the colonial discourse, they were judged as lazy, devious and malicious, as they generally succeeded in evading colonial labour discipline if they felt the wish to do so. This leads to the second reason why the plantations' labour supply in the *Lindi* district was insufficient most of the time. As the colonial administration had only very limited resources in exerting comprehensive rule, beyond its governmental centres of administration, both the political and economic infrastructure were concentrated along the coastal strip, north and south of the port town of Lindi, and were very isolated from the hinterland. Thus, vast areas of the *Lindi* district remained largely untouched by the colonial state, and colonial officials could therefore only seldomly pressure the majority of the locally administrating *Jumbes, Akidas, Liwalis* or Chiefs to send workers to the plantations. These deficient resources of the colonial administration to recruit sufficient workers for the plantation economy are strongly intertwined with the third reason why labour recruitment failed among the Wamakonde and the Wamuera. The Wamakonde lived isolated on the difficult-to-reach *Makonde Plateau*, stretching from German East Africa's south widely into Mozambique. Both societies organised themselves in a decentralised manner: They lived overwhelmingly in small villages, which were only loosely connected with each other, and they had no central figure who had authority over every, or even numerous settlements. The German colonial officials were consequently not able to order any local authority to pressure their subordinates to work – or if this was possible, it only applied to fairly small villages with few inhabitants who could potentially be recruited as workers.[44]

Constituting the decisive background for analysing labour supply at the Tendaguru Expedition, there are several conclusions to be drawn from Aas' analysis of the labour supply for plantation businesses in the *Lindi* district between ca. 1905 and 1914. First of all, Aas' work has shown that when the Tendaguru Expedition started in April 1909, the general labour supply of workers in the *Lindi* district was sufficient for large-scale plantations located along the coast. Aas' findings thus indicate that at this beginning stage, labour supply for the Tendaguru Expedition likewise must have been sufficient, as it took place in the same time period and in the same region. Secondly, the labour supply for these plantations of the *Lindi* district remained sufficient until 1912, whereas most of the palaeontological excavations at

44 Cf. Aas. *Koloniale Entwicklung*, pp. 141–163.

the Tendaguru ended as early as 1911. Thirdly, the Wayao and the Wangoni were the most popular plantation workers and tended to take up work to a greater extent voluntarily, and in greater numbers, than the Wamuera and the Wamakonde, whose reputation as plantation workers was very low among the colonial planters. As fourth observation, in times of labour shortage, the colonial officials succeeded in forcing labour from the local populations of *Lindi*, despite their limited resources. Given the porous character of the German colonial state, it is however rather unlikely that the increased pressure on the local populations to work could have been sustained for many years. Although this very last observation must remain rather speculative for now, there is no evidence to the contrary. The 'labour calamity' appears to have been solved by 1914. But as WWI ended German colonial rule in East Africa, it is impossible to ascertain whether the colonial administration would have been able to exert such pressure comprehensively in the entire *Lindi* district and for longer than a few weeks or a few months. All these four aspects are decisive for analysing and understanding the phenomenon of labour at the Tendaguru Expedition in German East Africa's *Lindi* district, especially between 1909 and 1911. They comprise the background to be kept in mind for all the sections to follow.

5.4 The Dependency on East African Expertise

5.4.1 No Minerals but Dinosaurs: East African Discoveries

> [. . .] Have I already written to you that one of our people – bang there's someone again, [. . .] because he reports bone finds 8 h east of here, at the foot of the Likonde Plateau and also brings a piece with him. This fits perfectly with the finds I was about to report: One of our people also saw bones in the Lukuledi Valley during the rainy season, about 6 h up from Lindi [. . .]! [. . .] Thus the enormous complex is once again multiplied many times over and, just as naturally, our task. [. . .] Our main concern now is: how do we get rid of the plateaus? A kingdom for a faith that moves mountains! [. . .]
>
> Edwin Hennig – Letter to his mother, Whitsunday 1910.[45]

Stories of discoveries and exploration in European (colonial) contexts have predominantly been established as hero stories of single *white* European men. Accordingly, such heroes endured a great variety of hardships for the sake of God, science or their nation. Already in the Early Modern period, but particularly in the mass media societies of the nineteenth century, these hero stories were welcomed by media producers like publishing houses, and by their audiences all over European societies. The legends of European explorers largely contributed

45 UAT. 407/2,2, pp. 321–322.

to the master narrative of western global primacy over the rest of the world and had and still have "the power to influence the way we see the world, its regions and its inhabitants". Yet, "exploration cannot fully be understood without exemplifying the multiple contexts in which they operated".[46] Therefore, each exploration tale, particularly in colonial contexts, must be (re-)assessed by investigating the role of the local people who have remained largely invisible in European historiography and in the history of science. In stark contrast to the traditional European myths, local people played a decisive, if not the predominant role, not only regarding European explorations, but also in other discoveries of relevance for science like fossil discoveries. This holds true for several palaeontological discoveries since the sixteenth century in North America, and also for palaeontological discoveries in Africa: including the discovery of the gigantic dinosaur fossils found at the foot of the Tendaguru Mountain in early 1907 in German East Africa.[47]

In this respect, Holger Stoecker has demonstrated recently that the old established narrative of the Tendaguru discovery is incomplete at best. It has turned out that this flimsy narrative has been passed on for many decades since it was established during the German colonial period. Accordingly, it was the engineer Bernhard Sattler who, while searching for new raw material fields to exploit for his *Lindi Schürfgesellschaft,* failed constantly to find any minerals, but then suddenly discovered curious fossils on the ground. After the news disseminated, all wheels were turned in Berlin and Dar es Salaam to establish the Tendaguru Expedition.

---

46 Kennedy, Dane. 'Introduction: Reinterpreting Exploration'. *Reinterpreting Exploration. The West in the World.* 1–20. Ed. Dane Kennedy. Oxford: 2014, pp. 6, 8.

47 Cf. Kennedy. 'Introduction', pp. 1–12. For the East African context cf. Rockel, Stephen J. 'Decentring Exploration in East Africa'. *Reinterpreting Exploration. The West in the World.* 172–194. Ed. Dane Kennedy. Oxford: 2014. For western ignorance regarding indigenous knowledge about fossil finds in North America cf. Mayor, Adrienne. 'Suppression of Indigenous Fossil Knowledge: From Claverack, New York, 1705 to Agate Springs, Nebraska, 2005'. *Agnotology. The Making and Unmaking of Ignorance.* 163–182. Eds. Robert N. Proctor and Londa Schiebinger. Stanford: 2008. Cf. Mayor, Adrienne. *Fossil Legends of the First Americans.* Princeton: 2005. For a case study regarding map making and cartography that highlights the significance of indigenous knowledge to European explorations and discoveries in the Indian colonial context. Cf. Raj, Kapil. *Relocating Modern Science. Circulation and the Construction of Knowledge in South Asia and Europe, 1650–1900.* New York: 2007, pp. 60–94. Regarding the negotiating character of colonial knowledge production and the significance of local Indian knowledge for British imperial or rather colonial expertise cf. Sivasundaram, Sujit. 'Trading Knowledge: The East India Company's Elephants in India and Britain'. 27–63. *The Historical Journal,* 48, 1. Cambridge: 2005. For a general critical assessment on the role of the invisible individuals involved in science cf. Shapin, Steven. 'The Invisible Technician'. 554–563. *Scientist,* 77, 6. Harvard: 1989. Web. http://nrs.harvard.edu/urn-3:HUL.InstRepos:3425945 (2 November 2017). Thanks to Verena Bunkus, Erik Liebscher and Anna-Maria Hünnes (all University of Erfurt) for recommending most of the works cited in this footnote!

Since then, this narrative has contributed to establishing the image of the Tendaguru Expedition as being an up-to-date and immensely successful palaeontological excavation that brought honour to not only German science but also to the German nation. In the 1920s and 1930s, during the Weimar Republic and National Socialism, the Tendaguru Expedition's success was thus a ready-at-hand argument for German colonial advocates to counter the regulations of the Treaties of Versailles, which denied any colonial possessions to Germany in the future. Using the Tendaguru Expedition as an example of successful German colonisation in Africa and the German ability to exert Europe's allegedly civilising mission on the continent, the dinosaur bones of the Tendaguru were turned into artefacts intended to perpetuate the ideal of resuming German colonialism (in East Africa), until the end of WWII. Indeed, even recent research about the Tendaguru has kept many aspects of this colonial narrative. Admittedly, demands to re-establish German colonies overseas quickly vanished in the course of depoliticising policies of the German Democratic Republic after WWII. But the story of Bernhard Sattler being the actual discoverer of the dinosaur bones at Tendaguru remains tenacious.[48]

In fact, the existence of the dinosaur fossils of the Tendaguru had been known to the East African population long before Bernhard Sattler's visit. Stories about the gigantic bones were embedded in the culture of all the populations resident in the *Lindi* district. Accordingly, folk tales reported about an ancient gigantic animal named *majimwi, mazimwi* or *ma'imi*, which walked either on two or four legs, was very dangerous, and had threatened the lives of many people in the colony's south. Although the stories were not uniform and often contradictory, even Edwin Hennig himself was convinced that they were somehow connected to the petrified dinosaur fossils found at the Tendaguru hill.[49] Apart from these folk tales, Holger Stoecker has also convincingly succeeded in correcting the history of the Tendaguru bones' discovery. His research has outlined that Bernhard Sattler had actually not discovered the fossils but was directed to the 'dinosaur cemetery' by one of his East African employees. Of course, there is no doubt that Sattler was an important figure in the events leading to the ultimate establishment of the Tendaguru Expedition and during the initial weeks of excava-

48 Cf. Heumann, Ina et al. 'Dinosaurier und Provenienz. Konjunkturen des Kolonialen, 1909–2018'. *Dinosaurier Fragmente. Zur Geschichte der Tendaguru-Expedition und ihrer Objekte 1906–2008.* 255–273. Eds. Ina Heumann et al. Göttingen: 2018. Cf. Stoecker. 'Maji-Maji-Krieg und Mineralien', pp. 26–37. Cf. Maier. *African Dinosaurs*, pp. 1–22, 83–93, 309–334. Cf. Mogge. '"Im Deutschen Boden Afrikas."', pp. 125–144. Cf. Mogge. *Wilhelm Branco,* p. 201. Cf. Kretschmann. 'Noch ein Nationaldenkmal?'. pp. 200–212. For further research gaps regarding Eberhard Fraas and the Museum of Natural History in Stuttgart cf. Rösser. 'Knotenpunkte des Kolonialen', pp. 56–61.

49 Cf. Hennig. *Am Tendaguru,* p. 134. Cf. UAT 407/80, pp. 63–64.

tions. But in fact, the attention he brought to the petrified bones lying on the surface of the East African ground, not just as ordinary stones, but as dinosaur fossils, was directed by one of his East African employees. Attempting to save his *Lindi Schürfgesellschaft* from bankruptcy, Sattler attempted to find promising raw material deposits that would ensure profitability in the future. Yet, his attempts, starting in 1906, were unsuccessful and remained not very promising for almost a year. According to the available sources, one of Sattler's East African employees felt the engineer's increasing disappointment and sorrow resulting from the unsuccessful quest for raw materials and directed him to a remote place where several huge bones stood out from the sandy soil. Sattler drew a sketch of the scene and sent this picture with a letter to his business partner, Wilhelm Arning, living in Hannover, in March 1907. Arning, as a former colonial officer and member of the *Reichstag*, used his connections in the *Reich's* influential circles to highlight the scientific importance of the fossil finds, besides saving his friend's company from bankruptcy. The palaeontologist, Eberhard Fraas, who happened to be in German East Africa's north as a geological advisor for Heinrich Otto's planned cotton business near *Nyanza* ('Lake Victoria'; cf. Chapter 4), thus inspected the fossils near the Tendaguru and confirmed their quality. Consequently, Germany's academic circles reacted determinedly and it was, particularly, Wilhelm Branca, director of Berlin's Museum of Natural History, who left no stone unturned to enable the Tendaguru Expedition to start its excavations by April 1909. From this moment onwards, contemporary publications and publications of the postcolonial era silenced the decisive role of the East African employee who had actually directed Sattler's attention to the fossils and kept on retelling the story of Sattler's alleged 'discovery'. In fact, directing Sattler to the very remote place of the Tendaguru, which is still barely accessible today, involved not only detailed knowledge of the environment as such. It also needed an awareness of the fact that the petrified dinosaur bones were indeed something uncommon and an almost singular occurrence. Hence, the lion's share of the discovery must be attributed to Sattler's East African employee, whose name is unfortunately not recorded in the sources.[50] In addition, many of the discoveries made during the Tendaguru Expedition were genuinely not made by Europeans, but by East Africans. Of course, Edwin Hennig and Werner Janensch were the leading palaeontologists, but they were almost the only Europeans among 500 working East Africans, who would discover numerous bones in the area around the Tendaguru and beyond. The majority of the discoveries were made by the many East African workmen, overseers and the preparators.

50 Cf. Stoecker. 'Maji-Maji-Krieg und Mineralien', pp. 28–37.

As revealed by Hennig's letter to his mother quoted above, the excavation area had expanded rapidly from spring 1909 onwards and therefore entailed a dependency on further East African intuition and knowledge for new fossil discoveries. During the ca. two and a half years of excavations, the palaeontologists Edwin Hennig and Werner Janensch employed by Wilhelm Branca's museum in Berlin were the only two Europeans who resided at the Tendaguru permanently. Only in the very first four weeks were they assisted by Bernhard Sattler and Mr Besser of the *DOAG*, and later joined by the geologist, Hans Reck, and the intellectual, Walter Furtwängler, who would also only stay for a few weeks with Janensch and Hennig. For the very isolated area of the Tendaguru Mountain, where the "nearest village Nanundo was two h away",[51] this meant that keeping a mere overview of the entire area and the huge number of fossil find locations was one of the biggest challenges for the palaeontologists. This excludes any mention of close supervision of the East Africans who were working and excavating independently most of the time. By the beginning of September 1909, "a tour of all the workplaces [. . .] [took] up the whole morning and there [were] still new locations"[52] where Hennig would have liked to start digging right away. The area under excavation expanded gradually and forced the Europeans to soon split up and to lead the excavations at two locations that were far away from each other. By July 1910, Hennig wrote to his mother:

> The two most distant ditches are now a long day's march apart. We dig in Kindope 1 h away, Ubolelo 3 h away, and Mtapaia or Kijengere 2–3 h away. I have to add another map. Of course, we cannot check there daily, but we have sent reliable supervisors there. In Mtapaia, I myself was there from 9–11 to get the work going, to Ubolelo, Janensch wants to go tomorrow. In both places we leave one tent all the time, so that we can have lunch without taking a large number of porters with us or stay overnight.[53]

Only two months later, in early September 1910, the most distant places like Ubolelo could not be visited on a daily basis anymore. Janensch and Hennig were happy if they could pay them a visit every month. From this very same month onwards, it often took the two German palaeontologists several days to be able to even take a brief look at the spectacular fossil finds, not only because of the ever rising number of finds, but especially because of the ever expanding area under excavation.[54] In the course of excavations between 1909 and 1911, finds were reported from places as far away as Masasi (ca. eighty km), places in the neighbour-

51 UAT. 407/2,1, p. 138.

52 UAT. 407/2,1, p. 172. Cf. UAT. 407/80, pp. 9, 11, 35, 78.

53 UAT. 407/2,2, p. 353. Cf. UAT. 407/80, pp. 35, 78. Cf. UAT. 407/81, pp. 10–11, 33.

54 Cf. UAT. 407/2,2, pp. 373, 384.

ing *Kilwa* district (ca. 150 km) and also from Ngerengere, a station of the newly built *Central Railway*, which was ca. 600 km away from the Tendaguru Mountain.[55] The distance of these find locations from the Tendaguru often meant that Janensch and Hennig had to leave the mountain for many weeks at a time. Of course, not all of these distant places – maybe except for Masasi – were part of the Tendaguru Excavations proper, but they show that close supervision and control of the work of East Africans was simply impossible. It is therefore more than obvious that not only Hennig and Janensch made the spectacular dinosaur fossil finds. Quite the contrary: The majority of the fossils, including the most spectacular ones like the skull of the *Brachiosaurus*, were found by East African overseers and ordinary workers. In contrast to the colonial myths, Janensch and Hennig would sit in the camp at the Tendaguru most of the time and do the paperwork, where their employees would approach them to report another fossil find, as shown in the incident quoted above. Thus, not only the initial bones resulting in the Tendaguru Expedition were discovered thanks to an East African. Moreover, the Tendaguru Expedition relied heavily on East African agency, knowledge and intuition for discovering new dinosaur fossils throughout the entire endeavour. Although Janensch and Hennig also found some bones every now and then themselves, their work was in essence limited to administration, bookkeeping and science, while the actual discoveries were made by East Africans.

Besides the vastness of the territory under excavation, the weather required Hennig and Janensch to rely on East Africans as well. Just like at the *Otto* plantation or at the *Central Railway*'s construction sites, the excavations at the Tendaguru could only be carried out in the absence of heavy rainfalls. Especially during the big rainy season – *masika* – starting in March and ending in May, hardly any excavations could be conducted, because the occasional large downpours filled the ditches with water regularly and made any palaeontological work impossible. Also, during the small rainy season between October and November with comparably low precipitation, the German palaeontologists left the Tendaguru. Particularly during *masika*, however, not only did Hennig and Janensch leave for vacations in the northern districts of *Usambara*, for example, but their workers also travelled long distances to plant the fields at their homes. In turn, the months-long absences of the two German palaeontologists and the vast majority of workers meant that only a small number of the staff stayed at the Tendaguru to protect the ditches, the entire camp, its provisions and their storage, away from weather, animals and man. As a result, during *masika*, the population of the Tendaguru excavation camp declined from its maximum of ca. 800 people

---

55 Cf. UAT. 407/81, pp. 119–135. Cf. UAT. 407/82, pp. 3–27. Cf. UAT. 407/2,2, pp. 325–330, 490–500.

(including the workers' families) to only a dozen. During these months, the expedition was entirely the responsibility of Hennig's and Janensch's East African senior overseers and preparators, who played not only an outstanding role during the rainy season but also during the dry season when the largest share of work was done.[56] The following section deals with their central role.

5.4.2 East African Overseers and Preparators

> I visited the trenches along the way first. Found a long-serving overseer asleep who was extremely surprised by my appearance.
>
> Edwin Hennig. Diary Entry. 12th June 1910.[57]

The work at the Tendaguru Expedition required a large number of skilled men. Those who bore the lion's share of the Tendaguru excavations were East Africans whom Janensch and Hennig either described as 'overseers' or 'preparators'. The labels are somewhat misleading as there was no clear-cut boundary between the occupation of an overseer or preparator. As far as the sources can tell, overseers and foremen generally had longer experience at the Tendaguru Expedition than the ordinary workers under supervision. Most of them were among the very first men who had been delivered to Janensch and Hennig by Sattler, when the two German palaeontologists arrived at the port of Lindi in April 1909. If the workers proved themselves reliable, Janensch and Hennig delegated tasks of higher responsibility to them gradually, until they were trusted and described as 'foremen' or 'overseers'. In general, the overseer's task was to put into practice the German palaeontologists' plan of excavating the fossil-prone ditches in the right order and in the right manner. Each overseer was generally in charge of one ditch. He had to report regularly about new fossil finds, the overall digging progress and had to instruct as well as correct the work of their subordinate men digging for dinosaur bones. Sometimes, overseers were the very first to put an eye on a newly found fossil far away from the main camp, often drawing a sketch of it and delivering a

---

56 Cf. UAT. 407/81, pp. 1–4, 119–129. Cf. UAT. 407/2,2, pp. 303–320. Cf. UAT. 407/2,1, pp. 193–194, 223, 238–239, 265–266. Cf. Hennig. *Am Tendaguru*, p. 43. Cf. Stoecker, Holger. 'Koloniales Kronland und Ausfuhrverbot. Wie die Fossilien vom Tendaguru für die deutsche Wissenschaft gesichert wurden'. *Dinosaurier Fragmente. Zur Geschichte der Tendaguru-Expedition und ihrer Objekte. 1906–2018.* 38–57. Eds. Ina Heumann et al. Göttingen: 2018, p. 53.
57 UAT. 407/81, p. 17.

report to the camp. On top of this, the overseers also recruited new workers or porters needed for the Tendaguru Expedition, if they were urgently required.[58]

Of course, the tasks of an overseer included the extraction and preparation of fossils in order to transport them to the coast. Janensch and Hennig completely relied on the work of these foremen as the vast area under excavation entailed the relative absence of the two German palaeontologists. Yet, just like any scientific endeavour, the Tendaguru excavations also required a certain amount of supervision. Given the vast distances between the ditches, Hennig and Janensch had to delegate many of their tasks to the skilled and experienced overseers. Like any African share in colonial labour processes, the role of the skilled East African overseers and palaeontological preparators has long been absent in research about the Tendaguru. While Hennig did express appreciation of African labour in his book about the expedition published in 1912, few historians have ever investigated more deeply into the issue. One exception is the article published by Michael Ohl and Holger Stoecker that analyses the naming of the dinosaurs and dinosaur fossils that were found at the Tendaguru. Many dinosaur fossils were initially named after these East African overseers who had discovered them in the first place. Only afterwards were they renamed according to the nomenclatures of European science and the customs of the German society. Almost all the bones initially carrying the names of East African overseers and preparators working at the Tendaguru were ultimately renamed. Today, they mostly bear the names of famous German palaeontologists, major donors of the Tendaguru Expedition or 'colonial heroes' like General Paul von Lettow-Vorbeck.[59]

Whereas the actual procedure of how dinosaurs are named is clearly regulated, the choice of the name itself is arbitrary. Generally, scientists do not name dinosaur fossils immediately at the find location, but they follow a labour-intensive procedure. After the newly found fossils have undergone detailed investigations, they must be compared and classified in accordance with those species known so far. Only afterwards is the ultimate scientific name applied to a recently found fossil. Sometimes, this process requires decades. For instance, the biggest dinosaur skeleton currently exhibited at the Berlin's Museum of Natural history, the *Brachiosaurus Brancai*, consists of two parts: *Brancai* is the name of Wilhelm Branca, head of Berlin's Museum of Natural History during and after the Tendaguru Expedition, and the scientific nomenclature *Brachiosaurus*, which indicates the dinosaur's palaeontological species and genus. But initially, after the immediate discovery of a

58 Cf. UAT. 407/80, pp. 87, 91. Cf. UAT. 407/81, p. 76. Cf. UAT. 407/82, p. 15. Cf. UAT. 407/2,2, pp. 353, 384. Cf. Hennig. *Am Tendaguru*, pp. 31, 36–37, 39–40.

59 Cf. Hennig. *Am Tendaguru*, pp. 7–11. Cf. Ohl and Stoecker. 'Taxonomien am Tendaguru', pp. 233–237.

dinosaur fossil at the Tendaguru, it was given an interim name, bearing aspects of the local context, for example being named after the East African preparator who had discovered the fossil first. Yet, the farther the recently discovered dinosaur fossil was moved from its initial find location to places like Berlin's Museum of Natural History, and the more time that passed after the fossils' discovery, the more a fossil became part of the European scientific museal context and blurred the immediate context of discovery. Through this process described as 'translocation' by Ohl and Stoecker, the name of the dinosaur fossil is changed according to the standards of the museal European context.[60] As far as the phenomenon of labour at the Tendaguru is concerned, the different nomenclatures are tell-tale. Especially the interim names initially given to the dinosaur fossils highlight the importance and the agency of the East Africans involved in the excavations, and reveal much about the global history of labour. As a matter of fact, the interim names reveal the context of their actual excavation. Such interim names were also of great importance to Janensch and Hennig, when working at Tendaguru. On the spot, the interim name of a fossil helped the palaeontologists keep an overview of the finds and an accurate record of the specific find locations in the areas under excavation. Although the interim names used by Hennig and Janensch for the Tendaguru dinosaur fossils vanished over the years and did not go into the books of palaeontology, science, or history for over 100 years, these interim names give significant information about those East African foremen and preparators who were indispensable for the German palaeontologists during the Tendaguru Expedition.[61]

The place names of the find locations, like Mtapaia, Nterego and Ligoma, provided the dinosaur interim names *Ligomasaurus, Nteregosaurus Oedipus* and *Mtapoiasaurus* for the corresponding dinosaur skeletons. Apart from revealing the actual find locations, such interim names often also revealed the presence and the agency of East African protagonists at Tendaguru. Among others, there was the *Nyororosaurus*, bearing the name of the overseer Seliman Nyororo, who discovered a skeleton on 24 September 1909. Another skeleton was named after the trusted preparatory, Salim. According to Hennig's diary, Salim had already discovered an "exceptionally fortunate find location [. . .] by himself at the northeastern side of the Tendaguru" two months earlier on 22 June and "exposed it splendidly". By September of the same year, this find location had "proven itself repeatedly" and finally "turned out more and more to be a treasure chest."[62] The *Mohammadisaurus* received its name from the overseer Mohammadi Keranje,

60 Cf. Ohl and Stoecker. 'Taxonomien am Tendaguru', pp. 233–237.

61 Cf. Ohl and Stoecker. 'Taxonomien am Tendaguru', pp. 234–236.

62 UAT. 407/80, pp. 31, 33. Cf. Ohl and Stoecker. 'Taxonomien am Tendaguru', p. 237. Cf. Maier. *African Dinosaurs*, p. 35.

who discovered two large skeletons in August 1909, whereas the *Salesisaurus* was exposed under the surveillance of the overseer Salesi in September 1909. Then, there was the *Selimanosaurus*, named after the preparator, Seliman Kawinga, who led the excavations from October 1909 onwards. In fact, apart from these names, there exists hardly any other source that could provide more details about the actual role of these overseers. Yet, these interim names are still enough evidence to prove the indispensability of the overseers involved at the excavation works at Tendaguru.[63]

Sometimes, however, the interim names of the dinosaurs rather veil the agency of the African protagonists involved. This applies for the skeleton, which was initially called *Blancocerosaurus*, and whose bones would ultimately become the largest parts of the *Brachiosaurus Brancai*, named after Wilhelm Branca. It turned out to be the largest skeleton of the Tendaguru and is still standing in the centre of the Atrium of Berlin's Museum of Natural History. Despite the nomenclature currently in use, this skeleton was unearthed by the Tendaguru head supervisor, Boheti bin Amrani, from October 1909 onwards. Boheti was the leading overseer and preparator with the greatest authority and autonomy, who worked not only for Hennig and Janensch from the very beginning, between 1909 and 1911, but also until the very end of the German expedition to the Tendaguru in 1913 under Hans von Staff and Hans Reck. Whenever the German palaeontologists left the Tendaguru for holidays or for other business in Lindi, they were represented by their "virtuous Boheti" or "our Boheti",[64] as Hennig as well as Janensch call him repeatedly in their diaries and letters. In turn, whenever Boheti left the Tendaguru himself, for example for the Ramadhan holiday, Hennig longed for his return, as on 29 October 1910: "Boheti comes back to the camp. At last! His absence is a part of our time that really seemed long!" It is therefore not very surprising that Boheti was trusted with the preparation of the skeletons that appeared the most spectacular, especially when they promised parts of or a complete dinosaur skull. Moreover, Boheti discovered many new dinosaur fossils himself and Hennig also named one entire excavation spot the "Boheti ditch".[65]

As early as 1909, the two German palaeontologists even wondered if it was possible to take Boheti to Germany, as Boheti himself was curious about life in Europe and his knowledge of the Tendaguru fossils had really prepared him for

---

63 Cf. Ohl and Stoecker. 'Taxonomien am Tendaguru', p. 237. Cf. Maier. *African Dinosaurs*, p. 35.

64 UAT. 407/81, p. 147. MfN. HBSB. 9.2, p. 8. UAT. 407/2,2, p. 369.

65 MfN. HBSB. 5.1, p. 86, cf. p. 215. UAT. 407/80, p. 83. UAT. 407/81, p. 76. Cf. UAT. 407/80, p. 10, 19–20, 83. Cf. UAT. 407/81, p. 145. UAT. 407/2,2, pp. 374, 479. Cf. UAT. 407/80, pp. 147, 164. Cf. UAT. 407/2,2, p. 374, 479. Cf. Ohl and Stoecker. 'Taxonomien am Tendaguru', p. 239. Cf. Maier. *African Dinosaurs*, pp. 42, 81.

further preparation work in the Museum of Natural History in Berlin – a thought that never materialised, however. Nevertheless, when Hennig and Janensch left East Africa for good and returned to Germany in early summer 1911, Boheti would also be put in charge of several unfinished tasks: He and a few dozen experienced workers finished the excavation of some pits and organised the transport of the unearthed dinosaur bones via the network of the *DOAG* to Germany. As soon as Branca and his team in Berlin had gathered another 50,000 Marks for another smaller Tendaguru Expedition between 1912–1914, which was primarily concerned with geographical research and complementary excavations only, Boheti remained indispensable for the German palaeontologists as an able and experienced local point of contact. Later, instead of Janensch and Hennig, Boheti welcomed the geologist Hans von Staff and even later, the volcanologist, Hans Reck, and introduced them to the East African work environment. After WWI, when the vast majority of the former German East Africa had become a territory of the League of Nations under the supervision of Great Britain, British palaeontologists resumed excavations in the Tendaguru area between 1923–1931 and turned to Boheti's expertise. In turn, this means that Boheti was one of the very few people – or maybe even the only person – who had worked for all palaeontological Tendaguru Expeditions throughout almost twenty years. Whereas all the other interim names used by Hennig and Janensch mentioned East African expertise only for a very short period of time before the fossils were baptised with European names, Boheti was permanently honoured by the palaeontologist Kristian Remes in 2007. Establishing a new species of dinosaurs 100 years after its excavation at the Tendaguru, Remes used the epithet *Australodocus Bohetii* to honour Boheti's palaeontological work in East Africa. However, the decisive role of most of the East African overseers and preparators is still veiled by the scientific nomenclature, which honours people like Janensch, Branca and Hennig instead.[66]

Besides the scientific nomenclature that honoured almost exclusively Europeans, the interim names could also veil the agency of East African individuals: Whereas the interim name of the *Mtapoiasaurus* bears the name of the place where it was found, Mtapaia, it does not reveal the name of the overseer, Salim Tombali, who not only discovered it in September 1909 but who would also become responsible for the subsequent excavation of the entire ditch in which the skeleton was found. Finally, there were also names that point to other aspects

66 Cf. Maier. *African Dinosaurs,* pp. 40, 85–107, 215, 217, 221–241. Cf. Ohl and Stoecker.'Taxonomien am Tendaguru'. pp. 241–253. Cf. Heumann, Ina et al. 'Gespräch. 225 Tonnen Gestein. Ein Gespräch mit Daniela Schwarz, Kustodin der Tendaguru-Sammlung'. *Dinosaurier Fragmente. Zur Geschichte der Tendaguru-Expedition und ihrer Objekte 1906–2008*. 276–291. Eds. Ina Heumann et al. Göttingen: 2018, pp. 287–288.

that are decisive for analysing the phenomenon of labour at the Tendaguru as they reveal the role of East African administrators in the service of the colonial administration. The *Abdallahsaurus*, for instance, was either discovered by the preparator Abdallah Kimbamba or by Sefu Abdallah. The latter not only worked as preparator at the Tendaguru Expedition, but he was also a governmental *Jumbe* and later also Janensch's *boy*. Sefu Abdallah's occupation as *Jumbe* was decisive in declaring potential find locations around the Tendaguru, as so-called *Kronland* (crown land), turning it from private property into property of the colonial government in German East Africa. To prevent foreign colonial powers like Great Britain from sending their own scientists to excavate the dinosaur fossils, the crown land declaration aimed at keeping foreigners out of the colony and thereby reserved the best bits of the dinosaur sensation for the honour of the German *Reich.* Turning the vast area of 3,500 ha into crown land also meant that East African people were not allowed to reside on the land without special permission. The surviving files suggest that while the Maji Maji War had led to massive population loss in this region, some people still living there were indeed expelled from the excavation area. Serving as *Jumbe* at the lowest levels of the colonial administration, Sefu Abdallah – along with his fellow *Jumbes,* the *Akida* Saadallah, and *Lindi*'s District Officer Wendt – signed the document that ultimately turned the area into crown land and implicitly forced the local people off their land.[67]

This raises the question of the backgrounds of those East Africans who actually became overseers or preparators at the Tendaguru Expedition, and how they were situated in the colonial context. Although this question cannot be finally settled in this study, as the sources do not provide for all-encompassing results, it seems that a substantial number of the overseers and preparators were people who had already collaborated with the German colonial administration before the beginning of the Tendaguru Expedition. This is of course the case regarding the former *Jumbe,* preparator, and *boy* Sefu Abdallah, but also applies to the preparator Sadallah. Although nothing is known either of Sadallah's work at the Tendaguru as such, or his life before the palaeontological excavations, the remaining sources tell us that Sadallah had been loyal to the German forces during the Maji Maji War, for instance. In contrast to this patchy research result, there are some details available regarding the life of Sefu Abdallah. Accordingly, he had lived on the East African island of Mafia, off the Tanganyikan coast, in the 1890s, where he had owned fifty-five slaves. Moreover, he had owned a "small plot of land" in the *Lindi* district before and during the German colonial rule. Just as Sadallah's and

67 Cf. Stoecker. 'Koloniales Kronland', pp. 38–55. Cf. Ohl and Stoecker. 'Taxonomien am Tendaguru', pp. 232–253.

Sefu Abdallah's names suggest an Arabic background, the same can be assumed for Hennig's and Janensch's superintendent Boheti: According to the historian Maier, Boheti had been "[p]art Arab",[68] suggesting that he, like Sadallah and Sefu Abdallah, was a member of the coastal Arab-Swahili elite that had dominated East African societies as well as its economy and politics in pre-colonial times. After the Swahili-Arab elite had to surrender, as they had been defeated by German troops in the late 1880s and early 1890s, a substantial number tended to become involved in the lower ranks of the German colonial administration, either as *Jumbe, Akida* or *Liwali.*[69] The assumption that most of the overseers and preparators were either Swahili or Arab is further supported by a partial list kept by Janensch in 1910 that sets out the quarries and their responsible overseers. Although it is almost impossible to separate the Swahili language entirely from Arabic, as nearly forty per cent of the Swahili vocabulary derives from Arabic, Janensch's list of overseers may help to indicate the origin of these most important East Africans at the Tendaguru. In total, the list has twenty-two names of East African overseers. Of those twenty-two, only the name of the overseer Laa Tatu[70] has no obvious Arabic element, whereas eight have clearly Arabic sounding names, like the overseer Issa bin Salim. The remaining eleven names obtain one element from Arabic and another from an African Bantu language, like the name of the overseer Mohammed Ngaranga.[71] Especially, members of this last group may have been Wanyamwezi, for example originating from central Tanganyika, who may have adopted the Muslim faith and, therefore, took an Arabic name. Nevertheless, their conversion to Islam, indicated by their name alone, already shows their relative proximity to the Swahili Arabic elite of the East African coast and their relative cultural distance from the people of the hinterland.

But other groups loyal to the German colonisers seem to have been involved at the Tendaguru, too. It is worth noting that Edwin Hennig reported of a "few overseers" at the Tendaguru Expedition who had been *Askari* of the German colonial military before coming to the Tendaguru. This further suggests that especially

68 Maier. *African Dinosaurs*, p. 25.

69 According to the colonial military officer Hans Paasche, the involvement of the Arab-Swahili elite in the German colonial administration was the reason why they became targets of Maji Maji attacks. Cf. Paasche. '"Der Aufstand"', pp. 52, 66, 74. Cf. Glassman. *Feasts and Riot*, pp. 1–54, 249–270. Cf. Casco. *Utenzi*, pp. 183–238.

70 Laa tatu (Swahili): La(a) = no!; tatu = three; Laa Tatu = "three times no!"; "La" also means "no" in colloquial Arabic, however. Thanks to my colleague Sarah al-Taher (Max-Weber-Centre University of Erfurt) for her help in this respect.

71 Cf. Maier. *African Dinosaurs*, p. 66. Cf. also Letter of Hennig to Janensch 30 July 1911 featuring five porters and one craftsman, who were employed for the Tendaguru Expedition. Five of them have clearly Arabic names. UAT. 407/2,2, p. 492.

those East Africans who had already established closer connections to the colonial administration would become overseers or preparators at the Tendaguru.[72] The same can be said for Hennig's scribe Claudio, who was probably neither an *Askari* nor an Arab, nor a Swahili. Yet, Claudio also had relative proximity to German colonialists before coming to the Tendaguru. He was one of up to three scribes working for Hennig and Janensch who "kept worker attendance records, marked packing crates, and maintained an inventory of excavation tools. They were required to record the quantity and sale of grain in camp as well."[73] The Christian name, Claudio, suggests he was a Christian convert and/or former missionary pupil, who were popular among colonialists for their reading and writing skills. Unfortunately, Claudio's individual background and those of the other two scribes – one of the others was named Matiri – must remain in speculation for now, as only patchy files and one photo survives in the archives under investigation.[74] Nevertheless, they were probably working in close coordination with Hennig and Janensch, just like the already mentioned overseers and preparators and the *boys* Sefu, Wilhelm and Ali. As the *boys*' role will be illustrated in the following section, it is important to highlight here that there were also numerous preparators, overseers and foreman, whose backgrounds and names are not conveyed by the files. They either appear as "old overseers" – meaning long-serving overseers – in Hennig's diary and letters, or as "Wangoni overseers", for instance. Whereas one Wangoni overseer, who had named himself "Tendaguru", is referred to in person in Hennig's documents, it is beyond doubt that many African preparators, having had decisive roles at the Tendaguru excavations, are not mentioned in the sources at all.[75]

Furthermore, obtaining a decisive role in the Tendaguru Expedition does not mean that general mechanisms of colonial rule did not still apply. Although Janensch and Hennig relied on their East African overseers and workers, colonial hierarchies prevailed and characterised the relationships between the German palaeontologists and their leading East African employees. When excavating in the *Kilwa* region in August 1911, Hennig enquired about work statuses and asked his "preparators, whether anyone want[ed] to return to the Tendaguru, because there [was] not enough work [in Kilwa] yet; answer: 'Man does not want to die,

72 UAT. 407/2,1, p. 175. Hennig was delighted that they allegedly instilled some "Prussian drill" into the ordinary workers. For a detailed analysis of the Askari cf. Moyd. *Violent Intermediaries*. Cf. Michels. *Schwarze Deutsche Kolonialsoldaten*.

73 Maier. *African Dinosaurs*, p. 32.

74 Cf. UAT. 407/2,2, p. 500. Cf. MfN. HBSB. Tendaguru Expedition. Konvolut Tendaguru (1694), Expeditionsverlauf- und dokumentation (421), Fotoalben (193), "Schreiber Claudio und Matiri mit Packern vor dem Knochenmagazin".

75 UAT. 407/80, pp. 28, 89–90 cf. p. 87. UAT. 407/81, pp. 11, 135, cf. p. 87.

but God lets him die. You are God here, what are you asking us?'". The answer left Hennig puzzled and made him complain about "the power [. . .] they put in our hands themselves."[76] In fact, Hennig used his power as a member of a German colonial endeavour every day to fulfil his tasks. This prevalence of colonial power at the Tendaguru Expedition is revealed by taking a closer look at both the topography of the Tendaguru (worker) camp, and the work relationships between Hennig and his personal servants.

5.5 'We Could Have Employed Many More': Labour and Command at the Tendaguru

5.5.1 Residing on the Tendaguru: A Colonial City Upon a Hill?

> With joyful astonishment I see that culture may penetrate but does not destroy. Europe and Africa live sharply separated from each other. Popular life [. . .] shows itself everywhere with full immediacy. In Dar es Salaam we [had] the incredibly interesting sight of the 'goma' (dances) for the unveiling ceremony of [Herrmann von Wissmann's] monument. The wretches probably do not know that they celebrate their oppressor.
>
> Edwin Hennig. Letter to his mother. On board the 'Feldmarshall' April 5th, 1909.[77]

The camp at the Tendaguru resembled the topography of other colonial settlements. Like Clement Gillman's construction camp at the *Central Railway* and the arrangement of *Otto's* cotton plantation near Kilossa, at the heart of any ideal-typical colonial settlement was the idea of racial segregation that would separate the colonisers from the colonised, to maintain and represent the racist colonial hierarchy. The perceived necessity to separate European from African was deduced from popular racist and Social Darwinist theories and for so-called 'hygienic considerations'. Accordingly, a too close interaction between the races would allegedly harm the *whiteness* of the Europeans and the colonisers, who therefore feared they would 'degenerate' to a lower racial level. Whereas all these ideas about such a colonial topography could be found in the design of the settlement at the Tendaguru Mountain throughout the entire excavation process, there seem to have been two major phases: The first phase lasted from the arrival of the Europeans Sattler, Besser, Hennig and Janensch at the Tendaguru in April 1909 until the end of the first *masika* at the turn of April to May 1910. The second phase started in spring 1910 and lasted until the very end of the palaeontological excavations of the Tendaguru Expe-

76 UAT. 407/2,2, p. 500.
77 UAT. 407/2,1, p. 87.

dition. Before the initial arrival of Sattler, Hennig and Janensch at the excavation site in early 1909, they had sent a caravan of ca. forty porters to the Tendaguru Mountain to prepare a camp for the European palaeontologists and their East African overseers, preparators and ordinary workers. As soon as this caravan had arrived at the excavation site, they cleared the ground, built bamboo huts as shelter for the workers, erected (food) storages and a kitchen in the same manner, and covered these with braided grass roofs. When the party of Europeans arrived some days later, the new arrivals pitched their tents next to the huts and dwelled close to the workers for the time being. This place remained at the foot of the Tendaguru Mountain because the vast majority of the abundant deposits of dinosaur fossils lay nearby. The Tendaguru hill is roughly 100 metres high and was about a quarter of an hour's walk north and sat enthroned over the palaeontological camp, which was situated in an isolated area, roughly two hours away from the nearest village. With an increasing number of workers and the steady arrival of their women and children, footpaths were cut into the surrounding bush, and further land was cleared to enlarge the camp. By the end of April, the crew oversaw the erection of the so-called 'bone hut' that sheltered both the often-porous fossils from weather and the workers who used the space to pack fossil loads for porterage to the coast.[78] Moreover,

> [a] round grass roofed shelter with open sides served as a workplace for the Germans [and] Sattler arranged the laborers' huts according to tribal affiliation to avoid conflicts. [These 'tribal' districts] were built in long orderly rows near the tents of the Germans, with sufficient space left between dwellings to prevent the spread of fire.[79]

In the end, there were five different quarters for the workers that each housed one specific ethnicity or 'tribe': One for the Wayao, one for the Wangoni, one for the Wamakwa, one for the Wadonde and one for the Wamuera. To enjoy the view from the top of the Tendaguru hill over the flat bushland surrounding the single mountain, superintendent Boheti gave an order to create steps for a stair leading uphill from the camp. On the top of the Tendaguru, the European crew and their servants would occasionally dine alone or with other European visitors, celebrate birthdays or Christmas, finish administrative work, or pursue hobbies like painting for recreation. After the first rainy season, Boheti, together with roughly a dozen men, remained in the camp to guard the tools, the grain stocks, and two hundred fossil loads ready for transport to the coastal town of Lindi.

---

78 Cf. Maier. *African Dinosaurs*, pp. 24–27, 46–47, 53. Cf. Hennig. *Am Tendaguru*, pp. 18–20, 25. Cf. UAT. 407/80, pp. 11–12. Cf. UAT. 407/81, pp. 2–3, 71. Cf. UAT. 407/2,1, pp. 100–101. Cf. MfN. HBSB. 9.2, pp. 10–11. Cf. MfN. HBSB. 5.1, pp. 4–7, 74, 86. Cf. MfN. HBSB. Tendaguru Expedition 10.4. Druckmedien, pp. 133–134.

79 Maier. *African Dinosaurs*, p. 27.

Moreover, these men repaired the huts and prepared everything for further excavations and an anticipated increasing number of excavated fossils. They thus built a larger 'bone hut' to store the bones ready for transport. More importantly, regarding the colonial topography, the rainy season crew was ordered to erect buildings for the Germans at the top of the Tendaguru hill.[80]

This location, which Hennig regarded as a "gift from the gods",[81] was not only turned into the new residence for the German palaeontologists for the sake of the splendid view and the enjoyment of their free time. Rather, colonial discourses about hygiene that intermingled with rational considerations about health and safety were decisive for the relocation. Up on the hill, the wind protected Hennig and Janensch from malaria-prone mosquitoes and other insects as well as from potential fires in the workers camp, which had once come close to the palaeontologists' tents. In addition to these points, the Germans also wanted to isolate themselves deliberately from the noises of potential workers' *ngomas* and to live a distinguished colonial life in the countryside of German East Africa:[82]

> [N]ow we are living in our precious seat again. We are the East African nobility: [. . .] 'The Lords of Tendaguru'. In proper style we now build our castle on the hill that was born for it. On the top of the hill is our magnificent viewing pavilion and on the south foot we set up our personal camp, two small houses for the tents, one for the boys, kitchen and pantry. A few steps lead up to the dining room, the same round pavilion as we used to live in. So, an incredibly homely and stately castle is being built, which offers a beautiful view to the east and south and will itself be quite picturesque. A wide ramp leads quite steeply up. All the preparatory work has been done with skill and taste by Boheti in our absence and we are busy with the difficult work of drawing up the plans.[83]

The self-perception of belonging to a local colonial elite that ruled over a perceived quasi-kingdom was widespread in written testimonials of Germans and other Europeans living in the colonies. Frequently, this view found its expression in representative buildings situated on a hill, enabling the colonial ruler to observe the land quasi-majestically.[84] Hennig's statement reveals that he and Janensch apparently shared this perception with their fellow Germans living in East Africa, as Hennig also described himself as "absolute ruler of the Tendaguru",

---

80 Cf. Maier. *African Dinosaurs*, pp. 24–27, 46–47, 53. Cf. Hennig. *Am Tendaguru*, pp. 18–20, 25. Cf. UAT. 407/80, pp. 11–12. Cf. UAT. 407/81, pp. 2–3, 71. Cf. UAT. 407/2,1, pp. 100–101. Cf. MfN. HBSB. 9.2, pp. 10–11. Cf. MfN. HBSB. 5.1, pp. 4–7, 74, 86. Cf. MfN. HBSB. 10.4, pp. 133–134.

81 UAT. 407/2,1, p. 100.

82 Cf. Maier. *African Dinosaurs*, p. 53. Cf. UAT. 407/80, pp. 28–29. Cf. MfN. HBSB. 5.1, pp. 74, 86.

83 UAT. 407/2,2, p. 308.

84 Cf. Rösser. 'Juristisches Seminar'. Cf. Itandala. 'African Response', pp. 19–25. Cf. Tambila, Kapepwa, I. 'The German Invasion and Occupation of East Africa. Policies, Processes and Tactics'.

when 'co-souverain' Janensch had gone to Lindi, leaving Hennig behind for two weeks as the only European at the excavations.[85]

As well as establishing this 'majestic residence', relocating the European camp up on the hill entailed distancing the two German palaeontologists from their East African workers. This social distance prevailed at the Tendaguru from after the first rainy season until the end of the excavation. It was in line with other colonial topographies, typical for colonial towns, such as Gillman's *Central Railway* construction camp or the design of the *Otto* plantation near Kilossa. Describing his 'homely and stately castle' on the Tendaguru hill, Hennig does not give any clues that would reveal his general agenda to segregate Europeans from Africans in the Tendaguru camp. Yet, other passages of his self-narratives suggest that the establishment of a racist colonial topography for the Tendaguru camp was indeed an important aspect for Hennig. Echoing Central European discourses claiming that the sphere of the African continent emanated from Mediterranean countries like Greece or Italy, Hennig likewise complained bitterly about the "complete mixture of races that knows no home" as soon as he had reached the harbours of Naples and Marseilles on his voyage from Germany to East Africa in spring 1909. Hennig's discontent grew steadily, especially when his steamer anchored in Port Said and in Aden. When hearing from his fellow passengers on board that "the [. . .] order of German East African ports [. . .] ma[de] an exception among all other colonies", Hennig, himself part of a German colonial endeavour, rejoiced of course, and felt at home immediately in the allegedly well-ordered German sphere in Dar es Salaam, where the races lived "sharply separated from each other".[86]

Hence, on Hennig's part, clearly separating the European sphere from the African residential area in the Tendaguru camp was not only done for the enjoyment of the marvellous view. It was certainly also done for the sake of establishing a camp near the excavation site that followed the ideals of colonial topographies. That Hennig and Janensch further allotted each ethnic group employed as workers at the Tendaguru their own residential areas, further strengthens this argument. Just as major colonial settlements like Dar es Salaam created separate residential areas for Europeans, Indians and Africans, Hennig and Janensch established dis-

Studien zur Geschichte des deutschen Kolonialismus in Afrika. Festschrift zum 60. Geburtstag von Peter Sebald. 501–520. Eds. Peter Heine and Ulrich van der Heyden. Pfaffenweiler: 1995, pp. 503–513. Cf. Pesek. *Koloniale Herrschaft*, pp. 190–265.

85 UAT. 407/2,1. p. 193. Cf. Hennig. *Am Tendaguru*, pp. 34.

86 UAT. 407/2,1, pp. 54, 60–61, 68, 87, cf. 21, 54, 60–61, 67, 78, 93. Cf. citation above. Cf. Pesek, Michael. 'Passage to Africa. Steamship travels of Germans to East Africa in early 20th century'. *Academia.edu.* Web. https://uni-hamburg.academia.edu/MichaelPesek (15 April 2020), pp. 7–16.

tinct residential areas for each 'tribe' accordingly. The German palaeontologists' residential policies implemented in the Tendaguru camp can thus be regarded as an expression of a colonial topography that attempted to establish a racially segregated living environment and to resemble and establish a racist colonial order. The only difference between major colonial cities like Dar es Salaam and the camp at the Tendaguru was a matter of scale. Yet, Hennig's and Janensch's residential colonial order did not concord with East African realities but rather with a colonial ideal and was therefore predominantly a phantasy of the two German palaeontologists. As the 'tribes' in the *Lindi* district had had many interrelationships of history and culture, separating them artificially in the Tendaguru camp was an act of tribalisation, typical for any European power trying to establish and secure its colonial rule.[87]

For Janensch and Hennig themselves, work and life at the Tendaguru might have resembled that of a colonial city upon a hill. This 'city' was characterised by challenging yet incredibly satisfying and fascinating palaeontological tasks for the two scientists. Besides their palaeontological work, their camp life at the Tendaguru offered the typical enjoyments of Germans in the East African colony such as hunting, travelling, good food and drink, and marvellous views from their privileged residence at the top of the Tendaguru hill. Just like Clement Gillman's construction camp at the *Central Railway* and Kaundinya's cotton plantation, Janensch and Hennig's living and working environment at the Tendaguru reflected German colonial command. Yet, with Hennig clearly valuing the skill and ability of his overseers, preparators and simple workers, and with even himself describing German colonialism as 'oppression', the colonial order prevalent at the Tendaguru appears on its face to have been comparatively benevolent compared to many other colonial contexts of labour. In fact, despite their skill and ability as well as Janensch's and Hennig's appreciation for it, all East Africans working at the Tendaguru were nevertheless exposed to several despotisms of German colonial rule in East Africa, as a closer look at the labour relationships at the Tendaguru reveal. Yet, the Tendaguru's colonial command was never comprehensive and left many niches for agency, which were not only found but also created by the East African overseers, preparators and ordinary workers at Tendaguru themselves. This also holds true for Hennig's and Janensch's personal servants. Contrary to the imagined European segregated sphere

87 Cf. UAT. 407/2,2, p. 500. Cf. Aas. *Koloniale Entwicklung*, pp. 88–94. Cf. Eckert, Andreas. *Kolonialismus*. Frankfurt o.M.: 2006, pp. 66–70. Cf. Singh, Gajendra. 'Finding those men with 'GUTS'. The Ascription and Re-ascription of Martial Identities in India after the Uprising'. *Mutiny at the Margins. New Perspectives on the Indian Uprising of 1857. Volume 4. Military Aspects of the Indian Uprising*. 113–134. Eds. Gevin Rand and Crispin Bates. New Dehli: 2013. Cf. Maier. *African Dinosaurs*, pp. 53–54.

of the Tendaguru's colonial topography, its African *boys* and cooks were integral to the 'colonial city upon a hill'.

5.5.2 *Boys'* Two Men: Personal Servants at the Heart of the Tendaguru

The segregation of Europeans and Africans at the Tendaguru was never complete. Despite their separated allotments, the entire workforce of the Tendaguru interacted regularly in the camp near the excavation sites, just like at the labour camps at the *Central Railway* or at the *Otto* plantation. Exchange between all of the workers happened not only during daily work, but also in the evenings at *ngomas.* At such events, respectable Tendaguru preparators joined the crowd of simpler workers in their dances regularly.[88] Moreover, the self-declared 'absolute rulers' of the Tendaguru were never alone in their 'castle'. As demonstrated above, Hennig and Janensch were largely dependent on their overseers and preparators, and therefore had to cooperate with them constantly in any task related to the excavation process.

Apart from interacting with the leading excavating personnel, the German palaeontologists' 'royal household' required the constant presence of personal servants (*'boys')* and chefs. As both *boys* and chefs were generally integral to the functioning of any colonial society, the Tendaguru was no exception, of course. Although the figure of the *boy* as domestic and personal servant flares up frequently in sources and narrations written by European colonialists, historiography has not yet examined their role comprehensively.[89] In fact, Janensch's and Hennig's *boys* were integral for the functioning of the 'European sphere' of the Tendaguru as the entire excavation would have been impossible without meeting the demands of the palaeontologists' households. Having anticipated a meagre

88 Cf. UAT. 407/80, pp. 28–29.

89 There are only some passages in research about the *boys*' role in colonial history, e.g. Cf. Lindner. *Koloniale Begegnungen. Deutschland und Großbritannien als Imperialmächte in Afrika 1880–1914.* Frankfurt o.M. and New York: 2011, pp. 385, 394. Cf. Söldenwagner. *Spaces*, pp. 180–185. Cf. Gräbel, Carsten. *Die Erforschung der Kolonien. Expeditionen und koloniale Wissenskultur deutscher Geographen, 1884–1919.* Bielefeld: 2015, pp. 128–133, 143–145, 153–154, 163, 166, 181, 189, 207, 271, 285. Cf. Natermann. *Persuing Whiteness*, pp. 84–85, 98. For *boys* in the context of the colonial military cf. Michels, Stefanie. *Schwarze deutsche Kolonialsoldaten*, pp. 115, 199, 212, 224. For a very brief general overview cf. Aitken. 'Forgotten Histories', pp. 139–150. There are furthermore various pieces of African literature dealing with the figure of the *boy:* cf. Oyono, Ferdinand. *Houseboy.* Oxford: 1990. Cf. Saro-Wiwa, Ken. *Sozaboy.* Munich: 1997. For a rather European novelistic perspective, cf. Lessing, Doris. *Afrikanische Tragödie.* Frankfurt o.M.: 1989. For the general role of African agency as interpreters, clerks and other intermediaries cf. Klein. 'African Participation',

standard of living in German East Africa before arriving in the colony, right after his arrival at the Tendaguru in April 1909, Hennig was more than satisfied with his formidable provisions. He wrote to his mother:

> If I myself had expected to have to do without some things, I have now gained the impression that I will come home very spoiled in every respect: the many black waiters, who only need a hint or infinitive to provide me with every comfort and who constantly [. . .] perform work without any special order, are already indispensable to me. Also the food and drink is not only here in the base, but was already on the march a worthy continuation of life on board. [. . .] All this is so quiet, fast and without supervision that I feel like a Prince Charming.[90]

But not only was this beginning a positive surprise for Hennig: the supplies allocated and treatment given to all Europeans residing at the Tendaguru remained splendid throughout the entire expedition process. By contrast, Hennig and Janensch had some difficulties purchasing food supplies for their workers, especially in the beginnings of the third dry season in 1911, resulting from the meagre precipitation during the preceding *masika.*[91] In charge of serving the European palaeontologists at the Tendaguru were Janensch's and Hennig's personal servants – their so-called *boys* – named Ali, Wilhelm and Sefu, as well as their two chefs, whose names are not conveyed in the sources. The fact that the chefs' names are not conveyed points to a historiographical blank space: only very few works have investigated the role of personal servants such as *boys* or chefs in European colonies.

Robbie Aitken, whose minor article is the most comprehensive study on personal servants in imperial Germany, elucidates some general trends about *boys* serving in the German colonies. He observes first that the vast majority of all the colonialists' servants were male and that the personal servants' status in the colonial hierarchy was comparatively high: In general, they established and maintained a close relationship to their European employers and often served as interpreters or cultural brokers, who introduced European newcomers to the colonial society. Similar to the Tendaguru's preparators and overseers, most of the *boys* In German East Africa originated from the coastal Swahili-Arab elite. In addition, especially in the beginning of German colonial rule in the 1890s, many had often been slaves, formerly owned by an Arab or a Swahili plantation owner or trader. In comparison to plantation or railway workers, the *boys'* work was physically less demanding,

pp. 273–288. Except for Lindner's, Söldenwagner's, Natermann's and Klein's work, I owe these references to Yagmur Karakis and especially Stefanie Michels.

90 UAT. 407/2,1, pp. 99–100.

91 Cf. Maier. *African Dinosaurs,* pp. 75–77. Cf. Hennig. *Am Tendaguru,* pp. 42–43. Cf. MfN. HBSB. 5.1, pp. 131–134.

whereas their wages were relatively high. With a German industrial worker making ca. twenty-five Marks a week in 1913, a personal servant in German East Africa could make up to the equivalent of ca. five Marks a week (ca. four Rupees). A *boy* was certainly not as well paid as an *Askari* or an African cook but was many times better off than an ordinary dinosaur fossil excavator employed at the Tendaguru. Moreover, many personal servants were internationally experienced, as travelling with their European employers was simply part of their job. Their occupation often brought them not only to various other colonies, but also to European countries such as the German *Reich*. As privileged as these benefits might make them appear initially, being a personal servant of a coloniser also included several disadvantages. Although the terminology of *boy* generally reflects that they were often recruited around the very young age of sixteen, it also reveals that the colonisers intended to assign their personal servants an inferior societal status despite their relatively high economic benefits. By calling their closest employees, *boys*, Europeans living in colonial Africa expressed a feeling of paternalist superiority that included the idea of educating or rather 'civilising' their personal servants constantly. Apart from this humiliation induced by the colonisers, most African societies regarded domestic service as female labour. Being a coloniser's *boy* could therefore threaten the masculine identity of a personal servant not only in the eyes of the Europeans, but also in the view of African societies. The realities of the colonial society thus relativised the *boys'* higher societal status gained through high payment and proximity to the highest circles of a colonial society. Analysing the European settler societies in German East Africa that included *boys*, Philippa Söldenwagner is thus convinced that both the occupation as a *boy* and as a cook bore a very ambivalent character: On the one hand, experienced and competent *boys* were indeed valued for their service by their employer, often resulting in years-long employment relationship and sometimes even resulting in a relationship with a high degree of mutual trust. On the other hand, working closely with a European colonialist always entailed the danger of brutal corporal punishment and abuse for any failure or misbehaviour, no matter if 'justified' or not. Due to their centrality in a European colonial household and their intimate knowledge of their 'master's' lives, personal servants furthermore often experienced not only trust, but also mistrust from their employers. Any well-intended gesture in a *boy's* daily service could be interpreted as a cheeky attempt by the personal servant to be granted benefits such as extra pay or vacations. In German East Africa, many Europeans even feared that their personal servants might poison them, either as an act of revenge or for any other irrational reason. As a result, personal servants in German East Africa had to fear the possibility of their employer's pre-emptive strikes at any time, making their employment a precarious existence indeed.[92]

Many of these aspects of the relationship between *boys* and their European employers also apply to Janensch's and Hennig's relationship to their *boys* in service at the Tendaguru. Given the source material, which was primarily produced by Edwin Hennig, there is an imbalance in the available information about the German palaeontologists' *boys*, with it focussing on Hennig's personal servants. In any case, an analysis of Hennig's employment relationship to his *boys* alone already contributes to a better understanding of the phenomenon of labour at the Tendaguru that goes not only beyond types of manual tasks of excavations performed by the simple workers, but also beyond the skilled work of experienced overseers and fossil preparators at the Tendaguru. The tasks of the *boys* and cooks were fundamental indeed, as employing personal servants was one of the immediate priorities for Hennig when arriving in German East Africa: "[two] boys and one cook [were] the usual minimum for [one] European" in the colony, because there was "enough to do all day" in a German colonial household. Whereas the cook's task centred on food preparation such as purchasing ingredients, keeping the kitchen and its firing material ready, and the actual preparation of food, Hennig regarded his *boys* as "maid for everything".[93] The occupation of his two *boys* named Ali and Sefu was to be at Hennig's service at any time for a great variety of tasks. These ranged from serving the food, acting as a waiter during meals, sewing, laundry, housekeeping, and packing as well as unpacking all the luggage necessary for any *safari*. Moreover, Hennig's *boys* accompanied him on all his travels around the Tendaguru and German East Africa. Furthermore, they were his regular guides who assisted Hennig in one of his favourite pastimes in German East Africa: The (big) game hunt.[94]

Particularly during his first months in German East Africa, Hennig's *boy* Ali was also of incalculable benefit as a personal Swahili teacher and cultural broker

92 Aitken states much higher wages for personal servants, namely 19 Marks per week, i.e. ca. 100 Rupees per month. This is in stark contrast to the numbers provided by Söldenwagner, who reports of 15 Rupees per month. Gillman, providing for a list of items purchased in Dar es Salaam in 1905, confirms the number of 15 Rupees a month for one personal servant. I thus deem 15 Rupees/month as correct. Cf. Gillman Diaries. Mss. Afr. S. 1175/1,2_1_no. 8, pp. 61–62. Cf. Söldenwagner. *Spaces*, pp. 180–185. Cf. Aitken. 'Forgotten Histories', pp. 139–150. Cf. Gunn. *Outsourcing*, pp. 7–9. Discussing the role of women who face competition from male domestic workers cf. Coquery. *African Women*, pp. 113–115. On domestic labour in (colonial) Africa cf. Bryceson. 'Domestic Work', pp. 301–332.

93 UAT. 407/2,2, p. 406. UAT. 407/2,1, p. 199, cf., pp. 82, 93, 99–102. Cf. Paasche. '"Der Aufstand"', p. 57.

94 Cf. Hennig. *Am Tendaguru*, pp. 60–72.

in various ways.[95] As Hennig had received the offer to become part of the Tendaguru Expedition at a very short notice, the preparations for his journey and stay were hasty. Thus, Hennig's Swahili language acquisition started during his journey to East Africa on board the steamer taking him to the German colony. On this voyage, Hennig received his first Swahili language instructions from one of the East African dragomans employed at Berlin's *Seminar für Orientalische Sprachen* ('Seminar for Oriental Languages'),[96] who happened to be returning to his home on the same ship as Hennig. Of course, these Swahili classes continued in Dar es Salaam as soon as Ali (cf. Figure 8) had become Hennig's *boy*, thus enabling Hennig to orient himself quickly in German East Africa, right after his arrival to the German colony. Apart from this, Ali was generally an indispensable source of knowledge for Hennig, as the German had never set foot on the African continent or any other (German) colony before. Undoubtedly, Hennig valued the experience of his personal servant:

> Anyway, my Ali will be a good guide for me, who knows not only literally all German East Africa, but also a good part of the English colonies and has been gliding around on the small cruiser 'Bussard' for [two] years, so that even Seychelles, Madagascar or Cape Town would be nothing new to him.[97]

---

95 Cf. Connell-Szasz, Margaret (Ed.). *Between Indian and White Worlds. The Cultural Broker.* Oklahoma: 2001. Cf. Klein. 'African Participation', pp. 273–288. Cf. Lawrence et al. (Eds.). *Intermediaries, Interpreters, and Clerks.*

96 The *Seminar für Orientalische Sprachen* was the most important institute in Germany, delivering classes in foreign languages spoken in the German colonies to future colonial officials. Swahili was one of the most prominent languages taught at this institution. The employment of East Africans at the Institute in Berlin was a common occurrence, as were their travels between Germany and East Africa. Cf. Rösser, Michael. 'Nachricht von Gott? Das Gratulationstelegramm von Selim bin Abakari an Hermann von Wißmann Anlässlich seiner Hochzeit am 20.11.1894'. *(Dis-)Locating Hermann von Wissmann.* 16–25. Ed. Stefanie Michels. Düsseldorf: 2018, pp. 22–25. Cf. Bromber, Katrin. 'German Colonial Administrators, Swahili Lecturers and the Promotion of Swahili at the Seminar for Orientalische Sprachen in Berlin'. 39–54. *Sudanic Africa,* vol. 15. Sudanic Africa (2004). Web. *Jstor.* https://www.jstor.org/stable/25653412?Search=yes&resultItemClick=true&searchText=bromber&searchText=katrin&searchText=orientalische&searchUri=%2Faction%2FdoBasicSearch%3FQuery%3Dbromber%2Bkatrin%2Borientalische%26amp%3Bacc%3Doff%26amp%3Bwc%3Don%26amp%3Bfc%3Doff%26amp%3Bgroup%3Dnone&ab_segments=0%2Fbasic_SYC5152%2Fcontrol&refreqid = search%3A42e2cef246d239906a9a270efa599fdc&seq=1 (21 April 2020). Cf. Pugach, Sarah. *Africa in Translation. A History of Colonial Linguistics in Germany and Beyond, 1814–1945.* Ann Arbor: 2015, pp. 66–70, 149–150.

97 UAT. 407/2,1, p. 199, cf. p. 14. Cf. Maier. *African Dinosaurs,* p. 23.

Figure 8: “Ali”.
Source: UAT. 407/91. Nachlass Hennig (1882–1977) Fotoalbum.

Unfortunately, Hennig does not give any details about Ali’s occupation, neither regarding his work in the English colonies nor on the German steamer *Bussard*. It is therefore not clear whether Ali was occupied in menial tasks on board a steamer that was central to the global transport system of the nineteenth century,[98] or whether he had already been employed as a *boy* serving a European person on board the ship. Yet, as each *boy* had to keep a book of references listing the assessments of all European employers, it appears likely that Ali had already been working as a *boy* for a long time before coming to the Tendaguru. At least, Hennig refers to such a book of references in his self-narratives. It is thus very likely that Ali had worked as a *boy* either in British colonies or on the *Bussard* or both before meeting Hennig in Dar es Salaam in April 1909. Remarkably, with Ali’s previous employment on the *Bussard*, the *boy* must have known many more German colonies than Edwin Hennig would ever visit in his entire life. It is very likely that Ali had established precious networks within European and especially German colonial circles on board the *Bussard* before coming to the Tendaguru

98 Cf. Cole and Hart. ‘Trade, Transport and Services’, pp. 279–282. Cf. Gunn. *Outsourcing*, pp. 12, 30–31.

Expedition, where he became fundamental in enabling Edwin Hennig's palaeontological work.

In any case, the information about Ali's previous employers contained in Hennig's self-narratives seems to be correct, as a closer look at the history of the steamer *Bussard* reveals. Built in 1890 and taken out of action in late 1912, the *SMS Bussard* was one of the very few German military steamers that saw action in many colonial battles during the heyday of German colonialism: Stationed in East Asia initially, she had her first military operations in New Guinea (*Kaiser-Wilhelms-Land)* to put down an uprising of the local population in 1892. One year later, she went on to Samoa for similar reasons before she proceeded to northern China, carrying German reinforcements to support the international troops putting down the Yihetuan Movement (the so-called 'Boxer War') between 1899 and 1901. When the Maji Maji War seriously challenged the German colonial rule in East Africa between 1905 and 1908, it was again the *Bussard* that reinforced the German colonial forces with marines. On her way from East Asia to German East Africa, the *SMS Bussard* left the German colony Tsingtau (China) in April 1904, passed by Hong Kong, Sabang (Indonesia) and Colombo, as well as Mahé (Seychelles), and was stationed ashore Dar es Salaam from June 1904 onwards.[99] As the *Bussard's* route resembles Ali's CV as reported by Edwin Hennig in April 1909, there can be no doubt about Ali's qualifications as a *boy* in the environment of the 'colonial globality' around 1900. Seen through the coloniser's eyes, Ali had certainly been judged as reliable because East Africans appearing dubious to German colonial officials would have certainly never had the chance to board one of the most significant military vessels crossing the oceans from one German colony to another. Moreover, it was the well-connected and highly experienced Bernhard Sattler who conveyed the *boys* Ali and Sefu as well as the East African cooks to the German palaeontologists, Hennig and Janensch. This further supports the argument that, with Ali as his *boy*, Hennig had employed not only a very experienced but also a highly skilled man as his personal servant at the Tendaguru excavations.[100] It is therefore not very surprising that Hennig indeed highly val-

99 Cf. Buchholz, Bernhard. 'Erlebnisse des Maschinisten Otto Gehring von SMS "Bussard" während des Maji-Maji-Aufstandes in Deutsch-Ostafrika'. N.p. Ed. *Traditionsverband ehemaliger Schutz- und Überseetruppen. Freunde der früheren deutschen Schutzgebiete e.V.* Web. http://www.traditionsverband.de/download/pdf/ bussard_buchholz.pdf (21 April 2020). Cf. Paasche. '"Der Aufstand"', pp. 48–50. Cf. Fellmann, Ulrich (Ed.). *Von Schwaben in den Bismarckarchipel. Tagebücher der Missionsfrau Johanna Fellmann aus Deutsch-Neuguinea 1896–1903.* Wiesbaden: 2009, pp. 119–129. Cf. Rösser. '"Den Seegedanken zu pflegen"?'

100 Cf. UAT. 407/2,1, pp. 82, 93, 96, 108. Cf. Maier. *African Dinosaurs*, p. 23.

ued his *boys'* experience and skills and described both Sefu and particularly Ali as 'clever' and 'capable' employees.[101]

Yet, little details could trigger conflicts between Hennig and his *boys* and the German palaeontologist certainly solved them in a colonial manner. After ca. six months in service, Hennig dismissed Sefu in October 1909 because the *boy* had committed "all kinds of small, but daily incapacities and sins of omission", and hired a young Mgoni named Wilhelm, who had been educated by a French mission, who remained in Hennig's service until the very end of the palaeontologist's stay at the Tendaguru.[102] Tangible conflicts also arose between the allegedly 'irreplaceable' Ali and Hennig for minor infringements as well. On one occasion in March 1911, Hennig "boxed" Ali "on the ear" for his "idling", resulting in the *boy's* passive resistance being provoked by Hennig's violence. Hennig thus turned furious and hurried to sentence Ali for his refusal to work as soon as possible. Subsequently, he "spread out [ten] strokes [. . .] in the camp" to publicly punish this "offence against" the German palaeontologist. As Sattler, Hennig's role model for treating African employees, had dealt out twenty-five strokes even for minor offences, Hennig believed his punishment to be comparatively mild. Even more so, as Hennig had initially planned to deal out fifteen instead of ten strokes but responded to Ali's pleadings and "had [also] let [the *boy*] keep his pants on"[103] during the public corporal punishment. Although Ali declared subsequently his wish to leave his employment for good because of Hennig's abuse, the *boy* apparently remained in Hennig's service until the end of the Tendaguru Expedition. Unfortunately, there are no further details available that could shed more light on the employment relationship between Ali and Hennig in the sources under investigation.[104]

Besides illustrating general abuse against East African employees, Ali's conflict with Hennig also reveals means of resistance to colonial command at the Tendaguru. Although the *boy* would ultimately remain at the palaeontological excavation site, Ali's case shows his options for resisting colonial orders. These ranged from refusal to work to the open threat of desertion. Furthermore, Ali was indeed able to reduce Hennig's sentence by verbal opposition, which also later caused Hennig to reassess his severity of punishment, stating in his diary that he "would like to punish less"[105] in the evening after the castigation. Not only did Ali's volition influence Hennig's intentions, but also the much younger Wilhelm appears to have expressed his own desires, repeatedly. For example, Wil-

101 UAT. 407/2,1, p. 34.

102 UAT. 407/2,1, pp. 88, 198. Cf. UAT. 407/2,2, pp. 341, 380. Cf. Maier. *African Dinosaurs,* pp. 254.

103 UAT. 407/81, p. 118.

104 Cf. UAT. 407/81, pp. 118–119.

105 UAT. 407/81, p. 118.

helm wished to see Dar es Salaam and the coast, which led to Hennig even pondering whether he could take his personal servant to Germany one day: a plan not uncommon in German colonial history as many colonisers took their personal servants to the German *Reich*, especially in the first half of the formal German colonial rule in Africa. Yet the plan to take Wilhelm to Germany never materialised,[106] and for Wilhelm's case, there is hardly any more information to be found in the consulted sources.[107]

Even less information is provided about the palaeontologist's cooks. Their role is rarely made explicit in Hennig's self-narratives. Yet, Hennig's documents reveal that becoming the personal servant of a German in colonial East Africa as a chef was not necessarily a popular option, even though it offered a comparatively high salary. Having fired one of his first cooks and trying to employ a new one, Hennig initially

> wanted to have a coast boy to help the [remaining other] cook and train himself thereby as a chef. Of course, there was nobody [t]here and only one of [the] youngest people agreed to take this risk. The recruitment went something like this (shortened): "Can you cook?" "No". "But you will learn?" "No." "Well, you'll try, won't you?" "Yes." "Then you will learn." "No." "Don't you have any brains at all? "Hapana kabisa mimi ni muera [–] not in the least, I am a Muera!" We [accepted him anyway], because that kind of self-awareness was a sure-fire sign to get better. But he was right after all [. . .] because [he didn't get anywhere]. [. . .] By the way, that modest [']Civis Romanus Sum['] of the Muera is often heard, it's touching![108]

Apart from the obvious fact that the potential cook was very reluctant to become Hennig's personal servant, there are several conclusions to be drawn from this incident. Besides the Mwera's constant verbal opposition to his recruitment as a cook for Hennig, it points to other strategies of resistance to colonial command at the Tendaguru and in German East Africa in general. First of all, it shows the general tendency of many colonial populations to opt for passive resistance as soon as active or open resistance failed to show any results. Regarding the district of *Lindi,* especially the Mwera people were extremely successful in pursuing this strategy. Given their loosely organised societal structure, the German colonial administration had never been able to gain influence over one powerful Mwera chief, who would have been able to control his people for the German colonists' sake. Although maintaining a complex network with both fellow Mwera dwellings and other societies, most of the Mwera lived in autonomously ruled villages, numbering a few huts only. Hence, as soon as the colonial administration sought to

106 Cf. UAT. 407/2,1, pp. 265–266. Cf. UAT. 407/2,2, p. 380.
107 There are few photographs that show a very young man named "Wilhelm" Cf. UAT. 407/91, "Wilhelm".
108 UAT. 407/2,1, p. 198.

win power over any Mwera community, it was very easy for such a village to leave their very settlement for good and start another in an area less accessible to the colonisers. As masters of passive resistance, the Mwera soon acquired the reputation of a 'reluctant', 'incapable', and 'lazy' people in the colonial discourse; a discourse that was also endorsed by Hennig, who judged the Mwera to be not as clever as other people living in German East Africa.[109] As the Mwera cook was well aware of this colonial discourse and as he apparently did not want to become Hennig's chef at all, he drew on this very colonial discourse to fend off the disliked employment at the Tendaguru. The further he resisted the disliked employment by pretending that any Mwera was unsuited to become a cook and continued his refusal by not working properly during the actual employment, the closer this Mwera succeeded in re-establishing his freedom as a man without any closer contact to the German coloniser.

Apart from illustrating the successful means of resistance against becoming a personal servant in colonial East Africa, the excerpt from Hennig's self-narrative quoted above points to another aspect of German colonial rule in East Africa. Especially its jocular tone illustrates that the use of humour may reveal certain tacit colonial realities. Jokes and humour in historical sources of colonialism often express scenes of absurdity that reveal "moments of violence and misunderstandings" in the colonial encounter. According to Michael Pesek, such moments of absurdity in colonial encounters were a substitute for speechlessness, which resulted from insecurities of colonial rule. Accordingly, both the coloniser and the colonised experienced the realities of colonial rule in a state of crisis. In such a crisis, old established patterns of behaviour would not apply to enable the pair to reach any mutual understanding. The colonised experienced this crisis frequently as a colonial rule characterised by sudden, unjustified, or irrational outbreaks of violence on the part of the coloniser: Like in Ali's case illustrated above, minor mistakes could result in numerous *kiboko* strokes.[110] Seen in this light, the young *Mwera*'s strategy – using racist colonial stereotypes to ward off potential corporal punishment for his reluctance to become Hennig's cook – was successful indeed. In this scene, absurdity marked by humour was the right strategy to prevent colonial abuse by "creating connections without creating common ground."[111]

---

109 Cf. Aas. *Koloniale Entwicklung*, pp. 29–31, 88–96, 147–155. Cf. Maier. *African Dinosaurs*, pp. 53–54. Cf. Hennig. *Am Tendaguru*, pp. 107–116.

110 Cf. Pesek, Michael. 'Die Absurdität kolonialer Repräsentationswelten. Humor und Gewalt in Deutsch-Ostafrika, 1889–1918'. 1–13. *Academia.edu*. Web. https://www.academia.edu/3648430/Die_Absurdit%C3%A4t_kolonialer_Repr%C3%A4sentationswelten._Humor_und_Gewalt_in_Deutsch-Ostafrika_1889-1918 (23 April 2020), pp. 1–8.

111 Pesek. 'Die Absurdität', p. 8.

5.6 Labour, Command and the Daily Life of the Workers

5.6.1 Female Labour

It was not only the preparators, overseers, and Hennig's and Janesch's personal servants who made the Tendaguru Expedition one of the most successful palaeontological excavations in the world around 1900. Without up to 500 other East Africans working and living with their families at the Tendaguru camp, the whole endeavour would have been doomed to failure. In an analogy to the decisive roles of the overseers and preparators, the importance of the ordinary workers is also illustrated by the interim names given to some dinosaur fossil skeletons found at the Tendaguru. Take the skeleton of the *Wagonisaurus* as an example: The *Wagonisaurus* describes a dinosaur skeleton found just north of the Tendaguru camp on 6 September 1909. It bore the expedition's largest and heaviest cervical vertebra, but it was in a very bad state of conservation and finally had to be left behind in the East African soil. It was named after the Wangoni, who were popular workers, not only among planters in the *Lindi* district but also at the *Central Railway*. Their skill and character were also greatly appreciated by Hennig and Janensch and they were one of the three largest groups of workers at the Tendaguru. Interimly naming one of the largest skeletons found at the Tendarugu after an East African group of workers illustrates two major aspects: First of all, it shows the German palaeontologists' respect towards the Wangoni's work performance in general.[112] As far as the sources can tell, a party of Wangoni not only discovered the skeleton, but also exposed it subsequently, as Hennig noted on Sunday, 19 September 1909: "Together with Janensch we visit the mighty skeleton, which has been well worked out by the Wangonis. So far it has [ten] trunk vertebrae with outrageous ribs and [four] very adventurous and valuable cervical vertebrae."[113] Besides Hennig's and Janensch's respect towards their Wangoni workers, the epithet *Wagonisaurus* reveals secondly that the individual role of many other workers at the Tendaguru is not made explicit in the sources. This holds not only true for the many individual Wangoni workers but also for many other East Africans present at the Tendaguru: women in particular.

Besides the Wangoni, there were also Wayao, Wamuera, Wadonde and Wamakwa, working and living at the Tendaguru. With the sources reporting a maximum of 500 workers, it must be stressed that the wives and families of most of the

---

112 Cf. UAT. 407/80, pp. 28, 89–90. Cf. UAT. 407/81, pp. 11, 87, 135. Cf. Ohl and Stoecker. 'Taxonomien', p. 237.
113 UAT. 407/80, p. 68.

male workers accompanied their husbands to the palaeontological excavations. This leads to an overall number of almost 800–900 people living in the camps at the Tendaguru. That implies that more than one-third of the people present at the camp were either children or women, making them a substantial part of the entire endeavour. Yet, it is difficult to assess the role of women and children regarding labour at the Tendaguru as they appear only scarcely in both Edwin Hennig's diary and in the files held in Berlin's Museum of Natural History. Yet, these sources suggest that just as Hennig and Janensch relied on their *boys* and cooks to maintain their households, the work capacities of the Tendaguru's male workers largely depended on the work of their wives and the other women present at the palaeontological excavation site. Although general research about female labour in (East) Africa has shown that women's work was not necessarily limited to the domestic sphere, but also included, for example, being a *chief,* a railway or road construction worker, as well as being a (petty-) trader,[114] the sources consulted for the Tendaguru suggest that the women and children were primarily occupied with tasks generally referred to as 'reproductive labour'. 'Reproductive labour' means that the work of the women sustained the working capabilities of their men by arranging anything necessary to enable the male's absence from home and his presence at work. It included predominantly childcare, food preparation and the collection of firewood. Of course, meals were generally eaten together in the camp in the evening after work but often, women or children delivered meals to the excavation ditches during work: This enabled the male workers to have their food during shorter breaks and prevented them from leaving the actual workplace to eat. Apart from the preparation and delivery of food for members of their own households, women at the Tendaguru also had other tasks fundamental to the overall expedition: The major task of women and children at the Tendaguru was to ensure sufficient water supply (cf. Figure 9). Water was crucial for the entire expedition in general, but especially because wells were scarce around the Tendaguru hill. Despite the problem of discovering water sources as such, most of the wells were not

114 Cf. Coquery. *African Women,* pp. 9–20, 32–33, 34–44. For the role of women at the Central railway in German East Africa cf. Chapter 3. Cf. Koponen. *People and Production,* pp. 268–333. For the role of women during WWI in German East Africa cf. Vokalavene, Yovita. *The Role of African Women in the First World War (1914–1918) in German East Africa.* Dissertation project at the University of Göttingen. Web. https://www.uni-goettingen.de/en/promotionen/561451.html (28 April 2020). For the history of women in southwest Tanzania, where also the Wangoni workers came from cf. Kinunda, Nives. *Negotiating Women's Labour: Women Farmers, State, and Society in the Southern Highlands of Tanzania, 1885–2000.* Unpublished Dissertation submitted at the University of Göttingen: August 2017. Web. https://ediss.uni-goettingen.de/bitstream/handle/11858/00-1735-0000-002E-E57A-9/Nives%20PhD2.pdf?sequence=1 (28 April 2020), pp. 112–115, 175–178, 278–286.

rich and some dried up during the dry season. In this case, women and children had to walk up to an hour to fill their vessels with the precious commodity before they could return to the camp again, needing another hour to come back. When precipitation was exceptionally low, a few trips a day to the wells were not enough. Instead, children and women had to walk day and night to the sources to haul water in order to guarantee the Tendaguru Expedition's constant water supply. Not only human beings were affected by the water scarcity, but wild animals also often frequented the few watering places and posed a threat to the water deliverers. On one occasion, a female water carrier was (almost) attacked by a lion when on her way to the water source, further illustrating the difficulties of maintaining a decent water supply to the Tendaguru and thus, the importance of female labour there.[115]

It seems that there were no women involved in any excavation work at the Tendaguru. This contrasts with the situations at the *Central Railway*, where women also performed several menial tasks of railroad construction and at the *Otto* plantation, where women were also part of the 'living machine'. Moreover, the archival sources do not report of any women working as sex workers or beer brewers at the Tedaguru Expedition, whereas there are reports of women working in these roles at the construction sites of the *Central Railway* and at *Otto's* plantation in Kilossa. Yet, as *pombe* (locally brewed beer) was central to *ngomas* (feasts), which also occurred at the Tendaguru camp, it is very likely that women were involved in the production and sale of alcoholic beverages at the Tendaguru as well.[116] Hence, female work seems to have been (largely) exempt of any wage labour at the palaeontological excavation site at the Tendaguru. This is, of course, in stark contrast to male labour, which was characterised by relatively constant wage payments and comparatively regular working hours.

5.6.2 Male Workers at the Tendaguru: The Popularity of Excavation Works

In contrast to the women at the Tendaguru, male workers were almost exclusively occupied with tasks either directly related to palaeontological excavation work or the subsequent transportation of the fossils to Lindi. They either dug for bones in the soil, or packed the fossils ready for transport, or carried them to the

115 Cf. Maier. *African Dinosaurs*, pp. 32, 38, 63, 79. Cf. Hennig. *Am Tendaguru*, pp. 37–39, 43, 61–62, 66–68, 111, 116, 127, 144. Cf. UAT. 407/80, pp. 10, 12, 51. Cf. UAT. 407/81, p. 35. Cf. UAT. 407/82, p. 30. Cf. UAT. 407/2,2, pp. 359–361, 369, 380, 408, 422, 496. Cf. MfN. HBSB. 10.4, pp. 133–134. There are also a few visual sources displaying female water carriers. Cf. UAT. 407/91, "Wasserholerinnen". Cf. MfN. HBSB. (1694), (421), (193), "Frauen mit Wassertöpfen".
116 Cf. UAT. 407/80, pp. 28–29. Cf. UAT. 407/2,2, pp. 389–390. Cf. UAT. 407/2,1, p. 87.

Figure 9: Female water carriers.
Source: UAT. 407/91.

coast for shipment to Europe. What regulated the labour of these men most was nature: For any working task, the most intense activity took place in the dry season, whereas activity regressed to a minimum in the rainy season. During *masika*, only the most important tasks like conservation and general surveillance of the area under excavation were carried out. This seasonal fluctuation was also reflected in the number of male workers employed at the Tendaguru Expedition in the year 1909: “Sixty local men had been engaged by April 23. [. . .] This grew to 70 and 80 in the [following] two months. [. . .] At the height of the season [in July], the Expedition employed 420 men. The number fell to 230 in November, to 200 at the start of December and to 170 in the course of [the same] month."[117] Ultimately, there remained only a few dozen people under superintendent Boheti when Hennig and Janensch were absent for several weeks between New Year and the end of April 1910, during *masika*. The maximum number of 500 male workers was only reached in the third year, when the entire area in which excavations were carried out spanned over ca. thirty km^2. Overall, the numbers given reflect only the general trends of seasonal fluctuations. In fact, the number of workers was neither rising nor falling constantly, but the number of workers employed fluctuated frequently. These minor swings were the result of various reasons: Sometimes, workers wanted to leave the Tendaguru to farm the fields in their home villages or had other reasons for requesting holidays. Occasionally, Janensch and Hennig also fired workers for varying reasons, mostly related to alleged lack of work discipline. Sometimes, the German palaeontologists were not sure if there were enough funds left in Berlin to pay a larger workforce, and thus refrained from hiring any new ones. This was especially the case in the third and final excavation season in 1911, when Hennig and Janensch refrained from (re-)hiring workers as they feared insufficient monetary supplies.[118]

In any case, it must be stressed that most of the funds collected for the Tendaguru Expedition were spent on the workers' wages. In total

> the expedition [. . .] spent 183,607.45 marks [between 1909 and 1911], of which 127,325.70 had been donated by private individuals. [. . .] Wages for the indispensable Africans, though cheap by European standards, amounted to almost 90,000 marks, or almost 50 percent of all the funds received.[119]

Remarkably, the wages paid at the Tendaguru for simple excavators were not only low, compared to European standards, but also compared to the wages paid at plantations or at the *Central Railway* in German East Africa: Hennig and Janensch themselves received ca. 266 Rupees (ca. 355 Marks) a month, whereas personal servants like their *boys* could make up to ca. fourteen Rupees a month (ca. nineteen Marks). A Tendaguru overseer or preparator received ten to eleven Rupees a month (ca. fifteen Marks), whereas one of Janensch's and Hennig's simple workers received nine Rupees a month only (ca. twelve Marks). In fact, of these nine Rupees, only five Rupees were the actual wage, whereas the other four Rupees were so-called *posho*, the food allowance. The *posho* of four rupees was paid

117 Maier. *African Dinosaurs*, pp. 27, 60.

118 Cf. Maier. *African Dinosaurs*, pp. 54–56. Cf. Hennig. *Am Tendaguru*, pp. 49, 93–94. Cf. MfN. HBSB. 5.1, pp. 18, 25, 40, 55, 60, 64–66, 74, 86–87, 91–93, 104–108, 129, 137, 184, 192, 201–205.

119 Maier. *African Dinosaurs*, p. 84, cf. pp. 49, 81, 84–85. Cf. Stoecker. 'Über Spenden', pp. 87–91. Cf. Hennig. *Am Tendaguru*, p. 8. Cf. MfN. HBSB. 5.1, p. 10.

in installments once a week. That means each worker received one Rupee to buy himself food for his daily meals every seven days.[120]

In fact, these comparatively low wages paid at the Tendaguru were not undisputed, and newly arriving workers attempted to raise them repeatedly. In the first place, the workers' striving to negotiate their working conditions is reflected in the names they had given to themselves such as "work to eat", "mind to talk", "three o'clock", "bad work" or "lion". All of these names indicate either their preference for their working hours, the reason why they actually took up an employment, or their staunch mind to fight for decent wages.[121] Secondly, especially those workers who had migrated to the Tendaguru from faraway places like the 700 km distant Lake *Nyassa*, "enquired about the salary and sought to raise them every time", before they finally decided to take up work at the palaeontological excavations. Moreover, they "did not want to commit themselves for a certain period of time, but wanted to be sure that the right of both parties to terminate the contract would be safeguarded."[122] Their insistence on the freedom of their working contracts allowed the workers to leave the Tendaguru either if the working conditions did not please them or if they just wanted to leave the work place, return to their villages or have a rest. Remarkably, the wages paid for workers performing simple tasks at the Tendaguru Expedition were not attractive compared to the wages paid by larger plantations in the *Lindi* district, which were not very far from the Tendaguru. These plantations, which were almost exclusively located along the coast, were only about 100 km away from the Tendaguru, and paid between twelve and thirteen Rupees a month for a male plantation worker between 1900 and 1907. Later, the amount rose slowly between 1907 and 1914.[123] Yet, despite this pay-gap between *Lindi*'s coastal plantations and the Tendaguru Expedition and the fact that the daily costs of living were somewhat higher along the coast than in the hinterland, it is still striking that this pay-gap was not reflected in the labour supply at the Tendaguru at all. Quite the contrary: Hennig and Janensch witnessed very reliable labour supply during their entire stay in German East Africa.

Whereas East Africans living in the catchment areas of the Moravian Mission tended to leave work that was provided by the missionary stations, immediately as soon as railway construction sites offered better pay (cf. Chapter 3), the work-

120 Cf. Hennig. *Am Tendaguru*, p. 41. Cf. UAT. 407/2,1, p. 152. Cf. MfN. HBSB. 10.4, pp. 124–125. Cf. MfN. HBSB. Tendaguru Expedition 6.7. Finanzierung (Löhne und Gehälter). Cf. MfN. HBSB. Tendaguru Expedition 6.2. Finanzierung. Cf. Maier. *African Dinosaurs*, p. 33. Cf. Söldenwagner. *Spaces*, pp. 180–183. Cf. Gillman Diaries. Mss. Afr. S. 1175/1,2_1_no. 8, pp. 61–62.
121 UAT. 407/2,1, p. 167.
122 UAT. 407/2,2, pp. 337–338.
123 Cf. Aas. *Koloniale Entwicklung*, pp. 141–147, 222–226. Cf. Maier. *African Dinosaurs*, p. 33.

ers at the Tendaguru remained at the palaeontological excavations despite the fact that payment remained very low throughout the entire excavation process. Overall, neither the published nor the archival sources report any shortage of labour at the Tendaguru at any time. This is a remarkable fact that scarcely ever occurred at any other colonial endeavour in German East Africa. Normally, any colonial enterprise in German East Africa would complain about labour scarcity every now and then and would consequently request the colonial administration to send the local population to work even by force, if necessary. This was also the case for the district of *Lindi*, where the planters even demanded that pressure be placed on starving people to work during the Maji Maji War, and repeatedly pressured the colonial administration to urge the local populations to work in times of peace (cf. above). By contrast, the German palaeontologists hardly ever experienced such labour scarcity, which would have threatened the Tendaguru Expedition's success. At the beginning of the Tendaguru Expedition, its excellent labour supply was not very surprising. It started in a well-organised manner and with the right people in charge of labour recruitment. The first sixty workers starting at the Tendaguru in April 1909 were initially recruited by Bernhard Sattler, who had known them for a relatively long time. They were not only able-bodied men, but they had also been trained as miners by the prospector Sattler himself and were therefore the perfect people to receive further education as fossil excavators by Hennig and Janensch. With Sattler, and later also *DOAG's* Besser, sharing the responsibilities with Janensch and Hennig in the first weeks of setting up the Tendaguru Expedition, language barriers between the Germans and the East Africans could therefore be avoided. This helped to establish a work environment that bore the potential of mutual understanding in this first instance. Secondly, with Sattler refraining from exerting excessive violence against his workers, he set the standards for Hennig and Janensch, reminding them that excessive use of force was counterproductive to ever becoming and remaining successful colonial employers. Generally, excesses of violence at any endeavour in German East Africa would ultimately lead to the most widespread means of African resistance to unpopular employments: namely, desertion from the workplace, which often threatened an employer's entire economic existence.[124]

The catchment area of the Tenaguru workers expanded constantly in the course of the excavation. In the beginnings of the expedition, besides those workers initially provided by Sattler, the people living in the surrounding areas of the Tendaguru would be the first to become fossil excavators. As far as the sources

---

124 Cf. UAT. 407/2,1, pp. 99–104, 108–109, 120–121, 126, 132, 140–141, 193, 238. Cf. Maier. *African Dinosaurs*, pp. 11, 19–20, 24, 27, 28, 36. Cf. UAT. 407/80, pp. 6, 8, 9, 10, 11, 38–39, 87.

can tell, these people living close to the Tendagauru did not avoid the palaeontological work but joined the excavations quickly. With them taking up work at the Tendaguru steadily, the excavating equipment available soon failed to keep up with the ever-rising number of workers. In May 1909, Hennig noted: "as soon as we have more tools, we will be happy to hire more." Strikingly, Hennig noted further: "There is certainly no lack of supply, almost daily we have to turn away more job seekers."[125] In the following month, the job hunters arrived at the Tendaguru from even more faraway places, and Hennig and Janensch initially had to refrain from employing these migratory workers too. In June 1909, Hennig noted:

> [five] Wayaos want[ed] work on the grounds that they have marched a full month for this purpose. When I asked them who had sent them, I was told that they had 'only heard about it'. Unfortunately, we had already hired 17 men and rejected 15 more. Our work seems to be very popular indeed.[126]

Given the ostensible popularity of Tendaguru's palaeontological work, resuming the excavations in the second season in April 1910 went smoothly. Hennig could not only count on the returning workers, he also had to send some of the newly arriving migratory workers away yet again, because he expected further "Wayao and Wangoni" to arrive soon. This time, workers even came as far as from 700 km distant Lake *Nyassa* to find employment at the Tendaguru between April and July 1910.[127] Whereas many European settlers, particularly in the north of German East Africa, generally suffered from insufficient labour supplies at this time, and were happy if only one-third of the demanded workforce would appear at their workplace in the morning, absenteeism at the excavation ditches at the Tendaguru almost did not occur at all. According to Hennig, the "discipline at Tendaguru would be the envy of the northern planters."[128] Having investigated the Tendaguru Expedition, the historian Gerhard Maier is of the very same opinion. Maier even claims that cutting wages or dismissing workers because of poor work performance or unauthorised absenteeism was "the most serious punishment" for the workers at the Tendaguru.

---

125 UAT. 407/2,1, p. 109, cf. pp. 99–104, 108–109, 120–121, 126, 132, 140–141, 193, 238. Cf. Maier. *African Dinosaurs*, pp. 11, 19–20, 24, 27, 28, 36. Cf. UAT. 407/80, pp. 6, 8, 9, 10, 11, 38–39, 87.
126 UAT. 407/80, pp. 33–34, cf. pp. 6, 8, 9, 10, 11, 38–39, 87. UAT. 407/2,1, p. 109, cf. pp. 99–104, 108–109, 120–121, 126, 132, 140–141, 193, 238. Cf. Maier. *African Dinosaurs*, pp. 11, 19–20, 24, 27, 28, 36.
127 UAT. 407/81, p. 5, cf. pp. 2, 5, 9, 30. Cf. UAT. 407/2,2, pp. 312, 325, 332–337, 348, 359. Cf. Maier. *African Dinosaurs*, pp. 54, 56.
128 UAT. 407/2,2, p. 367. Cf. Hennig. *Am Tendaguru*, p. 41.

Moreover, Maier even goes on to say that the "interaction between Europeans and Africans appears to have generally been positive."[129]

This is almost a singular finding compared to the vast majority of reliable studies investigating colonial labour regimes not only in German East Africa, but also in other colonies. Generally, colonial labour regimes were often characterised by force and abuse of workers. Thus, the 'positive interaction' between the European coloniser and the East African colonised at the Tendaguru turns the so-called 'labour question' in German East Africa upside down. Instead of the perpetuated discourses about the alleged African 'work-shyness', general labour scarcity and forced labour policies in German East Africa,[130] Hennig was convinced that the workers were not primarily concerned about the wages paid at the Tendaguru and did not need to be coerced through the imposition of colonial taxes. Instead, their motivations were simple – a desire for consumer goods such as clothing, for example – and they arrived out of their own initiative. It can thus be seen why Hennig also rejected the image of the 'lazy African' repeatedly in his self-narratives. He really believed that the African workers "were easy to treat and willing – just as willing as any European is at work."[131] As if this was not enough, the German palaeontologist went even further:

> As a former student, I know how to appreciate the precious freedom of choice about whether to work or not. And apart from the students, only one person has this freedom at his disposal: someone who sits on his own land. This little subjugated people [in German East Africa] is 1,000 times freer than our proletariat of world power. If only we would not rob them of their marvellous property with our rule! All the serenity of his being is rooted in this independence! Someone in our region really no longer needs to 'educate the Negro'; their already awakened need for clothes, perhaps even the old one for conviviality, leads them to the European.[132]

Moreover, Hennig also stated repeatedly his impression that the workers also came to the palaeontological excavations site because of their genuine interest in the work at the Tendaguru. The palaeontologist appreciated the workers' interest in his subject and its significance as an almost singular event. Compared to European societies where Hennig had "always sensed a certain resistance" and "a certain sluggishness in getting into" the scientific details of palaeontology and geology, he sensed that a palaeontologist could "only wish to always deal with such an audience" with profound interest in scientific questions as he had met in German East

129 Maier. *African Dinosaurs*, pp. 34, 49.

130 Cf. Conrad. *Globalisation*, pp. 77–143. Cf. Sippel. '"Wie erzieht man"', pp. 311–333. Cf. Koponen. *Development*, pp. 321–440.

131 UAT. 407/2,1, p. 121, cf. pp. 109–111, 120–121, 250.

132 UAT. 407/2,2, p. 419, cf. 361. Cf. UAT. 407/2,1, p. 164.

Africa and not only with mere demand for entertainment as he was used to in Germany.[133] Certainly, without the skill, interest and understanding of the Tendaguru's workers, overseers and preparators, the entire endeavour would not have been successful at all. Yet, Hennig's picture of colonial labour is certainly far too rosy and bears a good deal of his romanticising about life in the German colony. This is especially evident when he compares colonial labour relationships to the life of a European student. In the end, the truth is found somewhere in between the perpetuated discourses and Hennig's views. To generate a more nuanced picture of labour at the Tendaguru, a closer look into the sources is thus required.

The actual tasks of labour at the Tendaguru excavations were manifold and shuffled amongst the workforce, depending on the urgency of the task. Whereas, water carriers were predominantly female, the sources suggest that there were also occasionally men who were assigned to the task. Undoubtedly, the most important task for male workers at the Tendaguru was digging the soil with spades, shovels, pickaxes and hoes to expose the petrified dinosaur fossils slumbering in the ground. This comparatively simple but physically demanding work then gave way to more complex tasks. Depending on the size of the dinosaur skeleton under excavation and its depth in the soil, the initial ditches and trenches could develop into proverbial excavation pits. These pits could be as deep as ten meters and therefore required reinforcements made from wood to prevent the walls from collapsing. At quarry 'S', a fully encompassing retaining wall had to be built from wood, as Hennig and Janensch feared the walls' slippage. Both the construction materials, primarily, bamboo and rope, and the design of the reinforcing walls were based on East African techniques of house construction. Hence, Hennig and Janensch relied on the collective expertise of their workers once again. After the actual excavations, the two German palaeontologists had to train their workforce in several skills before the East African staff could work independently. As soon as the fossils were exposed, plaster casts were made before the petrified bones were ready to be ultimately removed from their find location. As a considerable number of bones were porous and their future transport required a certain amount of stability, measures of conservation had to be applied to any find. Rubber lotions were applied to bridge cracks and to make the fossils resistant to shocks. As there was no plaster available in German East Africa and imports from Europe soon proved either very costly or defective, Hennig and Janensch used East Africa's rich resource of red clay as a substitute for plaster casts. Apart from this fusion of European and African fossil conservation techniques, transporting the dinosaur bones required additional ingenuity. Already in the beginnings of

133 UAT. 407/2,2, p. 361, UAT. 407/2,1, p. 165.

the expedition, Berlin's Museum of Natural History had contacted the railway constructing company *Philipp Holzmann* to enquire whether it was worth considering using modern lorries to transport tons of bones from the Tendaguru to Lindi's port on the coast. Ultimately, the answer was negative: *Holzman's* trial using lorries to transport the materials needed for railway construction had failed, as the early motor vehicles had survived neither the East African climate nor its road conditions. As the sleeping sickness regularly killed any beast of burden in the colony, transport by mules, donkeys, oxen or horses was impossible as well. Hence, human porterage remained the only possible means of transportation.[134]

This form of transportation impacted the realities of transport profoundly. As one human porter was only able to carry ca. thirty kg over a long period, big bones either had to be cut into pieces or attached to wooden bars so that a party of up to twenty-five men could carry the load together by grasping the bars or lifting them onto their shoulders. If this was not enough to protect the sensitive fossils from damage, each piece was wrapped in a bamboo cask that was padded inside with dry grass. Caravans of several dozen porters would then transport their loads to the district capital of Lindi within two to three days and unload their cargo there. In Lindi, the casks were packed into crates made from imported Scandinavian lumber and manufactured by East African pupils at the governmental crafts school run by the German colonial administration in Lindi. Except for constructing and packing the shipping crates, each work step had to be carried out at the Tendaguru and performed by the East African workforce employed there. Except for porterage, which was physically hard enough, all other tasks required a high amount of local knowledge, diligence and craftsmanship. Initially instructed by Hennig and Janensch, it was the East African preparators and overseers led by Boheti who taught the rest of the workforce how to accomplish these tasks. Furthermore, the overseers and preparators would also delegate these complex tasks to the workers of the Tendaguru Expedition as part of the daily work routine.[135]

5.6.3 Work Routine at the Tendaguru

The general work rhythm was divided into a rainy and a dry season. During the dry season, the most active work period, work started at sunrise between five

134 Cf. Hennig. *Am Tendaguru,* pp. 23–29, 31, 34–40, 44–46, 49, 52, 54–56, 92–93. Cf. Maier. *African Dinosaurs,* pp. 27, 30–32, 42–44, 77, 83, 89–98. Cf. Vennen. 'Arbeitsbilder', pp. 56–75. Cf. MfN. HBSB. 1.3, "Schreiben von Gwinner, Berlin, den 15. February 1909."

135 Cf. Hennig. *Am Tendaguru,* pp. 23–29, 31, 34–40, 44–46, 49, 52, 54–56, 92–93. Cf. Maier. *African Dinosaurs,* pp. 27, 30–32, 42–44, 77, 83, 89–98. Cf. Vennen. 'Arbeitsbilder', pp. 56–75.

and six o' clock in the morning. It then lasted until two o'clock in the afternoon without break. The workers assembled for the morning roll call in the camp, where they were allotted into groups of ten to twenty-five men for each overseer responsible for one excavation ditch. After this routine, they would leave the camp for work at the trenches and return to the camp in the afternoon. Generally, there were six days of labour per week, with Sundays being the only day off. Like at Gillman's railway camp, exceptions were sometimes made: for example if time pressured, the palaeontologists called for work on an exceptionally bright Sunday only a few weeks ahead of *masika*. In contrast to railway or plantation labour, at Tendaguru, a workday totalling eight uninterrupted hours was preferred to the alternative of piecework for one major reason: the special nature of palaeontological work. Although "the unusual work with hoe and shovel [. . .] was certainly no less physically demanding than the various types of work on the plantations", excavating at the Tendaguru required "quality work" from all the preparators, overseers and 'simple workers'. The "work of searching required constant attention even to the smallest piece of bone" and thus a certain amount of skill and concentration – which also made it rather inherently satisfying, compared to other colonial occupations. This unusual level of care was just as necessary for the subsequent exposure, removal, shock-resistant packaging and final transportation of the fossils. Moreover, as the excavations soon spread over several square kilometres, the workers would have needed over an hour to reach their allotted ditch and therefore up to two hours would have been wasted if the workers returned to the camp for lunch.[136] As this quality work in the tropical East African climate required constant concentration, Hennig tolerated some minutes of rest or a short lunch break at the ditch. If the German palaeontologist judged the output insufficient, however, he would demand either some extra hours until four o'clock or until the evening of the same day. Sometimes, Hennig also used the free Sundays to make up for any omissions. Given this overall quite gruelling work routine, I, thus, would not entirely concur with Gerhard Maier's opinion that "work discipline was rarely harsh"[137] at the Tendaguru, although Hennig's views on colonialism might have been more nuanced than those of most of his contemporaries.

Yet, analysing Hennig's self-narratives, one is initially puzzled not only by his general appreciation of his workers' performance – something that is only rarely expressed in any source produced in a colonial context – but also by Hennig's criticism of European culture and German colonialism. For instance, in a letter to

---

136 Hennig. *Am Tendaguru*, pp. 38–39, cf. p. 40. UAT. 407/2,2, p. 341. Cf. UAT. 407/2,1, pp. 150–152, 184. Cf. UAT. 407/80, p. 117.

137 Maier. *African Dinosaurs*, p. 34.

his mother in August 1910, Hennig compared the Tendaguru's formidable labour supply and the workers' performance to those he had heard of in German East Africa's northern districts:

> Admittedly, it's easy for us to say: our funds are plentiful and they don't go to our own coffers. We can certainly [. . .] turn a blind eye to all of that. But the planter who struggles for his existence [. . .] must be more buttoned up. And anyone who, like most, sits on corporate plantations, has to earn the sum that is dictated to him, if not from the soil, then from the workers: the shareholders want their dividends. That is the terrible slavery we bring to the country in place of its latent, often hardly recognizable serfdom, which is to be abolished eagerly by all possible "humane" associations and personalities and is carried on by the states as a cultural mission of the first order. The fact that such slavery in our industry is often far more intolerable at home is a dismal consolation.[138]

This lament echoes Hennig's statement on the occasion of the inauguration ceremony of the Wissmann Statue right after his arrival to Dar es Salaam, when he had described German colonialists literally as the 'oppressor'. These views of the palaeontologist are often to be found in his self-narratives, raising questions about Hennig's and Janensch's roles as colonisers, and their views on German colonialism in general. As already demonstrated for the overseers, preparators and personal servants working at the Tendaguru, typical characteristics of German colonial rule in East Africa also applied there, despite the palaeontologists' generally positive appraisals of the work of their East African employees. Regarding the ordinary workforce, Hennig's deeds speak louder than his words as far as the treatment of his workers is concerned.

Undoubtedly, Hennig and Janensch valued not only the work of the preparators, overseers and personal servants, but also that of the workers performing either simpler tasks or having fewer responsibilities. Certainly, the palaeontologists' views on the impact of European colonialism in Africa might have been more nuanced than those of numerous other contemporary colonial diehards. Yet, just as for the East African *boys*, preparators and overseers, the simple workers at the Tendaguru were also subject to the realities of colonial command at the excavation sites. This is certainly reflected in the daily work routine: The workforce's labour rarely actually stopped at the end of eight hours of excavation work. To prepare their dinner after work in the camp, they first needed to collect firewood or water and sometimes needed to repair their huts, if it seemed necessary. This extra workload for so-called 'reproductive labour' after eight hard hours of hard physical work in the excavation ditches was unavoidable, especially for single men who had come to the Tendaguru without their wives or children, or if they could not afford

138 UAT. 407/2,2, pp. 366–367.

the services of a *boy*. Given the case that some men lived relatively close by to the Tendaguru, they would commute from their home village to the Tendaguru every day, walking several hours in the afternoon to finally reach their homes at night. Of course, they then had to get up in the middle of the night to reach the Tendaguru by sunrise again. If they failed to be on time and could not produce a proper excuse, they were fired, had their wages cut or they were "whacked either 15" strokes, had to work on "Sunday", "or both".[139] The same applied to any other forms of absenteeism, and ill men were generally also expected to come to the morning roll call to report sick. Fifteen *kiboko* strokes or face slaps, dismissal, wage cuts or a combination of all these punishments were also applied for offences that appeared to challenge either work discipline or the order of the camp. Besides absenteeism, for Hennig, such offences included gambling, slowdowns at work or porterage, theft, sexual affairs with fellow workers that led to scenes of jealousy within the workers' camp, or 'disrespectful behaviour' against the German palaeontologists.[140]

Despite the fact that a large number of workers migrated to the Tendaguru seeking work on their own initiative, Hennig and Janensch also relied on the whole arsenal of German colonial command in East Africa, if necessary, for their sufficient labour supply.

5.6.4 Policies of Labour Recruitment at the Tendaguru

Although the labour supply was generally good at the Tendaguru, Hennig and Janensch sometimes relied on their more experienced workers to recruit additional workers for them. As was also done at any other colonial enterprise, the employer – here, the German palaeontologists – would ask one or a few of its longer serving employees to act as quasi-labour recruiters when returning to his or their homes during *masika*, or during other days free of work. Back in the home village, they would ask their fellow villagers to follow them to their employment. Of course, this form of labour recruitment could have many varying facets. Successful recruitment could certainly occur, when the experienced African worker had really been satisfied with his employment and would, therefore, persuade some people to follow him. But in reality, this form of recruitment had also many gateways for abuse. This abuse ranged from making false promises about labour conditions or payment at the employment, up to the open threat or use of physical

139 UAT. 407/2,2, p. 368, cf. p. 341.

140 Cf. UAT. 407/2,1, pp. 150–152, 184. Cf. UAT. 407/80, pp. 24, 51, 72. Cf. UAT. 407/81, pp. 28, 71. Cf. Hennig. *Am Tendaguru*, pp. 38–40.

violence to force others to leave home for a distant place of work. Many of these aspects also occurred in the process of labour recruitment for the Tendaguru. Even though the labour supply was generally not a big challenge for Hennig and Janensch, it was sometimes not enough to simply wait for new workers to pour into the camp at the Tendaguru. Once, Hennig ordered two of his experienced overseers to recruit new men from as far away as neighbouring Mozambique. Returning only with thirteen men from the neighbouring colony, the two experienced Tendaguru men were not very successful on this occasion. But as new workers had arrived at the excavations, on their own, in the meantime, no labour scarcity ultimately occurred in this instance.[141]

Yet, if time was a pressure and people were needed urgently, like in November 1909, Hennig was ready to change his tunes and use the means, typical for many colonial employers. When a local *Jumbe* rejected Hennig's call for the provision of porters, the "vigorous and industrious overseer Mohammadi commandeered" a sufficient number of men: "By being on his feet from Sunday afternoon 4 o'clock until Monday morning at 9 o'clock; he walked through the villages, knocked on every house, woke the sleeping people with the friendly invitation: 'haia Safari!' and sent them to the camp at night."[142] It is not entirely clear what Hennig means by 'Mohammadi's friendly invitation', but reading between the lines and behind Hennig's euphemistic expression 'friendly invitation', it seems that the overseers of the Tendaguru were entitled to exert force, if necessary. On a similar occasion in March 1910, when the palaeontologist was working close to the *Central Railway*, Hennig is more explicit when stating that his *boy* "Ali and one man [went] out to commandeer porters, i.e., seize them while working in the[ir] field, do not even give them time to say goodbye to the woman, [and] do not even find the slightest resistance."[143] But since this sort of thing was an ordinary occurrence in German East Africa, Hennig did not feel disturbed by this forceful recruitment. To him, it was just normal, as shown when he observed the following scenes of labour recruitment:

> An Askari has an order from the district office to gather 60 men for certain Jumbes, and can only fulfil this order by roaming the villages at night, and since all the people flee into the Pori [bush], warned by the children's guards, dragging the women with them; the next morning the Jumbe is allowed to pick up his better half [here: his wife] at the [governmental] station – against the obligation to register [for work]![144]

141 Cf. UAT. 407/2,2, pp. 312–313, 348. Cf. MfN. HBSB. 5.1, p. 177.
142 UAT. 407/80, p. 91.
143 UAT. 407/80, p. 148.
144 UAT. 407/80, p. 148.

As long as this was the reality in German East Africa, Hennig was satisfied that "[t]he social tone [was] a bit rough" and this meant that he and his men would not "attract attention when [they] 'search[ed]' for carriers by force"[145] themselves. Apart from using physical means of labour recruitment on their part, Hennig and Janensch could also always count on the German colonial administration if anything threatened the excavation process at the Tendaguru hill. In this respect, especially the district office in *Lindi*, with its District Officer Wendt, played a crucial role. Whenever the palaeontologists needed any assistance, the district office exerted their power to provide the necessary logistics through forced labour, including finding porters to carry dinosaur fossils from the Tendaguru to the coast. In September 1910, Hennig even requested District Officer Wendt to build a new road from the Tendaguru to the coast, as many heavy loads of dinosaur fossils were too big to be carried on the existing narrow foot paths. In response to this request, the district office of *Lindi* did not hesitate one second. To acquire the labour needed to build this new road, the representatives of the colonial administration went to several villages in the region, whose populations were then forced to construct the new infrastructure, sustaining the future transportation of huge loads of dinosaur fossils.[146]

Particularly, this incident regarding road construction reveals how deeply Hennig and Janensch were embedded in colonial hierarchies and mechanisms of colonial command. However, the incident also points to the comparative benevolence of the Tendaguru Expedition as a colonial employer. In a letter to his mother, Hennig wrote about his experiences at the road constructions:

> I slept one night down at the Noto [. . .] to visit the works and to dismiss the Liwali, the highest black official, who was in charge of the works. It was a little difficult for me to preserve the dignity of the Reich when he told me that the people were running away from him despite his beatings and imprisonment, because they had to do the work for free and I must confess that I would have been angry as well. To compensate them [the workers] I shot a berappi [. . .].[147]

Compensating the unpaid quasi-tributary labour for road construction with the provision of berappi meat, Hennig attempted to make amends for the local population's forced labour with the Tendaguru Expedition on his own accord. At the same time however, this 'compensation' appears to have been primarily symbolic as Hennig himself and his palaeontological team were the real reason why District Officer Wendt recalled the populations of the *Lindi* district for unpaid forced

145 UAT. 407/80, p. 148. Cf. UAT. 407/81, p. 106.
146 Cf. UAT. 407/80, p. 81. Cf. UAT. 407/81, p. 37. Cf. UAT. 407/82, pp. 3, 26. Cf. UAT. 407/2,1, pp. 193–194. Cf. UAT. 407/2,2, pp. 356–366, 374–375, 413–414, 494, 496.
147 UAT. 407/2,2, p. 375.

road construction work, which was accompanied by physical violence exerted by the *Liwali*. Moreover, this incident shows how much power a German palaeontologist working in German East Africa could attain: Without having any official office at the colonial administration at all, Hennig felt, and was indeed, entitled to dismiss the local *Liwali*, who was only a subordinate to the German District Officer Wendt, but still superior to the *Akida*, *Jumbe* and the local African population, of course.

Yet, it seems that particularly the *Lindi* district was special in this regard. Hennig himself was aware of this fact and attributed it to the governmental policies of *Lindi*'s District Officer Wendt. When excavating in the neighbouring *Kilwa* district around the town of Makangaga, Hennig faced comparably stauncher resistance against the Tendaguru Expedition's demand for porterage from not only the local populations, but also from the East African *Jumbes*, *Akidas* and *Liwalis*, who repeatedly would not accept Hennig's orders. When Hennig left East Africa for good in summer 1911, he was convinced that the situation in the *Kilwa* district was, compared to the *Lindi* district, "really like day and night. The Tendaguru was unusually well situated for [the] expedition!"[148] This held true not only for the overall setting but, particularly, regarding the labour supply and the competences of the East African workers at the Tendaguru Expedition. Both seem to have been exceptional for any contested place of labour in German East Africa, as in *Lindi* – or rather at the area surrounding the Tendaguru – an exceptional situation regarding labour supply prevailed between 1909 and 1911.

148 UAT. 407/2,2, p. 494, cf. pp. 413–414, 494, 496.

6 Conclusion and Outlook

6.1 Conclusion

The phenomenon of labour takes the character of a prism. Labour is therefore always context-dependent and constituted through the actions of all protagonists involved in any labour relationship. On the basis of three case studies in colonial German East Africa – the construction of the *Central Railway* (1905–1916), the *Otto* Plantation in Kilossa (1907–1916) and the palaeontological Tendaguru Expedition (1909–1911) – labour and labour relations were analysed. The focus lay on labour by hitherto neglected actors and groups of actors in the colonial context of East Africa. These were especially German companies and their staff, white subaltern railway sub-contractors and labour recruiters, Indian skilled workers and (qualified) East African workers. Furthermore, all three sites of labour proved to have their individual logics and characteristics. But all of them were in tension between the 'global' and the 'local', coercion and voluntariness, machine and manual labour, skilled and unskilled labour, and reproductive and wage labour, as well as between *black* and *white*.

With the Indian Ocean experiencing its integration into the globalising world of the 'long nineteenth century', on the one hand major characteristic features of the Indian Ocean Area proved resilient. Generally, the monsoon winds regulated the East African climate and divided it into rainy and dry seasons. Most of the labour under investigation was limited to the dry season, as heavy rainfalls made railway, plantation or excavation work largely impossible. On the other hand, with East Africa being an integral part of the Indian Ocean Area, many characteristics of the Indian Ocean world changed. British and German colonialism were both especial perpetrators of this change. With Europeans having been only one player among many others until the early nineteenth century, the most profound changes in the Indian Ocean were certainly related to the British dominance in the seas between East Africa and Oceania, starting from the nineteenth century. As the British Empire had abandoned trading in unfree labour, that is slavery, at the beginning of the nineteenth century, she devoted much of her energy to ousting 'illegitimate trade' and economic activity in the Indian Ocean. In practice, that meant supplanting especially slave trade and slave labour from the area, which was dominated by regional players, and not by Britain. By means of this agitation, British economic policies slowly but surely ensured the Empire's dominance in the Indian Ocean. In the lee of this approach, British dominance followed the central role of India as the Empire's jewel in the crown, and the colonisation of East African territories, especially in Kenya, Uganda and Zanzibar. The Suez Canal

https://doi.org/10.1515/9783111218090-006

was primarily financed by British and French capital and fostered economic and British ties to India, the Red Sea and the Strait of Hormuz. As these areas becames major access points to the Indian Ocean, they also became focal points of British dominance. With the German *Reich* seeking for colonies in Africa, the beginnings of German colonial rule in East Africa in 1884 were embedded in this context: especially because the replacement of the chartered colonising company *DOAG* by the direct colonisation of the *Reich* was the result of the Anglo-German Agreement of 1890. Of course, this imperial trade-off disintegrated the existing East African economy as it cut the Zanzibar Archipelago off from its hinterland that subsequently became German East Africa. Nevertheless, old-established characteristics of the Indian Ocean remained intact. Economic ties with India and Indian migration to both British East Africa and German East Africa continued to increase. Likewise, the significance of the Arabian Peninsula for East Africa remained intact but adapted to the new circumstances. With Omani rule over Zanzibar since the early nineteenth century, there had long been decisive links between the Near East and East Africa. German colonial influence and imperial infrastructure building now altered these links, however. It was German financing institutions (esp. *Deutsche Bank*) and companies (esp. *Philipp Holzmann*) alongside German colonial policy makers that planned and constructed both the *Bagdadbahn* in the Ottoman Empire and the *Central Railway* in German East Africa. Whereas the *Bagdadbahn* was intended as a demonstration of German engineering skills, it also challenged the British dominance of access to the Middle East and, especially, India via the Suez Canal. The *Central Railway* in German East Africa was primarily intended to compensate the socio-economic loss of Zanzibar for the East African mainland and to enhance the colonial economy. Simultaneously, this new imperial infrastructure in the German colony must be regarded primarily as an enhancement of existing pre-colonial trading routes, as the *Central Railway* only followed the established East African caravan routes to the Congo Basin, which had been dominated by Arab-Swahili merchants since the beginning of the nineteenth century.

Construction of the *Baghdadbahn* had already begun in the 1890s and continued in the following decades. The railway project was financed by the *Deutsche Bank*, while the *Philipp Holzmann* Company, also from Frankfurt a.M., was entrusted with the construction. Both houses were also in charge of the *Central Railway* in German East Africa. The construction project in the German colony *in* the Indian Ocean was an extremely international undertaking. In addition to some German engineers, numerous others came from various countries in Europe as well as from North and South America. The same applied to other European personnel such as foremen and overseers. Of the Europeans involved in the construction, however, the largest group consisted of South(-East) European sub-contractors. In order to save construction costs, *Holzmann* outsourced most of the construction work to some Italian and German, but mainly to Greek sub-contractors. The majority of these sub-contractors migrated to East Africa via *Holzmann's* company networks. This was because most of the South(-East) Europeans had been employed in similar positions on the *Baghdadbahn* in the Middle East before their involvement with the *Central Railway*. Furthermore, railway sub-contractors were fundamental not only for the general colonial labour market in need of, for example, plantation workers for companies like *Otto*, but especially for the recruitment of railway workers. To be awarded one route section by *Philipp Holzmann* a railway sub-contractor required an accompanying workforce of at least twenty people: thus, the occupations of labour recruiter and railway sub-contractor were closely intertwined. Labour recruitment was mostly a dubious and very violent business in German East Africa. Recruiters applied various strategies that were barely legal, even according to colonial law. They faked governmental documents that were required by the colonial administration to convince local chiefs to provide workers for the railway or for other colonial companies such as *Otto's* cotton plantation in Kilossa. Other labour recruiters not only used overt physical violence to literally kidnap railway workers. The sources also reveal the recruiters' extravagant promises made to entice people to railway work. Such promises ranged from very high wages and bonuses to the provision of sex workers, feasts and *pombe*. With railway sub-contractors outsourcing parts of their own route sections to sub-sub-contractors, it is not very surprising that similar outsourcing also occurred in the field of labour recruitment. For the most part, such sub-labour recruiters were of East African descent. They often belonged to the Arab-Swahili elite, who had dominated East Africa's politics and economy in pre-colonial times.

People of Indian origin were essential for the construction of the *Central Railway* as well. They were mainly used as skilled labourers and did more demanding work as carpenters, blacksmiths, locksmiths or office clerks. While some of this group were recruited from the East African diaspora, others migrated directly from the Indian sub-continent to the German colony. The rest came to German East Africa from the neighbouring colony of British East Africa, having previously worked at the *Uganda Railway*. Yet, by far the largest part of the up to 20,000 people who worked on railway construction were East African workers who came from all areas of the German colony on the Indian Ocean.

In fact, the *Central Railway* stimulated German East Africa's colonial economic activity, as intended by major policy makers like Colonial State Secretary Bernhard Dernburg. Consequently, more German businesses settled along the line. One of them was the cotton plantation of the *Otto* Company near the town of Kilossa. The Swabian textile company from Unterboihingen, near Stuttgart, decided to establish its own plantation in German East Africa for several reasons. Firstly, since its foundation at the beginning of the nineteenth century, the company had been dependent on imports of the raw material cotton from the USA and thus on global fluctuations in the world market price, and sought independence as far as raw material supply was concerned. Secondly, in this case, *Otto's* entrepreneurial interest converged with the policy of the Imperial Colonial Office in Berlin. Since about 1900, fostering cotton production in its own colonies had been one of the main goals of German colonial policies, which in German East Africa contributed to the outbreak of one of the largest colonial wars ever: the Maji Maji War of 1905–1908. In this war, approximately 180,000 East Africans, primarily civilians, died as a result of the German colonial military's 'scorched earth' policies. Similar to the interests of the *Otto* Company, the aim of the colonial administration was to establish as self-sufficient a supply as possible of the central raw material, cotton. The raw material was crucial for the national economy of the German Empire in order to escape the vagaries of the world market and the dependency on US-American raw cotton production. As one of the largest textile producers in the world, this branch of industry was a matter of national interest for the German *Reich* at that time. Analogically to the involvement of US-American Tuskegee cotton experts in German colonial Togo, the colonial administration in German East Africa, alongside the *Kolonialwirtschatliche Komittee (KWK)*, sought North American expertise and hired a German-Texan cotton expert team to facilitate the production of this cash crop.

Besides the choice of location directly on the new railway in German East Africa, the selection of suitable personnel for the plantation in Kilossa was central to the *Otto* Company. In his search for a plantation manager, the devout company patriarch, Heinrich Otto, made use of networks that had their origins in the Pietist faith and reached as far as the UK, North America and India. For decades, German women from the Unterboihingen area had been married to missionaries, who were sent out into the world under the direction of the Protestant Basel Mission. From this context, the German-Indian missionary family Kaundinya had long been known to the Otto family. Deriving from these Pietist connections, Ranga Kaundinya, who had spent large parts of his youth in the Unterboihingen area, but later also worked in India, became head of the *Otto* plantation in German East Africa. Due to his Christian faith, his long-standing connection to the company and his experience as a so-called tropical planter in India, the German-Indian started his service in Kilossa in 1907.

In addition to setting up the plantation in Kilossa, *Otto* was also interested in mining fossil raw materials in German East Africa. Therefore, at the same time as Kaundinya's employment, the company engaged the renowned Stuttgart geologist and palaeontologist Eberhard Fraas, who was to prove possible mineral resources in the colony as an expert. During this work, however, Fraas received sensational news: in the difficult-to-access area around Tendaguru Mountain in the south of the colony, an African foreman of a colonial company had alerted his employer to huge fossils, the quality of which Fraas was now to assess. The find at the Tendaguru turned out to be a sensation and was to mark the beginning of the largest excavation of dinosaur fossils the world had seen so far, which considerably boosted the prestige of the German Empire as a colonial power and scientific nation. Furthermore, the excavation soon proved the perfect means to refurbish the blemished reputation of German colonialism within German society in the aftermath of the war against the Ovaheroro and Nama in German South West Africa and the Maji Maji War in German East Africa between 1904 and 1908. Even today, the skeleton of the Brachiosaurus Brancai in the atrium of the Berlin Museum of Natural History bears witness to the excavations in German East Africa.

It was the predecessor institution of the Berlin Natural History Museum that took over the patronage of the corresponding Tendaguru Expedition. During the principal excavation period between 1909 and 1911, the two German palaeontologists, Werner Janensch and Edwin Hennig, were in charge. During these years, they were mostly the only Europeans at Tendaguru. While they were mainly responsible for the scientific management and administration of the excavations, the majority of the fossils were discovered and uncovered by East African preparators and foremen, and transported to the coastal town of Lindi, about 100 km away. From there, tons of fossils were shipped to Germany to be scientifically examined in Berlin. In addition to their qualified East African excavators, fossil preparators and porters, Hennig and Janensch were also dependent on their personal servants. These so-called *boys* and chefs of East African origin did the daily housework for the palaeontologists and thus made the work of the German scientists in the remote region around the Tendaguru possible, in the first place. The international experience of these personal servants and their knowledge of local conditions also made it easier for the palaeontologists to find their way around German East Africa. In addition to their daily work, the personal servants functioned, among other things, as language teachers of Swahili and as travel and hunting guides.

Similar dependencies regarding reproductive labour existed at the *Otto* cotton plantation and at the *Central Railway* construction sites. While European engineers like the Anglo-German Clement Gillman had their own personal servants, many East African workers brought their wives or partners with them to the work sites, where about a third of the people present were female. As a rule, the women were responsible for domestic and care work, while their husbands pursued (wage) labour for ten to twelve hours a day. Especially at the *Central Railway*, many women also worked self-employed as beer-brewers, petty traders or sex workers. Regarding sex work, the boundaries between prostitution and sexualised violence were generally blurred. While women did not work at Tendaguru in the excavations *per se*, there were quite a few women who also did railway construction work and were employed in cotton plantation work at Kilossa.

Regardless of gender, the qualifications of a worker were central. As initial plans to lower the costs of African labour by the introduction of the latest technology to grow cotton on a large scale via steam ploughs failed miserably, East African labour remained crucial for any cotton production in Kilossa. Plantation managers like Kaundinya were aware that experienced East African cotton workers produced up to ten times more raw cotton than unskilled staff. Not surprisingly, other colonial plantation companies repeatedly tried to poach these experienced cotton workers from Kilossa. If another place of work seemed to offer the workers better conditions or higher wages, they were usually willing to change employers.

The staff of the *Central Railway* also took advantage of the competitive situation of the colonial economy. Literate office staff and qualified craftsmen were especially essential for *Holzmann*. Since the Indian skilled workers were more expensive for the construction company, compared to similarly qualified East African personnel, East African mission school graduates were increasingly recruited. Especially, former students of the Moravian Mission trained in handicraft or in reading, writing and accounting worked as craftsmen and office clerks for the colonial railway. An important reason for this employment was that the construction company paid the qualified personnel higher wages and granted more personal freedom when at work than the mission itself.

The migration of skilled labour to all three places of work under investigation was hardly associated with colonial coercion. For the Tendaguru Expedition, this can hardly be proven. The majority of ca. 500 workers came to the palaeontological excavation sites independently and out of their own initiative from as far away as *Lake Nyassa*, a distance of 700 km to the west. Sometimes, Hennig and Janensch even had to reject newly arriving volunteer workers. The overall sufficient labour supply at the Tendaguru is even more surprising as East African workers received lower wages excavating dinosaur bones than they would have received working at the 100-km-distant coastal plantations of the *Lindi* district. It is striking that despite this pay gap, the coastal plantations of the *Lindi* district frequently complained about a shortage of labour, whereas the Tendaguru Expedition experienced an oversupply of workers. In contrast, physical abuse of all kinds, including manslaughter, was commonplace both during labour recruitment and during labour deployment at the *Central Railway* and the *Otto* plantation. In addition to arbitrary beatings with or without the use of a whip, false promises, inadequate food, accommodation and medical treatment, withholding of wages or forced detention at the place of work after the end of the employment contract were the order of the day at both places of work.

There were constant disputes about who was responsible for these grievances, especially at the *Central Railway* construction sites. While the colonial administration held *Holzmann* responsible, the construction company constantly referred to its numerous sub-contractors: to *Holzmann's* view, they alone were responsible for the proper treatment of the East African workers. As many of *Holzmann's* sub-contractors outsourced their own railway sections even to another level and hired sub-sub-contractors to act on their behalf, clear responsibilities about labour conditions along the railroad further dissolved. In the course of this dispute, however, the working conditions remained scandalous until the end of formal German colonial rule in East Africa. Only the discourse around blame changed. German politicians, especially competing German railway construction sub-contractors in German East Africa, increasingly held their Greek colleagues responsible for any grievances. In doing so, they used racist clichés of the supposedly lazy, deceitful and uncivilised South(-East) European, who due to his culture and origin, was closer to the colonised population of Africa than to a Central European or German coloniser.

Similar discourses were also served up at the *Otto* Plantation in Kilossa. There were several reasons for this: for one thing, the enterprise was never profitable during its existence. Secondly, the plantation was staffed by poorly qualified German overseers who behaved violently towards the plantation workers and consumed a lot of alcohol. However, the plantation manager Kaundinya was primarily blamed for these abuses. Similar to the Greek sub-contractors in railway construction, the Indo-German was accused of lacking qualifications, especially because of his origin and his status as an alleged 'half-caste man'. Both Kaundinya and the Greek sub-contractors thus occupied a conflictual intermediate position between *black* and *white* in German East Africa's colonial society, qualifying them as white subalterns. In this field of tension, discourses about colonial labour were combined with those about origin and identity. The devaluation of anything non-Central European was linked to the German claim to cultural superiority in Europe and in other parts of the world, which at the same time legitimised colonial rule in racist terms.

All three places of work exerted colonial command in German East Africa as well. Given the ephemeral character of the colonial administration, comprehensive rule could only be exerted in the direct environments of governmental *bomas*, or centres of administrative offices. The farther away from such a centre, the less colonial claims to power were effective. With German economic and scientific undertakings in German East Africa also representing colonial claims on the East African territory, the construction sites of the *Central Railway*, the *Otto* plantation in Kilossa and the excavation sites of the Tendaguru Expedition may all be regarded as representatives of colonial rule. All of them were almost the only representation of a European presence on their spot and all were thus also representatives of colonial command. This is especially demonstrated by the fact that all the European protagonists of labour felt entitled to represent and exert colonial dominance at the three places of work.

Although each place of work had its own characteristics and dynamics, their individual claim as a site of colonial rule is reflected by the topography of each place of labour, in the first place. Similarly to colonial towns and larger settlements, the three places of labour also attempted to represent colonial hierarchies *en miniature.* The allotment of the accommodations at the exemplary construction camp of the Anglo-German railway engineer, Clement Gillman, reflects the colonial hierarchy clearly. Gillman, as the only middle-European and middle-class man, positioned his hut at the very centre of the construction camp. This privileged position was enhanced, as his dwelling was protected from the sun by a large tree, and had sanitary facilities nearby. Moreover, provisions were in his direct environment and sometimes Gillman's ruling position was underscored by the presence of an *Askari* living right next to him, who enhanced his means of asserting colonial power. A few metres away from the engineer's hut lived his South(-East) European foremen, who were on a lower level of the colonial hierarchy as white subalterns. As shown by Gillman's sketch of the construction camp, the East African workforce lived in the direct environment of the uncleared bush, reflecting the colonial ideology claiming African people as less civilised than Europeans. Further emphasising that the colonisers valued primarily the local population's physical strength, the workforce lived close to the actual site of construction where the railway was being built. The topographies of the *Otto* plantation in Kilossa and at the Tendaguru Expedition reflect the claims of colonial rule as well. In contrast to Gillman's railway camp, colonial hierarchies there were not reflected by centrality, but by elevation. At both places, the dwellings of the Europeans were ultimately built at a higher altitude than those of the African workforce. Reflecting colonial notions of health and hygiene, the colonisers at the Tendaguru and in Kilossa reserved the supposedly healthiest altitudes for the Europeans, and attempted to live spatially separated from their East African workforce. But the topographies of the places of work also reveal other rather inconclusive and precarious facets of colonial rule.

Apart from the workplace's topography, the performance of labour was also always an arena of colonial command. As long as labour was functional, forced labour and other means of coercion were comparatively low. In turn, whenever the smooth functioning of colonial labour was threatened, force and coercion intensified. If *Philipp Holzmann* had not enough workers for railway construction, they turned to the colonial administration first to ease the shortage. The colonial administration was ready to increase the pressure on the local population, if demanded by the construction company, accordingly. If the colonial authorities failed to provide workers *Holzmann* turned to freelance labour recruiters, who often exerted coercion on the local population. If this attempt also failed, *Holz-*

mann's own personnel engaged in coercive recruitment. Therefore, the question is not simply whether the ordinary, that is, comparatively unskilled, East African railway workers experienced forced labour or coercion, but rather who exerted it, to what degree and at which points in time. It appears that the most intense coercion occurred in times of intense colonial warfare, such as during the Maji Maji War, when POWs performed convict labour, and during economic upturns. At times of stirred economic activity, the general demand for workers rose correspondingly. As far as railway construction is concerned, increased pressure to work after the Maji Maji War was especially exerted between 1912 and 1914, when the colony experienced an economic upturn.

The findings on labour and labour supply at the *Otto* plantation further support these arguments. When Indo-German plantation manager, Ranga Kaundinya, arrived in Kilossa in 1907, the Maji Maji War was experiencing its last skirmishes. Luckily for the Indo-German plantation manager, *Holzmann* had just finished their construction works between Dar es Salaam and Morogoro and would only resume railway building in 1909. With the cooperation between *Holzmann* and Kaundinya in 1907, railway workers were turned into plantation workers for *Otto*. Yet, Kaundinya experienced labour shortages as soon as *Holzmann* resumed construction work in 1909: It is thus very likely that *Holzmann* got their initial railway men back, as East Africans generally preferred railway labour over plantation work. There is another important aspect regarding the origin of the workers and the character of their employment, however. With *Holzmann* employing POWs as punitive workers along the railroad during the Maji Maji War, it might be the case that Kaundinya had employed exactly those convict workers, which he was obligated to return to *Holzmann* as soon as the company from Frankfurt ordered them back when resuming railway construction. In subsequent labour competition with *Holzmann* in 1909, Kaundinya thus had to turn to freelance labour recruiters who delivered workers to Kilossa from the central *Iringa* and *Tabora* regions. With the economy in German East Africa experiencing an upturn from ca. 1911 onwards, the demand for workers remained also high in Kilossa. As the court files against the plantation owner, Walter Grund, in 1914 reveal, many plantation workers had been forced to stay in Kilossa longer than they had actually wanted. This meant that labour was particularly scarce when the colonial economy flourished and many enterprises sought for workers accordingly.

The Tendaguru Expedition provides both similarities and major differences regarding labour and command. Compared to the *Otto* plantation and the *Central Railway*, forced labour and coercion was largely absent. With voluntary workers pouring to the Tendaguru Mountain, hardly any shortage of labour occurred. Hence, no coercion was needed to recruit sufficient labour. Like the plantation manager Kaundinya, the palaeontologists Hennig and Janensch were initially supplied with workers – in this case, by the established colonial mining employer, Bernhard Sattler. Hence, in the direct aftermath of the Maji Maji War, when the Tendaguru Expedition started in 1909, no labour recruitment was necessary for this undertaking. At this point in time, the German colonial military's 'scorched earth' policies during the war had caused many thousands of deaths and led to widespread famine in southeast German East Africa, with the *Lindi* district being among the hardest hit. With the destruction of villages and food stuffs, especially *Lindi's* surviving population had lost everything during the war. Likewise, most colonial businesses had been destroyed. Although there were people who resisted colonial employment, even in the face of starving to death, research on the local economy shows that labour supply was best in the years directly after the war. Especially women, whose husbands had either died in battle or had been detained, readily took up work at colonial plantations to survive. Hence, as a result of destroyed colonial businesses, there existed a war-ridden economy experiencing a downturn (reducing competition for labour), coupled with demand for employment on the part of the local populations. As a result, there was no labour shortage in the *Lindi* district between ca. 1907 and 1911. In this very period, the Tendaguru Expedition carried out its major excavation works between 1909 and 1911. The conclusion to be drawn is that the good labour supply at the Tendaguru Expedition resulted largely from the local one-off effect that the famine after the Maji Maji War had caused more demand for colonial wage labour among the African population of *Lindi*. When the economy of German East Africa experienced an upturn from 1911 onwards until WWI, large-scale excavation works had already ceased at the Tendaguru and only a handful of workers were needed for smaller excavations until 1913. Thus, as far as labour supply in the *Lindi* district is concerned, the Tendaguru Expedition took place in the perfect time frame, as between 1909 and 1911, competing labour demand by colonial enterprises was particularly low, as many plantations had been destroyed during the Maji Maji War and could not employ any workers.

Remarkably Hennig and Janensch, nevertheless, exerted recruitment coercion in the *Kilwa* district, where the aftershocks of anti-colonial resistance during the Maji Maji War were still felt. Moreover, in the very few cases where workers or porters were desperately needed, Hennig and Janensch reacted just like any other colonial employer in German East Africa: they called upon the colonial administration for help, sent their personal servants to raid nearby villages or exerted pressure on the local population themselves. Therefore, the excellent labour supply of the Tendaguru Expedition can neither exclusively be attributed to the interesting work tasks requiring skilled labour, nor exclusively to the relative appreciation of their workers on the part of Hennig and Janensch, nor to the favourable point in time regarding labour supply. It equally relied on means of colonial command. If these means were not exerted directly by Hennig and Janensch, who did indeed use the (violent) repertoire of any coloniser in need of workers, the two palaeontologists profited indirectly from colonial command in German East Africa. As far as labour supply is concerned, the years between 1909 and 1911 just happened to be the perfect time frame to search for workers in the war-ridden area of *Lindi*. There, East African demand for employment was high in the aftermath of the Maj-Maji War. Simultaneously, the colonial economy had suffered severely during the war, and the resulting economic downturn reduced competition for labour. Exactly in this period, the largest dinosaur bones the world had ever seen so far were found and excavated close to the Tendaguru Mountain. Hence, the Tendaguru Expedition saw not only exceptional fossil finds, but also an exceptional point in time as far as labour supply in German East Africa's district of *Lindi* was concerned.

6.2 Outlook

This global labour history has illuminated the role of neglected protagonists of labour in German East Africa. In the first place, South(-East) European sub-contractors and labour recruiters were central to railway construction in the German colony and for the entire labour market in the German colony. With the majority of these railway sub-contractors migrating directly from the *Bagdadbahn* to the *Central Railway* in German East Africa, many aspects of their background remain unclear. The selection of the archives and the sources under investigation set the focus on South(-East) Europeans migrating to and working in German East Africa. Yet, only little is known about their history when working at the *Bagdadbahn*. Furthermore, nothing is known about the patterns of the sub-contractors' migration to that most prestigious German imperial railway in the Ottoman Empire. With the sub-contractors' conflict-laden intermediate position as white subalterns in German East Africa, it is further not clear whether they occupied a similar status in the society of the Ottoman Empire, when working at the *Bagdadbahn*, and whether working conditions at this railway were comparable to those at the *Central Railway* in German East Africa at all. In addition, whether the largest part of labour recruitment for the *Bagdadbahn* also lay in the hands of South(-East) European sub-contractors must remain unclear for now and thus constitutes a promising field of research for future works on the history of labour (intermediation) and imperial infrastructure.

Moreover, as revealed by the constant conflicts between *Philipp Holzmann* and the supervisory bodies of the colonial administration, latest questions of the new history of capitalism may be addressed more profoundly. In this study, it became clear that as far as the construction sites of the *Central Railway* are concerned, outsourcing construction tasks was indeed one of the most important features of the workings of 'colonial capitalism in action'. Regarding the *Central Railway*, by outsourcing, *Holzmann* certainly attempted to cut costs and avoid as many liabilities, as far as labour protection rights were concerned, in order to ensure rapid railway construction and the highest profitability possible. Interestingly, although colonial discourses strongly devalued white subaltern labour, *Holzmann's* business interests ran counter to this racist-colonial trope. The construction company happily employed South(-East) European sub-contractors as they had proven to be cheaper, more effective and more qualified than their German counterparts, who were actually ranked first in the colonial (labour) hierarchy. To address these themes raised here more profoundly, further research especially in the archives of today's Turkey appears promising. To reveal the migratory patterns of, especially, Greek sub-contractors, files held at several European consulates, for example in today's Egypt, or archives in Greece may be consulted. These files could help to illuminate details of their emigration to the *Bagdadbahn* and to German East Africa. Regarding the Greek diaspora, the singular case of the Greek sub-contractor, John Zavellas, may inspire larger questions about the interrelationship between Greek or rather South(-East) European emigration with North America and colonial (German) Africa. At the same time, the central role of South(-East) European railway sub-contractors working almost simultaneously at prestigious imperial infrastructure projects in the Near East and in German colonial East Africa bears the potential to add another facet to the history of the Indian Ocean Area that has barely found any attention. Regarding the white subalternity of South(-East) European railway sub-contractors, the matter of skill and colonial discourse deserves further attention. Given the fact that the performance of the Greeks working at the *Central Railway* was indeed valued by *Holzmann*, for example, while the company still vilified them as 'second-rate whites', directs to the question whether skill and ability could in fact raise or preserve *whiteness* in (semi-)colonial societies.

As the centre of the Indian Ocean Area, India had had links to East Africa for centuries. With this study illuminating the decisive role of Indian craftsmen and clerks at the *Central Railway*, the dimension of skill has been added to global labour history, also in this respect. Yet, it is too simple to speak about 'Indian labour' as such. With India having always been a very diverse sub-continent, little is known about the backgrounds of the Indian craftsmen and clerks who worked at the *Central Railway* in German East Africa. This is especially problematic, as the colonial archives tend to subsume anybody coming from the sub-continent as 'Indian'. Yet, this label of 'Indian' falls short in the light of the sub-continent's diversity and complexity in terms of religion, ethnicity, caste, or its relationship to British colonial power. With the sources under investigation having revealed Indian (indentured) labour migration from both India and British East Africa to

German East Africa, many aspects remain understudied. For Indian migration from the sub-continent to German East Africa, it appears promising to consult further archives, especially in India. The same holds true for the migration of skilled Indian railway workers and office clerks from the British *Uganda Railway* to German East Africa. As the COVID-19 pandemic limited my research in the Railway Museum in Nairobi to four days only, investigating the files of the *Uganda Railway* held there could be one starting point. To further reveal the role of skilled Indian labour migration from British colonies to German East Africa, the National Archives in Kew, Britain, is another option as well as the National Archives in Zanzibar, as the archipelago had hosted a significant Indian minority since the middle of the nineteenth century.

Along with highlighting that Indians were employed particularly as skilled workers for the *Central Railway*, significant details about the role of East African qualified labour have emerged from this global labour history. Receiving their training at the Moravian Missions, East African skilled labour is seen to have links to global dimensions of the Moravian railway missions. As this study proved that the Moravian railway mission was inspired by other railway missions in South Africa, further research on missions to colonial railways in Africa and beyond are promising. Regarding global labour history, research questions might investigate whether other (railway) missions provided for skilled East African labour in German and other colonies. Regarding German East Africa, the first archives to visit appear those of the Berlin Mission, which ran a railway mission between Dar es Salaam and Kilossa, in analogy to that of the Moravians in *Unyamwezi.* Moreover, the connections between the European, or rather the German introduction of *Bahnhofsmissionen* at numerous railway stations in the *Reich*, to German East Africa should be studied. Studies, taking a global approach on the history of the *Banhofsmissionen* and similar institutions, could add a so far neglected facet to the history of infrastructures or the global history of missions pursued and/ or demanded by many historians around the globe at the moment.

With the Moravian Mission occupying an important role for the provision of skilled labour for the *Central Railway*, it must be stressed that the global dimensions of faith and denomination were also central aspects regarding the *Otto* plantation in Kilossa. Just as the Pietist global company networks of the *Otto* Company were a significant network within the 'empire of cotton', the upbringing of the Indo-German plantation manager Ranga Kaundinya in the context of the Pietist Basel Mission also mattered for his employment in Kilossa. Whether Pietist company networks and shared denominational convictions also mattered for other entrepreneurs in other colonial enterprises has largely been ignored by global (labour) historians. The entire complex of company networks in a global colonial economy and its significance for employment strategies could thus be investigated for various colonial plantations and other companies around the globe. This bears the potential to generate new perspectives on the interconnectedness of the Pietist or rather Protestant work ethos *à là* Max Weber and capitalist expansion within the 'empire of cotton', but also for other research fields regarding an increasingly globalised economy. As far as the *Otto* plantation is concerned, the first archives to consult would be those of the Basel Mission in Switzerland, which could provide additional information about the Kaundinya family and the involvement of the Otto family and *Otto* company with Basel's mission work and the (possible) importance of Pietism for the business of *Otto*, in general.

In the topic area of female labour and reproductive labour, this global labour history has revealed that female labour was central for all three places of work. Yet, many aspects remain hazy. Given a general lack of information in the sources, any new documents available to shed light on the issue should be consulted and examined closely to further highlight the role of women in railway and plantation labour as well as in scientific endeavours such as the Tendaguru Expedition. Of course, this is also relevant to reproductive labour, petty trading, and sex work. Regarding colonial labour environments and sex work, the issue of pimping has generally been ignored. Given the fact that especially railway sub-contractors and labour recruiters, searching for workers, were able to attract male railway workers by offering concubines and the availability of sex workers, research investigating the issue of pimping appears as a promising field of global labour history at the interface between sex, work, coercion and (sexualised) violence. As the files held at the Moravian archives suggest that pimps offered sex work to missionaries like Gaardee at the construction sites of the *Central Railway*, the files held in other missions to other colonial railways might be worth studying.

Of course, reproductive labour will remain at the heart of studies investigating female labour, but it also bears the potential to further illuminate the role of personal servants in global labour history. With only few historical works dealing with the role of *boys* or chefs in charge of the colonisers' households, the Tendaguru Expedition especially revealed further insights. Having shown the usefulness of drawing on the self-narratives of the palaeontologist Edwin Hennig to reveal the central role of his personal servants, further studies may also want to draw upon such sources to elucidate this neglected field of global labour history. In this respect, the investigation of self-narratives is especially important as files held in colonial archives are generally silent on personal servants.

Some peculiarities of the Tendaguru also point to larger questions of the global history of labour. Although the good labour supply at the Tendaguru Expedition must primarily be attributed to the special situation in the *Lindi* district between ca. 1907 and 1911, historians may wonder whether labour supply at scientific expeditions, like palaeontological excavation works, generally experienced better supply than economic endeavours such as railway construction sites or colonial plantations. Comparing the labour supply at other scientific endeavours to the Tendaguru Expedition, global labour history of this fashion might be able to contribute to the question of whether primarily economic or rather capitalist endeavours were more prone to exploitation and forced labour than scientific endeavours – as the palaeontologist Edwin Hennig suggested himself when working at the Tendaguru.

In terms of larger questions of global labour history, a combination with research questions of environmental history and area studies appears promising. As all three places of work under investigation – the construction sites of the *Central Railway*, the *Otto* plantation in Kilossa, and the Tendaguru Expedition – to a large extent proved to be at the mercy of environmental conditions, it appears that not only labour policies and the actions of so far neglected groups and individuals affected the characteristics of colonial labour in German East Africa. Environmental issues impacted the rhythms of labour, the topologies of the labour sites, the feasibility of modern technology and the practicalities of transport in the colony. Thus, future research on global labour history might investigate the interconnection between environmental history and labour history more profoundly. Furthermore, with the monsoon winds of the Indian Ocean having dominated the history of the Indian Ocean for millennia, the amalgamation of global labour history, environmental history and studies on the Indian Ocean Area might provide for a renewed reference framework for global labour history. With the present study on global labour history examining the history of three particular places of work *in* the Indian Ocean, some illuminating pieces are contributed to the bigger picture of the entire region.

Last but not least, the major result of this study that there was no such thing as colonial labour *per se* and no prototypical colonial worker as such, may well be connected to the recurring questions of the new history of global capitalism and the fairly recent discussions about capitalism 'as a historical concept'. These questions revolve around the findings that capitalism produced and featured a multitude of supposedly free forms of (wage) labour and many varieties of unfree labour such as (chattel) slavery. Studying forms of indentured labour and other varieties of coerced labour, not least in the context of colonial forced and/ or tax labour, highlights that this global labour history has the potential to inspire any further research investigating colonial 'capitalism in action':[1] Firstly, the fact that companies and banks such as *Otto, Philipp Holzmann* or *Deutsche Bank* were decisive for the places of labour under investigation, stresses the importance of intertwining business history with global labour history and even the global history of financial capitalism.[2] As this study further suggests that economic upturns favoured forced labour policies in a colonial economy as a result of intensified competition for (African) labour, general questions of the interconnection between basic mechanisms of capitalist economies, that is the relation between supply and demand, and labour must be addressed in future. As Andrea Komlosy has pointed out, capitalism is also based on the inclusion and interaction of different forms of labour regimes, such as commodified wage work and, generally, unpaid forms of reproductive labour – a point that has repeatedly been made for so-called informal labour relations in sub-Saharan Africa[3] – the chapters on female labour and personal servants of this study offer a starting point to take up larger and additional investigations on the characteristics and mechanisms of their mutual relationship. This also entails the matter of scope and space as all three places of labour under investigation feature patterns of labour migration – and intermediation – prominently ranging from internal migration in (German East) Africa via larger migratory patterns embedded in the Indian Ocean Area to even farther connections to Europe and the Americas.[4]

1 Beckert. 'The New History', p. 246.
2 Cf. Fridenson, Patrick. 'Is there a return of Capitalism in Business History?'. *Capitalism. The Reemergence of a Historical Concept.* 107–132. Eds. Jürgen Kocka and Marcel van der Linden. London et al.: 2016. Cf. James, Harold. 'Finance Capitalism'. *Capitalism. The Reemergence of a Historical Concept.* 133–164. Eds. Jürgen Kocka and Marcel van der Linden. London et al.: 2016.
3 Cf. Eckert. 'Capitalism and Labor', pp. 170–173. Cf. Cooper. 'Von der Sklaverei in die Prekarität?', pp. 3–11.
4 Cf. Komlosy. 'Work and Labour', pp. 34, 60–64. Cf. Beckert. 'The New History', p. 238.

List of Works Cited

Archival Sources

Berlin-Brandenburgisches Wirtschaftsarchiv (BBWA) Bildarchiv der Philipp Holzmann AG/Hauptverband der Deutschen Bauindustrie e.V.

U5/03/17, Nr. 177. “Bahnbau Deutschostafrika Strecke Tabora-Kigoma. 1912–13. Malagarassi-Brücke”.
U5/03/17, Nr. 181. “Bahnbau Deutsch-Ostafrika. Strecke Tabora-Kigoma 1912–1913. Grashütten der Bauarbeiter”.

Bundesarchiv Berlin (BArch)

R1001/116. Einsatz fremder Arbeiter, v. a. von Chinesen.
R1001/846. Evangelische Brüder-Unität in Herrnhut.
R155F/81406 Neg. Jahresberichte 1908. Ssongea, Tabora, Mahenge.
R155F/81413 Pos. Jahresberichte 1908. Mpapua, Morogoro, Muansa u. Shirati.
R155F/81414 Pos. Jahresberichte Iringa.

Geheimes Staatsarchiv Preußischer Kulturbesitz (GehStArch)

VI. HA. Nachlass Heinrich Schnee Nr. 72. Bekanntmachungen und Verordnungen in Suaheli und lateinischer Umschrift. Bezirksämter Wilhelmstahl, Bagamoyo, Tanga, Lindi 1906–1912.

Historisches Archiv der Deutschen Bank (HADB)

P8049. Anatolische Eisenbahngesellschaft. Diverse Listen ihrer Angestellten.
S 1514. Ostafrikanische Eisenbahn.
S 1515. Ostafrikanische Eisenbahn.
S 1516. Ostafrikanische Eisenbahngesellschaft Expedition 1903 Ausrüstung.
S 1518. Ostafrikanische Eisenbahn. Verhandlungen Koppel.
S 1521. Konsortium Ostafrikanische Eisenbahn.
S 1522. Konsortium Ostafrikanische Eisenbahn.
S 1523. Konsortium Ostafrikanische Eisenbahn. Stichbahn Ruanda.
S 1525. Konsortium Ostafrikanische Eisenbahn. Tabora-Kigoma.

Historisches Archiv/Museum der MAN AG Augsburg

Erzeugnisse Werk Gustavsburg. 42, 352/a/3-2.

https://doi.org/10.1515/9783111218090-007

Historisches Archiv der Firma Krupp (HA Krupp)

N 13/7. Gustav Neumann. Baumeister in Tanganyika und Ruanda.

WA 4/1771. Schienenlieferung an die Eisenbahngesellschaft für Deutsch-Ostafrika (Usambara-Linie) 1894/96/97.

WA 4/2589. Anschreiben und Denkschrift in 3 Teilen und 8 Abschnitten nebst einem Anhang von 9 Karten im zweiten Teil.

WA 16 g/4.3/231. Bau einer Brücke über den Sanaga-Fluss bei Edea, Kamerun.

WA 70/1471. Abkommen über Klemmplatten für Kolonial-Eisenbahnen zw. 27.12.09–05.03.12.

Museum für Naturkunde Berlin (MfN) – Historische Bild und Schriftgutsammlungen (HBSB)

Tendaguru Expedition 1.3. Vorbereitungen.

Tendaguru Expedition 2.2. Transport.

Tendaguru Expedition 2.3. Transport/Ausrüstung (Afrika 1910–1912).

Tendaguru Expedition 3.1. Versorgung/Alltag.

Tendaguru Expedition 4.3. Versorgung/Alltag (Jagd).

Tendaguru Expedition 4.5. Versorgung/Alltag.

Tendaguru Expedition 5.1. Korrespondenzen von Janensch und Hennig.

Tendaguru Expedition 6.2. Finanzierung.

Tendaguru Expedition 6.7. Finanzierung (Löhne und Gehälter).

Tendaguru Expedition 7.3. Finanzierung.

Tendaguru Expedition 7.4. Finanzierung.

Tendaguru Expedition 9.2. Expeditionsdokumentation Tagebuch Janensch.

Tendaguru Expedition 10.4. Druckmedien.

Tendaguru Expedition Konvolut Tendaguru (1694), Expeditionsverlauf- und dokumentation (421), Fotoalben (193).

Railway Museum Nairobi (RMN)
German Tanganyika Files (GTF)

R1. S9. Sanitätsdienststellen.

R1. S10. Umbau Daressalaam-Morogoro. Akt. VIII. Bd.1. Gesundheits- und Arbeiterverhältnisse.

R2. S10. I_6, 1913/14. Sewa Hadji Hospital, Rechnung.

R3. S5. 154. [no title].

R3. S5. 1.1.13. [no title].

R3. S8. Direktion. Behörden. Betriebsdirektion.

R3. S8. 157. Lohnauszahlungen.

R3. S10. 2. Sewa Hadji Hospital. Rechnung.

R3. S48. Diverse Vertraulich.

R4. S3. 98. Gouvernementskrankenhaus, Institut für Seuchenbekämpfung, Sewa Haji Hospital, Sanitätsdienststellen, Behörden.

Oxford - Bodleian Libraries

Micr. Afr. 446. Service in German East Africa & Germany Foreign Office 1902–33. Extracts Gunzert.

Gillman Diaries

Mss. Afr. S. 1175/1,2_1, no. II.
Mss. Afr. S. 1175/1,2_1, no. 8.
Mss. Afr. S. 1175/1,2_1, no. 9.
Mss. Afr. S. 1175/1,2_1, no. 10.
Mss. Afr. S. 1175/1,2_2, no. 13.
Mss. Afr. S. 1175/1,2_2, no. 14.

Stadtarchiv Frankfurt o.M.
Wirtschaftsarchiv. Philipp Holzmann

W1/2–278/1. Holzmann in Afrika.
W1/2–517. Verträge über den Bau der Ruanda-Bahn (ehem. Deutsch.Ost-Afrika 1908–1918) (Morogoro-Tabora, Tabora-Kigoma, Umbau Daressalam-Morogoro).

Stadtmuseum Wendlingen am Neckar

Diashow Kilossa 1907–1916. 20. Min. 151 Bilder mit Musik.
Konrad Steinert's private document collection, "Ranga Reinhardt Rao Kaundinya (1863–1919). Leiter der Otto-Pflanzung Kilossa (1907–1916)".
Konrad Steinert's private document collection. "Tagebuch von der Reise nach Kilossa. 26.6. - 18.9.1913 von Fritz Otto, Abschrift".
Konrad Steinert's private document collection, "Zum Stammbaum von Kaundinya".

Tanzania National Archives (TNA) - Dar es Salaam

G1/16. [Beziehungen zu den] deutschen konsularischen Vertretungen in Arabien und Ostindien [Aden, Bombay, Calcutta, Batavia, Mahé].
G1/95. Verstöße gegen die Arbeiterwerbeverordnung (Personenverzeichnis).
G4/75. [Bestellung der Mitglieder und Sitzungsprotokolle des] Bezirksrates der Kommune Lindi.
G5/38. Bemühungen um Entsendung eines Stationsarztes nach Kilossa (Petition der ansässigen Europäer).
G8/58. [Klärung allgemeiner Fragen hinsichtlich der] Anwerbung von Indern [als Handwerker und Gärtner für das Gouvernement von Deutsch-Ostafrika mit Hilfe des deutschen Generalkonsulates in Kalkutta].
G8/59. Anwerbung und Ansiedlung von Indern [Singhalesen und Eingeborenen]. Bd. 1.
G8/60. Anwerbung und Ansiedlung von Indern [Singhalesen und Eingeborenen]. Bd. 2.
G8/61. Anwerbung und Ansiedlung von Indern [Singhalesen und Eingeborenen]. Bd. 3.
G8/146. [Angelegenheiten der] Ostafrikanische Eisenbahngesellschaft (1913-)1916. Bd. 3.
G8/894. [Angelegenheiten der Pflanzung des] Kommerzienrates Heinrich Otto [Kilossa, Bez. Morogoro]. Bd. 1.

G8/904. [Angelegenheiten der Pflanzung des] Kommerzienrates Heinrich Otto [Kilossa, Bez. Morogoro]. Bd. 2.
G12/82. Bau der Eisenbahn Daressalaam-Morogoro Bd. 2. 1905.
G12/164. Bauberichte und -dispositionen der Tanganyika-Eisenbahn. 1909–1915.
G12/167. Allgemeine [Angelegenheiten der] Tanganyika-Eisenbahn. 1908–1912.
G12/176. [Verursachung von Betriebs-] Unregelmäßigkeiten beim Bau und Betrieb der Tanganyika-Eisenbahn [durch Unfälle und Betriebsstörungen sowie Beschwerde des Bauunternehmers C. Berger [. . .]. 1913–1916.
G12/188. [Durchführung der politischen, wirtschaftlichen und technischen Erkundungen und] Vorbereitungen [für den Bau der] Eisenbahn Tabora-Tanganyika-See. Bd. 1. 1910–1911.
G12/202. Bauberichte und -dispositionen der Tanganyika-Eisenbahn Tabora-Kigoma [sowie der projektierten Eisenbahn Tabora-Kagera-Fluß (Ruanda-Bahn)] 1911–13 Bd. 1.
G17/30. Berichte des Baubeamten Buchner [über den Fortgang der Arbeiten an der Tanganyika-Eisenbahn Morogoro-Tabora]. 1908–1910.
G17/63. Monatliche Berichte der örtlichen Baubeamten über den Fortgang der Bauarbeiten an der Tanganyika-Eisenbahn Morogoro-Tabora. Bd. 1. 1908–1910.
G17/64. Monatliche Berichte der örtlichen Baubeamten über den Fortgang der Bauarbeiten an der Tanganyika-Eisenbahn Morogoro-Tabora. Bd. 2. 1910–1911.
G17/65. Monatliche Berichte der örtlichen Baubeamten über den Fortgang der Bauarbeiten an der Tanganyika-Eisenbahn Morogoro-Tabora. 1908–1912.
G17/66. Arbeiterverhältnisse der Tanganyika-Eisenbahn Morogoro-Tabora. 1909–1911.
G17/81. [Personal- und Verwaltungsangelegenheiten der Tanganyika-Eisenbahn Morogoro-Tabora, vorwiegend allgem.] 1912–1914.
G17/118. Monatliche Berichte über den Fortgang der Bauarbeiten an der Tanganyika- Eisenbahn Tabora-Kigoma. Bd. 1. 1912–1913.
G17/119. Monatliche Berichte über den Fortgang der Bauarbeiten an der Tanganyika- Eisenbahn Tabora-Kigoma. Bd. 3. 1914–1915.
G17/120. Monatliche Berichte der örtlichen Baubeamten über den Fortgang der Bauarbeiten an der Tanganyika-Eisenbahn Tabora-Kigoma. Bd. 1. 1912–1913.
G17/121. Monatliche Berichte der örtlichen Baubeamten über den Fortgang der Bauarbeiten an der Tanganyika-Eisenbahn Tabora-Kigoma. Bd. 2. 1913–1914.
G17/122. Monatliche Berichte der örtlichen Baubeamten über den Fortgang der Bauarbeiten an der Tanganyika-Eisenbahn Tabora-Kigoma. Bd. 3. 1914–1916.
G17/123. Arbeiterverhältnisse der Tanganyika-Eisenbahn Tabora-Kigoma. Bd. 1. 1912–1913.
G17/124. Arbeiterverhältnisse der Tanganyika-Eisenbahn Tabora-Kigoma. Bd. 2. 1913–1915. Enthält vorwiegend: Gesundheitsdienst.
G17/125. Schlafkrankheitsbekämpfung an der Tanganyika-Eisenbahn Tabora-Kigoma. 1912–1914.
G17/153. Arbeiterverhältnisse der Ruanda-Eisenbahn. 1914.
G17/158. Allgemeine [Angelegenheiten der] Tanganyika-Eisenbahn Morogoro-Tabora. Bd. 3. 1909–1911.
G21/89. Strafsache gegen den Pflanzungsassistenten Paul Wörz, Kilossa, Bez. Morogoro, wegen Mißhandlung des Landwirtes Georg Buzello. 1914–1915.
G21/210. Strafsache gegen den ehemaligen Kanzleigehilfen, Heinrich Klemp, Morogoro, wegen Sittlichkeitsverbrechen [an der Tochter des gefangenen Sultans Masudi aus Tabora]. 1908–1911.
G21/262. Ermittlungssache gegen Aufseher der Firma Philipp Holzmann & ‚Cie., Frederic Sainsburg, Kondoa, Bez. Morogoro wegen fahrlässiger Tötung seines Dieners Amdallah [durch eine diesem zugänglich gemachten Pistole]. 1909.

G21/271. Ermittelungssache gegen den Zollhilfsbeamten Kurt Robscheit, Daressalaam, wegen Notzucht an der Binti Nasoro. 1909–1910.
G21/347. Ermittelungssache gegen den Polizeiwachtmeister Lindner, Daressalaam, wegen Vergewaltigung [der Mwatonya binti Hanyange]. 1911.
G21/361. Ermittelungssache gegen den Aufseher Henry Parsons, Itigi, Bez. Dodoma [wegen Verursachung einer Schlägerei zwischen seinen Arbeitern und denen der Beamten der OAEG Eredi und Kurbjeweit]. 1911.
G21/373. Ermittelungssache gegen den Aufseher Christo Antonio, Goweko, Bez. Tabora, wegen Vergehens gegen die Arbeiteranwerbeordnung. 1911–1912.
G21/403. Ermittelungssache gegen Unbekannt [wegen angeblicher Freiheitsberaubung, begangen an einer eingeborenen Prostituierten]. 1912.
G21/412. Ermittelungssache gegen den Arbeiteranwerber Michael Georgiades, Mkalama, Bez. Kondoa-Irangi, wegen Betruges, Körperverletzung, Freiheitsberaubung und Nötigung. 1911–1912.
G21/428. Ermittelungssache gegen den Gouvernements-Büroassistenten Thurmann Bezirksnebenstelle Kibata, Bez. Kilwa, wegen Notzucht [an der Frau seines Kochs Thumi sowie der Frau des Polizeiwachtmeisters Littmann, Kilwa]. 1912.
G21/545. Strafsache gegen den Pflanzungsassistenten Walter Grund, Pugu, Bez. Daressalaam, wegen Vergehens gegen die Arbeiter- und Anwerbeverordnung [vom 5.2.1913.] 1914.
G21/592. Strafsache gegen den Unternehmer Max Miersen, Daressalaam, wegen Versuchter Notzucht [an der Geliebten eines Askaris der 18. Feldkompanie, Habiba binti Mkondo]. 1915–1916.
G21/644. Ermittelungssache gegen den Stadtkassenbeamten Fernandes Persi, Daressalaam, wegen versuchter Notzucht [an der Andikalo binti Baruti]. 1915.
G21/645. Ermittelungssache gegen den Unternehmer George Koyakos, Kilossa, Bez. Morogoro, wegen Vergehens gegen die Arbeiteranwerbeverodnung [vom 5.2.1913]. 1915.
G21/680. Strafsache gegen den Landwirt Leopold Hierl, Dabaga bei Iringa [aufgrund einer Strafanzeige des Hauptmanns Tom v. Prince] wegen Unzucht [mit der minderjährigen Eingeborenen Mdene]. 1899–1900.
G21/686. Strafsache gegen den italienischen Unternehmer Marras Salvatore, km 412 der Tanganyika-Eisenbahn, wegen versuchter Notzucht und Mißhandlung [der Fatuma]. 1910–1911.
G23/40. Strafsache gegen den Goanesen Castro de Lobo, Muhesa, Bez. Tanga, wegen Unterschlagung [von Prämien zur Arbeiteranwerbung] 1914.
G27/27. Strafsache gegen den Unternehmer John Zavellas, Tabora, wegen Anstiftung [mehrerer Aufseher zur Freiheitsberaubung]. 1911.
G27/53. Strafsache gegen den Unternehmer Emanuel Jeronimakis, km 592 der Tanganyika-Eisenbahn, wegen Verführung [der angeblich minderjährigen Adaa und Verschuldung ihres Selbstmordes]. 1911–1912.
G27/73. Strafsache gegen den Unternehmer John Zavellas, Kilossa, Bez. Morogoro, wegen Vergehens gegen die Arbeiterverordnung [vom 5.2.1912 – Nichtführung von Lohnlisten] und Führung eines unrichtigen Namens. 1914–1915.
G51/1. [Angelegenheiten der] Usambara-Eisenbahn. Bd., 2. 1899–1902.

TECHNOSEUM – Landesmuseum für Technik und Arbeit in Mannheim (LTA)

871.1-otto-195. Deutsche Nyanza-Schiffahrtsgesellschaft.
871.1-otto-197. Geschäftskorrespondenz über die Baumwoll-Pflanzungsgesellschaft "Kilwa" im ehemaligen Deutsch-Ostafrika.
871.1-otto-198. 8 Schreiben mit Kriegsnachrichten aus Kilossa, Ostafrika. 1915–1918.
871.1-otto-199. Vergleichsregelung zwischen Fa. Otto und dem deutschen Reich.
871.1-otto-202. Schriftwechsel über die Planung einer Pflanzung in Deutsch-Ostafrika. 1926–1928.
871.1-otto-203. Kriegsentschädigung für Kolonialbesitz. 1926–1934.
871.1-otto-204. Korrespondenz Karl Oskar Kübel, Deutsche Kolonialgesellschaft, Cannstadt. 1928–1936.
871.1-otto-229. [Firmenjubiläum am 12. November 1936.]
871.1-otto-233. Chronik.

Unitätsarchiv Herrnhut/Moravian Archives Herrnhut (UAH)

"Bericht des Missions Departments an die Generalsynode 1899".
"Bericht der Missionsdirektion an die Generalsynode 1909".
FI. A2. 35. "Bericht der Missionsdirektion an die Generalsynode 1914".
MD 767. Personalakten Mission. Gaarde, Nis Hansen.
MD 893. Personalakten Mission. Löbner, Mads Hansen.
MD 1530. Missionsdirektion Unyamwezi. Jahresberichte der Provinz 1906–1940.
MD 1532. Missionsdirektion Unyamwezi. Briefwechsel mit dem Superintendenten u. Vorsteher 1909–1911.
MD 1537. Prov. Missionsdirektion. Stationsberichte. Ipole 1909–1916.
MD 1539. Missionsdirektion Pert. Unyamwesi. Stationsberichte Kitunda 1909–1918.
MD 1540. Missionsdirektion Unyamwesi/Tansania. Stationsberichte 4. Sikonge. 1909–1917.
MD 1541. Missionsdirektion. Unyamwesi. Stationsberichte Urambo 1909–1916.
MD 1542. Missionsdirektion Unyamwesi. Stationsberichte Usoke 1906–1914.
MD 1543. Prov.: Missionsdirektion Pert.: Unyamwesi/Tansania Stationsberichte. Bahnmission (Berichte u. Briefwechsel). 1910–1912.
MD 1544. Berichte der Missionsstation Tabora.
MD 1547–1533. Stationsbriefwechsel versch. Stationen. 3. Kitunda.
MD 1557. Missionsdirektion Unyamwesi. Schriftwechsel mit dem Kaiserlichen Gouverneur und dem Kaiserlichen Bezirksamt in Tabora 1900–1927.
MD 1560. Verschiedenes. 3. Briefwechsel mit Verschiedenen 1909–1915.

Universitätsarchiv Tübingen (UAT)

407/2,1. Nachlass Hennig (1882–1977). Brief-Tagebuch an die Familie, Teil 1.
407/2,2. Nachlass Hennig (1882–1977). Brief-Tagebuch an die Familie, Teil 2.
407/80. Nachlass Hennig (1882–1977). Tagebuch, Teil 1.
407/81. Nachlass Hennig (1882–1977). Tagebuch, Teil 2.
407/82. Nachlass Hennig (1882–1977). Tagebuch, Teil 3.
407/91. Nachlass Hennig (1882–1977). Fotoalbum.

Oral Sources

Interview with Reverend John*. Mwanza: 08/09/16, 1:14:20–1:20:41. * = name changed due to privacy reasons.

Libaba, P.M. 'The Maji Maji Rising in the Lindi District'. Maji Maji Research Project No. 7/68/2/1. Gwassa, G.C.K. and Iliffe, John (Eds.). *Records of the Maji Maji Rising*. Dar es Salaam: 1968.

Printed Sources

Allmaras, Franz. 'Ich baue 2000 km Eisenbahnen'. *Heiß war der Tag. Das Kolonialbuch für das junge Deutschland*. 35–55. Ed. Hans Ernst Pfeiffer. Leipzig: 1938.

Baltzer, Franz. *Die Kolonialbahnen mit besonderer Berücksichtigung Afrikas*. Berlin: 1916.

Berkhout, A.H. 'Ziele, Resultate und Zukunft der Indischen Forstwirtschaft'. 303–313. *Der Tropenpflanzer. Zeitschrift für Tropische Landwirtschaft*. 13. Jahrgang, no. 7. Berlin: July 1909.

Brahmputr, Ganga-rao. *Indien. Seine Stellung zum Weltkrieg und zu seiner Zukunft. Ein Beitrag zur Aufklärung über indische Verhältnisse der Jetztzeit: Indiens Stellung zum Weltkrieg, zum "Heiligen Krieg" aller Mohamedaner und zur Frage seiner Befreiung*. Tübingen: 1916.

Delegated Representatives of Master Cotton Spinners' and Manufacturer's Association. *Official Report of the Proceedings of the First International Congress*. Manchester: 1904.

Deutsche Kolonialgesellschaft Abteilung Stuttgart. *Kurzer Rückblick auf die Tätigkeit der deutschen Kolonialgesellschaft und des kolonialwirtschaftlichen Komitees seit seiner Gründung 1881 u. 1896*. Stuttgart: 1912.

——. *Mitgliederverzeichnis 1899*. Stuttgart: 1899.

Dernburg, Bernhard. *Baumwollfragen. Vortrag, gehalten auf Veranlassung des Deutschen Handelstages am 14. April 1910*. Berlin: 1910.

——. *Südwestafrikanische Eindrücke. Industrielle Fortschritte in den Kolonien. Zwei Vorträge*. Berlin: 1909.

——. *Koloniale Erziehung*. Munich: 1907.

——. *Koloniale Lehrjahre. Vortrag Gehalten in Stuttgart am 23. Januar 1907*. Stuttgart et al.: 1907.

——. *Zielpunkte des deutschen Kolonialwesens. Zwei Vorträge*. Berlin: 1907.

Dernburg, Friedrich. *Aus der weißen Stadt. Spaziergänge in der Chicagoer Weltausstellung und weitere Fahrten*. Berlin: 1893.

Fuchs, Paul. *Die wirtschaftlichen Erkundungen einer ostafrikanischen Südbahn*. Berlin: 1905.

German Imperial Commissioner (Ed.). *Official Catalogue of the Exhibition of the German Empire. International Exposition St. Louis 1904*. Berlin: n.Y.

Gillman, Clement. 'Dar es Salaam 1860–1940: A Story of Growth and Change'. 1–23. *Tanganyika Notes and Records*, no. 20. Dar es Salaam: 1945.

——. 'A Short History of the Tanganyika Railways'. 14–56. *Tanganyika Notes and Records*, no. 13. Dar es Salaam: 1942.

Götzen, Gustav Adolf Graf von. *Deutsch-Ostafrika im Aufstand 1905/06*. Berlin: 1909.

Grages, Ferdinand. 'Holzmann in Afrika'. *Philipp Holzmann Aktiengesellschaft im Wandel von Hundert Jahren. 1849–1949*. 285–298. Ed. Hans Meyer-Heinrich. Frankfurt o.M.: 1949.

Hagenbeck, Carl. *Von Tieren und Menschen*. Web. *Zeno.org*. *http://www.zeno.org/Naturwissenschaften/M/Hagenbeck,+Carl/Von+Tieren+und+Menschen* (26 February 2020).

Handbuch der deutschen Aktien-Gesellschaften: ein Hand- und Nachschlagebuch für Bankiers, Industrielle, Kapitalisten, Behörden etc. Berlin and Leipzig: 1943.
Hehl, R.A. *Eisenbahnen in den Tropen. Spurweiten, Bau und Betrieb.* Berlin: 1902.
Hennig, Edwin. *Gewesene Welten. Auf Saurierjagd im ostafrikanischen Busch.* Rüschlikon bei Zürich: 1955.
——. *Am Tendaguru. Leben und Wirken einer deutschen Forschungsexpedition zur Ausgrabung vorweltlicher Riesensaurier in Deutsch-Ostafrika.* Stuttgart: 1912.
Hutson, James. *Chinese Life in the Tibetan Foothills.* Shanghai: 1921.
Jöhlinger, Otto. 'Bernhard Dernburg. Ein kaufmännischer Minister'. 1–13. *Der Kaufmann und das Leben. Beiblatt zur Zeitschrift für Handelswissenschaft und Handelspraxis.* Eds. Arthur Schröter and Heinz Rühl. Leipzig and Kassel, no. 5: Mai 1911.
Jungblut, Carl. *Vierzig Jahre Afrika. 1900–1940.* Berlin: 1941.
Kaundinya, H.A. *Die Lebensgeschichte des in Mangalur bekehrten Brahminen Hermann Anandraja Kaundinja.* Basel: 1854.
Kaundinya, Otto. *Das Handballspiel. Technik, Taktik, Spielregeln, Training.* 1st. & 2nd. Edition. Leipzig: 1935 and 1941.
——. *Die sportliche Leistung. Ihre biologischen, rassischen und pädagogischen Voraussetzungen.* Leipzig: 1936.
Kaundinya, R. *Erinnerungen aus meinen Pflanzerjahren in Deutsch-Ostafrika.* Leipzig: 1918.
Kolonialausstellung Stuttgart 1928. *Amtlicher Ausstellungsführer.* Stuttgart: 1928.
Koloniale Reichsarbeitsgemeinschaft Berlin – Afrikahaus. *Protest der deutschen Wirtschaft gegen den Raub von Deutsch-Ostafrika.* Berlin: 1930
Kolonialpolitisches Aktionskomitee (Ed.). *Die Eisenbahnen Afrikas. Grundlagen und Gesichtspunkte für eine koloniale Eisenbahnpolitik in Afrika. Nach der gleichnamigen amtlichen Denkschrift.* Berlin: 1907.
Kolonial-Wirtschaftliches Komitee. (Ed.). *Unsere Kolonialwirtschaft in ihrer Bedeutung für Industrie und Arbeiterschaft.* Berlin: 1909.
——. 'Unsere Kolonialwirtschaft in ihrer Bedeutung für Industrie und Arbeiterschaft'. 45–56. Beiheft zum „Tropenpflanzer", Jahrgang XIII, Nr. 3. March 1909.
——. *Wirtschaftsatlas der deutschen Kolonien.* Berlin: 1906.
Langkopp, Heinrich. *22 Jahre im Innern Afrikas. Was ich erstrebte, erlebte, erlitt.* Gnötzheim b. Würzburg: 1929.
Marcus, August and Kolonialwirtschaftliches Komitee. (Eds.). *Kolonial Handels- und Adreßbuch. Mandatsgebiete in Afrika. 1936. 19. Jahrgang.* Berlin: 1936.
Methner, Wilhelm. *Unter drei Gouverneuren. 16 Jahre Dienst in deutschen Tropen.* Breslau: 1938.
Milton, John. *Das Verlorene Paradies.* Altenmünster: 2016.
Müllendorf, Prosper. *Ost-Afrika im Aufstieg.* Essen: 1910.
Noske, Gustav. *Wie ich wurde. Selbstbiographien volkstümlicher Persönlichkeiten.* Berlin: 1919.
——. 'Kolonialpolitik nach dem Kriege'. 481–488. *Die Neue Zeit. Wochenschrift der Deutschen Sozialdemokratie.* vol. 1, no. 21. 22th February 1918.
——. *Kolonialpolitik und Sozialdemokratie.* Stuttgart: 1914.
Oetker, Karl früher Leiter des Gesundheitsdienstes beim Bahnbau Daressalam-Morogoro (Ostafrika). *Die Neger-Seele und die Deutschen in Afrika. Ein Kampf gegen Missionen, Sittlichkeits-Fanatismus und Bürokratie vom Standpunkt moderner Psychologie.* Munich: 1907.
Paasche, Hans. '"Der Aufstand" und "Gefechte am Rufiyi" aus: "Im Morgenhlicht. Kriegs-, Jagd- und Reise-Erlebnisse in Ostafrika"'. Hans Paasche. Das Verlorene Paradies. *Ansichten vom Lenbensweg eines Kolonialoffiziers zum Pazifisten und Revolutionär.* 48–86. Eds. P. Werner Lange und Helga Paasche. Berlin: 2008.

Paasche, Hermann. *Deutsch-Ostafrika. Wirtschaftliche Studien*. Hamburg: 1913.
Pfeil, Joachim. *Vorschläge zur praktischen Kolonisation in Ost-Afrika*. Berlin: 1890.
Rathenau, Walther. 'Erwägungen über die Erschlieszung [sic!] des Deutsch-Ostafrikanischen Schutzgebietes'. *Reflexionen*. 143–198. Ed. Walter Rathenau. Leipzig: 1908.
Report by His Britannic Majesty's Government on the Mandated Territory of Tanganyika for the Year 1960. London: 1960.
Richter, Otto. 'Holzmann in Asien. Die Anatolische und die Bagdadbahn'. *Philipp Holzmann Aktiengesellschaft im Wandel von Hundert Jahren. 1849–1949*. 249–273. Ed. Hans Meyer-Heinrich. Frankfurt o.M.: 1949.
Roeder, Georg. 'Aus Indiens Kolonial-Technik'. 403–428. *Der Tropenpflanzer. Zeitschrift für Tropische Landwirtschaft*. 13. Jahrgang, no. 9. Berlin: July 1909.
Schanz, Moritz. 'Der koloniale Baumwollanbau und Deutschland'. 160–172. Ed. InternationalerVerband der Spinner und Webervereinigungen. *Offizieller Bericht des Achten Internationalen Kongresses der Baumwoll-Industrie*. Manchester et al.: 1911.
——. 'Die Negerfrage in Nordamerika'. 573–585. Ed. Kolonial-Wirtschaftliches Komitee. *Beiheft zum „Tropenpflanzer"*, Jahrgang XIII, Nr. 3. March 1909.
Supf, Karl. 'Deutsch-Koloniale Baumwoll-Unternehmungen. Bericht XI (Frühjahr 1909)'. 161–162. Ed. Kolonial-Wirtschaftliches Komitee. *Beiheft zum „Tropenpflanzer"*, Jahrgang XIII, no. 5, May 1909.
——. 'Deutsch-koloniale Baumwoll-Unternehmungen Bericht IV (Herbst 1904)'. 615–621. Ed. Kolonialwirtschaftliches Komitee. *Der Tropenpflanzer. Zeitschrift für Tropische Landwirtschaft*, no. 11. Berlin: November 1904.
——. 'Deutsch-koloniale Baumwoll-Unternehmnungen 1903/1904'. 411–417. Ed. Kolonial-Wirtschaftliches Komitee. *Der Tropenfplanzer. Zeitschrift für Tropische Landwirtschaft*. No. 8., August 1904.
Tholens, R. 'Zum Baumwollbau in Ägypten'. 567–573. *Der Tropenpflanzer. Zeitschrift für Tropische Landwirtschaft*. 13. Jahrgang, no. 7. Berlin: July 1909.
Zimmermann, Adolf. *Mit Dernburg nach Ostafrika*. Berlin: 1908.

German Colonial Newspapers

Deutsch Ostafrikanische Zeitung (DOAZ)

"Anwendung der Einwanderungsverordnung auf Farbige". *DOAZ*, XIV, no. 90. Daressalam: 09 November 1912.
"Arbeitserziehung und Arbeitszwang". *DOAZ*, VIII, no. 22. Daressalam: 02 June 1906.
"Aus Dar es Salaam und Umgebung. Ein Streikversuch der indischen Flotillen Handwerker". *DOAZ*, VIII, no. 2. Daressalam: 13 January 1906.
"Aus der Kolonie. Die Riesenplantage bei Kilossa". *DOAZ*, IX, no. 48. Daressalam: 07 September 1907.
"Aus der Kolonie. Vorläufig keine Chinesen". *DOAZ*, VIII, no. 35. Daressalam: 01 September 1906.
"Aus der Kolonie. 500 Chinesen kommen". *DOAZ*, VIII, no. 33. Daressalam: 18 August 1906.
"Aus der Kolonie. Bedingungen des Gouvernements für die Gestellung von Zwangsarbeitern". *DOAZ*, VIII, no. 23. Daressalam: 9 June 1906.
"Aus der Kolonie. Chinesen-Einfuhr". *DOAZ*, VIII, no. 19. Daressalam: 12 May 1906.
"Aus der Kolonie. Einfuhr von Chinesen". *DOAZ*, VIII, no. 7. Daressalam: 17 February 1906.
"Aus der Kolonie". *DOAZ*, VII, no. 13. Daressalam: 01 January 1905.
"Aus unserer Kolonie". *DOAZ*, XIV, no. 96. Daressalam: 30 November 1912.

"Aus unserer Kolonie. Offizielle Eröffnung der Mittellandbahn bis Tabora". *DOAZ*, XIV, no. 61. Daressalam: 31 July 1912.
"Aus unserer Kolonie. Von den Arbeitskarten im Bezirk Wilhelmstal". *DOAZ*, XII, no. 79. Daressalam: 05 October 1910.
"Aus unserer Kolonie. Die weiße Bevölkerung Deutsch-Ostafrikas". *DOAZ*, XII, no. 28. Daressalam: 08 April 1911.
"Aus unserer Kolonie. Morogoro. Streik". *DOAZ*, XI, no. 85. Daressalam: 27 October 1909.
"Aus unserer Kolonie. Kilossa". *DOAZ*, XI, no. 37. Daressalam: 12 May 1909.
"Aus unserer Kolonie. X. Kilossa". *DOAZ*, X, no. 63. Daressalam: 19 August 1908.
"Aus unserer Kolonie. Die Inder in Deutsch-Ostafrika". *DOAZ*, XIII, no. 22. Daressalam: 18 March 1911.
"Berliner Telegramme. Ein Wechsel in der Haltung der kaiserlichen Regierung zur Frage der staatlichen Arbeiteranwerbung?". *DOAZ*, XV, no. 72. Daressalam: 09 September 1913.
"Chinesische Arbeiter". *DOAZ*, VIII, no. 20. Daressalam: 19 May 1906.
"Das Deutsch-Belgische Wettrennen zum Tanganikasee". *DOAZ*, XIV, no. 88. Daressalam: 02 November 1912.
"Der wirtschaftliche Aufschwung im Bezirk Muansa und die Inder-Einwanderung". *DOAZ*, VII, no. 1. Daressalam: 07 January 1905.
"Deutsche Unternehmer für den Bahnbau Tabora-Tanganika". *DOAZ*, XIV, no. 8. Daressalam: 27 January 1912.
"Die Inder-Überschwemmung Deutsch-Ostafrikas". *DOAZ*, VII, no. 18. Daressalam: 06 May 1905.
"Die Ostafrikanische Eisenbahngesellschaft". *DOAZ*, IX, no. 28. Daressalam: 29 July 1907.
"Die wirtschaftlichen Verhältnisse des Bezirks Tabora im Jahre 1911". *DOAZ*, XIV, no. 92. Daressalam: 16 November 1912.
"Die Zunahme der Einwanderung unbemittelter Inder". *DOAZ*, XIII, no. 72. Daressalam: 09 September 1911.
Dr. H. Krauß. "Über die Gesundheitsverhältnisse in Deutsch-Ostafrika". *DOAZ*, X, no. 94. Daressalam: 05 December 1908.
"Ein Deutscher Kaufmann über die Inderfrage". *DOAZ*, XI, no. 62. Daressalam: 07 August 1909.
"Eine Ernste Gefahr für unser Prestige". *DOAZ*, VII, no. 12. Daressalam: 25 March 1905.
"Eine indische Kraftprobe". *DOAZ*, X, no. 99. Daressalam: 24 December 1908.
"Einfuhrzölle und Arbeiterfrage". *DOAZ*, VIII, no. 27. Daressalam: 07 July 1906.
"Gewissenlose Berichterstattung". *DOAZ*, IX, no. 60. Daressalam: 19 October 1907.
"Gouvernementsrat (4. Verhandlungstag)". *DOAZ*, XVI, no. 55. Daressalam: 08 July 1914.
"Indische Völkerwanderung nach Deutsch-Ostafrica". *DOAZ*, VII, no. 43. Daressalam: 28 October 1905.
Karstedt, F.O. Dr. "Beiträge zur Inderfrage in Deutsch-Ostafrika I". *DOAZ*, XV, no. 76. Daressalam: 20 September 1913.
——. "Beiträge zur Inderfrage in Deutsch-Ostafrika II. (Fortsetzung)". *DOAZ*, XV, no. 77. Daressalam: 24 September 1913.
——. "Beiträge zur Inderfrage in Deutsch-Ostafrika IV. (Schluß)". *DOAZ*, XV, no. 79. Daressalam: 01 October 1913.
"Kilossa". *DOAZ*, X., no. 90. Daressalam: 21 November 1908.
"Kilossa". *DOAZ*, X, no. 65. Daressalam: 26 August 1908.
Krauß, Dr. Ehemals Bahnbauarzt der Firma Holzmann & Cie. "Der Gesundheitsdienst beim Bahnbau Daressalaam – Morogoro". *DOAZ*, X, no. 82. Daressalam: 24 October 1908.
"Lernen wir von der Ugandabahn". *DOAZ*, VII, no. 1. Daressalam: 07 January 1905.
"Lokales. Personenschmuggel". *DOAZ*, XV, no. 94. Daressalam: 22 November 1913.

"Lokales. Streik bei der Ostafrikanischen Eisenbahngesellschaft". *DOAG*, XV, no. 70. Daressalam: 30 August 1913.
"Morogoro. Ungesunde Lohnverhältnisse". *DOAZ*, XIII, no. 65. Daressalam: 16 August 1911.
"Samassa über die Inderfrage". *DOAZ*, XI, no. 61. Daressalam: 04 August 1909.
"Sind die Europäer in den Tropen in wirtschaftlicher Beziehung dauernd den Indern überlegen?". *DOAZ*, VII, no. 17. Daressalam: 29 April 1905.
"Soll Deutsch-Ostafrika eine deutsche Kolonie werden oder eine Hamburg-indische Domäne bleiben? 5. Die Inderfrage und die Behandlung der Farbigen". *DOAZ*, VII, no. 31. Daressalam: 05 August 1905.
"Strafarbeiter aus Kilwa für die Bahn". *DOAZ*, VIII, no. 37. Daressalam: 15 September 1906.
"Strafarbeiter für den Bahnbau". *DOAZ*, VIII, no. 40. Daressalam: 06 October 1906.
"Streifzüge in Ostafrika". *DOAZ*, XI, no. 19. Daressalam: 10 March 1909.
"Thätigkeit des Arbeiterkommissariats". *DOAZ*, VIII, no. 33. Daressalam: 18 August 1906.
"Über den Fortgang der Arbeiten an der Eisenbahn Dar es Salaam – Morogoro". *DOAZ*, VIII, no. 27. Daressalam: 07 July 1906.
"Unser Wissen von den Kometenschweifen". *DOAZ*, XII, no. 17. Daressalam: 02 March 1910.
"Vermischte Nachrichten. Der Stammbaum des Kometen". *DOAZ*, XII, no. 20. Daressalam: 12 March 1910.
"Verschiffung von Arbeitern für die Nordbezirke". *DOAZ*, VIII, no. 23. Daressalam: 09 June 1906.
"Von Unserer Bahn". *DOAZ*, VII, no. 23. Daressalam: 10 June 1905.
"Was ich auf meiner Reise von Dar es Salaam nach Kilossa sah". *DOAZ*, VII, no. 28. Daressalam: 15 July 1905.
"Wie wir von gut unterrichteter Seite erfahren". *DOAZ*, VIII, no. 4. Daressalam: 27 January 1906.
"X. Kilossa. Dampfpflüge". *DOAZ*, X., no. 63. Daressalam: 19 August 1908.
"Zur Abwehr der Indergefahr". *DOAZ*, VII, no. 22. Daressalam: 03 June 1905.
"Zur Griechenfrage". *DOAZ*, XI, no. 42. Daressalam: 29 May 1909.
"Zur Inderfrage". *DOAZ*, X, no. 36. Daressalam: 16 May 1908.

Kiongozi. Habari kwa Watu wote wa Deutsch-Ostafrika

"Nyota wa Mkia", no. 58. Tanga: March 1910.

Koloniale Rundschau. Monatsschrift für die Interessen unserer Schutzgebiete und ihrer Bewohner

Dernburg, Friedrich. "Aus Bernhard Dernburg's Werdegang". 402–407, no. 7, Berlin: July 1910.

Online Sources

ETH-Bibliothek – *Schweizerische Bauzeitung*

Gillman, Clement. 'Vom Bau der ostafrikanischen Mittellandbahn'. 160–166. *Schweizerische Bauzeitung*, 61/62, no. 12. Zürich: 1913. Web. *ETH-Bibliothek*. http://doi.org/10.5169/seals-30784 (08 February 2018).
——. 'Vom Bau der ostafrikanischen Mittellandbahn'. 176–179. *Schweizerische Bauzeitung*, 61/62, no. 13. Zürich: 1913. Web. *ETH-Bibliothek*. http://doi.org/10.5169/seals-30786 (08 February 2018).

Reichstagsprotokolle

Noske, Gustav. '232. Sitzung. Dienstag, den 10. März 1914'. 7984–7993. *Verhandlungen des Reichstags. Bd. 294. 1914.* Berlin: 1914. Web. http://www.reichstagsprotokolle.de/Blatt_k13_bsb00003390_00080.html (21 June 2018).

Universitätsbibliothek Frankfurt o.M.

Deutsches Koloniallexikon

"Eisenbahnen". *Deutsches Koloniallexikon*, 1920, Band II, p. 529. Web. *University of Frankfurt o.M.* http://www.ub.bildarchiv-dkg.uni-frankfurt.de/Bildprojekt/Lexikon/Standardframeseite.php?suche=eisenbahn (26 November 2019).

"Eisenbahnaufsicht". *Deutsches Koloniallexikon*, 1920, Band I, p. 525. Web. *University of Frankfurt o.M.* http://www.ub.bildarchiv-dkg.unifrankfurt.de/Bildprojekt/Lexikon/php/suche_db.php?suchname=Eisenbahnaufsicht (26 October 2020).

"Eisenbahnbeamte". *Deutsches Koloniallexikon*, 1920, Band I, p. 528–529. Web. *University of Frankfurt o.M.* http://www.ub.bildarchiv-dkg.uni-frankfurt.de/Bildprojekt/Lexikon/php/suche_db.php?suchname=Eisenbahnbeamte (26 October 2020).

"Eisenbahnbehörden". *Deutsches Koloniallexikon*, 1920, Band I, p. 529. Web. *University of Frankfurt o.M.* http://www.ub.bildarchiv-dkg.uni-frankfurt.de/Bildprojekt/Lexikon/php/suche_db.php?suchname=Eisenbahnbeh%F6rden (26 October 2020).

"Eisenbahnkommissar". *Deutsches Koloniallexikon*, 1920, Band I, p. 544. Web. *University of Frankfurt o.M.* http://www.ub.bildarchiv-dkg.unifrankfurt.de/Bildprojekt/Lexikon/Standardframeseite.php?suche=Kommissar (26 October 2020).

"Krankenhäuser". *Deutsches Kolonial-Lexikon*, 1920, Band II, S. 372. Web. *University of Frankfurt o.M.* http://www.ub.bildarchiv-dkg.uni-frankfurt.de/Bildprojekt/Lexikon/Standardframeseite.php?suche=Sewa (14 October 2020).

"Mpanganya". *Deutsches Koloniallexikon*, 1920, Band II, p. 595. Web. *University of Frankfurt o.M.* http://www.ub.bildarchiv-dkg.uni-frankfurt.de/Bildprojekt/Lexikon/Standardframeseite.php (18 June 2019).

"Oswald & Co.". *Deutsches Koloniallexikon.* 1920, Band II, p. 691. Web. *University of Frankfurt o.M.* http://www.ub.bildarchiv-dkg.uni-frankfurt.de/Bildprojekt/Lexikon/Standardframeseite.php?suche=O%27Swald (09 July 2021).

"Schuckmann, v.". *Deutsches Koloniallexikon*, 1920, Band II, p. 306. Web. *University of Frankfurt o.M.* http://www.ub.bildarchiv-dkg.uni-frankfurt.de/Bildprojekt/Lexikon/Standardframeseite.php (05 February 2020).

"Shantung-Eisenbahn". *Deutsches Kolonial-Lexikon*, 1920, Band III, p. 259. Web. *University of Frankfurt o.M.* http://www.ub.bildarchiv-dkg.uni-frankfurt.de/Bildprojekt/Lexikon/Standardframeseite.php?suche=shantung (22 October 2020).

"Vageler". *Deutsches Koloniallexikon*, 1920, Band III, p. 598. Web. *University of Frankfurt o.M.* http://www.ub.bildarchiv-dkg.uni-frankfurt.de/Bildprojekt/Lexikon/Standardframeseite.php?suche=Vageler (23 July 2019).

World Newspaper Archive

The Indian Voice of British East Africa, Uganda and Zanzibar

"Notes of the Week". *The Indian Voice of British East Africa, Uganda and Zanzibar*. Nairobi: 06 September 1911, p. 8. Web. *African Newspapers*. http://public.maximus.newsbank.com//images/L00000005/cache/pdf/bitonal_tiff_g4/13D0F5BDA3FEA150_13D0F21E098FF7B0.pdf (24 January 2018).

"To Africa. By a Disgusted Indian Clerk on Retiring from the Service of the Railway". *The Indian Voice of British East Africa, Uganda and Zanzibar*. Nairobi: 19 April 1911, p. 6. Web. *African Newspapers*. http://public.maximus.newsbank.com//images/L00000007/cache/pdf/bitonal_tiff_g4/13D0F5904120B628_13CF496663BB9D10.pdf (24 January 2018).

"We Hear". *The Indian Voice of British East Africa*. Nairobi: 10 May 1911. Web. *African Newspapers*. http://public.maximus.newsbank.com//images/L00000007/cache/pdf/bitonal_tiff_g4/13D0F59812493A88_13CF57D782C56578.pdf (24 January 2018).

Literature

Aas, Norbert and Sippel, Harald. *Koloniale Konflikte im Alltag. Eine rechtshistorische Untersuchung der Auseinandersetzungen des Siedlers Heinrich Langkopp mit der Kolonialverwaltung in Deutsch-Ostafrika und dem Reichsentschädigungsamt in Berlin (1910–1929)*. Bayreuth: 1997.

Aas, Norbert. *Koloniale Entwicklung im Bezirksamt Lindi (Deutsch-Ostafrika): Deutsche Erwartungen und Regionale Wirklichkeit*. Bayreuth: 1989.

Achinger, Christine. 'Deutsche Arbeit und die Poetisierung der Moderne'. *«Deutsche Arbeit». Kritische Perspektiven auf ein ideologisches Selbstbild*. 252–284. Eds. Felix Axster and Nikolas Lelle. Göttingen: 2018.

Adams, Zuleiga. *Demitrios Tsafendas: Race, Madness and the Archive. A dissertation submitted for the degree of Doctor of Philosophy in History. University of the Western Cape, December 2011*. Web. https://etd.uwc.ac.za/xmlui/bitstream/handle/11394/2912/Adams_PHD_2011.pdf?sequence=1&isAllowed=y (09 December 2019).

Adelman, Jeremy. 'What is Global History Now?'. *Aeon*. N.d. Web. https://aeon.co/essays/is-global-history-still-possible-or-has-it-had-its-moment (01 December 2020).

Aitken, Robbie. 'Forgotten Histories: Recovering the precarious lives of African servants in imperial Germany'. *Locating African European Studies. Interventions, Intersections, Conversations*. 139–150. Eds. Felipe Espinoza Garrido et al. London: 2020.

Aiyar, Sana. *Indians in Kenya. The Politics of Diaspora*. Cambridge: 2015.

Akira Iriye. 'Japan's drive to great-power status'. *The Cambridge History of Japan. Volume 5. The Nineteenth Century*. 721–782. Ed. Marius B. Jansen. Cambridge: 1989.

Akurang-Parry, Kwabena Opare. 'Colonial Forced Labor Policies for Road Building in Southern Ghana and International Anti-Forced Labor Pressures 1900–1940'. 1–25. *African Economic History*, no. 28. N.P.: 2000. Web. *Jstore*. http://www.jstor.org/stable/3601647 (12 November 2017).

Akyeampong, Emmanuel and Ambler, Charles. 'Leisure in African History. An Introduction'. 1–16. *The International Journal of African Historical Studies*, vol. 35, no. 1. Boston: 2002. Web. *Jstor*. https://www.jstor.org/stable/3097363 (01 August 2018).

Allen, Richard B. *European Slave Trading in the Indian Ocean, 1500–1850*. Athens (Ohio): 2015.

Alpers, Edward A. *The Indian Ocean in World History*. Oxford: 2014.

——. *East Africa and the Indian Ocean*. Princeton: 2009.

Angermann, Erich. "Bassermann, Friedrich Daniel". 624–625. *Neue Deutsche Biographie*, 1. 1953. Web. https://www.deutsche-biographie.de/sfz35199.html#ndbcontent. (22 December 2017).

Arnold, Bernd. *Steuer und Lohnarbeit im Südwesten von Deutsch-Ostafrika 1891–1916*. Münster and Hamburg: 1994.

Aselmeyer, Norman. *The Shadow Line. Railway and Society in Colonial East Africa, ca. 1890–1914 (Provisional Title)*. Web. https://www.uni-bremen.de/institut-fuer-geschichtswissenschaft/personen/a-z/aselmeyer-norman (19 September 2021).

Auslander, Leora. 'Accommodation, Resistance, and *Eigensinn. Évolués and Sapeurs between Africa and Europe*'. *Alltag, Erfahrung, Eigensinn. Historisch-anthropologische Erkundungen*. 205–217. Eds. Belinda Davis et al. Frankfurt o.M. and New York: 2008.

Austin, Gareth. 'African Business History'. 141–158. Ed. John F. Wilson. *The Routledge Companion to Business History*. London: 2017.

——. 'The Return of Capitalism as a Concept'. *Capitalism. The Reemergence of a Historical Concept*. 207–234. Eds. Jürgen Kocka and Marcel van der Linden. London et al.: 2016.

Authaler, Caroline. *Deutsche Plantagen in Britisch-Kamerun. Internationale Normen und lokale Realitäten 1925 bis 1940*. Cologne: 2018.

Axster, Felix and Lelle, Nikolas (Eds.). *«Deutsche Arbeit». Kritische Perspektiven auf ein ideologisches Selbstbild.* Göttingen: 2018.

——. '«Deutsche Arbeit». Kritische Perspektiven auf ein ideologisches Selbstbild. Zur Einführung'. *«Deutsche Arbeit». Kritische Perspektiven auf ein ideologisches Selbstbild*. 7–36. Eds. Felix Axster and Nikolas Lelle. Göttingen: 2018.

Axter, Felix. 'Arbeit an der 'Erziehung zu Arbeit'. Oder: die Figur des guten deutschen Kolonisators'. *«Deutsche Arbeit». Kritische Perspektiven auf ein ideologisches Selbstbild*. 226–251. Eds. Felix Axster and Nikolas Lelle. Göttingen: 2018.

Bach, Christine. "Pferdmenges, Robert". *Konrad Adenauer Stiftung*. Web. https://www.kas.de/web/geschichte-der-cdu/personen/biogramm-detail/-/content/robert-pferdmenges-v1 (18 July 2019).

Bähr, Andreas et al. 'Räume des Selbst. Eine Einleitung'. *Räume des Selbst. Selbstzeugnisforschung transkulturell*. 1–25. Eds. Andreas Bähr et al. Cologne et al: 2007.

Bähr, Johannes et al. *MAN. The History of a German Industrial Enterprise*. Munich: 2009.

Bänziger, Peter-Paul. *Moderne als Erlebnis. Eine Geschichte der Konsum- und Arbeitsgesellschaft. 1840–1940.* Göttingen: 2020.

Bärwald, Annika. 'Bremer Baumwollträume. Bremer Wirtschaftsinteressen und das Streben nach Rohstoffautarkie im kolonialen Togo'. 1–30. *Bonjour Geschichte. Bremer online Journal*, no. 5. 2017.

Bahnhofsmission Deutschland e.V. '125 Jahre Bahnhofsmission'. *www.bahnhofsmission.de*. Web. https://www.bahnhofsmission.de/index.php?id=15 (05 August 2021).

Bald, Detlef. *Deutsch-Ostafrika. Eine Studie über Verwaltung, Wirtschaft und Interessensgruppen*. Munich: 1970.

Banfield, Jane. 'Federation in East Africa'. 181–193. *International Journal*, vol. 18, no. 2. N.P.: 1963. Web. *Jstor.* https://www.jstor.org/stable/40198786 (14 June 2021).

Bartmuss, Hartmut. *Bernhard Dernburg. Kolonialpolitiker der Kaiserzeit*. Berlin: 2014.

Bayly, Christopher. *The Birth of the Modern World. 1780–1914. Global Connections and Comparisons.* Oxford: 2014.

Becker, Felicitas. 'Sudden Disaster and slow Change: Maji Maji and the Long-Term History of Southeast Tanzania'. *Maji Maji. Lifting the Fog of War*. 295–322. Eds. James Giblin and Jamie Monson. Leiden: 2010.

——. 'Südost-Tansania nach dem Maji-Maji-Krieg. Unterentwicklung als Kriegsfolge?'. *Der Maji-Maji-Krieg in Deutsch-Ostfafrika 1905–1907*. 184–195. Eds. Felicitas Becker and Jigal Beez. Berlin: 2005.

——. and Beez, Jigal (Eds.). *Der Maji-Maji Krieg in Deutsch-Ostafrika 1905–1907.* Berlin: 2005.

Becker, Frank. 'Die Hottentotten-Wahlen (1907)'. *Kein Platz an der Sonne. Erinnerungsorte der deutschen Kolonialgeschichte*. 177–190. Ed. Jürgen Zimmerer. Bonn: 2013.

Becker, Judith. *Conversio im Wandel. Basler Missionare zwischen Europa und Südindien und die Ausbildung einer Kontaktreligiösität, 1834–1860*. Göttingen: 2015.

Becker, Peter. 'Bürokratie'. *Docupedia-Zeitgeschichte*. 30 August 2016. Web. http://docupedia.de/zg/Becker_buerokratie_v1_de_2016 (12 October 2021).

Beckert, Sven. 'The New History of Capitalism'. *Capitalism. The Reemergence of a Historical Concept.* 235–250. Eds. Jürgen Kocka and Marcel van der Linden. London et al.: 2016.

——. *Empire of Cotton. A New History of Global Capitalism*. New York: 2015.

Beese, Sebastian. *Experten der Erschließung. Akteure der deutschen Kolonialtechnik in Afrika und Europa 1890–1943*. Paderborn: 2021.

Behal, Rana and Linden, Marcel van der (Eds.). *Coolies, Capital, and Colonialism: Studies in Indian Labour History*. New York: 2006.

Bellucci, Stefano and Eckert, Andreas. 'The 'Labour Question' in Africanist Historiography'. *General Labour History of Africa. Workers, Employers and Governments, 20th–21st Centuries*. 1–16. Eds. Stefano Bellucci and Andreas Eckert. Exeter: 2019.

Bertz, Ned. *Diaspora and Nation in the Indian Ocean. Transnational Histories of Race and Urban Space in Tanzania*. Honolulu: 2015.

Biermann, Werner. *Tanganyika Railways – Carriers of Colonialism. An Account of Economic Indicators and Social Fragments*. Münster: 1995.

Bleifuß, Gerhard and Hergenröder, Gerhard. *Die "Otto-Plantage Kilossa" (1907–1914). Aufbau und Ende eines kolonialen Unternehmens in Deutsch-Ostafrika*. Wendlingen am Neckar: 1993.

Bösch, Frank. 'Der Ankläger. Erzberger und die Kolonialpolitik im frühen 20. Jahrhundert'. *Matthias Erzberger. Ein Demokrat in Zeiten des Hasses*. 47–71. Eds. Haus der Geschichte Baden-Württemberg in Verbindung mit der Landeshauptstadt Stuttgart. Karlsruhe: 2013.

Boonen, Sofie and Lagate, Johan. 'A City Constructd by *'des gens d'ailleurs'*. Urban Development and Migration Policies in Colonial Lubumbashi, 1910–1930'. *From Railway Juncture to Portal of Globalization: Making Globalization Work in African and South Asian Railway Towns*. 51–69. Ed. Geert Castrick. *Comparativ*, 25, 3. Leipzig: 2015.

Boris, Eileen. 'Subsistence and Household Labour'. *Handbook The Global History of Work*. 329–344. Eds. Karin Hofmeester and Marcel van der Linden. Berlin and Boston: 2018.

Bowen, John. 'Introduction'. Orwell, George. *Nineteen Eighty-Four*. vii–xxxi. Ed. John Bowen. Oxford: 2021.

Bromber, Katrin. 'German Colonial Administrators, Swahili Lecturers and the Promotion of Swahili at the Seminar for Orientalische Sprachen in Berlin'. 39–54. *Sudanic Africa*, vol. 15. Sudanic Africa: 2004. Web. *Jstor.* https://www.jstor.org/stable/25653412?Search=yes&resultItemClick=true&searchText =bromber&searchText=katrin&searchText=orientalische&searchUri=%2Faction%2FdoBasicSearch%3FQuery%3Dbromber%2Bkatrin%2Borientalische%26amp%3Bacc% 3Doff%26amp%3Bwc%3Don%26amp%3Bfc%3Doff%26amp%3Bgroup%3Dnone&ab _segments=0%2Fbasic_SYC5152%2Fcontrol&refreqid=search%3A42e2cef246d239 906a9a270efa599fdc&seq=1 (21 April 2020).

Bruneau, Michel. 'Hellénisme et diaspora grecque. De la Méditerranée orientale à la dimension mondiale'. 33–58. *CEMOTI*, no 30. n.p.: 2000. Web. https://doi.org/10.3406/cemot.2000.1550https://www.persee.fr/doc/cemot_0764-9878_2000_num_30_1_1550 (28 March 2018).

Brunnbauer, Ulf and Buchenau, Klaus. *Geschichte Südosteuropas*. Stuttgart: 2018.

Bryceson, Deborah Fahy. 'Domestic Work'. *General Labour History of Africa. Workers, Employers and Governments, 20th–21st Centuries*. 301–332. Eds. Stefano Becllucci and Andreas Eckert. Exeter: 2019.

Buchholz, Bernhard. 'Erlebnisse des Maschinisten Otto Gehring von SMS „Bussard" während des Maji-Maji-Aufstandes in Deutsch-Ostafrika'. N.p. Ed. *Traditionsverband ehemaliger Schutz- und Überseetruppen. Freunde der früheren deutschen Schutzgebiete e.V.* Web. http://www.traditionsverband.de/download/pdf/bussard_buchholz.pdf (21 April 2020).

Büschel, Hubertus. 'Das Schweigen der Subalternen. Die Entstehung der *Archiv*kritik im Postkolonialismus'. *Archiv – Macht – Wissen. Organisation und Konstruktion von Wissen und Wirklichkeiten in Archiven*. 73–88. Eds. Anja Horstmann und Vanina Kopp. Frankfurt o.M.: 2010.

Burke, Peter. 'The Invention of Leisure in Early Modern Europe'. 136–150. *Past & Present*, no. 146. Oxford: 1995. *Jstor.* Web. https://www.jstor.org/stable/651154 (01 August 2018).

Calic, Marie-Janine. *Südosteuropa. Weltgeschichte einer Region*. Munich: 2016.

Callebert, Ralph. *On Durban's Docks. Zulu Workers, Rural Households, Global Labor*. Rochester: 2017.

Campbell, Gwynn et al. (Eds.). *Women and Slavery, Volume One. Africa, the Indian Ocean World, and the Medieval North Atlantic*. Athens (Ohio): 2007.

Campbell, Joan. *Joy in Work, German Work. The National Debate, 1800–1945*. Princeton: 1989.
Casco, José Arturo Saavedra. *Utenzi, War Poems, and the German Colonial Conquest of East Africa. Swahili Poetry as a Historical Source*. Trenton and Asmara: 2007.
Castryck, Geert (Ed.). 'From Railway Juncture to Portal of Globalization: Making Globalization Work in African and South Asian Railway Towns'. *Comparativ. Zeitschrift für Globalgeschichte und vergleichende Gesellschaftsforschung*, 25, 3. Leipzig: 2015.
Chaldeos, Antonis. *The Greek Community in Tanzania*. Athens: 2019.
——. 'Τρίτη, 28 Μαΐου 2019. The Greek Constructors of the Railway in Tanzania'. *Greeks of Africa*. Web. http://greeksofafrica.blogspot.com/2019/05/. (11 September 2019).
Chang, Gordon H. et al. (Eds.). *The Chinese and the Iron Road. Building the Transcontinental Railraod*. Stanford: 2019.
"Changing Track. Redirecting Research on Colonial Railways. Workshop on Colonial Railways in Africa c. 1880–1960". *EUI Florence* (Online): 09 November 2020.
Chaudhuri, Rosinka. 'Introduction'. George Orwell. *Burmese Days*. vii–xxxii. Ed. Rosinka Chaudhuri. Oxford: 2021.
Chin, Gabriel J. and Yoon, Diana. "Chinese Exclusion Act of 1882". *Encyclopedia.com*, May 29 2018. Web. https://www.encyclopedia.com/history/united-states-and-canada/us-history/chinese-exclusion-act (01 June 2023).
Clasen, Sönke. *Die Angehörigen der Kaiserlichen Schutztruppe für Deutsch-Ostafrika zur Zeit des Ersten Weltkriegs. Ein biographisches Verzeichnis*. Norderstedt: 2021.
Clogg, Richard (Ed.). *The Greek Diaspora in the Twentieth Century*. Basingstoke: 2001.
——. 'The Greek Diaspora: the Historical Context'. *The Greek Diaspora in the Twentieth Century*. 1–24. Ed. Richard Clogg. Basingstoke: 2001.
Cobble, Dorothy Sue. 'The Promise and Peril of the New Global Labor History'. 99–107. *International Labor and Working-Class History*, Fall 2012, no. 82. Cambridge: 2012. Web. *Jstor*. https://www.jstor.org/stable/23391672 (04 June 2021).
Cohen, Robin. *Global Diasporas. An Introduction*. London and New York: 2008.
Cole, Peter and Hart, Jennifer. 'Trade, Transport, and Services'. *Handbook The Global History of Work*. 277–298. Eds. Karin Hofmeester and Marcel van der Linden. Berlin and Boston: 2018.
Cooper, Frederick. 'The 'Labour Question' in Africa and the World. *General Labour History of Africa. Workers, Employers and Governments, 20th– 21st Centuries*. 617–636. Eds. Stefano Bellucci and Andreas Eckert. Exeter: 2019.
——. 'Von der Sklaverei in die Prekarität? Afrikanische Arbeitsgeschichte im Globalen Kontext'. *Re: work. Arbeit Global – Historische Rundgänge*. 4–29. Eds. Andreas Eckert and Felicitas Hentschke. Berlin and Boston: 2019.
——. 'What is the Concept of Globalization Good for?. An African Historian's Perspective'. 189–213. *African Affairs*, vol. 100, no. 399. Oxford: 2001. Web. *Jstor*. https://www.jstor.org/stable/3518765 (12 March 2021).
Connell-Szasz, Margaret (Ed.). *Between Indian and White Worlds. The Cultural Broker*. Oklahoma: 2001.
Conrad, Sebastian. *What is Global History?* Princeton: 2016.
——. *Globalgeschichte. Eine Einführung*. Munich: 2013.
——. *Globalisation and the Nation in Imperial Germany*. Cambridge: 2010.
Coquery-Vidrovitch, Catherine. *African Women. A Modern History*. New York: 1997.
Crosbie, Barry. *Irish Imperial Networks. Migration, Social Communication and Exchange in Nineteenth-Century India*. Cambridge: 2012.
Dalachanis, Angelos. *The Greek Exodus From Egypt. Diaspora Politics and Emigration, 1937–62*. New York: 2017.

Damir-Geilsdorf, Sabine et al. (Eds.). *Bonded Labour. Global and Comparative Perspectives (18th–21st Century).* Bielefeld: 2016.
Darwin, John. *Das unvollendete Weltreich: Aufstieg und Niedergang des Britischen Empires, 1600–1997.* Frankfurt o. M.: 2013.
——. 'Imperialism in Decline? Tendencies in British Imperial Policy Between the Wars'. 657–679. *The Historical Journal*, vol. 23, no. 3. Cambridge: 1980.
Daughton, J.P. *In the Forest of No Joy. The Congo-Océan Railroad and the Tragedy of French Colonialism.* New York: 2021.
Decker, Julio. 'Lines in the Sand. Railways and the archipelago of colonial territorialization in German Southwest Africa, 1897–1914'. 1–36. Web. *Sciencedirect.com.* https://doi.org/10.1016/j.jhg.2020.09.002 (15 March 2021).
Dejung, Christof. 'From Global Civilizing Missions to Racial Warfare: Class Conflicts and the Representations of the Colonial World in European Middle-Class Thought'. *The Global Bourgeoisie. The Rise of the Middle Classes in the Age of Empire.* 251–272. Eds. Christof Dejung et al. Princeton: 2019.
——. et al. 'Worlds of the Bourgeoisie'. *The Global Bourgeoisie. The Rise of the Middle Classes in the Age of Empire.* 1–40. Eds. Christof Dejung et al. Princeton: 2019.
——. *Commodity Trading, Globalization and the Colonial World. Spinning the Web of the Global Market.* New York and London: 2018.
Demhardt, Imre Josef. *Deutsche Kolonialgesellschaft. 1888–1918. Ein Beitrag zur Organisationsgeschichte der deutschen Kolonialbewegung.* Wiesbaden: 2002.
Dennis, Carolyne. 'Women in African Labour History'. 125–140. *Journal of Asian and African Studies*, XXIII, 1–2. Leiden: 1988.
Deutsch, Jan-Georg. *Emancipation without Abolition in German East Africa, c. 1884–1914.* Oxford: 2006.
——. 'Inventing an East African Empire: The Zanzibar Delimitation Commission of 1885/86'. *Studien zur Geschichte des deutschen Kolonialismus in Afrika. Festschrift zum 60. Geburtstag von Peter Sebald.* 210–219. Eds. Peter Heine and Ulrich van der Heyden. Pfaffenweiler: 1995.
Diebold, Jan. *Hochadel und Kolonialismus im 20. Jahrhundert. Die imperiale Biographie des ‚Afrika Herzogs' Adolf Friedrich zu Mecklenburg.* Vienna et al.: 2019.
Diogo, Maria Paula and Laak, Dirk van. *Europeans Globalizing. Mapping, Exploiting, Exchanging.* New York: 2016.
Dittrich, Carl and Rieke-Müller, Annelore. *Carl Hagenbeck (1844–1913): Tierhandel und Schaustellungen im Deutschen Kaiserreich.* Berlin et al.: 1998.
Divall, Colin. 'Railway Imperialisms. Railway Nationalisms'. *Die Internationalität der Eisenbahn. 1850–1970.* 195–210. Eds. Monika Burri et al. Zürich: 2003.
Dousemetzis, Dimitri. *The Man who killed Apartheid. The Life of Dimitri Tsafendas.* Johannesburg: 2019.
Drayton, Richard. 'Race, Culture and Class: European Hegemony and Global Class Formation, circa 1800–1950'. *The Global Bourgeoisie. The Rise of the Middle Classes in the Age of Empire.* 339–358. Eds. Christof Dejung et al. Princeton: 2019.
—— and David Motadel. 'Discussion. The Futures of Global History'. 1–21. *Journal of Global History*, 13. Cambridge: 2018. Web. https://www.cambridge.org/core/terms. https://doi.org/10.1017/S1740022817000262. (01 August 2018).
Ebay Offer by second-hand bookshop *Tucholsklavier* (Theodor Schmidt, Berlin). 'Handball-Nationaltrainer OTTO KAUNDINYA: 3 Briefe von 1913 (u.a. über Zukunft). 04 August 18. Web. https://www.ebay.de/itm/Handball-Nationaltrainer-OTTO-KAUNDINYA-3-Briefe-von-1913-u-a-uber-Zukunft/302442788301?hash=item466afeb5cd:g:tCwAAOSwa4FZsCPW. (19 July 2019).

——. '36 dt. Briefe (188 S.) von 1902 aus INDIEN //Ananda H. & Helene KAUNDINYA'. 21 June 2018. Web. https://www.ebay.de/itm/36-dt-Briefe-188-S-von-1902-aus-INDIEN-Ananda-H-Helene-KAUNDINYA-/152825391361. (19 July 2019).

Eckart, Wolfgang U. 'The Colony as Laboratory: German Sleeping Sickness Campaigns in German East Africa and in Togo, 1900–1914'. *History and Philosophy of the Life Sciences*, vol. 24, no. 1. Napoli: 2002. Web. *Jstor.* https://www.jstor.org/stable/23332441 (01 June 2021).

——. *Medizin und Kolonialimperialismus. Deutschland 1884–1945*. Paderborn et al.: 1997.

Eckert, Andreas. 'Area Studies and the Development of Global Labor History'. *The Lifework of a Labor Historian: Essays in Honor of Marcel van der Linden*. 156–173. Eds. Ulbe Bosma and Karin Hofmeester. Leiden: 2018.

——. 'Capitalism and Labor in Sub-Sahara Africa'. *Capitalism. The Reemergenceof a Historical Concept*. 165–186. Eds. Jürgen Kocka and Marcel van der Linden. London et al.: 2016.

——. 'Why all the fuss about a Global Labour History?'. *Global Histories of Work*. 3–24. Ed. Andreas Eckert. Berlin and Boston: 2016.

——. *Kolonialismus*. Frankfurt o.M.: 2006.

Eckhart, Franz G. and Geissler, Peter (Eds.). *The United Republic of Tanzania. National Archive of Tanzania. Guide to the German Records. Vol. II. Prepared by National Archives of Tanzania and Archivschule Marburg – Insitut für Archivwissenschaft*. Second Edition. Dar es Salaam and Marburg: 1984.

——. *Das Deutsch-Ostafrika-Archiv. Inventar der Abteilung „German Records" im Nationalarchiv der Vereinigten Republik Tansania, Dar es Salaam. Band I. Einleitung, Zentralverwaltung.* Marburg: 1973.

Edwards, Andrew David et al. (Eds.). 'Capitalism in Global History'. E1–e32. *Past and Present*, vol. 249, Issue 1, November. Oxford: 2020. Web. https://academic.oup.com/past/article/249/1/e1/6007772 (15 May 2023).

Eggers, Erik (Ed.). *Handball. Eine deutsche Domäne*. Göttingen: 2007.

——. 'Handball im Nationalsozialismus'. *Handball. Eine deutsche Domäne*. 63–92. Ed. Erik Eggers. Göttingen: 2007.

——. 'Porträt. Otto Kaundinya – der erste Star des Handballs'. *Handball. Eine deutsche Domäne.* 73–76. Ed. Erik Eggers. Göttingen: 2007.

Ehlers, Sarah. *Europa und die Schlafkrankheit. Koloniale Seuchenbekämpfung, europäische Identitäten und moderne Medizin 1890–1950*. Göttingen: 2019.

——. 'Medical Missions – Racial Visions: Fighting Sleeping Sickness in Colonial Africa in the Early Twentieth Century'. *Health and Difference. Rendering Human Variation in Colonial Engagements*. 91–110. Eds. Alexandra Widmer and Veronika Lipphardt. New York: 2016.

Elkins, Caroline. *Imperial Reckoning. The Untold Story of Britain's Gulag in Kenya*. New York: 2005.

Epple, Angelika. 'Globalisierung/en'. *Docupedia-Zeitgeschichte*. 11 June 2012. Web.http://docupedia.de/zg/epple_globalisierung_v1_de_2012 (21 January 2021).

——. ''Global History' und 'Area Studies'. Plädoyer für eine weltgeschichtliche Perspektivierung des Lokalen'. *Area Studies und die Welt. Weltregion und neue Globalgeschichte.* 90–116. Ed. Birgit Schäbler. Vienna: 2007.

Ettlich, Guido. *Konsul Schwarz. Bankier, Bürger & Bahá'í in Stuttgart und Bad Mergentheim*. Berlin: 2019.

Fabian, Johannes. 'Appendix: On the Ethnography and Economies of Collecting from Leo Frobenius' Nochmals zu den Bakubavölkern'. *The Scramble for Art in Africa*. 101–108. Ed. Enid Schildkrout and Curtis A. Keim. Cambridge: 1998.

Fall, Babacar and Roberts, Richard L. 'Forced Labour'. *General Labour History of Africa. Workers, Employers and Governments, 20th– 21st Centuries.* 77–118. Eds. Stefano Bellucci and Andreas Eckert. Exeter: 2019.

Fellmann, Ulrich (Ed.). *Von Schwaben in den Bismarckarchipel. Tagebücher der Missionsfrau Johanna Fellmann aus Deutsch-Neuguinea 1896–1903*. Wiesbaden: 2009.
Fischer-Tiné, Harald. *'Low and Licentious Europeans'. Race, Class and "White Subalternity" in Colonial India*. New Dehli: 2009.
Frangos, Stavros K. *Greeks in Michigan*. Michigan: 2004.
Franzke, Jürgen (Ed.). *Bagdad- und Hedjazbahn. Deutsche Eisenbahngeschichte im Vorderen Orient*. Nuremberg: 2003.
Frenz, Albrecht. *Freiheit hat Gesicht. Anandapur – eine Begegnung zwischen Kodagu und Baden-Württemberg*. Stuttgart: 2003.
Freund, Bill. 'Sub-Saharan Africa'. *Handbook The Global History of Work*. 63–82. Eds. Karin Hofmeester and Marcel van der Linden. Berlin and Boston: 2018.
Fridenson, Patrick. 'Is there a return of Capitalism in Business History?'. *Capitalism. The Reemergence of a Historical Concept*. 107–132. Eds. Jürgen Kocka and Marcel van der Linden. London et al.: 2016.
Fried, Johannes. *Dies Irae. Eine Geschichte des Weltuntergangs*. Munich: 2016.
Froböse, Rolf. *Der Halleysche Komet*. Thun: 1985.
Fuhrmann, Malte. 'Die Bagdadbahn'. *Kein Platz an der Sonne. Erinnerungsorte der deutschen Kolonialgeschichte*. 190–207. Ed. Jürgen Zimmerer. Bonn: 2013.
——. 'Deutschlands Abenteuer im Orient. Eine Geschichte semi-kolonialer Verstrickungen'. *Türkisch-Deutsche Beziehungen. Perspektiven aus Vergangenheit und Gegenwart*. 10–33. Eds. Claus Schönig et al. Berlin: 2012.
——. 'Anatolia as a Site of German Colonial Desire and National Re-awakenings'. 117–150. *New Perspectives on Turkey*, no. 41. N.P.: 2009.
Fukuyama, Francis. *The End of History and the Last Man*. New York: 1998.
Gall, Lothar et al. *Die Deutsche Bank. 1870–1995*. Munich: 1995.
Gallant, Thomas W. *Modern Greece. From the War of Independence to the Present*. London: 2016.
Gaul, Patrick. *Ideale und Interessen. Die mitteleuropäische Wirtschaft im Amerikanischen Bürgerkrieg*. Stuttgart: 2021.
Genner, Julian et al. 'Muße und Arbeit'. Conference Report 12th–14th April 2018. *HSozKult*. Web. https://www.hsozkult.de/searching/id/tagungsberichte-7814?title=musse-und-arbeit&q=mu%C3%9Fe&page=2&sort=&fq=&total=163&recno=29&subType=fdkn (25 May 2021).
Geppert, Alexander C.T. 'Weltausstellungen'. *EGO – Europäische Geschichte Online*. Web. http://ieg-ego.eu/de/threads/crossroads/wissensraeume/alexander-c-t-geppert-weltausstellungen (29 June 20).
Giblin, James and Monson, Jamie (Eds.). *Maji Maji. Lifting the Fog of War*. Leiden: 2010.
Ginsburgh, Nicola. *Class, Work and Whiteness: Race and Settler Colonialism in Southern Rhodesia, 1919–79*. Manchester: 2020.
Glasman, Joel and Gerstenberger, Debora (Eds.). *Techniken der Globalisierung. Globalgeschichte meets Akteur-Netzwerk-Theorie*. Bielefeld: 2016.
Glassman, Jonathon. *Feasts and Riot. Revelry, Rebellion, and Popular Consciousness on the Swahili Coast, 1856–1888*. Portsmouth: 1995.
Gleixner, Ulrike. *Pietismus und Bürgertum. Eine historische Anthropologie der Frömmigkeit*. Göttingen: 2005.
"Global Dis/Connections". *CAS LMU. Center for Advanced Studie*. N.d. https://www.cas.uni-muenchen.de/schwerpunkte/global_dis_connections/index.html (12 March 2021).
Gottberg, Achim. *Unyamwesi. Quellensammlung und Geschichte*. Berlin: 1971.

Gräbel, Carsten. *Die Erforschung der Kolonien. Expeditionen und koloniale Wissenskultur deutscher Geographen, 1884–1919*. Bielefeld: 2015.
Grazia, Victoria de. 'The Crisis of Hyper-Consumerism: Capitalism's Latest Forward Lurch'. *Capitalism. The Reemergence of a Historical Concept.* 71–106. Eds. Jürgen Kocka and Marcel van der Linden. London et al.: 2016.
Gregory, David. 'Scripting Egypt. Orientalism and the Cultures of Travel'. *Writes of Passage. Reading travel Writing*. 114–150. Eds. James Duncan and David Gregory. New York: 1999.
Greiner, Andreas. 'Permanente Krisen. Opposition, Kooperation und Konkurrenz ostafrikanischer Träger in europäischen Expeditionen'. *Der Träger. Zu einer 'tragenden' Figur der Kolonialgeschichte*. 181–204. Eds. Sonja Malzner and Anne D. Peiter. Bielefeld: 2018.
Groß, Lothar. *Anmerkungen zu 'Made in Germany'. Deutschlands Wirtschaftsgeschichte von der Industrialisierung bis heute*. BoD (Books on Demand). N.P.: 2019.
Gründer, Horst. *Geschichte der deutschen Kolonien*. Paderborn: 2004.
——. "Lindequist, Friedrich von". *Neue Deutsche Biographie*, 14, p. 601. 1985. Web. https://www.deutsche-biographie.de/pnd117025259.html#ndbcontent (08 July 2020).
——. *Christliche Mission und deutscher Imperialismus. Eine politische Geschichte ihrer Beziehungen während der deutschen Kolonialzeit (1884–1914) unter besonderer Berücksichtigung Afrikas und Chinas*. Paderborn: 1984.
Guettel, Jens-Uwe. 'The Myth of a Pro Colonialist SPD: German Social Democracy and Imperialism before World War I'. 452–484. *Central European History*, vol. 45, no. 3. Cambridge: 2012. Web. *Jstor.* https://www.jstor.org/stable/23270519?seq=1 (26 October 2020).
Guglielmo, Thomas A. *White on Arrival. Italians, Race, Color, and Power in Chicago, 1890–1945.* Oxford: 2003.
Gunderson, Frank. *Sukuma Labor Songs. 'We never Sleep, we dream of Farming'*. Leiden: 2010.
Gunn, Jeffrey. *Outsourcing African Labor. Kru Migratory Workers in Global Ports, Estates and Battlefields until the End of the 19th Century*. Berlin and Boston: 2021.
Gupta, Ashin das (Ed.). *India and the Indian Ocean World. Trade and Politics*. Oxford: 2004.
Habermas, Rebekka. *Skandal in Togo. Ein Kapitel deutscher Kolonialherrschaft*. Frankfurt o.M.: 2016.
—— and Hölzl, Richard (Eds.). *Mission Global. Eine Verflechtungsgeschichte seit dem 19. Jahrhundert.* Cologne et al.: 2014.
——. 'Mission global – Religiöse Akteure und globale Verflechtung seit dem 19. Jahrhundert'. *Mission Global. Eine Verflechtungsgeschichte seit dem 19. Jahrhundert.* 10–28. Eds. Rebekka Habermas and Richard Hölzl. Cologne et al.: 2014.
Hainbuch, Dirk. *Das Reichsministerium für Wiederaufbau 1919–1924. Die Abwicklung des Ersten Weltkrieges: Reparationen, Kriegsschäden, Beseitigung, Opferentschädigung und der Wiederaufbau der deutschen Handelsflotte*. Frankfurt o.M.: 2016.
Haller, Lea. Review on Beckert, Sven*: King Cotton. Eine Geschichte des globalen Kapitalismus.* München: 2014. *H-Soz-Kult*. 29 January 2015. Web. www.hsozkult.de/publicationreview/id/rezbuecher-23097. (16 July 2019).
Hamann, Ulrike. *Prekäre Koloniale Ordnung. Rassistische Konjunkturen im Widerspruch. Deutsches Kolonialregime 1884–1914*. Bielefeld: 2016.
Harlaftis, Gelina. 'Mapping the Greek Maritime Diaspora from the Early Eighteenth to the Late Twentieth Centuries'. *Diaspora Entrepreneurial Networks*. 147–172. Eds. Ina Baghdiantz et al. Oxford and New York: 2005.
Harpur, Brian. *Halleys Komet. Das offizielle Buch der 'Halley's Comet Society'*. Frankfurt o.M.: 1985.
Hasse, Rolf. 'Das Testament des Sewa Hadji'. Ed. *Mitteilungsblatt des Traditionsverbandes ehemaliger Schutz- und Überseetruppen*, pp. 43–53, no. 90, 1/2004.

Hausschild-Thiessen, Renate. *'O'Swald, William'. Hamburgische Biografie. Band 2*. 310–311. Eds. Franklin Kopitzsch and Dirk Brietzke. Hamburg: 2003.

Headrick, Daniel R. *The Tools of Empire. Technology and European Imperialism in the Nineteenth Century*. New York and Oxford: 1981.

Heesen, Anke te. 'Vom naturgeschichtlichen Investor zum Staatsdienst. Sammler und Sammlungen der Gesellschaft Naturforschender Freunde zu Berlin um 1800'. *Sammeln als Wissen. Das Sammeln und seine wissenschaftliche Bedeutung*. 62–84. Eds. Anke te Heesen and E.C. Spary. Göttingen: 2002.

Hentschke, Felicitas. 'Labour and Leisure in Global History. Summer Academy'. Cfp. 27th March 2018. *HSozKult*. Web. https://www.hsozkult.de/searching/id/event-86591?title=labour-and-leisure-in-global-history-summer-academy&q=Labour%20and%20Leisure%20in%20Global%20History&sort=&fq=&total=39&recno=10&subType=event (12 March 2021).

Hergenröder, Gerhard. *Wendlingen am Neckar. Auf dem Weg zu einer Stadt. Die Geschichte von Wendlingen, Unterboihingen und Bodelshofen*. Wendlingen am Neckar: 1992.

Hertsch, Florian M. and Mutlu, R. (Eds.). *Die Bagdadbahn. Ein Umriss deutsch-türkischer Beziehungen. Gesammelte Beiträge*. Hamburg: 2016.

Herzig, Pascale. *South Asians in Kenya: Gender, Generation and Changing Identities in Diaspora*. Münster: 2006.

Heumann, Ina et al. 'Dinosaurier und Provenienz. Konjunkturen des Kolonialen, 1909–2018'. *Dinosaurier Fragmente. Zur Geschichte der Tendaguru-Expedition und ihrer Objekte 1906–2008*. 255–273. Eds. Ina Heumann et al. Göttingen: 2018.

——. 'Gespräch. 225 Tonnen Gestein. Ein Gespräch mit Daniela Schwarz, Kustodin der Tendaguru-Sammlung'. *Dinosaurier Fragmente. Zur Geschichte der Tendaguru- Expedition und ihrer Objekte 1906–2008*. 276–291. Eds. Ina Heumann et al. Göttingen: 2018.

Heyden, Ulrich van der and Becher, Jürgen (Eds.). *Mission und Gewalt. Der christliche Umgang mit Gewalt und die Ausbreitung des Christentums in Afrika und Asien in der Zeit von 1792 bis 1918/19*. Stuttgart: 2000.

Hill, M.F. *Permanent Way. The story of the Kenya and Uganda railway, being the official history of the development of the transport system in Kenya and Uganda*. Nairobi: 1976.

—— *Permanent Way. Vol II. The Story of the Tanganyika Railways*. Nairobi: 1957.

Hoefte, Roesemarijn. 'Indentured Labour'. *Handbook The Global History of Work*. 363–376. Eds. Karin Hofmeester and Marcel van der Linden. Berlin and Boston: 2018.

Hölzl, Richard. *Gläubige Imperialisten. Katholische Mission in Deutschland und Ostafrika (1830–1960)*. Frankfurt o.M.: 2021.

Hofmeester, Karin and Linden, Marcel van der. 'Introduction'. *Handbook The Global History of Work*. 1–12. Eds. Karin Hofmeester and Marcel van der Linden. Berlin and Boston: 2018.

Hofmeester, Karin et al. 'No Global Labour History without Africa: Reciprocal Comparison and Beyond'. 249–276. *History in Africa*, vol. 41, n.p.: 2014. *JSTOR*. Web. www.jstor.org/stable/26362091 (12 March 2021).

Hooper, Jane. *Feeding Globalization. Madagascar and the Provisioning Trade, 1600–1800*. Athens (Ohio): 2017.

Hopkins, G.A. *An Economic History of West Africa. Second Edition*. New York: 2020.

Hoyle, B.S. *Gillman of Tanganyika 1882–1946. The Life and Work of a Pioneer Geographer*. Avebury: 1987.

—— 'Clement Gillman, 1882–1946: Biographical Notes on a Pioneer East African Geographer'. 1–16. *East African Review*, no 3, n.p.: April 1965.

Huber, Valeska. 'Multiple Mobilities. Über den Umgang mit verschiedenen Mobilitätsformen um 1900'. 317–341. *Geschichte und Gesellschaft*, no. 36. Göttingen: 2010.
Hürlimann, Esther et al. *Das Fräulein vom Bahnhof. Der Verein Freundinnen junger Mädchen in der Schweiz.* Zürich: 2021.
Hüsgen, Jan. 'Die Herrnhuter Brüdergemeinde als globales Unternehmen'. 13–27. *Zeitschrift für Weltgeschichte*, Jahrgang 14, Heft 1. Berlin: 2013.
Hunter, Emma. 'Modernity, Print Media, and the Middle Class in Colonial East Africa'. *The Global Bourgeoisie. The Rise of the Middle Classes in the Age of Empire*. 105–122. Eds. Christof Dejung et al. Princeton: 2019.
Huws, Ursula. 'The reproduction of difference: gender and the global division of labour'. 1–10. *Work Organisation, Labour & Globalisation*, vol. 6, no. 1. N.p.: 2012. Web. *Jstor.* https://www.jstor.org/stable/10.13169/workorgalaboglob.6.1.0001 (04 June 2021).
Ignatiev, Noel. *How the Irish Became White*. New York and London: 2012.
Iliffe, John. *A Modern History of Tanganyika*. Cambridge: 1979.
——. 'The Spokesman. Martin Kayamba'. *Modern Tanzanians A Volume of Biographies*. 66–94. Ed. John Iliffe. Dar es Salaam: 1973.
——. (Ed.). *Modern Tanzanians. A Volume of Biographies*. Dar es Salaam: 1973.
——. *Tanganyika under German Rule. 1905–1912*. Cambridge: 1969.
—— and Gwassa, Gilbert (Eds.). *Records of the Maji Maji Rising*. Dar es Salaam: 1968.
Isobe, Hiroyuki. 'Eine rationale Kolonialpolitik? Die Bekämpfung der Schlafkrankheit im deutschen Schutzgebiet Ostafrika vor dem Ersten Weltkrieg'. *Peripulus 2001. Jahrbuch für Aussereuropäische Geschichte*. 115–132. Ed. Christoph Marx. Berlin: 2011.
Itandala, Buludu. 'African Response to German Colonialism in East Africa: The Case of Ussukuma, 1890–1918'. 3–29. *Ufahamu. A Journal of African Studies*, no. 20, 1. UCLA: 01 January 1992. Web. https://escholarship.org/uc/item/7nh0x2p1 (21 November 2019).
Jacob, Frank. *The Russo-Japanese War and its Shaping of the Twentieth Century*. London: 2018.
Jahn, Nicola. *Der gute Draht zum Nachbarn. Die deutsch-niederländische Kooperation im Telegrafenwesen ihrer Kolonien und Interessenssphären im pazifischen Raum 1899–1936.* Münster: 2020.
James, Harold. 'Finance Capitalism'. *Capitalism. The Reemergence of a Historical Concept.* 133–164. Eds. Jürgen Kocka and Marcel van der Linden. London et al.: 2016.
Jancke, Gabriele. 'Jüdische Selbstzeugnisse und Ego-Dokumente der frühen Neuzeit in Ashkenas. Eine Einleitung'. *Selbstzeugnisse und Ego-Dokumente frühneuzeitlicher Juden in Ashkenas. Beispiele, Methoden, Konzepte*. 9–26. Eds. Birgit E. Klein and Rotraud Ries. Berlin: 2011.
Jézéquel, Jean-Hervé. '"Collecting Customary Law": Educated Africans, Ethnographic Writings, and Colonial Justice in French West Africa'. *Intermediaries, Interpreters, and Clerks. African Employees in the Making of Colonial Africa*. 139–158. Eds. Benjamin N. Lawrence et al. Wisconsin: 2006.
Jones, David. 'Military Observers, Eurocentrism and World War Zero'. *The Russo-Japanese War in Global Perspective. World War Zero. Volume II.* 135–179. Ed. David Wolf et al. Leiden: 2007.
Johnson, Walter. 'On Agency'. 113–124. *Journal of Social History*, vol. 37, no.1. Oxford: 2003.
Kaloudis, George. *Modern Greece and the Diaspora Greeks in the United States*. Lexington: 2018.
Keighren, Innes M. et al. *Travels into Print. Exploration, Writing, and Publishing with John Murray, 1773–1859*. Chicago and London: 2015.
Kennedy, Dane. 'Introduction: Reinterpreting Exploration'. *Reinterpreting Exploration. The West in the World*. 1–20. Ed. Dane Kennedy. Oxford: 2014.
Klein, Jochen. *„In Unruh und Arbeit“. C.F. Klein-Schlatter. 150 Jahre Weberei. 1828–1979.* Ratingen: 2001.

Klein, Martin. 'African Participation in Colonial Rule: The Role of Clerks, Interpreters and other Intermediaries'. *Intermediaries, Interpreters, and Clerks. African Employees in the Making of Colonial Africa.* 273–288. Ed. Benjamin N. Lawrence et al. Wisconsin: 2006.

Klein-Arendt, Reinhard. 'Ein Land wird gewaltsam in Besitz genommen. Die Kolonie Deutsch-Ostafrika'. *Der Maji-Maji-Krieg in Deutsch-Ostafrika 1905–1907.* 28–48. Eds. Felicitas Becker and Jigal Beez. Berlin: 2005.

Kleinöder, Nina. '"A Place in the Sun"? German Rails and Sleepers in Colonial Railway Building in Africa, 1905 to 1914'. 1–23. *Zeitschrift für Unternehmensgeschichte*, 65, no. 1. Berlin: 2020.

Kilian, Dieter E. *Kai-Uwe von Hassel und seine Familie. Zwischen Ostsee und Ostafrika. Militär biographisches-Mosaik.* Norderstedt: 2013.

Kinunda, Nives. *Negotiating Women's Labour: Women Farmers, State, and Society in the Southern Highlands of Tanzania, 1885–2000.* Unpublished Dissertation submitted at the University of Göttingen: August 2017. Web. https://ediss.uni-goettingen.de/bitstream/handle/11858/00-1735-0000-002E-E57A-9/Nives%20PhD2.pdf?sequence=1 (28 April 2020).

Kocka, Jürgen. 'Introduction'. *Capitalism. The Reemergence of a Historical Concept.* 1–12. Eds. Jürgen Kocka and Marcel van der Linden. London et al.: 2016.

——. 'Arbeit im historischen Grundriss'. *Alltag, Erfahrung, Eigensinn. Historisch-anthropologische Erkundungen.* 445–457. Eds. Belinda Davis et al. Frankfurt o.M. and New York: 2008.

——. *Arbeitsverhältnisse und Arbeiterexistenzen. Grundlagen der Klassenbildung im 19. Jahrhundert.* Bonn: 1990.

Kokot, Waltraud. 'Themen der Forschung'. *Peripulus. Jahrbuch für Außereuropäische Geschichte.* 1–10. Ed. Christoph Marx. 14. Jahrgang. Münster: 2004.

Komlosy, Andrea. 'Work and Labor Relations'. *Capitalism. The Reemergence of a Historical Concept.* 33–70. Eds. Jürgen Kocka and Marcel van der Linden. London et al.: 2016.

Konitzer, Werner. "Rasse' und 'Arbeit' als dichte Begriffe'. *«Deutsche Arbeit». Kritische Perspektiven auf ein ideologisches Selbstbild.* 76–87. Eds. Felix Axster and Nikolas Lelle. Göttingen: 2018.

Konrad, Dagmar. *Missionsbräute. Pietistinnen des 19. Jahrhunderts in der Baseler Mission.* Münster et al.: 2001.

Koponen, Juhani. *Development for Exploitation. German Colonial Policies in Mainland Tanzania, 1884–1914.* Helsinki and Hamburg: 1994.

——. *People and Production in late precolonial Tanzania. History and Structures.* Helsinki: 1988.

Korma, Lena. 'The Historiography of the Greek Diaspora and migration in the twentieth century'. 47–73. *Historien*, 16. Web. http://dx.doi.org/10.12681/historein.8778. (22 January 2021).

Krause, Ingo Till. *"Koloniale Schuldlüge"? Die Schulpolitik in den afrikanischen Kolonien Deutschlands und Britanniens im Vergleich.* Hamburg: 2007.

Kretschmann, Carsten. 'Noch ein Nationaldenkmal? Die Deutsche Tendaguru Expedition 1909–1913'. *Inszenierte Wissenschaft. Zur Popularisierung von Wissen im 19. Jahrhundert.* 191–212. Ed. Stefanie Samida. Bielefeld: 2011.

Kreye, Lars. *«Deutscher Wald» in Afrika. Koloniale Konflikte um regenerative Ressourcen, Tansania 1892–1916.* Göttingen: 2021.

Kundrus, Birthe. *Moderne Imperialisten. Das Kaisserreich im Spiegel seiner Kolonien.* Cologne et al.: 2003.

——. 'Die Kolonien. Kinder des Gefühls und der Phantasie'. *Phantasiereiche. Zur Kulturgeschichte des deutschen Kolonialismus.* 7–18. Ed. Birthe Kundrus. Frankfurt o.M.: 2003.

Laak, Dirk van. '"Auf den Hochstraßen des Weltwirtschaftsverkehrs". Zur Ideologie der "Erschließung" im ausgehenden 19. und frühen 20. Jahrhundert'. 104–126. *Comparativ. Zeitschrift für Globalgeschichte und vergleichende Gesellschaftsforschung*, vol. 19, no. 5. Leipzig: 2009.

—— *Über alles in der Welt. Deutscher Imperialismus im 19. und 20. Jahrhundert.* Munich: 2005.
—— *Imperiale Infrastruktur. Deutsche Planungen für eine Erschließung Afrikas 1880 bis 1960.* Paderborn et al.: 2004.
Laiqing, Yang. 'Die Ereignisse von Gaomi und der Widerstand der Bevölkerung gegen den deutschen Eisenbahnbau'. *Kolonialkrieg in China. Die Niederschlagung der Boxerbewegung 1900–01.* 49–58. Eds. Mechthild Leutner and Klaus Mühlhahn. Berlin: 2007.
Lambert, David and Lester, Alan (Eds.). *Colonial Lives Across the British Empire: Imperial Careering in the Long Nineteenth Century.* Cambridge: 2010.
Lawrence, Benjamin N. et al. (Eds.). *Intermediaries, Interpreters, and Clerks. African Employees in the Making of Colonial Africa.* Wisconsin: 2006.
——. 'Introduction: African Intermediaries and the "Bargain" of Collaboration'. *Intermediaries, Interpreters, and Clerks. African Employees in the Making of Colonial Africa.* 3–36. Eds. Benjamin N. Lawrence et al. Wisconsin: 2006.
Ledderhose, Karl Friedrich. "Mögling, Hermann Friedrich". *Allgemeine Deutsche Biographie* 22, 1985, pp. 47–52. Web. *Neue Deutsche-Biographie.* https://www.deutsche-biographie.de/pnd119490633.html#adbcontent (20 June 2019).
Leonhard, Jörn and Steinmetz, Willibald. 'Von der Begriffsgeschichte zur historischen Semantik von 'Arbeit''. *Semantiken von Arbeit: Diachrone und vergleichende Perspektiven.* 9–59. Eds. Jörn Leonhard and Willibald Steinmetz. Cologne et al.: 2016.
Lessing, Doris. *Afrikanische Tragödie.* Frankfurt o.M.: 1989.
Linden, Marcel van der. *Workers of the World. Eine Globalgeschichte der Arbeit.* Frankfurt o.M. and New York: 2017.
——. 'Final Thoughts'. *Capitalism. The Reemergence of a Historical Concept.* 251–266. Eds. Jürgen Kocka and Marcel van der Linden. London et al.: 2016.
—— 'The Promise and Challenges of Global Labor History'. *Global Histories of Work.* 25–48. Ed. Andreas Eckert. Berlin and Boston: 2016.
Lindner, Ulrike. 'Indentured Labour in Sub-Saharan Africa (1880–1918): Circulation of Concepts between Imperial Powers'. 59–82. *Bonded Labour. Global and Comparative Perspectives (18th–21st Century).* Eds. Sabine Damir-Geilsdorf et al. Bielefeld: 2016.
——. *Koloniale Begegnungen. Deutschland und Großbritannien als Imperialmächte in Afrika 1880–1914.* Frankfurt o.M. and New York: 2011.
Lockman, Zachary (Ed.). *Workers and the Working Classes in the Middle East: struggles, histories, historiographies.* Albany (NY): 1994.
Löw, Martina. *Raumsoziologie.* Frankfurt o.M.: 2015.
Lucassen, Jan. 'Workers. New Developments in Labor History since the 1980s'. *The Lifework of a Labor Historian: Essays in Honor of Marcel van der Linden.* 22–46. Eds. Ulbe Bosma and Karin Hofmeester. Leiden: 2018.
Lüdtke, Alf. *Eigen-Sinn. Fabrikalltag, Arbeitererfahrungen und Politik vom Kaiserreich bis in den Faschismus.* Hamburg: 1993.
Lynskey, Dorian. *The Ministry of Truth: A Biography of George Orwell's 1984.* London: 2021.
MacKenzie, John M. 'Experts and Amateurs: tsetse, nangana, and sleeping sickness in East and Central Africa'. *Imperialism and the Natural World.* 187–212. Ed. John M. MacKenzie. Manchester: 1990.
Madacho, Pedro et al. (Eds). *Pearls, People, and Power. Pearling the Indian Ocean Worlds.* Athens (Ohio): 2020.
Maier, Gerhard. *African Dinosaurs unearthed. The Tendaguru Expeditions.* Indiana: 2003.
Mangat, J.S. *A History of the Asians in East Africa c. 1886 to 1945.* Oxford: 1969.

Mantzaris, E.A. 'The Greeks in South Africa'. *The Greek Diaspora in the Twentieth Century*. 120–136. Ed. Richard Clogg. Basingstoke: 2001.

——. 'Greek Workers in South Africa. The Case of the Railway Workers and Cigarette-makers. 1905–1914'. 49–63. *Journal of the Hellenic Diaspora*, vol. XIV, no. 3 & 4. N.P.: Fall/Winter: 1987.

Markovits, Claude. *The Global World of Indian Merchants, 1750–1947. Traders of Sind from Bukhara to Panama*. Cambridge: 2000.

Marsh, Zoe and Kingsnorth, G.W. *A History of East Africa. An Introductory Survey*. Cambridge: 1972.

Maß, Sandra. 'Constructing global missionary families: Absence, memory, and belonging before World War I'. 340–361. *Journal of Modern European History*, vol. 19, 3. N.P.: 2021. Web. https://journals.sagepub.com/doi/pdf/10.1177/16118944211019933 (03 March 2022).

——. *Ruhr-Universität Bochum*. Web.https://www.ruhr-uni-bochum.de/transhistory/ueberuns/prof/index.html.de (15 October 2019).

Mayor, Adrienne. 'Suppression of Indigenous Fossil Knowledge: From Claverack, New York, 1705 to Agate Springs, Nebraska 2005'. *Agnotology. The Making and Unmaking of Ignorance*. 163–182. Eds. Robert N. Proctor and Londa Schiebinger. Stanford: 2008.

——. *Fossil Legends of the First Americans*. Princeton: 2005.

McDow, Thomas F. *Buying Time. Debt and Mobility in the Western Indian Ocean*. Athens (Ohio): 2018.

Medick, Hans. 'Introduction. Relational Selves'. *Selbstzeugnis und Person. Transkulturelle Perspektiven*. 75–77. Eds. Claudia Ulbrich et al. Cologne et al: 2012.

Melber, Henning. '". . . dass die Kultur der Neger gehoben werde!" – Kolonialdebatten im deutschen Reichstag'. *Kolonialmetropole Berlin. Eine Spurensuche*. 67–72. Eds. Ulrich van der Heyden and Joachim Zeller. Berlin: 2002.

Metcalf, Thomas R. *Imperial Connections. India and the Indian Ocean Arena. 1860–1920*. Berkeley et al.: 2007.

Methfessel, Christian. *Kontroverse Gewalt. Die imperiale Expansion in der englischen und deutschen Presse vor dem Ersten Weltkrieg*. Cologne et al.: 2018.

Mettele, Gisela. *Weltbürgertum oder Gottesreich. Die Herrnhuter Brüdergemeinschaft als globale Gemeinschaft 1727–1854*. Göttingen: 2009.

Michels, Stefanie. *Schwarze deutsche Kolonialsoldaten. Mehrdeutige Repräsentationsräume und früher Kosmopolitismus in Afrika*. Bielefeld: 2009.

Middell, Matthias and Naumann, Katja. 'Global history and the spatial turn: from the impact of area studies to the study of critical junctures of globalisation'. 149–170. *Journal of Global History* 5. London School of Economics and Political Science: 2010. Web. https://cambridge.org/core/terms.https://doi.org/10.1017/51740022809990362 (27 March 2019).

Minawi, Mostafa. *The Ottoman Scramble for Africa. Empire and Diplomacy in the Sahara and the Hijaz*. Stanford: 2016.

Mishra, Amit Kumar. 'Sardars, Kanganies and Maistries: Intermediaries in the Indian Labour Diaspora during the Colonial Period'. *The History of Labour Intermediation. Institutions and Finding Employment in the Nineteenth and Early Twentieth Centuries*. 368–387. Eds. Sigrid Wadauer et al. New York and Oxford: 2015.

Mogge, Winfried. '"Im deutschen Boden Afrikas". Wilhelm Branca, die Tendaguru-Expedition und die Kolonialpolitik'. *Deutsch-Ostafrika. Dynamiken Europäischer Kulturkontakte und Erfahrungshorizonte im kolonialen Raum*. 125–144. Eds. Stefan Noack et al. Berlin et al.: 2019.

——. *Wilhelm Branco, (1844–1928). Geologe – Paläontologe – Darwinist. Eine Biographie*. Berlin: 2018.

Mohr, Erna. "Hagenbeck, Carl". *Neue Deutsche Biographie*, 7, 1966, pp. 487–488. Web. https://www.deutsche-biographie.de/pnd118700502.html#ndbcontent (26 February 20).

Monson, Jamie. *Africa's Freedom Railway. How a Chinese Development Project changed the Lives and Livelihoods of Tanzania*. Indiana: 2009.

Moyd, Michelle R. *Violent Intermediaries. African Soldiers, Conquest, and Everyday Colonialism in German East Africa*. Athens (Ohio): 2014.

Murphy, David T. *The Heroic Earth. Geopolitical Thought in Weimar Germany, 1918–1933.* Kent (Ohio) and London: 1997.

N.A. 'Pferdmenges: Geld aus dem Fenster'. *Der Spiegel*, 5/1954. 27th January 1954. Web. https://www.spiegel.de/spiegel/print/d-28955044.html (02 July 2020).

Nagel, Daniel. *Von republikanischen Deutschen zu deutsch-amerikanischen Republikanern. Ein Beitrag zum Identitätswandel der deutschen Achtundvierziger in den Vereinigten Staaten 1850–1861.* St. Ingbert: 2012.

Nagel, Jürgen G. 'Schifffahrt auf dem Indischen Ozean im 19. Jahrhundert. Technologie und Wissen in der Transportrevolution der Moderne'. 61–80. *Zeitschrift für Weltgeschichte*, Jahrgang 18, Heft 2. Berlin: 2017.

—— *Die Kolonie als wissenschaftliches Projekt. Forschungsorganisation und Forschungspraxis im deutschen Kolonialreich.* Habilitationsschrift an der FernUniversität in Hagen. Fakultät für Kultur- und Sozialwissenschaften. Mai 2013. Web.https://www.academia.edu/41830319/Die_Kolonie_als_wissenschaftliches_Projekt_Forschungsorganisation_und_Forschungspraxis_im_deutschen_Kolonialreich (21 June 2021).

Naranch, Bradly D. '"Colonized Body," "Oriental Machine": Debating Race, Railroads, and the Politics of Reconstruction in Germany and East Africa, 1906–1910'. 299–338. *Central European History*, vol. 33, no. 3. Cambridge: 2000. Web. *Jstor*. http://www.jstor.org/stable/4546983 (13 July 2018).

Nasar, Saima. '*The Indian Voice*: Connecting Self-Representation and Identity Formulation in Diaspora'. 99–124. *History in Africa*, vol. 40. Cambridge: 2013. Web. https://www.cambridge.org/core/terms. https://doi.org/10.1017/hia.2013.10 (26 January 2018).

Natermann, Diana Miryong. *Pursuing Whiteness in the Colonies. Private memories from the Congo Free State and German East Africa (1884–1914)*. Münster and New York: 2018.

Nebelin, Manfred. *Ludendorff. Diktator im Ersten Weltkrieg*. Munich: 2011.

Nieuwland, Ilja. *American Dinosaur Abroad. A Cultural History of Carnegie's Plaster Diplodocus.* Pittsburgh: 2019.

Nikles, Bruno W. *Soziale Hilfe am Bahnhof. Zur Geschichte der Bahnhofsmission in Deutschland (1894.1960)*. Freiburg i. Br.: 1994.

Nish, Ian. *The Origins of the Russo-Japanese War*. London: 1985.

Nöhre, Joachim. *Das Selbstverständnis der Weimarer Kolonialbewegung im Spiegel Ihrer Zeitschrift.* Münster: 1998.

Nuzzo, Luigi. 'Kolonialrecht'. *Europäische Geschichte Online (EGO).* Ed. Institut für Europäische Geschichte (IEG), Mainz, 2011-07-14. Web. http://www.ieg-ego.eu/nuzzol-2011-deURN:urn:nbn:de:0159-2011051270 (14 January 2020).

Ochsenwald, William. *The Hijaz Railroad*. Charlottesville: 1980.

O'Donnell, Anthony. ''Organizing the Labour Market' in a Liberal Welfare State: The Origins of the Public Employment Service in Australia'. *The History of Labour Intermediation. Institutions and Finding Employment in the Nineteenth and Early Twentieth Centuries*. 388–414. Eds. Sigrid Wadauer et al. New York and Oxford: 2015.

Oestermann, Tristan. 'Review on: Samarin, William J. *The Black Man's Burden. African Colonial Labor on the Congo and Ubangi Rivers, 1880–1900'*. New York: 2019. *HSozKult.* 30 August 2021. Web. https://www.hsozkult.de/searching/id/reb-96367?title=w-j-samarin-the-black-man-s-burden&q=oestermann&sort=&fq=&total=21&recno=1&subType=reb (06 September 2021).

Ohl, Michael and Stoecker, Holger. 'Taxonomien am Tendaguru. Wie die Berliner Saurier ihre Namen bekamen'. *Dinosaurier Fragmente. Zur Geschichte der Tendaguru-Expedition und ihrer Objekte 1906–2008*. 232–252. Eds. Ina Heumann et al. Göttingen: 2018.

Orwell, George. *The Road to Wigan Pier*. Ed. Selina Todd. London: 2021.

——. 'Marrakech'. *The Orwell Foundation.* Web. https://www.orwellfoundation.com/the-orwell-foundation/orwell/essays-and-other-works/marrakech/ (25 May 2021).

Osterhammel, Jürgen. *Die Flughöhe der Adler: historische Essays zur globalen Gegenwart*. Munich: 2017.

——. *Die Verwandlung der Welt. Eine Geschichte des 19. Jahrhunderts.* Munich: 2009.

Oyono, Ferdinand. *Houseboy*. Oxford: 1990.

Panel "Railway Imperialism Reconsidered" of the Society for the History of the History of Technology (SHOT) in Milan (Italy) in November 2019.

Papakyriacou, Marios. *Formulation and definitions of the Greek national ideology in colonial Egypt (1856–1919)*. Unpublished Dissertation. Freie Universität Berlin: 2014. Web. *Freie Universität Berlin.* https://refubium.fuberlin.de/bitstream/handle/fub188/3114/Dissertation_Papakyriacou_Marios_12_2014.pdf?sequence=1&isAllowed=y (12 October 2021).

Papastefanaki, Leda and Potamianos, Nikos (Eds.). *Labour History in the Semi-periphery. Southern Europe, 19th– 20th centuries*. Berlin and Boston: 2021.

—— and Kabadayi, Erden M. (Eds.). *Working in Greece and Turkey. A Comparative Labour History from Empires to Nation States, 1840–1940*. New York and Oxford: 2020.

Pawliková-Vilhanová, Viera. 'Crescent or Cross? Islam and Christian Missions in Nineteenth-Century East and Central Africa'. *Mission und Gewalt. Der Umgang christlicher Mission mit Gewalt und die Ausbreitung des Christentums in Afrika und Asien in der Zeit von 1792 bis 1918/19*. 79–96. Eds. Ulrich van der Heyden and Jürgen Becher. Stuttgart: 2000.

Pearson, Michael. *The Indian Ocean*. London and New York: 2006.

Pearson, M.N. (Ed.). *The World of the Indian Ocean, 1500–1800. Studies in Economic, Social and Cultural History.* Burlington: 2005.

Pepijn Brandon. Review on: *Robins, Jonathan E.: Cotton and Race across the Atlantic. Britain, Africa, and America, 1900–1920.* Martlesham. Web. *Connections. A Journal for Historians and Area Specialists*. 29 September 2019. www.connections.clio-online.net/publicationreview/id/reb-26130 (21 October 2019).

Pesek, Michael. 'Die Absurdität kolonialer Representationswelten. Humor und Gewalt in Deutsch-Ostafrika, 1889–1918'. 1–13. *Academia.edu.* Web. https://www.academia.edu/3648430/Die_Absurdit%C3%A4t_kolonialer_Repr%C3%A4sentationswelten._Humor_und_Gewalt_in_Deutsch-Ostafrika_1889-1918 (23 April 2020).

——. 'Passage to Africa. Steamship travels of Germans to East Africa in early 20th century'. *Academia.edu.* Web. https://uni-hamburg.academia.edu/MichaelPesek (15 April 2020).

——. *Koloniale Herrschaft in Deutsch-Ostafrika. Expeditionen, Militär und Verwaltung seit 1880.* Frankfurt o.M.: 2005.

——. 'Kreuz oder Halbmond. Die deutsche Kolonialpolitik zwischen Pragmatismus und Paranoia in Deutsch-Ostafrika 1908–1914'. *Mission und Gewalt. Der Umgang christlicher Mission mit Gewalt und die Ausbreitung des Christentums in Afrika und Asien in der Zeit von 1792 bis 1918/19*. 97–111. Eds. Ulrich van der Heyden and Jürgen Becher. Stuttgart: 2000.

Plumpe, Werner et al. *Deutsche Bank. Die globale Hausbank 1870–2020*. Berlin: 2020.

Pohl, Manfred. *Philipp Holzmann. Geschichte eines Bauunternehmens. 1849–1999*. Munich: 1999

——. *Von Stambul nach Bagdad. Die Geschichte einer berühmten Eisenbahn*. Munich: 1999.

Powell, Jim. *Losing the Thread. Cotton, Liverpool, and the American Civil War*. Liverpool: 2021.

Prass, Reiner. 'Briefe aus Äthiopien und dem Sudan. Die Briefkommunikation zwischen europäischen Reisenden und dem Kartographen August Petermann in Gotha, 1854–1880'. *Verbindung halten. (Post)Kommunikation unter schwierigen Verhältnissen*. 87–109. Ed. René Smolarski et al. Göttingen: 2021.
Preuss, Monika. 'Das Unsagbare sagen. Aussagen über Sexualität von Jüdinnen und Juden in amtlichen Verhörprotokollen'. *Selbstzeugnisse und Ego-Dokumente frühneuzeitlicher Juden in Ashkenas. Beispiele, Methoden, Konzepte*. 167–184. Eds. Birgit E. Klein and Rotraud Ries. Berlin: 2011.
Przyrembel, Alexandra. 'Empire, Medien und die Globalisierung von Wissen im 19. Jahrhundert. Einführung'. *Von Käfern, Märkten und Menschen. Kolonialismus und Wissen in der Moderne*. 197–220. Eds. Rebekka Habermas and Alexandra Przyrembel. Göttingen: 2013.
Pugach, Sarah. *Africa in Translation. A History of Colonial Linguistics in Germany and Beyond, 1814–1945.* Ann Arbor: 2015.
Quenstedt, Werner. "Fraas, Eberhard". *Neue Deutsche Biographie*, 5, 1961, pp. 307–308. Web. https://daten.digitalesammlungen.de/0001/bsb00016321/images/index.html?id=00016321&groesser=&fip=eayaqrsqrseayaenfsdrfsdrxsxdsydenxs&no=3&seite=323 (06 July 2020).
Raj, Kapil. *Relocating Modern Science. Circulation and the Construction of Knowledge in South Asia and Europe, 1650–1900*. New York: 2007.
Ratliff, William G. "Heligoland-Zanzibar Treaty of 1890". *Historical Dictionary of European Imperialism.* 279–280. Ed. James S. Olson et al. Westport: 1991.
Reichart-Burikukiye, Marianne. *Gari la Moshi – Modernität und Mobilität. Das Leben mit der Eisenbahn in Deutsch-Ostafrika*. Münster: 2005.
Reusch, Wolfgang. *Bahnhofsmission in Deutschland 1897–1987. Sozialwissenschaftliche Analyse einer diakonisch-charitativen Einrichtung im sozialen Wandel*. Frankfurt o.M. et al.: 1988.
Riello, Giorgo. *Cotton: The Fabric that made the Modern World*. Cambridge: 2013.
Rieppel, Lukas. *Assembling the Dinosaur. Fossil Hunters, Tycoons, and the Making of a Spectacle*. Harvard: 2019.
Re:work. *International Research Center. Work and Human Lifecycle in Global History*. Web. https://rework.huberlin.de/de/aktuelles.html. (21 July 2017).
Robins, Johnathan E. *Cotton and Race Across the Atlantic. Britain, Africa, and America, 1900–1920*. Rochester: 2016.
Rockel, Stephen J. 'Decentring Exploration in East Africa'. *Reinterpreting Exploration. The West in the World*. 172–194. Ed. Dane Kennedy. Oxford: 2014.
——. *Carriers of Culture. Labor on the Road in Nineteenth-Century East Africa*. Portsmouth: 2006.
Rösser, Michael. 'Von Afrika nach Eurasien? Deutsche Unternehmen zwischen kolonialem Eisenbahnbau und geopolitischer Planungsphantasie während des Ersten Weltkriegs'. 183–204. *Vierteljahrschrift für Sozial und Wirtschaftsgeschichte (VSWG)*, vol. 110 no 2. Stuttgart: 2023. doi.org/10.25162/vswg-2023-0005.
——. 'Die Firma Wilkins & Wiese in "Neu-Hornow". Ein Drahtseilakt zwischen Rhein/Ruhr, Weißer Elster und Ostafrika'. *Nordrhein-Westfalen und der Imperialismus*. 128–150. Eds. Marianne Bechhaus-Gerst et al. Berlin: 2022.
——. '"*Shenzi Ulaya*". Deutsch griechische Verflechtungen von der Bagdadbahn zum kolonialen Deutsch-Ostafrika'. *Online-Compedium der deutsch-griechischen Verflechtungen*. Zentrum Modernes Griechenland der Freien Universität Berlin: 02 March 2022. Web. https://comdeg.eu/compendium/essay/109893/. (02 March 2022).
——. '«Shenzi Ulaya» — Ελληνογερμανικές Διασταυρώσεις: Από τον Σιδηρόδρομο της Βαγδάτης στην Αποικία της Γερμανικής Ανατολικής Αφρικής'. *Online-Compedium der deutsch-griechischen*

Verflechtungen. Zentrum Modernes Griechenland der Freien Universität Berlin: 02 March 2022. Web.https://comdeg.eu/el/compendium/essay/109893/ (02 March 2022).
——. 'Transimperiale Infrastruktur? Personal, Unternehmer und Arbeit beim Bau der Zentralbahn in Deutsch-Ostafrika'. *Moderne Transimperialitäten. Rivalitäten, Kontakte, Wetteifer*. 274–289. Eds. Laurent Dedryvère et al. Berlin: 2021.
——. 'Knotenpunkte des Kolonialen.' *Vorstudie „Kolonialistisches Denken und Kolonialkultur in Stuttgart".* Ed. Stadtarchiv Stuttgart. Stuttgart: 19 July 2021. Web. https://archiv0711.hypotheses.org/files/2021/07/Stadtarchiv_Stuttgart_Kolonialistisches-DenkenStuttgart.pdf (10 September 2021).
——. '"Den Seegedanken zu pflegen"? Hagener Krieger- und Marinevereine. Krieg und Gewalt in China und im Kolonialen Afrika'. *Fernes Hagen. Kolonialismus und wir*. 14–29. Eds. Fabian Fechner and Barbara Schneider. Hagen: 2021.
——. et al. 'Baumwolle, die Firma Joh. Anton Lucius aus Erfurt und der koloniale Kapitalismus'. 9–12. *Heimat Thüringen*, 27. Jahrgang, Heft 1. Weimar: 2020.
——. Review on 'Natermann, Diana Miryong: Pursuing Whiteness in the Colonies. Private Memories from the Congo Freestate and German East Africa (1884–1914)'. Münster: 2018. *H-Soz-Kult*. 15 March 2019. Web. www.hsozkult.de/publicationreview/id/rezbuecher-30169 (26 July 2019).
——. 'Nachricht von Gott? Das Gratulationstelegramm von Selim bin Abakari an Hermann von Wißmann Anlässlich seiner Hochzeit am 20.11.1894'. *(Dis-)Locating Hermann von Wissmann.* 16–25. Ed. Stefanie Michels. Düsseldorf: 2018.
——. 'Juristisches Seminar. Theodor von Gunzert'. *Koloniale-spuren-heidelberg.de.* Web. http://www.koloniale-spuren-heidelberg.de/juristisches-seminar-theodor-gunzert/#1478787905103-829876ab-548d761b-259b8d7e-2b64 (05 December 2017).
——. *Forced Labour in 'German East Africa' – Between 'Colonial Amnesia' and Structural Similarities to WWI in Europe*. Regensburg: 2015. (unpublished *Zulassungsarbeit* (thesis)).
Roolf, Christoph. 'Dinosaurier-Skelette als Kriegsziel: Kulturgutraubplanungen, Besatzungspolitik und die deutsche Paläontologie in Belgien im Ersten Weltkrieg'. 5–26. *Berichte zur Wissenschaftsgeschichte*, 27. Weinheim: 2004.
Rothermund, Dietmar. 'Globalgeschichte als Interaktionsgeschichte: Von der Außereuropäischen Geschichte zur Globalgeschichte'. *Area Studies und die Welt. Weltregion und neue Globalgeschichte.* 194–216. Ed. Birgit Schäbler. Vienna: 2007.
Sabea, Hanan. 'Pioneers of Empire? The Making of Sisal Plantations in German East Africa, 1890–1917'. *German Colonialism Revisited. African, Asian and Oceanic Experiences*. 114–129. Eds. Nina Berman et al. Ann Arbor: 2017.
Sachiko, Hirakawa. 'Portsmouth Denied: The Chinese Attempt to attend'. *The Russo-Japanese War in Global Perspective. World War Zero. Volume II.* 531–550. Ed. David Wolf et al. Leiden: 2007.
Saha, Jonathan. 'Colonizing elephants: Animal agency, undead capital and imperial science in British Burma'. 169–189. *BJHS: Themes*, 2. 24 April 2017. Web. https://www.cambridge.org/core/journals/bjhs-themes/article/colonizing-elephants-animal-agency-undead-capital-and-imperial-science-in-british-burma/34A559317F45848054C76C384BEEB8F3/core-reader (18 June 2018).
Saro-Wiwa, Ken. *Sozaboy*. Munich: 1997.
Sauer, Michael. 'Selbstzeugnisse als historische Quellen'. 2–11. *Geschichte Lernen*. Heft 156. Seelze: 2013.
Schaper, Ulrike. *Koloniale Verhandlungen. Gerichtsbarkeit, Verwaltung und Herrschaft in Kamerun, 1884–1916.* Frankfurt o.M. and New York: 2012.
Schiefel, Werner. *Bernhard Dernburg. 1857–1937. Kolonialpolitiker und Bankier im wilhelminischen Deutschland.* Zürich: 1974.

Schildkrout, Enid and Keim, Curtis A. 'Objects and Agendas: re-collecting the Congo'. *The Scramble for Art in Africa*. 1–36. Ed. Enid Schildkrout and Curtis A. Keim. Cambridge: 1998.
Schilling, Britta. *Postcolonial Germany. Memoirs of Empire in a Decolonized Nation*. Oxford: 2014.
Schinzinger, Francesca. *Die Kolonien und das Deutsche Reich. Die wirtschaftliche Bedeutung der deutschen Besitzungen in Übersee*. Stuttgart: 1984.
Schmidt, Jürgen. *Arbeiter in der Moderne. Arbeitsbedingungen, Lebenswelten, Organisationen*. Frankfurt o.M.: 2015.
Schnepel, Burkhard. 'Konnektivität in Bewegung: Der Indische Ozean als maritime Kontakt- und Austauschzone'. *Forschungsbericht – Max Planck Institut für ethnologische Forschung*. 2016. Web. https://www.eth.mpg.de/4393439/research_report_10998872?c=2923387 (06 July 2021).
Schreiner, Hanna. 'Carl Friedrich Klein und Christine Klein'. 56–61. *Wuppertaler Biographien*, 5. Wuppertal: 1965.
Schröder, Hans-Crhistoph. *Gustav Noske und die Kolonialpolitik des Deutschen Kaiserreiches*. Berlin and Bonn: 1979.
Schröder, Iris. 'Von der Ordnung zur Unordnung zur Umordnung'. *Karten-Meere: eine Welterzeugung*. 87–107. Eds. Wolfgang Struck et al. Wiesbaden: 2020.
——. *Das Wissen von der ganzen Welt. Globale Geographien und räumliche Ordnungen Afrikas und Europas 1790–1870*. Paderborn: 2011.
—— and Höhler, Sabine. 'Welt-Räume: Annäherungen an eine Geschichte der Globalität im 20. Jahrhundert'. *Welt-Räume. Geschichte, Geographie und Globalisierung seit 1900*. 9–50. Eds. Iris Schröder and Sabine Höhler. Frankfurt o.M. and New York: 2005.
——. *Arbeiten für eine bessere Welt. Frauenbewegung und Sozialreform 1890–1914*. Frankfurt o.M. and New York: 2001.
Schröder, Martin. *Prügelstrafe und Züchtigungsrecht in den deutschen Schutzgebieten Schwarzafrikas*. Münster: 1997.
Schröder, Peter J. *Gesetzgebung und „Arbeiterfrage" in den Kolonien. Das Arbeitsrecht in den Schutzgebieten des Deutschen Reiches*. Berlin: 2006.
Schumacher, Martin, "Hilgard, Heinrich". *Neue Deutsche Biographie*, 9, 1972, p. 139. Web. https://www.deutsche-biographie.de/pnd119068605.html#ndbcontent (05 February 2020).
Schweighöfer, Ellinor. *Vom Neandertal nach Afrika. Der Streit um den Ursprung der Menschheit im 19. und 20. Jahrhundert*. Göttingen: 2018.
Seeberg, Martin. *Der Maji Maji Krieg gegen die deutsche Kolonialherrschaft*. Berlin: 1989.
Seemann, Martin. *Kolonialismus in der Heimat. Kolonialbewegung, Kolonialpolitik und Kolonialkultur in Bayern 1882–1943*. Berlin: 2011.
Seetah, Krish (Ed.). *Archaeology and the History in the Indian Ocean*. Athens (Ohio): 2018.
Seibert, Julia. 'Kazi. Konzepte, Praktiken und Semantiken von Lohnarbeit im kolonialen Kongo'. *Semantiken von Arbeit: Diachrone und vergleichende Perspektiven*. 209–223. Eds. Jörn Leonhard and Willibald Steinmetz. Cologne et al.: 2016.
Seifert, Annika and Moon, Karen (Eds.). *Dar es Salaam. A History of Urban Space and Architecture*. DARCH, Dar Centre for Architectural Heritage. Dar es Salaam: 2017.
Shapin, Steven. 'The invisible Technician'. 554–563. *Scientist*, 77, 6. Harvard: 1989. Web. http://nrs.harvard.edu/urn-3:HUL.InstRepos:3425945 (02 November 2017).
Singh, Gajendra. 'Finding those men with 'GUTS'. The Ascription and Re-ascription of Martial Identities in India after the Uprising'. *Mutiny at the Margins. New Perspectives on the Indian Uprising of 1857. Volume 4. Military Aspects of the Indian Uprising*. 113–134. Eds. Gevin Rand and Crispin Bates. New Dehli: 2013.

Sippel, Harald. 'Mission und Gewalt in Deutsch-Ostafrika. Das Verhältnis zwischen Mission und Kolonialverwaltung'. *Mission und Gewalt. Der Umgang christlicher Mission mit Gewalt und die Ausbreitung des Christentums in Afrika und Asien in der Zeit von 1792 bis 1918/19*. 525–538. Eds. Ulrich van der Heyden and Jürgen Becher. Stuttgart: 2000.

——. '"Wie erzieht man am besten den Neger zur Plantagen-Arbeit?" Die Ideologie der Arbeitserziehung und ihre rechtliche Umsetzung in der Kolonie Deutsch-Ostafrika'. *Arbeit in Afrika*. 311–333. Eds. Kurt Beck and Gerd Spittler. Hamburg: 1996.

Sivasundaram, Sujit. *Islanded. Britain, Sri Lanka, and the Bounds of an Indian Ocean Colony*. Chicago and London: 2013.

——. 'Trading Knowledge: The East India Company's Elephants in India and Britain'. 27–63. *The Historical Journal*, 48, 1. Cambridge: 2005.

Söldenwagner, Philippa. *Spaces of Negotiation. European Settlement and Settlers in German East Africa. 1900–1914*. Munich: 2006.

Sokoll, Thomas. 'Alteuropäisches Erbe, moderne Ausprägung und postmoderne Verwerfungen im Arbeitsbegriff'. *Semantiken von Arbeit: Diachrone und vergleichende Perspektiven*. 393–409. Eds. Jörn Leonhard and Willibald Steinmetz. Cologne et al.: 2016.

Soske, Jon. *Internal Frontiers. African Nationalism and the Indian Diaspora in Twentieth-Century South Africa*. Athens (Ohio): 2017.

Spivak, Gayatri Chakravorty. 'Can the Subaltern Speak?'. *Can the Subaltern Speak? Postkolonialität und subaltern Artikulation*. 17–118. Ed. Hito Steyerl et al. Vienna and Berlin: 2020.

Steinecke, Ernst-Christian. 'Die Ausgrabung von Babylon. Wissenschaftsförderung im Deutschen Kaiserreich am Beispiel der Archäologie'. *Von Käfern, Märkten und Menschen. Kolonialismus und Wissen in der Moderne*. 285–296. Eds. Rebekka Habermas and Alexandra Przyrembel. Göttingen: 2013.

Stiles, Erin E. and Thompson, Katrina Daly (Eds.). *Gendered Lives in the Western Indian Ocean. Islam, Marriage, and Sexuality on the Swahili Coast*. Athens (Ohio): 2015.

Stoecker, Holger. 'Koloniales Kronland und Ausfuhrverbot. Wie die Fossilien vom Tendaguru für die deutsche Wissenschaft gesichert wurden'. *Dinosaurier Fragmente. Zur Geschichte der Tendaguru-Expedition und ihrer Objekte. 1906–2018*. 38–57. Eds. Ina Heumann et al. Göttingen: 2018.

——. 'Maji-Maji-Krieg und Mineralien. Zur Vorgeschichte der Ausgrabung von Dinosaurier- Fossilien am Tendaguru in Deutsch-Ostafrika'. *Dinosaurier Fragmente. Zur Geschichte der Tendaguru-Expedition und ihrer Objekte 1906–2008*. 25–38. Eds. Ina Heumann et al. Göttingen: 2018.

——. 'Über Spenden und Sponsoren. Zur Finanzierung der „Deutschen Tendaguru Expedition"'. *Dinosaurier Fragmente. Zur Geschichte der Tendaguru-Expedition und ihrer Objekte. 1906–2018*. 79–93. Eds. Ina Heumann et al. Göttingen: 2018.

Stoler, Laura Ann. *Along the Archival Grain. Epistemic Anxieties and Colonial Common Sense*. Princeton: 2009.

——. 'Colonial Archives and the Arts of Governance'. 87–109. *Archival Science*, 2. N.P.: 2002.

——. 'Rethinking Colonial Categories: European Communities and the Boundaries of Rule'. *Colonialism and Culture*. 319–352. Ed. Nicolas B. Dirks. Ann Arbor: 1992.

Stoyke, Michael. 'Suche nach einem Europa *en miniature*: Chinas Städte in den Augen europäischer Reisender um 1900'. *Welt-Räume. Geschichte, Geographie und Globalisierung seit 1900*. 147–174. Eds. Iris Schröder and Sabine Höhler. Frankfurt o.M. and New York: 2005.

Struck, Wolfgang. 'Einleitung'. *Karten-Meere: eine Welterzeugung*. 7–21. Eds. Wolfgang Struck et al. Wiesbaden: 2020.

——. 'Von der Schwierigkeit, eine Linie zu ziehen'. *Karten-Meere: eine Welterzeugung*. 125–135. Eds. Wolfgang Struck et al. Wiesbaden: 2020.

Sunseri, Thaddeus. *Vilimani. Labor Migration and rural Change in early colonial Tanzania*. Oxford: 2002.
——. '"Dispersing the Fields": Railway Labor and Rural Change in Early Colonial Tanzania'. 558–583. *Canadian Journal of African Studies/Revue Canadienne des Études Africaines*, vol. 32, no 3. N.P.: 1998. Web. https://www.jstor.org/stable/pdf/486328.pdf?refreqid=excelsior%3A219c27ca837ae53f96b249dce27189f7 (20 June 2018).
——. 'Labour Migration in Colonial Tanzania and the Hegemony of South African Historiography'. 581–598. *African Affairs*, vol. 95, no. 381. Oxford: 1996. Web. *Jstor*. http://www.jstor.org/stable/723445 (11 April 2018).
Tambila, Kapepwa I., 'The German Invasion and Occupaion of East Africa. Policies, Processes and Tactics'. *Studien zur Geschichte des deutschen Kolonialismus in Afrika. Festschrift zum 60. Geburtstag von Peter Sebald*. 501–520. Eds. Peter Heine und Ulrich van der Heyden. Pfaffenweiler: 1995.
Tamborini, Marco. 'Die Vermarktung der Tiefenzeit. Paläontologie im Umbruch'. *Dinosaurier Fragmente. Zur Geschichte der Tendaguru-Expedition und ihrer Objekte, 1906–2018*. 124–135. Eds. Ina Heumann et al. Göttingen: 2018.
Tamis, Anastasis Myrodis. *Greeks in the far Orient*. Thessaloniki: 2011
Tappe, Oliver and Lindner, Ulrike. 'Introduction: Global Variants of Bonded Labour'. *Bonded Labour. Global and Comparative Perspectives (18th– 21st Century)*. 9–34. Eds. Sabine Damir-Geilsdorf et al. Bielefeld: 2016.
Teichmann, Gabriele. "Pferdmenges, Robert". *Neue Deutsche Biographie*, 20, 2001, pp. 331–332. Web. https://www.deutsche-biographie.de/pnd118791729.html#ndb content (18 July 2019).
Tetzlaff, Rainer. *Koloniale Entwicklung und Ausbeutung. Wirtschafts- und Sozialgeschichte Deutsch-Ostafrikas 1885–1914*. Berlin: 1970.
Thiel, Jens. *„Menschenbassin Belgien". Anwerbung, Deportation und Zwangsarbeit im Ersten Weltkrieg*. Essen: 2007.
Thode-Arora, Hilke. 'Hagenbeck: Tierpark und Völkerschau'. *Kein Platz an der Sonne. Erinnerungsorte deutscher Kolonialgeschichte*. 244–256. Ed. Jürgen Zimmerer. Bonn: 2013.
Thomas, Lynn M. 'Historicising Agency'. 234–239. *Gender & History*, vol. 28, no. 2. Oxford: 2016.
Todd, Selina. 'Introduction'. George Orwell. *The Road to Wigan Pier*. vii–xxxiii. Ed. Selina Todd. Oxford: 2021.
Todzi, Kim Sebastian. 'Colonial Capitalism in Action. The New Social and Economic History of German Colonialism'. *HSozKult*. 14 April 2021. Web. https://www.hsozkult.de/searching/id/event-97072?title=colonial-capitalism-in-action-the-new-social-and-economic-history-of-german-colonialism&q=colonial%20capitalism%20in%20action&sort=&fq=&total=139&recno=1&subType=event (31 May 2021).
Tooze, Adam. *The Deluge. The Great War and the Remaking of the Global Order. 1916–1931*. London et. al.: 2014.
Treue, Wilhelm. 'Das Porträt. Robert Pferdmenges (1880–1962)'. 188–210. *Geschichte im Westen*, no. 2, pp. 188–205. N.P.: 1990. Web. http://www.brauweiler-kreis.de/wp-content/uploads/GiW/GiW1990_2/GiW_1990_2_TREUE_PFERDMENGES.pdf. (18 July 2019).
Trotha, Trutz von. *Koloniale Herrschaft. Zur soziologischen Staatsentstehung am Beispiel des »Schutzgebietes Togo«*. Tübingen: 1994.
Tziovas, Dimitris (Ed.). *Greek Diaspora and Migration Since 1700. Society, Politics and Culture*. Ashgate: 2009.
——. *Greece and the Balkans. Identities, Perceptions and Cultural Encounters Since the Enlightenment*. Ashgate: 2003.

Ulbrich, Claudia. 'Europäische Selbstzeugnisse in historischer Perspektive – neue Zugänge'. 1–20. *FU-Berlin.* Web. https://www.geschkult.fu-berlin.de/e/fmi/institut/arbeitsbereiche/ab_ulbrich/media/UlbrichEurop__ische_Selbstzeugnisse.pdf (10 May 2019).
——. et al. 'Selbstzeugnisse und Person. Transkulturelle Perspektiven'. *Selbstzeugnis und Person. Transkulturelle Perspektiven*. 1–20. Eds. Claudia Ulbrich et al. Cologne et al.: 2012.
Utermark, Sören. *"Schwarzer Untertan vs. schwarzer Bruder". Bernhard Dernburgs Reformen in den Kolonien Deutsch-Ostafrika, Deutsch-Südwestafrika, Togo und Kamerun*. Unpublished Dissertation. N.P.: 2011. Web. *Universität Kassel.* https://kobra.uni-kassel.de/bitstream/handle/123456789/2012082441677/DissertationSoerenUtermark.pdf?sequence=5&isAllowed=y (21 July 2021).
Varela, Raquel et al. (Eds.). *Shipbuilding and Ship Repair Workers around the World. Case Studies 1950–2010*. Amsterdam: 2017.
Vennen, Mareike. 'Arbeitsbilder – Bilderarbeit. Die Herstellung und Zirkulation von Fotografien der Tendaguru-Expedition'. *Dinosaurier Fragmente. Zur Geschichte der Tendaguru- Expedition und ihrer Objekte. 1906–2018*. 56–77. Eds. Ina Heumann et al. Göttingen: 2018.
——. 'Auf Dinosaurierjagd. Wissenschaft, Museum und Unterhaltungsindustrie'. *Dinosaurier Fragmente. Zur Geschichte der Tendaguru-Expedition und ihrer Objekte 1906–2008*. 208–231. Eds. Ina Heumann et al. Göttingen: 2018.
——. 'Wer hat den Größten? Zur Verwertung und Verteilung der ersten Tendaguru- Exponate'. *Dinosaurier Fragmente. Zur Geschichte der Tendaguru-Expedition und ihrer Objekte. 1906–2018.* 136–165. Eds. Ina Heumann et al. Göttingen: 2018.
——. 'Träger-Arbeiten. Die Zirkulation kolonialer Dinge und Bilder der Tendaguru- Expedition (1909–1913)'. *Der Träger. Zu einer 'tragenden' Figur der Kolonialgeschichte*. 157–180. Eds. Sonja Malzner and Anne D. Peiter. Bielefeld: 2018.
Vigna, Xavier et al. 'Gender history and labour history'. 176–203. *Clio. Women, Gender, History*, No. 38, Working women, working men. N. P.: 2013. Web. *Jstor*. https://www.jstor.org/stable/10.2307/26273601 (04 June 2021).
Vink, Markus P.M. 'The Ocean Studies and the 'new thalassology''. 41–62. *Journal of Global History*, 2. London: 2007. Web. *Cambridge.org*. doi:10.1017/S1740022807002033 (04 June 2019).
Vogel, Jakob. 'Public-private partnership. Das koloniale Wissen und seine Ressourcen im langen 19. Jahrhundert. Einführung'. *Von Käfern, Märkten und Menschen. Kolonialismus und Wissen in der Moderne*. 261–284. Eds. Rebekka Habermas and Alexandra Przyrembel. Göttingen: 2013.
Voigt-Graf, Carmen. *Asian Communities in Tanzania: A Journey to Past and Present Times*. Hamburg: 1998.
Vokalavene, Yovita. *The Role of African Women in the First World War (1914–1918) in German East Africa*. Dissertation project at the University of Göttingen. Web. https://www.uni-goettingen.de/en/promotionen/561451.html (28 April 2020).
Wadauer, Sigrid et al. 'Introduction: Finding Work and Organizing Placement in the Nineteenth and Twentieth Centuries'. *The History of Labour Intermediation. Institutions and Finding Employment in the Nineteenth and Early Twentieth Centuries*. 1–22. Eds. Sigrid Wadauer et al. New York and Oxford: 2015.
——. 'Concluding Remarks'. *The History of Labour Intermediation. Institutions and Finding Employment in the Nineteenth and Early Twentieth Centuries*. 415–420. Eds. Sigrid Wadauer et al. New York and Oxford: 2015.
Walther, Daniel J. *Sex and Control. Venereal Disease, Colonial Physicians, and indigenous Agency in German Colonialism, 1884–1914*. New York: 2015.
Watson, Julia. 'The Spaces of Autobiographical Narrative'. *Räume des Selbst. Selbstzeugnisforschung transkulturell*. 13–25. Eds. Andreas Bähr et al. Cologne et al.: 2007.

Webel, Mari k. 'Ziba Politics and the German Sleeping Sickness Camp at Kigarama, Tanzania 1907–14'. 399–423. *The International Journal of African Historical Studies*, vol. 47, no. 3. Boston: 2014. Web. *Jstor*. https://www.jstor.org/stable/24393436 (01 June 2021).
——. *The Politics of Disease Control. Sleeping Sickness in Eastern Africa, 1890–1920*. Athens (Ohio): 2019.
Wegmann, Heiko. *Vom Kolonialkrieg in Deutsch-Ostafrika zur Kolonialbewegung in Freiburg. Der Offizier und badische Veteranenführer Max Knecht (1874–1954)*. Freiburg i.Br.: 2019.
Wendels, Claudia. *Die Schantung-Eisenbahn. Das Interesse der Finanzwelt an der deutschen Bahnlinie in Ostchina*. Siegburg: 2012.
Wenzlhuemer, Roland. *Connecting the Nineteenth-Century World. The Telegraph and Globalization*. Cambridge: 2013.
Wette, Wolfgang. "Noske, Gustav". *Neue Deutsche Biographie*, 19, 1998, pp. 347–384. Web. https://www.deutsche-biographie.de/pnd118588761.html (01 July 2021).
Wetzel, Christa. 'Schreibend leben (1799–1892). Heinrich Witt und sein Tagebuch im Lima des 19. Jhs.'. *Selbstzeugnis und Person. Transkulturelle Perspektiven*. 139–154. Eds. Claudia Ulbrich et al. Cologne et al.: 2012.
Wilhelm, Friedrich. "Götzen, Adolf Graf von". *Neue Deutsche Biographie*, 6, 1964, pp. 593–594. Web. https://www.deutsche-biographie.de/pnd11907253X.html#ndbcontent (21 October 2019).
Wimmelbücker, Ludger. 'Verbrannte Erde. Zu den Bevölkerungsverlusten als Folge des Maji Maji Krieges'. *Der Maji Maji Krieg in Deutsch-Ostafrika. 1905–1907*. 87–99. Eds. Felicitas Becker and Jigal Beez. Berlin: 2005.
Woerden, Henk van. *Der Bastard. Die Geschichte des Mannes, der den südafrikanischen Premier ermordete*. Berlin: 2002.
Wurster, Gabriele. '*You have to balance*. Über die Verknüpfung von Beruf und Familie bei qualifizierten Frauen in Nairobi'. *Arbeit in Africa*. 275–287. Eds. Kurt Beck and Gerd Spittler. Hamburg: 1996.
Yekani, Minu Hashemi. *Koloniale Arbeit, Rassismus, Migration und Herrschaft in Tansania (1885–1914)*. Frankfurt o.M. and New York: 2019.
——. '"Inder und Chinesen werden unsere Kolonie nicht in die Höhe bringen". Arbeit, Klima und der 'Rasse'-Diskurs in Tansania (1885–1914)'. 209–225. Eds. Felix Axster and Nikolas Lelle. *«Deutsche Arbeit». Kritische Perspektiven auf ein ideologisches Selbstbild*. Göttingen: 2018.
Zimmerer, Jürgen. 'Kolonialismus und kollektive Identität: Erinnerungsorte deutscher Kolonialgeschichte'. *Kein Platz an der Sonne. Erinnerungsorte der deutschen Kolonialgeschichte*. 9–40. Ed. Jürgen Zimmerer. Bonn: 2013.
——. 'Deutscher Rassenstaat in Afrika. Ordnung, Entwicklung und Segregation in „Deutsch-Südwest" (1884–1915)'. *Von Windhuk nach Auschwitz? Beiträge zum Verhältnis von Kolonialismus und Holocaust*. 120–139. Ed. Jürgen Zimmerer. Berlin: 2011.
Zimmerman, Andrew. *Alabama in Africa. Booker T. Washington, The German Empire, and the Globalization of the New South*. Princeton: 2010.

Index

https://doi.org/10.1515/9783111218090-008